GREEN BUILDING PRODUCTS

3rd Edition

The GreenSpec® Guide to
Residential Building Materials

Alex Wilson and Mark Piepkorn · EDITORS

Nadav Malin · CO-EDITOR, GREENSPEC

Angela Battisto · GREENSPEC MANAGER

Jennifer Atlee · RESEARCH DIRECTOR

Brent Ehrlich · PRODUCT EDITOR

Frank Richter · ASSOC. PRODUCT EDITOR

Authoritative Information on Environmentally Responsible Building Design and Construction

NEW SOCIETY PUBLISHERS

Green Building Products 3rd Edition:
The GreenSpec® Guide to Residential Building Materials

Cataloging in Publication Data: A catalog record for this publication is available from the National Library of Canada.

Paperback ISBN-13: 978-0-86571-600-1

Cover photo by Randi Baird of a home designed and built by South Mountain Company, Martha's Vineyard, Massachusetts. Used by permission.

Product photos were provided by the manufacturers and are used by permission.

Production notes:

Text design by Joy Wallens-Penford. Layout by Julia Jandrisits. Cover design by DC Design.

In keeping with the copublishers' mission to build an ecologically sustainable society through their work and actions, this book is printed on acid-free paper that is FSC-certified, 100% old-growth forest free (100% post-consumer recycled), processed chlorine free, and printed with vegetable-based, low-VOC inks.

Printed in Canada.

Inquiries regarding requests to reprint all or part of this book should be addressed to BuildingGreen at the address below.

Copublished by:

BuildingGreen, 122 Birge Street, Suite 30, Brattleboro, VT 05301, USA   802-257-7300

BuildingGreen's mission is to provide accurate, unbiased, and timely information that will help building professionals improve the environmental performance of buildings and surrounding landscapes. For further information and to learn about our other information resources, please visit our website at: www.BuildingGreen.com.

New Society Publishers, P.O. Box 189, Gabriola Island, BC V0R 1X0, Canada   250-247-9737

New Society Publishers' mission is to publish books that contribute in fundamental ways to building an ecologically sustainable and just society, and to do so with the least possible impact on the environment, in a manner that models this vision. For further information, or to browse our full list of books and purchase securely, visit our website at: www.newsociety.com.

Contents

INTERIOR FINISH & TRIM 195

CAULKS & ADHESIVES 219

PAINTS & COATINGS 223

MECHANICAL SYSTEMS/HVAC 241

Foreword

by Sarah Susanka

The book you have in your hands is an important and much-needed tool in building a house that is green—a house that respects the value of our planet's natural resources, that protects its occupants, and that recognizes the impact and legacy it will leave for future generations.

When I first became an architect, back in the 1980s, I was a passive solar "nut," convinced that it was time to loosen our dependence on fossil fuels and embrace the abundant energy available from the sun. Then I moved to Minnesota and discovered that, though this might be an excellent strategy for warmer climates and lower latitudes, in Minneapolis in December there just aren't enough hours of sunlight, even on a really sunny day, to make passive solar strategies work effectively. So I turned into an energy-efficiency nut instead, learning everything I could about how to minimize heat loss in the winter and heat gain in the summer, while still designing homes that were comfortable as well as a delight to live in.

Over the twenty years I practiced residential architecture and energy-efficient design in the Twin Cities, my colleagues and I developed a strategy for building better, not bigger, which came to be known as building Not So Big. My first book, *The Not So Big House*, published in 1998 by Taunton Press, spelled out a recipe for a more sustainably made house—one that was about a third smaller than you thought you needed, with every space used every day. Such a house is filled with the special details of design and construction that make its structure last for centuries rather than decades, and with a character that encourages generations of inhabitants to take care of it, and make it their own, just like the homes of the Arts and Crafts movement did a century ago.

I believe that the very first step in building a green home is to build it just the right size for the way you want to live—you can read more about how to make this happen in the *Not So Big House* series of books, as well as my latest, *Home By Design*.

With a house design that's properly tailored to the activities of your life, and with spaces proportioned to fit our human scale, it is then time to select the products that support your efforts to make a healthy environment for your household, without hurting the planet in the process. For many years, this has presented a quandary. You've known what you WANT to be able to do—to make product selections that align with your values. You've known that you want to do what's best for the Earth and for future generations, and only purchase items that are in keeping with the natural order of things. But until now the problem has been how to find them. Simply having the values is not enough. You need a guide to help find the companies that share your goals and have made the effort to create sustainable products that can fulfill your dream for a truly green home.

This book is that guide. It's written in a way that makes it easy to find the information and product advice you need, and it's a must for anyone—builder, designer, architect, or homeowner—who wants to know the unbiased and unembellished truth about what's really "green." The editors at BuildingGreen, including Alex Wilson and Mark Piepkorn, are among the most knowledgeable people in the world on sustainability, energy efficiency, and environmental characteristics of building products. They provide an enormous service to all of us in documenting, in laypersons' language, the ins and outs of product selection for a green home.

Green Building Products provides the most comprehensive and useful resource for fulfilling the dreams that so many of us share for a sustainable future for our planetary—as well as our personal—home. Together we CAN make a difference, and this book points the way, giving us the tools to make the decisions that will ensure a better, though not necessarily bigger, future.

Sarah Susanka is an architect and author of the highly acclaimed Not So Big House *series of books, published by Taunton Press.*

Introduction

GREEN HOMES ARE SAFE TO LIVE IN, AFFORDABLE TO operate, and less damaging to the local, regional, and global environments.

Interest in green building has been growing by leaps and bounds in recent years for a number of reasons. Home-owners are alarmed by news about mold and asthma and about the alphabet soup of toxic chemicals that enters our homes through building products, furnishings, and consumer goods. We want the place where we live to be safe. We spend 90% of our time indoors and a significant chunk of that in our homes; these spaces should not make us sick. A green home is a healthy home.

Some people are worried that rising energy prices could make their homes too expensive to live in. In recent years, we have seen dramatic increases in the price of gasoline, natural gas, electricity, and heating oil. Evidence that worldwide oil production may be nearing a peak even as demand continues to grow leads to the concern that even higher prices may be just around the corner. (The prices of natural gas and electricity tend to rise and fall with the price of oil.) With more and more people nearing retirement age and facing the prospect of living on a fixed income, many are wisely concerned about the rising costs of operating their homes. This includes energy costs but also the costs of maintaining the home. A green home is affordable to operate—its energy use is low, and it is made with durable, low-maintenance materials.

Finally, more and more homeowners are beginning to recognize that their actions *can* make a difference. There is growing awareness about our impacts on the environment, and an increasing willingness to do something about it. Surveys show that efforts to make their homes more environmentally friendly are high priorities for homeowners and potential homebuyers—even if those measures increase costs.

Doing the right thing by creating a green home makes sense all around. It's good for your family's health, it saves money, and it's good for the environment.

Why Choose Green Building Products?

There are really three stakeholders to benefit from the use of green building products: the people who work with the materials (not only on the job site but also in the factories where the products are made); the homeowners who live with those materials; and the local, regional, and global environment that is protected through the production and use of these materials.

The direct benefits of green building products to workers and homeowners are the easiest to justify. Manufacturing facilities and construction companies can save money if employees don't have to use special protective gear and if they stay healthier, losing less time to sick leave. And the importance of a safe, healthy home goes almost without saying. Since we spend so much of our time indoors, it's imperative that our indoor environments don't make us sick. Asthma now affects one in eight children, and medical experts are increasingly pointing to homes—and the products we put in them—as the culprits that cause respiratory illnesses. Further, there are a slew of chemicals we introduce to our homes whose health effects we know almost nothing about, such as the plasticizers that make vinyl shower curtains and wallcoverings flexible, brominated flame retardants in foam cushions, and fluoropolymers such as Teflon® used to insulate some wiring and a component in some finishes. Some of these chemicals are now showing up in the blood of humans worldwide and are being linked to behavioral and developmental problems.

Homeowners benefit directly from many products in the operation of their homes: heating, cooling, water use, maintenance, and repairs. Some green building products are more energy-efficient or more water-efficient than conventional products; others are more durable or require less maintenance. These direct benefits will save people money or time over the life of their homes and can easily be justified on those grounds.

Selecting green products solely because they protect the environment can be more difficult to justify—but is no less important. While most homeowners will be sympathetic to concerns about rainforest destruction, ozone depletion, or toxic chemical releases from manufacturing plants, those impacts are far away, and most of them don't affect us directly. However, growing awareness about global warming is helping people understand the fact that actions in one place can have environmental impacts elsewhere. If, as most scientists believe, global warming is going to become a lot more apparent over the coming years and decades, it may become easier to draw the connection between our purchasing decisions and a wide range of impacts. If that happens, the environment could become a much bigger factor in the way we think, act, and make purchasing decisions.

When it comes to choosing green building products, both direct and indirect benefits are important. The relative priorities of these benefits, though, will vary significantly from person to person.

Product Selection Is Only One Part of Green Building

While this book focuses on the selection of products for building and remodeling to make a home more environmentally friendly, it is important to point out that green building is about much more than products. Green building is also about such issues as:

- Energy-efficient design and construction— where windows are located, how much insulation is installed, and how effectively air leakage is controlled;

- House size—not building a larger home than is needed;

- Where the house is built—so that use of automobiles can be minimized and important natural areas can be protected;

- Design and construction detailing to avoid moisture problems—the leading cause of indoor air quality problems in houses.

While the products and materials used in a home are often the most visible aspects of "green," these other issues are at least as important—and often significantly more important. Indeed, it is possible to build a compact, energy-efficient home close to alternative transportation that would be considered green by any measure with very few products and materials that are specifically considered "green." Conversely, a house could be built from 100% green products yet not be very green at all—because it isn't energy-efficient, because it's much bigger than necessary, or because building it damaged an ecologically sensitive area.

Selecting green building products is a very important aspect of green design, but it's not the whole story. Be sure to pay attention to the broader issues. For more information on green building, visit www.BuildingGreen.com.

What Makes a Product Green?

This is a very complicated question. Many different factors come into play in determining the "greenness" of products and materials; very often the distinctions are not black-and-white. Much of the complexity in examining the environmental and health impacts of materials results from the fact that the impacts can occur at different points in the *life cycle* of a product, and those impacts can vary tremendously from product to product.

The science of examining the environmental and health impacts of products is referred to as *life-cycle assessment*, or LCA. This process examines a product from "cradle to grave," considering environmental and health issues involved with all aspects of resource extraction, manufacture, use, and disposal. Instead of "cradle to grave," some prefer to think of this cycle as "cradle to cradle," recognizing the idea of taking a product at the end of its useful life and turning it into the raw material for something else—recycling.

A green product is one whose life-cycle impacts are low. A floor tile made from recycled glass is considered green because it is made from a waste material—something that would otherwise end up in a landfill. A mineral silicate paint is green because it is highly durable and won't require frequent recoating or other treatment throughout its life. Metal cabinets can be green if they don't emit VOCs (volatile organic compounds) or other pollutants. A compact fluorescent light bulb is green because it reduces energy consumption in the home. Sometimes, more than one environmental attribute apply to a product—for example, recycled plastic decking that is made from a waste product, is more durable than standard wooden decking, and doesn't release copper or other chemicals that can harm the environment (as can conventional pressure-treated wood).

A challenge in choosing green products is balancing all of these different—and often unrelated—considerations. A product might be made of recycled material but release harmful levels of VOCs; another might be durable but manufactured with chemicals that are significantly hazardous to the environment or to humans. We are often comparing apples to oranges when trying to decide which environmental impacts should carry greater weight. Fortunately, there are some efforts under way to quantify the environmental impacts of building materials using standardized measures.

Building for Environmental and Economic Sustainability (BEES) is a life-cycle assessment software tool that was developed by the National Institute of Standards and Technology (NIST). This tool helps architects, engineers, and environmental building consultants understand environmental and health impacts over a product's life cycle. While relatively few products have been assessed through BEES to date, it offers great promise for life-cycle assessment of building materials as the underlying database grows.

The nonprofit ATHENA™ Sustainable Materials Institute is amassing a comprehensive, public database of life-cycle *inventory* information about generic (as opposed to brand-specific) building materials. These inventories include detailed information on the environmental burdens that result from producing building materials.

Other organizations, including Green Seal, Scientific Certification Systems, NSF International, the Institute for Market Transformation to Sustainability, and others are developing sustainable product standards for various product categories, such as carpet and textiles.

As more rigorous and specific standards for green building products are developed, the selection criteria for product directories—such as this one—will become more quantitative. Until that time, the selection process for a product directory has to be based on the expertise of those creating it. Specifics of how products are selected for this directory are described below.

What Is *GreenSpec*?

GreenSpec® is the leading national directory of green building products. Included here are those *GreenSpec* products that are most relevant to home building. Our intent with *GreenSpec* is to highlight the *greenest* building products; we don't include some products with green attributes because there are similar products considered even greener. While we do our best to be comprehensive, there are doubtless many building products that would qualify for *GreenSpec* but are not yet included. If you have recommendations for products that should be considered, e-mail greenspec@BuildingGreen.com.

Manufacturers do not pay to be included in *GreenSpec*. Decisions about which products to include are based totally on criteria developed by the *GreenSpec* and *Environmental Building News* editorial team. This policy allows us to be nonbiased in selecting products—and in writing the descriptions of those products. Because manufacturers don't pay to be listed in *GreenSpec*, they can't control what is said about the products. In other words, what you read about products in this book is based on the research our staff has done; it is not written by the marketing staffs of manufacturing companies.

Product Selection Criteria Used in This Directory

BuildingGreen has been researching green building products and publishing information on them since 1992. Through writing hundreds of product reviews in the monthly newsletter *Environmental Building News*, and listing nearly 2,000 products in the comprehensive *GreenSpec*® database of green building products, BuildingGreen has developed specific criteria for what makes a product green. These criteria include:

PRODUCTS MADE WITH SALVAGED, RECYCLED, OR AGRICULTURAL WASTE CONTENT

The materials used to produce a building product, and where those materials come from, are important green criteria and probably the best known. When many people think of green building products, they think of products made from recycled materials.

- **Salvaged products.** Whenever we can *reuse* a product instead of producing a new one from raw materials—even if those raw materials are from recycled sources—we save resources and energy. Many salvaged materials used in buildings (including bricks, millwork, framing lumber, plumbing fixtures, and period hardware) are mostly sold on a local or regional basis by salvage yards. Fewer salvaged materials are marketed widely, and it is generally only these that are profiled in a national directory such as *GreenSpec*. Local and regional green product directories can really shine when it comes to finding salvaged materials. Certain salvaged products are not recommended, including toilets, faucets, and windows—because the water- and energy-savings of today's high-performance products offer far greater benefit than any there might be in using the old ones. With salvaged wood products, be aware that lead may be present. Test painted wood for lead paint or residue left from lead paint (easy-to-use test kits are available). If found, avoid the product or have the wood stripped and sealed.

• **Products with post-consumer recycled content.** Recycled content is an important feature of many green products. From an environmental standpoint, *post-consumer* is preferable to *pre-consumer* recycled content because post-consumer recycled materials are more likely to be diverted from landfills. For many product categories, there is currently no set standard for the percentage of recycled content required to qualify for inclusion in *GreenSpec*; such standards will increasingly be developed in the future as more products begin using higher percentages of recycled materials.

In some cases, products with recycled content are included with caveats regarding where they should be used. Rubber flooring made from recycled automobile tires is a good example—higher-emitting products should not be used in most fully enclosed indoor spaces due to potential offgassing of harmful chemicals.

In certain situations, from a life-cycle perspective, recycling has downsides. For example, energy consumption or pollution may be a concern with some collection programs or recycling processes. As more complete life-cycle information on recycled materials—and the process of recycling—becomes available, we will scrutinize recycled products more carefully.

• **Products with pre-consumer recycled content.** Pre-consumer (also called "post-industrial") recycling refers to the use of industrial byproducts—as distinguished from material that has been in consumer use. Examples of pre-consumer recycled materials used in building products include iron-ore blast furnace slag used in making mineral wool insulation; fly ash from the smoke stacks of coal-burning power plants used in making concrete; and PVC scrap from pipe manufacturing used in making roofing shingles. Usually excluded from this category is the use of scrap within the manufacturing plant where it was generated—material that would typically have gone back into the manufacturing process anyway. While post-consumer recycled content is

better than pre-consumer recycled content, the latter can still qualify a product for inclusion in *GreenSpec* in many product categories—especially those where there are no products available with post-consumer recycled content.

• **Products made from agricultural waste material.** A number of products are included in *GreenSpec* because they are derived from agricultural waste products. Most of these are made from straw—the stems left after harvesting cereal grains. Citrus oil, a waste product from orange and lemon juice extraction, is also used in some green products, but such products usually include other agricultural oils as well and are included under "Rapidly renewable products".

PRODUCTS THAT CONSERVE NATURAL RESOURCES

Aside from salvaged or recycled content, there are a number of other ways that products can contribute to the conservation of natural resources. Examples of these include products that use less material than the standard solution for a particular function; products that are especially durable or low-maintenance; wood products that carry third-party certification demonstrating well-managed forestry; and products made from rapidly renewable resources.

• **Products that reduce material use.** Products meeting this criterion may not be distinctly green on their own but are included in *GreenSpec* because of the resource efficiency benefits that they make possible. For example, drywall clips allow the elimination of corner studs in wood house framing; engineered stair stringers reduce lumber waste; pier foundation systems minimize concrete use; and concrete pigments can turn concrete slabs into attractive finished floors, eliminating the need for conventional finish flooring.

• **Products with exceptional durability or low maintenance requirements.** These products are environmentally attractive because they need to be replaced less frequently or their maintenance has very low impact. This criterion is highly variable by product type. Sometimes, durability is a contributing factor to the green designation—but not enough to distinguish the product as green on its own. Included in this category are such products as fiber-cement siding, fiberglass windows, slate shingles, and vitrified-clay waste pipe.

- **Certified wood products.** Third-party certification based on standards developed by the Forest Steward-ship Council (FSC) is the best way to ensure that wood products come from well-managed forests. Wood products must go through a chain-of-custody certification process to carry an FSC stamp. Manufactured wood products can meet the FSC certification requirements with less than 100% certified-wood content through *percentage-based claims* (30% certified-wood content is required if only virgin wood fiber is used; certified-wood content as low as 17.5% is allowable if the rest of the fiber content is from recycled sources). With a few special-case exceptions, any nonsalvaged solid-wood product must be FSC-certified to be included in *GreenSpec*. Engineered wood products in *GreenSpec* do not qualify by virtue of their resource efficiency benefits alone. A few manufactured wood products, including engineered lumber and particleboard or medium-density fiberboard (MDF), can be included if they have other environmental attributes—such as the absence of formaldehyde binders.

- **Rapidly renewable products.** Rapidly renewable materials are distinguished from wood by having a shorter harvest rotation—typically 10 years or less. They are biodegradable, often low in VOC emissions, and usually produced from agricultural crops. Because sunlight is generally the primary energy input (via photosynthesis), these products may be less energy-intensive to produce—though transportation and processing energy use should also be considered. Examples include natural linoleum; bamboo flooring; form-release agents made from plant oils; natural paints; geotextile fabrics from coir and jute; products made with bamboo or cork; and such textiles as or-ganic cotton, wool, and sisal. Note that not all rapidly renewable materials are included in GreenSpec—non-organic cotton, for example, is highly pesticide-inten-sive. In some cases, even though a product qualifies for GreenSpec by virtue of its natural raw materials, it may have negatives that render it inappropriate for certain uses—such as high VOC levels that cause problems for people with chemical sensitivities.

PRODUCTS THAT AVOID TOXIC OR OTHER EMISSIONS

Some building products are considered green because they have low manufacturing impacts, are alternatives to conventional products made from chemicals con-sidered problematic, or because they facilitate a reduction in polluting emissions from building main-tenance. In this *GreenSpec* criterion, a few product components were singled out for avoidance in most cases: substances that deplete stratospheric ozone, those associated with ecological damage or health risks, including mercury and halogenated compounds. In a few cases, these substances may be included in a "green" product, but that product has to have other significant environmental benefits (for example, , low energy or water use).

Substitutes for conventional products made with environmentally hazardous components may not, in themselves, be particularly green (i.e., they may be petrochemical-based or relatively high in VOCs), but *relative to the products being replaced* they can be considered green. Most of the products satisfying this criterion are in categories that are dominated by the more harmful products—such as foam insulation categories in which most products still contain HCFCs. We have created several subcategories here for green products:

- **Natural or minimally processed products.** Prod-ucts that are natural or minimally processed can be green because of low energy use and low risk of chemical releases during manufacture. These can in-clude wood products, agricultural or nonagricultural plant products, and mineral products such as natural stone and slate shingles. . Being minimally processed is not, in itself, enough to qualify a wood product for *GreenSpec*, however.

- **Alternatives to ozone-depleting substances.** Included here are categories in which the majority of products still contain or use HCFCs (hydrochlorofluoro-carbons), such as certain types of foam insulation and most compression-cycle heating and air-conditioning equipment. As ozone-depleting substances are phased out, the relative importance of this criterion drops (for example, polyisocyanurate insulation is no longer made with HCFC-141b as the blowing agent, so the environmental benefit of expanded polystyrene, EPS, over polyiso has disappeared).

- **Alternatives to hazardous products.** Some ma-terials provide a better alternative in an application dominated by products for which there are concerns about toxic constituents, intermediaries, or by-prod-ucts. Fluorescent lamps with low mercury levels are included here, along with form release agents that won't contaminate water or soils with toxicants. Also included here are alternatives to products made with chlorinated hydrocarbons such as polyvinyl chloride (PVC) and brominated fire retardants.

• **Products that reduce or eliminate pesticide treatments.** Periodic pesticide treatment around buildings can be a significant health and environmental hazard. The use of certain products can obviate the need for pesticide treatments, and such products are therefore considered green. Examples include physical termite barriers, borate-treated building products, and bait systems that can eliminate the need for broad-based pesticide applications.

• **Products that reduce stormwater pollution.** Porous paving products and green (vegetated) roofing systems result in less stormwater runoff and thereby reduce surface water pollution. Stormwater treatment systems reduce pollutant levels in any water that is released.

• **Products that reduce impacts from construction or demolition activities.** Included here are various erosion-control products, foundation products that eliminate the need for excavation, and exterior stains that result in lower VOC emissions into the atmosphere. Fluorescent lamp and ballast recyclers and low-mercury fluorescent lamps reduce environmental impacts during demolition (as well as renovation).

• **Products that reduce pollution or waste from operations.** Alternative wastewater disposal systems reduce groundwater pollution by decomposing organic wastes more effectively. Porous paving products and green (vegetated or "living") roofing systems result in less stormwater runoff and thereby reduce surface water pollution and sewage treatment plant loads. Masonry fireplaces and pellet stoves burn wood more completely with fewer emissions than conventional fireplaces and wood stoves. Recycling bins and compost systems enable occupants to reduce their solid waste generation.

PRODUCTS THAT SAVE ENERGY OR WATER

The ongoing environmental impacts that result from energy and water used in operating a building often far outweigh the impacts associated with its construction. Many products are included in *GreenSpec* for these benefits. There are several quite distinct subcategories:

• **Building components that reduce heating and cooling loads.** Examples include structural insulated panels (SIPs), insulated concrete forms (ICFs), autoclaved aerated concrete (AAC) blocks, and high-performance windows. As these energy-saving products gain market acceptance, our threshold for inclusion in *GreenSpec* may become more stringent. For example, we may begin including only SIPs and ICFs with steady-state R-values above a certain threshold or with other environmental features, such as recycled-content foam insulation. Some products, such as insulation, clearly offer environmental benefits but are so common that they need other environmental features to qualify for *GreenSpec*.

With windows, energy performance requirements for *GreenSpec* listing are based on the National Fenestration Rating Council (NFRC) *unit U-factors*; with U-factors, the lower the number, the better it insulates. The base standard for windows is a unit U-factor of 0.25 or lower for at least one product in a listed product line. If the windows are made from an environmentally attractive material (e.g., high recycled content or superb durability, such as fiberglass), the energy standard is less stringent: a U-factor of 0.30 or lower. If the frame material is nongreen, such as PVC (vinyl), the energy standard is more stringent: a U-factor of 0.20 or lower is required. There are a few exceptions to these standards, such as high-recycled-content windows made for unheated buildings.

• **Equipment that conserves energy.** With energy-consuming equipment such as water heaters, clothes washers, and refrigerators, the criteria for *GreenSpec* listing are based on energy performance ratings that rely on U.S. Department of Energy test standards. In most appliance categories, *GreenSpec* has a higher energy performance threshold than ENERGY STAR®—for example, exceeding those standards by 10% or 20%. With certain product categories, such as compact fluorescent lamps (CFLs), all products qualify from an energy standpoint, but some are eliminated due to performance problems.

• **Renewable energy and fuel cell equipment.** Equipment and products that enable us to use renewable energy instead of fossil fuels and conventionally generated electricity are highly beneficial from an environmental standpoint. Examples include solar water heaters, photovoltaic (PV) systems, and wind turbines. Fuel cells are also included here, even though fuel cells today nearly always use natural gas or another fossil fuel as the hydrogen source—they are considered green because emissions are lower than combustion-based equipment and because the use of fuel cells will help us eventually move beyond fossil fuel dependence.

- **Fixtures and equipment that conserve water.** All toilets and most showerheads today meet federal water efficiency standards—but not all of these products perform satisfactorily. With toilets, *GreenSpec* considers both water use and flush performance based on a standardized test procedure. To be listed in *GreenSpec* toilets must use at least 20% less water than the federally mandated 1.6 gallons per flush (gpf), a designation referred to as a high-efficiency toilet. Most toilets must also meet the minimum performance standards of the Uniform North American Requirements (UNAR) for toilets. With faucets, special controls that help conserve water are the usual basis for inclusion. Some other water-saving products, such as rainwater catchment systems, are also found here.

PRODUCTS THAT CONTRIBUTE TO A SAFE, HEALTHY INDOOR ENVIRONMENT

Houses should be healthy to live in, and product selection is a significant determinant of indoor environmental quality. Green building products that help to ensure a healthy indoor environment can be separated into several categories:

- **Products that don't release significant pollutants into the building.** Included here are zero- and low-VOC paints, caulks, and adhesives, as well as products with very low emissions, such as manufactured wood products made without formaldehyde binders. Just how low the VOC level needs to be for a given product to qualify for inclusion in *GreenSpec* depends on the product category. Ideally, those criteria should be based not on simple VOC content, but on resultant VOC concentrations in the space after a given period of time—the EPA has worked on such an approach for paints (including a way to factor in higher impacts for more toxic VOCs), but results from such research are not yet available.

- **Products that block the introduction, production, or spread of indoor contaminants.** Certain materials and products are green because they prevent the introduction (or development) of pollutants—especially biological contaminants—into the home. Duct mastic, for example, can block the entry of mold-laden air or insulation fibers into a duct system. "Track-off" systems for entryways help to remove pollutants from the shoes of people entering. Coated duct board—compared with standard rigid fiberglass duct board—prevents fiber shedding and helps control mold growth. And true linoleum naturally controls microbial contamination through the ongoing process of linoleic acid oxidation. (Note that vinyl flooring—which is PVC flooring—is often mistakenly referred to as linoleum. PVC is not considered a green product.)

- **Products that remove indoor pollutants.** Products that qualify for *GreenSpec* based on this criterion include certain ventilation products, filters, radon mitigation equipment, and other equipment that helps to remove pollutants or introduce fresh air. Because ventilation equipment is now fairly standard, only products that are particularly efficient or quiet, or that offer other environmental benefits, are included.

- **Products that warn occupants of health hazards in the building.** Included here are carbon monoxide (CO) detectors, lead paint test kits, and other indoor air quality (IAQ) test kits. Because CO detectors are so common, other features are needed to qualify these products for *GreenSpec*, such as evidence of superb performance.

- **Products that improve light quality.** A growing body of evidence suggests that natural daylight is beneficial to our health and productivity. Products that enable us to bring daylight into a building, such as tubular skylights, are included in *GreenSpec*.

- **Products that help control noise.** Noise, from both indoor and outside sources, adds to stress and discomfort. A wide range of products are available to help absorb noise, prevent it from spreading, mask it, and even reduce it with sound-cancellation technologies.

- **Products that enhance community well-being.** Beyond the walls of a building, many products can contribute to safer neighborhoods, increasing walkability and making high-density communities appealing.

Sitework & Landscaping

Sitework and landscaping are typically the first and last tasks, respectively, on a building site. Steps can be taken at the beginning of sitework that can increase the value—and reduce the cost—of landscaping after construction. Siting of the building itself usually has already occurred, but there is still often an opportunity to influence such issues as solar access and minimizing site disturbance.

A site survey should precede any sitework to identify sensitive areas and features to be protected, such as wetlands, trees, and other vegetation. It's well worth the effort to save trees if they are healthy and not too close to the structure. Mature trees on a lot can add more than 15% to the value of a house, and appropriately placed trees can reduce a building's conditioning needs by more than 40%.

A tree's root system extends quite a distance from the trunk—typically at least to the *drip line* of the farthest branches. Even just compacting the soil can harm the roots, so a large area around each protected tree needs to be fenced off. To ensure cooperation of subcontractors in this effort, one strategy is to specifically list in their contract the value of each mature tree and hold them responsible for that value if the tree is damaged.

Invasive plants introduced from other parts of the world can wreak havoc on the ecological balance of a region, so nonnative species should generally be avoided in landscaping (though noninvasive exotic species—those that don't spread and outcompete native plants—are less of a concern). Plants that are native to your area are also adapted to your climate, so they tend to need less care and maintenance, and require less watering—saving time and money. Most lawns are planted with nonnative turf grasses, such as Kentucky Bluegrass, which require watering in most U.S. climates. Hardy, native species such as buffalo grass and certain fescues should be used instead, or lawn areas should be replaced with other landscapes that require less water, fertilizer, herbicides, and maintenance.

Handling stormwater runoff can be a major design issue. Conventional solutions include concrete or PVC drainage pipes and, on larger projects, detention ponds; these are expensive and tend to increase the contamination of the water from surface pollutants. Softer solutions include the use of pervious surfaces to allow rainwater infiltration directly into the ground; these are far better environmentally and usually less expensive. Use of swales for rainwater instead of curbs and stormwater drains is also preferred.

Resource-efficient products and building materials for sitework and landscaping include porous paving systems suitable for driveways, walkways, courtyards, and parking areas; and landscaping timbers made from recycled plastics, which are more durable in ground contact than preservative-treated wood. Retaining walls and hardscape surfaces can often be made from salvaged materials, such as broken up concrete paving (which some green builders refer to as "urbanite").

Aggregate Surfacing

Salvaged and recycled materials, such as brick or glass chunks with softened edges, can be attractive surfacing materials in landscaping applications. Granulated rubber made from recycled tires can make a durable and highly resilient play environment when applied to a 6" depth; it creates a softer play environment than pea gravel and, unlike wood chips, will not rot or attract insects. Keep these areas separated from other landscaping materials, so that the nonbiodegradable aggregate can later be removed if uses change.

Brick Nuggets

Cunningham Brick Co., Inc.
701 N. Main St.
Lexington, NC 27292

Toll-free: 800-672-6181
Phone: 336-248-8541
www.cunninghambrick.com

Brick Nuggets are crushed waste bricks suitable for landscaping uses. They are available in 1/2 cubic foot bags.

Granulated Rubber

Rubber Granulators, Inc.
3831 152nd St. NE
Marysville, WA 98271

Phone: 360-658-7754
www.rubbergranulators.com

Rubber Granulators produces granulated rubber made from used tires available in 55-lb, 1,000-lb, and 2,000-lb sacks.

Perma-Turf Playground Safety Surface

TIREC Corporation
P.O. Box 604
Mullica Hill, NJ 08062

Phone: 856-478-4491
www.perma-turf.com

Perma-Turf® Playground Safety Surface is a fiber-reinforced rubber aggregate made from 100% recycled tires with the steel belting removed. Tirec guarantees its products to be 98% free of steel and backs them with a 50-year guarantee. Perma-Flex® High Performance Arena Footing is a similar product made for equestrian arenas.

Recycled Glass Aggregates and Powders

American Specialty Glass, Inc.
829 N. 400 W
North Salt Lake, UT 84054

Phone: 801-294-4222
www.americanspecialtyglass.com

American Specialty Glass, Inc., provides recycled-glass aggregate in a range of sizes and colors for terrazzo floors, pavers, and countertops. Sources include post-consumer bottle glass and post-industrial float glass cullet. Glass sand, a substitute for silica sand, is also available, as are powder fines that can be used as concrete coloring agents, providing a different effect than pigments. Polished or unpolished landscaping nuggets in a range of sizes are offered as well.

Recycled Glass for Landscaping

Conigliaro Industries, Inc.
701 Waverly St.
Framingham, MA 01702

Toll-free: 888-266-4425
Phone: 508-872-9668
www.conigliaro.com

Conigliaro Industries offers "barefoot-friendly" tumbled glass aggregates for decorative, landscape, and construction uses in 1/8" minus and 3/4" minus aggregate sizes. Appropriate for mulch replacement, road beds, flowable fills, backfills, and drainage projects, this aggregate made from 100% recycled glass bottles and plate glass is available in various color blends and in any quantity.

Recycled Glass for Landscaping

Heritage Glass, Inc.
130 W. 700 S. Bldg. E
Smithfield, UT 84335

Phone: 435-563-5585
www.heritageglass.net

Heritage Glass offers 1/2" to 2" recycled-glass aggregate with dulled edges and a range of colors for exterior and interior landscaping applications. Sources include post-industrial float glass cullet and post-consumer recycled bottle glass. Heritage also provides recycled-glass aggregate for terrazzo applications.

RubberStuff

ART (American Rubber Technologies, Inc.)
302 North Lane Ave.
Jacksonville, FL 32254

Toll-free: 800-741-5201
www.americanrubber.com

RubberStuff™, made from recycled-tire rubber, is a granulated-rubber safety surface for playground applications. The 1/4" rubber granules are usually installed at a 6" depth. The manufacturer has certified the following recycled-content levels (by weight): total recovered material 100% typical, 100% guaranteed; post-consumer material 100% typical, 100% guaranteed.

Tire Turf

Continental Turf Systems, Inc.
P.O. Box 389
Continental, OH 45831

Phone: 419-596-4242
www.continentalturf.com

Tire Turf is loose, granulated, 100% post-consumer recycled-tire-rubber ground cover for use in playgrounds, horse arenas, and as a landscaping mulch.

Brick Pavers

Recycled bricks are attractive and functional, and can be installed to have drainage voids along the installed edges as porous paving systems. Porous pavement needs to be installed above a "reservoir" of uniform-sized aggregate (for example, 1-1/2" crushed stone).

Green Leaf Brick

The Red Tree Group, Inc.
8615 Golf Ridge Dr.
Charlotte, NC 28277

Phone: 704-307-0930
www.greenleafbrick.com

Green Leaf Brick is a fired masonry brick made of 100% recycled materials. In addition to building brick, pavers are also available. Recycled materials include industrial waste from technical ceramic plants, mineral mining operations, and steel manufacturing; post-consumer content includes recycled glass, and incinerated sewage ash. Green Leaf Brick acquires materials from within 500 miles of its Salisbury NC plant, most within 100 miles.

Salvaged Brick

Gavin Historical Bricks
2050 Glendale Rd.
Iowa City, IA 52245

Phone: 319-354-5251
www.historicalbricks.com

Gavin Historical Bricks supplies salvaged bricks and cobblestones recovered from buildings and streets from around the country. Bricks are used in new construction to provide an antique look, as well as for historic restoration projects. Custom brick matching is available. The company also handcuts antique brick into 1/2" floor tile for a variety of applications. Shipping is provided nationwide, though the heavy weight reduces the practicality (and environmental attractiveness) of shipping large quantities long distances.

Erosion Protection

While polymer-based products dominate this market, alternatives made from natural fibers are available. These include coir (coconut-husk fiber obtained from coconut oil production) and jute, a fiber commonly used to make twine. The primary advantage of natural-fiber erosion control products is their biodegradability even after vegetation is established. Photodegradable products often fail to break down, as plant growth and other cover prevents light from hitting the material. And unlike polymer-based fabrics, natural-fiber products also absorb moisture and work like a mulch, benefiting seedling establishment. Products listed here are biodegradable.

Antiwash/Geojute and Geocoir DeKoWe

Belton Industries, Inc.
1205 Hamby Rd.
P.O. Box 127
Belton, SC 29627

Toll-free: 800-845-8753
Phone: 864-338-5711
www.beltonindustries.com

Antiwash®/Geojute® is woven in a 1/2" grid pattern that is suitable for moderate slopes sustaining runoff velocities of up to 8 ft/s. The jute fabric, available in 4'-wide by 225'- or 147'-long rolls, biodegrades in one to two years. Geocoir® DeKoWe®, made from coir, is stronger and more durable than jute geotextiles. This product is available in three different weights: 400, 700, and 900 g/m2; is typically used on steeper slopes; and may last from 4 to 5 years, depending upon the application.

BioFence

Environmental Research Corps
15 Mohawk Ave.
East Freetown, MA 02717

Phone: 508-763-5253
www.biofence.com

BioFence™ is a one-piece silt fence made from 100% biodegradable materials. Beech or maple stakes measuring 42" or 48" x 1-1/8" are sewn into 7- to 10-oz., 20-mesh seine weave Hessian Cloth composite stiffened with cornstarch. Aspen wood fiber matting is stitched to the front. This product installs more quickly than conventional silt fence/straw bale combinations and is cost-competitive. Custom fences are available for specific applications.

BioNet Erosion-Control Mats

North American Green
14649 Hwy 41 N
Evansville, IN 47725

Toll-free: 800-772-2040
Phone: 812-867-6632
www.nagreen.com

North American Green offers 100% biodegradable (as opposed to photodegradable) rolled erosion control blankets, including the netting and thread. The woven net structure reduces the risk of wildlife entrapment and prevents fiber loss. Matrices are agricultural straw or a combination of straw and coir (coconut fiber). Products are available to meet specific applications and functional longevities. 6.7' x 108' rolls cover 80 yd2. North American Green also offers erosion control blankets made with photodegradable polypropylene netting, and blanket pins made of biodegradable PLA plastic. North American Green is a wholly-owned, stand-alone subsidiary of Tensar International Corporation with headquarters in Atlanta, Ga.

Coir Erosion-Control Products

RoLanka International, Inc.
155 Andrew Dr.
Stockbridge, GA 30281

Toll-free: 800-760-3215
Phone: 770-506-8211
www.rolanka.com

RoLanka manufactures a full line of coir-based products for soil erosion control, sediment control, and streambank stabilization.

Curlex NetFree Erosion-Control Blankets

American Excelsior Company
850 Ave. H, E
Arlington, TX 76011

Toll-free: 800-777-7645
Phone: 817-385-3500
www.curlex.com

Curlex® NetFree™ is a 100% biodegradable excelsior erosion control blanket made with softly barbed, interlocking, curled, Great Lakes Aspen excelsior wood fibers (80% >6" long) stitched together with biodegradable thread. These blankets are free from weed seed, chemical additives, tackifiers, and paper products. These netless blankets will not entrap wildlife or pets, tangle in mowing equipment, present future environmental risk, or trip pedestrians. 8' wide X 90' long roll which equals 80 sq. yards of blanket per roll; NetFree can be used in low-flow channels up to 1-lb/ft2 shear stress; recommended for 3:1 maximum slopes. American Excelsior Company has 10 locations in the U.S. and over 100 distributor partners.

KoirMat and KoirLog

Nedia Enterprises, Inc.
22187 Vantage Pointe Pl.
Ashburn, VA 20148

Toll-free: 888-725-6999
Phone: 571-223-0200
www.nedia.com

Nedia Enterprises manufactures a full line of primarily coir-based erosion control products. KoirMat™ erosion control matting, made from 100% coir fiber, is suitable for a wide variety of applications. KoirLog™ is a 100% coconut fiber "log" for shoreline and stream channel erosion control applications. KoirLog is available in 12", 16", and 20" diameters and is typically 10' to 20' long.

Slopetame2

Invisible Structures, Inc.
1600 Jackson St., Ste. 310
Golden, CO 80401

Toll-free: 800-233-1510
Phone: 303-233-8383
www.invisiblestructures.com

Slopetame2 is a plastic grid product made from 100% injection-molded recycled HDPE with varying amounts of post-consumer and post-industrial content. Slopetame2 is designed to provide immediate erosion control in permanent installations on weak or eroding slopes by resisting undercutting water and soil movement. It has a geotextile backing.

Flexible Paving

While concrete is considered rigid paving, asphalt falls under the flexible paving label. Various materials can be added to or substituted for asphalt in pavement to improve environmental characteristics. Recycled tire rubber is the most common such additive. Though problems occurred in the past when recycled tire rubber was used to constitute 25% of the paving mixture, current mixtures with 18-20% of the material yield promising results. Recycled asphalt shingles have also been processed into flexible pavement components, and some natural-resin binders have been used in some pavement products.

Foamed Asphalt

Chamberlain Contractors, Inc.
162 Lafayette Ave.
Laurel, MD 20727

Toll-free: 866-670-1234
Phone: 301-725-4330
www.chamberlaincontractors.com

Foamed asphalt uses crushed, recycled asphalt pavement removed from existing roads or parking lots as aggregate for new paving. The aggregate is mixed with a small amount of water and hot bitumen oil, creating a foamed texture. No virgin aggregate is used, and the aggregate doesn't need to be kiln-dried or pre-heated, as is required with standard hot-mix asphalt. Foamed asphalt has slightly less structural strength than traditional hot-mix, so a slightly thicker application is required to meet the same performance standards; however, foamed asphalt costs substantially less to produce (financially and environmentally). A wear layer of standard hot asphalt is required. Popular overseas, foamed asphalt is making inroads in domestic markets.

Hydro-Mulching

Hydro-seeding is often the most effective way to sow grass seed over large areas. Cellulose mulch made from recycled newspaper is used as a primary component of hydro-seeding sprays. It prevents erosion, retains soil moisture, and encourages seed germination. There are slight differences among products, but all are similar.

A W I Mulch

All-Weather Insulation Co., LLC
19 W. Industry Dr.
Springfield, KY 40069

Phone: 859-336-3651

A W I Mulch contains recycled newspaper.

Applegate Mulch

Applegate Insulation Manufacturing
1000 Highview Dr.
Webberville, MI 48892

Toll-free: 800-627-7536
Phone: 517-521-3545
www.applegateinsulation.com

Applegate mulch is made from recycled paper. The manufacturer has certified the following recycled-content levels (by weight): total recovered material 99% typical, 99% guaranteed; post-consumer material 99% typical, 99% guaranteed.

Astro-Mulch

Thermo-Kool of Alaska
P.O. Box 230085
Anchorage, AK 99507

Phone: 907-563-3644

Astro-Mulch contains recycled newspaper. The manufacturer has certified the following recycled-content levels (by weight): total recovered material 99% typical, 85% guaranteed; post-consumer material 99% typical, 85% guaranteed.

Beno-Vert

Benolec, Ltd.
1451 Nobel St.
Sainte-Julie, QC J3E 1Z4 Canada

Phone: 450-922-2000
www.benolec.com

Beno-vert hydro-mulch contains recycled newspaper.

Climatizer Hydroseeding Mulch

Climatizer Insulation, Ltd.
120 Claireville Dr.
Etobicoke, ON M9W 5Y3 Canada

Toll-free: 866-871-5495
Phone: 416-798-1235
www.climatizer.com

Climatizer Hydroseeding Mulch contains recycled newspaper.

EcoSeries Hydromulch

Canfor Panel and Fibre
430 Canfor Ave.
New Westminster, BC V3L 5G2 Canada

Toll-free: 800-363-8873
Phone: 604-521-9650
www.canforpfd.com

A division of Canadian Forest Products Ltd., Canfor's EcoSeries of biodegradable hydromulches are made from long-strand softwood fibers (salvaged from logging operations), with varying amounts of nontoxic binder (guar gum, hydrocolloids) and mineral activators. The EcoAegis, EcoFibre, EcoMatrix, and EcoFlex lines accommodate variations of slope, expected weather conditions, anticipated germination speed, and the erosion susceptibility of the soil. Wood content varies between products from 90% to 100% by weight. The EcoFlex line (which is not available in the U.S. market) contains photodegradable (rather than biodegradable) polypropylene fibers and is not specified here.

EnviroGuard and Promat

Tascon, Inc.
7607 Fairview St.
P.O. Box 41846
Houston, TX 77241

Toll-free: 800-937-1774
Phone: 713-937-0900
www.tasconindustries.com

EnviroGuard™ landscape mulch, manufactured from recycled paper and plant materials, contains no chemical herbicides. It creates a solid layer when surface-applied as a weed block; tilled under, it provides organic matter. PROMAT is a hydro-seeding mulch manufactured from recycled paper. The manufacturer has certified the following recycled-content levels (by weight): total recovered material 85% typical, 85% guaranteed; post-consumer material 85% typical, 85% guaranteed.

Fiber Mulch

Thermoguard Insulation Co. LLC
125 N. Dyer Rd.
Spokane, WA 99212

Toll-free: 800-541-0579
Phone: 509-535-4600
www.service-partners.com

Thermoguard's hydro-mulch contains recycled newspaper.

Fiber Turf

Erie Energy Products, Inc.
1400 Irwin Dr.
Erie, PA 16505

Toll-free: 800-233-1810
Phone: 814-454-2828

Fiber Turf is made from recycled newspaper.

Fibrex

Paul's Insulation
P.O. Box 115
Vergas, MN 56587

Toll-free: 800-627-5190
Phone: 218-342-2800

Fibrex hydro-mulch is made from 100% post-consumer recycled newspaper.

Hydro-Spray

National Fiber
50 Depot St.
Belchertown, MA 01007

Toll-free: 800-282-7711
Phone: 413-283-8747
www.nationalfiber.com

Hydro-Spray hydro-seeding mulch contains a minimum of 99.5% recycled, over-issue newsprint. According to the manufacturer, it is guaranteed to be clean and free of plastics and other foreign material.

Hydro-Spray Mulch

Profile Products, LLC
750 Lake Cook Rd., Ste. 440
Buffalo Grove, IL 60089

Toll-free: 800-207-6457
Phone: 847-215-1144
www.profileproducts.com

Hydro-Spray Mulch contains recycled newspaper.

Natural-Fiber Hydromulch

Verdyol Plant Research Ltd.
5009 Concession 13, R.R. #4
Cookstown, ON L0L 1L0 Canada

Toll-free: 866-280-7327
Phone: 204-378-2142
www.verdyol.ca

Verdyol Plant Research offers hydromulches made with various mixtures of post-consumer recycled newsprint, weed-free natural straw fiber, raw cotton fiber, and vegetable gum carbohydrate stabilizer. Non-toxic liquid and powder tackifiers are also available.

Nu-Wool HydroGreen

Nu-Wool Co., Inc.
2472 Port Sheldon St.
Jenison, MI 49428

Toll-free: 800-748-0128
Phone: 616-669-0100
www.nuwool.com

Nu-Wool® HydroGreen™ hydroseeding mulch is made from 100% recycled paper fibers and contains an organic dye and wetting agent.

Irrigation

Over half of urban water use in the U.S. is for landscape irrigation. Before researching irrigation systems, consider water-saving landscapes with drought-hardy native plantings to reduce or eliminate water, energy, and chemical use. If irrigation is needed, high-tech, permanent irrigation systems that monitor soil and atmospheric conditions can save a great deal of water simply by not running when irrigation isn't needed. Drip irrigation systems release measured quantities of water directly to the soil surrounding the intended plants instead of spraying an entire area, using water more efficiently and greatly reducing evaporative loss. Look for products with intelligent sensing, long warranties that indicate good durability, and such environmental features as recycled content. Consider integrated systems that re-use water that would otherwise be sent down the drain.

Fiskars Soaker Hose and Sprinkler Hose

Fiskars, Inc. - Fiskars Garden Tools
780 Carolina St.
Sauk City, WI 53583

Toll-free: 800-500-4849
www.fiskars.com

Fiskars Soaker Hose and Sprinkler Hose, formerly Moisture Master, are products that contain 65% post-consumer recycled rubber from tires.

Graywater Treatment Systems

Clivus Multrum, Inc.
15 Union St.
Lawrence, MA 01840

Toll-free: 800-425-4887
Phone: 978-725-5591
www.clivusmultrum.com

Clivus Multrum custom-designs graywater irrigation systems for commercial and residential applications.

ReWater System

ReWater Systems, Inc.
P.O. Box 210171
Chula Vista, CA 91921

Phone: 619-421-9121
www.rewater.com

The ReWater® System is a graywater irrigation system comprised of two primary sections. A self-cleaning filter captures and pressurizes the water, which is then released through either a surface or subsurface drip irrigation network, depending on your state code. An electronic controller operates all 156 filtration and irrigation functions with 21 stations capable of being programmed for fresh water or drip of recycled water, with four independent irrigation programs. The electronic controller adds supplemental fresh water to recycling stations when required by the programs.

WeatherTRAK

HydroPoint Data Systems, Inc.
1726 Corporate Cir.
Petaluma, CA 94954

Toll-free: 800-362-8774
Phone: 707-769-9696
www.weathertrak.com

The WeatherTRAK irrigation control systems (available in commercial and residential models) automatically create watering schedules based on parameters that include plant and soil types, sun exposure, and slope. Each watering zone is subsequently adjusted automatically each day based on analyzed NOAA weather data received from HydroPoint's ET Everywhere™ satellite communications service, which eliminates the need for a standalone weather station by delivering geographically specific weather data. Remote management and monitoring via the internet is available. The system is also compatible with rain sensors that can override watering instructions (i.e., not irrigate if the ground is wet).

Landscape Edging

Landscape edging products are good applications for recycled plastics and tire-rubber. The material is impervious, resistant to root penetration, will not rot, and structural requirements are minimal.

Lawn Edging and Tree Rings

Phoenix Recycled Products, Inc.
360 W. Church St.
Batesburg, SC 29006

Phone: 803-532-4425
www.permamulch.com

Phoenix Recycled Products fabricates lawn edging and tree rings from recycled tire-rubber. (Tree rings are a mat that forms a weed barrier around trees.) The manufacturer has certified the following recycled-content levels, by weight: total recovered material 85% typical, 85% guaranteed; post-consumer material 85% typical, 85% guaranteed.

Recycled-Plastic Landscape Products

Master Mark Plastics
One Master Mark Dr.
P.O. Box 662
Albany, MN 56307

Toll-free: 800-535-4838
Phone: 320-845-2111
www.mastermark.com

Master Mark makes a variety of landscape products, such as lawn edging, lattice, downspout splash blocks, and privacy fencing from recycled HDPE plastic. According to the manufacturer, they currently recycle over 1 billion post-consumer HDPE plastic containers per year, and boast over 50 million feet of quality landscape edging installed every year. The manufacturer has certified the following recycled-content levels (by weight): post-consumer material 100% typical, 100% guaranteed.

Landscape Timbers

Landscape timbers provide an appropriate use of low-grade, commingled recycled plastics that little else can be produced from. Lighter-weight hollow extrusions, generally made from HDPE, require less energy for shipping. Many manufacturers of recycled plastic lumber also produce landscape timbers.

Aztec Recycled-Plastic Lumber

Amazing Recycled Products, Inc.
P.O. Box 312
Denver, CO 80201

Toll-free: 800-241-2174
Phone: 303-699-7693
www.amazingrecycled.com

Amazing Recycled Products manufactures lumber, timber, parking stops and bollards with recycled HDPE. Their Aztec line of park furnishings includes benches, chairs, picnic tables, and trash receptacles. The manufacturer has certified the following recycled-content levels (by weight): total recovered material 100% typical, 100% guaranteed; post-consumer material 80% typical, 75% guaranteed.

Barco Recycled-Content Products

Barco Products
11 N. Batavia Ave.
Batavia, IL 60510

Toll-free: 800-338-2697
Phone: 630-879-0084
www.barcoproducts.com

Barco Products offers site furnishings, landscape timbers, and traffic devices made with recycled content, including dozens of styles of picnic tables and park benches made with recycled commingled HDPE and LDPE averaging 40% post-consumer, as well as planters and waste receptacles made from recycled HDPE (90 to 100% post-consumer). Landscape Timbers are made from 100% recycled commingled HDPE and LDPE, sized as railroad ties with premolded holes for rebar reinforcement and interlocking edges for stacking stability. Each timber weighs 42 lbs, about half that of most plastic landscape timbers. 100% recycled tire rubber speed bumps and 100% recycled plastic speed bumps are offered, and colored wheel stops made of 95% recycled commingled HDPE and LDPE. Gray wheel stops contain 85% recycled PVC. Bollards are made from 96% recycled commingled LDPE and HDPE (50 to 80% post-industrial).

Bedford Technology Recycled-Plastic Products

Bedford Technology, LLC
2424 Armour Rd.
P.O. Box 609
Worthington, MN 56187

Toll-free: 800-721-9037
Phone: 507-372-5558
www.plasticboards.com

Bedford Technology offers plastic lumber and other products made with post-consumer recycled HDPE and LDPE. Their lumber is available in a variety of dimensions, including 5/4 decking, two-by, and large timbers up to 12x12, in black, brown, gray, and cedar with other colors available. Parking stops and speed bumps are also offered, as well as plastic paneling that can be used as a substitute for plywood. Bedford's ForeSite Designs(R) line of recycled-plastic site furnishings includes picnic tables, benches, and waste receptacles. The manufacturer has certified the following recycled-content levels (by weight): total recovered material 99% typical, 99% guaranteed; post-consumer material 65% typical, 50% guaranteed.

Ecoboard Plastic Lumber

Trelleborg Engineered Products, Inc.
3470 Martinsburg Pike
P.O. Box 98
Clearbrook, VA 22624

Phone: 540-667-5191
www.trelleborg.com

Ecoboard lumber is manufactured in a wide array of dimensions and colors. These products contain recycled HDPE and LDPE, as well as UV-stabilization, flame-retardant, and strength additives. Landscape timbers in 4x4, 5x5, and 6x6 contain fiberglass reinforcing. Ecoboard marine pilings have been tested as a friction pile where load-bearing capability needed to exceed 15 tons of vertical loading with a minimum of "creep" or failure, according to the manufacturer; the pilings tested to a 60-ton load, at which time the test was stopped. The manufacturer has certified the following recycled-content levels (by weight): total recovered material 100% typical, 100% guaranteed; post-consumer material 90% typical, 80% guaranteed.

EPS Recycled-Plastic Lumber and Outdoor Furniture

Engineered Plastic Systems
885 Church Rd.
Elgin, IL 60123

Phone: 847-289-8383
www.epsplasticlumber.com

Engineered Plastic Systems (EPS) Bear Board plastic lumber is typically made from a minimum 51% post-consumer recycled HDPE and is available in a variety of sizes and colors, with a smooth or wood-grain finish. Fiberglass-reinforced structural plastic lumber is also available. Their plastic landscape timbers (from the same feedstock) are available in a wide variety of colors and sizes. Durapoly plastic "plywood" is available in white and gray, in thicknesses ranging from 1/4" to 1-1/2". All of these products are covered by a 50-year limited warranty.

Landscape Timbers

American Recycled Plastic, Inc.
1500 Main St.
Palm Bay, FL 32905

Toll-free: 866-674-1525
Phone: 321-674-1525
www.itsrecycled.com

American Recycled Plastic manufactures landscape timbers from recycled HDPE plastic. The manufacturer has certified the following recycled-content levels (by weight): total recovered material 100% typical, 100% guaranteed; post-consumer material 80% typical, 80% guaranteed.

PlasTEAK Plastic Lumber

PlasTEAK
3563 Copley Rd.
P.O. Box 4290
Akron, OH 44321

Toll-free: 800-320-1841
Phone: 330-668-2587
www.plasteak.com

PlasTEAK is made with 100% post-consumer recycled HDPE in a paraffin base the boards become more slip-resistant when wet. Stock material includes solid (molded) and hollow (extruded) dimension lumber in a variety of sizes and colors. Trim and sheet goods are also available. Landscape timbers of 6 x 6 x 8' have a structural ribbed design that allows them to weigh less than half as much as wood timbers while maintaining strength. Landscape timbers have pre-molded holes for rebar reinforcement to facilitate installation.

Recycled-Plastic Decking, Docks, and Timbers

Plastic Lumber Yard, LLC
220 Washington St.
Norristown, PA 19401

Phone: 610-277-3900
www.plasticlumberyard.com

Plastic Lumber Yard, LLC, manufactures recycled-plastic lumber. The Forever Deck and ForeverDock Floating Dock Kits are constructed with recycled plastic lumber made from 100% recycled HDPE. Landscape grade plastic lumber in various profiles and colors is also available. The manufacturer has certified the following recycled-content levels (by weight): total recovered material 100% typical, 100% guaranteed; post-consumer material 30% typical.

Recycled-Plastic Posts

XPotential Products Inc.
St. Boniface Postal Sta.
P.O. Box 126
Winnipeg, MB R2H 3B4 Canada

Toll-free: 800-863-6619
Phone: 204-224-3933
www.xpotentialproducts.com

XPotential offers parking stops, landscape timbers, and fence posts made with recycled materials, including auto shredder residue as well as HDPE and LDPE plastics. Impact-Curb parking stops are approximately 5-1/4" x 8" in 6' or 8' lengths, and 4" x 6" in 6' or 8' lengths. Interlocking landscape timbers measure 2-1/2" x 3-1/2" x 95" and weigh 36 lbs. each. Impact-Post comes in two sizes (6" x 6" x 8' and 4" x 4" x 8') and is appropriate for landscaping and fencing posts. All the XPotential products come with a limited lifetime warranty. The manufacturer has certified the following recycled-content levels (by weight): total recovered material 100% typical, 100% guaranteed; post-consumer material 85% typical, 85% guaranteed.

Recycled-Plastic Products

American Recreational Products
1535 Locust Avenue
Bohemia, NY 11716

Toll-free: 800-663-4096
Phone: 631-244-0011
www.americanrecreational.com

American Recreational Products offers benches, picnic tables, landscape ties, wheel stops, speed bumps, and marine docks made from 100% recycled commingled plastics. Products are typically made from 50% post-consumer plastic and 50% pre-consumer plastic.

Recycled-Plastic Products

American Recycled Plastic, Inc.
1500 Main St.
Palm Bay, FL 32905

Toll-free: 866-674-1525
Phone: 321-674-1525
www.itsrecycled.com

American Recycled Plastic manufactures a range of products from recycled HDPE, including lumber and timbers, car stops, speed bumps and humps, and vehicle barriers. They also offer a wide variety of recycled-HDPE site furnishings, including benches, outdoor tables, waste receptacles, mailboxes, planters, custom wildlife structures, and bicycle racks. The manufacturer has certified the following recycled-content levels (by weight): total recovered material 100% typical, 100% guaranteed; post-consumer material 80% typical, 80% guaranteed.

Site Furnishings and Materials

Inteq Corp.
35800 Glen Dr.
Eastlake, OH 44095

Phone: 440-953-0550
www.4-inteqcorp.com

Inteq's benches and picnic tables are made from recycled HDPE plastic. Tables are either standard 6' or 8' length or hexagonal. Benches come in a variety of styles and can be custom designed. Inteq's waste receptacles and planters contain recycled HDPE plastic and are available in many styles including custom production. All are offered in a variety of colors. Recycled content is up to 100% (minimum 20% post-consumer). Inteq nonstructural landscape timbers are available in multiple colors up to 12' in length in standard sizes of 4x4, 4x6, and 6x6. Decking and railing material is also made from recycled HDPE plastic and is available in multiple colors.

SmartTie

Curb Appeal Materials, LTD
3824 N. Johnsburg Rd.
McHenry, IL 60050

Phone: 815-344-7926
www.vortexcomposites.com

SmartTie is made with 100% commingled plastics, including synthetic carpet material, from post-consumer and industrial sources in a patented cold-extrusion process. Colorants can be added for aesthetic effect. The material is more dense than wood, and has a lower burn rate; it doesn't warp or degrade, and is recyclable. It cuts and machines with woodworking tools. SmartTie is available in solid, hollow, and channeled versions in many dimensions. SmartTie can be used to control noise from highways and other sources. The manufacturer indicates that the material is not affected by freeze-thaw cycling.

The Plastic Lumber Company

The Plastic Lumber Company, Inc.
115 W. Bartges St.
Akron, OH 44311

Toll-free: 800-886-8990
Phone: 330-762-8989
www.plasticlumber.com

The Plastic Lumber Company offers approximately 20 different profiles of dimensional plastic lumber available in 12 different colors. Sizes range from 1/2" x 2-1/2" to 4x6. Commercial and residential decking is also available. Recycled content is 97% post-consumer.

Native Plants and Seeds

Landscaping with native plants adapted to your local climate and not requiring irrigation, fertilizers, or pesticides will result in lower environmental impact than conventional lawns and landscaping with nonnative plantings. Included here are several of the leading suppliers of native seed and seedlings. While these companies can be good sources, you should start by looking for native plant nurseries in your immediate area, as they're likely to have specific genotypes best adapted to your region.

Native Plant Supplier

Bitterroot Restoration, Inc.
445 Quast Ln.
Corvallis, MT 59828

Toll-free: 888-892-4991
Phone: 406-961-4991
www.bitterrootrestoration.com

Bitterroot Restoration maintains extensive offerings of native plants appropriate to the western U.S. The company, founded in 1986, provides restoration design and planning services in addition to selling plants. "Plant salvage" is among the services offered—transplanting of plants from land that will be developed. Comprehensive website; catalog available. Locations also in California and Washington.

Native Plant Supplier

The Reveg Edge/Ecoseeds
P.O. Box 609
Redwood City, CA 94064

Phone: 650-325-7333
www.ecoseeds.com/nature.html

The Reveg Edge, a division of the Redwood City Seed Company, is a unique supplier of native plants in that its plants are custom-grown with seeds supplied by the buyer that were collected from the ecosystem for which the plants are intended. In this way, the established plantings will be appropriate to the intended microclimate. This process allows the company to supply native plants to any place in the United States. The company, founded in 1971, also offers a wide range of hard-to-find and heirloom vegetable, herb, and medicinal plants under the Ecoseeds™ brand name, in addition to in-depth classes and consulting on establishment of native plants.

Native Seed and Plant Supplier

Ernst Conservation Seeds
9006 Mercer Pike
Meadville, PA 16335

Toll-free: 800-873-3321
Phone: 814-336-2404
www.ernstseed.com

Ernst Conservation Seeds is one of the few native seed and plant suppliers in the Northeast. The company was founded in 1963 and specializes in native wildflowers and grasses, legumes, cover crops, bioengineering materials, wetland restoration and wildlife habitat mixes, and naturalized conservation species.

Native Seed and Plant Supplier

Ion Exchange, Inc.
1878 Old Mission Dr.
Harpers Ferry, IA 52146

Toll-free: 800-291-2143
www.ionxchange.com

Ion Exchange was founded in 1988 and supplies seedlings and/or seed of more than 250 native grasses and wildflowers. Their selection of grasses, sedges, and rushes is particularly large, with over 40 species—most of which are available in plugs, pots, or seed (by the packet, ounce, or pound). The company has both a printed catalog and an online catalog, which allows searches based on ecosystem, type of plant, and so forth.

Native Seed and Plant Supplier

LaFayette Home Nursery, Inc.
RR 1 Box 1A
LaFayette, IL 61449

Phone: 309-995-3311
lafayettenursery.com

One of the oldest suppliers of seed and plants, LaFayette Home Nursery was founded in 1887 and is now run by third- and fourth-generation family members. The company's Prairie Department, which focuses on native plants, was established in 1970.

Native Seed and Plant Supplier

Native American Seed
127 N. 16th St.
Junction, TX 76849

Toll-free: 800-728-4043
www.seedsource.com

Serving Texas and the arid Southwest, Native American Seed has a superb website with extensive information, including photos of most of the native plant species they sell. The company, founded in 1974, is committed to supplying seeds that were produced using source seed harvested from sites within the ecoregion being served. In this way, they are able to retain the original genetic integrity of the plants. The parent company is Neiman Environments, Inc., which specializes in large-scale restoration projects of abused, neglected, and/or overgrazed land. The company supplies seed only (from seedlings) from more than 171 species.

Native Seed and Plant Supplier

Prairie Nursery, Inc.
P.O. Box 306
Westfield, WI 53964

Toll-free: 800-476-9453
www.prairienursery.com

Founded in 1972, Prairie Nursery's mission is "to preserve native plants and animals by helping people create attractive, nonpolluting natural landscapes that can support a diversity of wildlife." The company offers over 100 wildflowers and dozens of grasses, sedges, and bulrushes in seed form, individual plants, or both, as well as many seed mixes and collections of plants for special purposes. Their free, 66-page catalog and planting guide includes more specific information.

Native Seed and Plant Supplier

Prairie Restorations, Inc.
P.O. Box 327
Princeton, MN 55371

Phone: 763-389-4342
www.prairieresto.com

Prairie Restorations supplies native seed and plants for prairie restoration work in the Upper Midwest, offering distribution within a 200-mile radius of their two facilities in Princeton and Hawley, Minnesota—including parts of Wisconsin, Iowa, and the Dakotas. Installation, land management, and consultation services are also available.

Native Seed and Plant Supplier

S&S Seeds, Inc.
P.O. Box 1275
Carpinteria, CA 93014

Phone: 805-684-0436
www.ssseeds.com

Founded in 1975, S&S Seeds is a wholesale producer and supplier of more than 900 plant species including wildflowers, native grasses, and erosion-control seed mixes. The company also offers a line of erosion-control products, including EarthGuard, Flexterra, Bonded Fiber Matrices, Greenfix Erosion Control Blankets, and soil stabilizers.

Native Seed and Plant Supplier

Taylor Creek Restoration Nurseries
17921 Smith Rd.
Brodhead, WI 53520

Phone: 608-897-8641
www.appliedeco.com

Taylor Creek Restoration Nurseries was founded in the late 1970s as the companion company to Applied Ecological Services, an ecological consulting and restoration contracting firm. Taylor Creek Nurseries offers more than 400 species of native plants that are grown on 300 acres and supplied throughout the Midwest. Seeds, plants, trees and shrubs are available.

Operation and Maintenance of Plantings

Maintenance products for plantings include such things as soil amendments. Look first to nonchemical, water- and energy-saving landscapes. Use organic fertilizers or fertilizers produced from wastes diverted from landfills. Due to the shipping energy use (and costs), regional sources are generally preferred.

Cedar Grove Compost

Cedar Grove Composting, Inc.
7343 E. Marginal Way S.
Seattle, WA 98108

Toll-free: 888-832-3008
Phone: 206-832-3000
www.cedar-grove.com

Cedar Grove Composting, Inc. operates the largest independently owned yard waste composting facility in the U.S. The company started by making composted products from a curbside yard-waste collection program in Seattle. Its technology successfully includes pre- and post-consumer food wastes collected in major metropolitan areas. The manufacturer has certified the following recycled-content levels (by weight): total recovered material 100% typical.

EnviroGuard and Promat

Tascon, Inc.
7607 Fairview St.
P.O. Box 41846
Houston, TX 77241

Toll-free: 800-937-1774
Phone: 713-937-0900
www.tasconindustries.com

EnviroGuard™ landscape mulch, manufactured from recycled paper and plant materials, contains no chemical herbicides. It creates a solid layer when surface-applied as a weed block; tilled under, it provides organic matter. PROMAT is a hydro-seeding mulch manufactured from recycled paper. The manufacturer has certified the following recycled-content levels (by weight): total recovered material 85% typical, 85% guaranteed; post-consumer material 85% typical, 85% guaranteed.

Premium Compost and Lawn Topdressing

Central Maui Landfill / Maui Eko-Systems
P.O. Box 1065
Puunene, HI 96784

Phone: 808-572-8844

Premium Compost and Lawn Topdressing are soil amendments that are batch-tested by independent labs and certified by the Hawaii Department of Health. These products are available in 1-1/2 ft3 bags, 1 yd3 bulk bags, and in bulk.

Parking Bumpers (Car Stops)

Recycled plastics and rubber can be used for parking stops, diverting material from the waste stream and providing products with lower embodied energy than portland cement-based concrete products. In addition, the lighter weight of plastic parking bumpers (40-50 lbs. versus 250-300 lbs.) reduces transportation energy consumption and cost of shipping. Plastic parking stops are easily installed with 5/8" rebar stakes, and they never need painting.

Aztec Plastic Parking Stops and Bollards

Amazing Recycled Products, Inc.
P.O. Box 312
Denver, CO 80201

Toll-free: 800-241-2174
Phone: 303-699-7693
www.amazingrecycled.com

Amazing Recycled Products manufactures parking stops as well as flat-top, plateau-top, and chamfered-top bollards (also available customized) from recycled HDPE. The parking stops are 6'–8' long and are offered as industrial heavy duty and standard. Custom lengths are also available. Colors include brown, yellow, gray, blue, white and black. The manufacturer has certified the following recycled-content levels (by weight): total recovered material 100% typical, 100% guaranteed; post-consumer material 80% typical, 75% guaranteed.

Barco Recycled-Content Products

Barco Products
11 N. Batavia Ave.
Batavia, IL 60510

Toll-free: 800-338-2697
Phone: 630-879-0084
www.barcoproducts.com

Barco Products offers site furnishings, landscape timbers, and traffic devices made with recycled content, including dozens of styles of picnic tables and park benches made with recycled commingled HDPE and LDPE averaging 40% post-consumer, as well as planters and waste receptacles made from recycled HDPE (90 to 100% post-consumer). Landscape Timbers are made from 100% recycled commingled HDPE and LDPE, sized as railroad ties with premolded holes for rebar reinforcement and interlocking edges for stacking stability. Each timber weighs 42 lbs, about half that of most plastic landscape timbers. 100% recycled tire rubber speed bumps and 100% recycled plastic speed bumps are offered, and colored wheel stops made of 95% recycled commingled HDPE and LDPE. Gray wheel stops contain 85% recycled PVC. Bollards are made from 96% recycled commingled LDPE and HDPE (50 to 80% post-industrial).

Bedford Technology Recycled-Plastic Products

Bedford Technology, LLC
2424 Armour Rd.
P.O. Box 609
Worthington, MN 56187

Toll-free: 800-721-9037
Phone: 507-372-5558
www.plasticboards.com

Bedford Technology offers plastic lumber and other products made with post-consumer recycled HDPE and LDPE. Their lumber is available in a variety of dimensions, including 5/4 decking, two-by, and large timbers up to 12x12, in black, brown, gray, and cedar with other colors available. Parking stops and speed bumps are also offered, as well as plastic paneling that can be used as a substitute for plywood. Bedford's ForeSite Designs(R) line of recycled-plastic site furnishings includes picnic tables, benches, and waste receptacles. The manufacturer has certified the following recycled-content levels (by weight): total recovered material 99% typical, 99% guaranteed; post-consumer material 65% typical, 50% guaranteed.

Car Stops

ECG, Inc.
104 Corporate Dr.
Elizabeth City, NC 27909

Phone: 252-333-1002
www.glass-recycling.com/home.asp

ECG manufactures DOT Class B fiber- and rebar-reinforced concrete car stops using recycled glass (principally from post-consumer sources) as the aggregate. Normal car stop profiles are 6"h x 8"w x 72" and weigh 180 lbs; low-profile stops are 4"h x 6"w x 72" and weigh 80 lbs. The mounting holes contain PVC sleeves to prevent freeze/thaw damage caused by standing water. Eight standard integral colors are available; custom colors may be ordered. ECG offers a variety of cast-concrete products made with recycled-glass aggregate.

Car Stops

Kay Park Recreation Corp.
1301 Pine St.
P.O. Box 477
Janesville, IA 50647

Phone: 319-987-2313
www.kaypark.com

Kay Park Recreation's Car Stops are made from 96% post-consumer recycled, commingled plastic.

Car Stops and Speed Bumps

Plastic Recycling of Iowa Falls, Inc.
10252 Hwy. 65
Iowa Falls, IA 50126

Toll-free: 800-338-1438
Phone: 641-648-5073
www.hammersplastic.com

Plastic Recycling of Iowa Falls, formerly Hammer's Plastic Recycling, manufactures yellow, blue, and gray car stops and yellow speed bumps from recycled commingled HDPE, LDPE, LLDPE, and other miscellaneous plastics. The manufacturer has certified the following recycled-content levels (by weight): total recovered material 100% typical, 100% guaranteed; post-consumer material 50% typical, 50% guaranteed.

Parking Stops and Speed Bumps

The Plastic Lumber Company, Inc.
115 W. Bartges St.
Akron, OH 44311

Toll-free: 800-886-8990
Phone: 330-762-8989
www.plasticlumber.com

The Plastic Lumber Company's Parking Stops are made from recycled plastic, are available in 3', 4', or 6' lengths, and come in yellow, white, gray, blue, and black. Bright yellow Speed Bumps are 4', 6', or 9' in length. The manufacturer has certified the following recycled-content levels (by weight): post-consumer material 95% typical, 70% guaranteed.

Parking Stops, Speed Bumps, and Bollards

Litchfield Industries
4 Industrial Dr.
Litchfield, MI 49252

Toll-free: 800-542-5282
Phone: 517-542-2988
www.litchfieldindustries.com

Litchfield Industries manufactures parking stops, speed bumps, and bollards made from 100% post-consumer plastic. Parking stops are 3', 4', or 6' long and are available in yellow, blue, white, gray, and black. Speed bumps are 3', 6', or 9' long and yellow in color.

Parking Stops, Speed Bumps, and Bollards

Recycled Plastic Man, Inc.
P.O. Box 609
Placida, FL 33946

Toll-free: 800-253-7742
Phone: 941-698-1060
www.recycledplasticman.com

Recycled Plastic Man manufactures parking stops, speed bumps, and bollards from post-consumer recycled plastics (primarily HDPE). The manufacturer has certified the following recycled-content levels (by weight): total recovered material 100% guaranteed; post-consumer material 100% guaranteed.

Park-It and Easy Rider

GNR Technologies, Inc.
990 Upton
LaSalle, QC H8R 2T9 Canada

Toll-free: 800-641-4143
Phone: 514-366-6116
www.gnrtech.com

Park-It and Easy Rider are 100% recycled-rubber parking stops and speed bumps, respectively. These durable products are black with reflective yellow tape markings.

Pilot Rock Site Furnishings

R. J. Thomas Manufacturing Co., Inc.
P.O. Box 946
Cherokee, IA 51012

Toll-free: 800-762-5002
Phone: 712-225-5115
www.pilotrock.com

Pilot Rock Site Furnishings are made from recycled HDPE and LDPE plastic. The Pilot Rock line includes benches, picnic tables, waste receptacles, and car stops. The manufacturer has certified the following recycled-content levels (by weight): total recovered material 100% typical, 100% guaranteed; post-consumer material 75% typical, 60% guaranteed.

PlasTEAK Traffic Control Devices

PlasTEAK
3563 Copley Rd.
P.O. Box 4290
Akron, OH 44321

Toll-free: 800-320-1841
Phone: 330-668-2587
www.plasteak.com

PlasTEAK's parking stops, speed humps, and signage are made with 100% post-consumer recycled HDPE. The stops are available in 4', 6', and 8' lengths, as well as 20" wheel chocks, in standard colors yellow, gray, and blue; white, brown, and black are available by special order. Speed humps come in yellow only, in 4', 6', and 9' lengths. A five-year warranty is provided. Signage is available in a wide range of colors and styles.

Recycled-Plastic Parking Stops

Everlast Plastic Lumber
800 W. Market St.
P.O. Box 367
Auburn, PA 17922

Phone: 570-754-7440
www.everlastlumber.com

Everlast parking stops are made with 100% recycled HPDE (80% post-consumer). They are 6-1/2' long, weigh about 40 lbs, and are available in blue, silver-gray, and yellow.

Recycled-Plastic Posts

XPotential Products Inc.
St. Boniface Postal Sta.
P.O. Box 126
Winnipeg, MB R2H 3B4 Canada

Toll-free: 800-863-6619
Phone: 204-224-3933
www.xpotentialproducts.com

XPotential offers parking stops, landscape timbers, and fence posts made with recycled materials, including auto shredder residue as well as HDPE and LDPE plastics. Impact-Curb parking stops are approximately 5-1/4" x 8" in 6' or 8' lengths, and 4" x 6" in 6' or 8' lengths. Interlocking landscape timbers measure 2-1/2" x 3-1/2" x 95" and weigh 36 lbs. each. Impact-Post comes in two sizes (6" x 6" x 8' and 4" x 4" x 8') and is appropriate for landscaping and fencing posts. All the XPotential products come with a limited lifetime warranty. The manufacturer has certified the following recycled-content levels (by weight): total recovered material 100% typical, 100% guaranteed; post-consumer material 85% typical, 85% guaranteed.

Recycled-Plastic Products

American Recreational Products
1535 Locust Avenue
Bohemia, NY 11716

Toll-free: 800-663-4096
Phone: 631-244-0011
www.americanrecreational.com

American Recreational Products offers benches, picnic tables, landscape ties, wheel stops, speed bumps, and marine docks made from 100% recycled commingled plastics. Products are typically made from 50% post-consumer plastic and 50% pre-consumer plastic.

Recycled-Plastic Products

American Recycled Plastic, Inc.
1500 Main St.
Palm Bay, FL 32905

Toll-free: 866-674-1525
Phone: 321-674-1525
www.itsrecycled.com

American Recycled Plastic manufactures a range of products from recycled HDPE, including lumber and timbers, car stops, speed bumps and humps, and vehicle barriers. They also offer a wide variety of recycled-HDPE site furnishings, including benches, outdoor tables, waste receptacles, mailboxes, planters, custom wildlife structures,

and bicycle racks. The manufacturer has certified the following recycled-content levels (by weight): total recovered material 100% typical, 100% guaranteed; post-consumer material 80% typical, 80% guaranteed.

Recycled-Rubber Parking Curbs

Dinoflex Manufacturing, Ltd.
5590 - 46th Ave. SE
P.O. Box 3309
Salmon Arm, BC V1E 4S1 Canada

Toll-free: 877-713-1899
Phone: 252-832-7780
www.dinoflex.com

Park-Right Parking Curbs are made from 100% recycled tire rubber. These flexible, lightweight curbs can also be used indoors—mounted on the floor or walls—to prevent damage by forklifts, pallet jacks, dollies, and other plant machinery. They will not warp, crack, chip, or rot.

Road and Parking Appurtenances

Traffic & Parking Control Co., Inc. (TAPCO)
800 Wall St.
Elm Grove, WI 53122

Toll-free: 800-236-0112
Phone: 262-814-7000
www.tapconet.com

TAPCO distributes parking control devices made from recycled plastic and rubber, such as wheel stops, bollard covers, speed bumps, and speed humps. The manufacturer has certified the following recycled-content levels (by weight): total recovered material 100% typical, 100% guaranteed; post-consumer material 100% typical, 100% guaranteed.

Traffic and Parking Delineators and Devices

Inteq Corp.
35800 Glen Dr.
Eastlake, OH 44095

Phone: 440-953-0550
www.4-inteqcorp.com

Inteq produces a number of traffic and parking accoutrements. Their Parking Stops and Speed Bumps are made from 100% post-consumer recycled HDPE plastic; speed bumps are yellow, and parking stops are yellow, white, gray, black, or blue. They also produce traffic cones and safety delineators with bases of 100% post-consumer rubber or PVC; tops are made from virgin vinyl to maintain proper safety color. Inteq's A-Frame Barricades are made from 100% post-consumer recycled HDPE in 4' to 16' lengths. Highway Barrels are made from virgin LDPE to maintain safety color, but the barrels' ballasts contain recycled truck-tire rubber. The recycled-content levels for Highway Barrels (by weight) is 80-85% post-consumer material. Type I, II, and III Barriers are made from 75% post-consumer recycled HDPE plastic. The manufacturer has certified the following recycled-content levels (by weight): total recovered material 100% typical, 100% guaranteed; post-consumer material 100% typical, 95% guaranteed.

Pest Control Devices

Termite control in buildings has traditionally been accomplished with pesticides—in the past with chlordane and heptachlor, and more recently with chlorpyrifos. With all of these pesticides no longer in use because of health and environmental concerns, there's tremendous interest in alternatives. Products listed here include totally nontoxic termite barrier systems as well as less toxic, or more precisely targeted, chemical treatments. Termite barriers and full-control bait systems are generally quite expensive.

Basaltic Termite Barrier

Ameron Hawaii
2344 Pahounui Dr.
P.O. Box 29968
Honolulu, HI 96820

Phone: 808-832-9200
www.ameronhawaii.com

Basaltic Termite Barrier is a regionally available product made from basaltic aggregates (a coarse sand) on the Hawaiian Islands. These aggregates, when graded to a specific size, shape, and weight, form an effective, nontoxic barrier to standard subterranean and Formosan termite entry. The aggregates are too large and heavy for termites to move and the spaces between too small to move through.

Exterra

Ensystex, Inc.
P.O. Box 2587
Fayetteville, NC 28302

Toll-free: 888-398-3772
www.exterra.com

The Exterra® Termite Interception and Baiting System is similar to the Sentricon System, using a chitin synthesis-inhibitor called diflubenzuron. A unique feature of Exterra's bait station, the Labyrinth, is the ability to install pesticide in the bait core without disturbing termites feeding on the bait box perimeter.

Mite-Out

Hohmann & Barnard, Inc.
30 Rasons Ct.
P.O. Box 5270
Hauppauge, NY 11788-0270

Phone: 631-234-0600
www.h-b.com

Mite-Out from Hohmann & Barnard is a soft copper termite flashing adhered to a closed-cell polyethylene foam sill seal, providing termite protection while contributing to the airtightness of the building envelope in a location that can be troublesome to detail. The flexible, asphalt-free product is compatible with any adhesive, caulk, or sealant. Mite-Out is available in 8-, 10-, and 12-inch widths, in 50-foot long rolls.

Roach and Ant Baits

Blue Diamond, LLC
P.O. Box 953
Rogersville, TN 37857

Phone: 423-585-6312
www.bluediamonddistribution.com

Blue Diamond offers a number of dustless roach and ant baits in paste or gel formulations for residential, commercial, and industrial applications. The manufacturer claims that insects cannot build up resistance to the boric acid in these products, while they can with many chemical insecticides. The baits are spot-applied, odorless, noncombustible, and effective for a year after application. These products work outdoors, but must be protected from rain. The roach baits are not available in all U.S. states.

Sentricon Termite Colony Elimination System

Dow AgroSciences, LLC
9330 Zionsville Rd.
Indianapolis, IN 46268

Toll-free: 800-352-6776
www.sentricon.com

The Sentricon® Termite Colony Elimination System eliminates termites with a highly targeted noviflumuron-based bait. This bait is considered to be highly targeted because worker termites carry it back to the colony to feed others. The chemical affects chitin formation in termites. In a management-intensive approach that limits environmental impact, the noviflumuron pesticide is employed only when regularly inspected bait stations reveal termite activity. The Sentricon System is offered as part of an ongoing service contract.

Termimesh System

Termimesh, LLC
9519 N IH 35
Austin, TX 78753

Phone: 512-997-0066
www.termimesh.com

The Termimesh™ System is a termite barrier from Australia made from a tight-weave stainless steel mesh. Proper installation of Termimesh may avoid the repeated application of pesticides. Currently this system is available only in a few Southern states.

Plastic Fences and Gates

Conventional wood fencing—even that made from pressure-treated wood—is prone to degradation and has a short life. This is a good application for recycled plastics and agrifiber-plastic composites because such products are more durable than those made from wood, and the structural requirements are minimal. Recycled-plastic fencing products are significantly greener than virgin-polymer products.

Aeolian Plastic Lumber & Fences

Aeolian Enterprises, Inc.
P.O. Box 888
Latrobe, PA 15650

Toll-free: 800-269-4672
Phone: 724-539-9460
www.aeo1.com

Aeolian Enterprises manufactures hollow and solid-profile plastic lumber made from recycled HDPE (recycled content varies with color). Solid-profile products are planed to achieve a uniform flat surface and texture during fabrication. Various dimensions offered include nominal 1x4, 1x6, and 5/4x6. Aeolian also fabricates corral, privacy, and picket fencing products made from recycled HDPE.

Fencing

Inteq Corp.
35800 Glen Dr.
Eastlake, OH 44095

Phone: 440-953-0550
www.4-inteqcorp.com

Inteq manufactures recycled HDPE plastic fencing (10-100% post-consumer content). The capped hollow posts will accept two, three, or four hollow rails. Inteq's fencing products are available in white, gray, weathered (tan), and black. Picket and Privacy fence is also available. Orange safety fence and Snow fence are available in diamond or rectangular shapes and three additional colors.

PlasTEAK Fencing

PlasTEAK
3563 Copley Rd.
P.O. Box 4290
Akron, OH 44321

Toll-free: 800-320-1841
Phone: 330-668-2587
www.plasteak.com

PlasTEAK fencing, available in more than two dozen styles, is made with 100% post-consumer recycled HDPE.

Recycled-Plastic Landscape Products

Master Mark Plastics
One Master Mark Dr.
P.O. Box 662
Albany, MN 56307

Toll-free: 800-535-4838
Phone: 320-845-2111
www.mastermark.com

Master Mark makes a variety of landscape products, such as lawn edging, lattice, downspout splash blocks, and privacy fencing from recycled HDPE plastic. According to the manufacturer, they currently recycle over 1 billion post-consumer HDPE plastic containers per year, and boast over 50 million feet of quality landscape edging installed every year. The manufacturer has certified the following recycled-content levels (by weight): post-consumer material 100% typical, 100% guaranteed.

Recycled-Plastic Net Fencing

Masternet Ltd.
690 Gana Ct.
Mississauga, ON L5S 1P2 Canada

Toll-free: 800-216-2536
Phone: 905-795-0005
www.masternetltd.com

Vexar® fencing from Masternet is an extruded plastic netting composed of 97% post-consumer recycled HDPE, 3% color, and ultraviolet (UV) stabilizers. Products include yard fence (an alternative to chain-link) and a lighter-weight border fence; safety, construction, and barrier fences; and drift fences. A number of roll sizes are available. Masternet purchased the Vexar® technology from DuPont Canada in 1993.

Recycled-Plastic Posts

XPotential Products Inc.
St. Boniface Postal Sta.
P.O. Box 126
Winnipeg, MB R2H 3B4 Canada

Toll-free: 800-863-6619
Phone: 204-224-3933
www.xpotentialproducts.com

XPotential offers parking stops, landscape timbers, and fence posts made with recycled materials, including auto shredder residue as well as HDPE and LDPE plastics. Impact-Curb parking stops are approximately 5-1/4" x 8" in 6' or 8' lengths, and 4" x 6" in 6' or 8' lengths. Interlocking landscape timbers measure 2-1/2" x 3-1/2" x 95" and weigh 36 lbs. each. Impact-Post comes in two sizes (6" x 6" x 8' and 4" x 4" x 8') and is appropriate for landscaping and fencing posts. All the XPotential products come with a limited lifetime warranty. The manufacturer has certified the following recycled-content levels (by weight): total recovered material 100% typical, 100% guaranteed; post-consumer material 85% typical, 85% guaranteed.

SuperPicket

Curb Appeal Materials, LTD
3824 N. Johnsburg Rd.
McHenry, IL 60050

Phone: 815-344-7926
www.vortexcomposites.com

SuperPicket™ fencing is made with 100% post-consumer recycled materials—nylon carpet waste with some commingled plastic, stabilized with a small amount of carbon black. It's offered as a maintenance-free fencing material that doesn't rot, warp, splinter, split, or harbor insects—at a cost significantly below that of vinyl. The product comes in a charcoal color, and weathers to an aged-cedar gray. It also accepts paints and stains. Most nail guns won't penetrate the dense material; use screws for assembly. Note that this product consists of the pickets only, which are designed to install on standard cedar or treated posts. For fences taller than 4', three rails and decreased post spacing are recommended due to the weight of the product.

Porous Pavers, Plastic

Porous paving seeks to combine the load-carrying capacity we expect of paved areas with the water-infiltration qualities of natural ground cover. With plastic porous paving systems, look for recycled content—and avoid systems that can't be easily removed later (such as free fibers that are mixed with the soil) if needs change. These pavers are available in a variety of shapes, sizes, and colors, and some are interlocking. They should be installed above a "reservoir" of uniform-sized aggregate (for example, 1-1/2" crushed stone). In addition to infiltrating stormwater, porous paving systems planted with grass also minimize contributions to the urban heat-island effect while providing visually appealing outdoor space.

Ecogrid

Terrafirm Enterprises
23778 24th Ave.
Langley, BC V2Z 3A2 Canada

Toll-free: 866-934-7572
Phone: 604-534-7572
www.terrafirmenterprises.com

Ecogrid products from Terrafirm Solutions are made from 100% recycled post-consumer HDPE. The lock-together trays may be filled with planting medium or gravel. EcoGrid e30 is suitable for moderate vehicle traffic, walkways, and playgrounds. EcoGrid e50 will accommodate heavy vehicle traffic and parking areas. EcoGrid s50 is for slope stabilization. They are available in black, green, and brown, and may also be used for green roof applications to prevent soil compaction in growing areas while providing a barrier between the roofing membranes and pedestrian traffic.

MODI Porous Paving Grid

Green Innovations, Ltd
3700 Salem Rd. N
Pickering, ON L1Y 1E8 Canada

Toll-free: 888-725-7524
Phone: 416-725-7524
www.greeninnovations.ca

The modular, reversible MODI Porous Paving Grid from Green Innovations is made from 100% post-consumer HDPE. It can be used to create parking, driving, and nonslip walking surfaces on lawns or sand bases, or to create gravel surfaces. The flexible grid parts, which were designed to be reused, can be individually removed, and may be shaped with a saw or grinding disc. The grids will support heavy trucks, according to the manufacturer. Accessories (made of acetyl resin) include marker plugs and holding rings. The system comes in a dark green color; light grey or light beige are available on request.

Porous Pavers, Precast Concrete

As the proportion of land covered with impervious surfaces continues to grow, dealing with stormwater in the built environment is increasingly costly, demanding, and important. Natural environments are able to absorb most stormwater loads, maintaining a healthy hydrologic balance. Porous unit pavers made from concrete include open-grid products that can be filled with aggregate or plantings. Solid unit pavers are often used in porous pavement systems, installed to have drainage voids along the installed edges. Porous pavement needs to be installed above a "reservoir" of uniform-sized aggregate (for example, 1-1/2" crushed stone). In addition to infiltrating stormwater, porous paving systems planted with grass also minimize contributions to the urban heat-island effect while providing visually appealing outdoor space.

Concrete Porous Pavers

Capitol Ornamental Concrete Specialties, Inc.
90 Main St.
P.O. Box 3249
South Amboy, NJ 08879

Toll-free: 800-254-5098
Phone: 732-727-5460
www.capitolconcrete.com

Capitol Ornamental Concrete Specialties offers a number of concrete pavers suitable for porous paving installations, including the Ecologic™ Paver System—an engineered permeable pavement system that uses 4" x 8" and 4" x 4" interlocking concrete pavers installed over an air-entrained soil media.

Drain Stone and Turf Stone

Oldcastle Architectural Product Group
375 Northridge Rd., Ste. 250
Atlanta, GA 30350

Toll-free: 800-899-8455
Phone: 770-804-3363
www.belgardhardscapes.com

Drain Stone and Turf Stone by Belgard are concrete porous paving products. Drain Stone has an octagonal pattern (3-1/8" x 4" x 8") that allows water to infiltrate between adjoining pavers. Turf Stone is a larger, precast unit covering 2-2/3 ft2 each. The 40% open, basketweave pattern supports grass growth in and between the pavers. Both products have a compressive strength greater than 8,000 psi and meet or exceed ASTM tests for water absorption and freeze-thaw stability (C-936 and C-67).

EcoGrid Porous Pavers

Hanover Architectural Products
240 Bender Rd.
Hanover, PA 17331

Toll-free: 800-426-4242
Phone: 717-637-0500
www.hanoverpavers.com

EcoGrid™ Pavers are pervious interlocking concrete paving units which allow moderate vehicle traffic. Each unit is 11-3/4" x 11-3/4" x 4". EcoGrid Pavers contain a percentage of fly ash.

EP Henry ECO Pavers

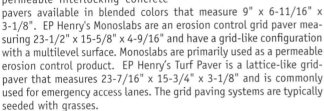

EP Henry Corporation
201 Park Ave.
P.O. Box 615
Woodbury, NJ 08096

Toll-free: 800-444-3679
www.ephenry.com

EP Henry manufactures ECO Pavers, permeable interlocking concrete pavers available in blended colors that measure 9" x 6-11/16" x 3-1/8". EP Henry's Monoslabs are an erosion control grid paver measuring 23-1/2" x 15-5/8" x 4-9/16" and have a grid-like configuration with a multilevel surface. Monoslabs are primarily used as a permeable erosion control product. EP Henry's Turf Paver is a lattice-like grid-paver that measures 23-7/16" x 15-3/4" x 3-1/8" and is commonly used for emergency access lanes. The grid paving systems are typically seeded with grasses.

Grasstone I and InfiltraStone

Pavestone Company
4835 LBJ Fwy., Ste. 700
Dallas, TX 75244

Phone: 972-404-0400
www.pavestone.com

Grasstone I is an interlocking concrete paver with an open-void lattice design in a figure-8 pattern to accommodate plant growth; it may also be used for permanent erosion control on slopes. InfiltraStone is a brick-shaped concrete paver with quarter-round voids at each corner, and a half-round void on each long edge. Pavestone Corporation has a number of production facilities in several states that can reduce shipping energy use.

SF-RIMA

Nicolock
640 Muncy Ave.
Lindenhurst, NY 11757

Toll-free: 800-669-9294
Phone: 631-669-0700
www.nicolock.com

Nicolock's environmental paving stones, SF-RIMA™, are made from no-slump concrete with a compressive strength of 8,000 psi. These square pavers (7-3/4" x 7-3/4") can be installed with either wide or narrow spacing, depending upon the orientation of integral spacers. Widely spaced pavers can be seeded with grasses, which may mitigate heat island effects and stormwater runoff. Nicolock has manufacturing facilities in Lindenhurst, NY, Frederick, MD, and North Haven, CT.

UNI Eco-Stone

UNI-Group U.S.A.
4362 Northlake Blvd.,
Ste. 204
Palm Beach Gardens, FL
33410

Toll-free: 800-872-1864
Phone: 561-626-4666
www.uni-groupusa.org

UNI Eco-Stone® is a 3-1/8"-thick interlocking concrete porous paver that measures approximately 9" long by 5-1/2" at its widest point. These pavers can be installed in running bond, basketweave, and herringbone patterns. UNI-Group U.S.A. licenses over two dozen companies around the country to manufacture these pavers.

Precast Concrete Pavers

Look for high recycled content, such as flyash and alternative aggregates. Consider the use of porous pavers that promote healthy hydrologic balance in the built environment.

Recycled-Glass-Aggregate Concrete Pavers

ECG, Inc.
104 Corporate Dr.
Elizabeth City, NC 27909

Phone: 252-333-1002
www.glass-recycling.com/home.asp

ECG manufactures commercial-grade pavers with decorative cast patterns using 82% recycled-glass aggregate (principally from post-consumer sources) for such applications as sidewalks, courtyards, and driveways. They may be installed on a concrete sub-base using mortar or grout, or on compacted gravel/sand. Available in eight standard integral colors (custom colors may be ordered), the pavers are 18" x 18" x 2" and weigh 36 lbs. ECG offers a variety of cast-concrete products made with recycled-glass aggregate.

Rigid Paving

Rigid, fluid-installed paving can double as a porous pavement (to provide excellent stormwater drainage) by using specialized formulas of concrete or asphalt that leave the "fines" out so that the cured pavement remains porous. Detailed specifications are available that will help your local concrete and asphalt mixing plants satisfy your needs; with these materials, look for a paving contractor familiar with porous pavement, as the installation is quite different.

Rubbersidewalks

Rubbersidewalks, Inc.
2622 W. 157th St.
Gardena, CA 90249

Phone: 310-515-5814
www.rubbersidewalks.com

Rubbersidewalks is a modular sidewalk system made from recycled tires with a polyurethane binder and colorant, and is particularly intended for use near trees. The high-density pavers, anchored together with self-gripping dowels and locked into a restraint chassis, can be removed for root or other maintenance and then reset, eliminating the need for concrete breakout and replacement. The reversible pavers don't expand in hot weather, and they absorb and retain less heat than concrete. The system has been freeze-thaw tested according to ASTM C1026 with good performance characteristics exhibited, and is also ADA compliant for pedestrian and wheeled traffic. While the pavers aren't considered porous themselves, the system provides immediate drainage at the module seams.

StoneyCrete

Stoney Creek Materials, LLC
25 Stoney Creek Cove
Austin, TX 78734

Phone: 512-261-0821
www.stoneycreekmaterials.com

StoneyCrete™ is a pervious concrete pavement installed by trained and certified contractors. The mix includes a proprietary additive that improves elasticity and strength: 4,000 psi at 28 days. Where available, some of the portland cement in the mix is replaced by fly ash (up to 20%) or blast-furnace slag (up to 40%).

Sound Barriers

Sound barriers should have low embodied energy, long useful lives, and be effective at blocking and/or absorbing noise. Look for high recycled content. Graffiti management, freeze-thaw effects, and damage by cars may be considerations.

EverQuiet Wall

New Frontier Industries, Inc.
P.O. Box 1360
Milton, NH 03851

Toll-free: 866-637-7888
Phone: 603-652-7888
www.newfrontierindustries.com

The EverQuiet Wall is a lightweight assembly of snap-together tongue-and-groove plastic "timbers" mounted in H-beams (polyester-fiberglass, steel, or galvanized steel). The maintenance-free 3-1/2" thick X 8" tall hollow boards are made from mixed recycled plastic with a thin, UV-protected PVC wear layer. Total post-consumer content is 95%. The sound transmission class (STC) rating is 42 (slightly better than a 4" concrete block wall). No foundation or footing is required. A variety of colors and simulated wood tones and textures are available. Per the manufacturer, most graffiti will clean by pressure washing with water. This product is re-usable, and comes with a 25-year transferable warranty.

SmartTie

Curb Appeal Materials, LTD
3824 N. Johnsburg Rd.
McHenry, IL 60050

Phone: 815-344-7926
www.vortexcomposites.com

SmartTie is made with 100% commingled plastics, including synthetic carpet material, from post-consumer and industrial sources in a patented cold-extrusion process. Colorants can be added for aesthetic effect. The material is more dense than wood, and has a lower burn rate; it doesn't warp or degrade, and is recyclable. It cuts and machines with woodworking tools. SmartTie is available in solid, hollow, and channeled versions in many dimensions. SmartTie can be used to control noise from highways and other sources. The manufacturer indicates that the material is not affected by freeze-thaw cycling.

Turf and Grasses

Lawn maintenance is a major source of air pollution and contaminated runoff from fertilizers and pesticides. Close to 40 million gas-powered mowers are used on the lawns of America. While domestic manufacturers have decreased their products' emissions significantly (as required by EPA regulations), an hour of mowing the lawn with a current gas-powered machine still pollutes about as much as driving a late-model car for 13 hours. Compounding the problem, fertilizer runoff from lawns is one of our most significant non-point-source water pollution problems; also, lawn pesticides are commonly applied at rates up to 20 times that of agricultural pesticides. Landscaping that requires less mowing, fertilizing, and pesticide use has significant environmental advantages.

No Mow

Prairie Nursery, Inc.
P.O. Box 306
Westfield, WI 53964

Toll-free: 800-476-9453
www.prairienursery.com

No Mow turfgrass mix consists of six native cool-season fescue varieties for seeding in the northern U.S. and southern Canada. No Mow requires only monthly or annual mowing. These drought-tolerant grasses require minimal irrigation and fertilization, and are appropriate for shady locations. Other prairie wildflowers and grasses for a variety of planting conditions are available.

Outdoor Structures

Outdoor structures include freestanding built items such as fences, tables, benches, planters, playground equipment, and other items that are installed or used out-of-doors, such as exterior sun-shade systems. Green criteria for products in this category include durability, low maintenance, and recycled content.

Prefabricated site furniture, landscaping timbers, fencing, and other outdoor products made with recycled plastic and wood-plastic composite lumber are available from many sources; they are more durable than wood, require less maintenance, and make use of materials that might otherwise end up in landfills. Products made with durable, rot-resistant, FSC-certified hardwoods such as Ipé can also be a good choice. (Certification from the Forest Stewardship Council—FSC—means that the wood has been sustainably harvested from well-managed resources.)

Architectural trellises can contribute to reduced solar gain and improved light quality in buildings, increased comfort for outdoor spaces, and are visually appealing. Combined with quick-growing seasonal vines, solar benefit in winter and solar shading in summer are both achieved.

For aquatic applications such as docks and pilings, avoid treated wood in favor of recycled plastic, which is impervious to marine borers and will not leach toxic chemicals. Though generally somewhat more expensive than treated wood, they will last longer—an important consideration in light of the expense of the more frequent replacement needs of wooden components.

Exterior Sun Control Devices

Products that can be used to selectively block out solar gain, including those that support vegetation along walls, can provide important energy conservation benefits while improving light quality for the occupants.

Econom

Elero GmbH
Linearantriebstechnik
Naßäckerstraße 11
D-07381, Pößneck   Germany

Phone: +49 (0) 3647-4607-0
www.elero-linear.com

Elero's Econom is a maintenance-free line of electric linear actuators for active façade systems that control building heating loads and glare, and improve occupant viewscapes. These stainless-steel-clad, weather-resistant actuators are appropriate for outdoor or indoor use, and can also be components of natural ventilation systems. Used in Europe and Asia for many years, but new to the North American market, the slender, 2.5-inch diameter devices have load-bearing capacities of as much as 675 foot-pounds. The Econom line is manufactured by the German company Elero GmbH, which specializes in drive units and control systems for roller shutters, sun protection systems, and gates.

Greenscreen Trellising System

Greenscreen
1743 S. La Cienega Blvd.
Los Angeles, CA 90035

Toll-free: 800-450-3494
Phone: 310-837-0526
www.greenscreen.com

Greenscreen™ is a three-dimensional, welded-wire trellis system that can be installed freestanding or wall-mounted. The basic trellis module is 4' wide, 2" or 3" thick, and 6', 8', 10', or 12' long. Custom-sized panels can be ordered in 2" increments. Greenscreen is available in a wrinkled matte finish of green or black, as well as a glossy finish of green, black, silver, or white. Various accessories, such as planter straps, edge trim, and specialty shapes, are also available. Thoughtful plant selection may be important for success of the system. In addition to the numerous environmental benefits of encouraging the growth of vegetation and that of energy savings from shading, Greenscreens can also play an important role in making the most of growing area in small-space and rooftop applications.

Marine Construction and Equipment

Treated-wood pilings may introduce hazardous chemicals to marine ecosystems, and their periodic replacement is expensive. Recycled-content plastic pilings are impervious to marine borers and are an appropriate solution for building durable docks and piers. These pilings are usually extruded around steel or fiberglass reinforcing rods and treated with UV inhibitors and antioxidants. While more expensive than wooden pilings, if maintenance and durability are considered, recycled-plastic pilings often have lower life-cycle costs. Docks and other construction in marine environments should avoid all pressure-treated wood in favor of components that are inherently resistant to water and microbial growth. Products listed here are made from recycled plastic, rubber, and fiberglass.

Ecoboard Plastic Lumber

Trelleborg Engineered Products, Inc.
3470 Martinsburg Pike
P.O. Box 98
Clearbrook, VA 22624

Phone: 540-667-5191
www.trelleborg.com

Ecoboard lumber is manufactured in a wide array of dimensions and colors. These products contain recycled HDPE and LDPE, as well as UV-stabilization, flame-retardant, and strength additives. Landscape timbers in 4x4, 5x5, and 6x6 contain fiberglass reinforcing. Ecoboard marine pilings have been tested as a friction pile where load-bearing capability needed to exceed 15 tons of vertical loading with a minimum of "creep" or failure, according to the manufacturer; the pilings tested to a 60-ton load, at which time the test was stopped. The manufacturer has certified the following recycled-content levels (by weight): total recovered material 100% typical, 100% guaranteed; post-consumer material 90% typical, 80% guaranteed.

PlasTEAK Plastic Paneling

PlasTEAK
3563 Copley Rd.
P.O. Box 4290
Akron, OH 44321

Toll-free: 800-320-1841
Phone: 330-668-2587
www.plasteak.com

PlasTEAK is made with 100% post-consumer recycled HDPE in a paraffin base—the boards become more slip-resistant when wet. Boatboard extruded HDPE panels meet the requirements of marine and outdoor environments. Limarpa is a lightweight alternative to plywood, also appropriate for marine use. PlasTEAK also makes UV-stabilized, 1' x 4' x 1.25"-thick, recycled-plastic grates for such applications as boardwalks, dune walkovers, nature walks, and floating docks; these grates provide 60% light and visual penetration for such uses as boardwalks, dune walkovers, and nature walks. Trim and lumber goods are available as well.

Recycled-Plastic Decking, Docks, and Timbers

Plastic Lumber Yard, LLC
220 Washington St.
Norristown, PA 19401

Phone: 610-277-3900
www.plasticlumberyard.com

Plastic Lumber Yard, LLC, manufactures recycled-plastic lumber. The Forever Deck and ForeverDock Floating Dock Kits are constructed with recycled plastic lumber made from 100% recycled HDPE. Landscape grade plastic lumber in various profiles and colors is also available. The manufacturer has certified the following recycled-content levels (by weight): total recovered material 100% typical, 100% guaranteed; post-consumer material 30% typical.

Recycled-Plastic Lumber Products

Recycled Plastic Man, Inc.
P.O. Box 609
Placida, FL 33946

Toll-free: 800-253-7742
Phone: 941-698-1060
www.recycledplasticman.com

Recycled Plastic Man manufactures extruded plastic lumber and marine-quality pilings from commingled, recycled HDPE in a variety of profiles and colors. The manufacturer has certified the following recycled-content levels (by weight): total recovered material 100% guaranteed; post-consumer material 100% guaranteed.

Recycled-Plastic Products

American Recreational Products
1535 Locust Avenue
Bohemia, NY 11716

Toll-free: 800-663-4096
Phone: 631-244-0011
www.americanrecreational.com

American Recreational Products offers benches, picnic tables, landscape ties, wheel stops, speed bumps, and marine docks made from 100% recycled commingled plastics. Products are typically made from 50% post-consumer plastic and 50% pre-consumer plastic.

Trimax

Trimax Building Products, Inc.
2600 W. Roosevelt Rd.
Chicago, IL 60608

Toll-free: 866-987-4629
www.trimaxbp.com

Trimax Decking consists of decking, rail, and stair parts containing 90% post-consumer HDPE by weight. Decking lumber and stair treads are also available in a knurled, nonskid finish. Trimax structural lumber and marine pilings contains 90% recycled material by weight, including post-consumer recycled HDPE (65%) and post-industrial recycled fiberglass. Trimax Structural Lumber comes in gray, and is available by special order in green, tan, redwood, and white; pilings come in gray and are available by special order in light gray, green, tan, redwood, and white.

Outdoor Seating and Tables, Other

Products listed here embody creative reuse, or use non-standard recycled content to make durable alternatives to wood or plastic outdoor furnishings.

Ski and Snowboard Furniture

Reeski, Inc.
P.O. Box 781
Aspen, CO 81612

Toll-free: 800-826-5447
Phone: 970-948-3491
www.reeski.com

Reeski manufactures chairs, benches, coat racks, and more from used skis and snowboards. Reeski offers many durable and creative designs; custom orders are welcome. Furniture often includes 100% recycled plastic lumber. Uncertified redwood is used for some items. The manufacturer has certified the following recycled-content levels (by weight): post-consumer material 99% typical, 99% guaranteed.

Outdoor Seating and Tables, Plastic

Recycled plastic is a durable material for outdoor furniture. Recycled plastic site furnishings are most commonly made from either HDPE or commingled plastics. Recycled commingled plastics may have slightly inconsistent properties, but this is a lower-grade waste material that is generally more of a disposal problem. Products listed here contain recycled content.

2nd Site Systems

Victor Stanley, Inc.
P.O. Drawer 330
Dunkirk, MD 20754

Toll-free: 800-368-2573
Phone: 301-855-8300
www.victorstanley.com

2nd Site Systems utilizes a patented slat design of 100% recycled plastic lumber reinforced with recycled steel bar. Products include park benches, picnic tables, and trash receptacles.

Barco Recycled-Content Products

Barco Products
11 N. Batavia Ave.
Batavia, IL 60510

Toll-free: 800-338-2697
Phone: 630-879-0084
www.barcoproducts.com

Barco Products offers site furnishings, landscape timbers, and traffic devices made with recycled content, including dozens of styles of picnic tables and park benches made with recycled commingled HDPE and LDPE averaging 40% post-consumer, as well as planters and waste receptacles made from recycled HDPE (90 to 100% post-consumer). Landscape Timbers are made from 100% recycled commingled HDPE and LDPE, sized as railroad ties with premolded holes for rebar reinforcement and interlocking edges for stacking stability. Each timber weighs 42 lbs, about half that of most plastic landscape timbers. 100% recycled tire rubber speed bumps and 100% recycled plastic speed bumps are offered, and colored wheel stops made of 95% recycled commingled HDPE and LDPE. Gray wheel stops contain 85% recycled PVC. Bollards are made from 96% recycled commingled LDPE and HDPE (50 to 80% post-industrial).

Bedford Technology Recycled-Plastic Products

Bedford Technology, LLC
2424 Armour Rd.
P.O. Box 609
Worthington, MN 56187

Toll-free: 800-721-9037
Phone: 507-372-5558
www.plasticboards.com

Bedford Technology offers plastic lumber and other products made with post-consumer recycled HDPE and LDPE. Their lumber is available in a variety of dimensions, including 5/4 decking, two-by, and large timbers up to 12x12, in black, brown, gray, and cedar with other colors available. Parking stops and speed bumps are also offered, as well as plastic paneling that can be used as a substitute for plywood. Bedford's ForeSite Designs(R) line of recycled-plastic site furnishings includes picnic tables, benches, and waste receptacles. The manufacturer has certified the following recycled-content levels (by weight): total recovered material 99% typical, 99% guaranteed; post-consumer material 65% typical, 50% guaranteed.

Benches and Picnic Tables

Polly Products, LLC
12 N. Charlotte St.
Mulliken, MI 48861

Toll-free: 877-609-2243
Phone: 517-649-2243
www.recycletechproducts.com

RecycleTech Products manufactures park benches and picnic tables from recycled HDPE. The manufacturer has certified the following recycled-content levels (by weight): total recovered material 95% typical, 95% guaranteed; post-consumer material 80% typical, 60% guaranteed.

Benches, Picnic Tables, and Planters

Cascades Re-Plast, Inc.
1350 chemin Quatre Saisons
Bon Conseil, QC J0C 1A0
Canada

Toll-free: 888-313-2440
Phone: 888-313-2440
www.cascadesreplast.com

Cascades Re-Plast manufactures an assortment of recycled-plastic outdoor furniture and accessories in brown, beige, green, gray, and black. Re-Plast plastic wood contains mixed polymers including HDPE, polypropylene, polystyrene, and PET from post-consumer sources.

Benches, Picnic Tables, and Recycling Receptacles

Eagle One Site Furnishings
1340 N. Jefferson St.
Anaheim, CA 92807

Toll-free: 800-448-3160
Phone: 714-983-0050
www.eagleoneproducts.com

EagleOne Site Furnishings offers site amenities, including benches, picnic tables, and recycling receptacles, made from recycled HDPE plastic.

Benches, Picnic Tables, Waste Receptacles, and Planters

Kay Park Recreation Corp.
1301 Pine St.
P.O. Box 477
Janesville, IA 50647

Phone: 319-987-2313
www.kaypark.com

Kay Park Recreation manufactures picnic tables, benches, waste receptacles, and planters containing 96% post-consumer recycled commingled plastics.

Conservancy Series - Benches, Picnic Tables, and Recycling Receptacles

Florida Playground and Steel Co.
4701 S. 50th St.
Tampa, FL 33619

Toll-free: 800-444-2655
Phone: 813-247-2812
www.fla-playground.com

Conservancy Series benches, picnic tables, and recycling receptacles are made from recycled plastic/wood composite materials and steel.

Earthcare Series

Litchfield Industries
4 Industrial Dr.
Litchfield, MI 49252

Toll-free: 800-542-5282
Phone: 517-542-2988
www.litchfieldindustries.com

The Earthcare Series of site furnishings is made from 100% post-consumer recycled plastic. The Series includes picnic tables, benches, and trash receptacles.

Eco Outdoor Series

Ecologic, Inc.
921 Sherwood Dr.
Lake Bluff, IL 60044

Toll-free: 800-899-8004
Phone: 847-234-5855
www.ecoinc.com

Ecologic is a large producer of furniture based on recycled HDPE plastic. They have an extensive range of outdoor furniture suitable for residential and public spaces, ranging from individual Adirondack chairs and ottomans to tables, benches, trash receptacles (designed to take standard Rubbermaid inserts), and fan trellises. Some of these products contain recycled steel to add stiffness. The entire line is manufactured with 97.5% recycled content. UV protection is integral to the plastic in each component.

EPS Recycled-Plastic Lumber and Outdoor Furniture

Engineered Plastic Systems
885 Church Rd.
Elgin, IL 60123

Phone: 847-289-8383
www.epsplasticlumber.com

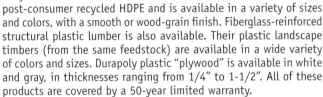

Engineered Plastic Systems (EPS) Bear Board plastic lumber is typically made from a minimum 51% post-consumer recycled HDPE and is available in a variety of sizes and colors, with a smooth or wood-grain finish. Fiberglass-reinforced structural plastic lumber is also available. Their plastic landscape timbers (from the same feedstock) are available in a wide variety of colors and sizes. Durapoly plastic "plywood" is available in white and gray, in thicknesses ranging from 1/4" to 1-1/2". All of these products are covered by a 50-year limited warranty.

Perennial Park Outdoor Furniture

Engineered Plastic Systems
885 Church Rd.
Elgin, IL 60123

Phone: 847-289-8383
www.epsplasticlumber.com

Environmental Plastic Systems manufactures Perennial Park outdoor furniture and accessories from 100% recycled HDPE (typically 100% post-consumer content). Products include benches and picnic tables, planter benches, and serving tables. Kid-sized and handicapped-accessible tables, as well as custom orders, are also available. Colors currently include white, gray, redwood, forest green, black, cedar, and tan. All EPS plastic products come with a 50-year limited warranty.

Picnic Tables and Benches

Plastic Recycling of Iowa Falls, Inc.
10252 Hwy. 65
Iowa Falls, IA 50126

Toll-free: 800-338-1438
Phone: 641-648-5073
www.hammersplastic.com

Plastic Recycling of Iowa Falls, formerly Hammer's Plastic Recycling, manufactures several park benches and picnic tables, including ADA-compliant products, of commingled recycled HDPE, LDPE, LLDPE, and other miscellaneous plastics. The manufacturer has certified the following recycled-content levels (by weight): total recovered material 100% typical, 100% guaranteed; post-consumer material 50% typical, 50% guaranteed.

Pilot Rock Site Furnishings

R. J. Thomas Manufacturing Co., Inc.
P.O. Box 946
Cherokee, IA 51012

Toll-free: 800-762-5002
Phone: 712-225-5115
www.pilotrock.com

Pilot Rock Site Furnishings are made from recycled HDPE and LDPE plastic. The Pilot Rock line includes benches, picnic tables, waste receptacles, and car stops. The manufacturer has certified the following recycled-content levels (by weight): total recovered material 100% typical, 100% guaranteed; post-consumer material 75% typical, 60% guaranteed.

Poly-Wood

Poly-Wood Inc.
1001 W. Brooklyn St.
Syracuse, IN 46567

Toll-free: 877-457-3284
Phone: 574-457-3284
www.polywoodinc.com

Poly-Wood manufactures outdoor residential furniture from 98% recycled HDPE plastic.

Recycle Design Site Furnishings

Trimax Building Products, Inc.
2600 W. Roosevelt Rd.
Chicago, IL 60608

Toll-free: 866-987-4629
www.trimaxbp.com

The award-winning Recycle Design site furnishings are made with Durawood PE plastic lumber that contains 90% post-consumer recycled HDPE by weight, and steel or aluminum structural components. The Recycle Design line includes benches, picnic tables, and waste receptacles.

Recycled-Plastic Products

American Recreational Products
1535 Locust Avenue
Bohemia, NY 11716

Toll-free: 800-663-4096
Phone: 631-244-0011
www.americanrecreational.com

American Recreational Products offers benches, picnic tables, landscape ties, wheel stops, speed bumps, and marine docks made from 100% recycled commingled plastics. Products are typically made from 50% post-consumer plastic and 50% pre-consumer plastic.

Recycled-Plastic Products

American Recycled Plastic, Inc.
1500 Main St.
Palm Bay, FL 32905

Toll-free: 866-674-1525
Phone: 321-674-1525
www.itsrecycled.com

American Recycled Plastic manufactures a range of products from recycled HDPE, including lumber and timbers, car stops, speed bumps and humps, and vehicle barriers. They also offer a wide variety of recycled-HDPE site furnishings, including benches, outdoor tables, waste receptacles, mailboxes, planters, custom wildlife structures, and bicycle racks. The manufacturer has certified the following recycled-content levels (by weight): total recovered material 100% typical, 100% guaranteed; post-consumer material 80% typical, 80% guaranteed.

Recycled-Plastic Products

BJM Industries, Inc.
12478 U.S. Route 422
Kittanning, PA 16201

Toll-free: 800-683-3810
Phone: 724-548-2440
www.bjmindustries.com

BJM Industries manufactures site furnishings, such as picnic tables, park and garden benches, and planters, from Millennium Lumber - a combination of 100% post-consumer recycled HDPE and post-industrial recycled cellulose (from diaper factory trimmings).

Recycled-Plastic Site Amenities

DuMor, Inc.
P.O. Box 142
Mifflintown, PA 17059

Toll-free: 800-598-4018
Phone: 717-436-2106
www.dumor.com

DuMor offers a wide array of site amenities made from recycled HDPE plastic lumber. Products include benches, picnic tables, planters, and waste receptacles. The HDPE used in DuMor's recycled plastic furnishings is derived from post-consumer bottle waste resulting in a product that is more than 90% recycled. The manufacturer has certified the following recycled-content levels (by weight): total recovered material 95% typical, 95% guaranteed; post-consumer material 95% typical, 95% guaranteed.

Recycled-Plastic Site Amenities

The Plastic Lumber Company, Inc.
115 W. Bartges St.
Akron, OH 44311

Toll-free: 800-886-8990
Phone: 330-762-8989
www.plasticlumber.com

The Plastic Lumber Company offers site furnishings, playground equipment, and signage made with recycled plastic. Commercial-grade benches, picnic tables, and waste receptacles/recycling centers are available in a variety of color combinations and are made with 97% post-consumer recycled content. Signage products have a post-industrial recycled content level up to 40% depending on color selection. (The Digital DeSigns line of signs does not contain recyled content).

Recycled-Plastic Site Furnishings

Plastic Lumber Yard, LLC
220 Washington St.
Norristown, PA 19401

Phone: 610-277-3900
www.plasticlumberyard.com

Plastic Lumber Yard, LLC manufactures a wide range of outdoor site furnishings from 100% recycled plastic. Products include picnic tables and benches, chairs (Adirondack and others), "gliders" and porch swings, as well as hexagonal, rectangular, and wheelchair-accessible tables.

Site Furnishings

Doty & Sons Concrete Products, Inc.
1275 E. State St.
Sycamore, IL 60178

Toll-free: 800-233-3907
www.dotyconcrete.com

Doty & Sons Concrete Products uses recycled HDPE plastic in its precast concrete site amenities, including benches and table sets, recycling and waste receptacles.

Site Furnishings and Materials

Inteq Corp.
35800 Glen Dr.
Eastlake, OH 44095

Phone: 440-953-0550
www.4-inteqcorp.com

Inteq's benches and picnic tables are made from recycled HDPE plastic. Tables are either standard 6' or 8' length or hexagonal. Benches come in a variety of styles and can be custom designed. Inteq's waste receptacles and planters contain recycled HDPE plastic and are available in many styles including custom production. All are offered in a variety of colors. Recycled content is up to 100% (minimum 20% post-consumer). Inteq nonstructural landscape timbers are available in multiple colors up to 12' in length in standard sizes of 4x4, 4x6, and 6x6. Decking and railing material is also made from recycled HDPE plastic and is available in multiple colors.

Outdoor Seating and Tables, Wood

Forest Stewardship Council (FSC) certification involves third-party evaluation and monitoring of sustainable forestry practices and chain-of-custody certification to ensure that labeled products were derived from FSC-certified forests. Products listed here are FSC-certified or made from salvaged materials.

Certified Teak Outdoor Furniture

SCI Interiors LLC / Skagerak
Denmark
133 Elm St.
Winooski, VT 05404

Toll-free: 866-596-6707
Phone: 802-846-5560
www.skagerak-denmark.com

SCI Interiors LLC is the North American distributor for Skagerak Denmark teak furniture. Three of the company's lines of park and garden furniture—Drachmann, Vitas Bering, and Selandia, a line of folding chairs and tables—have products available for an upcharge in FSC-certified teak. Skagerak Denmark is ISO 14001-certified.

Plastic Fences and Gates

Conventional wood fencing—even that made from pressure-treated wood—is prone to degradation and has a short life. This is a good application for recycled plastics and agrifiber-plastic composites because such products are more durable than those made from wood, and the structural requirements are minimal. Recycled-plastic fencing products are significantly greener than virgin-polymer products.

Aeolian Plastic Lumber & Fences

Aeolian Enterprises, Inc.
P.O. Box 888
Latrobe, PA 15650

Toll-free: 800-269-4672
Phone: 724-539-9460
www.aeo1.com

Aeolian Enterprises manufactures hollow and solid-profile plastic lumber made from recycled HDPE (recycled content varies with color). Solid-profile products are planed to achieve a uniform flat surface and texture during fabrication. Various dimensions offered include nominal 1x4, 1x6, and 5/4x6. Aeolian also fabricates corral, privacy, and picket fencing products made from recycled HDPE.

Fencing

Inteq Corp.
35800 Glen Dr.
Eastlake, OH 44095

Phone: 440-953-0550
www.4-inteqcorp.com

Inteq manufactures recycled HDPE plastic fencing (10-100% post-consumer content). The capped hollow posts will accept two, three, or four hollow rails. Inteq's fencing products are available in white, gray, weathered (tan), and black. Picket and Privacy fence is also available. Orange safety fence and Snow fence are available in diamond or rectangular shapes and three additional colors.

PlasTEAK Fencing

PlasTEAK
3563 Copley Rd.
P.O. Box 4290
Akron, OH 44321

Toll-free: 800-320-1841
Phone: 330-668-2587
www.plasteak.com

PlasTEAK fencing, available in more than two dozen styles, is made with 100% post-consumer recycled HDPE.

Recycled-Plastic Landscape Products

Master Mark Plastics
One Master Mark Dr.
P.O. Box 662
Albany, MN 56307

Toll-free: 800-535-4838
Phone: 320-845-2111
www.mastermark.com

Master Mark makes a variety of landscape products, such as lawn edging, lattice, downspout splash blocks, and privacy fencing from recycled HDPE plastic. According to the manufacturer, they currently recycle over 1 billion post-consumer HDPE plastic containers per year, and boast over 50 million feet of quality landscape edging installed every year. The manufacturer has certified the following recycled-content levels (by weight): post-consumer material 100% typical, 100% guaranteed.

Recycled-Plastic Net Fencing

Masternet Ltd.
690 Gana Ct.
Mississauga, ON L5S 1P2 Canada

Toll-free: 800-216-2536
Phone: 905-795-0005
www.masternetltd.com

Vexar® fencing from Masternet is an extruded plastic netting composed of 97% post-consumer recycled HDPE, 3% color, and ultraviolet (UV) stabilizers. Products include yard fence (an alternative to chain-link) and a lighter-weight border fence; safety, construction, and barrier fences; and drift fences. A number of roll sizes are available. Masternet purchased the Vexar® technology from DuPont Canada in 1993.

Recycled-Plastic Posts

XPotential Products Inc.
St. Boniface Postal Sta.
P.O. Box 126
Winnipeg, MB R2H 3B4 Canada

Toll-free: 800-863-6619
Phone: 204-224-3933
www.xpotentialproducts.com

XPotential offers parking stops, landscape timbers, and fence posts made with recycled materials, including auto shredder residue as well as HDPE and LDPE plastics. Impact-Curb parking stops are approximately 5-1/4" x 8" in 6' or 8' lengths, and 4" x 6" in 6' or 8' lengths. Interlocking landscape timbers measure 2-1/2" x 3-1/2" x 95" and weigh 36 lbs. each. Impact-Post comes in two sizes (6" x 6" x 8' and 4" x 4" x 8') and is appropriate for landscaping and fencing posts. All the XPotential products come with a limited lifetime warranty. The manufacturer has certified the following recycled-content levels (by weight): total recovered material 100% typical, 100% guaranteed; post-consumer material 85% typical, 85% guaranteed.

SuperPicket

Curb Appeal Materials, LTD
3824 N. Johnsburg Rd.
McHenry, IL 60050

Phone: 815-344-7926
www.vortexcomposites.com

SuperPicket™ fencing is made with 100% post-consumer recycled materials—nylon carpet waste with some commingled plastic, stabilized with a small amount of carbon black. It's offered as a maintenance-free fencing material that doesn't rot, warp, splinter, split, or harbor insects—at a cost significantly below that of vinyl. The product comes in a charcoal color, and weathers to an aged-cedar gray. It also accepts paints and stains. Most nail guns won't penetrate the dense material; use screws for assembly. Note that this product consists of the pickets only, which are designed to install on standard cedar or treated posts. For fences taller than 4', three rails and decreased post spacing are recommended due to the weight of the product.

Recycling Equipment

Enabling commercial and public building and campus occupants to be good environmental stewards is important. Systems that make it easy to recycle wastes should be provided in offices, institutions, parks, and other public spaces. Many of the products described here are themselves made from recycled waste materials.

Curbside or Work-Area Recycling Bins

Microphor
452 E. Hill Rd.
Willits, CA 95490

Toll-free: 800-358-8280
Phone: 707-459-5563
www.microphor.com

Microphor recycling bins, made from plastic, are designed for curbside or office-paper recycling. These stackable bins have large handles and measure 12-1/4" x 12-1/2" x 20-1/2". Standard colors are white, navy blue, blue, red, green, and yellow.

Feeny Lidded Waste and Recycle and Rotary Recycling Center

Knape & Vogt Manufacturing Company
2700 Oak Industrial Dr. NE
Grand Rapids, MI 49505

Toll-free: 800-253-1561
Phone: 616-459-3311
www.knapeandvogt.com

Knape & Vogt offers two products for residential recyclable collection. The Feeny Lidded Waste and Recycle is intended for base cabinet applications; it has up to 3 bins and rolls out. The Feeny Rotary Corner Recycling Center has 3 bins and works like a lazy susan.

Recycling Equipment

Recy-CAL Supply Co.
42597 De Portola Rd.
Temecula, CA 92592

Toll-free: 800-927-3873
Phone: 951-302-7585
www.recy-cal.com

Recy-CAL Supply is a distributor of recycling containers, waste receptacles, and mobile collection containers. Many styles and sizes of products from more than 30 manufacturers are available to fit various needs, budgets, and decors.

This Space is Available for Your Notes

Decking

Until 2004, most preservative-treated wood was pressure-treated with CCA (chromated copper arsenate). Concerns about arsenic and chromium leaching from decks and fences led to the removal of CCA-treated lumber from the market. Disposal of the existing billions of board feet of CCA-treated wood already in use will be an ongoing problem as it reaches the end of its useful life. Degradation of CCA-treated wood leaves residual toxins; burning it results in airborne toxins or, if burned in controlled incinerators, highly toxic ash.

Direct substitutes for CCA-treated wood include less toxic products such as ACQ (ammoniacal copper quaternary) and CBA (copper boron azole). ACQ is corrosive to standard steel over time—so stainless steel screws and nails and double-coated, hot-dipped galvanized hangers and hardware are typically recommended. CBA is less corrosive to steel. Aluminum hardware shouldn't be used with either. Both ACQ and CBA rely on copper as the active ingredient, and copper is highly toxic to many aquatic organisms; for this reason neither should be used on boardwalks, docks, or decks overhanging ponds, marshes, or other aquatic locations. Neither ACQ nor CBA are approved for saltwater applications. For wood that isn't exposed to weather, borate-based preservatives (without copper) are effective against insects while being much less toxic than other chemicals. Treatments using sodium silicate followed by heat offers a very attractive alternative to conventional copper-based treatments.

There are also problems associated with using naturally rot-resistant wood species, such as redwood and cedar. Clear-heart redwood is generally cut from old-growth forests. Redwood trees take a long time to mature, and there are very few remaining stands of privately owned redwood. Small but increasing amounts of redwood and cedar are available from certified, well-managed forests. The quick-growing second-growth redwood and cedar, with wide growth rings, is less resistant to rot and insects than old-growth wood. Sustainably harvested, long-lasting exotic hardwoods such as Ipé, imported from Brazil and Bolivia, are increasingly available; look for third-party FSC certification. Forest Stewardship Council (FSC) certification involves third-party evaluation and monitoring of sustainable forestry practices—and chain-of-custody verification that wood products were derived from certified forests.

In some settings, a patio made from local stone makes an attractive alternative to a wood deck.

For exposed applications, recycled plastic lumber is an excellent alternative that will handily outlast most wooden decking materials: 50-year warranties aren't uncommon. Products combining recycled plastic with wood fiber offer a more wood-like feel and less thermal expansion in the sun. Prefabricated picnic tables, benches, and garbage can enclosures made with these materials are available.

Certified Wood Decking

Products listed here are produced from FSC-certified wood. Forest Stewardship Council (FSC) certification involves third-party evaluation and monitoring of sustainable forestry practices.

Certified Decking

Cascadia Forest Goods, LLC
38083 Wheeler Rd.
Dexter, OR 97431

Phone: 541-485-4477
www.cascadiaforestgoods.com

Cascadia Forest Goods (CFG) is a supplier of FSC-certified and re-cycled forest products, including cedar and redwood decking. CFG also supplies FSC-certified flooring and decking from Central and South America, including ipe, machiche, and pucte (ironwood).

Certified Decking

Disdero Lumber Company
12301 SE Carpenter Dr.
P.O. Box 469
Clackamas, OR 97015

Toll-free: 800-547-4209
Phone: 503-239-8888
www.disdero.com

Disdero Lumber Company offers FSC-certified decking made with wood from Collins Pine Company, the first privately owned timber management company in the U.S. to receive FSC certification.

Certified Decking

Forest World Group
P.O. Box 852
Bethany Beach , DE 19930

Phone: 302-541-4541
www.forestworldgroup.com

Forest World Group, formerly Sylvania Certified, sells decking lumber of FSC-certified ipe and lesser-known naturally durable tropical species as alternatives for pressure-treated wood decking.

Certified Decking

Harwood Products
PO Box 224
Branscomb, CA 95417

Toll-free: 800-441-4140 (CA only)
Phone: 707-984-6181
www.harwoodp.com

Harwood Products offers certified redwood decking and timbers, Douglas fir lumber and timbers, and white fir lumber.

Certified Decking

Randall Custom Lumber, Ltd.
3530 S.E. Arcadia Rd.
Shelton, WA 98584

Phone: 360-426-8518

Randall Custom Lumber manufactures FSC-certified decking, flooring, hard and softwood lumber, and stair parts. Some of their certified species are ash, red cedar, red alder, Douglas fir, madrone, and maple.

Certified Iron Woods Decking

Cecco Trading, Inc.
600 E. Vienna Ave.
Milwaukee, WI 53212

Phone: 414-445-8989
www.ironwoods.com

Iron Woods® is a brand of ipe decking from the Brazilian forest that is offered FSC-certified with an upcharge. Iron Woods' natural durability rating of 25+ years is the highest of woods tested by the U.S. Forest Products Lab. The product is available in all standard decking, porch flooring, and dimensional lumber sizes from 2x2 to 4x12 and up to 20' long in standard even lengths. Iron Woods decking is Class A fire-rated and comes with a 25-year fully transferable limited warranty.

Certified Tropical Hardwood Decking

Sustainable Forest Systems, LP
995 Castaway Blvd.
Vero Beach, FL 32963

Phone: 772 234 3482

Sustainable Forest Systems has operated tropical hardwood timberlands and associated processing since 1994. They offer a wide range of FSC-certified tropical hardwood products.

Certified Wood Decking

AltruWood, Inc.
P.O. Box 3341
Portland, OR 97208

Toll-free: 877-372-9663
www.altruwood.com

AltruWood, chain-of-custody certified by SGS, only sells and distributes FSC-certified new domestic (including oak, pine, cherry and Douglas Fir) and tropical wood (including Jatoba, Ipe, and Massaranduba). Sourced and shipped from multiple locations, transportation costs and impacts are minimized. A custom cutting service allows the specification of exact sizes and dimensions, minimizing waste. AltruWood also sells reclaimed lumber.

Plastic Lumber

In 2003, the EPA estimated that 26.7 million tons of the municipal U.S. solid waste stream was plastics. Just 1.4 million tons of it was recycled; the rest went to landfills, where it occupies about 25% of the overall landfill space. Plastic lumber makes good use of recycled plastic and is an effective replacement for pressure-treated lumber, protecting timber resources and preventing the use of chemical lumber treatments. Plastic lumber won't rot, absorb water, splinter, or crack; it's also resilient to shock, making it an extremely durable component in exterior and marine applications. It can accept most types of fasteners and is workable with standard saws and carbide blades. Plastic lumber usually isn't a suitable replacement for load-bearing structural components, however; the physical characteristics of plastic polymers, while durable, don't provide the rigidity necessary for primary structural support. Some companies have addressed this weakness by reinforcing their products with fiberglass or steel. In addition, plastic lumber experiences greater rates of thermal expansion and contraction, which can give rise to problems in certain applications.

Aeolian Plastic Lumber

Aeolian Enterprises, Inc.
P.O. Box 888
Latrobe, PA 15650

Toll-free: 800-269-4672
Phone: 724-539-9460
www.aeo1.com

Aeolian Enterprises manufactures hollow and solid-profile plastic lumber made from recycled HDPE (recycled content varies with color). Solid-profile products are planed to achieve a uniform flat surface and texture during fabrication. Aeolian offers various dimensions including nominal 1x4, 1x6, and $^5/_4$x6.

Aloha Plastic Lumber

Aloha Plastics Recycling
75 Amala Pl.
Kahului, HI 96732

Phone: 808-877-0822
www.aloha-recycling.com

Aloha Plastics Recycling manufactures a variety of plastic products including plastic lumber from 100% post-consumer HDPE. Aloha Plastic Lumber is available in brown, green, black, and gray in a variety of dimensions and profiles.

American Recycled Plastic Lumber

American Recycled Plastic, Inc.
1500 Main St.
Palm Bay, FL 32905

Toll-free: 866-674-1525
Phone: 321-674-1525
www.itsrecycled.com

American Recycled Plastic manufactures lumber from recycled HDPE plastic. The manufacturer has certified the following recycled-content levels (by weight): total recovered material 100% typical, 100% guaranteed; post-consumer material 80% typical, 80% guaranteed.

Aztec Recycled-Plastic Lumber

Amazing Recycled Products, Inc.
P.O. Box 312
Denver, CO 80201

Toll-free: 800-241-2174
Phone: 303-699-7693
www.amazingrecycled.com

Aztec Recycled-Plastic Lumber is a molded HDPE product that includes a small percentage of waste-paper content. The waste paper imparts some slip-resistant qualities to the matte-finished product. Aztec is available in standard dimensions and lengths of 6', 8', 10', and 12', as well as some 16' lengths. The manufacturer has certified the following recycled-content levels (by weight): total recovered material 100% typical, 100% guaranteed; post-consumer material 80% typical, 75% guaranteed.

Bedford Technology Plastic Lumber

Bedford Technology, LLC
2424 Armour Rd.
P.O. Box 609
Worthington, MN 56187

Toll-free: 800-721-9037
Phone: 507-372-5558
www.plasticboards.com

Bedford Technology offers plastic lumber made from post-consumer recycled HDPE and LDPE. It is available in a variety of dimensions, including $^5/_4$ decking, two-by lumber, and large timbers up to 12x12. Bedford's standard product colors are black, brown, gray, and cedar with other colors available. The manufacturer has certified the following recycled-content levels (by weight): total recovered material 99% typical, 99% guaranteed; post-consumer material 65% typical, 50% guaranteed.

Better Than Wood

American Ecoboard, LLC
200-C Finn Ct.
Farmingdale, NY 11735

Phone: 631-753-5151
www.americanecoboard.com

American Ecoboard manufactures fiberglass-reinforced dimension lumber from recycled HDPE, LDPE, and PP plastics.

Ecoboard Plastic Lumber

Trelleborg Engineered Products, Inc.
3470 Martinsburg Pk.
PO Box 98
Clearbrook, VA 22624

Phone: 540-667-5191
www.recycledplastic.com

Ecoboard® lumber is manufactured in a wide array of dimensions and colors. These products contain recycled HDPE and LDPE, as well as UV-stabilization, flame-retardant, and strength additives. The manufacturer has certified the following recycled-content levels (by weight): total recovered material 100% typical, 100% guaranteed; post-consumer material 90% typical, 80% guaranteed.

Environmental Recycling Plastic Lumber

Environmental Recycling, Inc.
8000 Hall St.
St. Louis, MO 63147

Phone: 314-382-7766

Environmental Recycling offers a full line of 100% recycled HDPE plastic lumber in common dimensions and gray, redwood, and black colors. They specialize in flooring systems for commercial trucks.

EPS Plastic Lumber

Engineered Plastic Systems
740 B Industrial Dr., Ste. B
Cary, IL 60013

Phone: 847-462-9001
www.epsplasticlumber.com

Environmental Plastic Systems (EPS) Bear Board plastic lumber is typically made from 100% post-consumer recycled HDPE and is available in a variety of sizes with a smooth or wood-grain finish. Available colors include white, gray, redwood, forest green, black, cedar, and tan. All EPS plastic products come with a 50-year limited warranty. Fiberglass-reinforced structural plastic lumber is also available.

EverGrain

Epoch Composite Products, Inc.
P.O.Box 567
Lamar, MO 64759

Toll-free: 800-253-1401
www.evergrain.com

Epoch's EverGrain composite decking and railing products are made with post-consumer recycled HPDE, LPDE, and wood flour. Nominal sizes include $1/2$x12, 1x6, 2x2, 2x4, and 2x6 in lengths ranging from 12' to 20'. Post sleeves and caps are also available. EverGrain has a 10-year warranty.

Everlast Plastic Lumber

Everlast Plastic Lumber
1000 S. 4th St.
Hamburg, PA 19526

Phone: 610-562-8336
www.everlastlumber.com

Everlast nonstructural plastic lumber is made with 100% recycled HPDE (80% post-consumer). Nominal sizes include 1-$1/2$ x 1-$1/2$ x 8; 2 x 2 x 8; $5/4$ x 6 x 8; $5/4$ x 6 x 12; 2 x 4 x 12; 2 x 6 x 12; 4 x 4 x 12; 6 x 6 x 12. Conventional carpentry tools with carbide blades are used for cutting and routing. Nails are not sufficient for fastening due to expansion and contraction ($1/4$" per 8 board feet); screws must be used. This product has a 50-year warranty.

Everlasting Lumber

Great Lakes Specialty Products
206 Enterprise Rd.
Delafield, WI 53018

Toll-free: 800-505-7926
Phone: 262-646-9470
www.greatlakesspecialty.com

Everlasting Lumber™ is made with 95% recycled #2 HDPE from consumer and industrial sources, impregnated with UV inhibitors and non-metallic colorants. A foamless manufacturing process is claimed to significantly enhance the material's usable life. The solid, pultruded products are manufactured with a slight wood grain texture; a coarser anti-skid surface is also available. Its weight is comparable to oak. Floor and railing boards, spindles, posts, and fascia skirting are available in standard and special sizes. Great Lakes Specialty Products supplies commercial and significant private enterprises including golf courses, theme parks, and campuses.

Impact-Post

XPotential Products, Inc.
St. Boniface Postal Sta.
P.O. Box 126
Winnipeg, MB R2H 3B4
Canada

Toll-free: 800-863-6619
Phone: 204-224-3933
www.xpotentialproducts.
com

Impact-Post™ is a plastic-composite product manufactured with recycled materials including auto shredder residue as well as HDPE and LDPE plastics. Impact-Post comes in two sizes (6" x 6" x 8' and 4" x 4" x 8'). The manufacturer has certified the following recycled-content levels (by weight): total recovered material 100% typical, 100% guaranteed; post-consumer material 85% typical, 85% guaranteed.

Inteq Plastic Lumber

Inteq Corp.
33010 Lakeland Blvd.
Eastlake, OH 44095

Phone: 440-953-0550

Inteq manufactures a variety of recycled HDPE plastic lumber. Nonstructural landscape timbers are available in multiple colors up to 12' in length in standard sizes of 4x4, 4x6, and 6x6. Decking and railing material is also made from recycled HDPE plastic and is available in multiple colors. Additionally, Inteq offers structural and nonstructural recycled plastic lumber in standard dimensions. Nonstructural is 100% HDPE, and structural contains 15% recycled fiberglass. Inteq asks customers to consult with them before utilizing the structural lumber. The manufacturer has certified the following recycled-content levels (by weight): total recovered material 100% typical, 100% guaranteed; post-consumer material 100% typical, 100% guaranteed.

Leisure Deck

The Plastic Lumber Company, Inc.
115 W. Bartges St.
Akron, OH 44311

Toll-free: 800-886-8990
Phone: 330-762-8989
www.plasticlumber.com

Leisure Deck™ is available in 1x6 and $^5/_4$x6 boards in plank, tongue-and-groove, or groove-and-groove, in seven colors. Several railing, post, and trim options are available, as is a line of outdoor furniture. Leisure Deck boards and accessories are made from 100% recycled HDPE, 97% post-consumer.

Marine Lumber

Plastic Pilings, Inc.
1485 S. Willow Ave.
Rialto, CA 92376

Phone: 909-874-4080
www.plasticpilings.com

Plastic Pilings manufactures various structural plastic lumber products including members from 3" x 6" to 12" x 20" and up to 50' in length. This recycled plastic product is reinforced with steel or fiberglass re-bar. The manufacturer has certified the following recycled-content levels (by weight): total recovered material 50% typical; post-consumer material 50% typical.

Millennium Lumber

BJM Industries, Inc.
R.R. 1, Box 257A
Kittanning, PA 16201

Phone: 724-548-2440
www.bjmindustries.com

Millennium Lumber is manufactured from a combination of 100% post-consumer recycled HDPE and post-industrial recycled cellulose (from diaper factory trimmings). Millennium Lumber is available in standard lengths from 8' to 16' and up to 30' by special order in a variety of colors and profiles.

Perma-Deck

Cascades Re-Plast, Inc.
772 Sherbrooke St. W,
Ste. 400
Montreal, QC H3A 1G1
Canada

Toll-free: 888-703-6515
Phone: 514-284-9850
www.cascadesreplast.
com

Perma-deck® is 100% recycled HDPE decking and lumber available in light gray, sandstone brown, redwood, and beige.

Perma-Deck Plastic Lumber

Environmental Building Products, Inc.
P.O. Box 261310
Highlands Ranch, CO 80163

Phone: 303-470-7555
www.environmentalbldgprod.com

Environmental Building Products markets and distributes plastic lumber throughout the Rocky Mountain region and western United States. Perma-Deck is a wood-grained plastic lumber made from recycled HDPE, PP, and PS plastic, and it comes in sandstone brown, beige, redwood, and light gray. The product has a 50-year limited warranty against splitting, warping, peeling, rot, and insect infestation. The manufacturer has certified the following recycled-content levels (by weight): total recovered material 100% typical, 90% guaranteed; post-consumer material 50% typical, 30% guaranteed.

Plasboard

Northern Plastic Lumber, Inc.
77 St. David St.
Lindsay, ON K9V 1N8

Toll-free: 888-255-1222
Phone: 705-878-5700
www.northernplasticlumber.com

Plasboard plastic lumber is made with commingled post-consumer recycled plastics (approximately 96% HDPE/LDPE/PP, 2% PET, 1% P.S., 1% other). A wide range of stock dimensions and profiles are available ranging from $^7/_8$" x 3-$^3/_8$" to 4" x 4", and including round stock in 2" to 6" diameters. Custom-size orders can be quoted. The Premium Plus line is available in white, cedar, sandstone, orange, yellow, and red. The Premium consumer-quality line is available in brown, light gray, forest green, and blue. Plasboard Standard comes in range of gray only; and a low-priced Utility line is available for applications where function is more important than issues of color and visual quality.

PlasTEAK Plastic Lumber

PlasTEAK
3563 Copley Rd.
P.O. Box 4290
Akron, OH 44321

Toll-free: 800-320-1841
Phone: 330-668-2587
www.plasteak.com

PlasTEAK is made with 100% post-consumer recycled HDPE in a paraffin base—the boards become more slip-resistant when wet. Stock material includes solid (molded) and hollow (extruded) dimension lumber in a variety of sizes and colors. Trim and sheet goods are also available.

Plastic Lumber

Taylors Recycled Plastic Products, Inc.
581 Hwy. 28
Bailieboro, ON K0L 1B0 Canada

Phone: 705-939-6072
www.taylorsplasticlumber.com

Taylors Recycled Plastic Products, Inc. produces nonstructural recycled-plastic lumber primarily from post-consumer recycled plastic in a variety of sizes, with gray as the standard color. Other colors are available on volume orders.

Recycled Plastic Man Plastic Lumber

Recycled Plastic Man, Inc.
P.O. Box 609
Placida, FL 33946

Toll-free: 800-253-7742
Phone: 941-698-1060
www.recycledplasticman.com

Recycled Plastic Man manufactures extruded plastic lumber of commingled HDPE for marine and residential use in a variety of profiles and colors. The manufacturer has certified the following recycled-content levels (by weight): total recovered material 100% guaranteed; post-consumer material 100% guaranteed.

Recycled-Plastic Lumber

Plastic Recycling of Iowa Falls, Inc.
10252 Hwy. 65
Iowa Falls, IA 50126

Toll-free: 800-338-1438
Phone: 641-648-5073
www.hammersplastic.com

Plastic Recycling of Iowa Falls, formerly Hammer's Plastic Recycling, manufactures a full line of recycled plastic lumber (in lengths up to 12') and assembled products (picnic tables, park benches, etc.) in a variety of colors of commingled recycled HDPE, LDPE, LLDPE, and miscellaneous plastics. The manufacturer has certified the following recycled-content levels (by weight): total recovered material 100% typical, 100% guaranteed; post-consumer material 50% typical, 50% guaranteed.

Re-Source Plastic Lumber

Re-Source Building Products
1685 Holmes Rd.
Elgin, IL 60123

Toll-free: 800-585-4988
Phone: 847-931-4771
www.plastival.com

Re-Source Building Products manufactures plastic lumber from 98% recycled HDPE in 30 different profiles including deck and railing components.

Rumber Lumber

Rumber Materials Inc.
3420 Executive Center Dr., Ste. 200
Austin, TX 78731

Toll-free: 877-786-2371
Phone: 940-759-4181
www.rumber.com

Rumber® Lumber, made from recycled HDPE plastic and recycled-tire rubber, is available in 2x2, 2x4, 2x6, 2x8, 2x12, and 4x4 dimensions in standard lengths of 6' to 24'. The manufacturer has certified the following recycled-content levels (by weight): total recovered material 100% typical, 100% guaranteed; post-consumer material 50% typical, 50% guaranteed.

SeaTimber

Seaward International, Inc.
3470 Martinsburg Pike
Clearbrook, VA 22624

Toll-free: 800-828-5360
Phone: 540-667-5191

SeaTimber® recycled plastic lumber with fiberglass reinforcement was developed as an alternative to preservative-treated lumber for marine applications. SeaTimber contains UV inhibitors, is impervious to marine borers, and has been U.S. government-approved for structural marine applications.

The Forever Deck

Plastic Lumber Yard, LLC
220 Washington St.
Norristown, PA 19401

Phone: 610-277-3900
www.plasticlumberyard.com

The Forever Deck® is constructed with recycled plastic lumber made from 100% recycled HDPE. The manufacturer has certified the following recycled-content levels (by weight): total recovered material 100% typical, 100% guaranteed; post-consumer material 30% typical.

The Plastic Lumber Company

The Plastic Lumber Company, Inc.
115 W. Bartges St.
Akron, OH 44311

Toll-free: 800-886-8990
Phone: 330-762-8989
www.plasticlumber.com

The Plastic Lumber Company offers approximately 20 different profiles of dimensional plastic lumber available in 12 different colors. Sizes range from $1/2$" x 2-$1/2$" to 6x6. Commercial and residential decking is also available. Recycled content is 97% post-consumer.

Trimax Decking

Trimax Building Products, Inc.
2600 W. Roosevelt Rd.
Chicago, IL 60608

Toll-free: 866-987-4629
www.trimaxbp.com

Trimax Decking consists of decking, rail, and stair parts containing 90% post-consumer HDPE by weight. Decking lumber and stair treads are also available in a knurled, nonskid finish.

Trimax Structural

Trimax Building Products, Inc.
2600 W. Roosevelt Rd.
Chicago, IL 60608

Toll-free: 866-987-4629
www.trimaxbp.com

Trimax Structural Lumber contains 90% recycled material by weight, including post-consumer recycled HDPE (65%) and post-industrial recycled fiberglass. Trimax Structural Lumber comes in gray, and is available by special order in green, tan, redwood, and white.

VERDURA Deck

New Frontier Industries, Inc.
P.O. Box 1360
Milton, NH 03851

Toll-free: 866-637-7888
www.newfrontierindustries.com

VERDURA Deck is a strong, lightweight, engineered decking product made with 95% post-consumer mixed plastic (mostly ABS, polycarbonate and high impact polystyrene) with a thin, UV-protected PVC wear layer. The interlocking 6" x 1.5" tongue-and-groove engineered modules install onto joists using regular deck screws. The maintenance-free, slip-resistant, wood-textured surface is ribbed to channel water off the deck. A variety of colors and simulated wood tones are available. This product is re-usable and recyclable, according to the manufacturer, and comes with a 25-year transferable warranty. The "recyclable" claim is questionable, given the mix of polymer types going into the manufacture, especially the PVC topcoat.

Preservative-Treated Wood and Treatment Products

see Structural Systems & Components: Preservative-Treated Wood and Treatment Products.

Wood-Plastic Composite Lumber

Wood-plastic composite lumber incorporates some of the characteristics of wood with those of plastic lumber. Recycled plastic resin (usually polyethylene) is combined with wood fiber—which may be post-industrial recycled content or virgin fiber—to create a product that has various advantages over both solid wood and solid plastic. Like plastic lumber, it will not rot, crack, or splinter, while the wood fiber adds considerable strength. Wood-plastic composite materials generally have a more natural coloring and appearance than 100%-plastic materials. The wood fibers, however, may absorb water and fade in color over time. Some wood-plastic composite lumber is graded for structural use, primarily as deck substructure and for marine use. This is not true of all wood-plastic composites, so check with the manufacturer for specific product indications.

ChoiceDek

AERT, Inc.
(Advanced Environmental Recycling Technologies, Inc.)
P.O. Box 1237
Springdale, AR 72765

Toll-free: 800-951-5117
Phone: 479-756-7400
www.aertinc.com

AERT manufactures ChoiceDek™, a decking product composed of 48% recycled plastic and 52% recycled wood fibers. ChoiceDek is offered in 4 colors. The underside of a ChoiceDek board has large corrugations to improve the strength-to-weight ratio. The manufacturer has certified the following recycled-content levels (by weight): total recovered material 100% typical, 95% guaranteed; post-consumer material 10-20% typical, 0% guaranteed. ChoiceDek is available only at Lowe's Home Centers.

CorrectDeck

Correct Building
Products
8 Morin St.
Biddeford, ME 04005

Toll-free: 877-332-5877
Phone: 207-284-5600
www.correctdeck.com

CorrectDeck™ biocomposite decking is made with a combination of virgin and reclaimed polypropylene (minimum 25% recycled, up to 50%), reclaimed hardwood fiber (up to 60% of the total composition), and UV-inhibited pigmenting. CorrectDeck Classic™ has a solid profile and fastens with decking screws; CorrectDeck Channeled has a side-grooved profile to accommodate a hidden fastener system that eliminates screw holes. Both profiles have embossed wood grain and are slightly crowned to shed water; come in 12', 16', and 20' lengths; and are available in Grey, Cedar, Acadia, and Mahogany integral colors. Posts, rails, fascia and other accessories are also available. CorrectDeck DCL (dimensional composite lumber) is the same material as the decking, available in several dimensions and lengths including 2x4, 2x6, and 4x4. CorrectDeck offers a 25-year warranty.

MoistureShield Composite Trim

AERT, Inc.
(Advanced Environmental Recycling Technologies, Inc.)
P.O. Box 1237
Springdale, AR 72765

Toll-free: 800-951-5117
Phone: 479-756-7400
www.aertinc.com

AERT manufactures MoistureShield® CornerLoc™ composite trim and trim board from recycled hardwood fiber and recycled polyethylene plastic. MoistureShield can be ripped, routed, or molded to fit custom applications such as 45-degree corners. The product comes with a factory-applied tie-coat primer and offers either a textured or smooth surface. MoistureShield comes with a limited lifetime warranty against decay and insect damage. The manufacturer has certified the following recycled-content levels (by weight): total recovered material 100% typical, 95% guaranteed; post-consumer material 10-20% typical, 0% guaranteed.

Nexwood

Nexwood Industries, Ltd.
1327 Clark Blvd.
Brampton, ON L6T 5R5
Canada

Toll-free: 888-763-9966
Phone: 905-799-9686
www.nexwood.com

Nexwood™ is a 98%-recycled HDPE and cellulose fiber (rice hulls) composite decking product. Unlike similar products, this three-celled, hollow-core material is rigid. For residential decks Nexwood is suitable for installation on 24" centers with the 2x6 profile. For commercial decks, boardwalks, and docks, 16" on-center support is recommended. Nexwood is currently available in 2x6 and ⁵/₄ tongue-and-groove, ⁵/₄ radius edge board, as well as fence and rail components in 4x4, 2x4, 2x2, and fascia board. End caps are also available in all profiles except 2x4.

Rhino Deck

Master Mark Plastics
One Master Mark Drive
P.O. Box 662
Albany, MN 56307

Toll-free: 800-535-4838
Phone: 320-845-2111
www.mastermark.com

Rhino Deck® composite deck building components include lumber, posts, spindles, a rail system, and planks in 12', 14' and 20' lengths. Decking products are made from 50% recycled HDPE plastic and 50% recycled wood fibers from cabinet/furniture making operations. The manufacturer has certified the following recycled-content levels (by weight): total recovered material 50% typical, 50% guaranteed; post-consumer material 50% typical, 50% guaranteed.

Trex

Trex Company, Inc.
160 Exeter Dr.
Winchester, VA 22603

Toll-free: 800-289-8739
Phone: 540-542-6300
www.trex.com

Trex® was the first wood-plastic composite product brought to market. Available in a number of common dimensions, seven colors, and three finishes, Trex is a wood-polymer lumber made from post-consumer and/or post-industrial reclaimed plastic and waste wood. According to the manufacturer, the reclaimed plastic comes primarily from grocery sacks and stretch film, and the waste wood is from woodworking manufacturers. The manufacturer has certified the following recycled-content levels (by weight): total recovered material 97% typical, 94% guaranteed; post-consumer material 68% typical, 65% guaranteed.

WeatherBest Decking

LP
414 Union St., Ste. 2000
Nashville, TN 37219

Toll-free: 877-744-5600
www.lpcorp.com

WeatherBest™ Basic and WeatherBest Select are smooth-faced composite decking products that weather to varying shades of grey or ivory. WeatherBest Premium has a reversible, random wood-grained pattern over rough-sawn boards and is available in five colors with minimal fading. All three lines are made with 100% recycled wood and HDPE; the MSDS lists 55-90% wood flour, 5-35% HDPE, and less than 5% talc. These lines have a limited 10-year warranty. Available sizes include standard 8', 12', 16', and 20' lengths in a nominal $5/_4$x6 solid plank for 16" on-center installations. Fascia, post sleeves, post caps, balusters, and side rails are available in all colors.

This Space is Available for Your Notes

This Space is Available for Your Notes

Foundations, Footers, & Slabs

Conventional foundations, footers, and slabs use a lot of concrete, which is energy-intensive and polluting to produce—up to a ton of CO_2 is released in producing a ton of cement. Admixture components such as calcium chloride (an accelerator), gypsum (a retarder), and sulfonated melamine formaldehyde (SMF, a plasticizer) also affect the environmental impact of the concrete. Depending on the chemical, the impact may be on-site or at the plant. Also, concrete foundations and slabs do not provide much by way of thermal insulation, though they can provide thermal storage. Foundations, footers, and slabs should always be detailed to reduce thermal bridging as much as possible.

Forming can account for a significant portion of the total cost of poured concrete. Essentially, things get built twice: once in forms and again in concrete. Plywood has been the mainstay of concrete-forming companies for many years, though some companies have invested in reusable, durable forms—a more resource-efficient solution that is still relatively labor-intensive. Reusable forms also require form-release agents, most of which are petrochemical-based and offgas large amounts of volatile organic compounds (VOCs). Vegetable-based form-release oils are available.

For large buildings and some sites with poor soil conditions, foundations are engineered to specific structural requirements, and fairly extensive use of concrete may well be necessary. For certain applications, replacing up to 50% of the cement in a concrete mixture with fly ash from coal-burning power plants will reduce the environmental impact of producing the material, and this substitution can actually strengthen the concrete. Fine-ground blast-furnace slag from metal foundries can have similar properties to those of fly ash.

For homes and smaller buildings, alternative foundation systems are available that can reduce concrete use and increase energy efficiency. Many such products consist of stay-in-place insulating concrete forms (ICFs) made of polystyrene foam or a cementitious matrix of recycled foam or recycled wood fibers. Expanded polystyrene (EPS) foam should be preferred until extruded polysterene (XPS) foam insulation becomes available without ozone-depleting HCFCs. Some EPS foam products have an integral borate treatment, which helps keep damaging insects out of the foam. The brominated flame retardants used in most EPS foam have health and environmental risks that are generating significant concern.

Precast concrete foundation walls are available in some areas. They use less concrete than site-cast foundations and are designed to accommodate interior insulation.

The depth of a foundation wall (and thus the amount of material required) can be reduced by raising the frost line, generally by placing foam insulation horizontally (usually extending about 4') around the foundation. These "frost-protected shallow foundations" can save money and materials where crawl-space or slab-on-grade foundations are used in cold climates. "Rubble trench" foundations are another option—one that was favored by Frank Lloyd Wright. Pier foundations, which can reduce excavation requirements and concrete use significantly, may also be an appropriate choice.

Non-asphalt-based dampproofing reduces the risk of introducing chemicals into local aquifers and VOCs into the building, and they can be longer lasting.

In some parts of the country, rigid mineral wool panels are available that help insulate foundation walls while also providing effective drainage. Mineral wool typically includes iron-ore slag—a pre-consumer waste product. And recycled aggregate or crushed glass can be used as aggregate in the concrete or as backfill for foundation drains.

Foundations can also be designed with termite shields or be backfilled with special termite-proof sand, so that toxic soil treatments are not required. Pesticides commonly used around foundations introduce hazardous chemicals to the environment and must be periodically reapplied.

Autoclaved Aerated Concrete Blocks

Commercial production of autoclaved aerated concrete (AAC) began in 1930 in Europe, where it has been widely used for decades. Concrete masonry units (CMUs) made from AAC are lighter than conventional CMUs, generally have no cores, and provide higher insulation levels (R-values of up to 1.25 per inch, an order of magnitude higher than standard concrete). The insulating value of AAC allows it to function simultaneously as structure and insulation system. It has about 20% of the density—though only about 10% of the compressive strength—of regular concrete. Manufacturers may increase the product's strength by including reinforcing steel rods or mesh. Structural applications of unreinforced AAC are limited to low-rise buildings; in high-rise buildings it may be used in partition and curtain walls. AAC has very good sound-absorbing characteristics and can be worked with conventional carpenter's tools, making site modifications relatively easy. It's also nontoxic, fire-resistant, insect-proof , and can be produced using coal fly ash as a substitute for some of the sand in conventional AAC. But because AAC is a porous material, it must be protected from moisture with claddings or coatings. AAC is not a 1:1 substitution for conventional CMU in terms of installation; greater care must be taken in installation because the shallow mortar bed does not allow for alignment adjustments easily made with the deeper mortar beds of conventional CMUs.

ACCOA

ACCOA Aerated Concrete Corporation of America
3351 W. Orange Blossom Trl.
Apopka, FL 32712

Phone: 407-884-0051
www.accoaac.com

ACCO AAC blocks, lintels, and panels are made by Aerated Concrete Corporation of America.

Contec AAC

XELLA AAC Texas, Inc.
1535 Brady Blvd., Ste. 2
San Antonio, TX 78237

Toll-free: 877-926-6832
Phone: 210-402-3223
www.texascontec.com

Contec AAC, formed in 1995, manufactures Autoclaved Aerated Concrete (AAC) at its plant in Monterrey, Mexico. Texas Contec is their U.S. distributor and offers a full line of AAC products, accessories, and technical services.

E-Crete

E-Crete
2151 E. Broadway Rd. #115
Tempe, AZ 85282

Toll-free: 877-351-4448
Phone: 480-596-3819 x11
www.e-crete.com

E-Crete has been producing autoclaved aerated concrete (AAC) blocks in a plant near Phoenix, Arizona since December 2000. The company uses sterile mine tailings from an adjacent closed copper mine to substitute for the silica content, which represents 25% of the dry weight content. E-Crete reports a steady-state insulating value of approximately R-1.04 per inch for their most common block (density of 32 lbs/ft3). E-Crete has a UL Classified 4-hour fire rating and is mold resistant.

SafeCrete AAC

SafeCrete AAC
6652 Hwy. 41 North
PO Box 1129
Ringgold, GA 30736

Phone: 706-965-4587
www.safecrete.com

In June 2001, Babb International acquired Matrix (a licensee of the Hebel AAC process). SafeCrete, a Babb Company, offers many block and panel sizes of AAC, including blocks larger than standard CMU-size, larger "jumbo" units, panels, and a variety of specially manufactured shapes and pre-assembled wall sections—00with integral reinforcement. AAC products are made from a mixture of poured concrete, fly ash, and sand. Babb products can be used for interior and exterior applications. In exterior wall applications, they must not be exposed but can be painted with a textured paint, coated with a stucco finish specially made for AAC, or clad with standard siding.

Bentonite Waterproofing

Bentonite is a highly expansive natural clay. When exposed to moisture, it swells "shut," providing effective waterproofing. Products are available in sheets or panels.

Bentonite Waterproofing Systems

CETCO - Building Materials Group
1500 W. Shure Dr.
Arlington Heights, IL 60004

Toll-free: 800-527-9948
Phone: 847-392-5800
www.cetco.com

CETCO produces several waterproofing membranes using sodium bentonite, a natural clay with extremely low permeability and self-sealing properties. These membranes may be used beneath concrete slabs, against backfilled foundation walls, and for property line construction, such as lagging and metal sheet piling retention walls. Also, CETCO provides bentonite-based concrete joint waterstops that activate and swell to form a positive seal. CETCO claims that the products typically contain no VOCs and require no solvent-based primers or adhesives. Bentonite waterproofing can be installed on "green" concrete as soon as the forms are removed in a wide range of weather conditions, including freezing temperatures.

Cast-in-Place Concrete

Cement production is energy-intensive and polluting; concrete mixtures incorporating recycled-content, performance-enhancing, portland-cement-reducing admixtures such as fly ash are desirable. Recycled materials used in place of mined stone aggregate—such as slag, a byproduct of steel production—ease landfill burdens and can improve the concrete's strength-to-weight ratio and thermal properties. Products listed here incorporate recycled content or have other desirable environmental qualities.

Lafarge Lightweight Concrete Aggregate

Lafarge North America (Chicago and Hamilton Slag)
139 Windermere Rd.
Hamilton, ON L8H 3Y2 Canada

Phone: 219-378-1193
www.lafargenorthamerica.com

Lafarge Lightweight Concrete Aggregate is blast furnace slag aggregate--the recovered nonmetallic mineral components from iron blast furnaces. It can reduce portland cement concrete's weight while improving its compressive strength. The slag is inert and is otherwise typically landfilled. A finer grind of this slag has properties similar to fly ash.

Cast-in-Place Concrete Forms

Cement production requires about 6 million Btus per ton of cement produced; most of that energy is used in coal-fired cement kilns, resulting in high carbon dioxide, nitrous oxide, and sulfur emissions. It's been calculated that producing a ton of cement releases a ton of CO2 into the atmosphere. Judicious use of concrete is an important green-building consideration. Concrete pier foundations greatly reduce concrete use compared with full-height frost walls; while most commonly used for decks, outdoor stairs, and the like, they are also used for entire buildings and can be particularly appropriate on ecologically fragile sites. Products listed here are less resource-intensive than conventional concrete-forming products, permit the construction of foundations using less concrete, or are made from recycled-content materials or plywood certified according to the standards of the Forest Stewardship Council (FSC). Concrete construction tubes made from recycled paper, in conjunction with recycled-plastic or fabric footing forms, offer a quick, resource-efficient means of pouring structural piers.

Bigfoot System Footing Forms

Bigfoot Systems Inc.
6750 Hwy. #3
Martin's Point, NS B0J 2E0 Canada

Toll-free: 800-934-0393
Phone: 902-627-1600
www.bigfootsystems.com

The Bigfoot System® is a one-piece, lightweight, recycled, high-density polyethylene (HDPE) form for site-forming pier footings. The funnel-shaped form replaces site-built solid-wood footings. The construction tube and the footing pour as one unit. Bigfoot Systems will accept all 6", 8", 10", 12", 14", 16", and 18" cardboard construction tubes. Tubes are attached to the Bigfoot Systems using four screws.

Caraustar Concrete Column Forms

Caraustar ICPG Corp.
5000 Austell-Powder Springs Rd., Ste. 300
Austell, GA 30106

Phone: 770-948-3101
www.caraustar.com

Caraustar (formerly Smurfit) Concrete Column Forms are recycled-paper concrete forms with a polyethylene-impregnated virgin kraft interior layer (to aid release) and a waxed exterior. The recycled-paper content is estimated to be 90% from mixed, post-industrial, and post-consumer sources, according to the company. Caraustar Concrete Column Forms are available from 6" to 48" in diameter (2" increments up to 24").

Fastfoot, Fastbag, and Fast-Tube Fabric Forms

Fab-Form Industries Ltd.
Unit #212, 6333 148th St.
Surrey, BC V3S 3C3 Canada

Toll-free: 888-303-3278
Phone: 604-596-3278
www.fab-form.com

Fastfoot® is a fabric concrete footing form system for linear foundations. Specially designed steel "yokes" hold pairs of 2x4s, which hold the fabric in a trough formation. After the 2x4s are leveled, the trough is filled with concrete. The 2x4s can be nailed to the partially cured concrete as bracing for the foundation forms or removed for reuse. Fastfoot is well suited to rocky or uneven ground. Fastfoot Lite is a simplified version, which uses the same fabric with 2x4s and stakes. Fastbag®, for pier footings, is a nonwoven polypropylene "pillowcase" with a hole in the top that is nailed to the ground and filled with concrete. As the plastic fabric forms are not removed, there may be some indoor air quality benefits from the capillary break between footings and soil. The company also now offers Fast-Tube™ for forming concrete columns.

Geotube Reusable Plastic Column Forms

Geoproducts Corp.
11-110 Jardin Dr.
Concord, ON L4K 4R4 Canada

Toll-free: 877-GEOTUBE
Phone: 905-760-2256
www.geoproductscorp.com

Geotube reusable plastic forms for square, rectangular, and round columns are made with recycled polypropylene. Since concrete doesn't stick to plastic, these forms do not require release agents, lubricants, or cleaning detergents. The modular formworks, which can be stored in damp environments without damage, connect together with nylon handles. The manufacturer guarantees 100 reuses.

GreenCore Plyform

ROMEX World Trade Company, LLC - sales agent for ROM
P.O. Box 1110
Alexandria, LA 71309

Toll-free: 800-299-5174
Phone: 318-445-1973
www.royomartin.com

GreenCore Plyform® FSC-certified concrete forming panels are available in BB grade and 19/32" and 23/32" thicknesses. These panels are edge-sealed and oiled with NOX-CRETE Concrete Forming Oil, a petroleum-based product made by Chemtrec in Omaha, Nebraska. The mill also produces industrial plywood. GreenCore Plyform is certified using partial-content rules for certification (some fiber used in the mill comes from land not owned by the company), but 100% FSC-certified product can be provided. Roy O. Martin Lumber Management, LLC (ROM) is the first company to receive FSC-certification in the state of Louisiana, and they offer the first FSC-certified OSB and FSC-certified utility poles.

Recycled-Paper Formworks/Brick Ledger Void Forms

SureVoid Products, Inc.
1895 W. Dartmouth Ave.
Englewood, CO 80110

Toll-free: 800-458-5444
Phone: 303-762-0324
www.surevoid.com

SureVoid® produces a range of corrugated paper construction products, referred to commonly as "void forms" or "carton forms." These forms create a space between concrete structures and expansive soils (soils high in clay content that expand when wet) to isolate the concrete from the swelling ground. They can also provide a temporary support platform until the grade beam or structural slab has set and can support itself across drilled piers, pads, or intermittent footings. As the corrugated paper eventually absorbs ground moisture and loses strength, it creates a space for wet soil to expand into without causing damage. An alternative use for these products is to displace concrete volume as a means of reducing weight and cost.

Sonotubes Concrete Forms

Sonoco Products Co.
1 North Second St.
Hartsville, SC 29550

Toll-free: 888-875-8754
Phone: 843-383-7000
www.sonotube.com

Sonotube® concrete forms are made from recycled paperboard and are available from 6" to 60" in diameter. In addition to traditional round forms, the product line includes Sonotube Commercial, Sonotube Square, and Sonotube FinishFree for a smooth, architectural finish.

The Footing Tube

The Footing Tube
28 Amberwood Ln.
Fredericton, NB E3C 1L7 Canada

Toll-free: 888-929-2011
Phone: 506-452-8919
www.foottube.com

The Footing Tube™ is a tapered, one-piece, 100% recycled polyethylene footing and pier form primarily for decks and additions. The 62"-high form, which can hold a volume of 4.8 ft3 of concrete, has a diameter of 24" at the base of the footing and 8" at the top of the pier. According to the company, the taper and smooth plastic of the sides of a properly installed tube increases resistance to frost uplift in comparison to typical cylindrical formwork. The Footing Tube works in frost-prone areas to 5' depths.

Concrete Accessories

Concrete accessories include such items as anchors, inserts, expansion joints, waterstops, and products that prevent soil contamination from truck overages. Filling the expansion joints in concrete construction is a good use of panels made from recycled newspaper or waste agricultural materials, because the strength requirements are minimal (though for radon control, less permeable joint sealants may be preferable). Waterstops must be highly durable and corrosion resistant; plasticized PVC is the most common waterstop material, though alternatives are available to a limited degree. Rebar supports for concrete formwork hold rebar in place during pours; they have minimal structural requirements, making them good candidates for manufacturing with recycled waste plastic. Products listed here have high recycled content or some other significant attribute.

Earth Shield Chemical Resistant Waterstop

JP Specialties, Inc.
551 Birch St.
Lake Elsinore, CA 92530

Toll-free: 888-836-5778
Phone: 951-674-6869
www.jpspecialties.com

Earth Shield is a thermoplastic vulcanizate, an alloy of EPDM rubber for flexibility and polypropylene for processability and weldability. It contains no additives, such as fillers, stabilizers, or plasticizers, and is designed to withstand highly demanding conditions. The company claims that Earth Shield is the only embedded waterstop that has been certified to meet NSF Standard 61 for direct contact with drinking water.

EnviroSac Bag

Enviro-Systems, Inc.
1869 S. Cobb Industrial Blvd.
Smyrna, GA 30082

Toll-free: 800-851-3082
Phone: 770-333-0206
www.envirosys.us

EnviroSac™ woven polypropylene bags collect overage waste during clean-out of concrete ready-mix trucks, concrete pump rigs, and hoppers. The concrete can be left to cure for pick-up by loader, forklift, crane, or hoist. Lightweight EnviroSac bags come in several sizes, include high-strength lifting straps, and fold for compact storage. Bags may be made of lined, urethane coated, or uncoated material. Moisture will bleed through the uncoated material; waterproof liners are recommended for applications in which the alkaline runoff is not acceptable. EnviroSystems also has a program for recycling EnviroSac™ bags and provides customers with a national list of concrete recyclers for the excess concrete.

Homex 300

Homasote Company
932 Lower Ferry Rd.
P.O. Box 7240
West Trenton, NJ 08628

Toll-free: 800-257-9491
Phone: 609-883-3300
www.homasote.com

Homex® 300 can be used both as an expansion joint filler and a clean, curvable light-duty forming material for concrete slabs. This non-bituminous 98% post-consumer waste paper material with weather- and termite-resistant additives conforms to ASTM D-1751, and is available in a variety of lengths, widths, and thicknesses.

Rebar Supports

Eclipse Plastic, Inc.
12504 Roosevelt Rd.
Snohomish, WA 98290

Toll-free: 800-278-4276
Phone: 360-863-9213
www.eclipseplastic.com

Eclipse Plastic manufactures and sells directly a variety of rebar support devices made from 100% recycled engineering-grade plastic.

Concrete Blocks

Like many conventional products, CMUs can be used in "green" ways—for example, using a decorative type of block that eliminates additional finish materials. Products listed here exhibit superior energy performance (innovative web designs with specially designed expanded polystyrene insulation inserts), reduced material use by way of a finished exterior face (such as split-faced block), or post-industrial recycled content (such as fly ash or ground blast-furnace slag).

Grey Block and GlasStone

Clayton Block Company
515 Rte. 528
Lakewood, NJ 08701

Toll-free: 888-662-3044
Phone: 732-919-6009
www.claytonco.com

Clayton manufactures a regular and a lightweight gray concrete block containing respectively, 50% and 35% recovered block and concrete. Clayton also manufactures GlasStone™, a terrazzo-like architectural block made of approximately 80% recycled glass that is 1/2 post-industrial and 1/2 post consumer material. Clayton's manufacturing plants are in NJ and product is distributed regionally in the mid-Atlantic states.

Omni Block

Omni Block, Inc.
15125 N. Hayden Rd. #123
Scottsdale, AZ 85260

Phone: 480-661-9009
www.omniblock.com

Omni Block is a uniquely molded concrete block (not foam) available in 8" and 12" sizes designed to minimize thermal bridging and to receive molded EPS insulation inserts. Omni Block is reinforced with rebar and grout in some of the interior cells as determined per structural engineering. All electrical and plumbing are run within the block so no furring or sheetrock is required for a finished wall.

Concrete Curing

Concrete curing agents are coatings or admixtures that aid the set and cure of freshly poured concrete. They generally use coalescing agents to retard evaporation. Conventional products use a petroleum hydrocarbon resin base. Products listed here are made with biobased materials, are low-solvent, low-VOC (50 g/l or less), water-based, or some combination of those.

Concrete Curing Compounds

Kaufman Products, Inc.
3811 Curtis Ave.
Baltimore, MD 21226

Toll-free: 800-637-6372
Phone: 410-354-8600
www.kaufmanproducts.net

Kaufman Products offers several low-VOC industrial concrete curing and sealing compounds. Thinfilm 422 Wax Base is a zero-VOC water-emulsion membrane compound formulated especially for highways, but also appropriate for driveways, sidewalks, curbs, and gutters; available pigmented or clear in pails, drums, and bulk. Krystal 15 emulsion and Krystal 25 emulsion are water emulsion acrylic polymer curing and sealing compounds with 9 g/l VOC, available in drums and pails. Cure 100 is a water-emulsion, resin-based membrane compound with 14 g/l VOC, available in drums and pails. Cure & Seal 309 emulsion is a water-emulsion, acrylic-modified resin curing and sealing compound with 60 g/l VOC.

Cure and Seal

Natural Soy, LLC
P.O. Box 489
123 N. Orchard St.
Brooklyn, IA 52211

Toll-free: 888-606-9559
Phone: 641-522-9559
www.soyclean.biz

Natural Soy's Cure and Seal, made from
soy oil and other natural ingredients, is
designed to retain the hydration water
in freshly worked concrete. It also repels
water and assists in the prevention of surface scaling of concrete
induced by freeze-thaw cycles and the impact of deicing salts. Cure
and Seal will not prevent the penetration of motor or other heavier
oils. It is available in 5-, 55-, and 250-gallon containers and should
be applied at a rate of 1 gal/200 ft2.

Med-Cure and 1600-White Concrete Curing Compounds

W. R. Meadows, Inc.
300 Industrial Dr.
P.O. Box 338
Hampshire, IL 60140

Toll-free: 800-342-5976
Phone: 847-214-2100
www.wrmeadows.com

W.R. Meadows offers a variety of low-VOC concrete curing compounds.
Med-Cure is an economical, zero-VOC, general-purpose construction
curing compound used for curing, hardening, and dustproofing exposed
concrete floor slabs, sidewalks, driveways, etc. The 1600-White series,
with 31 g/l VOC, are white-pigmented curing compounds formulated
for exterior horizontal applications such as highways, airports, and
street paving. A water-based emulsion, 1600-White was specifically
developed to eliminate the use of hydrocarbon solvents.

Quantum-Cure

Atlas Construction Supply, Inc.
4640 Brinell St.
San Diego, CA 92111

Phone: 858-277-2100
www.atlasform.com

Atlas Quantum-Cure™ is a water-based, zero-VOC, concrete curing
compound that forms a moisture-retaining membrane for proper cement hydration. The ready-to-use, non-staining cure is spray-applied
on freshly placed concrete and does not need to be removed prior
to application of subsequent materials. Quantum-cure is NSF/ANSI
certified to be safe for potable water containment projects.

Vocomp-20, 25, 30

W. R. Meadows, Inc.
300 Industrial Dr.
P.O. Box 338
Hampshire, IL 60140

Toll-free: 800-342-5976
Phone: 847-214-2100
www.wrmeadows.com

Vocomp-20, -25, and -30, are low-VOC, water-based acrylic curing and
sealing compounds, with VOC levels of 4, 46, and 31 g/l, respectively.
Vocomp-20 has short application and drying times. Vocomp-25 and -30
are formulated to provide a medium to high sheen, with Vocomp-30
forming a thicker film. These products were developed as water-based
emulsions to eliminate the use of hydrocarbon solvents.

Concrete Form-Release Agents

*Conventional form-release oils can be a major source of VOCs, soil
contamination, and human health risks. Increasingly, biodegradable, nonpetroleum alternatives are available. These products
contain just a fraction of the federally permitted VOC limit for
concrete form-release agents. Many of these products produce a
smoother finished surface with fewer "bug holes." Products listed
here are made with agricultural crops, are typically water-based
and biodegradable, and have less than 60 grams per liter VOC.*

BEAN-e-doo Asphalt Release

Franmar Chemical, Inc.
P.O. Box 5565
Bloomington, IL 61702

Toll-free: 800-538-5069
Phone: 309-452-7526
www.franmar.com

Franmar makes soy-based asphalt and concrete form-release agents.

Bio-Form

Universal Building Products Inc.
840 25th Ave.
Bellwood, IL 60104

Phone: 708-544-4255
www.universalbuildingproducts.com

Bio-Form® is a biodegradable, zero-VOC concrete form-release agent
made primarily from rapeseed oil (in food-grade form known as Canola
oil). It can be used below freezing point and covers 2,000 ft2/gal on
pretreated high-density overlay forms. Bio-Form is available in 5- and
55-gallon containers and 275-gallon tanks. Though more expensive
than conventional products, it has been reported to perform better.

BioGuard Form Release Agent

Atlas Construction Supply, Inc.
4640 Brinell St.
San Diego, CA 92111

Phone: 858-277-2100
www.atlasform.com

Atlas Bio-Guard is a water-borne, zero-VOC, biodegradable, soy-derived
form-release agent that can be used on many types of concrete forms
and liners, including plywood, steel, aluminum, polystyrene, fiberglass,
etc. It is available in ready-to-use 5-, 55-, and 275-gallon containers.
Atlas offers 100% guaranteed satisfaction.

Crete-Lease 20-VOC

Cresset Chemical Company
One Cresset Center, Box 367
Weston, OH 43569

Toll-free: 800-367-2020
Phone: 419-669-2041
www.cresset.com

Crete-Lease 20-VOC is a water-based form-release agent. Available in 5- and 55-gallon containers and 275-gallon totes.

Duogard II

W. R. Meadows, Inc.
300 Industrial Dr.
P.O. Box 338
Hampshire, IL 60140

Toll-free: 800-342-5976
Phone: 847-214-2100
www.wrmeadows.com

Duogard II, a water-emulsion concrete form-release agent with a VOC content of 55 g/l, is available in 5- and 55-gallon containers.

Enviroform and Aquastrip

Conspec
4226 Kansas Ave.
Kansas City, KS 66106

Toll-free: 800-348-7351
Phone: 913-279-4800
www.conspecmkt.com

Enviroform is a 100% biodegradable, plant-oil-based, zero-VOC form-release agent. Aquastrip is a water-based, solvent-containing, VOC-compliant release agent.

Ezkote Green

US Mix Products Company
112 S. Santa Fe Dr.
Denver, CO 80223

Toll-free: 800-397-9903
Phone: 303-778-7227
www.usmix.com

Ezkote Green is a non-petroleum based, biodegradable form release agent made from agricultural oils. Ezkote Green contains zero VOCs and is part of the US SPEC line of concrete products from US Mix Co.

Farm Fresh Form Release Agent

Unitex
3101 Gardner
Kansas City, MO 64120

Toll-free: 800-821-5846
Phone: 816-231-7700
www.unitex-chemicals.com

Farm Fresh is a water-borne, zero-VOC, biodegradable, soybean oil, form-release agent for plywood, steel, aluminum, polystyrene and fiberglass forms and liners. Farm Fresh Plus is a solvent-borne version,

also made from soybean oil, for use in sub-freezing conditions. Both are available in 5-gallon pails, 55-gallon drums, and 275-gallon totes. The manufacturer offers 100% guaranteed satisfaction.

FormKote Emulsion

Kaufman Products, Inc.
3811 Curtis Ave.
Baltimore, MD 21226

Toll-free: 800-637-6372
Phone: 410-354-8600
www.kaufmanproducts.net

FormKote Emulsion is a water-based, freeze-thaw-stable, low-VOC (5 g/l), emulsified-chemical form-release agent offering a high coverage rate. Available in 55-gallon drums and five-gallon pails, this biodegradable product applies white and dries clear.

Formshield WB

The Euclid Chemical Company
19218 Redwood Rd.
Cleveland, OH 44110

Toll-free: 800-321-7628
Phone: 216-531-9222
www.euclidchemical.com

Formshield WB (formerly Aquaform) is a water-based form-release agent available in 5- and 55-gallon containers.

Greenplus Form Release Agent ES

Greenland Corporation
7016-30 St. SE
Calgary, AB T2C 1N9 Canada

Toll-free: 800-598-7636
Phone: 403-720-7049
www.greenpluslubes.com

Greenland Corporation manufactures the Greenplus line of rapidly biodegradable, vegetable oil-based lubricants suitable for a wide variety of lubricating applications. Customized products are also available, as well as technical support for the proper product choice, and ongoing support. Included in the line is Greenplus Form Release Agent ES for use with metal, wood, plastic, and fiberglass forms. Greenplus Form Release Agent does not react with portland cement or its common admixtures.

Soy Form Release and Natural Form Oil

Natural Soy, LLC
P.O. Box 489
123 N. Orchard St.
Brooklyn, IA 52211

Toll-free: 888-606-9559
Phone: 641-522-9559
www.soyclean.biz

Natural Soy produces Soy Form Oil form-release agent containing soy oil, surfactant, and water. It prevents the adhesion of concrete to forms and molds and can be used to clean forms for reuse. It is sprayable, cleans up with water, and has no VOCs or other hazards. It is available in 5-, 55-, and 250-gallon containers. 1 gallon covers approximately 300 ft2. Natural Form Oil is a nonwater-based version for use in freezing conditions.

SOYsolv Concrete Form Release Agent

SOYsolv
6154 N. CR 33
Tiffin, OH 44883

Toll-free: 800-231-4274
Phone: 419-992-4570
www.soysolv.com

Water-based, nonflammable, nontoxic SOYsolv® Concrete Form Release is made from soybean oil and cleans up with soap and water.

Concrete Maintenance and Rehabilitation

Concrete is a long-lasting material, but can require maintenance and repair—particularly when it is exposed to severe weather conditions and in structure-as-finish applications where appearance is almost as important as structural integrity. Covering up concrete with additional cosmetic layers can increase maintenance needs significantly over the life of the structure. Products listed here include concrete maintenance and cleaning agents made with biodegradable, biobased materials; and concrete-repair mortars with high fly-ash content.

Concrete & Masonry Cleaner and Sealer

Envirosafe Manufacturing Corporation
7634-B Progress Cir.
W. Melbourne, FL 32904

Toll-free: 800-800-5737
www.envirosafemfg.com

Trojan Masonry Sealer, a penetrating sealer for permanently waterproofing masonry, is a water-dispersed polyester polymer that dries to form a monolithic barrier filling voids and coating the interior particles of concrete to block moisture transmission. Trojan Masonry Sealer releases no VOCs, is nontoxic, nonflammable, noncaustic, and is suitable for use indoors or out on concrete, cement, brick, stucco, plaster, mortar, terrazzo, and most natural stones. Envirosafe NuLook Concrete & Masonry Cleaner #40-44 is a fluid-applied cleaner that removes dirt, oil, and stains from concrete. NuLook is biodegradable, noncarcinogenic, and water-soluble with a pH of less than 1.0. NuLook Gel is slightly more viscous for vertical surfaces. Envirosafe also has a production plant in Wenatchee, Washington.

Emaco T415 and Emaco T430

BASF Corporation
889 Valley Park Dr.
Shakopee, MN 55379

Toll-free: 800-433-9517
www.corporate.basf.com

Emaco T415 and Emaco T430 are concrete-repair mortars with high levels of fly ash content, an industrial waste product from coal-fired power plants. These products were formerly produced by Degussa Building Systems acquired by BASF in March of 2006.

Concrete Pigments

Coloring pigments in concrete add architectural interest using very little additional material—turning concrete into finished surfaces, which avoids the need for additional products and coatings, eliminating the environmental impacts associated with manufacturing and maintaining those materials. Products listed here include recycled materials and mineral byproducts of industry.

Davis Colors

Davis Colors
3700 E. Olympic Blvd.
Los Angeles, CA 90023

Toll-free: 800-356-4848
Phone: 323-269-7311
www.daviscolors.com

Davis Colors produces color additives for portland cement-based concrete paving and finished floor surfaces, concrete products, and structures. Made from recycled or reclaimed steel and iron, Davis Colors are added to the concrete mix with the company's Chameleon™ computer-operated automatic dosing system or with Mix-Ready® bags that dissolve when tossed directly into an operating ready-mix truck. With integral color, the high embodied energy of concrete is offset by the dual structural and finish floor role of the colored concrete.

EnvironOxide Pigments

Hoover Color Corporation
2170 Julia Simpkins Rd.
P.O. Box 218
Hiwassee, VA 24347

Phone: 540-980-7233
www.hoovercolor.com

Hoover Color Corporation, in partnership with Iron Oxide Recovery, Inc. (IOR), produces a range of earth-tone pigments made with EnvironOxide™, a natural iron oxide product recovered from abandoned coal mine drainage. Settling ponds and constructed wetlands are used in a patented process to contain the mine runoff. The process yields a premium quality pigment that is nontoxic, nonbleeding, and weather-resistant while cleaning water that would otherwise pollute the receiving stream. The product can be used as a colorant in a wide range of building products, including concrete, cement block, paint, wood stain, and brick. For general information, contact IOR at 412-571-2204; for sales, contact Hoover Color at 540-980-7233. Iron oxide pigments made from EnvironOxide must be specifically requested.

Recycled Glass Aggregates and Powders

American Specialty Glass, Inc.
829 N. 400 W
North Salt Lake, UT 84054

Phone: 801-294-4222
www.americanspecialtyglass.com

American Specialty Glass, Inc., provides recycled-glass aggregate in a range of sizes and colors for terrazzo floors, pavers, and countertops. Sources include post-consumer bottle glass and post-industrial float glass cullet. Glass sand, a substitute for silica sand, is also available, as are powder fines that can be used as concrete coloring agents, providing a different effect than pigments. Polished or unpolished landscaping nuggets in a range of sizes are offered as well.

Foundation and Load-Bearing Elements

Conventional foundation excavation can disturb plantings and soil, and cause sediment runoff and erosion. In fragile environments, such as boardwalks and decking in wetlands, and in erosion-prone areas, consider foundation-anchor systems that don't require excavation.

Diamond Pier

Pin Foundations, Inc.
8607 58th Ave. NW
Gig Harbor, WA 98332

Phone: 253-858-8809
www.pinfoundations.com

Diamond Pier™ DP-100 and DP-50 permit installation of pier foundations with neither excavation nor site-poured concrete. These products provide structural foundation systems for decks, outbuildings, and boardwalks. Held in place with four steel pins driven at angles through the piers and deep into the ground, they are particularly appropriate for frost conditions, fragile ecosystems, heaving soils, or difficult access sites. The company's Butterfly™ and Speed Pile™ systems are no longer offered.

Instant Foundation System

A. B. Chance, Division of Hubbell Power Systems, Inc.
210 N. Allen St.
Centralia, MO 65240

Phone: 573-682-8414
www.abchance.com

A. B. Chance manufactures the Instant Foundation®, a unique screw-anchor foundation system for supporting walkways in ecologically sensitive areas. The steel piers are screwed into the ground or wetland using portable rotary augering equipment, eliminating the need for any excavation or concrete. A. B. Chance also manufactures galvanized-steel hardware to complete the installations.

Foundation and Slab Drainage

Permanent installations, generally polymeric, that improve drainage around foundations and slabs increase the durability of buildings by enabling water to drain from around the structure. Products listed here have high recycled content or unique properties.

Delta-MS and Delta-Dry

Cosella Dörken Products Inc.
4655 Delta Way
Beamville, ON L0R 1B4
Canada

Toll-free: 888-433-5824
Phone: 905-563-3255
www.deltams.com

Delta-Dry is a stiff, egg-carton-textured, 5/16"-thick, vapor-impermeable housewrap made with 22-mil, virgin HDPE. When properly installed, the weather-resistive barrier creates a ventilated rainscreen, while blocking moisture migration through the wall assembly. Similarly, Delta-MS for subsurface use is an air-gap membrane constructed from 6 mm-thick HDPE, with a pattern of dimples molded into the surface. When installed, the membrane is held off the wall to allow any moisture in the concrete to migrate to the outer surface, condense on the inside surface of the membrane, and flow into the foundation drain. Because HDPE is impervious, soil moisture is unable to penetrate but will also flow to the foundation drain.

DrainBoard

Roxul Inc.
551 Harrop Dr.
Milton, ON L9T 3H3 Canada

Toll-free: 800-265-6878
Phone: 905-878-8474
www.roxul.com

Roxul offers DrainBoard™, a durable, rigid mineral wool insulation board that is water repellent and environmentally stable used as an insulating foundation drainage system. It is designed for use with a dampproofing layer on commercial applications up to 12' below grade. The non-directional fiber structure allows the system to be installed horizontally or vertically, providing an insulating drainage plane for foundation walls and structural concrete. Roxul's mineral wool is made from approximately equal amounts of natural basalt rock and recycled slag (with 1%-6% urea extended phenolic formaldehyde binder).

Enkadrain 3000 Series

Colbond Inc.
1301 Sand Hill Rd.
P.O. Box 1057
Enka, NC 28728

Toll-free: 800-365-7391
Phone: 828-665-5050
www.colbond-usa.com

Enkadrain® Subsurface Drainage Composite relieves hydrostatic pressure from backfill abutting below-grade structures including foundations and slabs, plaza decks, and retaining walls. It can also be used as a drainage plane for green roofs and roof gardens. It protects waterproofing during and after backfill, and will conform to irregular surfaces and corners. It consists of a post industrial recycled polypropylene drainage core of fused, entangled filaments and a geocomposite fabric bonded to one or two sides. The entangled filaments are molded into a square waffle pattern. Colbond is currently converting its entire product line to include high levels of recycled content.

J-DRain Prefabricated Drainage System

JDR Enterprises, Inc.
292 South Main St., Ste. 200
Alpharetta, GA 30004

Toll-free: 800-843-7569
Phone: 770-442-1461
www.j-drain.com

J-DRain replaces conventional crushed stone and perforated pipe used to provide drainage for a variety of horizontal and vertical construction applications including foundations, retaining walls, sub-slab layers, and green roofs. J-DRain consists of a geosynthetic filter fabric which holds back the soil and allows water to enter and flow through the 3-dimensional dimpled or honeycombed polymeric core. The J-DRain product line includes single-sided composites (200, 400, and 700 series) and multi-sided composites (SWD series), which, depending on the product, may contain some post-industrial recycled polypropylene, polystyrene, or high density polyethylene.

LowFlow Vertical Drainage System

Polyguard Products, Inc.
3801 S. Business 45
P.O. Box 755
Ennis, TX 75120

Toll-free: 800-541-4994
Phone: 972-875-8421
www.polyguardproducts.com

LowFlow™ is a 100% post-industrial recycled-content plastic geotextile that provides drainage and protection for foundation waterproofing at sites with low transmissivity clay soils. The manufacturer has certified the following recycled-content levels (by weight): total recovered material 100% typical, 100% guaranteed.

Masonry Mortaring

The portland cement content of conventional masonry mortar is high, making most masonry mortars high in embodied energy. Products listed here have some or all of their portland cement content substituted with industrial and agricultural waste products, such as fly ash, ground blast-furnace slag, or rice-hull ash.

MRT Blended Hydraulic Cement

Mineral Resource Technologies, LLC Inc.
2700 Research Forest Dr., Ste. 150
The Woodlands, TX 77381

Toll-free: 800-615-1100
Phone: 281-362-1060
www.mrtus.com

MRT Blended Hydraulic Cement, an alternative to portland cement, is made from Class C fly ash and other ingredients. It is available in bulk for ready-mix plants or in bags for mixing on-site. The manufacturer has certified the following recycled-content levels (by weight): total recovered material 83% typical, 80% guaranteed; post-consumer material 83% typical, 80% guaranteed.

St. Astier Natural Hydraulic Lime

TransMineral USA, Inc.
201 Purrington Rd.
Petaluma, CA 94952

Phone: 707-769-0661
www.limes.us

St. Astier Natural Hydraulic Lime, or NHL, is a 100% natural product that has been in production since 1851. St. Astier NHL Mortar is widely used in the restoration of old buildings. This natural hydraulic lime mortar imported from France allows stone to "breathe" naturally. Used in construction as plaster, stucco, mortar, and paint, its high level of vapor exchange and mineral composition can help reduce the risk of mold development and dry rot. NHL products are highly permeable, elastic, low shrinking, zero VOC, self-healing, and recyclable. Transmineral USA also offers Le Decor Selection, a line of high-end, all-natural interior/exterior limestone finishes which require trained installers and crushed limestone aggregate imported from France instead of the domestically available aggregate used for the St. Astier NHL products.

Moisture-Proofing

Products listed here help prevent moisture from penetrating the envelope.

Astec Coatings

Insulating Coatings Corp. (ICC)
103 Main St.
Binghamton, NY 13905

Toll-free: 800-223-8494
Phone: 607-723-1727
www.icc-astec.com

Astec Coatings are water-based ceramic, elastomeric building coatings with superior energy performance. White Astec coatings reflect solar radiation, as does the ceramic radiant barrier within the coating. ICC products are applied with a paint roller or spray equipment.

QuickFlash Weatherproofing Products

QuickFlash Weatherproofing Products, Inc.
4129 Wagon Trail Ave.
Las Vegas, NV 89118

Toll-free: 800-963-6886
Phone: 702-614-6100
www.quickflashproducts.com

A line of products from QuickFlash offers prefabricated thermoplastic flashing for exterior wall protrusions on buildings, including plumbing, electrical, gas, and HVAC penetrations. The polyethylene or rubber panels friction fit around a protrusion, helping prevent moisture, air, and insect entry. A variety of products in QuickFlash's plumbing and HVAC lines accommodate 1/2- and 3/4-inch pipes, up to 4" and 6" sheet metal duct. The electrical line offers specific solutions for single-gang, pancake, and round boxes, as well as depth variations for different exterior cladding. The products carry a 10-year warranty.

Precast Concrete Panels

Precast structural and architectural concrete products tend to have optimized geometries, can speed construction, and can contribute to reduced environmental damage on the construction site as compared with pouring concrete on-site. Waste from overage is also eliminated through precasting at a plant. Through aeration, the weight of precast concrete components can be reduced by up to a third while improving its insulation value; substitution of fly ash or other post-industrial waste materials can further improve environmental performance. Some panels are cast with integral foam insulation. Products listed here contain recycled materials, contribute to appropriate thermal design, or have other compelling environmental features.

CarbonCast Insulated Wall Panels

Altus Group
P.O. Box 10097
Lancaster, PA 17605

Toll-free: 866-462-5887
www.altusprecast.com

CarbonCast Insulated Wall Panels are precast panels comprised of two concrete wythes separated by rigid foam insulation and connected by C-GRID™ carbon fiber shear trusses. CarbonCast panels can be made in various thicknesses and with a variety of insulation types, including EPS and mineral wool, providing steady-state R-values from R-8 to R-30. The epoxy-coated, carbon-fiber C-GRID trusses reduce the structural concrete needs while allowing more insulation to be used, improving energy performance and reducing the weight of the panels. Panels are available as vertical load-bearing and non-loadbearing units in thicknesses of 7" to 12", with widths up to 15' and heights of over 50'. Horizontally-installed non-load-bearing panels are available in thicknesses of 6" to 12", widths of up to 15' and lengths of up to 40'. Until XPS has been reformulated to eliminate the ozone-depleting HCFC blowing agent, that insulation option should be avoided.

Oasis Foundation Wall System

Oldcastle Precast, Inc., A Division of CRH plc
1002 15th St., Ste. 110
Auburn, WA 98001

Toll-free: 866-423-4810
Phone: 253-833-2777
www.oasiswall.com

Oasis Foundation Wall System, manufactured and installed by Oldcastle Precast (a division of Oldcastle), is a 6000-psi precast concrete foundation system prefinished with EPS foam insulation and DensArmor® Plus paperless wallboard. DensArmor Plus incorporates fiberglass mat facings and a moisture- and mold-resistant gypsum core. The EPS foam minimizes thermal bridging and contributes to a total assembly rating of R-10. Oasis walls are 8'6" tall, using approximately 1/3 less concrete than typical 7'10" precast foundations. The concrete contains 15% flyash, a post-industrial recycled material. Top-access utility chases are provided 24 inches on center. Oldcastle Precast provides a lifetime warranty against structural defects and a 15-year warranty against water penetration.

Superior Walls

Superior Walls of America, Ltd.
937 East Earl Rd.
New Holland, PA 17557

Toll-free: 800-452-9255
www.superiorwalls.com

Superior Walls™ is a custom precast foundation wall system with integrated footer, concrete "studs," and bond beam that is insulated at the factory with extruded polystyrene (currently made with ozone-depleting HCFC-141b). Superior Wall Panels are lifted by crane into place and locked together. The R-5 line has 1" of rigid insulation to achieve an R-value of 5, which may be increased with additional insulation to R-24. The Xi line has 2-1/2" of rigid insulation for R-12.5, which may be increased with additional insulation to R-31.5.

Sheet Waterproofing

Sheet waterproofing is usually made from rubberized asphalt, isobutylene-isoprene rubber, or EPDM. Products listed here are manufactured using alternative materials, such as the more environmentally benign HDPE.

Delta-MS and Delta-Dry

Cosella Dörken Products Inc.
4655 Delta Way
Beamville, ON LOR 1B4
Canada

Toll-free: 888-433-5824
Phone: 905-563-3255
www.deltams.com

Delta-Dry is a stiff, egg-carton-textured, 5/16"-thick, vapor-impermeable housewrap made with 22-mil, virgin HDPE. When properly installed, the weather-resistive barrier creates a ventilated rainscreen, while blocking moisture migration through the wall assembly. Similarly, Delta-MS for subsurface use is an air-gap membrane constructed from 6 mm-thick HDPE, with a pattern of dimples molded into the surface. When installed, the membrane is held off the wall to allow any moisture in the concrete to migrate to the outer surface, condense on the inside surface of the membrane, and flow into the foundation drain. Because HDPE is impervious, soil moisture is unable to penetrate but will also flow to the foundation drain.

Underseal Termite-Resistant Membranes

Polyguard Products, Inc.
3801 S. Business 45
P.O. Box 755
Ennis, TX 75120

Toll-free: 800-541-4994
Phone: 972-875-8421
www.polyguardproducts.com

Underseal waterproofing membranes from Polyguard resist termites, radon, pesticide migration, soil fungi, puncture, and tearing while providing waterproofing and stress relief for slabs and concrete or IFC walls. Underseal Protected Wall Membrane is a peel-and-stick sheet membrane applied to the outside of finished flat concrete walls. Underseal Blindside has a nonwoven textile top layer that bonds with the concrete when monolithic walls are poured.

Stay-in-Place Insulating Concrete Forms

Insulating concrete forms (ICFs) provide a labor-efficient means of making insulated poured-concrete walls, floors, and roof decks. ICFs are permanent forms—they aren't disassembled after the concrete has cured. Most of these products are made from expanded polystyrene (EPS) foam produced with a non-ozone-depleting blowing agent; a couple are made from a composite of wood waste or EPS beads and portland cement. To protect against potential damage from wood-boring insects, some EPS foam used in ICFs contains borates, which are benign to humans and the environment; however, the brominated flame retardants used in most EPS foam have health and environmental risks that are generating significant concern. The environmental advantages of ICF walls include higher R-values, and their use can result in reduced concrete content compared with conventionally formed concrete walls. Be aware that the R-values claimed by ICF manufacturers are not always arrived at in a consistent manner and may be misleading. For comparison purposes, "steady-state" R-values should be used when that information is available. Mass-enhanced or "effective" R-values are only relevant in certain climates or under certain conditions, but they're often listed in product literature in a way that fails to distinguish them clearly from steady-state R-values.

Amazon Grid-Wall ICFs

Amazon Forms One, Inc.
19068 Marbach Ln.
San Antonio, TX 78266

Toll-free: 866-651-3322
Phone: 210-651-3322
www.amazongridwall.com

Amazon Grid-Wall™ is an insulated concrete form system made from polystyrene (85% by volume, 100% of which is post-consumer recycled) and cement. The standard form measures 4' long x 10" thick x 16" tall with 6" diameter voids running horizontally and vertically 16" o.c. Grid-Wall forms are dry stacked but must be spot glued with a polystyrene-compatible adhesive to keep the forms from shifting during the concrete pour. Grid-Wall does not require drywall on the interior; stucco can be applied to the exterior using only one coat and no wire lath. Grid-Wall forms are termite- and fire-resistant and can be molded with power tools or a rasp.

Amvic ICF Building System

Amvic Building System
501 McNicoll Ave.
Toronto, ON M2H 2E2 Canada

Toll-free: 877-470-9991
Phone: 416-410-5674
www.amvicsystem.com

Amvic ICFs consist of two 2-1/2"-thick interlocking expanded polystyrene (EPS) form panels with a density of 1.5 lb/cf on a 6" on-center polypropylene web. At R-4 per inch, the EPS panels provide an R-value of 20, so the overall wall R-value would be slightly higher than that. This web has a rebar holding system designed to eliminate the need for tie downs. The completely reversible 48"x16" panels use a Amvic's FormLock TM interlocking system designed to eliminate the need for glue or ties, and come with 4", 6", 8", or 10" spacers to create insulated concrete walls with corresponding concrete core thicknesses.

Arxx Walls & Foundations

Arxx Building Products
800 Division St.
Cobourg, ON K9A 5V2 Canada

Toll-free: 800-293-3210
Phone: 905-373-0004
www.arxxwalls.com

Arxx standard 6" ICFs are comprised of two 2-3/8"-thick EPS panels separated by 99% post-industrial recycled polypropylene plastic webbing on 8" centers. The webbing serves as strapping for attachment of interior and exterior finishes and as support for steel reinforcing rods within the wall. Each standard interlocking Arxx block is 4' long, 16-3/4" high, and 11-1/2" thick with a steady-state R-value of 22.1. Other thicknesses (4", 8", and 10") and configurations are available, as are a number of accessories that facilitate construction.

Baleblock System

Celestial Construction, Inc.
1599 Luisa St.
Santa Fe, NM 87505

Phone: 505-820-2818
www.birkaniarchitects.com

The Baleblock™ system uses straw bales with two predrilled 4" holes to form an insulating straw-bale wall with a "post-and-beam" reinforced-concrete structure. This technique was developed by Erem Birkan, an architect in Sante Fe, New Mexico.

Cempo Form

Cempo Forms, Inc.
P.O. Box 9300
Pahrump, NV 89060

Phone: 775-727-6565
www.cempo.com

Cempo Form is a 100% recycled EPS and cement-composite permanent form system. The standard forms are available in 8", 10", and 12" thicknesses in a 32" x 48" block (approximately 150 lbs. and most often chosen by owner-builders) and a 32" x 96" block (300 lbs. and more commonly used by contractors). Cempo Form can be easily worked with hand tools, and can be cut and shaped for a variety of details. The company is in the process of testing for R-value.

Durisol Wallforms

Durisol Building Systems Inc.
67 Frid St.
Hamilton, ON L8P 4M3
Canada

Phone: 905-521-0999
www.durisolbuild.com

Durisol Wallforms are the original stay-in-place concrete forms introduced in 1945. They are made from a composite of mineralized wood chips and portland cement. Each wallform provides approximately 3 ft2 of wall. Mineral wool insulation inserts are available in several sizes to provide steady-state R-values up to R-28. The structural design permits use in multistory buildings. The Durisol material can also be specified in custom shapes for use as precast noise-absorption panels, retaining walls, floor forms, and roof panels. The manufacturer has certified the following recycled-content levels (by weight): total recovered material 40% typical, 35% guaranteed; post-consumer material 0% typical, 0% guaranteed.

ECO-Block ICFs

ECO-Block, LLC
11220 Grader St., Ste. 700
Dallas, TX 75238

Toll-free: 800-503-0901
Phone: 214-503-1644
www.eco-block.com

ECO-Block® EPS ICFs have embedded HDPE webs that serve as recessed furring strips on the exterior and as attachment points on the interior. Connectors (4", 6", 8", and 10") can be used singly or spliced together, allowing for concrete thicknesses from 4" to 24" or greater. With 5" of EPS in the wall profile, ECO-Blocks have an R-value of 22. The ECO-Block system includes straight panels, 90-degree corners (4", 6", and 8"), 45-degree corners, and brick ledge panels, and is amenable to tilt-up construction with insulation on one side only. ICF blocks are shipped unassembled (to save freight) and assembled on-site. The total recycled content by weight is approximately 40%, per the

manufacturer. The ECO-Block team offers support for installation, code compliance, design assistance, and building science.

Faswall Wallforms

K-X Faswall Corp.
P.O. Box 88
Windsor, SC 29865

Toll-free: 800-491-7891
Phone: 803-642-8142
www.faswall.com

Faswall® is a fiber-cement block ICF. These ICFs are made of cement with optional fly ash content and K-X Aggregate (waste wood chips treated with mineral solutions to improve durability and cementitious bonding). A standard wallform block measures 16" x 8" x 11-1/2" with a 6"-deep core and weighs 22 lbs. Split-double, large-core, and corner wallforms are also available.

Fox Blocks

Fox Blocks
6110 Abbott Dr.
Division of Airlite Plastics Company
Omaha, NE 68110

Toll-free: 877-369-2562
www.foxblocks.com

Fox-Blocks™ is an ICF block system including reversible, pre-assembled ICF blocks with interlocking key-way block connections, ties, and corner brackets designed to add strength and facilitate application of veneer finishes. The ties are 100% recycled material. The EPS foam core has a steady-state R-value of 4.55 per inch, and the manufacturer claims a total R-value for the block of 35 or greater.

Greenblock ICF

Greenblock Worldwide Corp.
759 S. Federal Hwy., Ste. 213
Stuart, FL 34994

Toll-free: 800-216-1820
Phone: 772-223-8045
www.greenblock.com

Greenblock™ is an insulating concrete form made from EPS and held together by plastic webs for structural integrity and minimal thermal bridging. Greenblock's 6" core and 8" core blocks have 2-5/8" of foam on the interior side of the block and 2-5/8" on the exterior side. Greenblock forms have been used for over 30 years.

I.C.E. Block Insulated Concrete Forms

Southwest I.C.E. Block
501 East Plaza Cir., Ste. F
Litchfield Park, AZ 85340

Toll-free: 800-423-2557
Phone: 623-935-5428
www.iceblockinc.com

The I.C.E. Block™ System utilizes 16" x 48" x 9-1/4"-wide (or 11"-wide) tongue-and-groove EPS foam blocks with 6" (or 8") concrete cores. Steel studs are embedded on 12" centers within the blocks to facilitate attachment of interior and exterior finishes. Thermal bridging is minimized because the studs are not exposed. Concrete

Capacity: one yard fills 13 blocks of 6" core; or 10 blocks of 8" core; or 12 blocks of 6-8" Super Duty.

ICF Block System

ICF Industries, Inc.
570 S. Dayton - Lakeview Rd.
New Carlisle, OH 45344

Toll-free: 877-423-4800
Phone: 937-845-8347
www.iceblock.net

The ICF Block™ System utilizes 16" x 48" x 9-1/4"-wide (or 11"-wide) EPS foam blocks with 6" (or 8") concrete cores. Steel studs are embedded on 12" centers within the blocks to facilitate attachment of interior and exterior finishes. Thermal bridging is minimized because the studs are not exposed on the exterior of the EPS block.

iForm

Reward Wall Systems, Inc.
9931 S. 136th St., #100
Omaha, NE 68138

Toll-free: 800-468-6344
Phone: 402-592-7077
www.rewardwalls.com

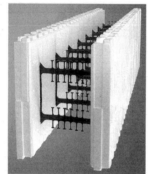

Reward Wall Systems manufactures the iForm™ flat wall form used in residential and commercial structures including large-scale high-rise projects. Reward's iForm is made from two 2.4"-thick premolded 48" x 16" slabs of EPS held together with plastic ties that are embedded in the EPS. The ties provide strength while the concrete is poured and serve as a nailing surface for interior and exterior finishes such as drywall and siding. The forms remain in place and become part of the wall providing a steady-state R-value of 22 and, according to the manufacturer, an effective R-value of more than 32.

Insul-Deck ICFs for Floors, Roofs, and Walls

Insul-Deck
935 Main St.
Ste. A2
Safety Harbor, FL
34695

Toll-free: 800-475-6720
www.insul-deck.org

Insul-Deck® is an interlocking ICF for joisted concrete floors, roofs, tilt-walls, and precast walls. Molded from EPS with integral steel functioning as support beams and receptors for drywall attachment, Insul-Deck can span up to 30' or more, allowing for clear-span basements. Integral channels (approximately 4-3/4" in diameter) for utility lines enable ducting within the insulated space and improved energy performance. Panels are available in any length, with variable thicknesses for R-values from 16 to 34. According to the manufacturer, the finished Insul-Deck system is 30-40% lighter than comparable poured-in-place slab floor systems and provides the same load capacity.

IntegraSpec ICF

Phil-Insul Corp o/a IntegraSpec ICF
11U - 735 Arlington Park Place
Kingston, ON K7M 8M8 Canada

Toll-free: 800-382-9102
Phone: 613-634-1319
www.integraspec.com

IntegraSpec® ICF consists of two 2-1/2"-thick interlocking expanded polystyrene form panels (48" long x 12-1/4" high interlocked) held together with High Impact Polystyrene (HIPS) plastic spacers of 4", 5", 6", 8", 10", or 12" to create insulated concrete walls with corresponding concrete core thicknesses. The spacers can be combined to increase core thickness and also function as furring strips/studs. The patented, completely reversible panels are shipped flat. IntegraSpec ICF has an R-value of 22+ per ASHRAE Fundamentals (1997) and is manufactured in both Canada and the U.S.

Lite-Form and Fold-Form

Lite-Form
1950 W. 29th St.
South Sioux City, NE 68776

Toll-free: 800-551-3313
www.liteform.com

Lite-Form ICFs are comprised of two EPS rigid-foam planks measuring 4' x 8' x 2" held together by plastic spacer ties that can be sized to offer concrete thicknesses from 4" to 24" (in 2" increments). Lite-Form is available in EPS or XPS foam. Only the EPS is being specified here. Fold-Form is an interlocking, foldable ICF. The forms are made from two 1' x 4' x 2" sheets of rigid EPS foam insulation held together with plastic spacer ties. Fold-Form folds flat for more compact shipping and storage. Form widths are available to create concrete thicknesses of 4" to 16" (also in 2" increments). Both Lite-Form and Fold-Form have calculated R-values of 26 for finished walls. In-Wall bracing is available for all walls over 4' in height.

Logix Insulated Concrete Forms

Logix
801 Klahanie Dr., Ste. 327
Port Moody, BC V3H 5K4 Canada

Toll-free: 888-415-6449
www.logixicf.com

Logix ICFs are heavier duty and more energy efficient than most, with two 2-3/4"-thick interlocking expanded polystyrene (EPS) form panels with a nominal R-value of 24 on an 8" on-center polypropylene web. The 48"x16" panels come with 4", 6", 8", 10" or 12" spacers to create insulated concrete walls with corresponding concrete core thicknesses.

NUDURA

NUDURA Corporation
27 Hooper Rd., Unit 10
Barrie, ON L4N 9S3 Canada

Toll-free: 866-468-6299
Phone: 705-726-9499
www.nudura.com

Nudura ICF's hinged plastic webs allow compact pre-assembled shipping. The modular, interlocking, reversible EPS units are unfolded at the site and stacked. Standard form size is 8' x 18", in five widths ranging from 9.25" to 17.25". Foam width is 2-5/8" on each side. The webbed polypropylene cross-ties are on 8" centers, with integral hangers for steel reinforcement. The webs are embedded in the foam, providing attachment strips for wall coverings. A variety of specialized forms and accessories are available, including end caps, tapers, corners, height adjusters, T-junctions, and lintels. Factory-cut radius walls are also available. The cross-tie and fastening strip components are made with 100% recycled HDPE from post-consumer and post-industrial sources. Hinge pins in the webbing are made with 100% recycled post-industrial steel alloy. Recycled content, by weight, ranges from 57% to 63% depending on overall width.

Pentstar Concrete Form Masonry Units

Pentstar, Corp.
6840 Shingle Creek Pkwy.
Unit 11
Minneapolis, MN 55430

Toll-free: 877-645-9704
Phone: 763-566-5400
www.pentstar.com

Pentstar® Concrete Form Masonry Units, a hybrid of unit masonry and ICF construction, are comprised of two masonry faces tied together by post-industrial recycled reinforced nylon connectors. Between the two masonry faces (starting on the outside) is a 1" dead-air space weep cavity and 2" of rigid foam (EPS or Celotex) that creates a 5-1/2" cavity for the concrete pour. The units are designed to be laid up with mortar, creating a hollow form that works like an ICF. With the insulation to the outside of the concrete pour and inner masonry, thermal mass effects are a significant part of the wall's thermal performance. An additional benefit is that the forms can also serve as the finish on both exterior and interior surfaces.

Perform Wall Panel System

Perform Wall, LLC
5776 N. Mesa St.
El Paso, TX 79912

Toll-free: 800-761-8590
Phone: 915-587-8885
www.performwall.com

Perform Wall Panels are made from 85% (by volume) post-consumer EPS and 15% portland cement molded into 8.5"-, 10"-, 12"-, and 14"- thick blocks. Flat stock is available in 2" or 4" thicknesses. Because of the insulating beads, the insulating value is considerably higher than that for concrete alone.

PolySteel Forms

American PolySteel, LLC
6808 Academy Pkwy. East, NE
Building C-2
Albuquerque, NM 87109

Toll-free: 800-977-3676
Phone: 505-345-8153
www.polysteel.com

American PolySteel manufactures a variety of ICF products utilizing expanded polystyrene foam form pieces and steel connectors/attachment studs rather than the much more common plastic ties. In 2002 the company reconfigured its forms so that the steel connectors are now recessed 1/2" below the surface of the form, thereby improving thermal performance. PolySteel manufactures both a "waffle-grid" and "flat-wall" form, as well as an insulated concrete deck form. The company also incorporates AFM Corporation's Perform Guard® borate treatment in their forms to protect against insect damage.

QUAD-LOCK Insulating Concrete Forms

QUAD-LOCK Building Systems Ltd.
7398 - 132nd St.
Surrey, BC V3W 4M7 Canada

Toll-free: 888-711-5625
Phone: 604-590-3111
www.quadlock.com

QUAD-LOCK® is a system of interlocking expanded polystyrene (EPS) panels connected with HDPE plastic ties. The panels are 12" high, 48" long, and either 2-1/4" or 4-1/4" thick; 10 wall configurations in any desired wall width. The manufacturer claims R-values of 22, 32, or 40.

R-Control ICF System

Advance Foam Plastics, Inc. - Colorado Division
5250 N. Sherman St.
Denver, CO 80216

Toll-free: 800-525-8697
Phone: 303-297-3844
www.afprcontrol.com

Advance Foam Plastics is a licensed manufacturer of AFM Corporation's R-Control® ICF System. The R-Control system consists of 1' x 8' R-Control PerformGuard® insect-resistant EPS foam panels joined by plastic form ties on 12" centers. Ties vary in length to create 4", 6", 8", and 10" walls with a nominal R-value of 20.

R-Control ICF System

Advance Foam Plastics, Inc. - Utah Division
111 W. Fireclay Ave.
Murray, UT 84107

Toll-free: 877-775-8847
Phone: 801-265-3465
www.afprcontrol.com

Advance Foam Plastics is a licensed manufacturer of AFM Corporation's R-Control® ICF System. The R-Control system consists of 1' x 8' R-Control PerformGuard® insect-resistant EPS foam panels joined by plastic form ties on 12" centers. Ties vary in length to create 4", 6", 8", and 10" walls with a nominal R-value of 20.

R-Control ICF System

Big Sky Insulations, Inc.
P.O. Box 838
Belgrade, MT 59714

Toll-free: 800-766-3626
Phone: 406-388-4146
www.bsiinc.com

Big Sky Insulations manufactures the R-Control® ICF System. The R-Control system consists of 1' x 8' R-Control Perform Guard® insect-resistant EPS foam panels joined by plastic form ties on 12" centers. Ties vary in length to create 4", 6", 8", and 10" walls with a nominal R-value of 20.

Reddi Form

Reddi Form, Inc.
10 Park Pl., Ste. 5-B
Butler, NJ 07405

Toll-free: 800-334-4303
Phone: 973-283-0055
www.reddiform.com

Reddi Form is a one-piece, screen-grid block insulating concrete form made entirely from expanded polystyrene (EPS). Available in two basic sizes, the 6" concrete-core form with 5 vertical cells (9.6" W x 48" L x 12" H) weighs 3 lbs. and can be used for most residential buildings. The 8" concrete-core form with 4 vertical cells (12" W x 48" L x 12" H) is used for commercial applications. Both foam forms have an R-value of 21. Reddi-Form warrants pours of up to 10' of wall height to be free of blow-outs.

Reddi-Deck Floor and Roof-Deck ICFs

Reddi Form, Inc.
10 Park Pl., Ste. 5-B
Butler, NJ 07405

Toll-free: 800-334-4303
Phone: 973-283-0055
www.reddiform.com

Reddi-Deck™ is a stay-in-place, self-supporting insulating concrete forming system for joisted concrete floor and roof decks. The Reddi-Deck panels are produced by a continuous molding production line integrating the insulating capabilities of EPS with the structural strength of metal inserts. According to the manufacturer, the systems are half the weight of comparable hollow-core, precast systems, which in turn reduces the load on walls and foundations.

SmartBlock

ConForm Pacific Inc.
1376 W. 8040 S, Ste. 2
West Jordan, UT 84088

Toll-free: 800-266-3676
Phone: 801-562-9050
www.smartblock.com

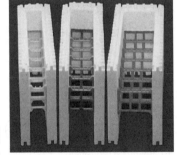

SmartBlocks, made from EPS, are available to form a solid concrete wall in 4", 6", 8", 10", and 12" nominal sizes or as a screen concrete wall measuring 40" x 10" x 10" with a 6-1/2" wide (standard size) post-and-beam concrete-core structure. SmartBlock walls possess superior acoustic insulation and use plastic connectors with 100% recycled content. ConForm Pacific Inc. claims R-22 to R-24 insulation values.

Standard ICFs

Standard ICFs
425 Second Ave. SW
Oronoco, MN 55960

Toll-free: 800-925-3676
Phone: 507-367-2183
www.standardicf.com

Standard ICF Corporation®, formerly Therm-O-Wall, manufactures the 895 ICFs™ System. The system consists primarily of two forms; a standard form made from two 2-3/8"-thick EPS panels separated by recycled-HDPE plastic brackets; and a corner form of the same materials. Standard panels are 48" L x 16" H x 11-1/4" W, providing for a concrete thickness of 6-1/2". The imbedded brackets are placed 12" on center and also function as furring strips for finish material attachment. The company claims an R-value of 26.

Tech Block

Tech Block International, LLC
P.O. Box 9954
Denver, CO 80209

Phone: 720-221-3912
www.techblock.com

Tech Blocks are patented exterior wall blocks composed of a mixture of polystyrene beads and cement. Bonded to the blocks is OSB sheathing, which becomes the inside surface of the wall and acts as an attachment surface for drywall. Underneath the drywall, the OSB acts as backing for hanging cabinetry, drape hardware, base, casing, etc. The exterior of the blocks is ready for stucco without the need for wire mesh. The Tech Block Wall System resists fire, sound, water, and termites. Each Tech Block weighs about 85 lbs. and measures 48" x 16" x 11" thick, with a steady-state R-value of 47.5, according to the manufacturer. Tech Block International, LLC, is an Energy Star® Partner with plants in Arizona, California, and Georgia, and has plans for plants in Texas and New Mexico.

TF System Vertical ICFs

ACH Foam Technologies, LLC - Colorado Division
5250 N. Sherman St.
Denver, CO 80216

Phone: 303-297-3844
Toll-free: 800-525-8697
Fax: 303-292-2613

The TF System Vertical ICF is an insulating concrete wall form designed for both above-grade and below-grade use in residential and commercial construction.

TF System Vertical ICFs

TF System - The Vertical ICF
3030C Holmgren Way
Green Bay, WI 54304

Toll-free: 800-360-4634
Phone: 920-983-9960
www.tfsystem.com

TF System® - The Vertical ICF manufactures vertically oriented insulated concrete forms. The system utilizes a standard 2-1/2" x 12" x 8' expanded polystyrene plank (or custom planks variable in height up to 12') and preformed corner planks. The planks are joined by 26-gauge galvanized steel I-Beam studs, which enable planks to slide up to allow access to the inside of the forms until a top cap is installed. Wall thicknesses of 4", 6", 8", 10", and 12" are possible, with the company claiming an R-value of 25. Forms are shipped flat. Bracing requirements are minimal, and compressive strength allows for the installation of floor systems before pouring.

Thermal Foams TF ICF

Thermal Foams, Inc.
2101 Kenmore Ave.
Buffalo, NY 14207

Phone: 716-874-6474
www.thermalfoams.com

Thermal Foams Inc. is an authorized manufacturer/distributor of the TF Insulated Concrete Building System. The TF ICF system is a vertical plank system that consists of Thermal Foams EPS foam panels joined together with PVC or metal I-beams that vary in height and are available in widths to create 4", 6", 8", 10", and 12" walls with a nominal R-value of 22.

VariantHouse ICFs

VariantHouse LLC
6625 Miami Lakes Dr. #243
Miami Lakes, FL 33014

Phone: 305-777-3849
www.varianthouse.com

VariantHouse uses BASF's Neopor® EPS to manufacture lightweight, thin, fire-retardant, ICF blocks that are targeted to the do-it-yourself market. VariantHouse's ICF blocks have naps and grooves that click together to create an insulating wall without thermal bridges that can be assembled and concrete-filled by a novice. VariantHouse provides a versatile set of blocks that can accommodate almost any architectural design and conventional finish (such as brick, stone, stucco, wood, and vinyl siding). VariantHouse is currently the only company in North America to use BASF's Neopor. The black Neopor beads contain microscopic flakes of graphite that reflect heat radiation, reducing the foam's thermal conductivity. Products made of silver-grey Neopor can achieve the same insulating performance as products using BASF's Styropor® with up to 20% less thickness and 50% less raw material. Neopor has an R-value of 5 per inch, which for Variant blocks of 9.8", 13.7", and 17.7" thicknesses, results in R-values of approximately 20, 38, and 57, respectively.

Water-Repellent Coatings

Fluid-applied waterproofing is commonly made of polyurethane-based or hot rubberized-asphalt materials. Products listed here have low VOC content, recycled content, exceptional durability, or some combination of these product attributes.

DynoSeal Waterproofing Sealer

American Formulating & Manufacturing (AFM)
3251 Third Ave.
San Diego, CA 92103

Toll-free: 800-239-0321
Phone: 619-239-0321
www.afmsafecoat.com

DynoSeal is an asphaltic emulsion waterproof sealer with a VOC content of less than 100 g/l for use on foundations and other wet applications. The product containers have over 90% post-consumer recycled-plastic content. The Dyno line of AFM coatings also includes driveway sealers and UV-stabilized rooftop coatings.

Rub-R-Wall Foundation Waterproofing

Rubber Polymer Corp.
1135 W. Portage Trl. Ext.
Akron, OH 44313

Toll-free: 800-860-7721
Phone: 330-945-7721
www.rpcinfo.com

Rub-R-Wall® foundation waterproofing is made from synthetic rubber. This product is spray-applied under high pressure (3,000 psi) and temperature (140 to 160 degrees F) by factory-certified professionals. The resulting rubber coating requires protection from backfilling with either 1/4" EPS foam or a woven geotextile. Rub-R-Wall has a lifetime limited warranty for residential applications and a 10-year warranty for commercial applications.

Water Repellents

Water repellents are clear liquid products that are usually solvent- or water-based silicone, acrylic, silane or siloxane based. Products listed here have VOC content well below the federal VOC content limit of 700 grams per liter for this category of products.

9400 and 9400W Impregnant

Palmer Industries, Inc.
10611 Old Annapolis Rd.
Frederick, MD 21701

Toll-free: 800-545-7383
Phone: 301-898-7848
www.palmerindustriesinc.com

9400 Impregnant is a water-repellent, UV-protective coating for masonry, concrete, and other cementitious materials, formulated without solvents for minimal toxicity. 9400W is a variant for wood surfaces.

Ashford Formula

Curecrete Distribution, Inc.
1203 W. Spring Creek Pl.
Springville, UT 84663

Toll-free: 800-998-5664
Phone: 801-489-5663
www.ashfordformula.com

Ashford Formula is a permanent, penetrating concrete hardener, densifier, dustproofer, and sealer for new or existing concrete. As it progressively seals, the concrete becomes watertight but remains breathable and will develop a shine through use or by scrubbing. The product also locks in salts to eliminate the formation of concrete dust. Ashford Formula is water-based, nontoxic, nonflammable, and releases no VOCs. It is effective on concrete, stucco, terrazzo, concrete block, and similar materials. This product is particularly intended for flooring applications.

Concrete & Masonry Cleaner and Sealer

Envirosafe Manufacturing Corporation
7634-B Progress Cir.
W. Melbourne, FL 32904

Toll-free: 800-800-5737
www.envirosafemfg.com

Trojan Masonry Sealer, a penetrating sealer for permanently water-proofing masonry, is a water-dispersed polyester polymer that dries to form a monolithic barrier filling voids and coating the interior particles of concrete to block moisture transmission. Trojan Masonry Sealer releases no VOCs, is nontoxic, nonflammable, noncaustic, and is suitable for use indoors or out on concrete, cement, brick, stucco, plaster, mortar, terrazzo, and most natural stones. Envirosafe NuLook Concrete & Masonry Cleaner #40-44 is a fluid-applied cleaner that removes dirt, oil, and stains from concrete. NuLook is biodegradable, noncarcinogenic, and water-soluble with a pH of less than 1.0. NuLook Gel is slightly more viscous for vertical surfaces. Envirosafe also has a production plant in Wenatchee, Washington.

Deck-O-Shield

W. R. Meadows, Inc.
300 Industrial Dr.
P.O. Box 338
Hampshire, IL 60140

Toll-free: 800-342-5976
Phone: 847-214-2100
www.wrmeadows.com

Deck-O-Shield is a ready-to-use, zero-VOC, water-based sealer and water repellent for use on natural stone, concrete, brick, stucco, and masonry surfaces. Deck-O-Shield is designed for use in or around swimming pools, providing a clear finish and also inhibiting the penetration of salts into the surface, reducing whitening or staining.

Enviroseal

BASF Corporation
889 Valley Park Dr.
Shakopee, MN 55379

Toll-free: 800-433-9517
www.corporate.basf.com

The Enviroseal® product line consists of single-component, water-based, water-repellent clear sealers. The VOC contents of these products is below 350 g/l. Enviroseal 20 and Enviroseal 40 are patented, penetrating silane sealers for concrete and masonry. Enviroseal 7 is an economical, blended silane/siloxane penetrating sealer for concrete, brick masonry, stucco, and many natural stones. Enviroseal Double 7 for Brick is a high-performance sealer developed for dense, vertical masonry surfaces such as hard-burnt brick, and also concrete, stone, and stucco. Enviroseal Surface Guard is a protective sealer designed

to repel water and oils from horizontal interior masonry surfaces. The Enviroseal product line was formerly produced by Degussa Building Systems acquired by BASF in March of 2006.

Intraseal

Conspec
4226 Kansas Ave.
Kansas City, KS 66106

Toll-free: 800-348-7351
Phone: 913-279-4800
www.conspecmkt.com

Intraseal is a penetrating, water-based, reactive siliconate concrete sealer, hardener, and dustproofer. Its VOC content is below 100 g/l. This product is for use on concrete floors.

Penetrating Waterstop

American Formulating & Manufacturing (AFM)
3251 Third Ave.
San Diego, CA 92103

Toll-free: 800-239-0321
Phone: 619-239-0321
www.afmsafecoat.com

Safecoat® Penetrating WaterStop is a zero-VOC sealer that increases water-repellency on brick walls, concrete foundations, stucco, stone, and most unglazed tile. It is nonflammable and free of formaldehyde and hazardous ingredients.

Seal-Krete Sealers

Seal-Krete, Inc.
Convenience Products
306 Gandy Rd.
Auburndale, FL 33823

Toll-free: 800-323-7357
Phone: 863-967-1535
www.seal-krete.com

Seal-Krete Original Waterproofing Sealer (SKWPS) is a water-based, very-low-VOC (less than 8 g/l), strong-binding, clear acrylic, penetrating sealer/primer for interior and exterior concrete and masonry surfaces. The product is available in 10% solids and 25% solids formulations. Seal-Krete Masonry Sealer is a waterborne, nonyellowing, clear acrylic emulsion sealer that can be used on both concrete and wood floors. It has a VOC content below 100 g/l. These sealers are for above-grade applications.

Seal-Once

New Image Coatings, LLC
150 Dow St.
Manchester, NH 03101

Phone: 603-669-8786
www.seal-once.com

Seal-Once™ is a water-based penetrating waterproofer for wood, concrete, masonry, and composite decking. It is colorless, UV-resistant, and paintable and contains no heavy metals, petroleum distillates, solvents, or VOCs. Seal-Once protects against mold, mildew, and freeze-thaw cycles and resists salts, chlorides, and UV damage yet allows water vapor to pass through. Clear and tinted formulas are available, as well as marine and industrial grades. The manufacturer claims the compound will not leach; is safe for aquatic environments; and will protect horizontal surfaces for 6 years and vertical surfaces for ten years.

SoySeal Wood Sealer

Natural Soy, LLC
P.O. Box 489
123 N. Orchard St.
Brooklyn, IA 52211

Toll-free: 888-606-9559
Phone: 641-522-9559
www.soyclean.biz

SoySeal is a water-based, nontoxic, nonflammable sealer suitable for exposed wood surfaces. It contains no VOCs or other known user hazards and cleans up with water. This product spreads water rather than beading it, which reduces the risk of UV magnification and damage, according to Natural Soy. Coverage is 150 to 300 ft2. This product complies with ASTM C-672 and is also used to seal concrete. It is available in 1-, 5-, 55-, and 250-gallon containers.

Weather-Bos Sealers

Weather-Bos International
316 California Ave., Ste. 1082
Reno, NV 89509

Toll-free: 800-664-3978
www.weatherbos.com

Weather-Bos sealers are made from natural, nontoxic vegetable oils and resins as well as other natural ingredients. These sealers are low-odor, water-reducible, nonflammable, and free of harmful fungicides. The small amount of pigment in some formulas provides UV protection. Masonry Boss™ waterproofs and protects brick, adobe, concrete, tile, and stone.

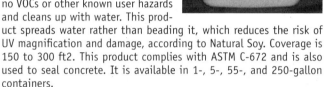

Waterproof Coatings for Concrete and Masonry

While most conventional concrete sealers and waterproofing agents have very high VOCs, some products react with the concrete or otherwise provide a seal without resorting to solvents that emit VOCs. Products listed here contain zero VOCs, either nominally or actually.

Aquafin-IC Crystalline Waterproofing

Aquafin, Inc.
505 Blue Ball Rd., Bldg. 160
Elkton, MD 21921

Toll-free: 888-482-6339
Phone: 410-392-2300
www.aquafin.net

Aquafin-IC is a penetrating, inorganic, cementitious material used to permanently waterproof and protect new or existing structurally sound concrete and concrete masonry by reacting with moisture and free lime in the concrete. Aquafin-IC resists strong hydrostatic pressure and can be used in both interior and exterior below-grade applications. It is "breathable," nontoxic, releases no VOCs, and is suitable for potable water storage applications. Aquafin-IC may take up to a month to reach full waterproofing potential.

Concrete & Masonry Cleaner and Sealer

Envirosafe Manufacturing Corporation
7634-B Progress Cir.
W. Melbourne, FL 32904

Toll-free: 800-800-5737
www.envirosafemfg.com

Trojan Masonry Sealer, a penetrating sealer for permanently waterproofing masonry, is a water-dispersed polyester polymer that dries to form a monolithic barrier filling voids and coating the interior particles of concrete to block moisture transmission. Trojan Masonry Sealer releases no VOCs, is nontoxic, nonflammable, noncaustic, and is suitable for use indoors or out on concrete, cement, brick, stucco, plaster, mortar, terrazzo, and most natural stones. Envirosafe NuLook Concrete & Masonry Cleaner #40-44 is a fluid-applied cleaner that removes dirt, oil, and stains from concrete. NuLook is biodegradable, noncarcinogenic, and water-soluble with a pH of less than 1.0. NuLook Gel is slightly more viscous for vertical surfaces. Envirosafe also has a production plant in Wenatchee, Washington.

Xypex Concentrate

Xypex Chemical Corporation
13731 Mayfield Pl.
Richmond, BC V6V 2G9 Canada

Toll-free: 800-961-4477
Phone: 604-273-5265
www.xypex.com

Xypex Concentrate is a nontoxic powder consisting of portland cement, very fine treated silica sand, and various active proprietary chemicals. Mixed with water to form a slurry, it penetrates the pores of concrete and masonry structures, plugging them with a nonsoluble crystalline formation that becomes an integral part of the structure. This product is approved for use on potable water structures and contains no VOCs. Xypex Concentrate is available in powder form in 20-lb. pails, 60-lb. pails, and 50-lb. bags. Other formulations for the protection and waterproofing of concrete are available. Xypex products also protect reinforcing steel.

This Space is Available for Your Notes

Structural Systems & Components

The structure of a building should be designed for durability and soundness—unless it's a temporary structure, in which case it should accommodate disassembly and reuse of the materials. Some structural materials may compromise the building's energy efficiency by creating thermal bridges from interior to exterior that allow heat to bypass the insulation; these should be addressed during building design.

For houses and small commercial buildings, wood is by far the most common framing material. Even with wood from certified, well-managed forests, measures should be taken to minimize the use of wood framing and maximize the amount of insulation in the building envelope. "Advanced framing" measures include framing at 24" on-center instead of 16", using single top plates (and lining up roof framing over the wall studs), using two- or three-stud corners, and insulating headers above openings.

Larger framing members, such as 2x10s and 2x12s, are made from mature trees that often come from scarce old-growth forests; engineered lumber products, such as trusses and I-joists, should be preferred. Finger-jointed lumber, which uses short pieces of wood that might otherwise become waste, makes straighter boards that are less prone to warp.

There are alternatives to wood. Light-gauge steel framing is used as a piece-for-piece substitute for wood framing. While it does contain some recycled content, the sheet steel used for light-gauge framing generally contains less recycled material than heavier types of steel. Steel is also quite energy-intensive to produce (high in embodied energy). Most important, however, is that steel conducts heat 400 times more readily than wood: steel framing can easily compromise a building's thermal performance unless insulation is specially designed to block thermal bridging.

Masonry construction is common in many areas. Hollow-core concrete masonry units (CMUs) are hard to insulate effectively. A special type of masonry block called autoclaved aerated concrete (AAC) insulates much better than standard concrete block. Other types of block should generally be insulated on the exterior, or between the concrete block and the exterior skin.

Concrete wall systems that are more typically used for foundations—including insulated concrete forms (ICFs)—can also be used to form above-grade walls. Making concrete is energy-intensive and polluting: the production of a ton of cement releases up to a ton of carbon dioxide. Admixture components also affect the environmental impact of concrete. Though concrete walls can provide thermal storage, they don't provide much thermal insulation; concrete walls for conditioned spaces should always be insulated.

Structural insulated panels (SIPs—sometimes called stress-skin or foam-core panels), usually made with foam insulation sandwiched between oriented-strand board (OSB) skins, are a viable alternative for houses and other small buildings. They insulate well, are usually quite airtight, and go up quickly. Some panels are available with mineral-wool insulation or compressed straw as the core instead of plastic foam.

Foam-core panels are often used to enclose post-and-beam or timber-frame structures. These heavy timber structures use a great deal of wood, but they're likely to be very durable—the finish materials and exterior skins can be replaced multiple times in the life of a solid timber frame. If the wood is local or from well-managed forests, this construction system can be a good choice. Some timber framers use salvaged timbers from buildings that are being demolished.

Other alternative structural systems include adobe, rammed earth, straw-bale construction, and cob construction (a hand-formed mixture of sand, clay, and straw). Log homes use a great deal of wood and don't insulate very well. Like their mainstream cousins, some proponents of alternative materials or methods claim mass-enhanced "effective R-values," which are relevant only under certain conditions.

Adobe Blocks

Adobe is a natural building material common to the U.S. Southwest. It can be very durable if protected from erosion; many Native American adobe structures built hundreds of years ago are still standing. Made from soil that has suitable sand and clay content and then air-dried in the sun, adobe bricks typically have extremely low greenhouse gas emissions and embodied energy. Most commercially available adobe bricks are "stabilized" with cement or asphalt additives, but adobe bricks are very commonly made on-site without stabilizers. Walls made of adobe bricks are most often protected from the weather with a parge coat of stucco or plaster, or large overhangs.

Adobe and Earth Plasters

Clay Mine Adobe, Inc.
6401 W. Old Ajo Hwy.
Tucson, AZ 85735

Phone: 520-578-2222
www.claymineadobe.com

Clay Mine Adobe, founded in 1996, manufactures adobe block with a custom portland cement stabilizer, wheat straw (optional), and washed coarse aggregate admixture. Clay Mine adobe block requires no sealing and retains the authentic look of unstabilized adobe. It is available in a variety of standard as well as custom sizes and natural custom colors including a burnt adobe look. Clay plaster, cement-stabilized and unstabilized in a variety of earth tones, is also available in 95-pound bags.

Adobe Factory

Adobe Factory
P.O. Box 510
Alcalde, NM 87511

Phone: 505-852-4131
www.adobefactory.com

Adobe Factory is northern New Mexico's main adobe manufacturer and supplier.

New Mexico Earth Adobes

New Mexico Earth Adobes
P.O. Box 10506
Albuquerque, NM 87184

Phone: 505-898-1271
www.newmexicoearth.com

New Mexico Earth Adobes is an adobe block supplier serving the central and northern New Mexico, and southern Colorado regions. Blocks are 4" x 10" x 14" and weigh approximately 30 lbs. each.

Old Pueblo Adobe

Old Pueblo Adobe Company
9353 N. Casa Grande Hwy.
Tucson, AZ 85743

Toll-free: 800-327-4705
Phone: 520-744-9268
www.oldpuebloadobe.com

Old Pueblo Adobe Company manufactures adobe and Southwestern building supplies as well as offering a variety of antique Mexican Ranchero furnishings, accessories, and building products for sale in their Tucson showroom.

Rio Abajo Adobe

Rio Abajo Adobe
7 Industrial Park Ln.
Belen, NM 87002

Phone: 505-864-6191

Rio Abajo Adobe manufactures adobe brick and offers consulting services for small to large adobe block manufacturing startups or people building adobe homes.

Autoclaved Aerated Concrete Blocks

Commercial production of autoclaved aerated concrete (AAC) began in 1930 in Europe, where it has been widely used for decades. Concrete masonry units (CMUs) made from AAC are lighter than conventional CMUs, generally have no cores, and provide higher insulation levels (R-values of up to 1.25 per inch, an order of magnitude higher than standard concrete). The insulating value of AAC allows it to function simultaneously as structure and insulation system. It has about 20% of the density—though only about 10% of the compressive strength—of regular concrete. Manufacturers may increase the product's strength by including reinforcing steel rods or mesh. Structural applications of unreinforced AAC are limited to low-rise buildings; in high-rise buildings it may be used in partition and curtain walls. AAC has very good sound-absorbing characteristics and can be worked with conventional carpenter's tools, making site modifications relatively easy. It's also nontoxic, fire-resistant, insect-proof , and can be produced using coal fly ash as a substitute for some of the sand in conventional AAC. But because AAC is a porous material, it must be protected from moisture with claddings or coatings. AAC is not a 1:1 substitution for conventional CMU in terms of installation; greater care must be taken in installation because the shallow mortar bed does not allow for alignment adjustments easily made with the deeper mortar beds of conventional CMUs.

ACCOA

ACCOA Aerated Concrete Corporation of America
3351 W. Orange Blossom Trl.
Apopka, FL 32712

Phone: 407-884-0051
www.accoaac.com

ACCO AAC blocks, lintels, and panels are made by Aerated Concrete Corporation of America.

Contec AAC

XELLA AAC Texas, Inc.
1535 Brady Blvd., Ste. 2
San Antonio, TX 78237

Toll-free: 877-926-6832
Phone: 210-402-3223
www.texascontec.com

Contec AAC, formed in 1995, manufactures Autoclaved Aerated Concrete (AAC) at its plant in Monterrey, Mexico. Texas Contec is their U.S. distributor and offers a full line of AAC products, accessories, and technical services.

E-Crete

E-Crete
2151 E. Broadway Rd. #115
Tempe, AZ 85282

Toll-free: 877-351-4448
Phone: 480-596-3819 x11
www.e-crete.com

E-Crete has been producing autoclaved aerated concrete (AAC) blocks in a plant near Phoenix, Arizona since December 2000. The company uses sterile mine tailings from an adjacent closed copper mine to substitute for the silica content, which represents 25% of the dry weight content. E-Crete reports a steady-state insulating value of approximately R-1.04 per inch for their most common block (density of 32 lbs/ft3). E-Crete has a UL Classified 4-hour fire rating and is mold resistant.

SafeCrete AAC

SafeCrete AAC
6652 Hwy. 41 North
PO Box 1129
Ringgold, GA 30736

Phone: 706-965-4587
www.safecrete.com

In June 2001, Babb International acquired Matrix (a licensee of the Hebel AAC process). SafeCrete, a Babb Company, offers many block and panel sizes of AAC, including blocks larger than standard CMU-size, larger "jumbo" units, panels, and a variety of specially manufactured shapes and pre-assembled wall sections--with integral reinforcement. AAC products are made from a mixture of poured concrete, fly ash, and sand. Babb products can be used for interior and exterior applications.

In exterior wall applications, they must not be exposed but can be painted with a textured paint, coated with a stucco finish specially made for AAC, or clad with standard siding.

Carpentry Accessories

Especially when structural requirements are minimal, look for recycled-content products.

EZ-Shim

EZ-Shim
P.O. Box 4820
Santa Barbara, CA 93140

Toll-free: 800-772-0024
Phone: 805-682-2155
www.ezshim.com

EZ-Shim™ is a load-bearing, injection-molded shim made from recycled ABS plastic with prescored grooves for breaking off excess shim stock after installation. EZ-Shim measures 1-3/16" x 7-7/8" x 5/16" at its thick end. There are 10 shims per sheet. The manufacturer has certified the following recycled-content levels (by weight): total recovered material 100% typical, 100% guaranteed.

Cast Concrete Roof Decks

Permanent, insulating concrete forms for roof decks are made from expanded polystyrene (EPS) foam produced with a non-ozone-depleting blowing agent. This labor-efficient approach provides improved thermal resistance and reduced concrete use.

Reddi-Deck Floor and Roof-Deck ICFs

Reddi Form, Inc.
10 Park Pl., Ste. 5-B
Butler, NJ 07405

Toll-free: 800-334-4303
Phone: 973-283-0055
www.reddiform.com

Reddi-Deck™ is a stay-in-place, self-supporting insulating concrete forming system for joisted concrete floor and roof decks. The Reddi-Deck panels are produced by a continuous molding production line integrating the insulating capabilities of EPS with the structural strength of metal inserts. According to the manufacturer, the systems are half the weight of comparable hollow-core, precast systems, which in turn reduces the load on walls and foundations.

Cementitious Reinforced Panels

Site-stuccoed insulation-core panels can be appropriate where the need for good R-values meets the need for extreme structural requirements where earthquake, hurricane, and tornado resistance are required. Products listed here provide superior energy performance, or use FSC-certified wood and other green materials.

Green Sandwich

Green Sandwich Technologies
8125 Lankershim Blvd.
North Hollywood, CA 91605

Phone: 866-695-3676
www.greensandwichtech.com

Green Sandwich Panels are site-finished structural concrete insulating panels consisting of an EPS core with a pre-engineered reinforcing cage surrounding and penetrating it. The panels are fastened together in the field, and a minimum 1.5" thickness of portland cement finish is machine- or hand-applied on both sides of the panel. The manufacturer specifies a 40% coal fly ash concentration for the skins. The EPS core is made with BASF's Greenguard-certified Styropor®. Locally-harvested biomass, such as straw, may be specified in place of EPS. The wire mesh contains 40% recycled steel. Panels are available up to 12' x 48', in 3" to 20" thicknesses.

Tridipanel

Hadrian Tridi-Systems
909 W. Vista Way, Ste. D
Vista, CA 92083

Phone: 760-643-2307
www.tridipanel.com

The Tridipanel consists of a rigid EPS core with 11-gauge steel welded wire 2" x 2" fabric mesh on both sides, held together with 9-gauge steel truss wires. The panels are fastened together in the field, and a minimum 1.5" thickness of portland cement finish is machine- or hand-applied on both sides of the panel. The standard panels are 4' x 8', but may be manufactured up to 40' in length in 8" increments. The EPS core is available in either 1- or 2-lb. density, in thicknesses ranging from 1.5" to 5" by half-inch increments. Polyisocyanurate foam may be specified in place of EPS. Wire gauges are available in 11, 12.5, and 14, in bright or galvanized. This building system is appropriate where extreme structural requirements for earthquake, hurricane, and tornado resistance are required.

Clay Blocks

Bricks are typically fired in large kilns at very high temperatures, which results in significant embodied energy. Reusing bricks is good because it saves that embodied energy. High temperature firing also enables waste materials—even toxic materials such as oil-contaminated soils—to be safely incorporated into certain brick products. Products listed here are salvaged for reuse in new brick veneer. Note that not all salvaged brick is suitable for reuse in new brick veneer—the salvaged brick's surface condition (residual mortar film), structural integrity (so-called "salmon" brick can be too soft and fragile for reuse in brick veneers) and water absorbancy need to be considered.

Cunningham Bricks

Cunningham Brick Co., Inc.
701 N. Main St.
Lexington, NC 27292

Toll-free: 800-672-6181
Phone: 336-248-8541
www.cunninghambrick.com

Cunningham Brick manufactures bricks that incorporate 1.3% manganese dioxide by weight, a toxic metal waste from battery production. Vitrified manganese imparts a darker color to the bricks and is considered safe after firing. The product may not be widely available.

Salvaged Brick

Gavin Historical Bricks
2050 Glendale Rd.
Iowa City, IA 52245

Phone: 319-354-5251
www.historicalbricks.com

Gavin Historical Bricks supplies salvaged bricks and cobblestones recovered from buildings and streets from around the country. Bricks are used in new construction to provide an antique look, as well as for historic restoration projects. Custom brick matching is available. The company also handcuts antique brick into 1/2" floor tile for a variety of applications. Shipping is provided nationwide, though the heavy weight reduces the practicality (and environmental attractiveness) of shipping large quantities long distances.

Thin-Sliced Salvaged Chicago Brick

Vintage Brick Salvage LLC.
1303 Harrison Ave.
Rockford, IL 61104

Toll-free: 800-846-8243
Phone: 847-714-3652
www.bricksalvage.com

Vintage Brick Salvage sells 1/2" and 3/4" thick antique brick that has been thin-sliced from antique common brick for use as flooring, paving, and veneer tile on walls. The brick installs like tile, using thin-set adhesive over a sub floor or backerboard, and can be sealed with polyurethane or a water-based terra cotta sealer. Some split-brick pieces may show saw marks or be flecked with iron deposits. Vintage Brick also sells full-size salvaged bricks and cobblestone pavers.

Concrete Blocks

Like many conventional products, CMUs can be used in "green" ways—for example, using a decorative type of block that eliminates additional finish materials. Products listed here exhibit superior energy performance (innovative web designs with specially designed expanded polystyrene insulation inserts), reduced material use by way of a finished exterior face (such as split-faced block), or post-industrial recycled content (such as fly ash or ground blast-furnace slag).

Grey Block and GlasStone

Clayton Block Company
515 Rte. 528
Lakewood, NJ 08701

Toll-free: 888-662-3044
Phone: 732-919-6009
www.claytonco.com

Clayton manufactures a regular and a lightweight gray concrete block containing respectively, 50% and 35% recovered block and concrete. Clayton also manufactures GlasStone™, a terrazzo-like architectural block made of approximately 80% recycled glass that is 1/2 post-industrial and 1/2 post consumer material. Clayton's manufacturing plants are in NJ and product is distributed regionally in the mid-Atlantic states.

Omni Block

Omni Block, Inc.
15125 N. Hayden Rd. #123
Scottsdale, AZ 85260

Phone: 480-661-9009
www.omniblock.com

Omni Block is a uniquely molded concrete block (not foam) available in 8" and 12" sizes designed to minimize thermal bridging and to receive molded EPS insulation inserts. Omni Block is reinforced with rebar and grout in some of the interior cells as determined per structural engineering. All electrical and plumbing are run within the block so no furring or sheetrock is required for a finished wall.

Engineered Lumber Products

While not free from ecological concerns, engineered lumber products can provide a significant environmental advantage over solid wood by efficiently utilizing fast-growing, small-diameter trees. Products listed here are limited to those that do not include formaldehyde binders; or, if they do, offer other green features such as FSC-certified content. Phenol-formaldehyde binders, while not emitting as much formaldehyde as urea-formaldehyde binders, still may pose an indoor air quality concern.

Certified Engineered Wood

Standard Structures, Inc.
5900 Pruitt Ave.
Windsor, CA 95492

Toll-free: 877-980-7732
Phone: 707-836-8100
www.standardstructures.com

Standard Structures was the first manufacturer of certified engineered wood products. The company can provide FSC-certified glulam beams, wood I-joists, and open-web trusses. Conventional phenol resorcinol formaldehyde binders are used in the manufacturing process. With some products, special orders may be required for certified-wood fabrication.

Engineered Finger-Joint Framing Studs

Innovative Wood Concepts
1087 E. Commerce Dr.
St. George, UT 84790

Phone: 435-674-4555

Innovative Wood Concepts (IWC) makes engineered finger-jointed studs for commercial and residential construction. IWC uses wood scraps recycled from construction sites and truss companies and processes them into studs using water-borne polyvinyl acetate (PVA, or white glue) adhesive. These studs are third-party monitored for quality and accepted by the SBCCI, ICC, and ICBO. Waste from their production is turned into mulch and animal bedding. According to the company, last year IWC kept over 3.5 million lineal feet of wood from reaching the landfill.

Insul-Beam

Premier Building Systems - Division of Premier Industries, Inc.
4609 70th Ave. East
Fife, WA 98424

Toll-free: 800-275-7086
Phone: 253-926-2020
www.pbspanel.com

Insul-Beam is an insulated header with laminated veneer lumber facings and a core of EPS foam insulation. EPS may contain up to 15% recycled content. Insul-Beam can be used in place of site-fabricated headers and will improve building envelope energy performance. This product is available for 2x4, 2x6, and 2x8 framing in lengths up to 24'. Engineering data is available from the company.

SWII, SWIII Headers

Superior Wood Systems
1301 Garfield Ave.
P.O. Box 1208
Superior, WI 54880

Toll-free: 800-375-9992
Phone: 715-392-1822
www.swi-joist.com

Superior Wood Systems SWII and SWIII headers are engineered, insulated headers that deliver superior thermal performance when compared to solid-wood, site-fabricated headers. SWII headers consist of solid 2" thick wood top and bottom chords and dual OSB web members that encase an EPS foam core. The SWIII headers have three OSB web members. The 5-1/2" wide headers insulate to R-18.

TimberStrand LSL Studs, Headers, and Rim Board

iLevel by Weyerhaeuser
2910 E. Amity Rd.
Boise, ID 83716

Toll-free: 888-453-8358
Phone: 208-364-1200
www.iLevel.com

Laminated Strand Lumber (LSL) is manufactured from fast-growing aspen and poplar trees that are debarked and shredded into strands.

The strands are coated with a formaldehyde-free MDI (methyl diisocyanate) binder and pressed into huge billets that are milled into dimensional lumber. LSL lumber is very consistent and stable; it does not warp and twist like solid wood. TimberStrand® LSL Studs and Headers are available in 2x4 and 2x6; Rim Boards are 2x10. Lengths up to 22' are available.

FSC-Certified Heavy Timber

Certified wood products are verified by a third party as originating from well-managed forests. GreenSpec recognizes the Forest Stewardship Council (FSC) standards as the most rigorous and the only certification system with well-established chain-of-custody certification. Some companies listed here sell both certified and noncertified wood products, or products that have been certified according to different, less stringent environmental standards. To make certain that you get environmentally responsible wood products, be sure to specify your interest in FSC-certified wood.

AltruWood Certified Wood Products

AltruWood, Inc.
P.O. Box 3341
Portland, OR 97208

Toll-free: 877-372-9663
www.altruwood.com

AltruWood, chain-of-custody certified by SGS, only sells and distributes FSC-certified new domestic (including oak, pine, cherry and Douglas Fir) and tropical wood (including Jatoba, Ipe, and Massaranduba). Sourced and shipped from multiple locations, transportation costs and impacts are minimized. A custom cutting service allows the specification of exact sizes and dimensions, minimizing waste. AltruWood also sells reclaimed lumber.

Certified Hardwood Lumber and Timbers

ROMEX World Trade Company, LLC - sales agent for ROM
P.O. Box 1110
Alexandria, LA 71309

Toll-free: 800-299-5174
Phone: 318-445-1973
www.royomartin.com

Roy O. Martin Lumber Management, LLC has received certification of its 585,000 acres of forestland and four mills according to standards of the Forest Stewardship Council (FSC). This is the first FSC certification of any forest management operation in Louisiana. Roy O. Martin produces FSC-certified lumber in red oak, white oak, ash, hackberry, pecan, sap gum (sweet gum), cypress, and several other species at the company's hardwood lumber mill in LeMoyen. While the majority of the mill's output is red oak, ROM has become one of the largest suppliers of southern ash and cypress. Lumber accounts for 75% of production, with the rest in timbers, railroad ties, and pallet cants.

Certified Lumber and Timbers

Harwood Products
P.O. Box 224
Branscomb, CA 95417

Toll-free: 800-441-4140 (CA only)
Phone: 707-984-6181
www.harwoodp.com

Harwood Products offers certified redwood decking and timbers, Douglas fir lumber and timbers, and white fir lumber.

Certified Redwood Lumber

Big Creek Lumber Company
3564 Hwy. 1
Davenport, CA 95017

Phone: 831-457-5023
www.big-creek.com

Big Creek harvests FSC-certified timber on its 6,800 acres of second- and third-growth forestland in the Santa Cruz Mountains of coastal California. They were the first wood products company operating a redwood forest to be awarded "Well Managed Forest" Certification by the Forest Conservation Program of Scientific Certification Systems (SCS). The family-owned lumber company runs five retail lumber yards on California's central coast; they also wholesale a wide variety of redwood Douglas-fir grades and dimensions, including 2x4 through 2x12, 4x4, 4x6 and 6x6. Larger timbers can be custom cut by special order.

Certified Wood Building Products

West Wind Hardwood, Inc.
P.O. Box 2205
Sidney, BC V8L 3S8 Canada

Toll-free: 800-667-2275
Phone: 250-656-0848
www.westwindhardwood.com

Family-owned and -operated West Wind Hardwood offers locally harvested, FSC-certified custom Douglas fir lumber, timbers, and flooring in clear and vertical grain. Other species, such as hemlock, pine, red oak, birch, and maple may be available, depending on supply. The company also offers SmartWood Rediscovered salvaged woods on request and availability. The dimensions and appearances of salvaged and recycled woods may vary due to the nature of the materials. The company specializes in Douglas fir, and is recognized for custom wood products for less usual applications.

Certified Wood Products

Cascadia Forest Goods, LLC
38083 Wheeler Rd.
Dexter, OR 97431

Phone: 541-485-4477
www.cascadiaforestgoods.com

Cascadia Forest Goods (CFG) is a supplier of FSC-certified and recycled forest products, including hardwood and softwood veneers, dimensional lumber and decking, timbers and beams, siding, flooring, paneling, and trim. CFG's woods come from the Pacific Northwest and British Columbia, and include the following species: douglas fir, incense and western red cedar, sitka and englemann spruce, ponderosa and sugar pine, and regional hardwoods (madrone, white and black oak, broadleaf maple, alder, chinkapin, and myrtlewood). FSC-certified and recycled-forest-product flooring species include madrone, white oak, clear vertical grain (CVG) Douglas fir, birch, big-leaf maple, and myrtlewood. CFG also supplies FSC-certified flooring and decking from Central and South America, including Santa Maria, catalox, chechen negro, jobillo, machiche, ramon blanco, sauche, ipe, pucte (ironwood), and others. CFG offers both solid and engineered wood flooring. CFG also supplies both FSC-certified hardwood and softwood veneers and lumber to window and door manufacturers.

Harmonized Tropical Wood

Harmonized Wood Products
5500 Prytania St., #143
New Orleans, LA 70115

Toll-free: 877-635-3362
Phone: 504-342-4250
www.harmonizedwood.com

Harmonized Wood Products offers a wide range of FSC-certified tropical hardwood products, specializing in Latin American hardwoods. Products include lumber, timber, decking, flooring, doors, veneer, and custom furniture.

Harrop-Procter Certified-Wood Building Products

Harrop-Procter Watershed Protection Society
101 3rd Ave.
P.O. Box 5
Procter, BC V0G 1V0 Canada

Phone: 250-229-2221
www.hpcommunityforest.org

The Harrop-Procter Community Forest in southeastern British Columbia, stewarded by The Harrop-Procter Watershed Protection Society and managed by The Harrop-Procter Community Co-operative, is FSC-certified. Species include Douglas fir, lodgepole pine, birch, aspen, larch, hemlock, balsam fir, and spruce. Rough green, tight-knot, cedar lumber and timbers are available in common dimensions. T&G indoor paneling is available in fir, pine, cedar, and larch. Fir and larch flooring, fir interior decking, cedar and larch exterior decking, and various profiles of cedar siding are offered. Custom orders over 1000 board feet can be quoted.

FSC-Certified Wood Framing Lumber

Certified wood products are verified by a third party as originating from well-managed forests. GreenSpec recognizes the Forest Stewardship Council (FSC) standards as the most rigorous and the only certification system with well-established chain-of-custody certification. Some companies listed here sell both certified and noncertified wood products, or products that have been certified according to different, less stringent environmental standards. To make certain that you get environmentally responsible wood products, be sure to specify your interest in FSC-certified wood.

AltruWood Certified Wood Products

AltruWood, Inc.
P.O. Box 3341
Portland, OR 97208

Toll-free: 877-372-9663
www.altruwood.com

AltruWood, chain-of-custody certified by SGS, only sells and distributes FSC-certified new domestic (including oak, pine, cherry and Douglas Fir) and tropical wood (including Jatoba, Ipe, and Massaranduba). Sourced and shipped from multiple locations, transportation costs and impacts are minimized. A custom cutting service allows the specification of exact sizes and dimensions, minimizing waste. AltruWood also sells reclaimed lumber.

Certified Hardwood and Softwood Lumber

Lashway Lumber, Inc.
22 Main St.
P.O. Box 768
Williamsburg, MA 01096

Phone: 413-268-7685
www.lashwaylumber.com

Lashway Lumber mills FSC-certified North American hardwood and softwood lumber. Species include white pine, white northern red oak, red pine, red sugar maple, and hard white ash.

Certified Hardwood Building Products

Maine Woods Company, LLC
Fish Lake Rd.
P.O. Box 111
Portage, ME 04768

Phone: 207-435-4393
www.mainewoods.net

Maine Woods Company, LLC, owned in part by Seven Islands Land Company, operates a state-of-the-art sawmill in northern Maine producing primarily hard maple and yellow birch lumber and flooring. Smaller quantities of American beech, red maple, and white ash are also produced. A portion of the mill output is FSC-certified.

Certified Hardwood Lumber

Allard Lumber Company
354 Old Ferry Rd.
Brattleboro, VT 05301

Phone: 802-254-4939
www.allardlumber.com

Allard Lumber is a manufacturer and wholesaler of FSC-certified northern hardwood lumber, including white hard maple, red oak, and cherry.

Certified Hardwood Lumber and Timbers

ROMEX World Trade Company, LLC - sales agent for ROM
P.O. Box 1110
Alexandria, LA 71309

Toll-free: 800-299-5174
Phone: 318-445-1973
www.royomartin.com

Roy O. Martin Lumber Management, LLC has received certification of its 585,000 acres of forestland and four mills according to standards of the Forest Stewardship Council (FSC). This is the first FSC certification of any forest management operation in Louisiana. Roy O. Martin produces FSC-certified lumber in red oak, white oak, ash, hackberry, pecan, sap gum (sweet gum), cypress, and several other species at the company's hardwood lumber mill in LeMoyen. While the majority of the mill's output is red oak, ROM has become one of the largest suppliers of southern ash and cypress. Lumber accounts for 75% of production, with the rest in timbers, railroad ties, and pallet cants.

Certified Iron Woods Lumber

Cecco Trading, Inc.
600 E. Vienna Ave.
Milwaukee, WI 53212

Phone: 414-445-8989
www.ironwoods.com

Iron Woods® is a brand of ipe decking and lumber from the Brazilian forest that is offered FSC-certified with an upcharge. Iron Woods' natural durability rating of 25+ years is the highest of woods tested by the U.S. Forest Products Lab. The product is available in all standard decking, porch flooring, and dimensional lumber sizes from 2x2 to 4x12 and up to 20' long in standard even lengths. Iron Woods decking is Class A fire-rated and comes with a 25-year fully transferable limited warranty.

Certified Lumber

Midwest Hardwood
Corporation
9540 83rd Ave. N
Maple Grove, MN 55369

Phone: 763-425-8700
www.midwesthardwood.
com

Midwest Hardwood Corporation's Sawmill Division offers some varieties of FSC-certified northern hardwood lumber. The wood is harvested from forests in Wisconsin, Michigan, and Minnesota.

Certified Lumber and Timbers

Harwood Products
P.O. Box 224
Branscomb, CA 95417

Toll-free: 800-441-4140 (CA only)
Phone: 707-984-6181
www.harwoodp.com

Harwood Products offers certified redwood decking and timbers, Douglas fir lumber and timbers, and white fir lumber.

Certified Lumber, Flooring, Wainscoting, and Veneer

McDowell Lumber Company, Inc.
Rte. 46 S
P.O. Box 148
Crosby, PA 16724

Phone: 814-887-2717
www.mcdowelllumber.com

McDowell Lumber deals in FSC-certified lumber, flooring, wainscoting, and veneer in over 15 species including red oak, cherry, hard and soft maple, ash, and a variety of other hardwoods harvested in Pennsylvania.

Certified Red Cedar

Mary's River Lumber Co.
4515 N.E. Elliott Cir.
Corvallis, OR

Toll-free: 800-523-2052
Phone: 541-752-0122
www.marysrvr.com

Mary's River Lumber offers FSC-certified, second-growth, tight-knotted, western red cedar products, including boards, decking, fencing, paneling, and siding in T&G, channel, bevel, and square-end.

Certified Redwood Lumber

Big Creek Lumber Company
3564 Hwy. 1
Davenport, CA 95017

Phone: 831-457-5023
www.big-creek.com

Big Creek harvests FSC-certified timber on its 6,800 acres of second- and third-growth forestland in the Santa Cruz Mountains of coastal California. They were the first wood products company operating a redwood forest to be awarded "Well Managed Forest" Certification by the Forest Conservation Program of Scientific Certification Systems (SCS). The family-owned lumber company runs five retail lumber yards on California's central coast; they also wholesale a wide variety of redwood Douglas-fir grades and dimensions, including 2x4 through 2x12, 4x4, 4x6 and 6x6. Larger timbers can be custom cut by special order.

Certified Spruce-Pine-Fir (SFP) Lumber

Materiaux Blanchet, Inc.
5055 W. Hamel Blvd., Ste. 225
Quebec City, QC G2E 2G6 Canada

Phone: 418-871-2626

Materiaux Blanchet, Inc. produces a full range of graded, kiln-dried, FSC-certified spruce-pine-fir dimensional lumber from Seven Islands Land Company timber.

Certified Wood Products

Cascadia Forest Goods, LLC
38083 Wheeler Rd.
Dexter, OR 97431

Phone: 541-485-4477
www.cascadiaforestgoods.com

Cascadia Forest Goods (CFG) is a supplier of FSC-certified and re-cycled forest products, including hardwood and softwood veneers, dimensional lumber and decking, timbers and beams, siding, flooring, paneling, and trim. CFG's woods come from the Pacific Northwest and British Columbia, and include the following species: douglas fir, incense and western red cedar, sitka and englemann spruce, ponderosa and sugar pine, and regional hardwoods (madrone, white and black oak, broadleaf maple, alder, chinkapin, and myrtlewood). FSC-certified and recycled-forest-product flooring species include madrone, white oak, clear vertical grain (CVG) Douglas fir, birch, big-leaf maple, and myrtlewood. CFG also supplies FSC-certified flooring and decking from Central and South America, including Santa Maria, catalox, chechen negro, jobillo, machiche, ramon blanco, sauche, ipe, pucte (ironwood), and others. CFG offers both solid and engineered wood flooring. CFG also supplies both FSC-certified hardwood and softwood veneers and lumber to window and door manufacturers.

Certified Wood Products

Randall Custom Lumber, Ltd.
3530 S.E. Arcadia Rd.
Shelton, WA 98584

Phone: 360-426-8518

Randall Custom Lumber manufactures FSC-certified decking, flooring, hard and softwood lumber, and stair parts. Some of their certified species are ash, red cedar, red alder, Douglas fir, madrone, and maple.

CollinsWood FSC-Certified Wood Products

The Collins Companies
1618 S.W. First Ave., Ste. 500
Portland, OR 97201

Toll-free: 800-329-1219
Phone: 503-417-7755
www.collinswood.com

The CollinsWood line includes FSC-certified western pine particleboard, FSC-certified TruWood engineered (hardboard) siding and trim, and FSC-certified hardwood and softwood lumber and millwork. TruWood products are made under FSC's partial-content rules (with an actual certified fiber content of 32%), and use a phenol formaldehyde binder. Millwork includes cherry, red oak, soft maple and poplar interior millwork, including casing, base, chair rail, crown, etc. In 1993, Collins Pine Company became the first privately owned timber management company to receive FSC certification in the U.S. CollinsWood has been a leader in the forest and wood products certification movement since its inception.

EarthSource Forest Products

EarthSource Forest Products/Plywood and Lumber Sales, Inc.
1618 28th St.
Oakland, CA 94608

Toll-free: 866-549-9663
Phone: 510-208-7257
www.earthsourcewood.com

EarthSource Forest Products, a division of Plywood and Lumber Sales, Inc., sells FSC-certified hardwood plywood and lumber of the following species: maple, cherry, red oak, white oak, ash, Honduras mahogany, walnut, machiche, amapola, and many more. EarthSource also sells salvaged and rediscovered lumber such as fir, redwood, and hickory.

F.D. Sterritt Certified-Wood Building Products

F.D. Sterritt Lumber Co.
110 Arlington St.
Watertown, MA 02472

Toll-free: 877-635-3362
Phone: 617-923-1480
www.sterrittlumber.com

F.D. Sterritt Lumber sells FSC-certified lumber, plywood, decking, hardwoods, and hardwood flooring. They have a variety of certified species in stock. Additional green building materials available, including low-VOC adhesives, caulking, sealants, and recycled drywall. F.D. Sterritt offers green building product consultations.

FSC-Certified Lumber, Plywood, and Products

Potlatch Corporation
601 W. First Ave., Ste. 1600
Spokane, WA 99201

Phone: 509-835-1500
www.potlatchcorp.com

In 2004, Potlatch Corporation became the first publicly traded U.S. timber company to certify timberland according to Forest Stewardship Council (FSC) standards. Potlatch is producing chain-of-custody FSC-certified Hem-Fir and Douglas Fir/Larch framing lumber, inland red cedar decking and siding, and Douglas fir and white fir plywood from three chain-of-custody-certified mills in Idaho. Potlatch has recently added over 400,000 acres of FSC certified timber in Arkansas which supports a chain-of-custody sawmill in Warren, Arkansas. Warren produces dimensional Southern Yellow Pine framing lumber. These products are stamped with the FSC logo when required for specific sales.

FSC-Certified Wood Products

Dwight Lewis Lumber / Lewis Lumber Products
30 S. Main St.
P.O. Box 356
Picture Rocks, PA 17762

Toll-free: 800-233-8450
Phone: 570-584-4460
www.lewislp.com

Dwight Lewis Lumber sells FSC-certified moldings, flooring, paneling, and hardwoods, subject to availability. Certified species are cherry, hard and soft maple, and red oak.

FSC-Certified Wood Products

Menominee Tribal Enterprises
Hwy. 47 N
P.O. Box 10
Neopit, WI 54150

Phone: 715-756-2311
www.mtewood.com

Menominee Tribal Enterprises (MTE) offers a full line of certified wood products harvested from the 220,000-acre Menominee Forest. MTE is continuing its development of value-added products from the 16 wood species harvested. Menominee forest lands were the first certified to FSC standards in North America.

Harmonized Tropical Wood

Harmonized Wood Products
5500 Prytania St., #143
New Orleans, LA 70115

Toll-free: 877-635-3362
Phone: 504-342-4250
www.harmonizedwood.com

Harmonized Wood Products offers a wide range of FSC-certified tropical hardwood products, specializing in Latin American hardwoods. Products include lumber, timber, decking, flooring, doors, veneer, and custom furniture.

Harrop-Procter Certified-Wood Building Products

Harrop-Procter Watershed Protection Society
101 3rd Ave.
P.O. Box 5
Procter, BC V0G 1V0 Canada

Phone: 250-229-2221
www.hpcommunityforest.org

The Harrop-Procter Community Forest in southeastern British Columbia, stewarded by The Harrop-Procter Watershed Protection Society and managed by The Harrop-Procter Community Co-operative, is FSC-certified. Species include Douglas fir, lodgepole pine, birch, aspen, larch, hemlock, balsam fir, and spruce. Rough green, tight-knot, cedar lumber and timbers are available in common dimensions. T&G indoor paneling is available in fir, pine, cedar, and larch. Fir and larch flooring, fir interior decking, cedar and larch exterior decking, and various profiles of cedar siding are offered. Custom orders over 1000 board feet can be quoted.

Horse- and Biodiesel-Harvested Hardwood and Softwood Lumber

JH Lumber & Wood Products
1701 Chase Rd.
Montpelier, VT 05602

Phone: 802-229-4148
www.jhlumber.net

JH Lumber & Wood Products mills kiln-dried North American hardwood and softwood lumber. Logging is done with horses and biodiesel-powered equipment and soon will occur on over 1,400 acres of forest land.

Particleboard, MDF, Plywood, Lumber, OSB

F.W. Honerkamp Co., Inc
500 Oak Point Ave.
Bronx, NY 10474

Toll-free: 800-999-8115
Phone: 718-589-9700
www.honerkamp.com

F.W. Honercamp distributes a number of no-added-formaldehyde (NAF) and FSC-certified panel products, including particleboard, medium density fiberboard, melamine panels, composite panels, and hardwood plywood (with veneer, particleboard, and MDF core options). Their NAF products use MDI, phenol-formaldehyde, or soy-based binders and polyvinyl acetate (PVA, or white glue) for finish veneers. The company also offers FSC-certified hardwood lumber and OSB, as well as class A fire-rated panels.

SmartChoice Wood Products

Certified Forest Products, LLC.
7 Los Conejos
Orinda, CA 94563

Phone: 925-258-4372
www.certifiedforestproducts.com

Certified Forest Products (CFP) is a distributor of SmartChoice, a collection of FSC-certified and reclaimed wood products from a variety of species including hardwoods, cedar, and redwood. Products include lumber, plywood, decking, siding, flooring, interior and exterior millwork.

FSC-Certified Wood Paneling

Certified wood products are verified by a third party as originating from well-managed forests. GreenSpec recognizes the Forest Stewardship Council (FSC) standards as the most rigorous and the only certification system with well-established chain-of-custody certification. Some companies listed here sell both certified and noncertified wood products, or products that have been certified according to different, less stringent environmental standards. To make certain that you get environmentally responsible wood products, be sure to specify your interest in FSC-certified wood.

Certified Red Cedar

Mary's River Lumber Co.
4515 N.E. Elliott Cir.
Corvallis, OR

Toll-free: 800-523-2052
Phone: 541-752-0122
www.marysrvr.com

Mary's River Lumber offers FSC-certified, second-growth, tight-knotted, western red cedar products, including boards, decking, fencing, paneling, and siding in T&G, channel, bevel, and square-end.

F.D. Sterritt Certified-Wood Building Products

F.D. Sterritt Lumber Co.
110 Arlington St.
Watertown, MA 02472

Toll-free: 877-635-3362
Phone: 617-923-1480
www.sterrittlumber.com

F.D. Sterritt Lumber sells FSC-certified lumber, plywood, decking, hardwoods, and hardwood flooring. They have a variety of certified species in stock. Additional green building materials available, including low-VOC adhesives, caulking, sealants, and recycled drywall. F.D. Sterritt offers green building product consultations.

FSC-Certified Wood Products

Dwight Lewis Lumber / Lewis Lumber Products
30 S. Main St.
P.O. Box 356
Picture Rocks, PA 17762

Toll-free: 800-233-8450
Phone: 570-584-4460
www.lewislp.com

Dwight Lewis Lumber sells FSC-certified moldings, flooring, paneling, and hardwoods, subject to availability. Certified species are cherry, hard and soft maple, and red oak.

Harrop-Procter Certified-Wood Building Products

Harrop-Procter Watershed Protection Society
101 3rd Ave.
P.O. Box 5
Procter, BC V0G 1V0 Canada

Phone: 250-229-2221
www.hpcommunityforest.org

The Harrop-Procter Community Forest in southeastern British Columbia, stewarded by The Harrop-Procter Watershed Protection Society and managed by The Harrop-Procter Community Co-operative, is FSC-certified. Species include Douglas fir, lodgepole pine, birch, aspen, larch, hemlock, balsam fir, and spruce. Rough green, tight-knot, cedar lumber and timbers are available in common dimensions. T&G indoor paneling is available in fir, pine, cedar, and larch. Fir and larch flooring, fir interior decking, cedar and larch exterior decking, and various profiles of cedar siding are offered. Custom orders over 1000 board feet can be quoted.

Particleboard, MDF, Plywood, Lumber, OSB

F.W. Honerkamp Co., Inc
500 Oak Point Ave.
Bronx, NY 10474

Toll-free: 800-999-8115
Phone: 718-589-9700
www.honerkamp.com

F.W. Honercamp distributes a number of no-added-formaldehyde (NAF) and FSC-certified panel products, including particleboard, medium density fiberboard, melamine panels, composite panels, and hardwood plywood (with veneer, particleboard, and MDF core options). Their NAF products use MDI, phenol-formaldehyde, or soy-based binders and polyvinyl acetate (PVA, or white glue) for finish veneers. The company also offers FSC-certified hardwood lumber and OSB, as well as class A fire-rated panels.

SmartChoice Wood Products

Certified Forest Products, LLC.
7 Los Conejos
Orinda, CA 94563

Phone: 925-258-4372
www.certifiedforestproducts.com

Certified Forest Products (CFP) is a distributor of SmartChoice, a collection of FSC-certified and reclaimed wood products from a variety of species including hardwoods, cedar, and redwood. Products include lumber, plywood, decking, siding, flooring, interior and exterior millwork.

Log Construction

Log and heavy timber construction has appeal in North America for its rustic qualities. Though the embodied energy of wood can be relatively low, heavy timber construction—such as in log houses—is rarely environmentally preferable compared with more conventional building systems. Conventional framing is more wood-efficient, and in most cases, results in a more energy-efficient building envelope. Products listed here have environmental features that separate them from conventional timber and log products.

EcoLog Homes

Haliburton Forest: EcoLog Concepts
Box 202, Kennisis Lake Rd.
R.R. 1
Haliburton, ON K0M 1S0 Canada

Phone: 705-754-2198
www.haliburtonforest.com

EcoLog Homes are built of certified hemlock logs from the 60,000-acre Haliburton Forest and Wildlife Reserve. Standard log buildings come with 8" squared wall timbers and 4"x10" heavy roof trusses. For lighter applications, such as seasonal use, 4"x8" wall members are also available. The company's annual capacity is limited by the sustainable yield of the forest to 20 building kits per year.

Masonry Accessories

Forces affecting the durability and performance of masonry wall systems include bulk water penetration, wicking of moisture, and solar-driven moisture movement. Products listed here are designed to improve the durability and performance of masonry wall systems. Masonry accessories that improve the durability and performance of masonry wall systems can include two-piece adjustable brick ties, brick veneer venting and clear cavity components. Note that clear cavity components represent a product solution that should be considered along with techniques for keeping the cavity space clear, such as loose sand and mortar cleanouts in the first course of the veneer.

CavClear Masonry Mat

Archovations, Inc.
P.O. Box 241
Hudson, WI 54016

Toll-free: 888-436-2620
Phone: 715-381-5773
www.cavclear.com

CavClear Masonry Mat is an airspace maintenance and drainage material designed to be installed full-height behind brick in exterior cavity wall construction. The matting prevents obstruction of the cavity airspace and also prevents formation of energy-conducting mortar bridges. CavClear is a nonwoven plastic mesh made from 100% recycled plastic (25% minimum post-consumer content) and is available in thicknesses of 1/2", 3/4", 1", 1-1/4" and 1-3/4". It is also available bonded to EPS insulation.

CavClear Weep Vents

Archovations, Inc.
P.O. Box 241
Hudson, WI 54016

Toll-free: 888-436-2620
Phone: 715-381-5773
www.cavclear.com

CavClear® Weep Vents are 100% recycled-plastic, nonwoven mesh vents with a flame-retardant binder designed for use in the vertical joints between brick masonry units at all flashing levels in cavity wall construction. Properly installed, CavClear Weep Vents promote greater ventilation and drainage than traditional rope wicks in brick cavity wall construction. The notched design facilitates faster drying than straight-cut weep vents, according to the manufacturer. The vents are available in a variety of colors to blend with mortar and brick colors, and are part of a complete line of products that aid in keeping cavity airspaces clear. These vents may also be used for venting at the top of the wall in a pressure-equalized cavity wall design.

CavityRock

Roxul Inc.
551 Harrop Dr.
Milton, ON L9T 3H3 Canada

Toll-free: 800-265-6878
Phone: 905-878-8474
www.roxul.com

CavityRock® is a non-combustible, lightweight, water repellent, semi-rigid, insulating drainage board for cavity wall applications. This mineral fiber product provides effective water drainage, and maintains its thermal resistance even when damp. A fire stop is not required because CavityRock® is a non-combustible insulation. According to the manufacturer, this product is compatible with all air/vapor barrier systems, adhesives, and wall ties. Roxul's mineral wool is made from approximately equal amounts of natural basalt rock and recycled slag (with 1%-6% urea extended phenolic formaldehyde binder).

Mortar Net Masonry Drainage and Flashing Products

Mortar Net USA, Ltd.
541 S. Lake St.
Gary, IN 46403

Toll-free: 800-664-6638
www.mortarnet.com

Mortar Net is a 90%-open, fibrous-mesh wall drainage system used to maintain airflow and allow moisture migration from behind masonry veneer facades. 2"-thick Mortar Net for Brick, Mortar Net Block, and Mortar Net Weep Vents are made from 50% recycled 200-dernier polyester; at least 17% is post-consumer and up to 33% is post-industrial polyester. Mortar Net is designed to keep mortar droppings from

blocking weep holes. Block-Flash is an embeddable flashing device for exterior single width C.M.U. wall systems.

Masonry Mortaring

The portland cement content of conventional masonry mortar is high, making most masonry mortars high in embodied energy. Products listed here have some or all of their portland cement content substituted with industrial and agricultural waste products, such as fly ash, ground blast-furnace slag, or rice-hull ash.

MRT Blended Hydraulic Cement

Mineral Resource Technologies, LLC Inc.
2700 Research Forest Dr., Ste. 150
The Woodlands, TX 77381

Toll-free: 800-615-1100
Phone: 281-362-1060
www.mrtus.com

MRT Blended Hydraulic Cement, an alternative to portland cement, is made from Class C fly ash and other ingredients. It is available in bulk for ready-mix plants or in bags for mixing on-site. The manufacturer has certified the following recycled-content levels (by weight): total recovered material 83% typical, 80% guaranteed; post-consumer material 83% typical, 80% guaranteed.

St. Astier Natural Hydraulic Lime

TransMineral USA, Inc.
201 Purrington Rd.
Petaluma, CA 94952

Phone: 707-769-0661
www.limes.us

St. Astier Natural Hydraulic Lime, or NHL, is a 100% natural product that has been in production since 1851. St. Astier NHL Mortar is widely used in the restoration of old buildings. This natural hydraulic lime mortar imported from France allows stone to "breathe" naturally. Used in construction as plaster, stucco, mortar, and paint, its high level of vapor exchange and mineral composition can help reduce the risk of mold development and dry rot. NHL products are highly permeable, elastic, low shrinking, zero VOC, self-healing, and recyclable. Transmineral USA also offers Le Decor Selection, a line of high-end, all-natural interior/exterior limestone finishes which require trained installers and crushed limestone aggregate imported from France instead of the domestically available aggregate used for the St. Astier NHL products.

Metal-Web Wood Joists

Metal-web wood joists are lightweight, high-strength framing members that can provide long, clear spans and don't require drilling for mechanical and electrical systems. Metal-web wood joists are also very resource-efficient.

Open-Web T-Series Trusses

iLevel by Weyerhaeuser
2910 E. Amity Rd.
Boise, ID 83716

Toll-free: 888-453-8358
Phone: 208-364-1200
www.iLevel.com

Trus Joist's new T-Series open-web trusses have a top chord made from TimberStrand® LSL, which is manufactured with fast-growing aspen and poplar trees that are debarked and shredded into strands. The strands are coated with a formaldehyde-free MDI (methyl diisocyanate) binder and pressed into huge billets that are milled into dimensional lumber. LSL lumber is very consistent and stable; it does not warp and twist like solid wood. TimberStrand® LSL also resists splitting, which increases the allowable nailing options. The bottom chord of these trusses is made from solid lumber, and steel-tube web members are in between. All trusses are custom-engineered and manufactured for specific applications.

Posi-Strut

MiTek Industries
14515 N. Outer 40 Dr., Ste. 300
Chesterfield, MO 63017

Toll-free: 800-325-8075
Phone: 314-434-1200
www.mii.com

Posi-Struts offer a high-strength 20-gauge steel alternative to wood webs for floor joists and roof rafters; their open-web configuration eliminates the need for cutting and drilling, and they feature standard 2' o.c. spacing to cut down on cost and labor over conventional webs.

SpaceJoist

Jager Metal Products
2711 - 61st Ave SE
Calgary, AB T2V 2X5 Canada

Toll-free: 888-885-2437
Phone: 403-259-0714
www.jagermetalproducts.com

The Jager SpaceJoist™ is a truss for wood-framed construction with solid-wood top and bottom flanges and open-metal web members. SpaceJoists can have trimmable, I-joist-type ends.

TrimJoist

TrimJoist
5146 Hwy. 182 E
P.O. Box 2286
Columbus, MS 39704

Toll-free: 800-844-8281
Phone: 662-327-7950
www.trimjoist.com

TrimJoist's open-web trusses are manufactured with solid-wood top and bottom chords and solid-wood web members joined with metal plate connectors. TrimJoists have trimmable, I-joist-type ends.

Precast Concrete Panels

Precast structural and architectural concrete products tend to have optimized geometries, can speed construction, and can contribute to reduced environmental damage on the construction site as compared with pouring concrete on-site. Waste from overage is also eliminated through precasting at a plant. Through aeration, the weight of precast concrete components can be reduced by up to a third while improving its insulation value; substitution of fly ash or other post-industrial waste materials can further improve environmental performance. Some panels are cast with integral foam insulation. Products listed here contain recycled materials, contribute to appropriate thermal design, or have other compelling environmental features.

CarbonCast Insulated Wall Panels

Altus Group
P.O. Box 10097
Lancaster, PA 17605

Toll-free: 866-462-5887
www.altusprecast.com

CarbonCast Insulated Wall Panels are precast panels comprised of two concrete wythes separated by rigid foam insulation and connected by C-GRID™ carbon fiber shear trusses. CarbonCast panels can be made in various thicknesses and with a variety of insulation types, including EPS and mineral wool, providing steady-state R-values from R-8 to R-30. The epoxy-coated, carbon-fiber C-GRID trusses reduce the structural concrete needs while allowing more insulation to be used, improving energy performance and reducing the weight of the panels. Panels are available as vertical load-bearing and non-loadbearing units in thicknesses of 7" to 12", with widths up to 15' and heights of over 50'. Horizontally-installed non-load-bearing panels are available in thicknesses of 6" to 12", widths of up to 15' and lengths of up to 40'. Until XPS has been reformulated to eliminate the ozone-depleting HCFC blowing agent, that insulation option should be avoided.

Oasis Foundation Wall System

Oldcastle Precast, Inc., A Division of CRH plc
1002 15th St., Ste. 110
Auburn, WA 98001

Toll-free: 866-423-4810
Phone: 253-833-2777
www.oasiswall.com

Oasis Foundation Wall System, manufactured and installed by Oldcastle Precast (a division of Oldcastle), is a 6000-psi precast concrete foundation system prefinished with EPS foam insulation and DensArmor® Plus paperless wallboard. DensArmor Plus incorporates fiberglass mat facings and a moisture- and mold-resistant gypsum core. The EPS foam minimizes thermal bridging and contributes to a total assembly rating of R-10. Oasis walls are 8'6" tall, using approximately 1/3 less concrete than typical 7'10" precast foundations. The concrete contains 15% flyash, a post-industrial recycled material. Top-access utility chases are provided 24 inches on center. Oldcastle Precast provides a lifetime warranty against structural defects and a 15-year warranty against water penetration.

Superior Walls

Superior Walls of America, Ltd.
937 East Earl Rd.
New Holland, PA 17557

Toll-free: 800-452-9255
www.superiorwalls.com

Superior Walls™ is a custom precast foundation wall system with integrated footer, concrete "studs," and bond beam that is insulated at the factory with extruded polystyrene (currently made with ozone-depleting HCFC-141b). Superior Wall Panels are lifted by crane into place and locked together. The R-5 line has 1" of rigid insulation to achieve an R-value of 5, which may be increased with additional insulation to R-24. The Xi line has 2-1/2" of rigid insulation for R-12.5, which may be increased with additional insulation to R-31.5.

Preservative-Treated Framing Lumber

The durability of preservative-treated wood is the most important advantage to its use. Extending the service life of wood products reduces the demands on forests for replacement timber. Sales of lumber treated with the preservative CCA (chromated copper arsenate) are banned for consumer applications. Disposal by incineration is the most significant environmental concern associated with the billions of board feet already in use that were treated with this preservative: toxins such as arsenic may become airborne, and those that don't get into the air end up in the ash, where they're highly leachable. Copper-based wood treatments such as ACQ (ammoniacal copper quaternary) and copper azole have replaced CCA as the standard product. Wood treated with copper should be avoided near aquatic ecosystems, since copper is highly toxic to many aquatic organisms. Copper-treated wood is also corrosive to steel fasteners; follow manufacturers' recommendations for fastener selection. Silica-based treatments are available that are not actually preservatives, but that have the same effect by rendering the wood inedible to insects and fungi. Borate treatments effectively protect wood from insects while offering low mammalian and environmental toxicity, however, most borate-treated products are only suitable in interior applications because the borates do not stay fixed in the wood when exposed to weather. Organic (carbon-based) pesticides, used in various combinations, also appear in treated wood, in both surface and pressure treatments. These pesticides, relatively new to wood preservation, offer a less-toxic alternative to copper-based treatments. Treated wood should not be chipped for mulch, or burned.

Advance Guard Borate Pressure-Treated Wood

Osmose Inc.
1016 Everee Inn Rd.
Griffin, GA 30224

Toll-free: 800-241-0240
Phone: 770-233-4200
www.osmose.com

Osmose introduced Advance Guard® lumber and plywood pressure-treated with Tim-Bor® sodium-borate in 1998. The product was developed to deal with the growing problem of termites and fungal decay in the southern U.S. and Hawaii. Advance Guard® is used for sill plate, furring strips, and other code driven applications. Advance Guard can be used for framing houses, though it costs significantly more than untreated lumber. Advance Guard treated lumber is offered with a lifetime residential limited warranty.

BluWood

WoodSmart Solutions, Inc.
3500 NW Boca Raton Blvd., Ste. 701 & 702
Boca Raton, FL 33431

Phone: 561-416-1972
www.bluwood.com

BluWood® framing lumber, trusses, and sheathing components are factory-treated against mold, rot, fungus, and wood-destroying insects with the WoodSmart Solutions two-part Perfect Barrier System: a water-repellent, vapor permeable, mold-resistant subsurface infusion film using a proprietary blend of fungicides, and a borate DOT (Disodium Octaborate Tetrahydrate) wood preservative. BluWood is appropriate in climates where houses are normally framed with treated wood. It is not for ground contact, or for use in exterior applications unless protected by paint, stain, or sealer. The blue-dyed BluWood can be stored uncovered at job sites for up to six months. The warranty against insect infestation requires soil treatment for the duration of the lifetime warranty. (The warranty is transferable within a 30-year initial period.)

EnviroSafe Plus

Wood Treatment Products, Inc.
P.O. Box 950445
Lake Mary, FL 32795

Toll-free: 800-345-8102
Phone: 407-330-0177
www.eswoodtreatment.com

ES+Wood is pressure-treated with Disodium Octaborate Tetrahydrate (DOT Borates) and EnviroSafe Plus®, a proprietary polymer binder that fixates the borates in the wood. According to the manufacturer, it is effective against such pests as termites (including Formosan), carpenter ants, beetles, silverfish, fleas, and cockroaches, in addition to possessing antifungal properties. ES+Wood pressure treated wood is non-corrosive, retains natural color characteristics and won't affect indoor air quality. It is approved for interior and exterior, code compliant applications and has a limited lifetime warranty. As of August 2007, ES+Wood is in the final process of obtaining an NER Number from the International Code Council (ICC).

FrameGuard

Arch Wood Protection, Inc.
1955 Lake Park Dr., Ste. 100
Smyrna, GA 30080

Toll-free: 877-442-5766
Phone: 770-801-6600
www.wolmanizedwood.com

FrameGuard framing lumber, trusses, and sheathing components are factory-treated against mold, rot, fungus, and wood-destroying insects with a surface coating of borate (disodium octaborate tetrahydrate) and a mix of three low-toxic organic fungicides. The borate component protects against decay and insects, while the organic compounds provide surface protection against mold. Green-dyed FrameGuard lumber is appropriate in climates where houses are normally framed with treated wood. It is not appropriate for ground contact, exterior applications, internal sill plates, or any other application where outdoor-exposure or ground-contact pressure-treated wood should be used. FrameGuard has been certified by Greenguard for low chemical emissions.

SafeLumber

Babb Technologies
7638 Nashville St.
Ringgold, GA 30736

Phone: 706-965-4587
www.babb.com

SafeLumber from Babb Technologies, a wood treater distributing wood through the southeast and midwest, is factory-treated against mold, rot, fungus, and wood-destroying insects using a borate DOT (Disodium Octaborate Tetrahydrate) wood preservative and a mold inhibitor. Safe-Lumber is appropriate in climates where houses are normally framed with treated wood, as an alternative to more toxic copper treatments. The blue-dyed wood is appropriate for interior framing and applications without exterior exposure or ground contact, and it does not corrode galvanized steel plates and fasteners. The warranty requires termiticide soil treatment for the duration of the lifetime warranty, including prior to construction, though GreenSpec does not endorse such treatments. The wood should be covered at job sites.

SillBor Borate-Treated Wood

Arch Wood Protection, Inc.
1955 Lake Park Dr., Ste. 100
Smyrna, GA 30080

Toll-free: 877-442-5766
Phone: 770-801-6600
www.wolmanizedwood.com

SillBor framing lumber is factory-treated against mold, rot, fungus, and wood-destroying insects with a borate DOT (Disodium Octaborate Tetrahydrate) wood preservative. SillBor is appropriate in climates where houses are normally framed with treated wood, as an alternative to more toxic copper treatments. The bluish-dyed wood is appropriate for interior framing and applications not exposed to the elements or ground contact, and it does not corrode galvanized steel plates and fasteners. The wood is sold at two retention levels, with the lower level not effective against the Formosan termite. The warranty requires termiticide soil treatment for the duration of the lifetime warranty, including prior to construction, though GreenSpec does not endorse such treatments. The wood should be covered at job sites.

TimberSIL Nontoxic Pressure-Treated Wood

Timber Treatment Technologies
7481 Huntsman Blvd., Suite 520
Springfield, VA 22153

Phone: 703-644-0391
www.timbersilwood.com

TimberSIL is a sodium-silicate-based treatment process for wood that relies on a micro-manufacturing technology rather than toxins to prevent infestations and decay. The patented process uses heat to change a proprietary formula from a soluble solution that is infused into the wood and turn it into a microscopic layer of amorphous glass throughout the wood, providing a permanent treatment with no dusting or leaching. The treated wood is non-toxic, odorless and nonvolatile, is not corrosive to fasteners, does not cause excessive wear on tools, and has a natural clear color. TimberSIL Decking and other exterior products carry a 40-year warranty and TimberSIL interior products can be stored for up to one year of outdoor exposure with no negative consequences. As of October 2005, this product was not yet listed with the International Code Council; approval for use is granted by local jurisdictions.

Preservative-Treated Wood and Treatment Products

Extending the service life of wood products reduces the demands on forests for replacement timber. Site-applied treatments can contribute to wood longevity as well as mold and insect prevention. Products listed here are low-toxic and low-VOC.

American MoldGuard

American MoldGuard, Inc.
30200 Rancho Viejo Rd., Ste. G
San Juan Capistrano, CA 92675

Toll-free: 877-665-3482
Phone: 949-240-5144
www.americanmoldguard.com

American MoldGuard offers a mold-inhibiting treatment program for new construction utilizing a proprietary, non-volatizing, non-migrating antimicrobial silicon polymer—a highly permeable, water-stabilized organosilane that inhibits the growth of mold, mildew, algae, and bacteria without the use of heavy metals or other conventional toxins. Certified applicators treat surfaces during three phases of construction: the first application occurs prior to drywall installation and treats all interior structural surfaces; a second application occurs after drywall is installed and prior to painting; the third application happens after all interior surfaces have been finished. The company provides a 10-year prevention warranty against mold infestation.

Bora-Care and Tim-Bor Professional

Nisus Corporation
100 Nisus Dr.
Rockford, TN 37853

Toll-free: 800-264-0870
Phone: 865-577-6119
www.nisuscorp.com

Bora-Care is a liquid borate-based termiticide, insecticide, and fungicide concentrate applied directly to wood and concrete. Treatment prevents termites from tubing across treated areas; it kills and prevents subterranean, Formosan, and drywood termites; wood boring beetles; carpenter ants; and fungal decay. Wood is removed as a food source. Bora-Care contains ethylene glycol and patented penetrants. Tim-bor Professional is a water soluble, glycol-free borate powder that acts as a wood preservative, fungicide, and insecticide to control and prevent wood decay fungi, drywood termites, wood boring beetles, and carpenter ants. Borate products will leach from wood exposed to running water, or extended or repeated flooding.

LifeTime Wood Treatment

Valhalla Wood Preservatives, Ltd.
P.O. Box 328
Salt Spring Island, BC V8K 2R7 Canada

Toll-free: 800-359-6614
Phone: 250-538-5516
www.valhalco.com

Valhalla claims LifeTime wood treatment as a nontoxic family recipe that outperforms pressure-treated wood. LifeTime, which can also be used as a wood stain, is packaged as a powder for mixing with water to create an acidic solution that can be applied by roller, brush, or sprayer. Some prominent green building experts have reported good success with LifeTime, though comprehensive test results have not been made available.

Preservative-Treated Wood Sheathing Panels

The durability of preservative-treated wood is the most important advantage to its use. Extending the service life of wood products reduces the demands on forests for replacement timber. Sales of lumber treated with the preservative CCA (chromated copper arsenate) are banned for consumer applications. Disposal by incineration is the most significant environmental concern associated with the billions of board feet already in use that were treated with this preservative: toxins such as arsenic may become airborne, and those that don't get into the air end up in the ash, where they're highly leachable. Copper-based wood treatments such as ACQ (ammoniacal copper quaternary) and copper azole have replaced CCA as the standard product. Wood treated with copper should be avoided near aquatic ecosystems, since copper is highly toxic to many aquatic organisms. Copper-treated wood is also corrosive to steel fasteners; follow manu-

facturers' recommendations for fastener selection. Silica-based treatments are available that are not actually preservatives, but that have the same effect by rendering the wood inedible to insects and fungi. Borate treatments effectively protect wood from insects while offering low mammalian and environmental toxicity, however, most borate-treated products are only suitable in interior applications because the borates do not stay fixed in the wood when exposed to weather. Organic (carbon-based) pesticides, used in various combinations, also appear in treated wood, in both surface and pressure treatments. These pesticides, relatively new to wood preservation, offer a less-toxic alternative to copper-based treatments. Treated wood should not be chipped for mulch, or burned.

Advance Guard Borate Pressure-Treated Wood

Osmose Inc.
1016 Everee Inn Rd.
Griffin, GA 30224

Toll-free: 800-241-0240
Phone: 770-233-4200
www.osmose.com

Osmose introduced Advance Guard® lumber and plywood pressure-treated with Tim-Bor® sodium-borate in 1998. The product was developed to deal with the growing problem of termites and fungal decay in the southern U.S. and Hawaii. Advance Guard® is used for sill plate, furring strips, and other code driven applications. Advance Guard can be used for framing houses, though it costs significantly more than untreated lumber. Advance Guard treated lumber is offered with a lifetime residential limited warranty.

BluWood

WoodSmart Solutions, Inc.
3500 NW Boca Raton Blvd., Ste. 701 & 702
Boca Raton, FL 33431

Phone: 561-416-1972
www.bluwood.com

BluWood® framing lumber, trusses, and sheathing components are factory-treated against mold, rot, fungus, and wood-destroying insects with the WoodSmart Solutions two-part Perfect Barrier System: a water-repellent, vapor permeable, mold-resistant subsurface infusion film using a proprietary blend of fungicides, and a borate DOT (Disodium Octaborate Tetrahydrate) wood preservative. BluWood is appropriate in climates where houses are normally framed with treated wood. It is not for ground contact, or for use in exterior applications unless protected by paint, stain, or sealer. The blue-dyed BluWood can be stored uncovered at job sites for up to six months. The warranty against insect infestation requires soil treatment for the duration of the lifetime warranty. (The warranty is transferable within a 30-year initial period.)

EnviroSafe Plus

Wood Treatment Products, Inc.
P.O. Box 950445
Lake Mary, FL 32795

Toll-free: 800-345-8102
Phone: 407-330-0177
www.eswoodtreatment.com

ES+Wood is pressure-treated with Disodium Octaborate Tetrahydrate (DOT Borates) and EnviroSafe Plus®, a proprietary polymer binder that fixates the borates in the wood. According to the manufacturer, it is effective against such pests as termites (including Formosan), carpenter ants, beetles, silverfish, fleas, and cockroaches, in addition to possessing antifungal properties. ES+Wood pressure treated wood is non-corrosive, retains natural color characteristics and won't affect indoor air quality. It is approved for interior and exterior, code compliant applications and has a limited lifetime warranty. As of August 2007, ES+Wood is in the final process of obtaining an NER Number from the International Code Council (ICC).

FrameGuard

Arch Wood Protection, Inc.
1955 Lake Park Dr., Ste. 100
Smyrna, GA 30080

Toll-free: 877-442-5766
Phone: 770-801-6600
www.wolmanizedwood.com

FrameGuard framing lumber, trusses, and sheathing components are factory-treated against mold, rot, fungus, and wood-destroying insects with a surface coating of borate (disodium octaborate tetrahydrate) and a mix of three low-toxic organic fungicides. The borate component protects against decay and insects, while the organic compounds provide surface protection against mold. Green-dyed FrameGuard lumber is appropriate in climates where houses are normally framed with treated wood. It is not appropriate for ground contact, exterior applications, internal sill plates, or any other application where outdoor-exposure or ground-contact pressure-treated wood should be used. FrameGuard has been certified by Greenguard for low chemical emissions.

Reclaimed-Wood Framing Lumber

As the demands on forest resources have increased, nonforest sources of wood have grown in importance. Reclaimed wood is usually salvaged from buildings slated for demolition, abandoned railroad trestles, and "sinker logs" that sank decades ago during river-based log drives. It can also be obtained from trees that have been recently harvested from urban or suburban areas (such as disease-killed trees). Reclaimed wood is often available in species, coloration, and wood quality that is no longer available in newly harvested timber. In some cases, reclaimed wood suppliers have only limited quantities with matching coloration or weathering patterns; ample lead time and accurate materials estimates can help ensure the availability of the desired wood. Lowering the uniformity standards for finished wood can also increase the potential for use of reclaimed wood. As with other resources, the supply of reclaimed wood is limited. Efficient and appropriate use of reclaimed wood is important for its long-term availability.

D. Litchfield Reclaimed Wood

D. Litchfield & Co. Ltd.
3046 Westwood St.
Port Coquitlam, BC V3C 3L7 Canada

Toll-free: 888-303-2222
Phone: 604-464-7525
www.dlitchfield.com

Litchfield carries a large, steady supply of all types of reclaimed lumber and beams salvaged through their deconstruction operations.

Georgian Bay Wet Wood

Georgian Bay Wet Wood Inc.
8520 Highway 93
Midland, ON L4R 4K4 Canada

Phone: 705-526-6912
www.georgianbaywetwood.com

Georgian Bay Wet Wood Inc. recovers submerged old-growth timber from Ontario's Georgian Bay of Lake Huron then mills it to produce veneers, flooring, and lumber. Birch, beech, birds-eye maple, and flame birch are typically recovered. Heritage Timber Veneers are available in two species, Flame Birch and Birds Eye Maple. Heritage Timber Engineered Flooring has a nominal 1/8" (3.2mm) sawn veneer of recovered Maple, Birch, or Oak in 4" wide, random length boards with tongue and groove sides, micro-bevel edges, and a 9mm, 7-ply, FSC-certified Birch plywood core. The flooring is pre-finished with an aluminum oxide, UV-cured, urethane coating. Overall, the product has greater than 70% FSC-certified wood. Georgian Bay Wet Wood's wood products come with a certificate of authenticity that verifies that the product is genuine Georgian Bay Wet Wood.

Heartwood Reclaimed-Wood Flooring

Heartwood Industries
3658 State Road 1414
Hartford, KY 42347

Phone: 270-298-0084
www.whiskeywood.com

Heartwood is an international distributor of dimension lumber and timbers salvaged from warehouses and whiskey distilleries. They specialize in flooring but also offer custom millwork and moldings in longleaf yellow pine, oak, chestnut, and cypress.

M. Fine Lumber Company

M. Fine Lumber Company
1301 Metropolitan Ave.
P.O. Box 37 701
Brooklyn, NY 11237

Phone: 718-381-5200
www.mfinelumber.com

M. Fine Lumber Company is a leading supplier of salvaged heavy timber and dimension lumber. Inventory is salvaged from buildings being demolished throughout the U.S. Species include longleaf yellow pine, oak, and Douglas fir.

Pinocchio's Reclaimed Lumber

Pinocchio's
18651 Hare Creek Ter.
Fort Bragg, CA 95437

Phone: 707-964-6272
www.pinocchioredwood.com

Pinocchio's offers raw and remilled lumber from Douglas fir and redwood in both standard-dimension and custom sizes.

Reclaimed Lumber and Timbers

R. W. Rhine Inc.
1124 112th St. E
Tacoma, WA 98445

Toll-free: 800-963-8270
Phone: 253-537-5852
www.rwrhine.com

R. W. Rhine stocks a wide variety of reclaimed lumber and beams supplied by its extensive deconstruction operations.

Reclaimed-Wood Building Products

Endura Wood Products, Ltd.
1303 S.E. 6th Ave.
Portland, OR 97214

Phone: 503-233-7090
www.endurawood.com

Endura Wood Products currently has access to over 3.5 million board feet of Douglas fir that is being reclaimed from the old Portland Dry Dock #2. Also available is a limited supply of Douglas fir with a distinct red hue that has been reclaimed from maraschino cherry vats.

Reclaimed-Wood Building Products

TerraMai
1104 Firenze St.
P.O. Box 696
McCloud, CA 96057

Toll-free: 800-220-9062
Phone: 530-964-2740
www.terramai.com

TerraMai produces several grades of flooring, ranging from clear tongue-and-groove to rough-cut plank, from reclaimed lumber and tropical hardwoods. All flooring is available in "Character" (with evidence of previous use) and "Select" (clear) grades. Douglas fir, ponderosa pine, and southern yellow pine are among their most popular species. TerraMai also mills various architectural woodwork products from their 700,000-board-foot inventory of reclaimed woods. All of TerraMai's varied products are from reclaimed wood and is FSC certified.

Reclaimed-Wood Building Products

Vintage Material Supply Co.
730 Shady Ln.
Austin, TX 78702

Phone: 512-386-6404
www.vintagematerialsupply.com

Vintage Material Supply Co. offers salvaged wood flooring available "as is" with edges cleaned, as well as new flooring milled from wood recovered from such sources as demolished buildings, ranch recovery, urban logging, and river bottoms. Primary species include old-growth longleaf pine, Tidewater cypress, mesquite, and walnut.

Reclaimed-Wood Building Products

West Wind Hardwood, Inc.
P.O. Box 2205
Sidney, BC V8L 3S8 Canada

Toll-free: 800-667-2275
Phone: 250-656-0848
www.westwindhardwood.com

Family-owned and -operated West Wind Hardwood offers SmartWood Rediscovered salvaged woods for flooring, planks, lumber, timber, and other applications. The dimensions and appearances of salvaged and recycled woods may vary due to the nature of the materials. The company also offers locally harvested, FSC-certified custom Douglas fir flooring in clear and vertical grain. Other species, such as hemlock, pine, red oak, birch, and maple may be available, depending on supply. The company specializes in Douglas fir, and is recognized for custom wood products for less usual applications.

Reclaimed-Wood Building Products

What It's Worth, Inc.
P.O. Box 162135
Austin, TX 78716

Phone: 512-328-8837
www.wiwpine.com

What It's Worth can provide reclaimed longleaf yellow pine flooring, cabinet stock, and timbers. They also offer tank cyprus (used for water tanks at the turn of the century) cut from salvaged first growth trees. Most of their products are harvested from pre-1900 structures that are being deconstructed.

Reclaimed-Wood Lumber and Products

Armster Reclaimed Lumber Co.
9 Old Post Rd.
Madison, CT 06443

Phone: 203-214-9705
www.woodwood.com

A Reclaimed Lumber Co. salvages wood from old water and wine tanks, mill buildings, bridge timbers, river-recovery log operations, and other sources and custom mills it into a variety of wood products including siding, plank flooring, millwork, paneling, shingles and shakes, stairs parts, and dimension lumber and timber. Available species include red cedar, redwood, beech, black cherry, chestnut, rock maple, red and white oak, Eastern hemlock, Douglas fir, mahogany and Longleaf heart pine. Wood is sourced from all over the country, much of it processed at their Connecticut mill; but the company makes an effort to provide wood that is local to the customer and will make arrangements to process it locally.

Reclaimed-Wood Products

Crossroads Recycled Lumber
57839 Rd. 225
P.O. Box 928
North Fork, CA 93643

Toll-free: 888-842-3201
Phone: 559-877-3645
www.crossroadslumber.com

Crossroads Recycled Lumber sells raw and remilled salvaged Douglas fir, sugar pine, ponderosa pine, cedar, and redwood lumber, timbers, flooring, paneling, and siding. They also offer doors made from this wood.

Resource Woodworks

Resource Woodworks, Inc.
627 E. 60th St.
Tacoma, WA 98404

Phone: 253-474-3757

Resource Woodworks specializes in Douglas fir, cedar, and redwood timbers salvaged from demolition projects and remilled to custom specifications, including decking, flooring, lumber, timbers, siding, paneling, and millwork.

Trestlewood

Trestlewood
292 N. 2000 W, Ste. A
Lindon, UT 84042

Toll-free: 877-375-2779
Phone: 801-443-4002
www.trestlewood.com

Trestlewood deals exclusively in reclaimed wood. Their wood comes from the Lucin Cutoff railroad trestle, which crosses the Great Salt Lake, and other salvage projects. Trestlewood products include flooring, millwork, timbers, decking, and siding. Available species include Douglas fir, redwood, southern yellow pine, longleaf yellow pine, oak, and other hardwoods.

Triton Underwater Wood

Triton Logging Inc.
6675 Mirah Rd.
Saanichton, BC V8M 1Z4 Canada

Phone: 250-652-4033
www.tritonlogging.com

Triton Logging harvests underwater, old-growth standing forests submerged decades ago by man-made lakes behind hydroelectric dams. Using its proprietary Sawfish™ unmanned logging submarine, Triton recovers Douglas Fir, Western Red Cedar, Western White Pine, Lodgepole Pine, Hemlock, and other species year-round in British Columbia, which is estimated to have five billion board feet of standing timber preserved in reservoirs. All Triton's product is certified SmartWood Rediscovered by the Rainforest Alliance.

Underwater Timber Salvage

Underwater Timber Salvage
1550 Railroad Ave.
St. Helens, OR 97051

Toll-free: 888-366-5353
Phone: 503-366-5353

Underwater Timber Salvage Corp. retrieves century-old "sinker logs" from the Columbia River Basin waterways for its custom mill. The company started out with removal of navigational hazards, but recognized the value of what they were removing. UTS offers clear, finished wood in standard dimensions, as well as rough-cut widths 24 inches (300 mm) and more, in lengths up to 20 feet (6 m). Trim packages cut entirely from a single log are available to ensure consistent quality and appearance. Species include fir, hemlock, cedar, ash, maple, alder, oak, pine, and others. Some of these woods are available in coloration and quality no longer available from today's second- and third-growth forests. Stock is dependent on what's come out of the water lately. UTS has applied for FSC certification through the "FSC Recycled" label, using the third-party certification organization SCS.

Wood Materials from Urban Trees

CitiLog
P.O. Box 685
Pittstown, NJ 08867

Toll-free: 877-248-9564
Phone: 908-735-8871
www.citilogs.com

CitiLog™, also known as D. Stubby Warmbold, is SmartWood-certified for the harvesting of trees in urban areas of New Jersey and Pennsylvania. Wood is sent by rail to Amish craftsmen in central Pennsylvania who take extra care to turn the lesser graded wood into higher quality products such as flooring, lumber, custom architectural millwork, furniture, and kitchen cabinets. Where appropriate, wood is now harvested using horses.

Reclaimed-Wood Heavy Timber

As the demands on forest resources have increased, nonforest sources of wood have grown in importance. Reclaimed wood is usually salvaged from buildings slated for demolition, abandoned railroad trestles, and "sinker logs" that sank decades ago during river-based log drives. It can also be obtained from trees that have been recently harvested from urban or suburban areas (such as disease-killed trees). Reclaimed wood is often available in species, coloration, and wood quality that is no longer available in newly harvested timber. In some cases, reclaimed wood suppliers have only limited quantities with matching coloration or weathering patterns; ample lead time and accurate materials estimates can help ensure the availability of the desired wood. Lowering the uniformity standards for finished wood can also increase the potential for use of reclaimed wood. As with other resources, the supply of reclaimed wood is limited. Efficient and appropriate use of reclaimed wood is important for its long-term availability.

AltruWood Reclaimed-Wood Products

AltruWood, Inc.
P.O. Box 3341
Portland, OR 97208

Toll-free: 877-372-9663
www.altruwood.com

AltruWood sells a variety of reclaimed-wood species and products, mostly salvaged from old buildings, barns, factories, warehouses and rivers in the U.S.—principally including domestic pine varieties, Douglas fir, oak, cedar, redwood, chestnut, cypress, and cherry. Products include flooring, timbers, siding, paneling, millwork, and lumber. The company will work with clients to locate recycled lumber from their region. A custom cutting service allows the specification of exact sizes and dimensions, minimizing waste. AltruWood also sells new domestic and tropical FSC-certified wood.

Appalachian Woods

Appalachian Woods, LLC
1240 Cold Springs Rd.
Stuarts Draft, VA 24477

Toll-free: 800-333-7610
Phone: 540-337-1801
www.appalachianwoods.com

Appalachian Woods reclaims and remills timber for a variety of custom millwork applications. Lumber is generally sold rough, but can be provided S4S and S2S. Lumber, flooring, and furniture is available in a variety of species including American chestnut, heart pine, and oak. Appalachian Woods has been a family-run business since 1976.

Barnstormers Reclaimed Hand-Hewn Beams

Barnstormers
166 Malden Tpke.
Saugerties, NY 12477

Phone: 845-661-7989
www.barnstormersflooring.com

Barnstormers sells antique hand-hewn beams from disassembled barns. Species include oak, chestnut, hemlock, and other hardwoods. The company also remills tongue-and-groove barnwood hardwood flooring and siding out of this reclaimed wood, using a technique called "skip planing" to mill the boards while leaving some of the original milling marks for aesthetic purposes.

D. Litchfield Reclaimed Wood

D. Litchfield & Co. Ltd.
3046 Westwood St.
Port Coquitlam, BC V3C 3L7 Canada

Toll-free: 888-303-2222
Phone: 604-464-7525
www.dlitchfield.com

Litchfield carries a large, steady supply of all types of reclaimed lumber and beams salvaged through their deconstruction operations.

Georgian Bay Wet Wood

Georgian Bay Wet Wood Inc.
8520 Highway 93
Midland, ON L4R 4K4 Canada

Phone: 705-526-6912
www.georgianbaywetwood.com

Georgian Bay Wet Wood Inc. recovers submerged old-growth timber from Ontario's Georgian Bay of Lake Huron then mills it to produce veneers, flooring, and lumber. Birch, beech, birds-eye maple, and flame birch are typically recovered. Heritage Timber Veneers are available in two species, Flame Birch and Birds Eye Maple. Heritage Timber Engineered Flooring has a nominal 1/8" (3.2mm) sawn veneer of recovered Maple, Birch, or Oak in 4" wide, random length boards with tongue and groove sides, micro-bevel edges, and a 9mm, 7-ply, FSC-certified Birch plywood core. The flooring is pre-finished with an aluminum oxide, UV-cured, urethane coating. Overall, the product has greater than 70% FSC-certified wood. Georgian Bay Wet Wood's wood products come with a certificate of authenticity that verifies that the product is genuine Georgian Bay Wet Wood.

Logs End Reclaimed-Wood Building Products

Logs End Inc.
1520 Triole St.
Ottawa, ON K1B3S9 Canada

Phone: 613-738-7851
www.logsend.com

Logs End, Inc., retrieves sinker logs in Canada's Upper Ottawa Valley area and processes them into lumber and timber, wide-plank flooring, paneling, siding, and trim in standard and custom dimensions. Old-growth, clear pine is typically recovered, though birch, red and white oak, and hard and soft maple are also available. Certificates of authenticity for educational purposes are issued by the company. Logs End lumber and timbers carry Smartwood "Rediscovered" certification.

M. Fine Lumber Company

M. Fine Lumber Company
1301 Metropolitan Ave.
P.O. Box 37 701
Brooklyn, NY 11237

Phone: 718-381-5200
www.mfinelumber.com

M. Fine Lumber Company is a leading supplier of salvaged heavy timber and dimension lumber. Inventory is salvaged from buildings being demolished throughout the U.S. Species include longleaf yellow pine, oak, and Douglas fir.

Michael Evans Natural Resources

Michael Evenson Natural Resources
P.O. Box 157
Petrolia, CA 95558

Phone: 707-629-3506
www.oldgrowthtimbers.com

Natural Resources dismantles buildings and remills salvaged lumber for resale. Available species include redwood, Douglas fir, and western red cedar.

Pinocchio's Reclaimed Lumber

Pinocchio's
18651 Hare Creek Ter.
Fort Bragg, CA 95437

Phone: 707-964-6272
www.pinocchioredwood.com

Pinocchio's offers raw and remilled lumber from Douglas fir and red-wood in both standard-dimension and custom sizes.

Reclaimed Lumber and Timbers

R. W. Rhine Inc.
1124 112th St. E
Tacoma, WA 98445

Toll-free: 800-963-8270
Phone: 253-537-5852
www.rwrhine.com

R. W. Rhine stocks a wide variety of reclaimed lumber and beams supplied by its extensive deconstruction operations.

Reclaimed-Wood Building Products

Conklin's Authentic Antique Barnwood
R.R. 1, Box 70
Susquehanna, PA 18847

Phone: 570-465-3832
www.conklinsbarnwood.com

Conklin's Authentic Antique Barnwood sells hand-hewn beams, barn boards, and flooring "as is" or remilled.

Reclaimed-Wood Building Products

Endura Wood Products, Ltd.
1303 S.E. 6th Ave.
Portland, OR 97214

Phone: 503-233-7090
www.endurawood.com

Endura Wood Products currently has access to over 3.5 million board feet of Douglas fir that is being reclaimed from the old Portland Dry Dock #2. Also available is a limited supply of Douglas fir with a distinct red hue that has been reclaimed from maraschino cherry vats.

Reclaimed-Wood Building Products

General Woodcraft, Inc.
531 Broad St.
New London, CT 06320

Phone: 860-444-9663
www.generalwoodcraftinc.com

General Woodcraft provides wood flooring and other products milled from beams and timbers salvaged from barns and factories built a century ago—often from old-growth timber. Species (as available) include pine, chestnut, and oak.

Reclaimed-Wood Building Products

J. Hoffman Lumber Co.
1330 E. State St.
Sycamore, IL 60178

Phone: 815-899-2260
www.hoffmanlumberco.com

J. Hoffman Lumber Co. is the Midwest's only sawmill company specializing in reclaimed antique heart pine, Douglas fir, and white pine. Reclaimed lumber is remilled into flooring, siding, and other millwork.

Reclaimed-Wood Building Products

Longleaf Lumber
115 Fawcett St.
Cambridge, MA 02138

Toll-free: 866-653-3566
Phone: 617-871-6611
www.longleaflumber.com

Longleaf Lumber, founded in 1997, remills antique timbers into millwork and flooring at the company's sawmill in southern Maine. Longleaf specializes in heart pine, but other salvaged woods such as chestnut, red and white oak, eastern white pine, and maple are also available from buildings dismantled in various locations around the New England region. Longleaf also sells unmilled reclaimed timbers and reclaimed barn siding. In addition to the sawmill, the company operates a retail store at their Cambridge, MA location.

Reclaimed-Wood Building Products

Mountain Lumber
6812 Spring Hill Rd.
P.O. Box 289
Ruckersville, VA 22968

Toll-free: 800-445-2671
Phone: 434-985-3646
www.mountainlumber.com

Mountain Lumber reclaims timbers from buildings slated for demolition and ships them to their mill in Virginia for remilling into wide-plank flooring, beams, rough-sawn cabinet lumber, and an extensive range of architectural millwork including stair parts and moldings. Species include heart pine, oak, American chestnut, maple, and elm.

Reclaimed-Wood Building Products

Pioneer Millworks
1180 Commercial Dr.
Farmington, NY 14425

Toll-free: 800-951-9663
Phone: 585-924-9970
www.pioneermillworks.com

Pioneer Millworks remills salvaged wood into flooring and a number of molding profiles, in addition to timbers, cabinetry, stair parts, doors, and trusses. The primary species is longleaf yellow pine; others that are often available include redwood, bald cypress, chestnut, white oak, Douglas fir, and white pine.

Reclaimed-Wood Building Products

Solid Wood Products
3756 Pineridge Dr.
Lac Le Jeune, BC V1S 1Y8 Canada

Phone: 250-320-0936
www.solidwoodpro.com

Solid Wood Products manufactures building and finish products, primarily wide-plank flooring from reclaimed Douglas fir. The one-inch flooring is available in 6" to 14" widths. Also offered are trim, wainscot, panels, and stair parts; timber-frame components including beams, braces, purlins, and rafters; as well as custom furniture.

Reclaimed-Wood Building Products

TerraMai
1104 Firenze St.
P.O. Box 696
McCloud, CA 96057

Toll-free: 800-220-9062
Phone: 530-964-2740
www.terramai.com

TerraMai produces several grades of flooring, ranging from clear tongue-and-groove to rough-cut plank, from reclaimed lumber and tropical hardwoods. All flooring is available in "Character" (with evidence of previous use) and "Select" (clear) grades. Douglas fir, ponderosa pine, and southern yellow pine are among their most popular species. TerraMai also mills various architectural woodwork products from their 700,000-board-foot inventory of reclaimed woods. All of TerraMai's varied products are from reclaimed wood and is FSC certified.

Reclaimed-Wood Building Products

Vintage Log and Lumber, Inc.
Glen Ray Rd.
Rt. 1, Box 2F
Alderson, WV 24910

Toll-free: 877-653-5647
Phone: 304-445-2300
www.vintagelog.com

Vintage Log and Lumber salvages the materials in log cabins and timber-frame barns in Kentucky, Ohio, Pennsylvania, and West Virginia. The company's inventory includes salvaged redwood, chestnut, oak, pine, and poplar boards, beams, flooring, and split rails. They also sell complete hand-hewn log cabins and timber-frame barns, as well as architectural salvage items.

Reclaimed-Wood Building Products

Vintage Material Supply Co.
730 Shady Ln.
Austin, TX 78702

Phone: 512-386-6404
www.vintagematerialsupply.com

Vintage Material Supply Co. offers salvaged wood flooring available "as is" with edges cleaned, as well as new flooring milled from wood recovered from such sources as demolished buildings, ranch recovery, urban logging, and river bottoms. Primary species include old-growth longleaf pine, Tidewater cypress, mesquite, and walnut.

Reclaimed-Wood Building Products

Vintage Timberworks
47100 Rainbow Canyon Rd.
Temecula, CA 92592

Phone: 951-695-1003
www.vintagetimber.com

Vintage Timberworks offers a wide range of reclaimed products made with wood salvaged from buildings in the U.S., Canada, and Australia that are typically at least 70 years old. Typical species include Douglas fir, cedar, and redwood. Reclaimed timber, beams, and flooring are available in a variety of species and are offered "as is," remilled, and/or refinished (distressed, hand-hewed, sandblasted, etc.). Douglas fir and oak flooring can be milled in a wide variety of widths and lengths. Most other species are limited in width and length to available stock. The company also can arrange for building demolition and material reclamation in the U.S. and Canada.

Reclaimed-Wood Building Products

West Wind Hardwood, Inc.
P.O. Box 2205
Sidney, BC V8L 3S8 Canada

Toll-free: 800-667-2275
Phone: 250-656-0848
www.westwindhardwood.com

Family-owned and -operated West Wind Hardwood offers SmartWood Rediscovered salvaged woods for flooring, planks, lumber, timber, and other applications. The dimensions and appearances of salvaged and recycled woods may vary due to the nature of the materials. The company also offers locally harvested, FSC-certified custom Douglas fir flooring in clear and vertical grain. Other species, such as hemlock, pine, red oak, birch, and maple may be available, depending on supply. The company specializes in Douglas fir, and is recognized for custom wood products for less usual applications.

Reclaimed-Wood Building Products

What It's Worth, Inc.
P.O. Box 162135
Austin, TX 78716

Phone: 512-328-8837
www.wiwpine.com

What Its Worth can provide reclaimed longleaf yellow pine flooring, cabinet stock, and timbers. They also offer tank cyprus (used for water tanks at the turn of the century) cut from salvaged first growth trees. Most of their products are harvested from pre-1900 structures that are being deconstructed.

Reclaimed-Wood Lumber and Products

Armster Reclaimed Lumber Co.
9 Old Post Rd.
Madison, CT 06443

Phone: 203-214-9705
www.woodwood.com

A Reclaimed Lumber Co. salvages wood from old water and wine tanks, mill buildings, bridge timbers, river-recovery log operations, and other sources and custom mills it into a variety of wood products including siding, plank flooring, millwork, paneling, shingles and shakes, stairs parts, and dimension lumber and timber. Available species include red cedar, redwood, beech, black cherry, chestnut, rock maple, red and white oak, Eastern hemlock, Douglas fir, mahogany and Longleaf heart pine. Wood is sourced from all over the country, much of it processed at their Connecticut mill; but the company makes an effort to provide wood that is local to the customer and will make arrangements to process it locally.

Reclaimed-Wood Materials

Big Timberworks
1 Rabel Ln.
P.O. Box 368
Gallatin Gateway, MT 59730

Phone: 406-763-4639
www.bigtimberworks.com

Big Timberworks offers custom-milled, reclaimed lumber and timbers in a variety of species. The company specializes in shipping timber frame houses all over the country for supervised construction but also sells custom-cut, reclaimed wood from their sawmill in Montana for residential and commercial applications such as siding, flooring, and millwork.

Reclaimed-Wood Materials

Black's Farmwood, Inc.
P.O. Box 2836
San Rafael, CA 94912

Toll-free: 877-321-9663
Phone: 415-454-8312
www.blacksfarmwood.com

Black's Farmwood sells reclaimed wood products from deconstructed buildings and river bottoms. Products are available in a variety of species and include salvaged timbers and beams, remilled flooring, and barn siding. The company has a showroom in San Rafael, CA and uses two mills, one in Kentucky and another in New York.

Reclaimed-Wood Products

Albany Woodworks, Inc.
P.O. Box 729
Albany, LA 70711

Toll-free: 1-800-551-1282
Phone: 225-567-1155
www.albanywoodworks.com

Albany Woodworks mills reclaimed woods, including heart pine and heart cypress, into various architectural woodwork products, including flooring, timber, and stair parts. Doors are also offered.

Reclaimed-Wood Products

Architectural Timber and Millwork
49 Mt. Warner Rd.
P.O. Box 719
Hadley, MA 01035

Toll-free: 800-430-5473
Phone: 413-586-3045
www.atimber.com

Architectural Timber and Millwork specializes in custom architectural millwork fabricated from reclaimed wood. They source their materials from different parts of the country, providing a widely varied species inventory. Wide-plank flooring is produced from wood salvaged from existing structures slated for demolition. Species include heart pine, chestnut, and oak.

Reclaimed-Wood Products

Centre Mills Antique Floors
P.O. Box 16
Aspers, PA 17304

Phone: 717-677-9698
www.centremillsantiquefloors.com

Centre Mills Antique Floors salvages, remills, and sells several species and types of wood products, many hand-hewn. Species include chestnut, oak, white pine, and fir. Centre Mills uses the old gristmill, built in 1841, in Centre Mills, Pennsylvania as their storage facility.

Reclaimed-Wood Products

Chestnut Specialists, Inc.
P.O. Box 304
Plymouth, CT 06782

Phone: 860-283-4209
www.chestnutspec.com

Chestnut Specialists dismantles buildings and remills reclaimed timbers for resale in a variety of products, including siding and flooring. Rough timber, planks, and beams in their original milled or hand-hewn condition are also available.

Reclaimed-Wood Products

Crossroads Recycled Lumber
57839 Rd. 225
P.O. Box 928
North Fork, CA 93643

Toll-free: 888-842-3201
Phone: 559-877-3645
www.crossroadslumber.com

Crossroads Recycled Lumber sells raw and remilled salvaged Douglas fir, sugar pine, ponderosa pine, cedar, and redwood lumber, timbers, flooring, paneling, and siding. They also offer doors made from this wood.

Reclaimed-Wood Products

Duluth Timber Co.
P.O. Box 16717
Duluth, MN 55805

Phone: 218-727-2145
www.duluthtimber.com

Duluth Timber reclaims and remills mainly Douglas fir and longleaf yellow pine, but also redwood and cypress. Demolition and salvage of warehouses and sheep-shearing sheds in

Australia has yielded a supply of Australian hardwoods such as jarrah and Mountain ash. Duluth has mills in Minnesota and Washington.

Resource Woodworks

Resource Woodworks, Inc.
627 E. 60th St.
Tacoma, WA 98404

Phone: 253-474-3757

Resource Woodworks specializes in Douglas fir, cedar, and redwood timbers salvaged from demolition projects and remilled to custom specifications, including decking, flooring, lumber, timbers, siding, paneling, and millwork.

Re-Tech Wood Products

Re-Tech Wood Products
1324 Russell Rd.
P.O. Box 215
Forks, WA 98331

Phone: 360-374-4141
www.retechwoodproducts.com

Re-Tech reclaims and remills timber for a wide variety of custom millwork and complete custom timber-frame packages for houses. They also make specialty cuts in timber to order.

River-Reclaimed Wood Products

Goodwin Heart Pine Company
106 S.W. 109th Pl.
Micanopy, FL 32667

Toll-free: 800-336-3118
Phone: 352-466-0339
www.heartpine.com

Goodwin manufactures antique wood flooring, millwork, stair parts, paneling, and siding made from antique heart pine and heart cypress logs—200 years old or older—recovered from Southern river bottoms. Flooring, siding, and paneling is kiln-dried, graded, and precision-milled. Decorative wood moldings are architecturally drawn and are designed to classic proportions. Stair parts include solid or laminated treads, and a full range of balusters, newels, and rails. Reclaimed timbers from old buildings are also available.

Timeless Timber

Timeless Timber, Inc.
2200 E. Lake Shore Dr.
Ashland, WI 54806

Toll-free: 1-888-653-5647
Phone: 715-685-9663
www.timelesstimber.com

Timeless Timber, Inc., formerly The Superior Water-Logged Lumber Company, harvests logs that sank during the log drives of the 1800s. Domestic species include red and white oak, maple, birch, white pine, basswood, elm, hickory, beech, ponderosa pine, and cypress. The company was certified in June of 2000 by Scientific Certification Systems as a producer of timber from 100% salvaged wood.

Trestlewood

Trestlewood
292 N. 2000 W, Ste. A
Lindon, UT 84042

Toll-free: 877-375-2779
Phone: 801-443-4002
www.trestlewood.com

Trestlewood deals exclusively in reclaimed wood. Their wood comes from the Lucin Cutoff railroad trestle, which crosses the Great Salt Lake, and other salvage projects. Trestlewood products include flooring, millwork, timbers, decking, and siding. Available species include Douglas fir, redwood, southern yellow pine, longleaf yellow pine, oak, and other hardwoods.

Triton Underwater Wood

Triton Logging Inc.
6675 Mirah Rd.
Saanichton, BC V8M 1Z4 Canada

Phone: 250-652-4033
www.tritonlogging.com

Triton Logging harvests underwater, old-growth standing forests submerged decades ago by man-made lakes behind hydroelectric dams. Using its proprietary Sawfish™ unmanned logging submarine, Triton recovers Douglas Fir, Western Red Cedar, Western White Pine, Lodgepole Pine, Hemlock, and other species year-round in British Columbia, which is estimated to have five billion board feet of standing timber preserved in reservoirs. All Triton's product is certified SmartWood Rediscovered by the Rainforest Alliance.

Underwater Timber Salvage

Underwater Timber Salvage
1550 Railroad Ave.
St. Helens, OR 97051

Toll-free: 888-366-5353
Phone: 503-366-5353

Underwater Timber Salvage Corp. retrieves century-old "sinker logs" from the Columbia River Basin waterways for its custom mill. The company started out with removal of navigational hazards, but recognized the value of what they were removing. UTS offers clear, finished wood in standard dimensions, as well as rough-cut widths 24 inches (300 mm) and more, in lengths up to 20 feet (6 m). Trim packages cut entirely from a single log are available to ensure consistent quality and appearance. Species include fir, hemlock, cedar, ash, maple, alder, oak, pine, and others. Some of these woods are available in coloration and quality no longer available from today's second- and third-growth forests. Stock is dependent on what's come out of the water lately. UTS has applied for FSC certification through the "FSC Recycled" label, using the third-party certification organization SCS.

Wood Materials from Urban Trees

CitiLog
P.O. Box 685
Pittstown, NJ 08867

Toll-free: 877-248-9564
Phone: 908-735-8871
www.citilogs.com

CitiLog™, also known as D. Stubby Warmbold, is SmartWood-certified for the harvesting of trees in urban areas of New Jersey and Pennsylvania. Wood is sent by rail to Amish craftsmen in central Pennsylvania who take extra care to turn the lesser graded wood into higher quality products such as flooring, lumber, custom architectural millwork, furniture, and kitchen cabinets. Where appropriate, wood is now harvested using horses.

Sheathing (including Plywood & OSB)

Sheathing comprises a significant portion of the materials used with many building types. Careful consideration of product selection and use can reduce the environmental impacts of a project. Wall sheathing is often used only as an additional layer of weather protection, although it may also be required for racking resistance. When let-in diagonal bracing is used to provide racking resistance, wood-panel sheathing can sometimes be eliminated or replaced with more resource-efficient or insulative products. Phenol-formaldehyde (PF) binders are used in plywood, while OSB can be made with PF or the non-formaldehyde-emitting methyl diisocyanate (MDI), a polyurethane binder. Paradoxically, exterior-rated products using PF binders are less of an offgassing concern than interior-grade panels made with urea-formaldehyde. Oriented-strand board (OSB) can be an efficient use of forest resources because it can be produced from small-diameter or low-grade tree species. Wood products can carry the "FSC Mixed" label under a percentage-based standard based on the average certified and non-certified throughput of the facility at which they are made. Products listed here have one or more of the following attributes: FSC-certification; nonformaldehyde binders; nontoxic (to humans) borate insect treatments; or other environmental advantages over conventional OSB and plywood.

4-Way Floor Deck, N.C.F.R., and Firestall Roof Deck

Homasote Company
932 Lower Ferry Rd.
P.O. Box 7240
West Trenton, NJ 08628

Toll-free: 800-257-9491
Phone: 609-883-3300
www.homasote.com

4-Way® Floor Deck, N.C.F.R.®, and Firestall® Roof Deck are structural high-density fiberboard panels made from 100% recycled newspaper, with paraffin binders and additives for pest and fire resistance. Panels are available in a variety of thicknesses. N.C.F.R. is a Class A fire-rated panel for interior and exterior use. 4-Way Floor Deck is a tongue-and-groove multi-ply subfloor that is structural, sound deadening, and moderately insulative (R-2.5/in.). Firestall Roof Deck is a tongue-and-groove Class A fire-rated panel manufactured with 1 to 4 plies of Homasote® and a face ply of N.C.F.R..

AdvanTech OSB

J. M. Huber Wood Products
One Resource Sq.
10925 David Taylor Dr., Ste. 300
Charlotte, NC 28262

Toll-free: 800-933-9220
Phone: 704-547-0671
www.huberwood.com

AdvanTech™ OSB from Huber is an OSB made primarily with formaldehyde-free MDI resin (a small quantity of phenolic resin is added to improve certain properties). Due to its greater moisture resistance than conventional OSB, AdvanTech carries a 50-year warranty. This product has been certified by Greenguard for low emissions.

Certified Pine Plywood

ROMEX World Trade Company, LLC - sales agent for ROM
P.O. Box 1110
Alexandria, LA 71309

Toll-free: 800-299-5174
Phone: 318-445-1973
www.royomartin.com

Roy O. Martin Lumber Management, LLC (ROM) has received Smart-Wood certification for its 585,000 acres of forestland and four mills according to standards of the Forest Stewardship Council (FSC). This is the first FSC certification of any forest management operation in Louisiana. ROM's FSC-certified pine plywood, formerly under the name of SmartCore®, is produced by Martco Plywood in Chopin, Louisiana. Sanded plywood is available in AA, AB, AC, BC, and A-Flat grades in 4' x 8' panels standard thicknesses of 1/4", 11/32", 15/32", 19/32" and 23/32". As is true for the company's OSB plant, some fiber used in the Chopin mill comes from non-company-owned land, but 100% FSC-certified product can be provided. ROM's pine plywood is also available sided with a foil radiant barrier, or printed with the company's new "GRID" panel marking system.

CollinsWood FSC-Certified Wood Products

The Collins Companies
1618 S.W. First Ave., Ste. 500
Portland, OR 97201

Toll-free: 800-329-1219
Phone: 503-417-7755
www.collinswood.com

The CollinsWood line includes FSC-certified western pine particleboard, FSC-certified TruWood engineered (hardboard) siding and trim, and FSC-certified hardwood and softwood lumber and millwork. TruWood products are made under FSC's partial-content rules (with an actual certified fiber content of 32%), and use a phenol formaldehyde binder. Millwork includes cherry, red oak, soft maple and poplar interior millwork, including casing, base, chair rail, crown, etc. In 1993, Collins Pine Company became the first privately owned timber management company to receive FSC certification in the U.S. CollinsWood has been a leader in the forest and wood products certification movement since its inception.

EarthSource Forest Products

EarthSource Forest Products/Plywood and Lumber Sales, Inc.
1618 28th St.
Oakland, CA 94608

Toll-free: 866-549-9663
Phone: 510-208-7257
www.earthsourcewood.com

EarthSource Forest Products, a division of Plywood and Lumber Sales, Inc., sells FSC-certified hardwood plywood and lumber of the following species: maple, cherry, red oak, white oak, ash, Honduras mahogany, walnut, machiche, amapola, and many more. EarthSource also sells salvaged and rediscovered lumber such as fir, redwood, and hickory.

F.D. Sterritt Certified-Wood Building Products

F.D. Sterritt Lumber Co.
110 Arlington St.
Watertown, MA 02472

Toll-free: 877-635-3362
Phone: 617-923-1480
www.sterrittlumber.com

F.D. Sterritt Lumber sells FSC-certified lumber, plywood, decking, hardwoods, and hardwood flooring. They have a variety of certified species in stock. Additional green building materials available, including low-VOC adhesives, caulking, sealants, and recycled drywall. F.D. Sterritt offers green building product consultations.

FreeForm

The Collins Companies
1618 S.W. First Ave., Ste. 500
Portland, OR 97201

Toll-free: 800-329-1219
Phone: 503-417-7755
www.collinswood.com

FreeForm is an FSC-certified particleboard produced with urea-formaldehyde-free melamine binder rather than the industry-standard urea-formaldehyde. While low-formaldehyde particleboard made with phenolic binders is darker than conventional UF-particleboard (due to the reddish color of phenol-formaldehyde), FreeForm is lighter in color, because melamine binder is white. All FreeForm particleboard carries the FSC certification for well-managed forests—rather than the certification being an option.

FSC-Certified Lumber, Plywood, and Products

Potlatch Corporation
601 W. First Ave., Ste. 1600
Spokane, WA 99201

Phone: 509-835-1500
www.potlatchcorp.com

In 2004, Potlatch Corporation became the first publicly traded U.S. timber company to certify timberland according to Forest Stewardship Council (FSC) standards. Potlatch is producing chain-of-custody FSC-certified Hem-Fir and Douglas Fir/Larch framing lumber, inland red cedar decking and siding, and Douglas fir and white fir plywood from three chain-of-custody-certified mills in Idaho. Potlatch has recently added over 400,000 acres of FSC certified timber in Arkansas which supports a chain-of-custody sawmill in Warren, Arkansas.

Warren produces dimensional Southern Yellow Pine framing lumber. These products are stamped with the FSC logo when required for specific sales.

Green Board

GreenImports, LLC
P.O. Box 60
North Stonington, CT 06359

Phone: 857-526-6091
www.wwieinc.com

Green Board is made from recycled Tetra Pak beverage cartons and is composed of 75% paper, 20% polyethylene, and 5% aluminum. It is water resistant, termite and borer resistant, and provides insulative and sound proofing qualities. Green Board has a textured surface, and can be formed into curves and other shapes. Marketed as a direct replacement for plywood in any application (including "roofing, boats, cabinets, shipping crates, sheathing, underlayment, furniture"), it can be sawn, molded, cut, glued, screwed, or nailed. Available from the importer by the container-load in 4x8 sheets in 10, 12, or 18 mm thicknesses. Each container holds 676, 250, or 354 sheets of the respective board thicknesses.

Microstrand

Environ Biocomposites, LLC
221 Mohr Dr.
Mankato, MN 56001

Toll-free: 800-324-8187
Phone: 507-388-3434
www.environbiocomposites.com

Microstrand is an industrial-grade replacement for particleboard or plywood, made from rapidly renewable wheat straw and formaldehyde-free polyurethane (MDI) resin. Though 10%–15% lighter than traditional particleboard, the panels offer better strength and impact resistance. The product accepts paints, stains, and lamination, and can be custom-engineered to meet specific requirements, including increased fire-resistance.

Particleboard, MDF, Plywood, Lumber, OSB

F.W. Honerkamp Co., Inc
500 Oak Point Ave.
Bronx, NY 10474

Toll-free: 800-999-8115
Phone: 718-589-9700
www.honerkamp.com

F.W. Honercamp distributes a number of no-added-formaldehyde (NAF) and FSC-certified panel products, including particleboard, medium density fiberboard, melamine panels, composite panels, and hardwood plywood (with veneer, particleboard, and MDF core options). Their NAF products use MDI, phenol-formaldehyde, or soy-based binders and polyvinyl acetate (PVA, or white glue) for finish veneers. The company also offers FSC-certified hardwood lumber and OSB, as well as class A fire-rated panels.

PureKor Certified Plywood and Manufactured Panels

Panel Source International
23 Rayborn Cres., 2nd Fl.
St. Albert, AB T8N 5B9 Canada

Toll-free: 877-464-7246
Phone: 780-458-1007
www.panelsource.net

PureKor Certified Hardwood Plywood Plus is FSC-certified and contains no added urea formaldehyde. The binder used for both the plywood substrate and for adhering the face veneer, according to Panel Source, is polyvinyl acetate (PVA). This plywood is available in a number of grades and species, including alder, ash, birch, cherry, pine, cedar, hickory, maple, okoume, red and white oak, white maple, mahogany, poplar, and walnut. With most products, the core veneers are FSC-certified and the face veneers are not. Panel Source International also offers particleboard and PureKor Platinum Grade MDF panels made with FSC-certified, pre-consumer recycled wood fiber and formaldehyde-free resin. They are available from 4 x 8 to 5 x 12, in thicknesses ranging from 1/4" to 1-1/2" in mill grade, M1, M2, and premium. Standard density is 45 lbs.

SierraPine Formaldehyde-Free Fiberboard

SierraPine Ltd.
3010 Lava Ridge Ct. #220
Roseville, CA 95661

Toll-free: 800-676-3339
Phone: 916-772-3422
www.sierrapine.com

SierraPine's Medex MDF, for use in interior high-moisture applications, and Medite II MDF, for interior non-structural applications, are manufactured with a polyurethane binder, methyl diisocyanate(MDI), rather than conventional formaldehyde-based resins. SierraPine's newest formaldehyde-free product, Arreis SDF (Sustainable Design Fiberboard), uses the same MDI binder more efficiently to lower cost premiums. SierraPine has earned certification from Scientific Certification Systems (SCS) for using up to 100% recovered and recycled wood fiber for their MDF products.

SkyBlend MDF

Roseburg Forest Products
P.O. Box 1088
Roseburg, OR 97470

Toll-free: 800-245-1115
Phone: 541-679-3311
www.rfpco.com

Skyblend MDF Plus is a light-colored, moisture-resistant, medium-density fiberboard (MDF) that can be used for laminates and veneers and can be shaped and finished without pitting. Skyblend is made from 100% recovered wood, as certified by Scientific Certification Systems (SCS), and uses phenol formaldehyde as a binder instead of the more common (and higher-formaldehyde-emitting) urea formaldehyde. The wood used in Skyblend is mostly Southern pine and does not carry FSC certification. Skyblend MDF is offered in thicknesses of 5/8", 11/16" and 3/4"; and in sizes 49" x 97", 49" x 145", and 61" x 97". Other thicknesses and sizes are available upon request.

SkyBlend UF-Free Particle Board

Roseburg Forest Products
P.O. Box 1088
Roseburg, OR 97470

Toll-free: 800-245-1115
Phone: 541-679-3311
www.rfpco.com

Roseburg SkyBlend™ is a general-use particleboard produced with phenol-formaldehyde (PF) binder instead of the industry-standard urea-formaldehyde (UF) binder. The company claims formaldehyde emissions of about 0.01 parts per million (ppm) under standard test conditions—comparable to natural levels in outdoor air. It is Green Cross-certified by Scientific Certification Systems (SCS) as being made from 100% recycled wood fibers (pre-consumer waste from lumber mills). The wood fiber is not FSC-certified. The particleboard core is tinted light blue for field identification. SkyBlend™ is available in industrial grade only, in seven thicknesses from 1/4" to 1-1/8". Standard dimensions for most thicknesses are 49" x 97", while the 3/4" and 1-1/8" panels are also available in larger sizes. Custom dimensions may be available for large orders.

SmartChoice Wood Products

Certified Forest Products, LLC.
7 Los Conejos
Orinda, CA 94563

Phone: 925-258-4372
www.certifiedforestproducts.com

Certified Forest Products (CFP) is a distributor of SmartChoice, a collection of FSC-certified and reclaimed wood products from a variety of species including hardwoods, cedar, and redwood. Products include lumber, plywood, decking, siding, flooring, interior and exterior millwork.

Tuff-Strand Certified OSB

ROMEX World Trade Company, LLC - sales agent for ROM
P.O. Box 1110
Alexandria, LA 71309

Toll-free: 800-299-5174
Phone: 318-445-1973
www.royomartin.com

Roy O. Martin Lumber Management, LLC (ROM) has gained FSC-certification of its 585,000 acres of forestland and four mills. In addition to this being the first FSC certification of any forest management operation in Louisiana, ROM has made available the first-ever FSC-certified oriented strand board (OSB). Tuff-Strand® is a fairly conventional OSB produced by the Martco Partnership plant in LeMoyen, Louisiana. The 4' x 8' panels are available in three standard thicknesses: 7/16", 15/32", and 19/32". The mill is fed by up to 70% company-owned timber, and while OSB is typically certified using FSC's partial-content rules, the company can provide 100% FSC-certified product. Tuff-Strand's binder is 100% phenol formaldehyde. FSC-certified Tuff-Strand is also now available sided with a foil radiant barrier, or printed with the company's new "GRID" panel marking system.

Versaroc Cement-Bonded Particleboard

U.S. Architectural Products
55 Industrial Cir.
Lincoln, RI 28730

Toll-free: 800-243-6677
www.architecturalproducts.com

Versaroc® from U.S. Architectural Products is a structural cement-bonded particleboard made with mineralized wood particles and portland cement. It can be worked with typical carpentry tools; fasteners should be treated for corrosion resistance. The formaldehyde-free, termite-resistant, noncombustible product is available in stock nominal ("uncalibrated") thicknesses of 10 mm (3/8"), 12 mm (1/2"), and 19 mm (3/4"); several other thicknesses may be special-ordered. "Calibrated" stock is sanded to more precise thicknesses for applications requiring tighter tolerances. These boards are available square-edged in 48" widths; or tongue-and-groove in 46-1/2" widths for thickness of 16 mm (5/8") or more. Stocked length is 96"; shorter or longer boards (up to 120") are available by special order, as are widths less than 48" square or 46-1/2" tongue-and-groove. All orders can be factory-sealed on all surfaces with an acrylic paint sealer. Due to the energy intensity of the cement content, this product should not be considered a green substitute for particleboard except where significant resistance to fire, moisture, termites, or vermin are required.

Viroc Cement-Bonded Particleboard

Allied Building Products Corp.
15 East Union Ave.
East Rutherford, NJ 07073

Toll-free: 800-541-2198
www.alliedbuilding.com

Viroc is a structural cement-bonded particleboard made with portland cement and mineralized wood particles (71% portland cement, 18.5% wood fibers). It can be machined and worked with typical carpentry tools. Viroc is available in 4x8 sheets from 5/16" to 1-5/8" thicknesses. 4x10 sheets come in 3 thicknesses of 5/16", 3/8", and 1/2". T&G, half-lap, and beveled edge are available. Due to the energy intensity of the cement content, this product should not be considered a green substitute for particleboard except where significant resistance to fire, moisture, termites, or vermin are required.

Stay-in-Place Insulating Concrete Forms

Insulating concrete forms (ICFs) provide a labor-efficient means of making insulated poured-concrete walls, floors, and roof decks. ICFs are permanent forms—they aren't disassembled after the concrete has cured. Most of these products are made from expanded polystyrene (EPS) foam produced with a non-ozone-depleting blowing agent; a couple are made from a composite of wood waste or EPS beads and portland cement. To protect against potential damage from wood-boring insects, some EPS foam used in ICFs contains borates, which are benign to humans and the environment; however, the brominated flame retardants used in most EPS foam have health and environmental risks that are generating significant concern. The environmental advantages of ICF walls include higher R-values, and their use can result in reduced concrete content compared with conventionally formed concrete walls. Be aware that the R-values claimed by ICF manufacturers are not always arrived at in a consistent manner and may be misleading. For comparison purposes, "steady-state" R-values should be used when that information is available. Mass-enhanced or "effective" R-values are only relevant in certain climates or under certain conditions, but they're often listed in product literature in a way that fails to distinguish them clearly from steady-state R-values.

Amazon Grid-Wall ICFs

Amazon Forms One, Inc.
19068 Marbach Ln.
San Antonio, TX 78266

Toll-free: 866-651-3322
Phone: 210-651-3322
www.amazongridwall.com

Amazon Grid-Wall™ is an insulated concrete form system made from polystyrene (85% by volume, 100% of which is post-consumer recycled) and cement. The standard form measures 4' long x 10" thick x 16" tall with 6" diameter voids running horizontally and vertically 16" o.c. Grid-Wall forms are dry stacked but must be spot glued with a polystyrene-compatible adhesive to keep the forms from shifting during the concrete pour. Grid-Wall does not require drywall on the interior; stucco can be applied to the exterior using only one coat and no wire lath. Grid-Wall forms are termite- and fire-resistant and can be molded with power tools or a rasp.

Amvic ICF Building System

Amvic Building System
501 McNicoll Ave.
Toronto, ON M2H 2E2 Canada

Toll-free: 877-470-9991
Phone: 416-410-5674
www.amvicsystem.com

Amvic ICFs consist of two 2-1/2"-thick interlocking expanded polystyrene (EPS) form panels with a density of 1.5 lb/cf on a 6" on-center polypropylene web. At R-4 per inch, the EPS panels provide an R-value of 20, so the overall wall R-value would be slightly higher than that. This web has a rebar holding system designed to eliminate the need for tie downs. The completely reversible 48"x16" panels use a Amvic's FormLock TM interlocking system designed to eliminate the need for glue or ties, and come with 4", 6", 8", or 10" spacers to create insulated concrete walls with corresponding concrete core thicknesses.

Arxx Walls & Foundations

Arxx Building Products
800 Division St.
Cobourg, ON K9A 5V2 Canada

Toll-free: 800-293-3210
Phone: 905-373-0004
www.arxxwalls.com

Arxx standard 6" ICFs are comprised of two 2-3/8"-thick EPS panels separated by 99% post-industrial recycled polypropylene plastic webbing on 8" centers. The webbing serves as strapping for attachment of interior and exterior finishes and as support for steel reinforcing rods within the wall. Each standard interlocking Arxx block is 4' long,

16-3/4" high, and 11-1/2" thick with a steady-state R-value of 22.1. Other thicknesses (4", 8", and 10") and configurations are available, as are a number of accessories that facilitate construction.

Baleblock System

Celestial Construction, Inc.
1599 Luisa St.
Santa Fe, NM 87505

Phone: 505-820-2818
www.birkaniarchitects.com

The Baleblock™ system uses straw bales with two predrilled 4" holes to form an insulating straw-bale wall with a "post-and-beam" reinforced-concrete structure. This technique was developed by Erem Birkan, an architect in Sante Fe, New Mexico.

Cempo Form

Cempo Forms, Inc.
P.O. Box 9300
Pahrump, NV 89060

Phone: 775-727-6565
www.cempo.com

Cempo Form is a 100% recycled EPS and cement-composite permanent form system. The standard forms are available in 8", 10", and 12" thicknesses in a 32" x 48" block (approximately 150 lbs. and most often chosen by owner-builders) and a 32" x 96" block (300 lbs. and more commonly used by contractors). Cempo Form can be easily worked with hand tools, and can be cut and shaped for a variety of details. The company is in the process of testing for R-value.

Durisol Wallforms

Durisol Building Systems Inc.
67 Frid St.
Hamilton, ON L8P 4M3
Canada

Phone: 905-521-0999
www.durisolbuild.com

Durisol Wallforms are the original stay-in-place concrete forms introduced in 1945. They are made from a composite of mineralized wood chips and portland cement. Each wallform provides approximately 3 ft2 of wall. Mineral wool insulation inserts are available in several sizes to provide steady-state R-values up to R-28. The structural design permits use in multistory buildings. The Durisol material can also be specified in custom shapes for use as precast noise-absorption panels, retaining walls, floor forms, and roof panels. The manufacturer has certified the following recycled-content levels (by weight): total recovered material 40% typical, 35% guaranteed; post-consumer material 0% typical, 0% guaranteed.

ECO-Block ICFs

ECO-Block, LLC
11220 Grader St., Ste. 700
Dallas, TX 75238

Toll-free: 800-503-0901
Phone: 214-503-1644
www.eco-block.com

ECO-Block® EPS ICFs have embedded HDPE webs that serve as recessed furring strips on the exterior and as attachment points on the interior. Connectors (4", 6", 8", and 10") can be used singly or spliced together, allowing for concrete thicknesses from 4" to 24" or greater. With 5" of EPS in the wall profile, ECO-Blocks have an R-value of 22. The ECO-Block system includes straight panels, 90-degree corners (4", 6", and 8"), 45-degree corners, and brick ledge panels, and is amenable to tilt-up construction with insulation on one side only. ICF blocks are shipped unassembled (to save freight) and assembled on-site. The total recycled content by weight is approximately 40%, per the manufacturer. The ECO-Block team offers support for installation, code compliance, design assistance, and building science.

Faswall Wallforms

K-X Faswall Corp.
P.O. Box 88
Windsor, SC 29865

Toll-free: 800-491-7891
Phone: 803-642-8142
www.faswall.com

Faswall® is a fiber-cement block ICF. These ICFs are made of cement with optional fly ash content and K-X Aggregate (waste wood chips treated with mineral solutions to improve durability and cementitious bonding). A standard wallform block measures 16" x 8" x 11-1/2" with a 6"-deep core and weighs 22 lbs. Split-double, large-core, and corner wallforms are also available.

Fox Blocks

Fox Blocks
6110 Abbott Dr.
Division of Airlite Plastics Company
Omaha, NE 68110

Toll-free: 877-369-2562
www.foxblocks.com

Fox-Blocks™ is an ICF block system including reversible, pre-assembled ICF blocks with interlocking key-way block connections, ties, and corner brackets designed to add strength and facilitate application of veneer finishes. The ties are 100% recycled material. The EPS foam core has a steady-state R-value of 4.55 per inch, and the manufacturer claims a total R-value for the block of 35 or greater.

Greenblock ICF

Greenblock Worldwide Corp.
759 S. Federal Hwy., Ste. 213
Stuart, FL 34994

Toll-free: 800-216-1820
Phone: 772-223-8045
www.greenblock.com

Greenblock™ is an insulating concrete form made from EPS and held together by plastic webs for structural integrity and minimal thermal bridging. Greenblock's 6" core and 8" core blocks have 2-5/8" of foam on the interior side of the block and 2-5/8" on the exterior side. Greenblock forms have been used for over 30 years.

I.C.E. Block Insulated Concrete Forms

Southwest I.C.E. Block
501 East Plaza Cir., Ste. F
Litchfield Park, AZ 85340

Toll-free: 800-423-2557
Phone: 623-935-5428
www.iceblockinc.com

The I.C.E. Block™ System utilizes 16" x 48" x 9-1/4"-wide (or 11"-wide) tongue-and-groove EPS foam blocks with 6" (or 8") concrete cores. Steel studs are embedded on 12" centers within the blocks to facilitate attachment of interior and exterior finishes. Thermal bridging is minimized because the studs are not exposed. Concrete Capacity: one yard fills 13 blocks of 6" core; or 10 blocks of 8" core; or 12 blocks of 6-8" Super Duty.

ICF Block System

ICF Industries, Inc.
570 S. Dayton - Lakeview Rd.
New Carlisle, OH 45344

Toll-free: 877-423-4800
Phone: 937-845-8347
www.iceblock.net

The ICF Block™ System utilizes 16" x 48" x 9-1/4"-wide (or 11"-wide) EPS foam blocks with 6" (or 8") concrete cores. Steel studs are embedded on 12" centers within the blocks to facilitate attachment of interior and exterior finishes. Thermal bridging is minimized because the studs are not exposed on the exterior of the EPS block.

iForm

Reward Wall Systems, Inc.
9931 S. 136th St., #100
Omaha, NE 68138

Toll-free: 800-468-6344
Phone: 402-592-7077
www.rewardwalls.com

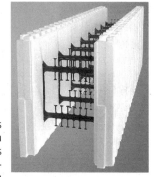

Reward Wall Systems manufactures the iForm™ flat wall form used in residential and commercial structures including large-scale high-rise projects. Reward's iForm is made from two 2.4"-thick premolded 48" x 16" slabs of EPS held together with plastic ties that are embedded in the EPS. The ties provide strength while the concrete is poured and serve as a nailing surface for interior and exterior finishes such as drywall and siding. The forms remain in place and become part of the wall providing a steady-state R-value of 22 and, according to the manufacturer, an effective R-value of more than 32.

Insul-Deck ICFs for Floors, Roofs, and Walls

Insul-Deck
935 Main St.
Ste. A2
Safety Harbor, FL 34695

Toll-free: 800-475-6720
www.insul-deck.org

Insul-Deck® is an interlocking ICF for joisted concrete floors, roofs, tilt-walls, and precast walls. Molded from EPS with integral steel functioning as support beams and receptors for drywall attachment, Insul-Deck can span up to 30' or more, allowing for clear-span basements. Integral channels (approximately 4-3/4" in diameter) for utility lines enable ducting within the insulated space and improved energy performance. Panels are available in any length, with variable thicknesses for R-values from 16 to 34. According to the manufacturer, the finished Insul-Deck system is 30-40% lighter than comparable poured-in-place slab floor systems and provides the same load capacity.

IntegraSpec ICF

Phil-Insul Corp o/a IntegraSpec ICF
11U - 735 Arlington Park Place
Kingston, ON K7M 8M8 Canada

Toll-free: 800-382-9102
Phone: 613-634-1319
www.integraspec.com

IntegraSpec® ICF consists of two 2-1/2"-thick interlocking expanded polystyrene form panels (48" long x 12-1/4" high interlocked) held together with High Impact Polystyrene (HIPS) plastic spacers of 4", 5", 6", 8", 10", or 12" to create insulated concrete walls with corresponding concrete core thicknesses. The spacers can be combined to increase core thickness and also function as furring strips/studs. The patented, completely reversible panels are shipped flat. IntegraSpec ICF has an R-value of 22+ per ASHRAE Fundamentals (1997) and is manufactured in both Canada and the U.S.

Lite-Form and Fold-Form

Lite-Form
1950 W. 29th St.
South Sioux City, NE 68776

Toll-free: 800-551-3313
www.liteform.com

Lite-Form ICFs are comprised of two EPS rigid-foam planks measuring 4' x 8' x 2" held together by plastic spacer ties that can be sized to offer concrete thicknesses from 4" to 24" (in 2" increments). Lite-Form is available in EPS or XPS foam. Only the EPS is being specified here. Fold-Form is an interlocking, foldable ICF. The forms are made from two 1' x 4' x 2" sheets of rigid EPS foam insulation held together with plastic spacer ties. Fold-Form folds flat for more compact shipping and storage. Form widths are available to create concrete thicknesses of 4" to 16" (also in 2" increments). Both Lite-Form and Fold-Form have calculated R-values of 26 for finished walls. In-Wall bracing is available for all walls over 4' in height.

Logix Insulated Concrete Forms

Logix
801 Klahanie Dr., Ste. 327
Port Moody, BC V3H 5K4 Canada

Toll-free: 888-415-6449
www.logixicf.com

Logix ICFs are heavier duty and more energy efficient than most, with two 2-3/4"-thick interlocking expanded polystyrene (EPS) form panels with a nominal R-value of 24 on an 8" on-center polypropylene web. The 48"x16" panels come with 4", 6", 8", 10" or 12" spacers to create insulated concrete walls with corresponding concrete core thicknesses.

NUDURA

NUDURA Corporation
27 Hooper Rd., Unit 10
Barrie, ON L4N 9S3 Canada

Toll-free: 866-468-6299
Phone: 705-726-9499
www.nudura.com

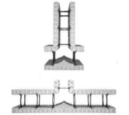

Nudura ICF's hinged plastic webs allow compact pre-assembled shipping. The modular, interlocking, reversible EPS units are unfolded at the site and stacked. Standard form size is 8' x 18", in five widths ranging from 9.25" to 17.25". Foam width is 2-5/8" on each side. The webbed polypropylene cross-ties are on 8" centers, with integral hangers for steel reinforcement. The webs are embedded in the foam, providing attachment strips for wall coverings. A variety of specialized forms and accessories are available, including end caps, tapers, corners, height adjusters, T-junctions, and lintels. Factory-cut radius walls are also available. The cross-tie and fastening strip components are made with 100% recycled HDPE from post-consumer and post-industrial sources. Hinge pins in the webbing are made with 100% recycled post-industrial steel alloy. Recycled content, by weight, ranges from 57% to 63% depending on overall width.

Pentstar Concrete Form Masonry Units

Pentstar, Corp.
6840 Shingle Creek Pkwy.
Unit 11
Minneapolis, MN 55430

Toll-free: 877-645-9704
Phone: 763-566-5400
www.pentstar.com

Pentstar® Concrete Form Masonry Units, a hybrid of unit masonry and ICF construction, are comprised of two masonry faces tied together by post-industrial recycled reinforced nylon connectors. Between the two masonry faces (starting on the outside) is a 1" dead-air space weep cavity and 2" of rigid foam (EPS or Celotex) that creates a 5-1/2" cavity for the concrete pour. The units are designed to be laid up with mortar, creating a hollow form that works like an ICF. With the insulation to the outside of the concrete pour and inner masonry, thermal mass effects are a significant part of the wall's thermal performance. An additional benefit is that the forms can also serve as the finish on both exterior and interior surfaces.

Perform Wall Panel System

Perform Wall, LLC
5776 N. Mesa St.
El Paso, TX 79912

Toll-free: 800-761-8590
Phone: 915-587-8885
www.performwall.com

Perform Wall Panels are made from 85% (by volume) post-consumer EPS and 15% portland cement molded into 8.5"-, 10"-, 12"-, and 14"-thick blocks. Flat stock is available in 2" or 4" thicknesses. Because of the insulating beads, the insulating value is considerably higher than that for concrete alone.

PolySteel Forms

American PolySteel, LLC
6808 Academy Pkwy. East, NE
Building C-2
Albuquerque, NM 87109

Toll-free: 800-977-3676
Phone: 505-345-8153
www.polysteel.com

American PolySteel manufactures a variety of ICF products utilizing expanded polystyrene foam form pieces and steel connectors/attachment studs rather than the much more common plastic ties. In 2002 the company reconfigured its forms so that the steel connectors are now recessed 1/2" below the surface of the form, thereby improving thermal performance. PolySteel manufactures both a "waffle-grid" and "flat-wall" form, as well as an insulated concrete deck form. The company also incorporates AFM Corporation's Perform Guard® borate treatment in their forms to protect against insect damage.

QUAD-LOCK Insulating Concrete Forms

QUAD-LOCK Building Systems Ltd.
7398 - 132nd St.
Surrey, BC V3W 4M7 Canada

Toll-free: 888-711-5625
Phone: 604-590-3111
www.quadlock.com

QUAD-LOCK® is a system of interlocking expanded polystyrene (EPS) panels connected with HDPE plastic ties. The panels are 12" high, 48" long, and either 2-1/4" or 4-1/4" thick; 10 wall configurations in any desired wall width. The manufacturer claims R-values of 22, 32, or 40.

R-Control ICF System

Advance Foam Plastics, Inc. - Colorado Division
5250 N. Sherman St.
Denver, CO 80216

Toll-free: 800-525-8697
Phone: 303-297-3844
www.afprcontrol.com

Advance Foam Plastics is a licensed manufacturer of AFM Corporation's R-Control® ICF System. The R-Control system consists of 1' x 8' R-Control PerformGuard® insect-resistant EPS foam panels joined by plastic form ties on 12" centers. Ties vary in length to create 4", 6", 8", and 10" walls with a nominal R-value of 20.

R-Control ICF System

Advance Foam Plastics, Inc. - Utah Division
111 W. Fireclay Ave.
Murray, UT 84107

Toll-free: 877-775-8847
Phone: 801-265-3465
www.afprcontrol.com

Advance Foam Plastics is a licensed manufacturer of AFM Corporation's R-Control® ICF System. The R-Control system consists of 1' x 8' R-Control PerformGuard® insect-resistant EPS foam panels joined by plastic form ties on 12" centers. Ties vary in length to create 4", 6", 8", and 10" walls with a nominal R-value of 20.

R-Control ICF System

Big Sky Insulations, Inc.
P.O. Box 838
Belgrade, MT 59714

Toll-free: 800-766-3626
Phone: 406-388-4146
www.bsiinc.com

Big Sky Insulations manufactures the R-Control® ICF System. The R-Control system consists of 1' x 8' R-Control Perform Guard® insect-resistant EPS foam panels joined by plastic form ties on 12" centers. Ties vary in length to create 4", 6", 8", and 10" walls with a nominal R-value of 20.

Reddi Form

Reddi Form, Inc.
10 Park Pl., Ste. 5-B
Butler, NJ 07405

Toll-free: 800-334-4303
Phone: 973-283-0055
www.reddiform.com

Reddi Form is a one-piece, screen-grid block insulating concrete form made entirely from expanded polystyrene (EPS). Available in two basic sizes, the 6" concrete-core form with 5 vertical cells (9.6" W x 48" L x 12" H) weighs 3 lbs. and can be used for most residential buildings. The 8" concrete-core form with 4 vertical cells (12" W x 48" L x 12" H) is used for commercial applications. Both foam forms have an R-value of 21. Reddi-Form warrants pours of up to 10' of wall height to be free of blow-outs.

Reddi-Deck Floor and Roof-Deck ICFs

Reddi Form, Inc.
10 Park Pl., Ste. 5-B
Butler, NJ 07405

Toll-free: 800-334-4303
Phone: 973-283-0055
www.reddiform.com

Reddi-Deck™ is a stay-in-place, self-supporting insulating concrete forming system for joisted concrete floor and roof decks. The Reddi-Deck panels are produced by a continuous molding production line integrating the insulating capabilities of EPS with the structural strength of metal inserts. According to the manufacturer, the systems are half the weight of comparable hollow-core, precast systems, which in turn reduces the load on walls and foundations.

SmartBlock

ConForm Pacific Inc.
1376 W. 8040 S, Ste. 2
West Jordan, UT 84088

Toll-free: 800-266-3676
Phone: 801-562-9050
www.smartblock.com

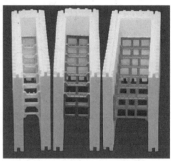

SmartBlocks, made from EPS, are available to form a solid concrete wall in 4", 6", 8", 10", and 12" nominal sizes or as a screen concrete wall measuring 40" x 10" x 10" with a 6-1/2" wide (standard size) post-and-beam concrete-core structure. SmartBlock walls possess superior acoustic insulation and use plastic connectors with 100% recycled content. ConForm Pacific Inc. claims R-22 to R-24 insulation values.

Standard ICFs

Standard ICFs
425 Second Ave. SW
Oronoco, MN 55960

Toll-free: 800-925-3676
Phone: 507-367-2183
www.standardicf.com

Standard ICF Corporation®, formerly Therm-O-Wall, manufactures the 895 ICFs™ System. The system consists primarily of two forms; a standard form made from two 2-3/8"-thick EPS panels separated by recycled-HDPE plastic brackets; and a corner form of the same materials. Standard panels are 48" L x 16" H x 11-1/4" W, providing for a concrete thickness of 6-1/2". The imbedded brackets are placed 12" on center and also function as furring strips for finish material attachment. The company claims an R-value of 26.

Tech Block

Tech Block International, LLC
P.O. Box 9954
Denver, CO 80209

Phone: 720-221-3912
www.techblock.com

Tech Blocks are patented exterior wall blocks composed of a mixture of polystyrene beads and cement. Bonded to the blocks is OSB sheathing, which becomes the inside surface of the wall and acts as an attachment surface for drywall. Underneath the drywall, the OSB acts as backing for hanging cabinetry, drape hardware, base, casing, etc. The exterior of the blocks is ready for stucco without the need for wire mesh. The Tech Block Wall System resists fire, sound, water, and termites. Each Tech Block weighs about 85 lbs. and measures 48" x 16" x 11" thick, with a steady-state R-value of 47.5, according to the manufacturer. Tech Block International, LLC, is an Energy Star® Partner with plants in Arizona, California, and Georgia, and has plans for plants in Texas and New Mexico.

TF System Vertical ICFs

TF System - The Vertical ICF
3030C Holmgren Way
Green Bay, WI 54304

Toll-free: 800-360-4634
Phone: 920-983-9960
www.tfsystem.com

TF System® - The Vertical ICF manufactures vertically oriented insulated concrete forms. The system utilizes a standard 2-1/2" x 12" x 8' expanded polystyrene plank (or custom planks variable in height up to 12') and preformed corner planks. The planks are joined by 26-gauge galvanized steel I-Beam studs, which enable planks to slide up to allow access to the inside of the forms until a top cap is installed. Wall thicknesses of 4", 6", 8", 10", and 12" are possible, with the company claiming an R-value of 25. Forms are shipped flat. Bracing requirements are minimal, and compressive strength allows for the installation of floor systems before pouring.

Thermal Foams TF ICF

Thermal Foams, Inc.
2101 Kenmore Ave.
Buffalo, NY 14207

Phone: 716-874-6474
www.thermalfoams.com

Thermal Foams Inc. is an authorized manufacturer/distributor of the TF Insulated Concrete Building System. The TF ICF system is a vertical plank system that consists of Thermal Foams EPS foam panels joined together with PVC or metal I-beams that vary in height and are available in widths to create 4", 6", 8", 10", and 12" walls with a nominal R-value of 22.

VariantHouse ICFs

VariantHouse LLC
6625 Miami Lakes Dr. #243
Miami Lakes, FL 33014

Phone: 305-777-3849
www.varianthouse.com

VariantHouse uses BASF's Neopor® EPS to manufacture lightweight, thin, fire-retardant, ICF blocks that are targeted to the do-it-yourself market. VariantHouse's ICF blocks have naps and grooves that click together to create an insulating wall without thermal bridges that can be assembled and concrete-filled by a novice. VariantHouse provides a versatile set of blocks that can accommodate almost any architectural design and conventional finish (such as brick, stone, stucco, wood, and vinyl siding). VariantHouse is currently the only company in North America to use BASF's Neopor. The black Neopor beads contain microscopic flakes of graphite that reflect heat radiation, reducing the foam's thermal conductivity. Products made of silver-grey Neopor can achieve the same insulating performance as products using BASF's Styropor® with up to 20% less thickness and 50% less raw material. Neopor has an R-value of 5 per inch, which for Variant blocks of 9.8", 13.7", and 17.7" thicknesses, results in R-values of approximately 20, 38, and 57, respectively.

Structural Insulated Panels

Most structural insulated panels (SIPs) consist of oriented strand board (OSB) sandwiching an insulating foam core. SIPs are gaining market share in the residential and light commercial building market because they're quick to assemble and provide excellent energy performance. The insulating core of SIPs is most commonly made from expanded polystyrene (EPS)—not to be confused with extruded polystyrene, which is not ozone safe—though in some cases polyurethane foam, or even compressed straw or mineral wool, is used. SIPs are manufactured in a range of thicknesses providing different R-values. In response to problems with insects burrowing in SIP foam cores, look for products that incorporate borate compounds, which can help deter them. Even with borate treatment, however, it may be necessary to use insect mesh, trap systems, and insecticides on an ongoing basis. SIP buildings can be quickly assembled, particularly when panels are factory-cut for door and window openings.

Agriboard

Agriboard Industries, L.C.
8301 E. 21st St. N
Suite 320
Wichita, KS 67206

Toll-free: 866-247-4267
Phone: 316-630-9223
www.agriboard.com

After being purchased by one of the original investors in the company, Agriboard™ Industries is back in business manufacturing an engineered insulated panel construction system; its straw core is bound only with high heat and pressure. 4" cores are laminated single- or double-ply between two sheets of OSB using a polyurethane adhesive, though Agriboard has plans to switch to a soy-based adhesive, as well as straw-based outer panels. According to the company, the structural wall panels offer excellent thermal and acoustical insulation, have up to a 2-hour fire transmission rating, and are lower in cost and two to three times stronger than conventional wood-frame construction in compressive load, racking, and bending. Agriboard also offers a new ceramic and fiberglass composite, water- and UV-resistant, factory-applied exterior coating.

Enercept Super Insulated Building System

Enercept, Inc.
3100 9th Ave. SE
Watertown, SD 57201

Toll-free: 800-658-3303
Phone: 605-882-2222
www.enercept.com

Enercept SIPs consist of a core of expanded polystyrene laminated between two sheets of oriented strand board (OSB).

EPS and Polyurethane SIPs

Winter Panel Corporation
74 Glen Orne Dr.
Brattleboro, VT 05301

Phone: 802-254-3435
www.winterpanel.com

Winter Panel produces structural insulated panels with either EPS or polyisocyanurate (polyurethane) foam cores. EPS has always been blown with non-ozone-depleting, non-global-warming pentane. Winter Panel's urethane foam uses HFC-245 as a blowing agent, which is also non-ozone-depleting. The 4-1/2"- or 6-1/2"-thick panels are available in Structurewall™ (a direct substitute for 2x4 or 2x6 framing using OSB as the outer skins), Curtainwall panels (nonstructural with gypsum wallboard on interior side, OSB on outside), and Woodclad™ (Structurewall panels with 1x8 v-groove pine cladding on interior finish side). The EPS-core panels are less expensive, while the polyurethane panels have a higher R-value. Panels with custom skins, cores, and thicknesses are also available.

Foard Structural Insulated Panels

Foard Panel
P.O. Box 185
West Chesterfield, NH 03466

Toll-free: 800-644-8885
Phone: 603-256-8800
www.foardpanel.com

Foard Panel, Inc. makes structural insulated panels (SIPs) with expanded polystyrene foam cores (ESP), which are ozone-safe. Foard SIPs are four feet wide, and eight to 24 feet long with nominal 4", 6", or 8" thick insulation cores. In additional to the structural panels, Foard also makes a curtainwall panel, with drywall on one side an oriented-strand board (OSB) on the other, and nailbase roof insulation panel, with OSB on one side only. Only products with an EPS core are being specified here.

Industry Representation

Structural Insulated Panel Association
P.O. Box 1699
Gig Harbor, WA 98335

Phone: 253-858-7472
www.sips.org

The Structural Insulated Panel Association (SIPA) represents the industry in promoting the advantages of SIPs to designers, contractors, and homeowners.

Insulspan SIPs

Insulspan
9012 E. U.S. Hwy. 223
P.O. Box 38
Blissfield, MI 49228

Toll-free: 800-726-3510
Phone: 517-486-4844
www.insulspan.com

Insulspan's SIPs are produced with EPS foam cores laminated between OSB sheathing.

Murus EPS and Polyurethane SIPs

The Murus Company, Inc.
3234 Rte. 549
P.O. Box 220
Mansfield, PA 16933

Phone: 570-549-2100
www.murus.com

Murus produces structural insulated panels offering several skin materials including OSB, cement board, and sound board, among others, with non-ozone depleting polyurethane or EPS foam cores. Both panel types are available in a variety of sizes, thicknesses, and application-specific configurations. The EPS SIPs are available with system R-Values of 16, 23, 30, 38, and 45 (the latter 12-1/4" thick), and are manufactured by cutting and laminating the pre-molded EPS core to the OSB skin with a urethane adhesive. The Polyurethane SIPs have a tongue and groove edge and unique cam-lock connectors. The Polyurethane SIPs are available with system R-values of 26, 33, and 40, and are manufactured by foaming the self-adhering expanding foam between the skins.

Polyurethane Structural Insulated Panels

Insulated Component Structures
Rocky Mountain, Inc. (ICS-RM)
5858 Wright Dr.
Loveland, CO 80538

Phone: 970-427-7477
www.ics-rm.net

ICS-Rocky Mountain produces structural insulated panels (SIPS) with polyurethane foam cores that provide above R-6 per inch and have ASTM Class 1 fire resistance rating. The foam is blown without ozone depleting substances and is injected between the skins, resulting in strong surface bonding. Products include corner, wall, roof, and specially shaped panels, as well as cladding (for adding insulation to the outside of an existing building). Panels include metal camlocks for ease of installation and are available in a variety of sizes and thicknesses. Wall and roof panels come in 4 1/2" (R-28+), and 6 1/2" (R-42+) thicknesses. Surface options include fiber-cement, OSB, fiber re-enforced plastic laminate, metal, and custom. ICS-Rocky Mountain, with its affiliate companies in Florida and North Carolina, manufactures and distributes nationally.

R-Control Panels

AFM Corporation
211 River Ridge Circle S., Ste. 102
Burnsville, MN 55337

Toll-free: 800-255-0176
Phone: 952-474-0809
www.r-control.com

R-Control® SIPs are made with Foam-Control EPS cores and OSB skins. Foam-Control EPS with Perform Guard is treated with a borate to provide termite resistance for the core. R-Control SIPs are also available with a Frameguard coating to protect against mold, mildew, and termites. Panel dimensions range from 4' x 8' to 8' x 24' in thicknesses of 4-1/2" to 12-1/4". R-Control SIPs are covered by an ICC-ES report to demonstrate building code compliance. AFM licenses manufacturers throughout the U.S. to produce R-Control SIPs.

Structural Insulated Panels

Extreme Panel Technologies, Inc.
475 E. Fourth St. N
P.O. Box 435
Cottonwood, MN 56229

Toll-free: 800-977-2635
Phone: 507-423-5530
www.extremepanel.com

Extreme Panel Technologies, Inc. manufactures structural insulated panels for residential, commercial, and agricultural applications. Panels are made with oriented strand board manufactured to APA standards for maximum strength and durability, and are available with expanded polystyrene cores.

Structural Insulated Panels

FischerSIPs, Inc.
1843 Northwestern Pkwy.
Louisville, KY 40203

Toll-free: 800-792-7477
Phone: 502-778-5577
www.fischersips.com

A FischerSIP® is made by laminating an expanded polystyrene foam core between two sheets of 7/16" oriented strand board (OSB). Panels can be manufactured in sizes ranging from 4' x 8' to 8' x 24'.

Structural Insulated Panels

Foam Laminates of Vermont
P.O. Box 102
Hinesburg, VT 05461

Toll-free: 800-545-6290
Phone: 802-453-3727
www.foamlaminates.com

Foam Laminates of Vermont started manufacturing structural insulated panels in 1982 in conjunction with their sister company, Vermont Frames. Exterior skins are generally plywood or OSB. Insulating cores are either expanded polystyrene (EPS) or polyisocyanurate. Only products with an EPS core are being specified here.

Structural Insulated Panels

General Panel Corporation
106 Perma R Rd.
Johnson City, TN 37604

Toll-free: 800-647-6130
www.generalpanel.com

General Panel Corporation, formerly Perma R and previously listed as Apache Products Company, produces an EPS-core SIP system.

Structural Insulated Panels

Pacemaker Building Systems
126 New Pace Rd.
P.O. Box 279
Newcomerstown, OH 43832

Toll-free: 800-551-9799
Phone: 740-498-4181
www.pacemakerbuildingsystems.com

Pacemaker Building Systems is a manufacturer of Structural Insulated Panels with full fire and structural testing, and related UL and building code listings. The panels are made with EPS cores and OSB skins. Dimensions range from 4' x 8' to 8' x 24' in thicknesses of 4-9/16" (R-16) to 12-9/16" (R-45).

Structural Insulated Panels

PORTERCorp
4240 N. 136th Ave.
Holland, MI 49424

Toll-free: 800-354-7721
Phone: 616-399-1963
www.portersips.com

PORTERCorp (formerly W. H. Porter) SIPs are made with an EPS foam core and come in any size that can be cut from a 4' x 8' or 8' x 24' sheet of oriented strand board. Panels with custom angles and/or cut-outs are also available. Panels are available in thicknesses of 4-1/2", 6-1/2", 8-1/4", 10-1/4", and 12-1/4" and provide R-values ranging from 15.8 to 45.7.

Structural Insulated Panels

Premier Building Systems - Division of Premier Industries, Inc.
4609 70th Ave. East
Fife, WA 98424

Toll-free: 800-275-7086
Phone: 253-926-2020
www.pbspanel.com

Premier Building Systems manufactures SIPs with borate-treated EPS foam insulation and OSB skins. Other substrates are available upon request. EPS may contain up to 15% recycled content. Panels are available in sizes of 4' x 8' up to 8' x 24' and range in thickness from 4" to 12" (with R-values of 15, 23, 30, 37, and 45). The company has SIP manufacturing plants in Fife, Washington, and Phoenix, Arizona.

Structural Insulated Panels

Shelter Enterprises, Inc.
8 Saratoga St.
P.O. Box 618
Cohoes, NY 12047

Toll-free: 800-836-0719
Phone: 518-237-4101
www.shelter-ent.com

Shelter custom-builds stress skin panels and interior wall panels in sizes up to 8' x 40'. Shelter produces their own EPS foam for the core. 98% of the EPS waste is recycled into other products. Other core materials are available upon request.

Thermal Foam SIPs

Thermal Foams, Inc.
2101 Kenmore Ave.
Buffalo, NY 14207

Phone: 716-874-6474
www.thermalfoams.com

Thermal Foams Inc. is a manufacturer of structural insulated panels made from Thermal Foams EPS cores and OSB Skins. Panel sizes range from 4' x 8' to 8' x 24' in thicknesses of 4-1/2" to 12-1/4". Thermal Foams has gone through full structural and fire testing of its systems with an approved model code testing facility.

Thermapan Structural Insulated Panels

Thermapan Structural Insulated
Panels Inc.
1380 Commerce Pkwy.
P.O. Box 429
Fort Erie, ON L2A 5M4 Canada

Toll-free: 877-443-9255
Phone: 905-994-7399
www.thermapan.com

Thermapan SIP, formerly known as The
Wall™, is an EPS-core structural insulated panel system.

Structural Plastic Lumber

*In 2003, the EPA estimated that 26.7 million tons of the munici-
pal U.S. solid waste stream was plastics. Just 1.4 million tons
of it was recycled; the rest went to landfills, where it occupies
about 25% of the overall landfill space. Plastic lumber makes
good use of recycled plastic and is an effective replacement for
pressure-treated lumber, protecting timber resources and preventing the use of chemical lumber treatments. Plastic lumber
won't rot, absorb water, splinter, or crack; it's also resilient to
shock, making it an extremely durable component in exterior and
marine applications. It can accept most types of fasteners and is
workable with standard saws and carbide blades. Plastic lumber
usually isn't a suitable replacement for load-bearing structural
components, however; the physical characteristics of plastic
polymers, while durable, don't provide the rigidity necessary for
primary structural support. Some companies have addressed this
weakness by reinforcing their products with fiberglass or steel.
In addition, plastic lumber experiences greater rates of thermal
expansion and contraction, which can give rise to problems in
certain applications.*

Trimax

Trimax Building Products, Inc.
2600 W. Roosevelt Rd.
Chicago, IL 60608

Toll-free: 866-987-4629
www.trimaxbp.com

Trimax Decking consists of decking, rail, and stair parts containing
90% post-consumer HDPE by weight. Decking lumber and stair treads
are also available in a knurled, nonskid finish. Trimax structural lumber and marine pilings contains 90% recycled material by weight,
including post-consumer recycled HDPE (65%) and post-industrial
recycled fiberglass. Trimax Structural Lumber comes in gray, and is
available by special order in green, tan, redwood, and white; pilings
come in gray and are available by special order in light gray, green,
tan, redwood, and white.

Structural Steel Framing

*Steel is both the most energy-intensive framing material, on
a pound-for-pound basis, and the most recyclable. Overall, the
steel industry's recycling rate is over 60%. Heavy-gauge structural
steel framing members, from almost all sources, commonly have
greater than 90% recycled content. The embodied energy of steel
averages about 19,200 Btu/lb; manufacture of structural steel
from recycled materials conserves 5,450 Btu/lb. In addition to
having lower embodied energy, high-recycled-content steel results
in lower impact associated with mining waste and pollution.
Products listed here contain at least 90% recycled content.*

Delta Stud and Mega-Joist

Steelform Building Products, Inc.
4104 69th Ave.
Edmonton, AB T6B-2V2

Toll-free: 866-440-4499
Phone: 780-440-4499
www.steelform.ca

Delta Studs and Mega-Joists from Steelform Building Products offer
a lightweight alternative to conventional steel studs and joists for
steel-frame construction. Regular stamped openings in the stud and
joist webs reduce weight and use of raw materials, as well as reducing
the need for cutting and drilling to accommodate electrical and piping installation. Flanges around each opening increase the product's
strength-to-mass ratio. When used in insulated building-envelope
applications, the openings in the web reduce thermal and acoustical
transference.

Tri-Chord

Tri-Chord Steel Systems, Inc.
3639 E. Superior
Phoenix, AZ 85040

Toll-free: 877-426-7100
Phone: 602-426-8700
www.tri-chordsteel.com

The Tri-Chord Stud and Truss Systems
were designed to minimize thermal
bridging. They have triangular sections at each edge, and discrete webs
spanning the wall cavity instead of a
solid heat-conducting steel web (90%
of the stud webbing is removed leaving 10% for thermal transference). The manufacturer claims to have the highest thermal, seismic,
acoustic and fire ratings for steel framing, and that it will meet the
thermal transference of wood. Tri-Chord EESI Thermal Steel Studs are
structural; 18 gauge will carry just under 7,000 lbs each. Tri-Chord also
manufactures wide-spanning, open-web floor trusses. These studs and
trusses contain up to 66% post-consumer recycled content.

Tri-Steel

Tri-Steel Homes
5400 S. Stemmons Fwy.
Denton, TX 76210

Toll-free: 800-874-7833
Phone: 940-497-7070
www.tri-steel.com

Tri-Steel Homes fabricates steel framing for residential construction. Over 66% of the steel content in the studs is recycled scrap material, such as from automobiles.

Wall Panels

Wall panels can be made of metal, a composition of fibers and asphalt, or other materials.

Durra Panel

Durra Building Systems
2747 State Highway 160
Whitewright, TX 75491

Toll-free: 866-364-1198
Phone: 903-364-1198
www.durra.com

Durra Panel is designed to replace standard stud and drywall construction for interior walls. These 2-1/4"-thick straw panels, measuring 4' wide, are bound together with only high heat and pressure using straw that originated from within a 50-mile radius of the manufacturing plant. The panels are tapered at the vertical edges to 2" with slots to receive biscuit connector disks for fastening panels together with screws. Joints can be taped and finished just like drywall. Two preformed 3/4" channels per panel are available for wiring. Durra Panel comes with a recycled paperboard finish and is resistant to mold, termites, and fire—with a Class A fire rating possible for commercial use and a Class B rating for residential use. Straw panels bound in this way are exceptionally strong and do not offgas pollutants. This product was previously marketed as Prestowall™ by Affordable Building Systems. Durra also makes acoustical solutions with strawboard.

kama Energy Efficient Building Systems

kama Energy Efficient Building Systems, Inc.
6012 Topaz St., Ste. 6
Las Vegas, NV 89120

Phone: 702-451-7155
www.kama-eebs.com

kama Energy Efficient Building Systems™ panels consist of EPS board-stock inside structural galvanized steel framing designed to have no thermal breaks. kama-eebs™ panels can be used as a structural wall, floor, or roof system and can be used with any roof system and any interior and exterior finish. Panels are available in all dimensional lumber sizes and custom thicknesses and are built to meet project specifications.

Wood Framing Fasteners

Let-in metal wall bracing, which provides racking resistance, can eliminate or reduce the need for wall sheathing in light-frame construction. Follow structural requirements carefully, and obtain a design review by a structural engineer if uncertain. Also check with a building official before substituting let-in bracing for structural sheathing.

S365, S366, S367 Wall Bracing

USP Structural Connectors
14305 Southcross Dr., Ste. 200
Burnsville, MN 55306

Toll-free: 800-328-5934
www.uspconnectors.com

S365, S366, and S367 Wall Bracing requires a shallow (1/2"-deep) kerf cut.

TWB and RCWB Wall Bracing

Simpson Strong-Tie Connectors
5956 W. Las Positas Blvd.
P.O. Box 10789
Pleasanton, CA 94588

Toll-free: 800-999-5099
Phone: 925-560-9000
www.strongtie.com

Simpson TWB and RCWB Wall Bracing are let-in metal bracing products available in both T and L cross-sections requiring 15/16" and 9/16" deep kerf cuts, respectively. They are designed to fulfill the same code bracing requirements as 1x4 let-in bracing. TWB and RCWB are available in lengths of 9'9", 11'4", and 14'2".

Wood Trusses

Roof and floor trusses are inherently more wood-efficient than dimension-lumber rafters and joists. Products listed here use FSC-certified wood or have other compelling environmental attributes.

BluWood

WoodSmart Solutions, Inc.
3500 NW Boca Raton Blvd., Ste. 701 & 702
Boca Raton, FL 33431

Phone: 561-416-1972
www.bluwood.com

BluWood® framing lumber, trusses, and sheathing components are factory-treated against mold, rot, fungus, and wood-destroying insects with the WoodSmart Solutions two-part Perfect Barrier System: a water-repellent, vapor permeable, mold-resistant subsurface infusion film using a proprietary blend of fungicides, and a borate DOT (Disodium Octaborate Tetrahydrate) wood preservative. BluWood is appropriate in climates where houses are normally framed with treated wood. It is not for ground contact, or for use in exterior applications unless protected by paint, stain, or sealer. The blue-dyed BluWood can be stored uncovered at job sites for up to six months. The warranty against insect infestation requires soil treatment for the duration of the lifetime warranty. (The warranty is transferable within a 30-year initial period.)

FrameGuard

Arch Wood Protection, Inc.
1955 Lake Park Dr., Ste. 100
Smyrna, GA 30080

Toll-free: 877-442-5766
Phone: 770-801-6600
www.wolmanizedwood.com

FrameGuard framing lumber, trusses, and sheathing components are factory-treated against mold, rot, fungus, and wood-destroying insects with a surface coating of borate (disodium octaborate tetrahydrate) and a mix of three low-toxic organic fungicides. The borate component protects against decay and insects, while the organic compounds provide surface protection against mold. Green-dyed FrameGuard lumber is appropriate in climates where houses are normally framed with treated wood. It is not appropriate for ground contact, exterior applications, internal sill plates, or any other application where outdoor-exposure or ground-contact pressure-treated wood should be used. FrameGuard has been certified by Greenguard for low chemical emissions.

Hayward Corporation

Hayward Corporation
10 Ragsdale Dr., Ste. 100
Monterey, CA 93940

Phone: 831-643-1900
www.haywardlumber.com

Hayward Corporation, formerly Hayward Lumber, with eight building supply centers in California, is reported to have the largest stock of certified lumber in the country. They also carry an expanding stock of other green building materials, including high-performance windows, ACQ- and borate-treated lumber, cotton insulation, and wood alternatives. In 2000, the company began producing its own line of FSC-certified roof trusses, now manufactured in a solar-powered LEED Gold facility.

This Space is Available for Your Notes

Sheathing

Sheathing generally serves as a secondary weather barrier behind the exterior finish. It can also be the primary substrate for attaching the finish layer, and often provides diagonal bracing for the structure.

The most common sheathing materials for residential and light commercial construction are plywood and oriented-strand board (OSB). Plywood requires trees of a diameter large enough for veneers to be peeled off as the cylindrical core is turned on a lathe. OSB can be manufactured from fast-growing trees of relatively low commercial value, and uses a higher percentage of the tree. OSB sheathing and wood *I-joist* framing, used together, can reduce wood requirements dramatically while providing superior structural integrity. Most OSB and plywood uses phenol-formaldehyde (PF) adhesive that offgasses less

formaldehyde than the urea-formaldehyde (UF) commonly used in interior particleboard and paneling. Some OSB uses primarily a polyurethane-type (MDI) resin for its adhesive; it emits no formaldehyde but is more toxic in its uncured state, placing factory workers at risk.

Recycled-content sheathing is available in various types. A sandwich material with aluminum foil facings over recycled paperboard is available that meets most wind load requirements and costs less than OSB. Exterior gypsum sheathing, typically made with recycled paper facings, is often used on commercial buildings and is particularly good under stucco for houses. Some exterior gypsum sheathing products use fiberglass facings or integral fibers that do not support mold growth.

Air Barriers

Products listed here are designed to limit air infiltration through discontinuities in the building envelope.

Energy Block

Pine Ridge Builders
613 2nd St. NE
Jamestown, ND 58401

Phone: 701-320-1111
www.energyblock.com

Energy Block is a 1.5 pound-density EPS block of foam insulation molded to fit tightly around electrical boxes, providing an air barrier around and behind. Installation with latex caulk can be quickly accomplished without electricians. Energy Blocks are available in three sizes—for single boxes, multiple gang (up to 4), and a block for ceiling fixtures.

Fireplace DraftStopper

Battic Door Energy Conservation Products
P.O. Box 15
Mansfield, MA 02048

Phone: 508-320-9082
www.batticdoor.com

The Fireplace DraftStopper™ is an inflatable urethane pillow that is installed beneath the fireplace damper to stop drafts that occur even when the damper is shut. After installation, the filling tube hangs down into the fireplace with an orange warning label to prevent fires from being lit when the unit is installed. Significant energy savings can be achieved, up to 30% according to the manufacturer. Available in 2 sizes to fit any masonry fireplace with a rectangular damper (Large) or any metal or zero-clearance fireplace with a round damper (Small).

The Battic Door Attic Stair Cover

Battic Door Energy Conservation Products
P.O. Box 15
Mansfield, MA 02048

Phone: 508-320-9082
www.batticdoor.com

The Battic Door is a simple and inexpensive product for weatherstripping attic hatches that have folding stairways. Essentially a heavy-duty cardboard box that embeds itself into foam weatherstripping installed on the top of the stairway frame, the unit allows easy access to the attic, while providing an airtight seal when dropped into place. Available in two sizes to fit 22" to 22-1/2" x 54" as well as 25" to 25-1/2" x 54" rough openings. A reflective insulation kit (R-7) and an encapsulated-fiberglass slip-on insulation kit (R-50) are also available.

The Energy Guardian

ESS Energy Products, Inc.
P.O. Box 400
Paoli, PA 19301

Phone: 610-993-9585
www.energysentrysolutions.com

Made from high-density EPS, The Energy Guardian™ is an insulating and air-sealing cover for attic hatches and pull-down ladders. These patent-pending units consist of a frame and a snug-fitting lid, which is simply put aside and then put in place again when entering and exiting the attic. The ladder-cover version fits any opening less than 35" x 63" and allows 7-1/2" clearance for a folded ladder. A second frame can be added for 16-1/2" total clearance. The attic hatch cover is designed to fit any opening measuring less than 28" x 32". For areas with little clearance, a 2" frame is available for 7" of total clearance; a 10" frame allows 15" of clearance. The manufacturer claims an R-value of 30 and offers a lifetime warranty. Significant energy savings can be achieved.

Fire-Resistant Sheathing Board

Products listed here have formaldehyde-free binders, are FSC-certified, or have other compelling environmental attributes.

4-Way Floor Deck, N.C.F.R., and Firestall Roof Deck

Homasote Company
932 Lower Ferry Rd.
P.O. Box 7240
West Trenton, NJ 08628

Toll-free: 800-257-9491
Phone: 609-883-3300
www.homasote.com

4-Way® Floor Deck, N.C.F.R.®, and Firestall® Roof Deck are structural high-density fiberboard panels made from 100% recycled newspaper, with paraffin binders and additives for pest and fire resistance. Panels are available in a variety of thicknesses. N.C.F.R. is a Class A fire-rated panel for interior and exterior use. 4-Way Floor Deck is a tongue-and-groove multi-ply subfloor that is structural, sound deadening, and moderately insulative (R-2.5/in.). Firestall Roof Deck is a tongue-and-groove Class A fire-rated panel manufactured with 1 to 4 plies of Homasote® and a face ply of N.C.F.R..

Microstrand

Environ Biocomposites, LLC
221 Mohr Dr.
Mankato, MN 56001

Toll-free: 800-324-8187
Phone: 507-388-3434
www.environbiocomposites.com

Microstrand is an industrial-grade replacement for particleboard or plywood, made from rapidly renewable wheat straw and formaldehyde-free polyurethane (MDI) resin. Though 10%–15% lighter than traditional particleboard, the panels offer better strength and impact resistance. The product accepts paints, stains, and lamination, and can be custom-engineered to meet specific requirements, including increased fire-resistance.

PyroBlock Fire-Retardant Particleboard, MDF, and Plywood

Panel Source International
23 Rayborn Cres., 2nd Fl.
St. Albert, AB T8N 5B9 Canada

Toll-free: 877-464-7246
Phone: 780-458-1007
www.panelsource.net

PyroBlock® PB Plus Particleboard PyroBlock MDF Plus, and Plywood Plus Fire-Retardant Panels are urea formaldehyde-free. Unlike conventional fire-retardant panels, in which a fire-retardant chemical is incorporated throughout the product, PyroBlock Panels rely on an intumescent coating. This coating expands and chars when subjected to heat and thereby insulates and protects the substrate from fire. According to the company, the product is inert when cured. PyroBlock meets applicable flame-spread standards (ASTM E-84(01) in the U.S., and CAN/ULC 102-M in Canada). Available sizes are 4' or 5' wide by 8', 9', or 10' long by 1/8" to 1-1/4" thick. PyroBlock FSC-certified fire-retardant composite panels are also available.

Insulating Sheathing

Products listed here provide insulating qualities, often through the incorporation of a radiant barrier. When they face a heat source, radiant barriers work by reflecting heat. When faced away from a heat source, radiant barriers function primarily by virtue of their low emissivity. This means that the surface does not radiate heat well. A radiant-barrier surface on roof sheathing, for example, heats up from the sunlight striking the roof, but that heat energy is not readily emitted into the attic space—so that attic remains cooler. This is why the radiant barrier seems to "reflect" heat back out of the building. An air space is required on at least one side of a radiant barrier in order for it to function as designed. Radiant barriers in attics are most beneficial in reducing cooling loads; their effectiveness in reducing heating loads is more limited. Radiant barrier products usually do not include significant recycled content, because of the lower reflectivity of recycled aluminum and the difficulty in producing very thin foils from recycled aluminum; the high embodied energy of virgin aluminum can be recovered through energy savings. When comparing products, look for the lowest emissivity (which corresponds to the highest reflectivity). Do not rely on "effective" or "equivalent" R-values, which are only relevant in certain climates or under certain conditions.

BarrierPanel, TechShield Radiant Barrier, and BarrierFloor OSB

LP
414 Union St., Ste. 2000
Nashville, TN 37219

Toll-free: 877-744-5600
www.lpcorp.com

Part of the SmartGuard™ family, a venture between LP Corp. and Osmose, these products are treated with zinc borate for resistance to termites, carpenter ants, and fungal decay. LP's BarrierPanel™ is an OSB sheathing product suitable for wall, roof, and (double-layer) subfloor applications in residential and light commercial buildings. TechShield™ Radiant Barrier is an OSB roof sheathing with a radiant-foil overlay to minimize radiant heat gain. LP's BarrierFloor™ T&G OSB subflooring is edge-coated to reduce swelling. All carry a 20-year transferable warranty.

EnerMax Radiant Barrier Sheathing

Building Products of Canada Corporation
9510 St. Patrick St.
LaSalle, QC H8R 1R9 Canada

Toll-free: 800-567-2726
www.bpcan.com

EnerMax™ is a 1/2"-thick, lightweight structural sheathing radiant barrier panel made from reclaimed sawdust and wood shavings with a nontoxic binder. The company claims that the product's vapor-resistant aluminum-foil skin can boost the wall R-value by 4.7 (this will depend on the application, however). EnerMax comes in 4' x 8' and 4.5' x 12' sizes with preprinted nailmarks at 8" intervals. The company also produces High Performance sheathing, which includes an asphalt coating on all six sides.

Fiberboard - Regular and High Density

Huebert Brothers Products, LLC
1545 E. Morgan St.
Boonville, MO 65233

Toll-free: 800-748-7147
Phone: 660-882-2704
www.huebertfiberboard.com

Huebert Fiberboard is made from waste wood chips and cellulose fiber with a carbon-based black emulsion surface coating. This insulating roof sheathing product for mopped roofs contains 40-60% recycled materials, of which 20% is post-consumer. The company claims R-values of roughly 2.78/in. for the 1/2"-, 1"-, and 2"-thick panels.

Fiberboard Insulating Sheathing

Knight-Celotex
One Northfield Plaza
Northfield, IL 60093

Phone: 847-716-8030
www.knightcelotex.com

Knight-Celotex Premium Insulating Sheathing is a vapor-permeable exterior sheathing alternative to plywood and OSB. It is made with 80% or more recovered fiber (hardwood or sugarcane, depending on which plant manufactures the product), and small percentages of starch, clay, paraffin, carbon black, and formaldehyde-free adhesive. SturdyBrace™ is a similar product with improved structural qualities; it contains 75% fiber, 22% asphalt, and small amounts of starch and wax. These 1/2" sheathing products cut with a knife, have a 1.3 R-value, and are most appropriate behind vented rainscreen and reservoir claddings. The high permeability is an important feature in climates where wall-cavity drying to the exterior is important.

Polar-Ply Radiant-Barrier

Superior Radiant Insulation
P.O. Box 247
San Dimas, CA 91773

Toll-free: 888-774-4422
Phone: 909-305-1450
www.superiorrb.com

Superior Radiant Insulation manufactures several radiant barrier and insulation products. Among them is Polar-Ply™ aluminum foil-faced OSB or plywood sheathing.

Thermo-Ply

Covalence Coated Products
700 Centreville Rd.
Constantine, MI 49042

Toll-free: 800-345-8881
Phone: 616-435-2425
www.covalencecoatedproducts.com

Thermo-ply® are thin, lightweight structural sheathing panels manufactured from 100% recycled cardboard and aluminum-foil facings. The plies are pressure-laminated with a special water-resistant, nontoxic adhesive. Thermo-ply is available in three grades: nonstructural, structural, and super strength. Although Thermo-ply structural is less than 1/8" thick, when properly secured with 3" fastener spacing on the perimeter and 3" spacing on intermediate studs, the racking strength meets building codes even in seismically active areas. Thermo-ply super strength is applicable with studs on 16" centers. Additionally, when Thermo-ply is overlapped 3/4", it may qualify as a weather-resistant barrier. All grades are available in the following sizes: 4' x 8', 4' x 9', 4'-3/4" x 8', and 4'-3/4" x 9'.

Sheathing (including Plywood & OSB)

Sheathing comprises a significant portion of the materials used with many building types. Careful consideration of product selection and use can reduce the environmental impacts of a project. Wall sheathing is often used only as an additional layer of weather protection, although it may also be required for racking resistance. When let-in diagonal bracing is used to provide racking resistance, wood-panel sheathing can sometimes be eliminated or replaced with more resource-efficient or insulative products. Phenol-formaldehyde (PF) binders are used in plywood, while OSB can be made with PF or the non-formaldehyde-emitting methyl diisocyanate (MDI), a polyurethane binder. Paradoxically, exterior-rated products using PF binders are less of an offgassing concern than interior-grade panels made with urea-formaldehyde. Oriented-strand board (OSB) can be an efficient use of forest

resources because it can be produced from small-diameter or low-grade tree species. Wood products can carry the "FSC Mixed" label under a percentage-based standard based on the average certified and non-certified throughput of the facility at which they are made. Products listed here have one or more of the following attributes: FSC-certification; nonformaldehyde binders; nontoxic (to humans) borate insect treatments; or other environmental advantages over conventional OSB and plywood.

4-Way Floor Deck, N.C.F.R., and Firestall Roof Deck

Homasote Company
932 Lower Ferry Rd.
P.O. Box 7240
West Trenton, NJ 08628

Toll-free: 800-257-9491
Phone: 609-883-3300
www.homasote.com

4-Way® Floor Deck, N.C.F.R.®, and Firestall® Roof Deck are structural high-density fiberboard panels made from 100% recycled newspaper, with paraffin binders and additives for pest and fire resistance. Panels are available in a variety of thicknesses. N.C.F.R. is a Class A fire-rated panel for interior and exterior use. 4-Way Floor Deck is a tongue-and-groove multi-ply subfloor that is structural, sound deadening, and moderately insulative (R-2.5/in.). Firestall Roof Deck is a tongue-and-groove Class A fire-rated panel manufactured with 1 to 4 plies of Homasote® and a face ply of N.C.F.R..

AdvanTech OSB

J. M. Huber Wood Products
One Resource Sq.
10925 David Taylor Dr., Ste. 300
Charlotte, NC 28262

Toll-free: 800-933-9220
Phone: 704-547-0671
www.huberwood.com

AdvanTech™ OSB from Huber is an OSB made primarily with formaldehyde-free MDI resin (a small quantity of phenolic resin is added to improve certain properties). Due to its greater moisture resistance than conventional OSB, AdvanTech carries a 50-year warranty. This product has been certified by Greenguard for low emissions.

Certified Pine Plywood

ROMEX World Trade Company, LLC - sales agent for ROM
P.O. Box 1110
Alexandria, LA 71309

Toll-free: 800-299-5174
Phone: 318-445-1973
www.royomartin.com

Roy O. Martin Lumber Management, LLC (ROM) has received Smart-Wood certification for its 585,000 acres of forestland and four mills according to standards of the Forest Stewardship Council (FSC). This is the first FSC certification of any forest management operation in Louisiana. ROM's FSC-certified pine plywood, formerly under the name of SmartCore®, is produced by Martco Plywood in Chopin, Louisiana. Sanded plywood is available in AA, AB, AC, BC, and A-Flat grades in

4' x 8' panels standard thicknesses of 1/4", 11/32", 15/32", 19/32" and 23/32". As is true for the company's OSB plant, some fiber used in the Chopin mill comes from non-company-owned land, but 100% FSC-certified product can be provided. ROM's pine plywood is also available sided with a foil radiant barrier, or printed with the company's new "GRID" panel marking system.

CollinsWood FSC-Certified Wood Products

The Collins Companies
1618 S.W. First Ave., Ste. 500
Portland, OR 97201

Toll-free: 800-329-1219
Phone: 503-417-7755
www.collinswood.com

The CollinsWood line includes FSC-certified western pine particleboard, FSC-certified TruWood engineered (hardboard) siding and trim, and FSC-certified hardwood and softwood lumber and millwork. TruWood products are made under FSC's partial-content rules (with an actual certified fiber content of 32%), and use a phenol formaldehyde binder. Millwork includes cherry, red oak, soft maple and poplar interior millwork, including casing, base, chair rail, crown, etc. In 1993, Collins Pine Company became the first privately owned timber management company to receive FSC certification in the U.S. CollinsWood has been a leader in the forest and wood products certification movement since its inception.

EarthSource Forest Products

EarthSource Forest Products/Plywood and Lumber Sales, Inc.
1618 28th St.
Oakland, CA 94608

Toll-free: 866-549-9663
Phone: 510-208-7257
www.earthsourcewood.com

EarthSource Forest Products, a division of Plywood and Lumber Sales, Inc., sells FSC-certified hardwood plywood and lumber of the following species: maple, cherry, red oak, white oak, ash, Honduras mahogany, walnut, machiche, amapola, and many more. EarthSource also sells salvaged and rediscovered lumber such as fir, redwood, and hickory.

F.D. Sterritt Certified-Wood Building Products

F.D. Sterritt Lumber Co.
110 Arlington St.
Watertown, MA 02472

Toll-free: 877-635-3362
Phone: 617-923-1480
www.sterrittlumber.com

F.D. Sterritt Lumber sells FSC-certified lumber, plywood, decking, hardwoods, and hardwood flooring. They have a variety of certified species in stock. Additional green building materials available, including low-VOC adhesives, caulking, sealants, and recycled drywall. F.D. Sterritt offers green building product consultations.

FreeForm

The Collins Companies
1618 S.W. First Ave., Ste. 500
Portland, OR 97201

Toll-free: 800-329-1219
Phone: 503-417-7755
www.collinswood.com

FreeForm is an FSC-certified particleboard produced with urea-formaldehyde-free melamine binder rather than the industry-standard urea-formaldehyde. While low-formaldehyde particleboard made with phenolic binders is darker than conventional UF-particleboard (due to the reddish color of phenol-formaldehyde), FreeForm is lighter in color, because melamine binder is white. All FreeForm particleboard carries the FSC certification for well-managed forests—rather than the certification being an option.

FSC-Certified Lumber, Plywood, and Products

Potlatch Corporation
601 W. First Ave., Ste. 1600
Spokane, WA 99201

Phone: 509-835-1500
www.potlatchcorp.com

In 2004, Potlatch Corporation became the first publicly traded U.S. timber company to certify timberland according to Forest Stewardship Council (FSC) standards. Potlatch is producing chain-of-custody FSC-certified Hem-Fir and Douglas Fir/Larch framing lumber, inland red cedar decking and siding, and Douglas fir and white fir plywood from three chain-of-custody-certified mills in Idaho. Potlatch has recently added over 400,000 acres of FSC certified timber in Arkansas which supports a chain-of-custody sawmill in Warren, Arkansas. Warren produces dimensional Southern Yellow Pine framing lumber. These products are stamped with the FSC logo when required for specific sales.

Green Board

GreenImports, LLC
P.O. Box 60
North Stonington, CT 06359

Phone: 857-526-6091
www.wwieinc.com

Green Board is made from recycled Tetra Pak beverage cartons and is composed of 75% paper, 20% polyethylene, and 5% aluminum. It is water resistant, termite and borer resistant, and provides insulative and sound proofing qualities. Green Board has a textured surface, and can be formed into curves and other shapes. Marketed as a direct replacement for plywood in any application (including "roofing, boats, cabinets, shipping crates, sheathing, underlayment, furniture"), it can be sawn, molded, cut, glued, screwed, or nailed. Available from the importer by the container-load in 4x8 sheets in 10, 12, or 18 mm thicknesses. Each container holds 676, 250, or 354 sheets of the respective board thicknesses.

Microstrand

Environ Biocomposites, LLC
221 Mohr Dr.
Mankato, MN 56001

Toll-free: 800-324-8187
Phone: 507-388-3434
www.environbiocomposites.com

Microstrand is an industrial-grade replacement for particleboard or plywood, made from rapidly renewable wheat straw and formaldehyde-free polyurethane (MDI) resin. Though 10%–15% lighter than traditional particleboard, the panels offer better strength and impact resistance. The product accepts paints, stains, and lamination, and can be custom-engineered to meet specific requirements, including increased fire-resistance.

Particleboard, MDF, Plywood, Lumber, OSB

F.W. Honerkamp Co., Inc
500 Oak Point Ave.
Bronx, NY 10474

Toll-free: 800-999-8115
Phone: 718-589-9700
www.honerkamp.com

F.W. Honercamp distributes a number of no-added-formaldehyde (NAF) and FSC-certified panel products, including particleboard, medium density fiberboard, melamine panels, composite panels, and hardwood plywood (with veneer, particleboard, and MDF core options). Their NAF products use MDI, phenol-formaldehyde, or soy-based binders and polyvinyl acetate (PVA, or white glue) for finish veneers. The company also offers FSC-certified hardwood lumber and OSB, as well as class A fire-rated panels.

PureKor Certified Plywood and Manufactured Panels

Panel Source International
23 Rayborn Cres., 2nd Fl.
St. Albert, AB T8N 5B9 Canada

Toll-free: 877-464-7246
Phone: 780-458-1007
www.panelsource.net

PureKor Certified Hardwood Plywood Plus is FSC-certified and contains no added urea formaldehyde. The binder used for both the plywood substrate and for adhering the face veneer, according to Panel Source, is polyvinyl acetate (PVA). This plywood is available in a number of grades and species, including alder, ash, birch, cherry, pine, cedar, hickory, maple, okoume, red and white oak, white maple, mahogany, poplar, and walnut. With most products, the core veneers are FSC-certified and the face veneers are not. Panel Source International also offers particleboard and PureKor Platinum Grade MDF panels made with FSC-certified, pre-consumer recycled wood fiber and formaldehyde-free resin. They are available from 4 x 8 to 5 x 12, in thicknesses ranging from 1/4" to 1-1/2" in mill grade, M1, M2, and premium. Standard density is 45 lbs.

SierraPine Formaldehyde-free Fiberboard

SierraPine Ltd.
3010 Lava Ridge Ct. #220
Roseville, CA 95661

Toll-free: 800-676-3339
Phone: 916-772-3422
www.sierrapine.com

SierraPine's Medex MDF, for use in interior high-moisture applications, and Medite II MDF, for interior non-structural applications, are manufactured with a polyurethane binder, methyl diisocyanate(MDI), rather than conventional formaldehyde-based resins. SierraPine's newest formaldehyde-free product, Arreis SDF (Sustainable Design Fiberboard), uses the same MDI binder more efficiently to lower cost premiums. SierraPine has earned certification from Scientific Certification Systems (SCS) for using up to 100% recovered and recycled wood fiber for their MDF products.

SkyBlend MDF

Roseburg Forest Products
P.O. Box 1088
Roseburg, OR 97470

Toll-free: 800-245-1115
Phone: 541-679-3311
www.rfpco.com

Skyblend MDF Plus is a light-colored, moisture-resistant, medium-density fiberboard (MDF) that can be used for laminates and veneers and can be shaped and finished without pitting. Skyblend is made from 100% recovered wood, as certified by Scientific Certification Systems (SCS), and uses phenol formaldehyde as a binder instead of the more common (and higher-formaldehyde-emitting) urea formaldehyde. The wood used in Skyblend is mostly Southern pine and does not carry FSC certification. Skyblend MDF is offered in thicknesses of 5/8", 11/16" and 3/4"; and in sizes 49" x 97", 49" x 145", and 61" x 97". Other thicknesses and sizes are available upon request.

SkyBlend UF-Free Particle Board

Roseburg Forest Products
P.O. Box 1088
Roseburg, OR 97470

Toll-free: 800-245-1115
Phone: 541-679-3311
www.rfpco.com

Roseburg SkyBlend™ is a general-use particleboard produced with phenol-formaldehyde (PF) binder instead of the industry-standard urea-formaldehyde (UF) binder. The company claims formaldehyde emissions of about 0.01 parts per million (ppm) under standard test conditions—comparable to natural levels in outdoor air. It is Green Cross-certified by Scientific Certification Systems (SCS) as being made from 100% recycled wood fibers (pre-consumer waste from lumber mills). The wood fiber is not FSC certified. The particleboard core is tinted light blue for field identification. SkyBlend™ is available in industrial grade only, in seven thicknesses from 1/4" to 1-1/8". Standard dimensions for most thicknesses are 49" x 97", while the 3/4" and 1-1/8" panels are also available in larger sizes. Custom dimensions may be available for large orders.

SmartChoice Wood Products

Certified Forest Products, LLC.
7 Los Conejos
Orinda, CA 94563

Phone: 925-258-4372
www.certifiedforestproducts.com

Certified Forest Products (CFP) is a distributor of SmartChoice, a collection of FSC-certified and reclaimed wood products from a variety of species including hardwoods, cedar, and redwood. Products include lumber, plywood, decking, siding, flooring, interior and exterior millwork.

Tuff-Strand Certified OSB

ROMEX World Trade Company, LLC - sales agent for ROM
P.O. Box 1110
Alexandria, LA 71309

Toll-free: 800-299-5174
Phone: 318-445-1973
www.royomartin.com

Roy O. Martin Lumber Management, LLC (ROM) has gained FSC-certification of its 585,000 acres of forestland and four mills. In addition to this being the first FSC certification of any forest management operation in Louisiana, ROM has made available the first-ever FSC-certified oriented strand board (OSB). Tuff-Strand® is a fairly conventional OSB produced by the Martco Partnership plant in LeMoyen, Louisiana. The 4' x 8' panels are available in three standard thicknesses: 7/16", 15/32", and 19/32". The mill is fed by up to 70% company-owned timber, and while OSB is typically certified using FSC's partial-content rules, the company can provide 100% FSC-certified product. Tuff-Strand's binder is 100% phenol formaldehyde. FSC-certified Tuff-Strand is also now available sided with a foil radiant barrier, or printed with the company's new "GRID" panel marking system.

Versaroc Cement-Bonded Particleboard

U.S. Architectural Products
55 Industrial Cir.
Lincoln, RI 28730

Toll-free: 800-243-6677
www.architecturalproducts.com

Versaroc® from U.S. Architectural Products is a structural cement-bonded particleboard made with mineralized wood particles and portland cement. It can be worked with typical carpentry tools; fasteners should be treated for corrosion resistance. The formaldehyde-free, termite-resistant, noncombustible product is available in stock nominal ("uncalibrated") thicknesses of 10 mm (3/8"), 12 mm (1/2"), and 19 mm (3/4"); several other thicknesses may be special-ordered. "Calibrated" stock is sanded to more precise thicknesses for applications requiring tighter tolerances. These boards are available square-edged in 48" widths; or tongue-and-groove in 46-1/2" widths for thickness of 16 mm (5/8") or more. Stocked length is 96"; shorter or longer boards (up to 120") are available by special order, as are widths less than 48" square or 46-1/2" tongue-and-groove. All orders can be factory-sealed on all surfaces with an acrylic paint sealer. Due to the energy intensity of the cement content, this product should not be considered a green substitute for particleboard except where significant resistance to fire, moisture, termites, or vermin are required.

Viroc Cement-Bonded Particleboard

Allied Building Products Corp.
15 East Union Ave.
East Rutherford, NJ 07073

Toll-free: 800-541-2198
www.alliedbuilding.com

Viroc is a structural cement-bonded particleboard made with portland cement and mineralized wood particles (71% portland cement, 18.5% wood fibers). It can be machined and worked with typical carpentry tools. Viroc is available in 4x8 sheets from 5/16" to 1-5/8" thicknesses. 4x10 sheets come in 3 thicknesses of 5/16", 3/8", and 1/2". T&G, half-lap, and beveled edge are available. Due to the energy intensity of the cement content, this product should not be considered a green substitute for particleboard except where significant resistance to fire, moisture, termites, or vermin are required.

This Space is Available for Your Notes

This Space is Available for Your Notes

Exterior Finish & Trim

The exterior finish is a building's first defense against the weather, and its most visible aspect.

Building systems that rely on the exterior finish as the sole weather barrier are susceptible to failure—especially in climates with wind-driven rain or without good drying conditions. The driving forces of wind and other air-pressure factors will force moisture through even the smallest openings. Because of this, siding or curtain wall systems designed around the *rain-screen* principle are much more effective and durable. This strategy uses a vented exterior finish and a tightly sealed secondary barrier that work together to equalize the pressure on both sides of the exterior finish, taking away the forces that would otherwise drive moisture inwards.

Recycled-wood-fiber composite siding and trim are more stable than materials made from natural wood, hold paint better, and generally cost less. Some hardboard products have had durability problems when improperly installed or when installed without adequate drying provisions in wet climates.

Fiber-cement siding is very durable, looks like wood when it's painted, and provides a fire-resistant surface. The wood fibers provide strength, elasticity, and good paint-holding ability.

Locally produced brick and stone are long-lasting, low-maintenance finishes that reduce transportation costs and environmental impacts. Molded cementitious stone replaces the environmental impacts of quarrying and dressing natural stone with the impacts of producing cement.

Air, Vapor, and Moisture Barriers

Weather barriers form a secondary drainage plane (the first in most cases being the exterior cladding) to assist in keeping assembly components to the interior protected from bulk water. Note that the vapor permeability of concealed weather barrier products can vary widely and the desirability of low or high or no vapor permeability is always in the context of the primary direction of wetting, the primary direction of drying, and the vapor permeability of all the other components in the assembly. Products listed here contribute to durability (generally by creating an air space) and/or reduce the potential for indoor air quality problems associated with moisture and mold.

Construction Film

Gempak
9611 James Ave. S
Bloomington, MN 55431

Toll-free: 800-328-4556
Phone: 952-881-8673

Gempak, formerly Strout Plastics, manufactures construction film that generally contains 100% recycled LDPE. With some production runs, contamination of recycled materials necessitates the addition of virgin resins to produce a quality product.

Delta-MS and Delta-Dry

Cosella Dörken Products Inc.
4655 Delta Way
Beamville, ON LOR 1B4
Canada

Toll-free: 888-433-5824
Phone: 905-563-3255
www.deltams.com

Delta-Dry is a stiff, egg-carton-textured, 5/16"-thick, vapor-impermeable housewrap made with 22-mil, virgin HDPE. When properly installed, the weather-resistive barrier creates a ventilated rainscreen, while blocking moisture migration through the wall assembly. Similarly, Delta-MS for subsurface use is an air-gap membrane constructed from 6 mm-thick HDPE, with a pattern of dimples molded into the surface. When installed, the membrane is held off the wall to allow any moisture in the concrete to migrate to the outer surface, condense on the inside surface of the membrane, and flow into the foundation drain. Because HDPE is impervious, soil moisture is unable to penetrate but will also flow to the foundation drain.

Home Slicker

Benjamin Obdyke Inc.
400 Babylon Rd.
Ste. A
Horsham, PA 19044

Toll-free: 800-523-5261
Phone: 215-672-7200
www.benjaminobdyke.com

Home Slicker® is a ventilating and self-draining rainscreen for use under siding, which provides a thermal break and moisture protection for sidewalls. Home Slicker's 3-dimensional, 0.25"-thick matrix provides a continuous space for drying, drainage, and pressure equalization. For use under sidings such as wood, fiber-cement, EIFS, brick, and vinyl, Home Slicker comes with a 50-year limited warranty.

Water Out Flashing

Water Out Flashing
8206-1200 Providence Rd.
Charlotte, NC 28277

Phone: 866-568-0050
www.wateroutflashing.com

Water Out window and door flashing products will fit openings of any width and are designed to be easy to install. The flexible polypropylene pans with integral, tapered drain channels and end-dams don't require precision cutting or adhesives, and they have wide flanges for proper integration with the envelope in both straight and radial fenestrations. These flashings are sold by the case, and are available in white, black, brown, and paintable white.

Weatherstripping and Gaskets

M-D Building Products
4041 N. Santa Fe Ave.
Oklahoma City, OK 73118

Toll-free: 800-654-8454
Phone: 405-528-4411
www.mdteam.com

M-D manufactures a wide range of weatherstripping and weatherization products.

Weatherstripping and Gaskets

Resource Conservation Technology, Inc.
2633 N. Calvert St.
Baltimore, MD 21218

Toll-free: 800-477-7724
Phone: 410-366-1146
www.conservationtechnology.com

Resource Conservation Technology specializes in building gaskets, weatherstripping, and air barriers.

Artificial Stone

Simulated stone products typically contain an high percentage of portland cement, a material with high embodied energy. As with all cementitious claddings adhered to the structural exterior wall, two layers of building paper or housewrap should be used, the first to serve as the bond break, and the latter to function as the weather-resistive barrier.

Products listed here have significant or total replacement of the portland cement content with agricultural or industrial waste materials, such as fly ash.

LodeStone

LodeStone Companies
2708 Glenwood
Denton, TX 76209

Phone: 940-483-1761
www.lodestoneproducts.com

LodeStone is designed to achieve the appearance of natural stone. These veneer blocks are 3" thick at the mortar joint and come in nominal sizes ranging from 12" x 8" to 32" x 16". A handful of trim profiles and end pieces are also available. LodeStone uses Class C coal fly ash to replace most the portland cement typically used in cast stone; portland cement accounts for 20% of the cement blend, while Class C fly ash constitutes 65%, and other industrial recycled materials comprise most of the remaining 15%.

Composition Siding

Composition siding products are environmentally attractive because they utilize low-grade or waste wood fiber (such as newsprint or sawdust), or strands of fast-growing wood mixed with binding agents and finishes. Although composition siding is resource-efficient relative to solid wood, some products in the past have demonstrated poor durability. Quality composition siding products, if durable, can be affordable green products.

CollinsWood FSC-Certified Wood Products

The Collins Companies
1618 S.W. First Ave., Ste. 500
Portland, OR 97201

Toll-free: 800-329-1219
Phone: 503-417-7755
www.collinswood.com

The CollinsWood line includes FSC-certified western pine particleboard, FSC-certified TruWood engineered (hardboard) siding and trim, and FSC-certified hardwood and softwood lumber and millwork. TruWood products are made under FSC's partial-content rules (with an actual certified fiber content of 32%), and use a phenol formaldehyde binder. Millwork includes cherry, red oak, soft maple and poplar interior millwork, including casing, base, chair rail, crown, etc. In 1993, Collins Pine Company became the first privately owned timber management company to receive FSC certification in the U.S. CollinsWood has been a leader in the forest and wood products certification movement since its inception.

LP SmartSide Siding and Exterior Trim Products

LP
414 Union St., Ste. 2000
Nashville, TN 37219

Toll-free: 877-744-5600
www.lpcorp.com

LP's SmartSide™ siding and exterior trim includes formaldehyde-free OSB-based (lap and panel), soffit, and fascia trim products treated during manufacture with zinc borate. A paint-based overlay enhances weather resistance. The 30-year transferable warranty includes 7-year 100% repair/replacement coverage, and a 30-year termite resistance guarantee is offered. Introduced in 1997, SmartSide Siding was joined in 2000 by other products in the LP SmartGuard® family of termite-resistant building products.

PaperStone Certified

KlipTech Composites
2999 John Stevens Way
Hoquiam, WA 98550

Phone: 360-538-9815
www.paperstoneproducts.com

PaperStone Certified is made with 100% FSC-certified, post-consumer recycled paper. The proprietary water-based resin system uses non-petroleum phenols, including cashew nut shell liquid derivatives. The finished product works easily with a triple-chip, carbide-tipped saw blade and carbide-tipped router bits. It has no detectable free formaldehyde, is Class A fire-rated, heat-resistant to 350 degrees, and stain-resistant. PaperStone comes in 30" and 60" widths, lengths of 8', 10', & 12', with thicknesses ranging from 1/4" - 2". The product is available in a variety of colors. The regular PaperStone product line is made with 50% post-consumer recycled content, versus 100% for PaperStone Certified.

Fiber-Cement Siding

Fiber-cement building materials earn green points for durability. Fiber-cement, the new generation of what was once an asbestos-containing material, is today made from portland cement, sand, clay, and wood fiber. Environmental concerns include the embodied energy of portland cement and the source of the wood fiber—some products use wood from such distant locations as New Zealand and Russia. Although the current generation of fiber-cement products isn't yet proven over the long haul, the material is quite stable, and products carry up to 50-year warranties. Most fiber-cement siding is available factory primed. It takes paint very well, and proper painting is important for long-term durability.

Cemplank and Cempanel

Cemplank, Inc.
26300 La Alameda, Ste. 250
Mission Viejo, CA 92691

Toll-free: 877-236-7526
www.cemplank.com

Cemplank lap siding and Cempanel vertical siding have cedar textures. Cemplank is 5/16" thick and 12' long and is available in widths from 6" (4-3/4" exposure) to 12" (10-3/4" exposure). Cemplank is a division of James Hardie Building Products, with manufacturing locations in Pennsylvania and South Carolina.

CertainTeed Fiber-Cement Siding

CertainTeed Corporation
750 E. Swedesford Rd.
P.O. Box 860
Valley Forge, PA 19482

Toll-free: 800-233-8990
Phone: 610-341-7000
www.certainteed.com

CertainTeed's fiber-cement WeatherBoards and ColorMax siding lines are available in lap, panel, and soffit products with smooth, cedar, or stucco (panel only) textures. Lap siding is available in widths from 6-1/4" to 12". Panel siding comes in 4' x 8', 9', or 10' sheets. The WeatherBoards and ColorMax lines include 30%–50% flyash in addition to wood fiber, portland cement, and other additives. According to CertainTeed, the manufacturing process provides 60% higher interlaminate bond strength for superior freeze/thaw protection. CertainTeed delivers the siding with FiberTect sealant, which penetrates the siding surface to provide moisture protection while acting as the base coat for painting. ColorMax is prefinished in a choice of 16 colors.

HardiePlank, HardiePanel, and HardieShingle

James Hardie Building Products, Inc.
26300 La Alameda, Ste. 250
Mission Viejo, CA 92691

Toll-free: 888-542-7343
Phone: 949-348-1800
www.jameshardie.com

HardiePlank™ lap siding is 12' long and is available in widths ranging from 6-1/4" (5" exposure) to 12" (10-3/4" exposure). Textures include Smooth, Select Cedarmill, Colonial Smooth, Colonial Roughsawn, Beaded Smooth, and Beaded Cedarmill. Straight-Edge Shingle Plank™ emulates the look of shingles in an embossed lap-siding product; it comes in 12' lengths and is 8-1/4" wide with a 7" exposure. HardiePanel™ vertical siding is available in 4' x 8', 4' x 9', and 4' x 10' sheets in Smooth, Stucco, or Sierra textures with vertical grooves at 8" spacings. HardiePlank and HardiePanel carry 50-year limited warranties. Available accessories include HardieSoffit™ and HardieTrim™. HardieShingle™ offers the look of cedar shingles in a fiber-cement siding, is available in a variety of styles and profiles, and comes with a 30-year limited warranty.

MaxiTile Fiber-Cement Siding

MaxiTile, Inc.
849 E. Sandhill Ave.
Carson, CA 90746

Toll-free: 800-338-8453
Phone: 310-217-0316
www.maxitile.com

MaxiPlank and MaxiPanel siding products are available in several surface textures and patterns. MaxiPlank is produced in 12' lengths and widths from 6-1/4" to 12". MaxiPanel measures 4' x 8', 4' x 9', and 4' x 10'.

Nichiha Fiber-Cement Rainscreen Siding

Nichiha USA, Inc.
6659 Peachtree Industrial Blvd.
Norcross, GA 30092

Toll-free: 866-424-4421
Phone: 770-805-9466
www.nichiha.com

Nichiha offers a line of panelized fiber-cement siding installed with special clips that hold the panels away from the sheathing to provide a rainscreen exterior to control water intrusion and increase the durability of the entire wall system. The panels are ship-lapped on four sides and have the appearance of bricks, shakes, or stone. (A lap siding is also available.) Most panels come in 6', 8', or 10' sections, in heights ranging from approximately 8" to 18" and thicknesses ranging from 1/2" to 1". Depending on the product, the manufacturer offers a 30-year or 50-year transferable warranty.

Weatherside

GAF Materials Corp.
1361 Alps Rd.
Wayne, NJ 07470

Toll-free: 800-223-1948
Phone: 973-628-3000
www.gaf.com

GAF manufactures Weatherside™ fiber-cement siding available with different textures and dimensions. WeatherSide™ shingles are fire-proof, durable, and resistant to freeze- thaw conditions — and backed by a 25 year limited warranty.

FSC-Certified Wood Siding

Certified wood products are verified by a third party as originating from well-managed forests. GreenSpec recognizes the Forest Stewardship Council (FSC) standards as the most rigorous and the only certification system with well-established chain-of-custody certification to ensure that products used were derived from certified forests. Some companies listed here sell both certified and noncertified wood products, or products that have been certified according to different, less stringent environmental standards. To make certain that you get environmentally responsible wood products, be sure to specify your interest in FSC-certified wood.

Certified Red Cedar

Mary's River Lumber Co.
4515 N.E. Elliott Cir.
Corvallis, OR

Toll-free: 800-523-2052
Phone: 541-752-0122
www.marysrvr.com

Mary's River Lumber offers FSC-certified, second-growth, tight-knotted, western red cedar products, including boards, decking, fencing, paneling, and siding in T&G, channel, bevel, and square-end.

Certified Wood Products

Cascadia Forest Goods, LLC
38083 Wheeler Rd.
Dexter, OR 97431

Phone: 541-485-4477
www.cascadiaforestgoods.com

Cascadia Forest Goods (CFG) is a supplier of FSC-certified and re-cycled forest products, including hardwood and softwood veneers, dimensional lumber and decking, timbers and beams, siding, flooring, paneling, and trim. CFG's woods come from the Pacific Northwest and British Columbia, and include the following species: douglas fir, incense and western red cedar, sitka and englemann spruce, ponderosa and sugar pine, and regional hardwoods (madrone, white and black oak, broadleaf maple, alder, chinkapin, and myrtlewood). FSC-certified and recycled-forest-product flooring species include madrone, white oak, clear vertical grain (CVG) Douglas fir, birch, big-leaf maple, and myrtlewood. CFG also supplies FSC-certified flooring and decking from Central and South America, including Santa Maria, catalox, chechen negro, jobillo, machiche, ramon blanco, sauche, ipe, pucte (ironwood), and others. CFG offers both solid and engineered wood flooring. CFG also supplies both FSC-certified hardwood and softwood veneers and lumber to window and door manufacturers.

F.D. Sterritt Certified-Wood Building Products

F.D. Sterritt Lumber Co.
110 Arlington St.
Watertown, MA 02472

Toll-free: 877-635-3362
Phone: 617-923-1480
www.sterrittlumber.com

F.D. Sterritt Lumber sells FSC-certified lumber, plywood, decking, hardwoods, and hardwood flooring. They have a variety of certified species in stock. Additional green building materials available, includ-ing low-VOC adhesives, caulking, sealants, and recycled drywall. F.D. Sterritt offers green building product consultations.

FSC-Certified Lumber, Plywood, and Products

Potlatch Corporation
601 W. First Ave., Ste. 1600
Spokane, WA 99201

Phone: 509-835-1500
www.potlatchcorp.com

In 2004, Potlatch Corporation became the first publicly traded U.S. timber company to certify timberland according to Forest Steward-ship Council (FSC) standards. Potlatch is producing chain-of-custody FSC-certified Hem-Fir and Douglas Fir/Larch framing lumber, inland red cedar decking and siding, and Douglas fir and white fir plywood from three chain-of-custody-certified mills in Idaho. Potlatch has recently added over 400,000 acres of FSC certified timber in Arkan-sas which supports a chain-of-custody sawmill in Warren, Arkansas. Warren produces dimensional Southern Yellow Pine framing lumber. These products are stamped with the FSC logo when required for specific sales.

FSC-Certified TruWood Siding

Collins Products, LLC
6410 Hwy. 66
Klamath Falls, OR 97601

Toll-free: 800-547-1793
Phone: 541-885-3289
www.collinswood.com

Collins Products, a subsidiary of Collins Companies, offers an FSC-certified version of its engineered TruWood siding and trim. It is made from FSC-certified wood chips (using FSC's partial-content rules, with an actual certified fiber content of 32%), phenol formaldehyde binder (5-6% by weight), paraffin wax, acrylic sealants, and finishes. The product is also certified by Scientific Certification Systems to con-tain a minimum of 40% recycled or recovered wood fiber (minimum 4% post-consumer recycled, 20% post-industrial recycled, and the remainder "recovered"). According to Collins, when compared with cedar siding, TruWood is less expensive, holds paint longer, has no knots or raised grain, and requires less paint to cover. TruWood siding comes with a limited 30-year warranty in a wide variety of both lap and panel products with various textures and finishes. Distributed by Weyerhaeuser in the western U.S. only.

SmartChoice Wood Products

Certified Forest Products, LLC.
7 Los Conejos
Orinda, CA 94563

Phone: 925-258-4372
www.certifiedforestproducts.com

Certified Forest Products (CFP) is a distributor of SmartChoice, a col-lection of FSC-certified and reclaimed wood products from a variety of species including hardwoods, cedar, and redwood. Products include lumber, plywood, decking, siding, flooring, interior and exterior millwork.

Insulated Metal Wall Panels

With a thin metal skin and foam insulation for a core, insulated metal wall panels provide excellent thermal protection and ef-ficient use of materials. The materials, themselves, however, have relatively high embodied energy.

Acsys Panel System

Acsys Inc.
1677 E. Miles Ave., Ste. 101
Hayden, ID 83835

Toll-free: 866-362-2797
Phone: 208-772-6422
www.acsys.net

The Acsys Building System is a structural insulated panel-type product employing an engineered 16- to 20-gauge corrugated galvanized steel endoskeletal core (rather than the more common exoskeleton of OSB). The steel is embedded in molded EPS, which offers R-values ranging from 25 to 50 (panel thicknesses of 6", 8", 10", and 12"). The EPS typically contains 7-10% recycled content from packaging waste, according to the manufacturer. Available in 2' and 4' widths up to 18' long, it may be used with steel framing or as a fully load-bearing system. The panels interconnect with ship-lap joints (secured by galvanized screws) and may be lifted into place by two people. 18-gauge galvanized steel top- and bottom-mounting tracks, as well as corner locater plates, are provided. Panels are typically finished on the exterior with acrylic stucco and on the interior with drywall.

Masonry Accessories

Forces affecting the durability and performance of masonry wall systems include bulk water penetration, wicking of moisture, and solar-driven moisture movement. Products listed here are designed to improve the durability and performance of masonry wall systems. Masonry accessories that improve the durability and performance of masonry wall systems can include two-piece adjustable brick ties, brick veneer venting and clear cavity components. Note that clear cavity components represent a product solution that should be considered along with techniques for keeping the cavity space clear, such as loose sand and mortar cleanouts in the first course of the veneer.

CavClear Masonry Mat

Archovations, Inc.
P.O. Box 241
Hudson, WI 54016

Toll-free: 888-436-2620
Phone: 715-381-5773
www.cavclear.com

CavClear Masonry Mat is an airspace maintenance and drainage material designed to be installed full-height behind brick in exterior cavity wall construction. The matting prevents obstruction of the cavity airspace and also prevents formation of energy-conducting mortar bridges. CavClear is a nonwoven plastic mesh made from 100% recycled plastic (25% minimum post-consumer content) and is available in thicknesses of 1/2", 3/4", 1", 1-1/4" and 1-3/4". It is also available bonded to EPS insulation.

CavClear Weep Vents

Archovations, Inc.
P.O. Box 241
Hudson, WI 54016

Toll-free: 888-436-2620
Phone: 715-381-5773
www.cavclear.com

CavClear® Weep Vents are 100% recycled-plastic, nonwoven mesh vents with a flame-retardant binder designed for use in the vertical joints between brick masonry units at all flashing levels in cavity wall construction. Properly installed, CavClear Weep Vents promote greater ventilation and drainage than traditional rope wicks in brick cavity wall construction. The notched design facilitates faster drying than straight-cut weep vents, according to the manufacturer. The vents are available in a variety of colors to blend with mortar and brick colors, and are part of a complete line of products that aid in keeping cavity airspaces clear. These vents may also be used for venting at the top of the wall in a pressure-equalized cavity wall design.

CavityRock

Roxul Inc.
551 Harrop Dr.
Milton, ON L9T 3H3 Canada

Toll-free: 800-265-6878
Phone: 905-878-8474
www.roxul.com

CavityRock® is a non-combustible, lightweight, water repellent, semi-rigid, insulating drainage board for cavity wall applications. This mineral fiber product provides effective water drainage, and maintains its thermal resistance even when damp. A fire stop is not required because CavityRock® is a non-combustible insulation. According to the manufacturer, this product is compatible with all air/vapor barrier systems, adhesives, and wall ties. Roxul's mineral wool is made from approximately equal amounts of natural basalt rock and recycled slag (with 1%-6% urea extended phenolic formaldehyde binder).

Mortar Net Masonry Drainage and Flashing Products

Mortar Net USA, Ltd.
541 S. Lake St.
Gary, IN 46403

Toll-free: 800-664-6638
www.mortarnet.com

Mortar Net is a 90%-open, fibrous-mesh wall drainage system used to maintain airflow and allow moisture migration from behind masonry veneer facades. 2"-thick Mortar Net for Brick, Mortar Net Block, and Mortar Net Weep Vents are made from 50% recycled 200-dernier polyester; at least 17% is post-consumer and up to 33% is post-industrial polyester. Mortar Net is designed to keep mortar droppings from blocking weep holes. Block-Flash is an embeddable flashing device for exterior single width C.M.U. wall systems.

Reclaimed-Wood Siding

Reclaimed-wood siding, though not commonly available, is environmentally attractive. It is generally milled from large timbers recovered from old buildings and other structures—not from wood that previously served as siding. Due to slower growth and straighter grain, quality, stability, and durability, reclaimed siding is often superior to new siding. However, the finite supply of reclaimed wood resources suggests that the material may be more suited to higher-visibility uses, such as furniture, interior trim, and flooring.

AltruWood Reclaimed-Wood Products

AltruWood, Inc.
P.O. Box 3341
Portland, OR 97208

Toll-free: 877-372-9663
www.altruwood.com

AltruWood sells a variety of reclaimed-wood species and products, mostly salvaged from old buildings, barns, factories, warehouses and rivers in the U.S.—principally including domestic pine varieties, Douglas fir, oak, cedar, redwood, chestnut, cypress, and cherry. Products include flooring, timbers, siding, paneling, millwork, and lumber. The company will work with clients to locate recycled lumber from their region. A custom cutting service allows the specification of exact sizes and dimensions, minimizing waste. AltruWood also sells new domestic and tropical FSC-certified wood.

Antique Woods & Colonial Restorations

Antique Woods & Colonial Restorations, Inc.
121 Quarry Rd.
Gouverneur, NY 13642

Toll-free: 888-261-4284
Phone: 610-913-0674
www.vintagewoods.com

Antique Woods & Colonial Restorations, Inc. (formerly Vintage Barns, Woods & Restorations) sells reclaimed and remilled wood products including flooring, siding, millwork, and whole barn frames.

Appalachian Woods

Appalachian Woods, LLC
1240 Cold Springs Rd.
Stuarts Draft, VA 24477

Toll-free: 800-333-7610
Phone: 540-337-1801
www.appalachianwoods.com

Appalachian Woods reclaims and remills timber for a variety of custom millwork applications. Lumber is generally sold rough, but can be provided S4S and S2S. Lumber, flooring, and furniture is available in a variety of species including American chestnut, heart pine, and oak. Appalachian Woods has been a family-run business since 1976.

D. Litchfield Reclaimed Wood

D. Litchfield & Co. Ltd.
3046 Westwood St.
Port Coquitlam, BC V3C 3L7 Canada

Toll-free: 888-303-2222
Phone: 604-464-7525
www.dlitchfield.com

Litchfield carries a large, steady supply of all types of reclaimed lumber and beams salvaged through their deconstruction operations.

Logs End Reclaimed-Wood Building Products

Logs End Inc.
1520 Triole St.
Ottawa, ON K1B3S9 Canada

Phone: 613-738-7851
www.logsend.com

Logs End, Inc., retrieves sinker logs in Canada's Upper Ottawa Valley area and processes them into lumber and timber, wide-plank flooring, paneling, siding, and trim in standard and custom dimensions. Old-growth, clear pine is typically recovered, though birch, red and white oak, and hard and soft maple are also available. Certificates of authenticity for educational purposes are issued by the company. Logs End lumber and timbers carry Smartwood "Rediscovered" certification.

Michael Evans Natural Resources

Michael Evenson Natural Resources
P.O. Box 157
Petrolia, CA 95558

Phone: 707-629-3506
www.oldgrowthtimbers.com

Natural Resources dismantles buildings and remills salvaged lumber for resale. Available species include redwood, Douglas fir, and western red cedar.

Pinocchio's Reclaimed Lumber

Pinocchio's
18651 Hare Creek Ter.
Fort Bragg, CA 95437

Phone: 707-964-6272
www.pinocchioredwood.com

Pinocchio's offers raw and remilled lumber from Douglas fir and redwood in both standard-dimension and custom sizes.

Poplar Bark Siding

Highland Craftsmen, Inc.
534 Oak Ave.
Spruce Pine, NC 28777

Phone: 828-765-9010
www.highlandcraftsmen.com

Highland Craftsmen offers Bark House™ chemical-free, kiln-sterilized siding made of tulip poplar or tulip tree (Liriodendron tulipifera) bark salvaged with hand tools during conventional logging practices. The "bark house" style was popular in the Appalachians a century ago. 75-year-old extant examples suggest good durability.

Reclaimed-Wood Building Products

Conklin's Authentic Antique Barnwood
R.R. 1, Box 70
Susquehanna, PA 18847

Phone: 570-465-3832
www.conklinsbarnwood.com

Conklin's Authentic Antique Barnwood sells hand-hewn beams, barn boards, and flooring "as is" or remilled.

Reclaimed-Wood Building Products

Endura Wood Products, Ltd.
1303 S.E. 6th Ave.
Portland, OR 97214

Phone: 503-233-7090
www.endurawood.com

Endura Wood Products currently has access to over 3.5 million board feet of Douglas fir that is being reclaimed from the old Portland Dry Dock #2. Also available is a limited supply of Douglas fir with a distinct red hue that has been reclaimed from maraschino cherry vats.

Reclaimed-Wood Building Products

J. Hoffman Lumber Co.
1330 E. State St.
Sycamore, IL 60178

Phone: 815-899-2260
www.hoffmanlumberco.com

J. Hoffman Lumber Co. is the Midwest's only sawmill company specializing in reclaimed antique heart pine, Douglas fir, and white pine. Reclaimed lumber is remilled into flooring, siding, and other millwork.

Reclaimed-Wood Building Products

Longleaf Lumber
115 Fawcett St.
Cambridge, MA 02138

Toll-free: 866-653-3566
Phone: 617-871-6611
www.longleaflumber.com

Longleaf Lumber, founded in 1997, remills antique timbers into millwork and flooring at the company's sawmill in southern Maine. Longleaf specializes in heart pine, but other salvaged woods such as chestnut, red and white oak, eastern white pine, and maple are also available from buildings dismantled in various locations around the New England region. Longleaf also sells unmilled reclaimed timbers and reclaimed barn siding. In addition to the sawmill, the company operates a retail store at their Cambridge, MA location.

Reclaimed-Wood Building Products

Pioneer Millworks
1180 Commercial Dr.
Farmington, NY 14425

Toll-free: 800-951-9663
Phone: 585-924-9970
www.pioneermillworks.com

Pioneer Millworks remills salvaged wood into flooring and a number of molding profiles, in addition to timbers, cabinetry, stair parts, doors, and trusses. The primary species is longleaf yellow pine; others that are often available include redwood, bald cypress, chestnut, white oak, Douglas fir, and white pine.

Reclaimed-Wood Building Products

TerraMai
1104 Firenze St.
P.O. Box 696
McCloud, CA 96057

Toll-free: 800-220-9062
Phone: 530-964-2740
www.terramai.com

TerraMai produces several grades of flooring, ranging from clear tongue-and-groove to rough-cut plank, from reclaimed lumber and tropical hardwoods. All flooring is available in "Character" (with evidence of previous use) and "Select" (clear) grades. Douglas fir, ponderosa pine, and southern yellow pine are among their most popular species. TerraMai also mills various architectural woodwork products from their 700,000-board-foot inventory of reclaimed woods. All of TerraMai's varied products are from reclaimed wood and is FSC certified.

Reclaimed-Wood Building Products

Vintage Log and Lumber, Inc.
Glen Ray Rd.
Rt. 1, Box 2F
Alderson, WV 24910

Toll-free: 877-653-5647
Phone: 304-445-2300
www.vintagelog.com

Vintage Log and Lumber salvages the materials in log cabins and timber-frame barns in Kentucky, Ohio, Pennsylvania, and West Virginia. The company's inventory includes salvaged redwood, chestnut, oak, pine, and poplar boards, beams, flooring, and split rails. They also sell complete hand-hewn log cabins and timber-frame barns, as well as architectural salvage items.

Reclaimed-Wood Lumber and Products

Armster Reclaimed Lumber Co.
9 Old Post Rd.
Madison, CT 06443

Phone: 203-214-9705
www.woodwood.com

A Reclaimed Lumber Co. salvages wood from old water and wine tanks, mill buildings, bridge timbers, river-recovery log operations, and other sources and custom mills it into a variety of wood products including siding, plank flooring, millwork, paneling, shingles and shakes, stairs parts, and dimension lumber and timber. Available species include red cedar, redwood, beech, black cherry, chestnut, rock maple, red and white oak, Eastern hemlock, Douglas fir, mahogany and Longleaf heart pine. Wood is sourced from all over the country, much of it processed at their Connecticut mill; but the company makes an effort to provide wood that is local to the customer and will make arrangements to process it locally.

Reclaimed-Wood Materials

Big Timberworks
1 Rabel Ln.
P.O. Box 368
Gallatin Gateway, MT 59730

Phone: 406-763-4639
www.bigtimberworks.com

Big Timberworks offers custom-milled, reclaimed lumber and timbers in a variety of species. The company specializes in shipping timber frame houses all over the country for supervised construction but also sells custom-cut, reclaimed wood from their sawmill in Montana for residential and commercial applications such as siding, flooring, and millwork.

Reclaimed-Wood Materials

Black's Farmwood, Inc.
P.O. Box 2836
San Rafael, CA 94912

Toll-free: 877-321-9663
Phone: 415-454-8312
www.blacksfarmwood.com

Black's Farmwood sells reclaimed wood products from deconstructed buildings and river bottoms. Products are available in a variety of species and include salvaged timbers and beams, remilled flooring, and barn siding. The company has a showroom in San Rafael, CA and uses two mills, one in Kentucky and another in New York.

Reclaimed-Wood Products

Centre Mills Antique Floors
P.O. Box 16
Aspers, PA 17304

Phone: 717-677-9698
www.centremillsantiquefloors.com

Centre Mills Antique Floors salvages, remills, and sells several species and types of wood products, many hand-hewn. Species include chestnut, oak, white pine, and fir. Centre Mills uses the old gristmill, built in 1841, in Centre Mills, Pennsylvania as their storage facility.

Reclaimed-Wood Products

Chestnut Specialists, Inc.
P.O. Box 304
Plymouth, CT 06782

Phone: 860-283-4209
www.chestnutspec.com

Chestnut Specialists dismantles buildings and remills reclaimed timbers for resale in a variety of products, including siding and flooring. Rough timber, planks, and beams in their original milled or hand-hewn condition are also available.

Reclaimed-Wood Products

Crossroads Recycled Lumber
57839 Rd. 225
P.O. Box 928
North Fork, CA 93643

Toll-free: 888-842-3201
Phone: 559-877-3645
www.crossroadslumber.com

Crossroads Recycled Lumber sells raw and remilled salvaged Douglas fir, sugar pine, ponderosa pine, cedar, and redwood lumber, timbers, flooring, paneling, and siding. They also offer doors made from this wood.

Reclaimed-Wood Products

Duluth Timber Co.
P.O. Box 16717
Duluth, MN 55805

Phone: 218-727-2145
www.duluthtimber.com

Duluth Timber reclaims and remills mainly Douglas fir and longleaf yellow pine, but also redwood and cypress. Demolition and salvage of warehouses and sheep-shearing sheds in Australia has yielded a supply of Australian hardwoods such as jarrah and Mountain ash. Duluth has mills in Minnesota and Washington.

Resource Woodworks

Resource Woodworks, Inc.
627 E. 60th St.
Tacoma, WA 98404

Phone: 253-474-3757

Resource Woodworks specializes in Douglas fir, cedar, and redwood timbers salvaged from demolition projects and remilled to custom specifications, including decking, flooring, lumber, timbers, siding, paneling, and millwork.

River-Reclaimed Wood Products

Goodwin Heart Pine Company
106 S.W. 109th Pl.
Micanopy, FL 32667

Toll-free: 800-336-3118
Phone: 352-466-0339
www.heartpine.com

Goodwin manufactures antique wood flooring, millwork, stair parts, paneling, and siding made from antique heart pine and heart cypress logs—200 years old or older—recovered from Southern river bottoms. Flooring, siding, and paneling is kiln-dried, graded, and precision-milled. Decorative wood moldings are architecturally drawn and are designed to classic proportions. Stair parts include solid or laminated treads, and a full range of balusters, newels, and rails. Reclaimed timbers from old buildings are also available.

Trestlewood

Trestlewood
292 N. 2000 W, Ste. A
Lindon, UT 84042

Toll-free: 877-375-2779
Phone: 801-443-4002
www.trestlewood.com

Trestlewood deals exclusively in reclaimed wood. Their wood comes from the Lucin Cutoff railroad trestle, which crosses the Great Salt Lake, and other salvage projects. Trestlewood products include flooring, millwork, timbers, decking, and siding. Available species include Douglas fir, redwood, southern yellow pine, longleaf yellow pine, oak, and other hardwoods.

Wood Materials from Urban Trees

CitiLog
P.O. Box 685
Pittstown, NJ 08867

Toll-free: 877-248-9564
Phone: 908-735-8871
www.citilogs.com

CitiLog™, also known as D. Stubby Warmbold, is SmartWood-certified for the harvesting of trees in urban areas of New Jersey and Pennsylvania. Wood is sent by rail to Amish craftsmen in central Pennsylvania who take extra care to turn the lesser graded wood into higher quality products such as flooring, lumber, custom architectural millwork, furniture, and kitchen cabinets. Where appropriate, wood is now harvested using horses.

Vapor-Retarding Coatings

Vapor retarders are generally sheet goods added to either the interior (cold climates) or exterior (hot and particularly hot humid climates) to restrict moisture moving by diffusion into wall, roof and foundation assemblies. Products listed here usually have superior performance in terms of variable vapor permeability based on their water content. Note that the placement of vapor retarders should always be done in the context of the vapor permeabilities of all the other components of the assembly and their vapor permeability, and the designated direction for drying of the assembly.

MemBrain Smart Vapor Retarder

CertainTeed Corporation
750 E. Swedesford Rd.
P.O. Box 860
Valley Forge, PA 19482

Toll-free: 800-233-8990
Phone: 610-341-7000
www.certainteed.com

MemBrain™ Smart Vapor Retarder is made from a transparent polyamide-based (Nylon-6) material, which changes permeability according to relative humidity and can increase the drying potential of closed building envelope systems. The 2-mil-thick, high-tensile-strength sheeting is as strong as a 6-mil sheet of polyethylene. Its moisture permeability varies from less than 1 perm at low relative humidity to more than 20 perms at high (95%) relative humidity. MemBrain is intended for use in heating and mixed climates, and is not suitable for cooling climates with high outdoor humidity or in buildings with high constant indoor relative humidity. Interior finish materials and cavity-fill insulation must also be highly permeable.

Wood Shingles and Shakes

Wood shingles and shakes are traditionally and most commonly made from old-growth western red cedar. Although the embodied energy of this product is quite low, the harvesting of western red cedar is, in most cases, unsustainable. If a wood shingle roof is desired and fire-related concerns aren't prohibitive, using certified eastern white cedar shingles, commonly used as wall siding, is an option. Some recycled-plastic shingles are manufactured to look like wood shingles.

Certified PR Shingles

Industries Maibec, Inc.
660 Lenoir St.
Sainte-Foy, QC G1X 3W3 Canada

Toll-free: 800-363-1930
Phone: 418-659-3323
www.maibec.com

PR® Shingles are made from eastern white cedar from the Seven Islands Land Company that is chain-of-custody certified by SCS. Shingles are available in three options: unfinished (natural); kiln-dried and factory-stained in gray, beige, or an unlimited choice of colors; and factory-treated with an oil finish. While most commonly used on walls, they may be appropriate in some roofing applications if installed more thickly.

Reclaimed-Wood Lumber and Products

Armster Reclaimed Lumber Co.
9 Old Post Rd.
Madison, CT 06443

Phone: 203-214-9705
www.woodwood.com

A Reclaimed Lumber Co. salvages wood from old water and wine tanks, mill buildings, bridge timbers, river-recovery log operations, and other sources and custom mills it into a variety of wood products including siding, plank flooring, millwork, paneling, shingles and shakes, stairs parts, and dimension lumber and timber. Available species include red cedar, redwood, beech, black cherry, chestnut, rock maple, red and white oak, Eastern hemlock, Douglas fir, mahogany and Longleaf heart pine. Wood is sourced from all over the country, much of it processed at their Connecticut mill; but the company makes an effort to provide wood that is local to the customer and will make arrangements to process it locally.

Wood-Alternative Trim

Pressures on timber supply are especially acute for high-visibility, solid-wood products like window sash and molding, which have traditionally been produced from old-growth trees. Molding made from plastic wastes is an excellent substitute for paint-grade moldings.

Timbron Molding

Timbron International, Inc.
1333 N. California Blvd., Ste. 545
Walnut Creek, CA 94596

Phone: 925-943-1632
www.timbron.com

Timbron produces interior molding in a variety of profiles made from at least 90% recycled polystyrene, along with small quantities of a coloring agent, a UV stabilizer, and a foaming agent. Timbron has earned certification from Scientific Certification Systems (SCS) for using a minimum of 75% post-consumer and 15% pre-consumer recycled material in its molding products, and claims the products are zero-VOC and recyclable. Timbron is highly durable, waterproof, termite-proof, paintable (though also suitable unpainted as white), and fully workable with carpentry tools.

Roofing

Roofs provide one of the most fundamental functions of a building: shelter from the elements. They must endure drastic temperature swings, long-term exposure to ultraviolet (UV) light, high winds, rain, hail and, depending on the climate, snow. In conflict with these performance and durability requirements, much of the roofing industry is driven by highly competitive economics and thin profit margins. Since shingles are rarely recycled, the 15- or 20-year typical life span of asphalt composite roofing products makes them highly resource-intensive. The National Roofing Contractors Association estimates that 75% of the dollars spent on roofing in the U.S. are for replacing or repairing existing roofs.

Durability is critical in roofing because a failure can mean serious damage not just to the roof itself but also to the building and its contents. Such damage multiplies the economic and environmental cost of less reliable roofing materials. Most roofing failures take place at joints and penetrations, so it's not just the roofing material that must be durable but the entire system, including flashings and edge treatments. Proper installation is vital.

Roofing can also have a significant impact on cooling loads—within the building and even in the surrounding community. Use of lighter colored, low-solar absorptance roofing surfaces is one of the key measures advocated in the "Cooling Our Communities" program of the U.S. EPA. Reflective roofing can significantly assist appropriate insulation in dramatically reducing summertime solar gain into the building and thereby lowering the cooling load. Roofs with high solar reflectance also help to minimize the "urban heat island" effect, which raises the ambient temperature in urbanized areas.

Low-slope roofs, more common on commercial buildings, are typically single-ply membranes or built-up asphalt with polyisocyanurate insulation underneath. When these roofs are replaced, the insulation usually has to be replaced as well, taking up landfill space and creating new resource demands for the replacement materials. Systems that separate the insulation from the membrane, and that use a polystyrene insulation which can get wet and dry out without deteriorating, are often preferable because the insulation can be reused. In "protected membrane" applications, the rigid insulation (usually extruded polystyrene, XPS) is actually installed on top of the roofing membrane, with concrete pavers on top of the insulation.

Most intriguing environmentally are green roofs (living roofs) in which soil and plantings are used over the waterproof membrane and specialized green roof components. These living layers help replace the ecological functions that are lost when a building footprint covers open land. By using drought-tolerant, low-growing sedums, the planting media requirements with a green roof are fairly minimal. A green roof does not eliminate the need for roof insulation.

Asphalt shingles with fiberglass or organic-fiber mats are still the most common choice for sloped roofing applications. Due to the durability concerns described above, only the heaviest-duty asphalt shingles (with a minimum 30-year warranty) should be considered. Alternatives are available in steel, plastic, rubber, and fiber-cement that use recycled-content materials and come in shake or shingle styles. Clay and concrete tiles are also an option, especially where hail isn't a serious threat. Weight is an issue with some of these products. Sheet steel is also increasingly popular on sloped roofs. Steel roofing should have a thick, galvanized or galvalume coating or be factory-coated with a highly durable finish, such as polyvinylidene fluoride (Kynar 500™), for maximum life.

The movement to integrate solar electricity generation into buildings—called Building-Integrated Photovoltaics (BIPV)—has reached the roofing industry with the introduction of photovoltaic (PV) shingles and larger integrated roofing panels. These are still quite pricey, and an electrician may have to work with the roofers during installation. Once installed, however, they produce electricity that can help power the building, and any excess can be sold to the utility company in most states.

Clay Roofing Tiles

Clay tiles are durable and made from abundant raw materials. As typically installed, roof tiles are also effective at preventing heat gain through the roof. In some climates and with some products, hail may be a concern. Some recycled-plastic shingles are manufactured to look like clay roof tiles.

Clay Roofing Tiles

Gladding, McBean & Co.
P.O. Box 97
Lincoln, CA 95648

Toll-free: 800-776-1133
Phone: 916-645-3341
www.gladdingmcbean.com

Gladding, McBean manufactures clay roofing tiles in a large variety of shapes, sizes, and fire-flashed blends, all of which are suitable for freeze/thaw climates.

Clay Roofing Tiles

Ludowici Roof Tile, Inc.
4757 Tile Plant Rd.
New Lexington, OH 43764

Toll-free: 800-945-8453
Phone: 740-342-1995
www.ludowici.com

Ludowici Clay Roof Tiles are available in 47 standard profiles and 43 standard colors in matte, gloss, weathered, sanded, and combed finishes. The company also offers an expanding lineup of larger, more affordable clay roofing tiles that reduce installation time and create less of a load for the roof deck. Recommended in freeze/thaw climates, all Ludowici standard grade tiles and fittings are covered by a 75-year limited warranty.

Clay Roofing Tiles

MCA Clay Tile
1985 Sampson Ave.
Corona, CA 92879

Toll-free: 800-736-6221
www.mca-tile.com

Among the tiles manufactured by MCA Clay Tile are a one-piece, S-shaped mission style tile in natural or glazed colors, the Corona Tapered Mission Tile available in standard and custom colors and blends, and an interlocking flat tile (MF 108 Flat) in Natural Red and glazed colors. MCA also manufactures Turret Tile®, which allows for a true turret- or fan-shaped installation. MCA's Oriental Style is an interlocking tile in the Japanese tradition. It is available in various glazed colors with many accessories and ornaments available. All MCA tiles have a limited 50-year warranty.

Claylite and ClayMax

US Tile Company
909 W. Railroad St.
Corona, CA 92882

Toll-free: 800-252-9548
Phone: 909-737-0200
www.ustile.com

Claylite® and ClayMax® are over 40% lighter than standard roofing tile. Claylite is configured in the traditional "S" tile shape, while ClayMax is in the form of a twin "S." US Tile® (UST) also manufactures tiles of standard weight. All UST tiles are a true tapered mission style to provide a tight fit; they are offered in over 20 colors and have a transferable lifetime limited warranty ($50 transfer fee).

Nu-Lok Slate Roofing System

Nu-Lok Roofing Systems
711 South Carson St., Ste. 4
Carson City, NV 89701

Toll-free: 800-946-8565
Phone: 802-287-9701
www.nu-lok.com

The Nu-Lok roofing system is a stainless-steel framework of battens, channels, and clips that holds natural slate or ceramic tile in place, reducing the amount of material needed for roofing installations. The system reduces the weight of the roof, reduces material use, and increases installation options while reducing labor costs. The system comes with a 50-year warranty and, according to the manufacturer, permits installation and repair of slate by standard roofing crews. The system is available with GreenStone Slate from a Vermont slate quarrier.

Reclaimed Natural Salvaged Slate and Clay Tile Roofing

Durable Slate Co.
1050 N. Fourth St.
Columbus, OH 43201

Toll-free: 800-666-7445
Phone: 614-299-5522
www.durableslate.com

Durable Slate Co. stocks well over 600,000 pieces of salvaged slate and 400,000 pieces of salvaged clay tiles. Durable Slate is able to match colors and styles of slate and tile that are no longer produced.

Salvaged Clay and Concrete Tile Roofing

Custom Tile Roofing, Inc.
4560 Columbine St.
Denver, CO 80216

Phone: 303-761-3831
www.customtileroofing.com

Custom Tile Roofing maintains an inventory of close to 400,000 pieces of reclaimed roofing tiles.

Salvaged Slate and Clay Tile Roofing

Alluvium Construction
200 Lake Shore Dr.
Marlton, NJ 08053

Phone: 856-767-2700
www.historicroofs.com

Alluvium Construction specializes in reclaimed slate and tile roofing in all quantities, types, and colors. Domestic or imported new slate may also be ordered. If purchasing new slate, domestic slate from nearby quarries is recommended.

Salvaged Slate and Clay Tile Roofing

Emack Slate Company, Inc.
9 Office Park Cir., Ste. 120
Birmingham, AL 35223

Phone: 205-879-3424
www.emackslate.com

Emack Slate maintains an inventory of salvaged slate and clay tiles. Domestic or imported new slate may also be ordered. If purchasing new slate, domestic slate from nearby quarries is recommended.

Salvaged Slate and Clay Tile Roofing

Reclaimed Roofs, Inc.
7454 Lancaster Pike #328
Hockessin, DE 19707

Phone: 302-369-9187
www.reclaimedroofs.com

Reclaimed Roofs provides salvaged roofing slates and tiles. Its owner sits on the Board of Directors for the National Slate Association.

Salvaged Slate and Clay Tile Roofing

Renaissance Roofing, Inc.
P.O. Box 5024
Rockford, IL 61125

Toll-free: 800-699-5695
Phone: 815-547-1725
www.claytileroof.com

Renaissance Roofing, Inc. is a supplier of salvaged clay tile and slate roofing materials.

Salvaged Slate and Clay Tile Roofing

The Roof Tile and Slate Company
1209 Carroll St.
Carrollton, TX 75006

Toll-free: 800-446-0220
Phone: 972-446-0005
www.claytile.com

The Roof Tile and Slate Company maintains a large inventory of salvaged slate and tile. New domestic slate and tile are also available.

Fiber-Cement Roofing Shingles

Fiber-cement building materials earn green points for their durability. The new generation of fiber-cement doesn't contain asbestos; it's made from portland cement, sand, clay, and wood fiber. Environmental concerns with fiber-cement include the embodied energy of portland cement and the source of the wood fiber—some fiber-cement products use wood from such distant locations as New Zealand and Russia. Although newer fiber-cement products are not yet proven over the long haul, the material is quite stable and typically carries a 50-year warranty. Of particular concern with roof shingle products in cold climates are the effects of freeze-thaw cycling; some products have coatings or polymer constituents to minimize water absorption.

Naturals Roofing

Re-Con Building Products, Inc.
4850 S.W. Scholls Ferry Rd., Ste. 203
Portland, OR 97225

Toll-free: 877-276-7663
Phone: 604-850-7353
www.naturalsroofing.com

Naturals™ roofing is a polymer-modified fiber-cement product available in Rustic Shake™ or Quarry Slate™ styles. Both products have high recycled content. Rustic Shake is available in three colors; Quarry Slate is available in six colors. These products are Class A fire-rated, Class IV hail-rated, and backed by a 50-year warranty.

Green Roof Components

Green roof systems for low-slope roofs protect the roof membrane, reduce stormwater flows, and help green the built environment through rooftop plantings. A green roof includes drainage, geotextile, soil, and vegetation layers. Products listed here can be used to create one or more of the elements of a green roof system.

Biotrays

Green Roof Solutions
4307 Regency Dr.
Glenview, IL 60025

Phone: 847-724-7936
www.greenroofsolutions.com

Biotrays are biodegradable trays for preplanted green roof media. Made with coconut husk fiber (coir) bound with natural vulcanized latex, the 17-inch-square, three-inch-deep carriers speed installation and provide nutrition as they decompose over time. Green Roof Solutions provides the media and regionally-appropriate plants for the Biotrays, or will consult with professional tradespeople to ensure appropriate use and installation.

Ecogrid

Terrafirm Enterprises
23778 24th Ave.
Langley, BC V2Z 3A2 Canada

Toll-free: 866-934-7572
Phone: 604-534-7572
www.terrafirmenterprises.com

Ecogrid products from Terrafirm Solutions are made from 100% recycled post-consumer HDPE. The lock-together trays may be filled with planting medium or gravel. EcoGrid e30 is suitable for moderate vehicle traffic, walkways, and playgrounds. EcoGrid e50 will accommodate heavy vehicle traffic and parking areas. EcoGrid s50 is for slope stabilization. They are available in black, green, and brown, and may also be used for green roof applications to prevent soil compaction in growing areas while providing a barrier between the roofing membranes and pedestrian traffic.

Enkadrain 3000 Series

Colbond Inc.
1301 Sand Hill Rd.
P.O. Box 1057
Enka, NC 28728

Toll-free: 800-365-7391
Phone: 828-665-5050
www.colbond-usa.com

Enkadrain® Subsurface Drainage Composite relieves hydrostatic pressure from backfill abutting below-grade structures including foundations and slabs, plaza decks, and retaining walls. It can also be used as a drainage plane for green roofs and roof gardens. It protects waterproofing during and after backfill, and will conform to irregular surfaces and corners. It consists of a post industrial recycled polypropylene drainage core of fused, entangled filaments and a geocomposite fabric bonded to one or two sides. The entangled filaments are molded into a square waffle pattern. Colbond is currently converting its entire product line to include high levels of recycled content.

GEOdren Roof Garden Units

Geoproducts Corp.
11-110 Jardin Dr.
Concord, ON L4K 4R4 Canada

Toll-free: 877-GEOTUBE
Phone: 905-760-2256
www.geoproductscorp.com

GEOdren, made from recycled polypropylene, is a modular system for creating green roofs. The interlocking trays combine water retention, drainage, and aeration, and are strong enough to withstand the weight of mini-excavators or small forklifts. Rounded feet allow the trays to be placed directly on the roof's waterproof liner without damage. The trays are intended to be filled with pumice or other porous drainage material, then overlaid with geotextile and covered with planting media.

Green Roof Blocks

Saint Louis Metalworks Company
11701 New Halls Ferry Rd.
Florissant, MO 63033

Phone: 314-972-8010
www.greenroofblocks.com

Green Roof Blocks are ready-to-install 22-gauge anodized aluminum 2' x 2' planters with 4" depths that are placed on a rooftop to create a living roof. Custom shapes, sizes and depths are available upon request. Saturated unit weights range from 17 to 51 lbs/sf. Live plants and growth media are included. Pads at each corner and in the center of the planters elevate them from the roof surface, allowing drainage and airflow. Green Roof Blocks are made with 80% recycled metal and 50% recycled rubber. The self contained units are portable, facilitating roof work and aesthetic rearrangement.

MODI Roof Garden

Green Innovations, Ltd
3700 Salem Rd. N
Pickering, ON L1Y 1E8 Canada

Toll-free: 888-725-7524
Phone: 416-725-7524
www.greeninnovations.ca

MODI Roof Garden trays are made from post-consumer recycled HDPP, come in two depths, and are suitable for use over any type of watertight membrane. The system has high compressive strength, allowing the use of small loaders or mini-excavators during installation or maintenance. The attachment system accommodates changing slopes and curved surfaces, and in conjunction with the optional MODI Paving Grill, can be used on roofs with slopes greater than 15%. The trays may be shaped with a saw or disc grinder.

Green Roof Planting Media

Green roof systems for low-slope roofs protect the roof membrane, reduce stormwater flows, and help green the built environment through rooftop plantings. A green roof includes drainage, geotextile, soil, and vegetation layers. Products listed here represent appropriate planting media for green (living) roofs.

Rooftop Planting Media

Midwest Trading - Horticultural Supplies, Inc.
48W805 Illinois Rte. 64
Virgil, IL 60151

Toll-free: 800-546-9522
Phone: 630-365-1990
www.midwest-trading.com

Midwest Trading is a regional supplier of mulch, mixes, and planting media, including media optimized for green roofs. Green roof planting media should have high absorptivity (high total pore space) and low organic content—properties appropriate for green roofs. A partner company, Midwest Groundcovers, has a number of sedums available for green roof applications.

Green Roof Plants

Green roof systems for low-slope roofs protect the roof membrane, reduce stormwater flows, and help green the built environment through rooftop plantings. A green roof includes drainage, geotextile, soil, and vegetation layers. Products listed here represent appropriate planting media for green (living) roofs. Products listed here are sources for appropriate plants for green (living) roofs.

Green Roof Plants

Green Roof Plants - Emory Knoll Farms
3410 Ady Rd.
Street, MD 21154

Phone: 410-452-5880
www.greenroofplants.com

Green Roof Plants (Emory Knoll Farms) is the only company in North America known to specialize solely in plants for extensive (low-profile) green roofs. In operation for six generations, the company has shifted production solely to green roof applications. The company's greenhouse is powered by a 3 kW PV system, and solar power also powers water pumping. The company has an organic growing focus and makes maximum use of reclaimed, recycled, recyclable, and natural materials. Much of the nutrients are provided by the farm's 25 llamas. The company propagates hundreds of species of sedum for green roof projects throughout North America. Green Roof Plants also provides horticultural consulting for extensive green roof projects.

Green Roof Plants

Intrinsic Perennial Gardens, Inc.
10702 Seaman Rd.
Hebron, IL 60034

Toll-free: 800-648-2788
Phone: 815-648-2788
www.intrinsicperennialgardens.com

Intrinsic Perennial Gardens offers over 100 varieties of sedum, as well as other hardy perennials appropriate for green roof applications, and primarily serves the Midwest.

Green Roof Plants

MotherPlants
863 Hayts Rd.
Ithaca, NY 14850

Phone: 607-256-2482
www.motherplants.net

MotherPlants grows a wide range of species, primarily Sedums, Delosperma, and Sempervivums. Plants are offered as plugs, cuttings, vegetated mats, or planted in modules. Any species not stocked can be acquired and grown to specification.

Green Roof Systems

Green roof systems for low-slope roofs protect the roof membrane, reduce stormwater flows, and help green the built environment through rooftop plantings. Green roofs, which are more common in Europe, can detain over 50% of rainwater from a typical storm: stormwater detention reduces the loads placed on storm sewers, making it a particularly attractive system in urban areas that have combined sewer overflow (CSO) events during heavy rains. Multilayered green roof systems are thicker than conventional roofs, and additional structural support is typically required. A green roof includes drainage, geotextile, soil, and vegetation layers; sedums or a thick sod of native grasses interspersed with wildflowers can be a wonderful architectural element which helps to reduce building heat gain and the urban heat island effect. Plantings also absorb CO_2.

AMERGREEN Roof Garden System

American Wick Drain Corporation
1209 Airport Rd.
Monroe, NC 28110

Toll-free: 800-242-9425
Phone: 704-238-9200
www.americanwick.com

The Amergreen™ Roof Garden System consists of a needle-punched, nonwoven polypropylene geotextile filter fabric with an optional copper hydroxide root-barrier coating, a polystyrene "drain core" with water-storing cones that also provides airflow, and another polypropylene geotextile separation layer. Their 50RS system has a 7/16"-deep drain core, while the 100RS has a 1" core. American Wick Drain also manufactures products appropriate for reducing hydrostatic pressure on earth-sheltered homes.

ELT Easy Green System

Elevated Landscape Technologies Inc.
245 King George Rd. Ste. 319
Brantford, ON N3R 7N7 Canada

Toll-free: 866-306-7773
www.eltgreenroofs.com

The ELT Easy Green System is a pre-grown green roof system comprised of an interlocking water retention / drainage layer, filter fabric, root reinforcement layer, and vegetation. Shallow (<6") and deep (>6") systems range from 8lbs/sf to more than 25lbs/sf, and are appropriate for residential or commercial installations.

EnviroTech Roof System

Building Logics, Inc.
2984 S. Lynnhaven Rd.,
Ste. 103
Virginia Beach, VA
23452

Phone: 757-431-3170
www.buildinglogics.com

Using the Famogreen name, Building Logics, Inc. supplies green roof systems with the German FAMOS APAO modified bitumen membrane and vegetation mats. Specialized versions of the membrane are available with a copper-impregnated spun-polyester root barrier and/or a lightweight hydrogel to retain water. Technical support for the design and specification of soil mixes and plants is available.

GreenScapes

CETCO - Building Materials Group
1500 W. Shure Dr.
Arlington Heights, IL 60004

Toll-free: 800-527-9948
Phone: 847-392-5800
www.cetco.com

Cetco, a company that specializes in waterproofing technology, offers the GreenScapes green roof system. The GreenScapes system uses a waterproofing membrane, root barrier, drainage, growing media, and plants, and is available in a variety of assemblies depending on need. GreenScapes can be "extensive" (lightweight, low-maintenance roofs that have a thin layer of growing media and shallow plant roots) or "intensive" (which can have growing media several feet thick to support bushes and small trees). GreenScapes takes advantage of Cetco's experience with waterproofing technology and comes with their Hydroshield warranty program, which covers both labor and materials.

LiveRoof

LiveRoof, LLC
P.O. Box 533
Spring Lake, MI 49456

Toll-free: 800-875-1392
www.liveroof.com

LiveRoof is a modular green roof system made from 100% pre-consumer recycled polypropylene. The modules come pre-filled with LiveRoof engineered planting medium and are delivered pre-planted with drought-resistant plants chosen based on client preference and local growing conditions. After installation, the soil and plants merge together with neighboring modules to form a single plant bed. The LiveRoof system does not include roof preparation, so waterproofing and a 45-60 mil. root barrier (or comparable system) must be installed by a qualified contractor prior to the LiveRoof. LiveRoof comes with a 20-year warranty.

Optigreen Green Roof System

Resource Conservation Technology, Inc.
2633 N. Calvert St.
Baltimore, MD 21218

Toll-free: 800-477-7724
Phone: 410-366-1146
www.conservationtechnology.com

Resource Conservation Technology sells a complete green roof system for up to 10,000 sf of roof that includes a sheet EPDM rubber membrane, a plastic drainage substrate, water-retaining lightweight soil, plants, and a rainwater collection system for irrigation in dry weather.

Roofmeadow

Roofscapes, Inc. (SM)
7114 McCallum St.
Philadelphia, PA 19119

Phone: 215-247-8784
www.roofmeadow.com

Roofscapes, Inc.(SM) is a design and consulting firm that specializes in lightweight green roofs. Services offered include design and consulting, installation, construction inspection, and service and maintenance. Roofscapes is affiliated with Optigreen (Optigruen International AG), a German company with over 30 years of green roof experience.

Gutters and Downspouts

Products that are effective at directing rainwater away from foundations increase building durability.

Rain Run

Presto Products Company
670 N. Perkins St.
P.O. Box 2399
Appleton, WI 54912

Toll-free: 800-548-3424
Phone: 920-738-1328
www.prestoproducts.com

Rain Run®, made with recycled plastic, is a splashblock for use at the base of gutter downspouts. The splashblock keeps rainwater away from the foundation and allows it to soak into the ground more effectively.

Rainhandler and Doorbrella

Savetime Corporation
2710 North Ave.
Bridgeport, CT 06604

Toll-free: 800-942-3004
www.rainhandler.com

Rainhandler is an aluminum, multilouvered, self-cleaning device designed to replace gutters. The product breaks up heavy sheets of water into smaller drops that are more easily absorbed into the ground, and spreads the water over a greater area to further facilitate absorption. Doorbrella is an accessory designed to channel water over unprotected doorways to Rainhandlers on each side of the door. Rainhandler is available in brown or white baked-on enamel or unfinished aluminum. Doorbrella is available in brown or aluminum. Both products come with a 25-year limited warranty and a one-year, money-back guarantee.

RainTube

GLI Systems, Inc.
215 S. 4th St.
Jacksonville, OR 97530

Toll-free: 866-724-6356
www.raintube.com

RainTube is a roof gutter debris filter-tube made from 100% post-consumer recycled high-density polyethylene (HDPE) plastic. The filter-tube does not significantly inhibit rainwater capture, allowing the capture of rainfall at more than 100 in/hr. The RainTube can be compressed to fit into narrower gutters. Installed, it crowns slightly above the roof surface. Maintenance consists of occasional light brushing or blowing to remove debris. The system may be useful with rainwater harvesting systems to keep leaves and other debris out of collected rainwater. By preventing clogging of gutters, it may also help to improve building durability.

Recycled-Plastic Landscape Products

Master Mark Plastics
One Master Mark Dr.
P.O. Box 662
Albany, MN 56307

Toll-free: 800-535-4838
Phone: 320-845-2111
www.mastermark.com

Master Mark makes a variety of landscape products, such as lawn edging, lattice, downspout splash blocks, and privacy fencing from recycled HDPE plastic. According to the manufacturer, they currently recycle over 1 billion post-consumer HDPE plastic containers per year, and boast over 50 million feet of quality landscape edging installed every year. The manufacturer has certified the following recycled-content levels (by weight): post-consumer material 100% typical, 100% guaranteed.

Metal Shingles

Metals are readily recyclable, and certain metal roofing products also have high recycled content. These products can be a part of a long-lasting roof when installed with appropriate fasteners and proper flashing. The use of dissimilar metals for roofing, flashing, and fastening isn't recommended because they're susceptible to galvanic corrosion in the presence of water. Metal is also a preferred material for roofs used in rainwater catchment systems. In northern climates, snow readily slides off metal roofs, avoiding the damage caused by ice dams.

MetalWorks Steel Shingles

Tamko Roofing Products, Inc.
220 W. 4th St.
P.O. Box 1404
Joplin, MO 64801

Toll-free: 800-641-4691
www.metalworksroof.com

MetalWorks (formerly AstonWood) Steel Shingles from Tamko are made from as much as 50% recycled material. The shingles consist of G90 galvanized steel with a Kynar 500® or Hylar 5000® coating. These wood and slate shingle look-alike products are 12" x 40" and interconnect on all four sides. Shingles are available in a variety of colors. Because of their light weight, these steel shingles can be installed over two existing layers of asphalt shingles. MetalWorks shingles carry a 50 year warranty.

Recycled-Metal Shingles

Zappone Manufacturing
2928 N. Pittsburg St.
Spokane, WA 99207

Toll-free: 800-285-2677
Phone: 509-483-6408
www.zappone.com

Zappone shingles are made from either recycled copper or aluminum. Both products contain a concealed nailing flange and a four-way interlocking mechanism. Shingles measure 9-1/8" x 15" with a 8" x 14-1/2" exposure. Aluminum shingles have a Kynar 500 finish in a choice of 6 colors. Recycled aluminum fasteners and accessories are also available. The manufacturer has certified the following recycled-content levels for copper shingles (by weight): total recovered material 85% typical, 85% guaranteed; post-consumer material 75% typical, 75% guaranteed. The manufacturer has certified the following recycled-content levels for aluminum shingles (by weight): total recovered material 100% typical, 100% guaranteed; post-consumer material 100% typical, 100% guaranteed.

Rustic Shingle

Classic Metal Roofing Systems
8510 Industry Park Dr.
P.O. Box 701
Piqua, OH 45356

Toll-free: 800-543-8938
Phone: 937-773-9840
www.classicroof.com

Rustic Shingle is made from an alloy with recycled-aluminum content (mostly beverage cans). The shingles are formed to resemble wood shakes and finished with a baked-on Kynar coating. The Rustic Shingle System consists of 12" x 24" interconnecting panels and matching preformed accessories. The shingles are available in 11 colors. The manufacturer has certified the following recycled-content levels (by weight): post-consumer material 98% typical.

Plastic and Rubber Shingles

Plastic roofing products, like plastic lumber, provide a use for plastics in the solid-waste stream. Products included here appear very durable, but as with plastic lumber, the long-term effects of UV light, and expansion and contraction of the material, are still unknown. Some of these products carry 50-year warranties—longer than those of asphalt shingles. Another environmental benefit of some of these products is their end-of-life recyclability. Rubber roofing shingles and tiles can provide exceptional durability without adding a lot of weight to the roof. Some products made from crumb rubber may use environmentally questionable binders.

Authentic Roof FR

Crowe Building Products Ltd.
116 Burris St.
Hamilton, ON L8M 2J5 Canada

Phone: 905-529-6818
www.authentic-roof.com

Authentic Roof™ was the first slate-look recycled polymer and rubber roofing material. This product's weight is only 25% that of slate and installs quickly. Authentic Roof FR is produced using a proprietary thermoplastic olefin (TPO) and is available in a choice of 5 colors and 3 slate patterns: full, mitered-edge, and beavertail. Authentic shingles have UL Class A, B, or C fire rating; Class 4 hail; pass 110 MPH wind tunnel; and carry a 50-year limited warranty.

Eco-Shake

Re-New Wood, Inc.
103 N.W. 8th St.
P.O. Box 1093
Wagoner, OK 74467

Toll-free: 800-420-7576
Phone: 918-485-5803
www.renewwood.com

Eco-shake® is a roofing shingle made from pre-consumer recycled PVC (recycled content varies due to market availability) and 100% reclaimed wood fibers. The product has the look of a wood shake and is available in three standard colors: umber, teak, and charcoal. Custom colors are also available.

Enviroshake

Wellington Polymer Technology Inc.
650 Riverview Dr., Unit #1
P.O. Box 1462
Chatham, ON N7M 5W8
Canada

Toll-free: 866-423-3302
Phone: 519-380-9265
www.enviroshake.com

Enviroshake® Composite Engineered Roofing shakes are manufactured from 95% recycled material by weight. Approximately 90% of the shake is comprised of roughly equal parts post-industrial recycled plastics and agricultural fiber waste, plus a small percentage of recycled tire rubber. The remaining portion is comprised of proprietary binders. Enviroshake starts out dark brownish grey and ages to a silver-gray that resembles weathered cedar shakes within 3 to 9 months. The 20"-long shakes come in bundles of mixed widths of 12", 8", 7", 6", 5", and 4" and carry a 50-year limited warranty. Custom molded ridge caps are also available.

EuroSlate and EuroShake

GEM, Inc.
9330 48 St. SE
Calgary, AB T2C 2R2 Canada

Phone: 403-215-3333
www.euroslate.ca

EuroSlate and EuroShake are interlocking roofing systems with the look of slate tiles and cedar shakes. They are made with 60-70% recycled tire crumb rubber, plus another 15% of a recycled component that the manufacturer will not divulge. The materials are heat-formed with a binder, also proprietary. The system is lightweight (under 4 lbs/ft2) and recyclable, and the manufacturer is in the process of obtaining Class A fire-resistance certification at this writing. Available colors for EuroSlate include black, slate grey, copper, dark brown, leather, and terra cotta and for EuroShake colors include weathered, black, grey, and redwood. Colors are integral, so those other than black may reduce the overall recycled content of the product. A licensed installer is required. The manufacturer indicates that installation time is significantly reduced over more common options.

Infinity Roof System

Inteq Corp.
35800 Glen Dr.
Eastlake, OH 44095

Phone: 440-953-0550
www.4-inteqcorp.com

Inteq Corp. manufactures the Infinity Roof System in simulated slate, wood shake, and terra cotta tile profiles from recycled HDPE. All three styles have uniform color throughout and come with a 50-year warranty. Slate and wood shake styles have a UL Class A fire rating; Terra Cotta style are rated Class C. Recycled content is 60% pre-consumer, with up to 15% post-consumer content available.

Majestic Slate Tiles

EcoStar
P.O. Box 7000
Carlisle, PA 17013

Toll-free: 800-211-7170
www.ecostar.carlisle.com

Majestic Slate Tiles are 98% post-industrial recycled and recyclable, lightweight shingles made from industrial rubber and plastics. The coloration of Majestic Slate varies slightly, imitating differences in color of natural slate. Preformed ridge slates are also available. EcoStar is a division of Carlisle SynTec, Inc.

Mooroof Recycled-Tire Roofing

Moore Enviro Systems
Box 1459
Squamish, BC V0N 3G0 Canada

Phone: 604-898-5683

Mooroof roof tiles are made of post-consumer recycled tire rubber treads. The sidewalls are removed during the manufacturing process; the tread is installed as roofing tiles with screws, either inside-out or tread-side-up. The tiles, which can be painted if desired, have a class C fire rating and a 50-year warranty.

Ny-Slate

NYCORE
200 Galleria Pkwy., Ste. 2000
Atlanta, GA 30339

Phone: 770-980-0000
www.nycore.com

Ny-Slate, made from 100% recycled post-consumer carpet, is a lightweight, mold- and bacteria-resistant replacement for slate, tile, cedar, or asphalt roofing. The proprietary manufacturing process generates a durable, extruded material that can be cut with standard saws, screwed, nailed, glued, and painted. It doesn't rot, deteriorate, or support mold or insects. According to the manufacturer, no waste is generated in the manufacturing process, and the product is recyclable. A 50-year manufacturer's warranty is offered. Considerations may include thermal expansion and cold-weather brittleness.

RoofRoc Synthetic Slate

RoofRoc Canada Ltd.
19483 Fraser Way
Pitt Meadows, BC V3Y 2V4 Canada

Toll-free: 877-465-5177
Phone: 604-465-5177
www.roofroc.com

RoofRoc is a roofing tile made with 15 – 20% post-consumer recycled HDPE and 80% calcium carbonate (limestone). Closely resembling natural slate in appearance and feel but with only one-third the weight (about 5.75 lbs/sf), it carries a Class A Fire Rating and a 50-year warranty. Its integral colors—black, grey, green, or brown—vary slightly, like natural slate. The standard tiles are approximately 10" x 16" inches, with four profiles to provide a random look. Hip and ridge caps are 5" x 16", with a beveled edge.

Ridge and Soffit Vents

Adequate ventilation of attic spaces helps keep buildings with pitched roofs cooler in the summer and reduces the risks of ice dams in the winter. Some evidence indicates that certain roofing materials experience less thermal stress and last longer on properly ventilated roofs, though this contention is hotly debated. Ridge vents in conjunction with soffit vents create an effective ventilation flow, with air entering at the soffits and exiting at the ridge. The ventilation performance of ridge and soffit vents is superior to either gable-end vents or rooftop ventilators. Insulated roofs require an air channel between the insulation and the roof sheathing. Ventilating underlayment products installed beneath roof shingles and tiles allows the roofing to dry uniformly between rain events—increasing life and minimizing mold growth.

Cedar Breather

Benjamin Obdyke Inc.
400 Babylon Rd.
Ste. A
Horsham, PA 19044

Toll-free: 800-523-5261
Phone: 215-672-7200
www.benjaminobdyke.com

Cedar Breather® is a fire-resistant underlayment for use with wood shingles or shakes, providing continuous airflow between the solid roof deck and shingles. Cedar Breather's 0.27"-thick, 3-dimensional nylon matrix allows the entire underside of the shingle to dry, eliminating excess moisture, preventing thermal cupping and warping, and reducing potential rotting. Cedar Breather eliminates the need for furring strips and comes with a 50-year warranty.

Cobra Ridge Vents

GAF Materials Corp.
1361 Alps Rd.
Wayne, NJ 07470

Toll-free: 800-223-1948
Phone: 973-628-3000
www.gaf.com

GAF's Cobra ridge vents are made from recycled fibers formed into an airy, fibrous mat that, when capped with asphalt shingles, provides a low-profile ridge vent.

Roof Accessories

Many different accessories are used to install roofing materials and facilitate access to the roof surface after it's installed. Products listed here have high recycled content.

Recycled-Rubber Roofing Underlayment

CETCO - Building Materials Group
1500 W. Shure Dr.
Arlington Heights, IL 60004

Toll-free: 800-527-9948
Phone: 847-392-5800
www.cetco.com

StrongSeal™ Recycled Rubberized Products manufactures roofing underlayments from 50% recycled tire crumb rubber, 40% off-spec Dow Engage, and 10% recycled polypropylene. StrongSeal DB (25 mils thick) is the company's nail-down version, and StrongSeal SA (40 mils) is a peel-and-stick version. These products do not contain asphalt and, according to the manufacturer, can be exposed to the elements for a period of 12 months. StrongSeal is backed by an industry leading material warranty.

Rolath

Bedford Technology, LLC
2424 Armour Rd.
P.O. Box 609
Worthington, MN
56187

Toll-free: 800-721-9037
Phone: 507-372-5558
www.plasticboards.com

Rolath is a 1-1/4"-wide strapping product made from recycled plastic. Most of the product's content is waste from Bedford Technology's other manufacturing operations, which uses post-consumer recycled HDPE and LDPE. Rolath is most often used to secure roofing felt but is also effective at securing polyethylene film and building wraps. The manufacturer has certified the following recycled-content levels (by weight): total recovered material 99% typical, 95% guaranteed; post-consumer material 0% typical, 0% guaranteed.

Roof Walkway Pads and Paving Risers

North West Rubber Mats, Ltd.
33850 Industrial Ave.
Abbotsford, BC V2S 7T9 Canada

Toll-free: 800-663-8724
Phone: 604-859-2002
www.northwestrubber.com

North West Rubber's Roof Walkway Pads are made from recycled-tire rubber for use in protecting low-slope membrane roofs. The pads are 3/8", 1/2", or 3/4" thick. Paving Risers, made from 100% recycled-tire-derived styrene butadiene rubber, come in squares (6" x 6" and 3/8" or 5/8" thick) or circles (4" in diameter and 1" thick) that are used to support cement roof pavers above the roof membrane surface.

Roof-Guard Pads

Humane Manufacturing LLC
805 Moore St.
P.O. Box 24
Baraboo, WI 53913

Toll-free: 800-369-6263
Phone: 608-356-8336
www.humanemfg.com

Roof-Guard Pads are made from recycled-tire rubber, are interlocking, and come in sizes ranging from 2' x 3' to 4' x 6'. They are available with either a raised button or impressed pattern. The manufacturer has certified the following recycled-content levels (by weight): total recovered material 93% typical, 93% guaranteed; post-consumer material 93% typical, 93% guaranteed.

Roofing Panels

Roof panels can be made of metal, a composition of fibers and asphalt, or other materials, but they must be durable enough to withstand the ultraviolet radiation and other elements experienced on a roof. Metal roofing, properly installed, is highly durable and readily recyclable at the end of its useful life. Using dissimilar metals for roofing, flashing, and fastening isn't recommended because they're susceptible to galvanic corrosion in the presence of water. Metal is also a preferred material for roofs used in rainwater catchment systems. In northern climates, snow readily slides off metal roofs, avoiding the damage caused by ice dams. In recent years, manufacturers have introduced low-slope metal roofing systems to complement more conventional steep-slope products.

kama Energy Efficient Building Systems

kama Energy Efficient Building Systems, Inc.
6012 Topaz St., Ste. 6
Las Vegas, NV 89120

Phone: 702-451-7155
www.kama-eebs.com

kama Energy Efficient Building Systems™ panels consist of EPS board-stock inside structural galvanized steel framing designed to have no thermal breaks. kama-eebs™ panels can be used as a structural wall, floor, or roof system and can be used with any roof system and any interior and exterior finish. Panels are available in all dimensional lumber sizes and custom thicknesses and are built to meet project specifications.

Met-Tile

Met-Tile
1745 E. Monticello Ct.
Ontario, CA 91761

Phone: 909-947-0311
www.met-tile.com

Met-Tile metal roofing is corrugated and detailed to give the appearance of clay roofing tiles. It is made from recycled steel with a "zincalume" (zinc-alloy) coating for durability and an additional water-based coating in a choice of 10 colors. It comes in lengths from 2' to 25'. Cool Roof panels that meet or exceed Energy Star requirements are available. Met-tile roofs are custom-designed to order.

Ondura

Tallant Industries, Inc.
4900 Ondura Dr.
Fredericksburg, VA 22407

Toll-free: 800-777-7663
Phone: 540-898-7000
www.ondura.com

Ondura corrugated asphalt roofing is composed of 50% asphalt and 50% cellulose fiber (by weight). The cellulose fiber is 100% post-consumer recycled mixed-paper waste. Ondura claims that their product is safe for rainwater collection systems. Ondura sheets measure 48" x 79" (4.5 sheets per square). Ondura tiles measure 48" x 19-3/4" (24 tiles per square). The manufacturer has certified the following recycled-content levels (by weight): total recovered material 50% typical, 50% guaranteed; post-consumer material 50% typical, 50% guaranteed.

Slate Shingles

Natural slate roofing is an excellent product from an environmental standpoint. Besides being a minimally processed material, slate also has superb durability: properly installed slate roofs last 70 to 100 or more years with only minor maintenance. Additionally, slates can easily be salvaged and reused on new building projects. However, they are heavy—proximity to slate quarries and adequately strong roof structures must be considered. Some recycled-plastic shingles are manufactured to look like slate shingles.

Nu-Lok Slate Roofing System

Nu-Lok Roofing Systems
711 South Carson St., Ste. 4
Carson City, NV 89701

Toll-free: 800-946-8565
Phone: 802-287-9701
www.nu-lok.com

The Nu-Lok roofing system is a stainless-steel framework of battens, channels, and clips that holds natural slate or ceramic tile in place, reducing the amount of material needed for roofing installations. The system reduces the weight of the roof, reduces material use, and increases installation options while reducing labor costs. The system comes with a 50-year warranty and, according to the manufacturer, permits installation and repair of slate by standard roofing crews. The system is available with GreenStone Slate from a Vermont slate quarrier.

Reclaimed Natural Salvaged Slate and Clay Tile Roofing

Durable Slate Co.
1050 N. Fourth St.
Columbus, OH 43201

Toll-free: 800-666-7445
Phone: 614-299-5522
www.durableslate.com

Durable Slate Co. stocks well over 600,000 pieces of salvaged slate and 400,000 pieces of salvaged clay tiles. Durable Slate is able to match colors and styles of slate and tile that are no longer produced.

Salvaged Slate and Clay Tile Roofing

Alluvium Construction
200 Lake Shore Dr.
Marlton, NJ 08053

Phone: 856-767-2700
www.historicroofs.com

Alluvium Construction specializes in reclaimed slate and tile roofing in all quantities, types, and colors. Domestic or imported new slate may also be ordered. If purchasing new slate, domestic slate from nearby quarries is recommended.

Salvaged Slate and Clay Tile Roofing

Emack Slate Company, Inc.
9 Office Park Cir., Ste. 120
Birmingham, AL 35223

Phone: 205-879-3424
www.emackslate.com

Emack Slate maintains an inventory of salvaged slate and clay tiles. Domestic or imported new slate may also be ordered. If purchasing new slate, domestic slate from nearby quarries is recommended.

Salvaged Slate and Clay Tile Roofing

Reclaimed Roofs, Inc.
7454 Lancaster Pike #328
Hockessin, DE 19707

Phone: 302-369-9187
www.reclaimedroofs.com

Reclaimed Roofs provides salvaged roofing slates and tiles. Its owner sits on the Board of Directors for the National Slate Association.

Salvaged Slate and Clay Tile Roofing

Renaissance Roofing, Inc.
P.O. Box 5024
Rockford, IL 61125

Toll-free: 800-699-5695
Phone: 815-547-1725
www.claytileroof.com

Renaissance Roofing, Inc. is a supplier of salvaged clay tile and slate roofing materials.

Salvaged Slate and Clay Tile Roofing

The Roof Tile and Slate Company
1209 Carroll St.
Carrollton, TX 75006

Toll-free: 800-446-0220
Phone: 972-446-0005
www.claytile.com

The Roof Tile and Slate Company maintains a large inventory of salvaged slate and tile. New domestic slate and tile are also available.

Salvaged Slate Roofing

Echeguren Slate
1620 Innes Ave.
San Francisco, CA 94124

Phone: 415-206-9343
www.echeguren.com

Echeguren Slate offers salvaged roofing slate in sizes from 8" x 12" to 12" x 24" and in thicknesses of 3/16" to 3/4". Domestic or imported new slate for roofing and flooring may also be ordered. If purchasing new slate, domestic slate from nearby quarries is recommended.

Slate Roofing Shingles

Hilltop Slate Inc.
Rte. 22A
P.O. Box 201
Middle Granville, NY 12804

Phone: 518-642-2270
www.hilltopslate.com

Hilltop Slate, in business since 1948, is a producer of slate roofing shingles with six quarries in New York and Vermont. Hilltop Slate is part of the Slate Products division of the Alfred McAlpine Group and a sister company to Penrhyn, the largest producer of slate products in the world.

Slate Roofing Shingles

Vermont Structural Slate Co., Inc.
3 Prospect St.
P.O. Box 98
Fair Haven, VT 05743

Toll-free: 800-343-1900
Phone: 802-265-4933
www.vermontstructuralslate.com

Vermont Structural Slate has been a producer of slate products since 1859. The company offers roofing shingles in several colors from their Vermont quarries as well as select top quality stones from around the world.

Slate Roofing Shingles

Virginia Slate Company
2471 Goodes Bridge Rd.
Richmond, VA 23224

Toll-free: 888-827-5283
Phone: 804-745-4100
www.virginiaslate.com

The Virginia Slate Company has been producing slate roofing shingles from its Buckingham County quarry since 1860. Slate can be purchased directly from their own quarry. Virginia Slate also offers slate from other producers in a variety of color choices. Their premium roofing slate carries a 100-year limited warranty.

Vermont Slate Roofing Shingles

North Country Slate
8800 Sheppard Ave. E
Toronto, ON M1B 5R4

Toll-free: 800-975-2835
Phone: 416-724-4666
www.northcountryslate.com

North Country Slate offers slate roofing shingles in a variety of colors from Canadian and Vermont quarries in the North Country.

Thermoplastic Membrane Roofing

Single-ply roofing membranes, typically used on large commercial buildings, are also occasionally used on homes and light-commercial buildings for low-slope roof areas and beneath upper-floor walk-out decks. They can be ballasted, mechanically fastened, or fully adhered. Thermoplastic membranes can be heat-welded at seams, minimizing use of solvent-based adhesives. PVC has long been the most common thermoplastic membrane material. For roof membranes, PVC requires plasticizers for flexibility; these chemicals, which may dissipate over time and cause brittleness, are a major cause of membrane failure. PVC is targeted by some environmental groups for its chlorine content and the risk of dioxin production in the event of an unintentional fire or during improperly controlled incineration. Phthalate plasticizers, commonly used with PVC, also may mimic natural hormones in humans and other animals, causing health problems. Concerns about the environmental and health impacts and performance characteristics of PVC have led to the development of thermoplastic olefin (TPO) membranes. Polyolefins are a class of polymers that includes polyethylene and polypropylene. These materials obtain their flexibility through the copolymers rather than plasticizers; however, without the addition of fire retardants, some do not pass necessary fire tests for unballasted applications.

Stevens EP

Stevens Roofing Systems
9 Sullivan Rd.
Holyoke, MA 01040

Toll-free: 800-621-7663
Phone: 413-533-8100
www.stevensroofing.com

Stevens Roofing Systems is one of the world's largest TPO producers. The Stevens EP family of nonhalogenated TPO membranes uses hydrated mineral salts as a fire retardant. Stevens EP membranes are available in nominal 45-, 60-, and 80-mil thickness, and in standard 76.5"-wide rolls. No solvents or adhesives are required, and no known toxins are released if the product is incinerated. The material is available in many colors and can be installed using several attachment methods. White Stevens EP is highly reflective, reducing energy loads and avoiding contributions to the urban heat island effect. It also meets the EPA Energy Star Roof Products guidelines.

UltraPly TPO

Firestone Building Products Company
250 W. 96th St.
Indianapolis, IN 46260

Toll-free: 800-428-4442
Phone: 317-575-7000

Firestone's UltraPly TPO is a heat-weldable, solar-reflective roofing material that meets fire codes without chlorine or other halogenated fire-retardants. This prevents the release of hydrochloric acid (HCl), dioxins, or related compounds in the event of fire.

Wood Shingles and Shakes

Wood shingles and shakes are traditionally and most commonly made from old-growth western red cedar. Although the embodied energy of this product is quite low, the harvesting of western red cedar is, in most cases, unsustainable. If a wood shingle roof is desired and fire-related concerns aren't prohibitive, using certified eastern white cedar shingles, commonly used as wall siding, is an option. Some recycled-plastic shingles are manufactured to look like wood shingles.

Certified PR Shingles

Industries Maibec, Inc.
660 Lenoir St.
Sainte-Foy, QC G1X 3W3 Canada

Toll-free: 800-363-1930
Phone: 418-659-3323
www.maibec.com

PR® Shingles are made from eastern white cedar from the Seven Islands Land Company that is chain-of-custody certified by SCS. Shingles are available in three options: unfinished (natural); kiln-dried and factory-stained in gray, beige, or an unlimited choice of colors; and factory-treated with an oil finish. While most commonly used on walls, they may be appropriate in some roofing applications if installed more thickly.

Reclaimed-Wood Lumber and Products

Armster Reclaimed Lumber Co.
9 Old Post Rd.
Madison, CT 06443

Phone: 203-214-9705
www.woodwood.com

A Reclaimed Lumber Co. salvages wood from old water and wine tanks, mill buildings, bridge timbers, river-recovery log operations, and other sources and custom mills it into a variety of wood products including siding, plank flooring, millwork, paneling, shingles and shakes, stairs parts, and dimension lumber and timber. Available species include red cedar, redwood, beech, black cherry, chestnut, rock maple, red and white oak, Eastern hemlock, Douglas fir, mahogany and Longleaf heart pine. Wood is sourced from all over the country, much of it processed at their Connecticut mill; but the company makes an effort to provide wood that is local to the customer and will make arrangements to process it locally.

Doors

Exterior doors are usually solid wood or foam wrapped in metal, or some other weather-resistant material. Most foam insulation in doors (polyisocyanurate) used to contain ozone-depleting HCFCs, but that is no longer the case.

Most insulated doors are relatively similar in energy efficiency since the market is so competitive; they're distinguished largely by the quality of their weather-stripping and threshold. Insulating values of R-5 to R-7 are common.

Interior doors are usually wood, molded hardboard, or hollow core. Since Lauan plywood comes from nonsustainably harvested rainforest wood, it should be avoided. Molded hardboard is often made with some recycled content and pressed into shape; some hardboard is made with urea-formaldehyde and should be avoided. While solid wood is beautiful and a natural, minimally processed product, clear stock is becoming harder to get and may come from old-growth forests.

An increasing number of manufacturers are offering doors using wood from certified sources. Certification to Forest Stewardship Council—FSC—standards involves third-party evaluation and monitoring of sustainable forestry practices.

Composite Doors

Products listed here are made with agrifiber cores.

Agrifiber Core Architectural Doors

VT Industries, Inc.
1000 Industrial Park
Box 490
Holstein, IA 51025

Toll-free: 800-827-1615
Phone: 712-368-4381
www.vtindustries.com

VT Industries manufactures architectural wood doors with agrifiber particleboard cores. The core material is manufactured from rapidly renewable materials such as wheat straw, soybean straw, and sunflower hulls, with formaldehyde-free binders. Agrifiber-core doors are available in a variety of sizes and finishes, with FSC certified veneer available by special order. The doors can be manufactured as non-fire-rated, or to meet Category-A 20-minute positive pressure fire ratings, with 45-minute and 60-minute fire ratings also available in limited sizes.

GreenDor Agfiber Doors

Lynden Door
2077 Main St.
P.O. Box 528
Lynden, WA 98264

Toll-free: 800-631-3667
Phone: 360-354-5676
www.lyndendoor.com

The Greencor™ core in these doors is made from wheat straw and/or rice straw, rapidly renewable and 100% recovered agricultural fibers. The agrifiber cores contain no added urea-formaldehyde. The LD2500 model has a bonded, sanded core and a maximum size of 4' x 10' (single door) and 8' x 10' (regular and double egress paired doors) for the nonrated doors. It is also available in 20-minute-positive- and neutral-pressure-rated models (PC3, PC5 and PC7) in heights up to 8'. The LD6500 one hour positive pressure category 'A' model comes in a maximum size of 3' x 8' (single door). Not recommended for exterior applications.

Wheatcore Doors and Cabinets

Humabuilt Healthy Building
Solutions
2305-C Ashland St. #511
Ashland, OR 97520

Phone: 541-488-0931
www.humabuilt.com

Humabuilt Wheatcore Doors are available in a wide variety of styles, sizes, wood-veneer species, and paint-grade finishes. The core is made from chopped wheat straw bound with waterproof, nonformaldehyle, MDI binder. These doors contain 85% rapidly renewable resource by volume. Lag-bolt construction at the door edges strengthens the styles and rails. Ultra-low-VOC

water-based adhesives are used for joining components and veneers. The competitively priced doors have a lifetime warranty to the original owner and a 5-year commercial warranty. Humabuilt Wheatcore production cabinets are available in a wide variety of styles, sizes, and wood-veneer species. These production cabinets are KCMA certified.

General Information, Windows and Doors

These listings are for industry representation and ratings organizations for doors and windows.

Industry Representation

National Fenestration Rating Council
6305 Ivy Ln., Ste. 140
Greenbelt, MD 20770

Phone: 301-589-1776
www.nfrc.org

The National Fenestration Rating Council (NFRC), a nonprofit research and educational organization, promulgates standards for determining the energy performance of fenestration products and administers a voluntary, uniform rating and labeling system for communicating the energy performance of windows, doors, curtain wall and storefront systems, and skylights. NFRC provides a freely accessible listing of fenestration products and their related energy performance ratings.

The Efficient Windows Collaborative

The Efficient Windows Collaborative
1850 M St., NW
Suite 600
Washington, DC 20036

Phone: 202-530-2254
www.efficientwindows.org

The Efficient Windows Collaborative is actively involved in promoting energy-efficient windows. A nonprofit coalition comprised of industry, government, and other interested groups, their website provides free resources and information.

Metal Doors and Frames

Even though steel conducts heat more readily than wood, steel entry doors that include foam insulation and are installed in wooden frames with quality weatherstripping generally provide better energy performance than wood entry doors. In choosing an insulated entry door, consider the R-value of the insulation, weatherstripping, and glazing materials.

Contours Steel Doors

Jeld-Wen, Inc.
401 Harbor Isles Blvd.
Klamath Falls, OR 97601

Toll-free: 800-535-3936
Phone: 541-882-3451
www.jeld-wen.com

The Contours steel entry door has an EPS foam core and is available with low-e coated insulating glass. By contrast, most insulation used in entry doors is polyurethane, which is made with ozone-depleting HCFCs. The Contours line replaces Jeld-Wen's Energy Saver line.

Operation and Maintenance of Doors and Frames

Innovative products can prolong the life of doors and improve their energy performance.

GenYDoors Resurfacing System

GenYDoors Inc.
145 Schoolhouse St., Ste. 28
Coquitlam, BC V3K 4X8 Canada

Phone: 604-551-1137
www.genydoors.com

Using a process developed in Finland, GenYDoors resurfaces existing flat-panel interior doors into paneled-door look-alikes—a more environmentally-friendly and cost-effective alternative to purchasing new doors for renovation projects (especially for non-standard sizes) that keeps old doors out of landfills and avoids the environmental debt of making new ones. The door coating and "panel" edges are made with high-impact polystyrene and adhered using a water-based, zero-VOC glue. Three finishes are offered: white, beech, and cherry. The system requires that the existing doors be brought to a GenYDoors shop location.

Wood Doors

Products listed here include doors made from FSC-certified wood or reclaimed wood. As with other wood products, specifying certified-wood doors promotes long-term forest management for the benefit of forest ecosystems, timber resources, and local economies. Reclaimed wood doors, like other reclaimed wood products, don't carry the environmental burdens of recent timber harvesting. Previously harvested woods remilled into wood doors can provide rich colors and beauty generally not available from today's faster-growing timber. From an energy performance perspective, wood entry doors are usually not the best option. Composite entry doors, like steel doors, are available with foam insulation; these doors far outperform traditional solid-wood doors in terms of energy conservation. Composite doors may also be made from recovered and/or recycled materials.

Certified Stave Core Doors

Marshfield DoorSystems
1401 E. 4th St.
P.O. Box 7780
Marshfield, WI 54449

Toll-free: 800-869-3667
Phone: 715-384-2141
www.marshfielddoors.com

Marshfield DoorSystems' Environmental-Class Architectural Wood Doors are FSC-certified stave core doors available for nonrated as well as 20-minute rated applications with either neutral- or positive-pressure fire labels. The composite products in this door do not contain any added urea-formaldehyde. Doors are available with a wide range of veneer options, Styled™ faces, medium-density overlay (MDO), or plastic laminate. Also available is the Enviroclad™ UV factory finish, which uses water-based stains and ultraviolet-cured topcoats, and releases no VOCs. Glue used in the stave core contains 1-5% formaldehyde, but, according to the manufacturer, the doors are encapsulated and will not release any formaldehyde.

Certified Wood Doors

Algoma Hardwoods, Inc.
1001 Perry St.
Algoma, WI 54201

Toll-free: 800-678-8910
Phone: 920-487-5221
www.algomahardwoods.com

Algoma Hardwoods manufactures and supplies FSC-certified interior wood doors for residential and commercial custom orders. Lead time for orders of 20 to 30 doors is 10 weeks. The primary species is red oak, with some birch and cherry available as well.

Certified Wood Doors

Eggers Industries
1 Eggers Dr.
P.O. Box 88
Two Rivers, WI 54241

Phone: 920-793-1351
www.eggersindustries.com

Eggers Industries manufactures architectural wood doors in flush as well as stile-and-rail styles that are SmartWood-certified according to the standards of the Forest Stewardship Council. The doors are certified by partial-content rules to contain over 70% certified wood. Current certified offerings include nonrated and 20-minute doors, negative or positive pressure. Some products, such as the wood composite doors, contain urea-formaldehyde resins; check with the manufacturer.

Certified Wood Doors

VT Industries, Inc.
1000 Industrial Park
Box 490
Holstein, IA 51025

Toll-free: 800-827-1615
Phone: 712-368-4381
www.vtindustries.com

VT Industries offers a line of architectural wood doors certified by SmartWood according to the standards of the Forest Stewardship Council.

Interior and Exterior Doors

Alternative Timber Structures, Inc.
1054 Rammell Mt. Rd.
Tetonia, ID 83452

Phone: 208-456-2711
www.alternativetimberstructures.com

The Bead & Batten Door specializes in custom-building of doors in unusual sizes and thicknesses from reclaimed and new woods.

Purekor Platinum Door Core

Panel Source International
23 Rayborn Cres., 2nd Fl.
St. Albert, AB T8N 5B9 Canada

Toll-free: 877-464-7246
Phone: 780-458-1007
www.panelsource.net

Purekor's FSC-certified particleboard door core contains no added urea formaldehyde, is made from 100% pre-consumer recycled wood fiber, and a contains a minimum of 17.5% FSC-certified wood fiber to meet FSC labeling requirements. This product meets the ANSI LD 2 specification for door core; has an average density of approximately 32 lbs per cubic foot; is a available in any thicknesses from 1" to 2"; and can be delivered cut to size.

Reclaimed-Wood Building Products

Vintage Log and Lumber, Inc.
Glen Ray Rd.
Rt. 1, Box 2F
Alderson, WV 24910

Toll-free: 877-653-5647
Phone: 304-445-2300
www.vintagelog.com

Vintage Log and Lumber salvages the materials in log cabins and timber-frame barns in Kentucky, Ohio, Pennsylvania, and West Virginia. The company's inventory includes salvaged redwood, chestnut, oak, pine, and poplar boards, beams, flooring, and split rails. They also sell complete hand-hewn log cabins and timber-frame barns, as well as architectural salvage items.

Reclaimed-Wood Carriage Doors

Real Carriage Door Company
9808 44th Ave NW
Ste. 102
Gig Harbor, WA 98332

Phone: 253-238-6908
www.realcarriagedoors.com

The "Green Line" of doors from Real Carriage Door includes garage or entry doors made from reclaimed wood. Reclaimed-wood doors are made from re-milled aged warehouse beams.

Reclaimed-Wood Products

Albany Woodworks, Inc.
P.O. Box 729
Albany, LA 70711

Toll-free: 1-800-551-1282
Phone: 225-567-1155
www.albanywoodworks.com

Albany Woodworks mills reclaimed woods, including heart pine and heart cypress, into various architectural woodwork products, including flooring, timber, and stair parts. Doors are also offered.

Reclaimed-Wood Products

Crossroads Recycled Lumber
57839 Rd. 225
P.O. Box 928
North Fork, CA 93643

Toll-free: 888-842-3201
Phone: 559-877-3645
www.crossroadslumber.com

Crossroads Recycled Lumber sells raw and remilled salvaged Douglas fir, sugar pine, ponderosa pine, cedar, and redwood lumber, timbers, flooring, paneling, and siding. They also offer doors made from this wood.

Recycled-Content Wood Doors

Executive Door Company
3939 W. Clarendon
Phoenix, AZ 85019

Phone: 602-272-8076
www.executivedoor.com

Executive Door Company manufactures Environmental residential and commercial interior and exterior doors from medium-density fiberboard (MDF). The doors are constructed of 100% recovered and recycled wood fibers with at least 30% post-industrial recycled waste content. Executive Door offers a lifetime warranty against splitting, cracking, or warping.

Windows

Windows are one of the most high-tech products in residential construction. Since the early 1980s, the energy performance of typical windows has increased by over 50%, the result of both improvements in glazing and in frame construction. The National Fenestration Rating Council (NFRC) publishes the energy performance of certified window products; in some states, manufacturers are required to label their windows with the NFRC's rating. These ratings are like the EPA mileage rating for cars—they may not provide actual energy consumption in a particular application, but are useful for comparison.

The emergence of energy-efficient windows is a key part of a breakthrough in the overall design of houses and light-commercial buildings. Glazed surfaces no longer have to lose a lot of heat or feel cold in winter, so heating systems can be much smaller and less expensive. For example, heating elements are no longer required beneath windows to compensate for the drafts and cold surfaces that windows used to generate. In a well-designed, highly energy-efficient house, central heating may no longer be necessary at all—though air distribution systems are still important to ensure good indoor air quality.

Low-e glass coatings, which increase the R-value of standard double-glazing from 2 to about 3, are gaining in market share each year. The premium of 10–20% for low-e easily pays for itself in a few years in most applications. The added benefit is a warmer window surface that's more comfortable to be near both in cold weather and in very hot weather. Double low-e and HeatMirror™ coatings on suspended films are available in premium windows, and can increase the center-of-glass insulating value up to R-9.

By careful selection of low-e coatings, windows can be "tuned" to optimize the performance of a structure—balancing heat loss, solar gain, and visible light transmission through the glass. In hot climates, coatings that transmit less solar gain should generally be preferred. In cold climates, where solar gain can be beneficial in winter, glazing that transmits more solar energy is preferable on the south side of a building. On the east and west, less solar gain is preferable even in cold climates, because solar gain is greatest on these orientations during the summer, when air conditioning is likely to be used.

Use of an inert, low-conductivity gas in the space between layers of glazing is another way to improve thermal performance. Most low-e windows have argon gas fill; some super-energy-efficient windows have krypton or a mix of argon and krypton between the glazing layers.

Although standard for many years, aluminum windows are disappearing from most cold-climate markets. If aluminum frames are used, they should be constructed with a *thermal break* between the inner and outer surfaces to improve energy performance. Aluminum windows are rapidly being replaced by vinyl frames.

Vinyl frames are much better than aluminum in terms of thermal performance, but there are some environmental concerns associated with the production and eventual disposal of PVC (polyvinyl chloride). Vinyl windows vary greatly in quality; many have weather-sealing problems over the life of the window due to the expansion and contraction of the plastic. They're better suited to sliders and double hung windows than casements, because those styles are prone to warping and sagging. There are also concerns about the PVC resin itself and various compounds that are added to it to provide UV stability, flexibility, and flame resistance.

Wood windows are still the standard for energy efficiency. Vinyl or aluminum cladding adds value in its low maintenance qualities. Wood window manufacturers are facing increasing difficulty in finding affordable, knot-free material from which to manufacture their product; some are using finger-jointed material with an interior coating and exterior cladding.

Other energy-efficient frame materials include fiberglass, with or without foam insulation in the hollow channels, and composites such as a combination of recycled vinyl and wood fibers.

With any window materials, durability of the edge seals and spacers that separate the layers of glass is extremely important, as failure of this seal will cause condensation inside the window (fogging), and the loss of any low-conductivity gas fill.

Composite Windows

Composite windows come in two basic types: fiberglass, and wood/plastic composite. Fiberglass has some distinct advantages over wood, vinyl, and metal for window frame and sash construction. As high-quality wood resources become scarce, fiberglass (a composite of polyester resin and glass fibers) is likely to become more common because of its energy performance and durability. Pultruded fiberglass frame members have a hollow profile that's usually insulated with fiberglass or polyurethane foam. Because the conduction through window frames is a significant source of heat loss, insulated fiberglass frames are an attractive option. The coefficient of thermal expansion of fiberglass is low, very similar to that of glass; limited differential expansion and contraction between the sash and glazing materials puts less stress on the glazing's edge seals. Durability of fiberglass as an exterior material is also good. Most fiberglass windows have factory-applied, baked-on coatings and can be repainted. To be included in GreenSpec, fiberglass and other composite window lines must include products with NFRC unit U-factors of 0.30 or lower.

Alpen Fiberglass Windows

Alpen Glass
5400 Spine Rd.
Boulder, CO 80301

Toll-free: 800-882-4466
Phone: 303-530-1150
www.alpeninc.com

In its high-performance fiberglass windows, Alpen Energy Group uses a combination of suspended low-emissivity (low-e) Heat Mirror films, low-e coatings directly deposited on the glass, low-iron glass (which increases visible light transmittance), low-conductivity gas fill (including krypton and xenon), pultruded fiberglass frames insulated with vacuum silica aerogel packets, and low-conductivity glazing spacers. These 1-3/8"-thick custom windows are available with a wide range of properties to meet different needs. Their highest performing windows have three suspended films (each with low-e coatings on both sides) and provide R-20 center-of-glass insulating value (unit R-value of 10, U-factor 0.10)—the highest performance of any window in the world. The majority of the company's products are used in projects in which different glazings are used for different wall orientations.

High-Performance Fiberglass Windows

Accurate Dorwin Company
1535 Seel Ave.
Winnipeg, MB R3T 1C6 Canada

Toll-free: 888-982-4640
Phone: 204-982-8370
www.accuratedorwin.com

Accurate Dorwin's pultruded fiberglass windows are double- or triple-glazed with one or two low-e coatings, extruded silicone spacers, and argon-filled cavities. U-factors for Accurate Dorwin windows range as low as 0.15 (corresponding to an R-value of 6.7).

High-Performance Fiberglass Windows

Comfort Line Ltd.
5500 Enterprise Blvd.
Toledo, OH 43612

Toll-free: 800-522-4999
Phone: 419-729-8520
www.comfortlineinc.com

Comfort Line manufactures fiberglass pultruded frame windows with multi-cavity, sealed-frame members. Comfort Line's most advanced glazing option is a triple-glazed, krypton-filled panel with two low-e coatings and warm edge spacers. All Comfort Line windows and doors are qualified by Energy Star® and NFRC.

High-Performance Fiberglass Windows

Duxton Windows & Doors
10 Higgins Ave.
Winnipeg, MB R3B 0A2 Canada

Phone: 204-339-6456
www.duxtonwindows.com

Duxton Windows & Doors manufactures advanced, high-performance windows and doors with pultruded-fiberglass frames. Glazing options include multiple low-e coatings on glass, suspended Heat Mirror films, and a 90:10 mixture of krypton and argon gas-fill. The highest-performance windows easily meet GreenSpec criteria for fiberglass windows, though NFRC unit U-factor testing has not been completed. The company lists center-of-glass R-values as high as 7.6.

High-Performance Fiberglass Windows

Fibertec Window & Door Mfg.
280 Bowes Rd.
Concord, ON L4K 1J9 Canada

Toll-free: 888-232-4956
Phone: 905-660-7102
www.fibertec.com

Fibertec™ fiberglass windows have foam-insulated frames and can include Heat Mirror™ or low-e coatings, argon gas-fill, and warm-edge spacers. Fibertec's Santoprene™ weather stripping is applied in three locations for more effective sealing against air infiltration.

High-Performance Fiberglass Windows

Inline Fiberglass Ltd.
30 Constellation Ct.
Toronto, ON M9W 1K1 Canada

Toll-free: 866-566-5656
Phone: 416-679-1171
www.inlinefiberglass.com

Inline Fiberglass, a world leader in pultrusion technology, manufactures fiberglass windows and doors. A number of units meet or exceed the 0.30 U-value threshold for GreenSpec with some quadruple-glazed, krypton-filled units rating as low as 0.18. The company also licenses their pultrusion technology to other manufacturers.

High-Performance Fiberglass Windows

Thermotech Fiberglass Fenestration
2121 Thermotech Rd.
Carp, ON K0A 1L0 Canada

Toll-free: 888-930-9445
Phone: 613-839-6158
www.thermotechfiberglass.com

Thermotech's most energy-efficient windows include silicone foam Super Spacers™, triple panes, and low-e glazing (Pilkington or AFG), resulting in some of the highest-performance windows in North America (many glazing options produce window unit U-factors below 0.20). Thermotech promotes the use of different glazings on different orientations to optimize energy performance. The company offers up to 4 different IG (insulating glass) options per project. Other features include: 15% post-industrial recycled-content fiberglass frames, near-zero-solvent waterborne paint, offcut-sourced polystyrene insulation, and river-bottom-recovered pine jamb extensions.

High-Performance Windows

Milgard Manufacturing, Inc.
965 54th Ave. E
Tacoma, WA 98424

Toll-free: 800-562-8444
Phone: 253-922-6030
www.milgard.com

Milgard is the largest window manufacturer in the West and produces vinyl, thermally broken aluminum, pultruded fiberglass windows, and fiberglass-clad wood windows. All Milgard windows are custom-manufactured, and the company offers a wide range of glazing options, including several that meet the GreenSpec energy performance criteria.

Integrity Fiberglass Windows

Integrity Windows and Doors - Marvin Marketing Office
2020 Silver Bell Rd., Ste. 15
Eagan, MN 55122

Toll-free: 888-419-0076
Phone: 218-386-1430
www.integritywindows.com

Integrity™ windows from Marvin feature exterior frame and sash components made from Ultrex™, a pultruded composite of fiberglass and polyester resin. Solid wood jambs are bonded to the interior of the Ultrex frame, giving the windows a natural-wood appearance. Integrity's glazing options are limited to low-e2 with argon insulating glass, but a few products meet the GreenSpec 0.30 U-factor threshold.

Renewal by Andersen Windows

Andersen Windows
9900 Jamaica Ave. S
Cottage Grove, MN 55016

Toll-free: 877-773-6392
Phone: 651-264-4000
www.renewalbyandersen.com

Andersen's Renewal by Andersen®
line of windows features frames

and sashes made from Fibrex® material, a post-industrial wood and waste-PVC composite with a coextruded virgin PVC exterior coating. High Performance™ Low-E4™ glass from Cardinal IG is standard in all products. The highest-performance Renewal by Andersen® windows in the NFRC Certified Products Directory have unit U-factors of 0.29 and qualify for GreenSpec because of their recycled content.

Domed Unit Skylights

There have been a number of innovations in the area of metal-framed skylights. Active skylighting systems rely on reflectors and sun-tracking mechanisms to increase daylight entry; these systems boost daylighting primarily during early-morning and late-afternoon hours when the sun is low and little direct sunlight typically enters a conventional skylight. Another technology, prismatic skylights, refracts sunlight to boost daylighting performance.

Natural Lighting Systems

DayStar Systems, LLC
14164 State Route 4
Campbell Hill, IL 62916

Toll-free: 866-732-9782
Phone: 618-426-1868

DayStar High Performance Natural Lighting Systems gather natural light and diffuse it into a broad, even pattern. These skylights feature a clear acrylic outer dome with an inner lens that minimizes winter heat loss and summer heat gain, and an insulated, highly reflective light shaft. Ceiling lenses include full spectrum or soft white. Typical installation for full illumination requires 1.75–3.5 percent of roof area, depending on the application. DayStar offers complete packages with nearly 150 curb styles and sizes designed to fit shingle, metal, or membrane roofs with pitches from 0 to 12/12. DayStar will manufacture to custom specifications.

General Information, Windows and Doors

These listings are for industry representation and ratings organizations for doors and windows.

Industry Representation

National Fenestration Rating Council
6305 Ivy Ln., Ste. 140
Greenbelt, MD 20770

Phone: 301-589-1776
www.nfrc.org

The National Fenestration Rating Council (NFRC), a nonprofit research and educational organization, promulgates standards for determining the energy performance of fenestration products and administers a voluntary, uniform rating and labeling system for communicating the energy performance of windows, doors, curtain wall and storefront systems, and skylights. NFRC provides a freely accessible listing of fenestration products and their related energy performance ratings.

The Efficient Windows Collaborative

The Efficient Windows Collaborative
1850 M St., NW
Suite 600
Washington, DC 20036

Phone: 202-530-2254
www.efficientwindows.org

The Efficient Windows Collaborative is actively involved in promoting energy-efficient windows. A nonprofit coalition comprised of industry, government, and other interested groups, their website provides free resources and information.

Glazing

Specifying glazing is common in commercial building applications and with some residential window products. The high-performance glazings listed here help control heating and cooling loads. Careful selection of glazing for specific applications (orientation, building type, etc.) is critical for optimum energy performance and building comfort.

Comfort E2, Comfort Ti, and Solar Glass

AFG Industries, Inc.
1400 Lincoln St.
Kingsport, TN 37660

Toll-free: 800-251-0441
Phone: 423-229-7200
www.afgglass.com

AFG Industries is a leading manufacturer of float glass and solar glass products. AFG manufactures Comfort E2 and Comfort Ti for the residential market and several specialized solar glass products for PV, passive, and active solar applications.

Heat Mirror Glass

Alpen Glass
5400 Spine Rd.
Boulder, CO 80301

Toll-free: 800-882-4466
Phone: 303-530-1150
www.alpeninc.com

Alpen Glass manufactures insulating glass with Heat Mirror™-coated films suspended between two panes of glass filled with argon or krypton gas. Alpen offers high-performance glazings with 99.5% reduction in UV transmission.

LoE2 and LoE3

Cardinal Glass Industries
775 Prairie Center Dr., Ste. 200
Eden Prairie, MN 55344

Toll-free: 800-843-1484
Phone: 952-229-2600
www.cardinalcorp.com

LoE2 is a soft-coat, low-e glazing. When combined with clear glass in a double-pane unit, thermal heat flow is significantly reduced, as is solar heat gain. In applications where passive solar heating is desired, a glazing with a higher solar heat gain coefficient is preferable. LoE3 366 ("Low-e cubed 366") offers a solar heat gain coefficient as low as many tinted low-e glazings while the visible light transmittance is nearly as high as the widely used LoE2 product. Cardinal is the largest manufacturer of coated glass for residential windows in North America. LoE3 glass is used by window and door manufacturers such as Milgard, Weather Shield, Kolbe & Kolbe, and Atrium - sometimes under their own tradenames, such as SunCoatMAX™ and Zo-e-shield™.

Pilkington Energy Advantage

Pilkington NA
811 Madison Ave.
P.O. Box 799
Toledo, OH 43697

Toll-free: 800-221-0444
Phone: 419-247-3731
www.pilkington.com

Pilkington® Energy Advantage is a hard-coat (pyrolytic), low-e glass with an emissivity of 0.15. In a double-pane unit, a SHGC of 0.7 is achieved. This is an excellent glazing for use in passive solar buildings on southern orientations where solar gain needs to be high.

SageGlass Insulated Glass Unit

SAGE Electrochromics, Inc.
One Sage Way
Faribault, MN 55021

Phone: 507-331-4848
www.sage-ec.com

SAGE Electrochromics manufactures SageGlass®, an electronically tintable exterior glazing that blocks solar heat gain while providing glare control and preserving views. SageGlass incorporates durable thin-film ceramic coatings and uses 0.28 W/ft2 to switch the glass from clear to tinted state and 0.1 W/ft2 to maintain a darkened state. Used with typical clear glass to fabricate an insulated unit, the tinting reduces the visible transmittance from 62% to 3.5%, while reducing the solar heat gain coefficient (SHGC) from 0.48 to 0.09. SAGE is partnering with window, skylight, and curtainwall manufacturers to produce efficient commercial and residential products that can be used to provide energy savings, control peak electricity demand, and possibly downsize HVAC systems, while improving occupant comfort and control.

Superglass Quad with Heat Mirror

Southwall Technologies
3788 Fabian Way
Palo Alto, CA 94303

Toll-free: 800-365-8794
Phone: 650-798-1200
www.southwall.com

Southwall developed and manufactures solar radiation control films, including Heat Mirror® with a range of performance properties. These films are fabricated into insulated-glass units (IGUs) and laminated glass by approximately 30 manufacturers in North America. Southwall's highest-performing Superglass® incorporates two Heat Mirror suspended films and three gas-filled cavities between dual panes of glass. Center-of-glass R-values above R-10 can be achieved with dual Heat Mirror films and low-conductivity gas-fill.

Metal-Framed Skylights

There have been a number of innovations in the area of metal-framed skylights. Active skylighting systems rely on reflectors and sun-tracking mechanisms to increase daylight entry; these systems boost daylighting primarily during early-morning and late-afternoon hours when the sun is low and little direct sunlight typically enters a conventional skylight. Another technology, prismatic skylights, refracts sunlight to boost daylighting performance.

SunOptics Skylights

SunOptics Skylights
6201 27th St.
Sacramento, CA 95822

Toll-free: 800-289-4700
Phone: 916-395-4700
www.sunoptics.com

SunOptics manufactures prismatic skylights in which tiny prisms are embedded in the skylight glazing to refract visible light into the skylight, while reflecting infrared and UV light to keep it out. SunOptics skylights transmit more visible light than conventional white-acrylic skylights. Available single-, double-, triple-, and quad-glazed, they are designed with thermal breaks in the frames to reduce heat loss and prevent condensation. SunOptics also makes photo-cell-controlled louvers.

Velux SageGlass Skylights

Velux
450 Old Brickyard Rd.
Greenwood, SC 29648

Toll-free: 800-888-3589
www.veluxusa.com

Velux offers skylights with SageGlass®, a dynamically tintable, electrochromic glazing that blocks glare and UV and controls solar heat gain while preserving views. The touch of a button activates an electrical current to switch the glass from clear to tinted state and to maintain a darkened state. A house with SageGlass skylights uses less energy than a single 40-watt light bulb on a daily basis while providing energy savings and heat and glare control. SageGlass technology is available for a range of skylight models and sizes. There is a substantial up-charge for this glazing.

Plastic Windows

Like vinyl, ABS is very low-maintenance. Because there's no chlorine in ABS, there's no risk of dioxin generation during an accidental fire or incineration at the end of the product's life.

Accent High-Performance Vinyl Windows

Accent Windows, Inc.
12300 Pecos St.
Westminster, CO 80234

Toll-free: 888-284-3948
Phone: 303-420-2002
www.accentwindows.com

Accent Windows is a Colorado manufacturer of vinyl replacement windows. The company uses low-e glass coatings (LoElite™) or suspended Heat Mirror™ films, along with argon or argon/krypton gas-fills to achieve some of the highest energy performance of any replacement windows. Unit U-factors are as low as 0.17. All Accent windows are custom-manufactured, so the dimensions will be optimized to the window opening. The company serves the mountain region from Billings, Montana to Albuquerque, New Mexico as well as Missouri and Illinois.

Gilkey High-Performance Vinyl Windows

Gilkey Window Company, Inc.
3625 Hauck Rd.
Cincinnati, OH 45241

Toll-free: 800-878-7771
Phone: 513-769-4527
www.gilkey.com

Gilkey Window manufactures custom vinyl replacement windows for Ohio, Kentucky, and the Upper Midwest. The company offers a wide range of glazing options and actively promotes super-high-performance windows as well as the strategy of using glazings specifically "tuned" to the orientation. Among the glazing options is a "quad" option with both a low-e coating on two glass panes and a suspended Heat Mirror® coating, with krypton gas-fill and warm-edge glass spacers. The NFRC Certified Products Directory lists products with unit U-factors as low as 0.19. Company sales reps carry Btu meters to explain and demonstrate energy savings potential to prospective customers, and a 20% energy savings guarantee is provided with certain windows.

Gorell High-Performance Vinyl Windows

Gorell Enterprises, Inc. Windows & Doors
1380 Wayne Ave.
Indiana, PA 15701

Toll-free: 800-9-GORELL
Phone: 724-465-1800
www.gorell.com

Gorell was founded as a manufacturer of vinyl windows in 1994. The company offers a number of energy-conserving glazing options for replacement and new-construction applications; many meet the GreenSpec criteria for vinyl windows. All Gorell windows feature heavy-duty construction with four-point fusion welding and the PPG Intercept spacer system. Gorell's best-performing glass is Thermal Master III, a triple-glazed unit with two low-e coatings and krypton gas-fill. The highest-performance Gorell products in the NFRC Certified Products Directory have unit U-factors as low as 0.17. More than 92% of Gorell's product line qualifies for the Energy Star label.

High-Performance Non-PVC Thermoplastic Windows

Thermal Line Windows, Inc.
3601 30th Ave. NW
P.O. Box 579
Mandan, ND 58554

Toll-free: 800-662-1832
Phone: 701-663-1832
www.tlwindows.com

A regional company (12-state Midwestern region) founded in 1984, Thermal Line produces both vinyl (PVC) windows and windows made from an engineered ABS plastic called Compozit™. This is a thermoplastic material engineered by GE Plastics division under the name Cycolac/Geloy. Performance is similar to PVC, and the material contains no chlorine. The highest-performance Compozit windows are triple-glazed with two low-e coatings and krypton gas-fill; they have NFRC-listed unit U-factors as low as 0.20 for residential-sized windows and 0.19 for commercial.

High-Performance Windows

Milgard Manufacturing, Inc.
965 54th Ave. E
Tacoma, WA 98424

Toll-free: 800-562-8444
Phone: 253-922-6030
www.milgard.com

Milgard is the largest window manufacturer in the West and produces vinyl, thermally broken aluminum, pultruded fiberglass windows, and fiberglass-clad wood windows. All Milgard windows are custom-manufactured, and the company offers a wide range of glazing options, including several that meet the GreenSpec energy performance criteria.

High-Performance Wood and Vinyl Windows

Paramount Windows, Inc.
105 Panet Rd.
Winnipeg, MB R2J 0S1 Canada

Toll-free: 800-519-0508
Phone: 204-233-4966
www.paramountwindows.com

Paramount Windows, founded in 1948, has been promoting highly energy-efficient windows for decades. The company introduced insulated-glass windows in 1957 and triple-glazed windows (Canada's first) in 1962. The company primarily produces wood and aluminum-clad wood windows but also offers vinyl windows—mostly for the replacement market. Several glazing options are available: EnerPlus 4 is triple-glazed with one low-e coating, argon gas-fill in one of the interpane spaces, and two energy-saving spacers. EnerPlus 6 is triple-glazed with two low-e coatings, and argon gas-fill in both interpane spaces. The lowest NFRC U-factor ratings are 0.22. The company's wood supplier has FSC certification, so FSC-certified wood windows can be special-ordered for larger jobs.

Kensington High-Performance Vinyl Windows

Kensington Windows, Inc.
1136 Industrial Park Dr.
Vandergrift, PA 15690

Toll-free: 800-444-4972
Phone: 724-845-8133
www.kensingtonwindows.com

Kensington manufactures fairly high-end vinyl replacement windows sold primarily through dealers east of the Rocky Mountains. The company emphasizes energy efficiency and offers dozens of products that exceed the GreenSpec criteria for super energy performance. The highest-performance windows have two panes with low-e coatings, plus a suspended Heat Mirror film (for a total of three low-e coatings), krypton gas-fill, and foam-filled vinyl frames.

Paradigm High-Performance Vinyl Windows

Paradigm Windows
P.O. Box 10109
Portland, ME 04104

Toll-free: 877-994-6369
Phone: 207-878-9701
www.paradigmwindows.com

Paradigm's premium double-hung and casement windows have unit U-values that meet the GreenSpec standard of .20 for vinyl windows. The highest-performing windows have three glazing layers with krypton fill and multiple low-e films. These windows meet American Architectural Manufacturers Association (AAMA) standards for structural performance, and air and water infiltration.

Schuco Homecraft High-Performance Vinyl Windows

SCHÜCO, LP
240 Pane Rd.
Newington, CT 06111

Toll-free: 877-472-4826
Phone: 860-666-0505
www.schuco-usa.com

Schuco Homecraft is the U.S. division of a large European manufacturer that has been producing windows for 40 years. The company offers triple-glazed windows with two low-e coatings and krypton gas-fill. They also use a unique thermoplastic edge spacer, which the company claims outperforms conventional metal spacers both in terms of energy performance and durability.

Stanek High-Performance Vinyl Windows

Stanek Vinyl Windows Corp.
4570 Willow Pkwy.
Cuyahoga Heights, OH 44125

Toll-free: 800-962-5512
Phone: 216-341-7700
www.stanekwindows.com

Stanek Windows is predominantly a regional manufacturer of vinyl replacement windows serving the Cleveland, Ohio area, though the company now sells product in some other areas of the East and Midwest. Included in its offerings are a number of remarkably high-energy-performance windows, including System 9 and System 13—the latter are 1-1/8"-thick quad-glazed windows with two Heat Mirror® suspended films, a low-e coating on one of the panes of glass, and krypton gas-fill. NFRC-based unit U-factors as low as 0.17 are listed in the NFRC Certified Products Directory. Styles offered include casement, double-hung, bays, bows, sliders, and patio doors. All products are custom-fabricated using reinforced vinyl extrusions.

Thermal Industries High-Performance Vinyl Windows

Thermal Industries, Inc.
5450 Second Ave.
Pittsburgh, PA 15207

Toll-free: 800-245-1540
www.ThermalIndustries.com

Thermal Industries, a subsidiary of the Atrium Company, is a Pittsburgh-based manufacturer of custom vinyl replacement windows serving many regions of the eastern U.S. The company's highest-performance glass package, Super Peak Performance™ Glass, has three layers of glass, two low-e coatings, krypton gas-fill, and low-conductivity warm-edge spacers between the panes of glass. The NFRC Certified Products Directory lists unit U-factors as low as 0.18.

UniFrame Maxuus 10

Great Lakes Window, Inc.
P.O. Box 1896
Toledo, OH 43603

Toll-free: 800-666-0000
www.greatlakeswindow.com

The UniFrame line of vinyl replacement windows from Great Lakes Window includes a Maxuus 10 option in every configuration (double-hung, slider, casement, awning, etc.). The Maxuus 10 option provides triple glazing with two low-e coatings and krypton gas fill, for a whole-unit U-value of 0.19 to 0.21, depending on the configuration. All UniFrame windows are made from unplasticized, impact-resistant polyvinyl chloride (uiPVC) frames with polyurethane foam insulation in the cores.

Roof Windows

Daylighting serves several green purposes. Studies show that natural daylighting can improve the general well-being of building occupants as well as provide such measurable benefits as increased workplace productivity and enhanced school performance. The energy benefit from daylighting generally comes from both savings in electric lighting and cooling-load avoidance. Not all daylighting systems save energy—careful energy modeling can help determine energy benefits in particular applications. As with window and glazing products, the energy performance of skylights and roof windows varies greatly among different products and should be carefully considered.

Roof Windows and Skylights

Insula-Dome
83 Horseblock Rd.
Yaphank, NY 11980

Phone: 631-924-7890
www.insula-dome.com

Insul-Dome skylights have double-glazed, low-e, argon-filled glazing. This product was formerly manufactured by Roto-Frank of America.

Roof Windows and Skylights

Velux
450 Old Brickyard Rd.
Greenwood, SC 29648

Toll-free: 800-888-3589
www.veluxusa.com

Velux roof windows and skylights are solid-wood framed and come standard with low-e2 coatings and argon gas-fill. Velux products are EPA Energy Star®-approved.

Solar-Control Window Film

Solar-control plastic window films have been used for decades as a retrofit measure to control solar heat-gain through windows. Dye-tinted films attempt to prevent solar gain by absorbing both light and heat, and are better at reducing light levels than heat gain. Spectrally-selective films rely on reflectivity and emissivity rather than absorption, blocking the infrared spectrum responsible for almost half the heat of sunlight while allowing much of the visible light through. Use of these films in commercial applications can result in rapid payback through lowered cooling costs. Always check with the window manufacturer before applying window films, or having them applied professionally; application of films may void the window's warranty.

Scotchtint Plus All Season Films

3M Specified Construction Products Department
3M Center 223-2S-24
St. Paul, MN 55144

Toll-free: 800-480-1704
www.3m.com

Scotchtint™ Plus All Season Films from 3M offer the same solar gain and glare control as their popular Scotchtint Sun Control Window Film line—but with cold-weather heat loss reduction ratings of 23% for silver, and 30% for amber, thanks to a low-e coating that reflects interior heat back to the interior. A ten-year commercial and governmental warranty is offered; residential applications are given a lifetime warranty.

V-Kool Window Film

V-KOOL, Inc.
13805 West Rd., Ste. 400
Houston, TX 77041

Toll-free: 800-786-2468
Phone: 713-856-8333
www.v-kool-usa.com

V-Kool® offers virtually colorless, spectrally-selective films that block up to 55% of solar gain while maintaining high optical clarity. Minimal visible light reflection avoids the "mirror" effect. V-Kool holds global distribution rights for the film, which is manufactured by Southwall Technologies. It had previously been marketed by Southwall as XIR, and by V-Kool as Solis. This film has been most widely used in OEM laminated automotive windows overseas, with millions of installations in place. A ten year-commercial warranty is offered, and a lifetime residential warranty.

Tubular Skylights

Tubular skylights, or light pipes, allow daylight to be transferred from the roof to occupied space below, even when there's a considerable distance involved (such as through an attic). The system is composed of three parts: an acrylic rooftop dome and flashing, a reflective light pipe, and an interior diffuser. With most of these products, the reflective tube can bend around obstructions, or connect nonaligned roof and ceiling penetrations. Some products include other features such as compact-fluorescent lights or ventilation fans.

Brighten Up and SolaMaster Tubular Skylights

Solatube International, Inc.
2210 Oak Ridge Way
Vista, CA 92081

Toll-free: 888-765-2882
Phone: 760-477-1120
www.solatube.com

Solatube is the world's leading manufacturer of tubular skylights. For residential and smaller commercial applications, the Brighten Up® series is available in 10" and 14" units and features Solatube's patented Spectralight® Infinity tubing material, and two patented technologies to intercept and collect low angle sunlight. The SolaMaster® Series, featuring a 21" unit, is suitable for commercial buildings and larger residential areas and accommodates a wide variety of ceilings. Installing one 21" SolaMaster can displace approximately two traditional light fixtures, each using three F032T8 fluorescent lamps, according to the manufacturer. Seamless one-piece flashing is available in both the Brighten Up and SolaMaster series. All Solatube skylights are offered with optional light kits, and the 10" Brighten Up unit is available with an optional ventilation fan. A motorized "Daylight Dimmer" butterfly baffle, which is controlled by a wall-mounted switch, is also available for all sizes, adjusting the skylight's output from 100% to approximately 2%.

HUVCO Skylights

HUVCO, Daylighting Solutions
P.O. Box 3
Rohrersville, MD 21779

Toll-free: 800-832-6116
Phone: 301-432-0678
www.huvco.com

HUVCO's High Performance Daylighting System utilizes a thermally broken, dual-prismatic dome and a highly reflective, insulated light well. Prismatic interior diffusers are available in flat, double-hip, and drop-pan. These systems are available in 4'x4', 2'x4', 2'x2', and custom sizes; the light well can be custom made in lengths up to thirty feet. Their High Performance Tubular Skylights (HPTS) come in five diameter sizes: 10", 13", 18", 21" and 24", with recommended maximum pipe lengths of up to 20+. The company offers a lifetime guarantee.

ODL Tubular Skylights

ODL, Inc.
215 E. Roosevelt Ave.
Zeeland, MI 49464

Toll-free: 866-635-4968
Phone: 616-772-9111
www.odl.com

ODL manufactures tubular skylights in 10" and 14" diameters. The light tube is coated with a highly reflective, atomically bonded, mirror-finish reflective film and comes with a standard prismatic light diffuser at the ceiling to improve light spread. The product is designed for either contractor or DIY installations. ODL offers the option of an electric light kit, which may reduce light output by approximately 2-3% (when the pipe is straight), according to the manufacturer.

Sun Tunnel Tubular Skylights

Velux
450 Old Brickyard Rd.
Greenwood, SC 29648

Toll-free: 800-888-3589
www.veluxusa.com

The Sun Tunnel has a flexible tube (most other tubular skylights offer only elbows to make slight bends). Double diffusion panes produce even light distribution and reduce the likelihood of condensation. The company indicates that thorough testing shows there is no appreciable heat gain or loss with the Sun Tunnel. It is available in 14" and 22" diameters and carries a 7-year warranty. These tubular skylights were formerly manufactured by Sun Tunnel Skylights, Inc.

Sun-Dome Tubular Skylights

Daylighting Technologies, Inc.
3520 Investment Ln., Ste. 4
Riviera Beach, FL 33404

Toll-free: 800-596-8414
Phone: 561-840-0095
www.sun-dome.net

Daylighting Technologies produces 10", 13", and 21" tubular skylights with aluminum flashing and high-impact Lexan polycarbonate domes

for both residential and commercial applications. The domes are large-missile impact-tested and Dade County hurricane-approved. The adjustable tubes provide up to 97% reflectivity, according to the company. Daylighting Technologies also provides lighting retrofit systems with fluorescent bulbs, electronic dimmable ballasts, and light sensors to provide constant light levels in all applications. Installations may be eligible for tax credits, according to the manufacturer.

SunPipe Tubular Skylights

Sun Pipe Co., Inc.
P.O. Box 5760
Elgin, IL 60121

Toll-free: 800-844-4786
Phone: 847-888-9222
www.sunpipe.com

Sun Pipe introduced tubular skylights to the U.S. in 1991. The lined, reflective aluminum pipe is offered in 9", 13", and 21" diameter, with the larger product directed toward the commercial market. SunPipe® Tubular Skylights are lined with real silver, which is more reflective than a mirror because there is no glass on top of it, according to the manufacturer. The company's light control damper, the Eclipse, is scheduled for release in late 2006.

SunScope Tubular Skylights

Sky-Tech Sky-Lights
11503 - 160 St.
Edmonton, AB T5M 3V9 Canada

Toll-free: 800-449-0644
Phone: 780-438-6770
www.sunscope.com

SunScope tubular skylights are available in 8-1/2" or 13" diameters, as well as a 21" commercial model, in lengths up to 20'. An optional motorized damper can control light levels. Roof units for multiple SunScopes are also available, allowing any combination of up to six 8-1/2" or 13" tubular skylights to be connected to one rectangular skylight unit, reducing the number of roof penetrations. Per the manufacturer, these tubular skylights do not contribute to heat loss in winter or solar heat gain in the summer.

Sun-Tek Tube

Sun-Tek Manufacturing
10303 General Dr.
Orlando, FL 32824

Toll-free: 800-334-5854
Phone: 407-859-2117
www.sun-tek.com

The Sun-Tek Tube® is a tubular skylight available in 10"-, 14"-, and 21"-diameter sizes. The company also manufactures a curb-mount tube and a multi-tubed skylight, the Spyder, that can illuminate multiple locations with only a single opening in the roof.

Tru-Lite Tubular Skylights

Tru-Lite Skylights, Inc.
13695 E. Davies Pl.
Centennial, CO 80112

Toll-free: 800-873-3309
Phone: 303-783-5700
www.tru-lite.com

Tru-Lite Tubular Skylights® are available in 12" and 16" diameters to illuminate up to 500 ft2. No structural modifications or roof curbing are needed. The tube can be raised above the roof plane to improve low-angle daylight collection.

Tubular Skylight

Tubular Skylight, Inc.
753 Cattlemen Rd.
Sarasota, FL 34232

Toll-free: 800-315-8823
Phone: 941-378-8823
www.tubular-skylight.com

Tubular Skylights are available in three sizes: 8", 13", and 21" diameter.

Window Shades

Window shades, blinds, and other treatments can control daylight penetration and significantly reduce heat loss or heat gain through windows. In commercial buildings, engineered window shading installations can be part of an integrated design strategy addressing glare, heat gain, and solar penetration. In residential buildings, insulating window blinds and quilts may be appropriate retrofits for older, leaky windows, when window replacement can't be justified. In new construction or when replacement can be justified, installing high-performance windows is usually a better option than investing in energy-conserving blinds or shades.

Duette Window Shades

Hunter Douglas Window Covering
1 Duette Way
Broomfield, CO 80020

Toll-free: 800-789-0331
Phone: 303-466-1848
www.hunterdouglas.com

Duette shades from Hunter Douglas offer significantly better energy performance than standard shades because of their unique accordion-fold design. When lowered, the fabric opens up providing pockets of trapped air. The Duette Architella line is a honeycomb-within-a-honeycomb design that creates multiple pockets of insulating trapped air, providing improved noise reduction and thermal resistance--up to R-7.7--for the 1.25-inch opaque version, which includes a reflective layer to boost energy performance.

Earthshade Natural Fiber Window Treatments

Earthshade Natural Window Fashions
P.O. Box 1003
Great Barrington, MA 01230

Toll-free: 866-528-5443
www.earthshade.com

Made from mostly wildcrafted grasses and reeds grown without the use of fertilizers or pesticides, Earthshade custom window treatments are handwoven in Mexico and assembled in Texas. The materials are handharvested, sundried, and if treated at all, bathed in hydrogen peroxide to meet import regulations. Glues are water-based, and the only finishes are a water-based stain on one pattern (others are baked to achieve their color) and an optional water-based flame retardant for commercial spaces. Nylon cords are used to operate the shades though the company is currently testing hemp as a replacement. Earthshade offers a comprehensive collection of PVC-, urea-formaldehyde-, and halogen-free fabrics for Spring, Clutch, or motorized roler shades. Earthshade natural window treatments are available in 10 operating styles and come with the industry standard lifetime limited warranty making them suitable for both contract and residential applications.

Handwoven Collection

Hartmann & Forbes
P.O. Box 1149
Tualatin, OR 97062

Toll-free: 888-582-8780
Phone: 503-692-9313
www.hfshades.com

Hartmann & Forbes produces handwoven window coverings made from natural materials, such as reeds, grasses, bamboos, and cotton string. The PapyrusWeave™ line includes woven roman shades, draperies, rollershades, and a panelscreen that operates on a track. There is no glue used in the weave; non-chlorine polyvinyl acetate (PVA) glue is used in assembly of the finished product. Hartmann&Forbes also has a Take-Back Initiative™ to collect and recycle used shades.

Sailshade Window Coverings

Sailshade/Cloth Construction
P.O. Box 3935
Westport, MA 02790

Phone: 508-677-3160
www.sailshadeyourhome.com

Sailshade® multilayer window coverings are estimated by the manufacturer to provide R-8 insulating values in combination with a double-glazed window. When not in use, they fold compactly in a "self-creating valance" to maximize solar gain. The standard face fabric is minimally processed 100% cotton twill (washed, but no chemical finishes); 100% hemp linen is an available option, or customer's own material may be supplied. The blackout lining is non-PVC (Roc-lon), and an interior layer of Reflectix® insulation is standard.

Shading Solutions

Lutron Electronics Co., Inc.
7200 Suter Rd.
Coopersburg, PA 18036

Toll-free: 888-588-7661
Phone: 610-282-3800
www.lutron.com

Lutron offers manual and motorized shading systems for residential and commercial interiors. A number of PVC- and halogen-free fabrics—made with various combinations of fiberglass, acrylic, cotton, and polyester—are available. Openness ranges from blackout to 10 percent, in widths from 69 to 92 inches. Lutron shading systems are designed for easy integration with electric lighting controls from the same company.

Warm Window Insulated Shade System

The Warm Company
5529 186th Place SW
Lynnwood, WA 98037

Phone: 425-248-2424
www.warmcompany.com

The Warm Window Insulated Shade System (previously Window Quilt) is an insulating blind for windows. Blinds roll up at the top of the window, and the edges fit into a track, making the blind fairly airtight. The product makes the most sense for older windows; with new construction or when windows are being replaced, investing in super-high-performance windows generally makes more sense. The Warm Company finalized the acquisition of Window Quilt®, a Vermont company, in early 2006.

Warm Windows

Cozy Curtains
4295 Duncan Dr.
Missoula, MT 59802

Toll-free: 800-342-9955
www.cozycurtains.com

Warm Windows® is a custom-made insulating Roman-shade system which folds above the window when not in use. The shades are made up of 4 layers: High Density Dacron Holofil II®, a polyethylene moisture vapor barrier, metalized Mylar®, and the customer's choice of fabric. The company reports an R-value of 7.69 for installations over single-pane and 8.69 over double-pane windows. Shades attach to a board over the window frame with Velcro® and are pulled up and down with a cord. Magnetic strips around the frame and concealed within the shade provide a magnetically tight seal. Cozy Curtains also offers individual components for sale for do-it-yourselfers.

Window Treatment Hardware

Products listed here have recycled content or specialized features that save energy or achieve other environmental benefits.

Windows

Drapery Rods

Antique Drapery Rod Co., Inc.
140 Glass St.
Dallas, TX 75207

Phone: 214-653-1733
www.antiquedraperyrod.com

Antique Drapery Rod Co. manufactures drapery rods from 100% recycled steel produced at an energy-efficient mini-mill. Other steel products contain minimum 65% post-consumer recycled content. Aluminum products are made from 100% post-consumer content. The company uses recycled wood for their drapery rods, brackets, and rings, as well as offering rods and rings made from bamboo. Wood stains are water-based and low-VOC. The bamboo "tortoise shell" finish is produced using only fire, earth, and water. Antique Drapery Rod minimizes packaging material and uses shipping materials with high recycled content.

Window Treatment Hardware

S&L Designs
P.O. Box 222325
Dallas, TX 75222

Toll-free: 800-788-0358
Phone: 214-742-6417
www.s-ldesigns.com

S&L Designs manufactures decorative window treatment hardware, including rods, finials, and tiebacks. Most products are handcrafted from recycled-content metals; items made from aluminum have 100% recycled content. The company donates part of its profits to environmental causes.

Wood Windows

As with other building products made from wood, the source of that wood should be an important consideration. Currently, only a very few manufacturers use FSC-certified wood as a standard frame material, though more use it in certain components or as a special-order option. (Certification to Forest Stewardship Council—FSC—standards involves third-party evaluation and monitoring of sustainable forestry practices.) Energy performance is the primary green consideration of windows, and new developments in window technology enable today's products to far outperform those of a few decades ago. Among the improvements are multiple glazing layers, low-conductivity gas fills, better seals on insulated glazing units, heat-reflective (low-emissivity) coatings, advanced weather-stripping, and new frame systems. Low-emissivity coatings which allow short-wavelength solar radiation (sunlight) to pass through but reflect long-wavelength radiation (heat) back into the conditioned space are now standard options from all major window manufacturers. Further improvement in energy performance is achieved with triple-glazing and multiple low-e coatings; sometimes an additional glazing layer is provided as a suspended polyester film. To qualify for GreenSpec, wood windows must achieve an NFRC-certified unit U-factor of 0.25

or lower and must not only be available, but actively marketed. The U-factor threshold is higher (less stringent) for fiberglass, certified-wood, or recycled-content frame materials—and more stringent (lower U-factors) for vinyl because of environmental concerns with PVC.

Certified Wood Windows

J.S. Benson Woodworking & Design, LLC
118 Birge St.
Brattleboro, VT 05301

Toll-free: 800-339-3515
Phone: 802-254-3515
www.jsbensonwoodworking.com

J.S. Benson Woodworking & Design is a manufacturer of high-end, custom, true-divided-lite windows both for the renovation and new construction market. Available in FSC-certified mahogany. The company offers dual-sealed insulated units using clear annealed glass. Energy features include low-e coatings, argon-fill, and warm-edge insulated glass spacers.

Heat Smart

Loewen Windows
77 Hwy. #52 W
Steinbach, MB R5G
1B2 Canada

Toll-free: 800-563-9367
Phone: 204-326-6446
www.loewen.com

Loewen Window's Heat Smart glazing is available in three versions: double-glazed with low-e coatings and argon gas-fill; triple-glazed with one low-e coating and one argon-filled cavity; and triple-glazed with two low-e coatings and two argon-filled cavities. All products are NFRC-rated. Loewen Windows is a founding member of the DOE Efficient Window Collaborative and is an Energy Star® window partner. Loewen windows offers Forest Stewardshp Council (FSC) chain-of-custody certification as an option for all of their product lines.

High-Performance Windows

Milgard Manufacturing, Inc.
965 54th Ave. E
Tacoma, WA 98424

Toll-free: 800-562-8444
Phone: 253-922-6030
www.milgard.com

Milgard is the largest window manufacturer in the West and produces vinyl, thermally broken aluminum, pultruded fiberglass windows, and fiberglass-clad wood windows. All Milgard windows are custom-manufactured, and the company offers a wide range of glazing options, including several that meet the GreenSpec energy performance criteria.

High-Performance Wood and Vinyl Windows

Paramount Windows, Inc.
105 Panet Rd.
Winnipeg, MB R2J 0S1 Canada

Toll-free: 800-519-0508
Phone: 204-233-4966
www.paramountwindows.com

Paramount Windows, founded in 1948, has been promoting highly energy-efficient windows for decades. The company introduced insulated-glass windows in 1957 and triple-glazed windows (Canada's first) in 1962. The company primarily produces wood and aluminum-clad wood windows but also offers vinyl windows—mostly for the replacement market. Several glazing options are available: EnerPlus 4 is triple-glazed with one low-e coating, argon gas-fill in one of the interpane spaces, and two energy-saving spacers. EnerPlus 6 is triple-glazed with two low-e coatings, and argon gas-fill in both interpane spaces. The lowest NFRC U-factor ratings are 0.22. The company's wood supplier has FSC certification, so FSC-certified wood windows can be special-ordered for larger jobs.

High-Performance Wood Windows

Jeld-Wen Windows & Doors, Willmar Collection
550 Munroe Ave.
Winnipeg, MB R2K 4H3 Canada

Toll-free: 888-945-5627
Phone: 204-668-8230
www.willmar.ca

Willmar Windows, part of the Jeld-Wen family, manufactures wood windows with 8 glazing options. Included in Willmar's selection are a number of dual-pane and triple-pane glazing options available with Solar Gain and Solar Shield low-e coatings featuring warm-edge Intercept spacers, and with low-conductivity gas-fill. In addition to solid wood, Willmar Windows are available in metal-clad and copper-clad models. The company also makes 100% vinyl windows.

High-Performance Wood Windows

Marvin Windows and
Doors
401 States Ave.
P.O. Box 100
Warroad, MN 56763

Toll-free: 888-537-7828
Phone: 218-386-1430
www.marvin.com

Marvin offers a High-R glazing option with its wood windows that includes triple glazing with two low-E coatings and argon gas-fill. U-factors as low as 0.18 for Marvin wood windows are found in the NFRC Certified Products Directory, with many products having U-factors below 0.25.

High-Performance Wood Windows

Weather Shield Manufacturing, Inc.
1 Weathershield Plz.
P.O. Box 309
Medford, WI 54451

Toll-free: 1-800-222-2995
Phone: 715-748-2100
www.weathershield.com

Weather Shield offers a wide range of wood window products and glazing options. The highest performing glazing options are Value R6 and Value R10. Value R6 is a triple-glazed, argon-filled panel with two low-e surfaces. Value R10 is similar to Value R6 but contains a krypton/argon gas mix. The foundation of the glazing program is a warm-edge spacer system that is used to enhance thermal performance. Among the lowest unit U-factors found in the NFRC Certified Products Directory are 0.16 for commercial-sized fixed windows and 0.17 for residential-sized. According to the manufacturer, colored and specialty glass may also be specified to meet SHGC, structural, or safety specs.

Pella Designer Series

Pella Corporation
102 Main St.
Pella, IA 50219

Toll-free: 800-847-3552
Phone: 641-621-1000
www.pella.com

Pella's Designer Series® wood windows and doors are made from ponderosa pine, eastern white pine, sugar pine, and some white fir. They are available with an interior hinged panel of glass and with an exterior panel of either single-pane or double-pane argon-filled, low-emissivity glazing. The exterior is clad with recycled aluminum finished with a baked-on EnduraClad™ coating. These windows are made with 21% post-industrial recycled content, per the manufacturer. A number of Pella windows have unit U-factors at or below 0.25.

This Space is Available for Your Notes

Insulation

Insulation is one of the most important components of any environmentally responsible building because it reduces energy consumption and the pollution that usually results. In this sense, any insulation material is a "green" product. Good design and appropriate levels of insulation can minimize, or even eliminate, the need for central heating and cooling in many buildings.

Insulation is a key part of the building envelope and an important element in the entire building as an integrated system. Choosing an insulation material should include considering how it works with the rest of the wall, roof, and floor system—and what additional functions, such as air-sealing, the material might serve.

Different types of insulation also have varying impacts in terms of their raw materials and manufacture. These life-cycle impacts should be considered along with factors such as R-value, air-sealing ability, and cost.

The *quality of installation* also makes a big difference in how well insulation performs. If insulation is not installed property, it will not achieve the energy savings its rated R-value would suggest; a California study concluded that a 4% void in fiberglass batts resulted in a 50% decrease in insulation effectiveness.

The type of structural framing also affects the performance of insulation. Steel studs conduct heat much more readily than wood studs, so they create *thermal bridging* that can bypass insulation installed in the cavities. Steel-framed exterior walls should have insulative sheathing installed over the framing members to reduce this problem—in fact, the U.S. Department of Energy recommends that insulative sheathing should be used with steel framing in all U.S. climates.

Fiberglass insulation is the standard in the industry today. High-density fiberglass makes the same wall cavity 15–20% more effective in reducing heat loss. Most fiberglass manufacturers now incorporate at least 30% recycled material; some products are third-party certified for their recycled-glass content. The potential for health problems due to fiber shedding is controversial; loose fill is a greater risk than batts in this regard. While concern has been expressed that airborne fibers might be carcinogenic, those concerns have been allayed to some extent in recent years. Most fiberglass batts are manufactured with phenol formaldehyde as a binder, though some products use alternative binders or no binder at all.

Cellulose insulation is primarily made out of recycled newspaper, though not always from post-consumer sources. When it is damp-sprayed into open cavities, or blown into closed cavities at relatively high density, it forms a good infiltration barrier that adds to the airtightness of the house—and it's less contractor-dependent for quality control in filling voids than fiberglass batts.

Rigid foam insulation applied to framing yields added infiltration resistance, reduced frame conduction losses, and higher overall wall R-value. Extruded polystyrene (XPS) and polyisocyanurate (polyiso) rigid foam insulation used to be made with ozone-depleting CFC blowing agents, but when ozone depletion was identified as a major environmental problem, the CFCs were replaced with HCFCs through international agreement. HCFCs were eliminated from polyiso insulation as of 2003, but they are not scheduled to be totally eliminated from XPS until 2020. Polyiso is currently produced with hydrocarbon blowing agents. Expanded polystyrene (EPS) rigid foam has long been made with non-ozone-depleting pentane rather than HCFCs.

Acoustic Blanket Insulation

Noise, both from indoor and outside sources, adds to stress and discomfort. A wide range of products are available to help absorb noise and prevent it from spreading. Products listed here are designed to provide acoustical isolation in addition to any thermal insulation properties they may have. If these products are also listed under thermal insulation, they must meet Green-Spec's criteria for that type of thermal insulation.

Formaldehyde-Free Insulation Batts

Johns Manville Corporation
P.O. Box 5108
Denver, CO 80217

Toll-free: 800-654-3103
Phone: 303-978-2000
www.jm.com

Johns Manville Corporation eliminated the use of formaldehyde in their insulation products in 2002. Their thermal- and sound-insulating fiberglass batts use an acrylic binder, and come in rolls either unfaced or with foil, FSK, or Kraft facing. ComfortTherm is a poly-encapsulated fiberglass insulation designed for metal- and wood-framing as well as for directly above suspended ceilings. Available in batts or rolls, R-values range from 11 to 38. ComfortTherm contains 20% post-consumer and 5% post-industrial recycled glass.

The Insulator

Bonded Logic, Inc.
411 E. Ray Rd.
Chandler, AZ 85225

Phone: 480-812-9114
www.bondedlogic.com

The Insulator™ Thermal-Acoustic Insulation is a 3/8"-thick thermal and acoustic insulation made from post-industrial denim and cotton fiber and faced on either one or both sides with an aluminum barrier (also available in a two- or three-ply version). The product is formaldehyde-free and comes in 4' x 6' or 4' x 75' rolls (in 3/8" thickness only). The Insulator is thermally bonded using a synthetic fiber binder and is treated with a boric acid antimicrobial agent. It is Class A fire-rated, and no protective clothing or gear is necessary for installation. The 3/8" pad has a noise reduction coefficient of 0.45 and an R-value of 1.47.

Air, Vapor, and Moisture Barriers

Weather barriers form a secondary drainage plane (the first in most cases being the exterior cladding) to assist in keeping assembly components to the interior protected from bulk water. Note that the vapor permeability of concealed weather barrier products can vary widely and the desirability of low or high or no vapor permeability is always in the context of the primary direction of wetting, the primary direction of drying, and the vapor permeability of all the other components in the assembly.

Products listed here contribute to durability (generally by creating an air space) and/or reduce the potential for indoor air quality problems associated with moisture and mold.

Construction Film

Gempak
9611 James Ave. S
Bloomington, MN 55431

Toll-free: 800-328-4556
Phone: 952-881-8673

Gempak, formerly Strout Plastics, manufactures construction film that generally contains 100% recycled LDPE. With some production runs, contamination of recycled materials necessitates the addition of virgin resins to produce a quality product.

Delta-MS and Delta-Dry

Cosella Dörken Products Inc.
4655 Delta Way
Beamville, ON L0R 1B4
Canada

Toll-free: 888-433-5824
Phone: 905-563-3255
www.deltams.com

Delta-Dry is a stiff, egg-carton-textured, 5/16"-thick, vapor-impermeable housewrap made with 22-mil, virgin HDPE. When properly installed, the weather-resistive barrier creates a ventilated rainscreen, while blocking moisture migration through the wall assembly. Similarly, Delta-MS for subsurface use is an air-gap membrane constructed from 6 mm-thick HDPE, with a pattern of dimples molded into the surface. When installed, the membrane is held off the wall to allow any moisture in the concrete to migrate to the outer surface, condense on the inside surface of the membrane, and flow into the foundation drain. Because HDPE is impervious, soil moisture is unable to penetrate but will also flow to the foundation drain.

Home Slicker

Benjamin Obdyke Inc.
400 Babylon Rd.
Ste. A
Horsham, PA 19044

Toll-free: 800-523-5261
Phone: 215-672-7200
www.benjaminobdyke.com

Home Slicker® is a ventilating and self-draining rainscreen for use under siding, which provides a thermal break and moisture protection for sidewalls. Home Slicker's 3-dimensional, 0.25"-thick matrix provides a continuous space for drying, drainage, and pressure equalization. For use under sidings such as wood, fiber-cement, EIFS, brick, and vinyl, Home Slicker comes with a 50-year limited warranty.

Water Out Flashing

Water Out Flashing
8206-1200 Providence Rd.
Charlotte, NC 28277

Phone: 866-568-0050
www.wateroutflashing.com

Water Out window and door flashing products will fit openings of any width and are designed to be easy to install. The flexible polypropylene pans with integral, tapered drain channels and end-dams don't require precision cutting or adhesives, and they have wide flanges for proper integration with the envelope in both straight and radial fenestrations. These flashings are sold by the case, and are available in white, black, brown, and paintable white.

Weatherstripping and Gaskets

M-D Building Products
4041 N. Santa Fe Ave.
Oklahoma City, OK 73118

Toll-free: 800-654-8454
Phone: 405-528-4411
www.mdteam.com

M-D manufactures a wide range of weatherstripping and weatherization products.

Weatherstripping and Gaskets

Resource Conservation Technology, Inc.
2633 N. Calvert St.
Baltimore, MD 21218

Toll-free: 800-477-7724
Phone: 410-366-1146
www.conservationtechnology.com

Resource Conservation Technology specializes in building gaskets, weatherstripping, and air barriers.

Blanket Insulation

Blanket insulation is typically made up of fiberglass, mineral wool, or cotton. Most fiberglass insulation is made primarily from silica spun into glass fibers and contains a phenol-formaldehyde (PF) binder— though formaldehyde-free products have been introduced. Most fiberglass insulation today has at least 30% recycled-glass content, with some plants using as much as 40% post-consumer recycled beverage glass as the raw material. Mineral wool insulation is made from either molten slag—a waste product of steel production—or natural rock, such as basalt and diabase. Mineral wool has a higher density than fiberglass, so it has better sound-blocking properties. It's also more fire-resistant than fiberglass. Cotton insulation is made from post-industrial recycled cotton textiles, such as denim, with synthetic fibers added to maintain loft. Nontoxic flame retardants similar to those used in clothing are added. Unlike fiberglass and mineral wool, there are no mineral microfibers as a potential cause of

respiratory problems. Products listed here have high recycled content, reduced indoor air quality concerns, or superior performance in particular applications based on their air tightness or management of moisture.

CertainTeed Batt Insulation

CertainTeed Corporation
750 E. Swedesford Rd.
P.O. Box 860
Valley Forge, PA 19482

Toll-free: 800-233-8990
Phone: 610-341-7000
www.certainteed.com

CertainTeed Building Insulation is manufactured with recycled glass cullet. CertainTeed uses an average of approximately 25% recycled glass depending on availability. These products carry the Greenguard certification for low emissions. The manufacturer has certified the following recycled-content levels (by weight): total recovered material 20% typical; post-consumer material 10% typical.

Climatizer Plus and Enviro-Batt

Climatizer Insulation, Ltd.
120 Claireville Dr.
Etobicoke, ON M9W 5Y3 Canada

Toll-free: 866-871-5495
Phone: 416-798-1235
www.climatizer.com

Climatizer Plus thermal and acoustical cellulose insulation contains recycled newspaper. It may be hand-poured or pneumatically placed with a blowing machine and delivery hose. Enviro-Batt™ contains less than 2% formaldehyde-free, no-VOC adhesive activated by a very small amount of water during pneumatic installation; moisture-loading is only 20% of that experienced with typical wet-cellulose applications. Both products contain at least 85% post-consumer recycled paper fibers.

Fiberglass Insulation

Ottawa Fibre, Inc.
1365 Johnston Rd.
Ottawa, ON K1V 8Z1
Canada

Phone: 613-247-7116
www.ofigroup.com

Ottawa Fibre L.P. fiberglass insulation is made from 65% recycled glass (typical), of which 30% is usually post-consumer content. Ottawa Fibre's Golden Glow Fiber Glass residential insulation is available in five configurations; unfaced, kraft-faced, foil-faced, FSK-faced, and flangeless. R-values range from R-8 to R-40, depending on density and thickness. The company also offers a wide range of fiberglass insulation products including commercial and industrial insulation and ceiling tiles for both residential and commercial markets.

Formaldehyde-Free Insulation Batts

Johns Manville Corporation
P.O. Box 5108
Denver, CO 80217

Toll-free: 800-654-3103
Phone: 303-978-2000
www.jm.com

Johns Manville Corporation eliminated the use of formaldehyde in their insulation products in 2002. Their thermal- and sound-insulating fiberglass batts use an acrylic binder, and come in rolls either unfaced or with foil, FSK, or Kraft facing. ComfortTherm is a poly-encapsulated fiberglass insulation designed for metal- and wood-framing as well as for directly above suspended ceilings. Available in batts or rolls, R-values range from 11 to 38. ComfortTherm contains 20% post-consumer and 5% post-industrial recycled glass.

InsulCot Cotton Insulation

Insulcot
411 S. Fox St.
Post, TX 79356

Phone: 806-777-2811
www.insulcot.com

InsulCot contains 75% cotton fibers and 25% polyester binder. Cotton fibers impregnated with a nontoxic phosphorous flame retardant is mixed with polyester and then heated, causing the polyester to melt. InsulCot, which has passed all federal tests for insulation, including fire and moisture resistance, is available in most standard widths and thickness in rolls or bats, with or without asphalted Kraft flanged facing. It is also available as a cellulose alternative for blow-in installations. InsulCot Cotton Insulation provides equivalent R-values to synthetic fibers per inch, but is lighter-weight. It meets the same Class 1 standards as fiberglass insulation.

Mineral Wool Insulation

Roxul Inc.
551 Harrop Dr.
Milton, ON L9T 3H3 Canada

Toll-free: 800-265-6878
Phone: 905-878-8474
www.roxul.com

Roxul offers the U.S. market commercial and industrial mineral wool products in faced and unfaced rigid and semi-rigid boards, blankets, and formed products for thermal, acoustical, and fireproofing insulation for wall, floor, curtain wall, pipe, and tank installations. Roxul's mineral wool—made from approximately equal amounts of natural basalt rock and recycled slag (with 1%-6% urea extended phenolic formaldehyde binder)—is vapor-permeable, water-repellant, and non-combustible. The dimensionally stable, chemically inert material doesn't degrade or support mold, and is made with CFC- and HCFC-free processes. Compressive strength of up to 877 psf (42 kPa) is available in rigid boards. R-values per inch range from 4 to 4.3. Roxul offers additional products for residential applications to the Canadian market.

PINK Fiberglas Building Insulation

Owens Corning
1 Owens Corning Pkwy.
Toledo, OH 43659

Toll-free: 800-438-7465
Phone: 419-248-8000
www.owenscorning.com

Owens Corning Pink fiber glass insulation products are certified by Scientific Certification Systems to contain at least 35% recycled glass (9% post-consumer and 26% post-industrial). A wide range of insulation products are manufactured by Owens Corning. This product carries the Greenguard certification for low emissions.

UltraTouch Natural Fiber Insulation

Bonded Logic, Inc.
411 E. Ray Rd.
Chandler, AZ 85225

Phone: 480-812-9114
www.bondedlogic.com

Bonded Logic makes UltraTouch from pre-consumer recycled denim and other cotton-fiber textile trimmings. This insulation contains no mineral fibers and carries no warning labels for installers or occupants. It is completely recyclable at the end of its useful life and has been ASTM tested for thermal resistance, surface-burning characteristics, water-vapor absorption, mold/fungi resistance, and odor emission. Available in batts that are either 16" or 24" wide, UltraTouch comes in 3-1/2" (R-13) or 5-1/2" (R-19) thicknesses. The manufacturer has certified the following recycled-content levels (by weight): total recovered material 75% typical, 75% guaranteed; post-consumer material 0% typical, 0% guaranteed.

Wool Insulation

Good Shepherd Wool
Insulation
R.R. #3
Site 14, Box 17
Rocky Mountain House,
AB T4T 2A3 Canada

Phone: 403-845-6705
www.goodshepherd-
wool.com

Good Shepherd Wool Insulation is sold in batts for frame houses (16" or 24" centers) and wool rope for log homes. The only additive is a boron-based fire retardant and vermin and insect repellent.

Board Insulation

Board insulation can be made up of glass fibers, mineral wool or rigid foam. Unlike most batt or blown-in insulation, rigid boards can be applied across the surface of walls, roofs, or foundations, reducing thermal bridging through the structure. Foam insulation products are all petroleum-derived with most foams require a blowing agent to create the foaming action. Extruded polystyrene (XPS) is still blown with HCFC-142b—although

European manufacturers have converted to non-ozone-depleting blowing agents. Only a few specialized XPS insulation materials in the U.S. are currently produced without HCFCs. Mineral wool insulation is made from either molten slag—a waste product of steel production—or natural rock, such as basalt and diabase. Mineral wool has a higher density than fiberglass, so it has better sound-blocking properties. Note that board insulation products vary widely in terms of more than just their resistance to conductive heat loss; consideration of each product's air tightness and moisture performance may be important as well. Products listed here have post-consumer and/or post-industrial recycled-content, reduced off-gassing, reduced or eliminated ozone-depleting potential blowing agents.

ACFoam

Atlas Roofing Corp.
2000 RiverEdge Pkwy.,
Ste. 800
Atlanta, GA 30328

Toll-free: 800-933-1476
Phone: 770-952-1442
www.atlasroofing.com

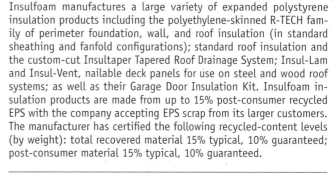

ACFoam® was the first North American polyisocyanurate foam insulation to be blown with hydrocarbons rather than HCFCs; it has zero ODP and zero GWP. ACFoam with ACUltra™ is sold under various brand names for both commercial and residential roofing and wall sheathing applications. This product also contains recovered materials and meets ASTM C-1289, UL, and FM standards. ACFoam-II (a roof insulation) contains between 16% and 43% recovered materials by weight, depending on thickness.

DrainBoard

Roxul Inc.
551 Harrop Dr.
Milton, ON L9T 3H3 Canada

Toll-free: 800-265-6878
Phone: 905-878-8474
www.roxul.com

Roxul offers DrainBoard™, a durable, rigid mineral wool insulation board that is water repellent and environmentally stable used as an insulating foundation drainage system. It is designed for use with a dampproofing layer on commercial applications up to 12' below grade. The non-directional fiber structure allows the system to be installed horizontally or vertically, providing an insulating drainage plane for foundation walls and structural concrete. Roxul's mineral wool is made from approximately equal amounts of natural basalt rock and recycled slag (with 1%-6% urea extended phenolic formaldehyde binder).

EPS Foam

Insulfoam (Division of Premier Industries, Inc.)
1019 Pacific Ave., Ste. 1501
Tacoma, WA 98402

Toll-free: 800-248-5995
Phone: 253-572-5111
www.insulfoam.com

Insulfoam manufactures a large variety of expanded polystyrene insulation products including the polyethylene-skinned R-TECH family of perimeter foundation, wall, and roof insulation (in standard sheathing and fanfold configurations); standard roof insulation and the custom-cut Insultaper Tapered Roof Drainage System; Insul-Lam and Insul-Vent, nailable deck panels for use on steel and wood roof systems; as well as their Garage Door Insulation Kit. Insulfoam insulation products are made from up to 15% post-consumer recycled EPS with the company accepting EPS scrap from its larger customers. The manufacturer has certified the following recycled-content levels (by weight): total recovered material 15% typical, 10% guaranteed; post-consumer material 15% typical, 10% guaranteed.

EPS Foam Insulation Components

BASF Corporation
889 Valley Park Dr.
Shakopee, MN 55379

Toll-free: 800-433-9517
www.corporate.basf.com

BASF produces components for manufacturing low-pentane foam insulation.

Foam-Control EPS

AFM Corporation
211 River Ridge Circle S., Ste. 102
Burnsville, MN 55337

Toll-free: 800-255-0176
Phone: 952-474-0809
www.r-control.com

Foam-Control EPS Insulation is a non-ozone-depleting foam insulation manufactured in various Types and sizes for many insulation applications. Foam-Control EPS Tapered is cut to achieve appropriate pitches for low-slope roofs. Foam-Control EPS with Perform Guard® is termite-resistant EPS formulated with a borate additive. Foam-Control EPS with Perform Guard is also used as the core material for R-Control SIPs (structural insulated panels). AFM licenses several manufacturers throughout the U.S. to produce these products.

Mineral Wool Insulation

Roxul Inc.
551 Harrop Dr.
Milton, ON L9T 3H3 Canada

Toll-free: 800-265-6878
Phone: 905-878-8474
www.roxul.com

Roxul offers the U.S. market commercial and industrial mineral wool products in faced and unfaced rigid and semi-rigid boards, blankets, and formed products for thermal, acoustical, and fireproofing insulation for wall, floor, curtain wall, pipe, and tank installations. Roxul's mineral wool—made from approximately equal amounts of natural basalt rock and recycled slag (with 1%-6% urea extended phenolic formaldehyde binder)—is vapor-permeable, water-repellant, and non-combustible. The dimensionally stable, chemically inert material doesn't degrade or support mold, and is made with CFC- and HCFC-free processes. Compressive strength of up to 877 psf (42 kPa) is available in rigid boards. R-values per inch range from 4 to 4.3. Roxul offers additional products for residential applications to the Canadian market.

Polar Guard Rigid EPS

Polar Industries
32 Grammar Ave.
Prospect, CT 06712

Toll-free: 800-237-3763
Phone: 203-758-6651
www.polarcentral.com

Polar Industries manufactures Polar Guard, a standard 1-lb. density EPS board manufactured with the pulfusion process. Polar Guard is available in 3/4", 1", and 2" thicknesses.

Styrofoam High Performance Underlayment

Dow Chemical Co., Styrofoam Brand Products
200 Larkin Ctr.
Midland, MI 48674

Toll-free: 800-441-4369
Phone: 989-636-1000
www.styrofoam.com

Styrofoam® High Performance Underlayment from Dow is the first U.S.-manufactured extruded polystyrene (XPS) foam board with zero ODP. This product, blown with HFC-152a, is designed for residential wall-sheathing applications. It comes in 4' x 50' fanfold sections, several different facings, and in thicknesses of 1/4" (R-1) and 3/8" (R-1.5).

Thermafiber Mineral Wool Insulation Products

Thermafiber, Inc.
3711 W. Mill St.
Wabash, IN 46992

Toll-free: 888-834-2371
Phone: 260-563-2111
www.thermafiber.com

Thermafiber makes a range of mineral-fiber insulation products made from pre-consumer recycled slag for commercial and residential thermal, sound attenuation, and fire-resistant applications. The products come in a wide variety of densities, facings, thicknesses, and R-values, as rigid or blanket material. These products have been evaluated by an independent testing facility for low pollutant emissions. ThermaTech products, according to the manufacturer, contain no added chemical fire retardants, are noncombustible, odor-free, will not absorb moisture or support mildew or fungus, and will not rot or decay. Phenolic resin content is less than 5% by weight.

Thermax

Dow Chemical
P.O. Box 3190
Marietta, GA 30062

Toll-free: 800-800-3626
Phone: 770-428-2684
www.itsgreatstuff.com

THERMAX is a brand of non-structural, rigid board insulation products consisting of a glass-fiber reinforced polyisocyanurate foam faced with aluminum foil. Depending on the product, the faces differ in thickness and are either embossed aluminum or embossed white acrylic-coated aluminum. THERMAX™ has an R-Value of 6.5/in and is designed for use in wall and roof assemblies, crawlspaces, and interior basement applications. Thermax products are made with non-ozone-depleting hydrocarbon blowing agents.

Foam Joint Sealants

The challenge of sealing building envelopes against air infiltration is made easier with foam sealants. Look for products with blowing agents that are non-ozone-depleting and have low global-warming potential. Be aware that a label "no CFCs" is not the same as "ozone-safe"; HCFC propellants/blowing agents, while not as bad as CFCs, still deplete ozone. Foam sealants are commonly available in high-expanding and low-expanding formulations; low-expanding foam is the material of choice for sealing window and door rough openings—it performs significantly better than fiberglass and will be less likely than high-expanding foams to swell the openings (which can make opening and closing difficult). Foam sealants are useful in many applications, especially in building renovation. Some products are available only in disposable cans; the use of bulk tanks and reusable dispensing guns can reduce the environmental costs of using these sealants by minimizing waste.

CF 116 Grip Filler Foam

Hilti, Inc.
P.O. Box 21148
Tulsa, OK 74121

Toll-free: 866-445-8827
Phone: 918-252-6000
www.us.hilti.com

CF 116 is a single-component, polyurethane-based foam sealant propelled by HFC-134a, propane, and isobutane blowing agents. This minimally expanding product is dispensed from a can with a reusable gun. According to the company, one can is equivalent to 46 ten-ounce tubes of caulk.

PurFil 1G

Todol Products
25 Washington Ave.
P.O. Box 398
Natick, MA 01760

Toll-free: 800-252-3818
Phone: 508-651-3818
www.todol.com

PurFil 1G uses HFC-134a as its propellant and a mix of propane and isobutane as the blowing agent. It is available in disposable cans with application guns.

Touch'n Foam

Convenience Products
866 Horan Dr.
Fenton, MO 63026

Toll-free: 800-325-6180
Phone: 636-349-5333
www.convenienceproducts.com

Touch'n Foam is an HCFC-free foam sealant that uses a mixture of propane and isobutane as the blowing agent. It is available in triple-expanding or low-expanding formulations in disposable cans.

Foamed-in-Place Insulation

With foamed-in-place insulation it is relatively easy (though not necessarily inexpensive) to fill wall and ceiling cavities completely, providing high R-values (3.6 to 6.5 per inch) and blocking air leakage very effectively. Installation requires special equipment, however, and must be done by licensed contractors. Most foamed-in-place insulation products are fairly high-density (2 lbs. per cubic foot) closed-cell polyurethanes. Open-cell, low-density polyurethane foams have been produced with water or carbon dioxide as the blowing agent for some time. Compared with closed-cell polyurethane, open-cell products also use significantly less material, making them attractive from a resource standpoint, but also lower in R-value per inch. Some of the low-density foam products are made in part from bio-based raw materials in place of petrochemicals. Products listed use blowing agents that are non-ozone depleting.

Air Krete Foam Insulation

Air Krete, Inc.
2710 E. Brutus St.
P.O. Box 380
Weedsport, NY 13166

Phone: 315-834-6609
www.airkrete.com

Air Krete is a lightweight, inorganic, cementitious foam insulation that is fireproof, nontoxic, pest-resistant, and moisture resistant. It does not support mold growth, and contains no fluorocarbons. Compressed air is mixed with an expanding agent, and the cement (magnesium oxide) is added to produce the final product. Air Krete, at standard density, has an R-value of 3.9/in. when tested at 75 degrees F. It is foamed in place in new or existing wall cavities by licensed Air Krete contractors. The foam density can be varied to withstand high-vibration environments, such as along busy roadways.

BioBased 501

Bio-Based Systems
1315 N 13th St.
Rogers, AR 72756

Toll-free: 800-803-5189
Phone: 479-246-9523
www.biobased.net

BioBased 501 soybean-oil-based polyurethane spray foam insulation functions much like petroleum-based polyurethane foam. The polyol component of the two-part urethane consists of about 40% soy-derived oil. The open-cell foam is installed at a density of 0.5 lbs/ft3 using CO_2 as the blowing agent. It expands to 100 times its original liquid size. The product has an R-value of 3.7/in. (R-13 at 3-1/2") and is applied with customized equipment by certified installers. BioBased 501 was named "Outstanding Green Product of the Year" in 2003 by the National Association of Homebuilders (NAHB) Green Builders Conference in Baltimore.

RTC Polyurethane Insulation

Resin Technology Division of Henry Co.
2270 Castle Harbor Pl.
Ontario, CA 91761

Toll-free: 800-729-0795
Phone: 909-947-7224
www.henry.com

Resin Technology formulates several water-blown, open-cell polyurethane foam insulation products with installed densities of 0.35 to 0.6 lbs/ft3, depending on specific requirements. The company reports an R-value of close to 3.4/in. As with all polyurethane foams, this insulation requires appropriate, professional precautions during installation.

Sealection 500

Demilec USA, Inc.
2925 Galleria Dr.
Arlington, TX 76011

Toll-free: 877-336-4532
Phone: 817-640-4900
www.sealection500.com

Sealection™ 500 is a low-density polyurethane foam that is 100% water-blown and contains no HCFCs or hydrocarbon blowing agents. The product insulates to R-3.8/in. This product has passed the established offgassing tests and is approved by the Environmental Choice Program (a private ecolabeling program in Canada). Like all polyurethane foams, Sealection is hazardous during installation.

SUPERGREEN FOAM

Foam-Tech, Division of Building Envelope Solutions, Inc.
P.O. Box 87, Rte. 5
N. Thetford, VT 05054

Phone: 802-333-4333
www.foam-tech.com

SuperGreen Foam™ is a closed-cell, high-density polyurethane foam containing no HCFCs. The blowing agent is HFC-134a. SuperGreen insulates to between R-6 and R-7/in. Like all polyurethane foams, SuperGreen is hazardous during installation. Foam-Tech is a foamed-in-place building insulation contractor that holds a patent license to produce SuperGreen using components manufactured by Preferred Foam Products.

The Icynene Insulation System

Icynene Inc.
6747 Campobello Rd.
Mississauga, ON L5N 2L7 Canada

Toll-free: 800-758-7325
Phone: 905-363-4040
www.icynene.com

The Icynene Insulation System® was the first water based, HCFC-free, low-density, open-cell polyurethane insulation to be introduced and is the most widely recognized brand in its kind. The foam is typically sprayed into open wall, ceiling, and floor cavities in a thin layer. It expands about 100 times its original volume to form an air barrier and is trimmed flush with the framing members before drywall is installed. With an R-value of about R-3.6/in., it can outperform fiberglass insulation with twice the R-value and minimizes airborne moisture problems such as mold and mildew due to its air sealing capability. A slightly different formulation of Icynene can be poured into closed wall cavities in retrofit applications.

HVAC Insulation

Air-supply and return ducts can be a medium for mold growth or (with insulated ducts) a source of fiber-shedding, both of which can pose significant indoor air quality concerns. Products listed here allow easy duct cleaning, or protect against mold growth or fiber-shedding. Also included are specialized insulation products for piping and other mechanical equipment. For hydronic heating pipes that experience high temperature (over 150 degrees F), inexpensive foam-plastic pipe insulation sleeves may not be adequate; high-temperature pipe insulation is required.

Cotton Insulating Duct Wrap

Payless Insulation, Inc.
1331 Seamist Dr.
Houston, TX 77008

Phone: 713-868-1021
www.superiorairducts.com

Superior R8 Cotton Duct Wrap™ is an insulating HVAC duct wrap for commercial or residential applications. It is made with 85% post-industrial fibers (2.2 lbs/ft3 density, borax-treated cotton) bonded to a metallized mylar jacket and is resistant to fungus, bacteria, fire, and moisture. Standard available size is 2" thick x 25' long x 5' wide. The cotton fiber is supplied by Bonded Logic, Inc.

Knauf Air-Handling Insulation Products

Knauf Insulation
One Knauf Dr.
Shelbyville, IN 46176

Toll-free: 800-825-4434
Phone: 317-398-4434
www.knaufusa.com

Knauf air-handling insulation products, including duct wrap, duct board, duct liner, and plenum liner contribute minimal levels of formaldehyde and other pollutants to the indoor environment. Duct wrap rolls are available with a variety of facings, including PSK (polypropylene-scrim-kraft); duct liner rolls have an airstream surface mat facing of tightly bonded fiberglass. Duct board is available with a nonwoven mat face; the rigid plenum liner has a polymer overspray on the airstream side.

ToughGard

CertainTeed Corporation
750 E. Swedesford Rd.
P.O. Box 860
Valley Forge, PA 19482

Toll-free: 800-233-8990
Phone: 610-341-7000
www.certainteed.com

CertainTeed's ToughGard™ fiberglass duct board is a ducting material with integral insulation. At 75 degrees F, the company claims an R-value of 4.3 for 1" board, 6.5 for 1-1/2" board, and 8.7 for 2" board. To prevent fiber shedding, ToughGard has both a nonwoven composite interior facing of textile fiberglass and polypropylene, and a reinforced foil-laminate exterior facing. The material's ship-lap design helps minimize air leakage at joints. This product carries the Greenguard certification for low emissions.

Insulated Metal Wall Panels

With a thin metal skin and foam insulation for a core, insulated metal wall panels provide excellent thermal protection and efficient use of materials. The materials, themselves, however, have relatively high embodied energy.

Acsys Panel System

Acsys Inc.
1677 E. Miles Ave., Ste. 101
Hayden, ID 83835

Toll-free: 866-362-2797
Phone: 208-772-6422
www.acsys.net

The Acsys Building System is a structural insulated panel-type product employing an engineered 16- to 20-gauge corrugated galvanized steel endoskeletal core (rather than the more common exoskeleton of OSB). The steel is embedded in molded EPS, which offers R-values ranging from 25 to 50 (panel thicknesses of 6", 8", 10", and 12"). The EPS typically contains 7-10% recycled content from packaging waste, according to the manufacturer. Available in 2' and 4' widths up to 18' long, it may be used with steel framing or as a fully load-bearing system. The panels interconnect with ship-lap joints (secured by galvanized screws) and may be lifted into place by two people. 18-gauge galvanized steel top- and bottom-mounting tracks, as well as corner locater plates, are provided. Panels are typically finished on the exterior with acrylic stucco and on the interior with drywall.

Insulation Baffles

In vented roof and attic assemblies, insulation baffles ensure that a properly sized cavity is maintained between the top of the insulation and the roof decking. Proper ventilation in attics and roofs is essential to maintaining insulation performance unless other measures have been taken to prevent heat-transfer moisture problems. Insulation performance suffers when moisture, trapped under the roof sheathing, condenses on the insulation below, and escaping heat can cause ice-damming. The highly conductive nature of water renders wet insulation much less effective—and wet insulation can also result in rotting wood framing members and mold growth. Insulation baffles can be made from corrugated cardboard with sizing, foam, or plastic. Products listed here have recycled content and avoid extruded polystyrene produced with HCFC blowing agents.

DUROVENT and proVent

ADO Products
21800 129th Ave. N
P.O. Box 236
Rogers, MN 55374

Toll-free: 866-240-4933
Phone: 763-428-7802
www.adoproducts.com

Durovent is made from EPS foam with up to 40% recycled content; proVent is made from polystyrene plastic and has up to 80% recycled content. Both products are 48" long and available for 16" and 24" rafter spacings. Durovent is for new construction, while proVent is designed for remodeling applications. The thinner profile of proVent allows this product to be shipped more compactly, and its greater durability results in less breakage and other damage than occurs with EPS foam.

Insul-Tray

Insulation Solutions, Inc.
401 Truck Haven Rd.
East Peoria, IL 61611

Toll-free: 866-698-6562
Phone: 309-698-0062
www.insulationsolutions.com

Insul-Tray insulation baffles are made from 100% recycled-content corrugated cardboard with or without a radiant-barrier foil facing for 16" and 24" on-center rafter bays and wall cavities. The radiant barrier reduces heat gain and heat loss through the roof as long as the baffles have an air space next to them.

PermaVent Attic Baffle

Perma "R" Products
2064 Sunset Dr.
P.O. Box 279
Grenada, MS 38902

Toll-free: 800-647-6130
Phone: 662-226-8075
www.leclairindustries.com

PermaVent Attic Baffles are insulation baffles for 16" and 24" on-center rafter bays. The product measures 3/8" x 22" x 48" for 24" o.c. rafters; break along center perforations for 16" o.c. installations.

StyroVent

DiversiFoam Products
9091 County Rd. 50
P.O. Box 44
Rockford, MN 55373

Toll-free: 800-669-0100
Phone: 763-477-5854
www.diversifoam.com

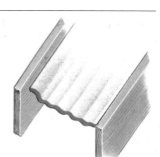

StyroVent Attic Ventilation Chute, made from RayLite brand EPS, comes in two sizes: StyroVent Mini is for 16" on-center construction and measures 15" W x 2-1/4" D x 48" L; StyroVent Maxi, for 24" on-center construction, measures 23-1/4" W x 2-1/2" D x 48" L.

TuffVENT and BaffleVENT

Weidmann Electrical Technology, Inc.
One Gordon Mills Way
St. Johnsbury, VT 05819

Phone: 800-242-6748
www.weidmann-industrial.com

TuffVENT is made from 100% unbleached post-industrial recycled paper fibers (from box clippings), with a mild sizing agent added for moisture resistance. Appropriate for new construction and remodeling, the sturdy, recyclable material resists staple blow-through, ripping, and damage, but cuts easily to accommodate pipes and conduits. TuffVENT provides a 2" air-channel depth, and is available for 16" or 24" on-center rafters, in 43" or 120" lengths. BaffleVENT is a similar product (16" o.c. only) with an integrated baffle that extends from the roof decking past the top plate, preventing blown-in insulation from blocking the soffit.

Vent-Rite Attic Vents

Plymouth Foam Incorporated
1800 Sunset Dr.
Plymouth, WI 53073

Toll-free: 800-669-1176
Phone: 920-893-0535
www.plymouthfoam.com

Vent-Rite attic vents are insulation baffles made from EPS foam for 16" and 24" on-center rafter bays. They are not known to contain recycled polystyrene. Plymouth Foam operates manufacturing plants in Plymouth, Wisconsin; Becker, Minnesota; and Newcomerstown, Ohio.

Loose-Fill Insulation

Loose-fill insulations include fiberglass, mineral wool or cellulose systems, among others. Cellulose insulation has several environmental advantages. Most contain 75-80% recycled newspaper (often post-consumer) and nontoxic borate and/or ammonium sulfate fire retardants. The energy performance is comparable to high-density fiberglass batts at roughly R-3.7 per inch, but cellulose insulation generally packs more tightly so is more effective at controlling air leakage. Health concerns with fiberglass have not been substantiated, but it is generally a good idea to install loose-fill fiberglass only if the fibers can be prevented from getting into occupied space or air distribution systems. Products listed here have recycled content, superior moisture or air leakage performance, or reduced indoor air quality concerns.

All-Weather Insulation

All-Weather Insulation Co., LLC
19 W. Industry Dr.
Springfield, KY 40069

Phone: 859-336-3651

All-Weather Cellulose Insulation contains recycled newspaper.

Applegate Loosefill and Stabilized Cellulose Insulation

Applegate Insulation Manufacturing
1000 Highview Dr.
Webberville, MI 48892

Toll-free: 800-627-7536
Phone: 517-521-3545
www.applegateinsulation.com

Applegate insulation is made with 80-85% recycled newsprint. The manufacturing process uses 1/5 the amount of energy as needed for fiberglass insulation, and generates almost no emissions. The manufacturer has certified the following recycled-content levels (by weight): total recovered material 85% typical, 80% guaranteed; post-consumer material 85% typical, 80% guaranteed.

AZ Energy Saver

Paul's Insulation
P.O. Box 115
Vergas, MN 56587

Toll-free: 800-627-5190
Phone: 218-342-2800

AZ Energy Saver is cellulose insulation made from 100% post-consumer recycled newspaper.

Benotherm

Benolec, Ltd.
1451 Nobel St.
Sainte-Julie, QC J3E 1Z4 Canada

Phone: 450-922-2000
www.benolec.com

Benotherm cellulose insulation contains recycled newspaper.

Cell-Pak Advantage

Cell-Pak, Inc.
204 McIntire Ln.
Decatur, AL 35603

Phone: 256-260-2151
www.cellpak.com

Cell-Pak Advantage cellulose insulation, formerly Celluguard Light Wallboard, contains 85% recycled newspaper.

Cellulose Insulation

Advanced Fiber Technology, Inc.
100 Crossroads Blvd.
Bucyrus, OH 44820

Phone: 419-562-1337
www.advancedfiber.com

Advanced Fiber Technology manufactures cellulose insulation from recycled wastepaper. The company would not disclose which fire retardant is used in this insulation. Advanced Fiber Technology is also a manufacturer of cellulose insulation processing equipment.

Cellulose Insulation

Can-Cell Industries, Inc.
14735 124th Ave.
Edmonton, AB T5L 3B2
Canada

Toll-free: 800-661-5031
www.can-cell.com

Can-Cell Industries manufactures Weathershield loose-fill cellulose, WallBAR stabilized cavity-fill cellulose, K-13 spray-applied thermal and acoustical insulation, and Sonaspray "fc" acoustical spray insulation from recycled newspaper. Typical post-consumer recycled content is 85%. Can-Cell Industries now manufactures K-13 and Sonaspray "fc" for the entire Canadian market.

Cellulose Insulation

Clayville Insulation
P.O. Box 713
Burley, ID 83318

Toll-free: 800-584-9022
Phone: 208-678-9791

Clayville insulation is made from recycled newspaper.

Cellulosic Fiber Insulation

Mountain Fiber Insulation
1880 E. Anvil Blvd.
Hyrum, UT 84319

Toll-free: 800-669-4951
Phone: 435-245-6081
www.mtfiberinsulation.com/

Mountain Fiber Insulation's cellulose insulation is made from recycled newspaper. The manufacturer has certified the following recycled-content levels (by weight): total recovered material 80% typical, 80% guaranteed; post-consumer material 80% typical, 80% guaranteed.

Climate Pro Blow-In Loose-Fill Insulation

Johns Manville Corporation
P.O. Box 5108
Denver, CO 80217

Toll-free: 800-654-3103
Phone: 303-978-2000
www.jm.com

Climate Pro® Blowing Wool is a formaldehyde-free loose-fill fiberglass insulation containing 20% post-consumer and 5% post-industrial recycled glass. Climate-Pro can achieve an R-value of R-70 over 1/2" ceiling drywall without exceeding ceiling weight limits.

Climatizer Plus and Enviro-Batt

Climatizer Insulation, Ltd.
120 Claireville Dr.
Etobicoke, ON M9W 5Y3 Canada

Toll-free: 866-871-5495
Phone: 416-798-1235
www.climatizer.com

Climatizer Plus thermal and acoustical cellulose insulation contains recycled newspaper. It may be hand-poured or pneumatically placed with a blowing machine and delivery hose. Enviro-Batt™ contains less than 2% formaldehyde-free, no-VOC adhesive activated by a very small amount of water during pneumatic installation; moisture-loading is only 20% of that experienced with typical wet-cellulose applications. Both products contain at least 85% post-consumer recycled paper fibers.

Cocoon Loose-Fill and Cocoon2 Stabilized Insulation

GreenFiber
2500 Distribution St., Ste. 200
Charlotte, NC 28203

Toll-free: 800-228-0024
Phone: 704-379-0644
www.us-gf.com

Cocoon® Loose-fill Insulation consists of 85% recycled paper fiber (at least 80% post-consumer paper content) that has been treated with borates to meet and exceed fire resistance requirements. Cocoon Insulation is blown into attics and is also used in retrofit sidewall applications. Cocoon2® products consist of 85% recycled paper fiber (at least 80% post-consumer paper content) and have an added adhesive for use in walls, attics, floors, ceilings, and other enclosed spaces.

Comfort-Zone

Mason City Recycling
P.O. Box 1534
Mason City, IA 50402

Toll-free: 800-373-1200
Phone: 641-423-1200
www.mcrecycling.com

Comfort-Zone cellulose insulation is manufactured from recycled newspaper. The manufacturer has certified the following recycled-content levels (by weight): total recovered material 80% typical, 80% guaranteed; post-consumer material 80% guaranteed.

Dry Pac Wall System

Par/PAC(TM)
53 Coveside Rd.
P.O. Box 153
South Bristol, ME 04568

Toll-free: 877-937-3257
www.parpac.com

The Par/PAC™ Dry Pac Wall System™ is a patented cellulose insulation in which a non-elastic, polyester-reinforced vapor retarder (Par/PAC poly) is stapled to wooden wall studs prior to drywalling and Good News-Reused™ cellulose insulation is dry-blown into the cavity at a high density. The poly layer allows inspection of the insulation to prevent voids. Cellulose insulation contains recycled newspaper.

Energy Control

Energy Control, Inc.
804 W. Mill St.
P.O. Box 327
Ossian, IN 46777

Toll-free: 800-451-6429
Phone: 260-622-7614

Manufactured under the brand names Energy Control II and Forest Wool, Energy Control cellulose insulation contains over 80% recycled newspaper.

EnviroPro, EnviroSmart, and Spray-On

Tascon, Inc.
7607 Fairview St.
P.O. Box 41846
Houston, TX 77241

Toll-free: 800-937-1774
Phone: 713-937-0900
www.tasconindustries.com

EnviroPro and EnviroSmart are residential insulation products for attic and wall applications. They are made from recycled paper and perform well to insulate and control sound. Spray-On, made from recycled paper, is applied to interior building walls and ceiling to insulate, prevent condensation, and control sound. The manufacturer has certified the following recycled-content levels (by weight): total recovered material 80% typical, 80% guaranteed; post-consumer material 80% typical, 80% guaranteed.

Fiberlite Cellulose Insulation

Fiberlite Technologies, Inc.
3605 E. 25th St.
Joplin, MO 64804

Toll-free: 800-641-4296
Phone: 417-781-6380
www.fiberlitetech.com

Fiberlite Technologies, Inc. offers several lines of cellulose insulation products containing at least 80% post-consumer recycled newspaper.

Fiber-lite, Fiber-lite Plus, and In-Cide® PC are residential products; SATAC is for commercial use. Wal-Mat is a residential product made with recycled cardboard.

Fibre-Wool Cellulose

Tri-State Insulation Co.
1003 Valley View Dr.
Vermillion, SD 57069

Toll-free: 800-658-3531
Phone: 605-624-6405
www.tri-stateinsulation.com

Tri-State's Fibre-Wool cellulose insulation contains 100% recycled newspaper (minimum 80% post-consumer).

Good News - Reused, House Blanket, Weather Blanket, and Comfort Control

Modern Insulation
1206 S. Monroe St.
Spencer, WI 54479

Phone: 715-659-2446

Modern Insulations' cellulose insulation products contain 80% post-consumer recycled newspaper.

Igloo Cellulose Insulation

Igloo Cellulose, Inc.
195 Brunswick
Pointe Claire, QC H9R 4Z1 Canada

Toll-free: 800-363-7876
Phone: 514-694-1485
www.cellulose.com

Contains 85% recycled newspaper and special natural additives.

InsulSafe SP

CertainTeed Corporation
750 E. Swedesford Rd.
P.O. Box 860
Valley Forge, PA 19482

Toll-free: 800-233-8990
Phone: 610-341-7000
www.certainteed.com

InsulSafe® SP is a formaldehyde-free, loose-fill, fiberglass insulation suitable for open-blow attic applications. InsulSafe SP contains recycled glass cullet (20% post-consumer or post-industrial). This product carries the Greenguard certification for low emissions. The manufacturer has certified the following recycled-content levels (by weight): total recovered material 20% typical; post-consumer material 10% typical.

Mono-Therm

Thermo-Kool of Alaska
P.O. Box 230085
Anchorage, AK 99507

Phone: 907-563-3644

Mono-Therm insulation contains recycled newspaper. The manufacturer has certified the following recycled-content levels (by weight): total recovered material 86% typical, 85% guaranteed; post-consumer material 86% typical, 85% guaranteed.

OPTIMA Fiberglass Insulation

CertainTeed Corporation
750 E. Swedesford Rd.
P.O. Box 860
Valley Forge, PA 19482

Toll-free: 800-233-8990
Phone: 610-341-7000
www.certainteed.com

Optima® is an insulation system composed of a nonwoven fabric facing behind which Optima is blown. Optima fiberglass is blown dry, without additives or moisture, and can be used in closed-cavity, retrofit applications. Some of the glass fibers are from recycled glass cullet. This product carries the Greenguard certification for low emissions. The manufacturer has certified the following recycled-content levels (by weight): total recovered material 20% typical; post-consumer material 10% typical.

Regal Wall Net and Insulweb

Regal Industries, Inc.
9564 E. County Rd. 600 S
Crothersville, IN 47229

Toll-free: 800-848-9687
Phone: 812-793-2214
www.regalind.com

Regal Industries offers two products that are stapled or glued to the interior face of stud framing to contain blown-in cellulose insulation prior to the installation of drywall. Regal Wall Insulweb is a clothlike product, while Regal Wall Net is a more expensive plastic netting. Glue is available either water-based latex by the gallon for warm weather, or solvent-based in a 5-gal. container for cold weather. The solvent-based adhesive has higher VOC emissions.

Therm Shield

Erie Energy Products, Inc.
1400 Irwin Dr.
Erie, PA 16505

Toll-free: 800-233-1810
Phone: 814-454-2828

Therm Shield cellulose insulation contains recycled newspaper.

Thermafiber Mineral Wool Insulation Products

Thermafiber, Inc.
3711 W. Mill St.
Wabash, IN 46992

Toll-free: 888-834-2371
Phone: 260-563-2111
www.thermafiber.com

Thermafiber makes a range of mineral-fiber insulation products made from pre-consumer recycled slag for commercial and residential thermal, sound attenuation, and fire-resistant applications. The products come in a wide variety of densities, facings, thicknesses, and R-values, as rigid or blanket material. These products have been evaluated by an independent testing facility for low pollutant emissions. ThermaTech products, according to the manufacturer, contain no added chemical fire retardants, are noncombustible, odorfree, will not absorb moisture or support mildew or fungus, and will not rot or decay. Phenolic resin content is less than 5% by weight.

Thermo-Cel and Cel-Pak

National Fiber
50 Depot St.
Belchertown, MA 01007

Toll-free: 800-282-7711
Phone: 413-283-8747
www.nationalfiber.com

Cel-Pak and NuWool WallSeal cellulose insulation are borate based and contain 83% recycled newspaper according to the manufacturer. Delivery is available to the 9 northeastern states. The manufacturer has certified the following recycled-content levels (by weight): total recovered material 83% typical, 82% guaranteed; post-consumer material 83% typical, 82% guaranteed.

Therm-O-Light

Therm-O-Comfort Co. Ltd.
75 S. Edgeware Rd.
St. Thomas, ON N5P 2H7 Canada

Toll-free: 877-684-3766
Phone: 519-631-3400
www.thermocomfort.ca

Therm-O-light cellulose insulation is a fiberized product made of 100% recycled newspaper (40% pre-consumer and 60% post-consumer) and a proprietary fire retardant. It is available in both loose fill and stabilized forms.

Thermolok and Thermospray

Hamilton Manufacturing, Inc.
901 Russet St.
Twin Falls, ID 83301

Toll-free: 800-777-9689
Phone: 208-733-9689
www.hmi-mfg.com

Thermolok and Thermospray cellulose insulation contain 100% boron and recycled newspaper.

Walkote Mix II, Loose Fill, and Craftkote

Western Fibers, Inc.
1601 E. Broadway
Hollis, OK 73550

Phone: 580-688-9223
www.westernfibers.com

Walkote Mix II, Loose Fill, and Craftkote cellulose insulation products contain recycled newspaper and cardboard.

Weather Blanket, House Blanket, Comfort Control, and Good News - Reused

Champion Insulation, Inc.
1249 S. Hickory St.
P.O. Box 1555
Fond du Lac, WI 54936

Phone: 920-322-8977
www.championinsulation.com

Champion Insulation's cellulose insulation products are manufactured using over 85% post-consumer recycled newsprint. The manufacturer has certified the following recycled-content levels (by weight): total recovered material 85% typical, 85% guaranteed; post-consumer material 85% typical, 85% guaranteed.

Weathershield

Thermo-Cell Industries, Ltd.
123 Clement Rd.
Vars, ON K0A 3H0 Canada

Toll-free: 800-267-1433
www.thermocell.com

Weathershield cellulose insulation contains 85% by weight recycled newspaper from a mix of post-consumer and post-industrial sources.

Xcell Cellulose Insulation

Central Fiber Corp.
4814 Fiber Ln.
Wellsville, KS 66092

Toll-free: 800-654-6117
Phone: 785-883-4600
www.centralfiber.com

Xcell cellulose insulation is made from recycled newspaper with a boric acid fire-retardant.

Preformed Joint Seals

Quality weatherstripping and gaskets are very important in achieving airtight, low-energy buildings. Specialized gaskets can also be used as a moisture-control strategy, as in the "Airtight Drywall Approach" for light-frame construction.

Weatherstripping and Gaskets

M-D Building Products
4041 N. Santa Fe Ave.
Oklahoma City, OK 73118

Toll-free: 800-654-8454
Phone: 405-528-4411
www.mdteam.com

M-D manufactures a wide range of weatherstripping and weatherization products.

Weatherstripping and Gaskets

Resource Conservation Technology, Inc.
2633 N. Calvert St.
Baltimore, MD 21218

Toll-free: 800-477-7724
Phone: 410-366-1146
www.conservationtechnology.com

Resource Conservation Technology specializes in building gaskets, weatherstripping, and air barriers.

Radiant Barrier Paints

When they face a heat source, radiant barriers work by reflecting heat. When faced away from a heat source, radiant barriers function primarily by virtue of their low emissivity. This means that the surface does not radiate heat well. A radiant-barrier surface on roof sheathing, for example, heats up from the sunlight striking the roof, but that heat energy is not readily emitted into the attic space—so that attic remains cooler. This is why the radiant barrier seems to "reflect" heat back out of the building. An air space is required on at least one side of a radiant barrier in order for it to function as designed. Radiant barriers in attics are most beneficial in reducing cooling loads; their effectiveness in reducing heating loads is more limited. When comparing low-emissivity aluminized paints, look for the lowest emissivity (which corresponds to the highest reflectivity), and low VOC levels. Do not rely on "effective" or "equivalent" R-values, which are only relevant in certain climates or under certain conditions.

E-Barrier Coating

The Sherwin-Williams Company Stores Group
101 Prospect Ave. NW
Cleveland, OH 44115

Toll-free: 800-524-5979
Phone: 216-566-2000
www.sherwin-williams.com

E-Barrier reflective coating for commercial or residential attic decking contains microscopic metal particles to create a low-e surface. Its emissivity when applied over wood is 0.32, and is 0.29 when applied over metal. The VOC content is under 300 g/l —below the 500 g/l limit for metallic pigmented coatings under California Rule 1113. It can be applied with brush, roller, or sprayer. A 2" minimum air space between E-Barrier and the next substrate is required for maximum effectiveness, according to the manufacturer. Energy savings will vary depending upon building materials, home location, and conditions.

Lo/Mit-II

SOLEC-Solar Energy Corp.
129 Walters Ave.
Ewing, NJ 08638

Phone: 609-883-7700
www.solec.org

Lo/Mit-II is a low-emissivity, silicone emulsion radiant barrier paint for interior use. Compared to similar products, it has an unusually low VOC content of 43 g/l, offering an emissivity of 0.21 to 0.26, depending on the substrate. Installs with standard spray equipment, low-nap rollers, or fine-bristle brushes. In buildings, low-e coatings are typically applied to the underside of roof sheathing, and are particularly helpful when retrofitting poorly insulated ceilings.

Radiant Barriers

When they face a heat source, radiant barriers work by reflecting heat. When faced away from a heat source, radiant barriers function primarily by virtue of their low emissivity, which reduces the amount of heat that radiates from them. Radiant barrier products can be foil-faced kraft paper, foil-faced polyethylene film, foil facings on rigid insulation or wood-fiber sheathing, or aluminized paints. If the radiant surface is touching another material it won't work--an air space is required on at least one side of a radiant barrier in order for it to function as designed. Radiant barriers in attics are most beneficial in reducing cooling loads; their effectiveness in reducing heating loads is more limited. Radiant barrier products usually do not include significant recycled content, because of the lower reflectivity of recycled aluminum and the difficulty in producing very thin foils from recycled aluminum; the high embodied energy of virgin aluminum can be recovered through energy savings. Products listed here have below average emissivity (which corresponds to the highest reflectivity), recycled-content in non-aluminum components of the product, or low VOC levels in the case of paints. A word of caution: Do not rely on blanket "effective" or "equivalent" R-values; they are only relevant in certain climates or under certain conditions.

Astro-Foil

Innovative Energy
10653 W. 181 Ave.
Lowell, IN 46356

Phone: 219-696-3639
www.insul.net

Astro-Foil has two layers of polyethylene film with air bubbles sandwiched between layers of reflective aluminum foil. The company claims the following insulation performance, based on ASTM C-236 Hot Box testing procedures, depending on the direction of heatflow: down, R-15; up, R-5.4; and horizontal, R-7.3.

F-2, FSKF, and Type 4, 5, & 6

Superior Radiant Insulation
P.O. Box 247
San Dimas, CA 91773

Toll-free: 888-774-4422
Phone: 909-305-1450
www.superiorrb.com

Superior Radiant Insulation manufactures several radiant barrier and insulation products. F-2 is 100-lb. kraft paper-faced with foil on both sides. Similarly, FSKF has two foil facings on 30-lb. kraft with a nylon or fiberglass mesh scrim layer. Type 4, 5, and 6 are multilayer radiant barriers with chipboard stapling flanges for use in 2x4 and 2x6 framing. Superior Radiant Insulation also manufactures an aluminum foil-faced OSB or plywood sheathing.

Fi-Foil Radiant Barriers

Fi-Foil Company, Inc.
612 Bridgers Ave. W.
P.O. Box 800
Auburndale, FL 33823

Toll-free: 800-448-3401
Phone: 863-965-1846
www.fifoil.com

Fi-Foil produces a number of low- and high-perm radiant sheet barrier products using metalized polyethylene films, recycled paper materials, and PVA hot-melt adhesives. Some products contain metalized PVC backings; those are not specified here. Applications include wood, metal, and masonry wall, roof, and floor systems.

K Shield Reflective Barrier

Key Solutions Marketing
7529 E. Woodshire CV
Scottsdale, AZ 85258

Toll-free: 800-776-9765
Phone: 480-948-5150
www.paintwithceramic.com

The K Shield Reflective Barrier is made from aluminum-foil facings with a core of either 100# kraft paper or plastic film. Available in 500 and 1,000 ft2 rolls, 25-1/2" and 51" wide.

Low-E Insulation

Environmentally Safe Products, Inc.
313 W. Golden Ln.
New Oxford, PA 17350

Toll-free: 800-289-5693
Phone: 717-624-3581
www.low-e.com

Low-E Insulation has a core of microcell polyethylene foam insulation, which has 40% recycled content, and facings of polished aluminum foil. The product is reported to reflect 97% of the radiant energy that strikes its surfaces. Based on the direction of heat flow, the company claims the following insulation performance (ASTM C-236) for the 1/4" version: down, R-10.74; up, R-7.55; and horizontal, R-7.75.

Reflectix Foil/Bubble Insulation

Reflectix, Inc.
1 School St.
P.O. Box 108
Markleville, IN 46056

Toll-free: 800-879-3645
Phone: 765-533-4332
www.reflectixinc.com

Reflectix® reflective-foil, air-cellular insulation consists of one or two layers of air-cellular material laminated between layers of aluminum foil. The company claims up to 97% radiant heat reflection for this insulation. Reflectix insulation is a Class A/Class 1 fire-retardant product. Reflectix, Inc. is a subsidiary of Sealed Air Corp.

The Insulator

Bonded Logic, Inc.
411 E. Ray Rd.
Chandler, AZ 85225

Phone: 480-812-9114
www.bondedlogic.com

The Insulator™ Thermal-Acoustic Insulation is a 3/8"-thick thermal and acoustic insulation made from post-industrial denim and cotton fiber and faced on either one or both sides with an aluminum barrier (also available in a two- or three-ply version). The product is formaldehyde-free and comes in 4' x 6' or 4' x 75' rolls (in 3/8" thickness only). The Insulator is thermally bonded using a synthetic fiber binder and is treated with a boric acid antimicrobial agent. It is Class A fire-rated, and no protective clothing or gear is necessary for installation. The 3/8" pad has a noise reduction coefficient of 0.45 and an R-value of 1.47.

Sprayed Acoustic Insulation

Noise, both from indoor and outside sources, adds to stress and discomfort. A wide range of products are available to help absorb noise and prevent it from spreading. Products listed here are designed to provide acoustical isolation in addition to any thermal insulation properties they may have. If these products are also listed under thermal insulation, they must meet Green-Spec's criteria for that type of thermal insulation.

Cellulose Insulation

Can-Cell Industries, Inc.
14735 124th Ave.
Edmonton, AB T5L 3B2
Canada

Toll-free: 800-661-5031
www.can-cell.com

Can-Cell Industries manufactures Weathershield loose-fill cellulose, WallBAR stabilized cavity-fill cellulose, K-13 spray-applied thermal and acoustical insulation, and Sonaspray "fc" acoustical spray insulation from recycled newspaper. Typical post-consumer recycled content is 85%. Can-Cell Industries now manufactures K-13 and Sonaspray "fc" for the entire Canadian market.

Fiberlite Cellulose Insulation

Fiberlite Technologies, Inc.
3605 E. 25th St.
Joplin, MO 64804

Toll-free: 800-641-4296
Phone: 417-781-6380
www.fiberlitetech.com

Fiberlite Technologies, Inc. offers several lines of cellulose insulation products containing at least 80% post-consumer recycled newspaper.

Fiber-lite, Fiber-lite Plus, and In-Cide® PC are residential products; SATAC is for commercial use. Wal-Mat is a residential product made with recycled cardboard.

K-13 and SonaSpray "fc" Insulation

International Cellulose Corporation
12315 Robin Blvd.
P.O. Box 450006
Houston, TX 77245

Toll-free: 800-979-4914
Phone: 713-433-6701
www.spray-on.com

K-13 is designed for surface-spray applications. It gives a rough finish and can be applied up to 5" thick. SonaSpray® "fc" gives a finished ceiling and can be applied 1" thick. Fire resistance is obtained by adding Borax. Both products, made from recycled ONP, OCC, and other papers, are available in standard colors or custom tints. K-13 has an insulation R-value of 3.8 per inch. SonaSpray "fc" has an NRC (noise reduction) of 0.65 at 1/2" and 0.90 at 1". The manufacturer has certified the following recycled-content levels (by weight): total recovered material 80% typical, 80% guaranteed.

Thermal-Pruf, Dendamix, and Sound-Pruf

American Sprayed Fibers, Inc.
P.O. Box 735
Crown Point, IN 46308

Toll-free: 800-824-2997
Phone: 219-690-0180
www.asfiusa.com

Thermal-Pruf™ is a blend of cellulose and premium rock wool insulation that can be spray-applied onto steel, aluminum, concrete, brick, block, or wood. In addition to achieving an R-value of 3.9/in., Thermal-Pruf also provides fireproofing and acoustical insulation. It can be applied to exterior as well as interior locations and be left textured, rolled to a smooth finish, or overcoated with approved weather-coating systems. American Sprayed Fibers also offers two additional spray-on systems that provide thermal insulation: Dendamix™, made specifically for fireproofing, and Sound-Pruf™ for soundproofing. The manufacturer has certified the following recycled-content levels (by weight): total recovered material 100% guaranteed; post-consumer material 100% guaranteed.

Sprayed Insulation

Many insulation materials that are installed as loose-fill can also be sprayed when mixed with moisture or a binding agent. Some are sprayed into cavities and then covered, as with damp-spray cellulose, or fiberglass with a binder, while others are sprayed onto exposed surfaces. These applications are often effective at reducing air leakage, in addition to reducing conductive heat loss or gain. Installers must carefully manage the moisture content of

damp-sprayed fiber products to ensure that they can dry quickly and avoid trapping moisture in building cavities. Products listed here have high recycled content and low-toxicity binders.

Applegate Loosefill and Stabilized Cellulose Insulation

Applegate Insulation
Manufacturing
1000 Highview Dr.
Webberville, MI 48892

Toll-free: 800-627-7536
Phone: 517-521-3545
www.applegateinsula-
tion.com

Applegate insulation is made with 80-85% recycled newsprint. The manufacturing process uses 1/5 the amount of energy as needed for fiberglass insulation, and generates almost no emissions. The manufacturer has certified the following recycled-content levels (by weight): total recovered material 85% typical, 80% guaranteed; post-consumer material 85% typical, 80% guaranteed.

Attic Insulation and Wall Cavity Spray

ThermoCon
12315 Robin Blvd.
Houston, TX 77045

Toll-free: 800-979-4914
www.thermocon.com

Attic Insulation and Wall Cavity Spray are cellulose insulations made from recycled newspaper.

Cellulose Insulation

Can-Cell Industries, Inc.
14735 124th Ave.
Edmonton, AB T5L 3B2
Canada

Toll-free: 800-661-5031
www.can-cell.com

Can-Cell Industries manufactures Weathershield loose-fill cellulose, WallBAR stabilized cavity-fill cellulose, K-13 spray-applied thermal and acoustical insulation, and Sonaspray "fc" acoustical spray insulation from recycled newspaper. Typical post-consumer recycled content is 85%. Can-Cell Industries now manufactures K-13 and Sonaspray "fc" for the entire Canadian market.

Climatizer Plus and Enviro-Batt

Climatizer Insulation, Ltd.
120 Claireville Dr.
Etobicoke, ON M9W 5Y3 Canada

Toll-free: 866-871-5495
Phone: 416-798-1235
www.climatizer.com

Climatizer Plus thermal and acoustical cellulose insulation contains recycled newspaper. It may be hand-poured or pneumatically placed with a blowing machine and delivery hose. Enviro-Batt™ contains less than 2% formaldehyde-free, no-VOC adhesive activated by a very small amount of water during pneumatic installation; moisture-loading is only 20% of that experienced with typical wet-cellulose applications. Both products contain at least 85% post-consumer recycled paper fibers.

EnviroPro, EnviroSmart, and Spray-On

Tascon, Inc.
7607 Fairview St.
P.O. Box 41846
Houston, TX 77241

Toll-free: 800-937-1774
Phone: 713-937-0900
www.tasconindustries.com

EnviroPro and EnviroSmart are residential insulation products for attic and wall applications. They are made from recycled paper and perform well to insulate and control sound. Spray-On, made from recycled paper, is applied to interior building walls and ceiling to insulate, prevent condensation, and control sound. The manufacturer has certified the following recycled-content levels (by weight): total recovered material 80% typical, 80% guaranteed; post-consumer material 80% typical, 80% guaranteed.

Fiberiffic 2000

Ark-Seal
2185 S. Jason St.
Denver, CO 80223

Toll-free: 800-525-8992
Phone: 303-934-7772
www.fiberiffic.com

Ark-Seal manufactures the Fiberiffic® 2000 spray equipment and supplies the latex binder to spray-on loose-fill insulation (cellulose is the greenest option) with a latex foam binder similar in composition to interior latex paint. This product contains no HCFCs. It can be troweled to a smooth surface or used in blown-in applications. R-values range from 4/in. with fiberglass to 3.6/in. with cellulose, to 3.5/in. with rockwool and cotton. It can be painted, waterproofed, or coated with stucco.

Fiberlite Cellulose Insulation

Fiberlite Technologies, Inc.
3605 E. 25th St.
Joplin, MO 64804

Toll-free: 800-641-4296
Phone: 417-781-6380
www.fiberlitetech.com

Fiberlite Technologies, Inc. offers several lines of cellulose insulation products containing at least 80% post-consumer recycled newspaper. Fiber-lite, Fiber-lite Plus, and In-Cide® PC are residential products; SATAC is for commercial use. Wal-Mat is a residential product made with recycled cardboard.

Isolite, Thermalite, and Isopro

Thermoguard Insulation Co. LLC
125 N. Dyer Rd.
Spokane, WA 99212

Toll-free: 800-541-0579
Phone: 509-535-4600
www.service-partners.com

Thermoguard offers a loose-fill cellulose insulation and two different spray-on adhesive insulations, one with a mesh backing. Both are designed for wet-spray installation. Thermoguard is UL-approved. Thermoguard insulation contains recycled newspaper.

K-13 and SonaSpray "fc" Insulation

International Cellulose Corporation
12315 Robin Blvd.
P.O. Box 450006
Houston, TX 77245

Toll-free: 800-979-4914
Phone: 713-433-6701
www.spray-on.com

K-13 is designed for surface-spray applications. It gives a rough finish and can be applied up to 5" thick. SonaSpray® "fc" gives a finished ceiling and can be applied 1" thick. Fire resistance is obtained by adding Borax. Both products, made from recycled ONP, OCC, and other papers, are available in standard colors or custom tints. K-13 has an insulation R-value of 3.8 per inch. SonaSpray "fc" has an NRC (noise reduction) of 0.65 at 1/2" and 0.90 at 1". The manufacturer has certified the following recycled-content levels (by weight): total recovered material 80% typical, 80% guaranteed.

Monoglass Spray-On Insulation

Monoglass, Inc.
922 - 1200 W. 73rd Ave.
Vancouver, BC V6P 6G5 Canada

Toll-free: 888-777-2966
Phone: 604-261-7712
www.monoglass.com

Monoglass® Spray-On Insulation is a combination of elongated, recycled-cullet glass fibers and water-based, nontoxic adhesives that can be spray-applied to virtually any surface or configuration. Without additional support, Monoglass can be applied overhead to a maximum of 5" (R-20) and applied vertically to 7" (R-28). Monoglass is white in color, noncombustible, and can be applied over fireproofing.

Monoglass contains no formaldehyde and does not support fungal growth or encourage infestation by pests. The manufacturer has certified the following recycled-content levels (by weight): total recovered material 37% typical, 37% guaranteed; post-consumer material 25% typical, 25% guaranteed.

Nu-Wool Engineered Cellulose Insulation

Nu-Wool Co., Inc.
2472 Port Sheldon St.
Jenison, MI 49428

Toll-free: 800-748-0128
Phone: 616-669-0100
www.nuwool.com

Nu-Wool cellulose insulation is made from recycled newspaper and contains an EPA Registered fungicide making it resistant to mold growth. The manufacturer has certified the following recycled-content levels (by weight): total recovered material 85% typical, 85% guaranteed; post-consumer material 85% typical, 85% guaranteed.

Thermafiber Mineral Wool Insulation Products

Thermafiber, Inc.
3711 W. Mill St.
Wabash, IN 46992

Toll-free: 888-834-2371
Phone: 260-563-2111
www.thermafiber.com

Thermafiber makes a range of mineral-fiber insulation products made from pre-consumer recycled slag for commercial and residential thermal, sound attenuation, and fire-resistant applications. The products come in a wide variety of densities, facings, thicknesses, and R-values, as rigid or blanket material. These products have been evaluated by an independent testing facility for low pollutant emissions. ThermaTech products, according to the manufacturer, contain no added chemical fire retardants, are noncombustible, odor-free, will not absorb moisture or support mildew or fungus, and will not rot or decay. Phenolic resin content is less than 5% by weight.

Thermal-Pruf, Dendamix, and Sound-Pruf

American Sprayed Fibers, Inc.
P.O. Box 735
Crown Point, IN 46308

Toll-free: 800-824-2997
Phone: 219-690-0180
www.asfiusa.com

Thermal-Pruf™ is a blend of cellulose and premium rock wool insulation that can be spray-applied onto steel, aluminum, concrete, brick, block, or wood. In addition to achieving an R-value of 3.9/in., Thermal-Pruf also provides fireproofing and acoustical insulation. It can be applied to exterior as well as interior locations and be left textured, rolled to a smooth finish, or overcoated with approved weather-coating systems. American Sprayed Fibers also offers two additional spray-on systems that provide thermal insulation: Dendamix™, made specifically for fireproofing, and Sound-Pruf™ for soundproofing. The manufacturer has certified the following recycled-content levels (by weight): total recovered material 100% guaranteed; post-consumer material 100% guaranteed.

Walkote Mix II, Loose Fill, and Craftkote

Western Fibers, Inc.
1601 E. Broadway
Hollis, OK 73550

Phone: 580-688-9223
www.westernfibers.com

Walkote Mix II, Loose Fill, and Craftkote cellulose insulation products contain recycled newspaper and cardboard.

Structural Insulated Panels

Most structural insulated panels (SIPs) consist of oriented strand board (OSB) sandwiching an insulating foam core. SIPs are gaining market share in the residential and light commercial building market because they're quick to assemble and provide excellent energy performance. The insulating core of SIPs is most commonly made from expanded polystyrene (EPS)—not to be confused with extruded polystyrene, which is not ozone safe—though in some cases polyurethane foam, or even compressed straw or mineral wool, is used. SIPs are manufactured in a range of thicknesses providing different R-values. In response to problems with insects burrowing in SIP foam cores, look for products that incorporate borate compounds, which can help deter them. Even with borate treatment, however, it may be necessary to use insect mesh, trap systems, and insecticides on an ongoing basis. SIP buildings can be quickly assembled, particularly when panels are factory-cut for door and window openings.

Agriboard

Agriboard Industries, L.C.
8301 E. 21st St. N
Suite 320
Wichita, KS 67206

Toll-free: 866-247-4267
Phone: 316-630-9223
www.agriboard.com

After being purchased by one of the original investors in the company, Agriboard™ Industries is back in business manufacturing an engineered insulated panel construction system; its straw core is bound only with high heat and pressure. 4" cores are laminated single- or double-ply between two sheets of OSB using a polyurethane adhesive, though Agriboard has plans to switch to a soy-based adhesive, as well as straw-based outer panels. According to the company, the structural wall panels offer excellent thermal and acoustical insulation, have up to a 2-hour fire transmission rating, and are lower in cost and two to three times stronger than conventional wood-frame construction in compressive load, racking, and bending. Agriboard also offers a new ceramic and fiberglass composite, water- and UV-resistant, factory-applied exterior coating.

Enercept Super Insulated Building System

Enercept, Inc.
3100 9th Ave. SE
Watertown, SD 57201

Toll-free: 800-658-3303
Phone: 605-882-2222
www.enercept.com

Enercept SIPs consist of a core of expanded polystyrene laminated between two sheets of oriented strand board (OSB).

EPS and Polyurethane SIPs

Winter Panel Corporation
74 Glen Orne Dr.
Brattleboro, VT 05301

Phone: 802-254-3435
www.winterpanel.com

Winter Panel produces structural insulated panels with either EPS or polyisocyanurate (poly-urethane) foam cores. EPS has always been blown with non-ozone-depleting, non-global-warming pentane. As of late 2003, Winter

Panel's urethane foam is using HFC-245 as a blowing agent, which is also non-ozone-depleting. The 4-1/2"- or 6-1/2"-thick panels are available in Structurewall™ (a direct substitute for 2x4 or 2x6 framing using OSB as the outer skins), Curtainwall panels (nonstructural with gypsum wallboard on interior side, OSB on outside), and Woodclad™ (Structurewall panels with 1x8 v-groove pine cladding on interior finish side). The EPS-core panels are less expensive, while the polyurethane panels have a higher R-value. Panels with custom skins, cores, and thicknesses are also available.

Foard Structural Insulated Panels

Foard Panel
P.O. Box 185
West Chesterfield, NH 03466

Toll-free: 800-644-8885
Phone: 603-256-8800
www.foardpanel.com

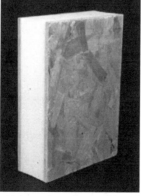

Foard Panel, Inc. makes structural insulated panels (SIPs) with expanded polystyrene foam cores (ESP), which are ozone-safe. Foard SIPs are four feet wide, and eight to 24 feet long with nominal 4", 6", or 8" thick insulation cores. In additional to the structural panels, Foard also makes a curtainwall panel, with drywall on one side an oriented-strand board (OSB) on the other, and nailbase roof insulation panel, with OSB on one side only. Only products with an EPS core are being specified here.

Industry Representation

Structural Insulated Panel Association
P.O. Box 1699
Gig Harbor, WA 98335

Phone: 253-858-7472
www.sips.org

The Structural Insulated Panel Association (SIPA) represents the industry in promoting the advantages of SIPs to designers, contractors, and homeowners.

Insulspan SIPs

Insulspan
9012 E. U.S. Hwy. 223
P.O. Box 38
Blissfield, MI 49228

Toll-free: 800-726-3510
Phone: 517-486-4844
www.insulspan.com

Insulspan's SIPs are produced with EPS foam cores laminated between OSB sheathing.

Murus EPS and Polyurethane SIPs

The Murus Company, Inc.
3234 Rte. 549
P.O. Box 220
Mansfield, PA 16933

Phone: 570-549-2100
www.murus.com

Murus produces structural insulated panels offering several skin materials including OSB, cement board, and sound board, among others, with non-ozone depleting polyurethane or EPS foam cores. Both panel types are available in a variety of sizes, thicknesses, and application-specific configurations. The EPS SIPs are available with system R-Values of 16, 23, 30, 38, and 45 (the latter 12-1/4" thick), and are manufactured by cutting and laminating the pre-molded EPS core to the OSB skin with a urethane adhesive. The Polyurethane SIPs have a tongue and groove edge and unique cam-lock connectors. The Polyurethane SIPs are available with system R-values of 26, 33, and 40, and are manufactured by foaming the self-adhering expanding foam between the skins.

Polyurethane Structural Insulated Panels

Insulated Component Structures
Rocky Mountain, Inc. (ICS-RM)
5858 Wright Dr.
Loveland, CO 80538

Phone: 970-427-7477
www.ics-rm.net

ICS-Rocky Mountain produces structural insulated panels (SIPS) with polyurethane foam cores that provide above R-6 per inch and have ASTM Class 1 fire resistance rating. The foam is blown without ozone depleting substances and is injected between the skins, resulting in strong surface bonding. Products include corner, wall, roof, and specially shaped panels, as well as cladding (for adding insulation to the outside of an existing building). Panels include metal camlocks for ease of installation and are available in a variety of sizes and thicknesses. Wall and roof panels come in 4 1/2" (R-28+), and 6 1/2" (R-42+) thicknesses. Surface options include fiber-cement, OSB, fiber re-enforced plastic laminate, metal, and custom. ICS-Rocky Mountain, with its affiliate companies in Florida and North Carolina, manufactures and distributes nationally.

R-Control Panels

AFM Corporation
211 River Ridge Circle S., Ste. 102
Burnsville, MN 55337

Toll-free: 800-255-0176
Phone: 952-474-0809
www.r-control.com

R-Control® SIPs are made with EPS cores and OSB skins. AMF's R-Control Perform Guard® panels incorporate Frameguard to protect against mold, mildew, and termites. Panel dimensions range from 4' x 8' to 8' x 24' in thicknesses of 4-1/2" to 12-1/4". AFM has conducted full structural and fire testing of its system, including relevant building code listings. AFM licenses manufacturers throughout the U.S. to produce R-Control SIPs. Currently, not all manufacturing facilities apply Frameguard.

Structural Insulated Panels

Extreme Panel Technologies, Inc.
475 E. Fourth St. N
P.O. Box 435
Cottonwood, MN 56229

Toll-free: 800-977-2635
Phone: 507-423-5530
www.extremepanel.com

Extreme Panel Technologies, Inc. manufactures structural insulated panels for residential, commercial, and agricultural applications. Panels are made with oriented strand board manufactured to APA standards for maximum strength and durability, and are available with expanded polystyrene cores.

Structural Insulated Panels

FischerSIPs, Inc.
1843 Northwestern Pkwy.
Louisville, KY 40203

Toll-free: 800-792-7477
Phone: 502-778-5577
www.fischersips.com

A FischerSIP® is made by laminating an expanded polystyrene foam core between two sheets of 7/16" oriented strand board (OSB). Panels can be manufactured in sizes ranging from 4' x 8' to 8' x 24'.

Structural Insulated Panels

Foam Laminates of Vermont
P.O. Box 102
Hinesburg, VT 05461

Toll-free: 800-545-6290
Phone: 802-453-3727
www.foamlaminates.com

Foam Laminates of Vermont started manufacturing structural insulated panels in 1982 in conjunction with their sister company, Vermont Frames. Exterior skins are generally plywood or OSB. Insulating cores are either expanded polystyrene (EPS) or polyisocyanurate. Only products with an EPS core are being specified here.

Structural Insulated Panels

General Panel Corporation
106 Perma R Rd.
Johnson City, TN 37604

Toll-free: 800-647-6130
www.generalpanel.com

General Panel Corporation, formerly Perma R and previously listed as Apache Products Company, produces an EPS-core SIP system.

Structural Insulated Panels

Pacemaker Building Systems
126 New Pace Rd.
P.O. Box 279
Newcomerstown, OH 43832

Toll-free: 800-551-9799
Phone: 740-498-4181
www.pacemakerbuildingsystems.com

Pacemaker Building Systems is a manufacturer of Structural Insulated Panels with full fire and structural testing, and related UL and building code listings. The panels are made with EPS cores and OSB skins. Dimensions range from 4' x 8' to 8' x 24' in thicknesses of 4-9/16" (R-16) to 12-9/16" (R-45).

Structural Insulated Panels

PORTERCorp
4240 N. 136th Ave.
Holland, MI 49424

Toll-free: 800-354-7721
Phone: 616-399-1963
www.portersips.com

PORTERCorp (formerly W. H. Porter) SIPs are made with an EPS foam core and come in any size that can be cut from a 4' x 8' or 8' x 24' sheet of oriented strand board. Panels with custom angles and/or cut-outs are also available. Panels are available in thicknesses of 4-1/2", 6-1/2", 8-1/4", 10-1/4", and 12-1/4" and provide R-values ranging from 15.8 to 45.7.

Structural Insulated Panels

Premier Building Systems - Division of Premier Industries, Inc.
4609 70th Ave. East
Fife, WA 98424

Toll-free: 800-275-7086
Phone: 253-926-2020
www.pbspanel.com

Premier Building Systems manufactures SIPs with borate-treated EPS foam insulation and OSB skins. Other substrates are available upon request. EPS may contain up to 15% recycled content. Panels are available in sizes of 4' x 8' up to 8' x 24' and range in thickness from 4" to 12" (with R-values of 15, 23, 30, 37, and 45). The company has SIP manufacturing plants in Fife, Washington, and Phoenix, Arizona.

Structural Insulated Panels

Shelter Enterprises, Inc.
8 Saratoga St.
P.O. Box 618
Cohoes, NY 12047

Toll-free: 800-836-0719
Phone: 518-237-4101
www.shelter-ent.com

Shelter custom-builds stress skin panels and interior wall panels in sizes up to 8' x 40'. Shelter produces their own EPS foam for the core. 98% of the EPS waste is recycled into other products. Other core materials are available upon request.

Thermal Foam SIPs

Thermal Foams, Inc.
2101 Kenmore Ave.
Buffalo, NY 14207

Phone: 716-874-6474
www.thermalfoams.com

Thermal Foams Inc. is a manufacturer of structural insulated panels made from Thermal Foams EPS cores and OSB Skins. Panel sizes range from 4' x 8' to 8' x 24' in thicknesses of 4-1/2" to 12-1/4". Thermal Foams has gone through full structural and fire testing of its systems with an approved model code testing facility.

Thermapan Structural Insulated Panels

Thermapan Structural Insulated Panels Inc.
1380 Commerce Pkwy.
P.O. Box 429
Fort Erie, ON L2A 5M4 Canada

Toll-free: 877-443-9255
Phone: 905-994-7399
www.thermapan.com

Thermapan SIP, formerly known as The Wall™, is an EPS-core structural insulated panel system.

Thermal Insulation

Thermal insulation products for buildings generally reduce the flow of heat by trapping air or some other gas in a matrix of loose-fill fibers or particles (glass, cellulose, mineral wool, cotton), sprayed in place foams, or rigid board products. Products listed here exhibit one or more of the following attributes: reduced off-gassing (particularly of formaldehydes), post-consumer recycled-content, less-processed formulations, post-industrial waste content, non-ozone depleting blowing agents, and reduced greenhouse gas emissions. Note that any product that manages conductive heat loss can also manage both energy loss by air infiltration and moisture flow; the selection process for insulation products should include consideration of these other hygrothermal properties.

Aerogel Insulation

Solar Components Corp.
121 Valley St.
Manchester, NH 03103

Phone: 603-668-8186
www.solar-components.com

Cabot's synthetic silica aerogel, Nanogel™, provides both high insulating value (R-8/inch) and high light transmissivity (53% with 1" thickness). The product is UV-stable, hydrophobic, and non-combustible. The lightweight microporous structure reduces sound transmission as well as heat conduction and convection. This aerogel provides diffuse daylighting without sacrificing energy performance, and has been used for a number of daylighting products. Solar Components Corporation sells this Aerogel in one- and five-gallon containers.

Industry Representation

North American Insulation Manufacturers Association
44 Canal Center Plz., Ste. 310
Alexandria, VA 22314

Phone: 703-684-0084
www.naima.org

The North American Insulation Manufacturers Association (NAIMA) is the trade association of North American manufacturers of fiberglass, rock wool, and slag wool insulation products. Insulation often incorporates recycled glass and iron slag. The manufacturer has certified the following recycled-content levels (by weight): total recovered material 70% typical; post-consumer material 40% typical.

This Space is Available for Your Notes

Flooring & Floorcoverings

Flooring and floorcoverings are subject to physical abuse from feet and heavy objects; and since they're the lowest spot in a room, they tend to collect dirt, moisture, and other contaminants. A good flooring material should be very durable—to reduce the frequency of replacement—and it should be easy to clean. At the same time, softer surfaces may be preferred for reasons of comfort, noise absorption, and style, setting up a potential conflict in choices. Raw material and manufacturing impacts must also be considered with many types of carpeting and other floorcoverings.

Carpet systems, including carpet pads and adhesives, have been identified by the EPA as a potential source of indoor air pollution. Testing and monitoring are ongoing; the Green Label and more stringent Green Label Plus programs of the Carpet and Rug Institute help prevent the most severe instances of toxic offgassing from new carpet. High-end commercial carpets tend to be more chemically stable than inexpensive residential-quality carpets; some manufacturers are willing to provide detailed air-quality testing data on their products. Carpets may also contribute to air quality problems by trapping pollutants and moisture, and damp carpeting can provide a medium for growth of mold, mildew, and dust mites. Flexible-foam carpet padding frequently contains brominated flame retardants (BFRs); these compounds, chemically similar to PCBs, are raising health concerns because they are being found in human blood and breast milk worldwide, and there is evidence of health effects. BFRs from carpet padding can be released into the living space, especially as the carpet padding ages. In residences, hard flooring surfaces with area rugs, which can be thoroughly cleaned, are often preferable to wall-to-wall carpeting.

Modular carpet tiles can be replaced selectively, reducing the cost and environmental impact of recarpeting an entire room when one area becomes worn or damaged. Some carpet tiles also contain a high percentage of recycled content, and others can be resurfaced and reused. Carpet tiles with random patterns allow easy replacement of individual tiles. Some companies now have extensive recycling programs; when installing new carpeting, it may be possible to have the old carpeting hauled away for recycling at a price no higher than the cost of disposal.

A wide variety of high quality carpet is made from recycled soda bottles (PET) and offers the feel and performance of conventional carpet in residential or other low-traffic settings. Natural-fiber carpet with jute backing can be a good alternative to synthetic fibers, particularly if the carpeting is made domestically. Imported wool carpet is typically treated with pesticides before it can enter the country. Some sources suggest that the lifecycle cost of wood carpet, which includes the agricultural degradation of grazing and other factors, may be quite high.

The underlayment used between a subfloor and floorcovering is often made from Lauan, a tropical hardwood that comes from unsustainable logging operations in Southeast Asia. Other underlayment products are available and should be chosen in consultation with your floorcovering supplier. For example, recycled-content, formaldehyde-free, gypsum-based underlayment is recommended by major tile manufacturers as a substrate. Under carpet, a recycled-newsprint-and-paraffin product is a good alternative. Wool underlayment is also available.

Vinyl flooring, whose primary component is polyvinyl chloride (PVC), may be a source of VOC offgassing, both from the flooring itself and from the adhesive. There's also concern about toxic byproducts, such as dioxin, which may be produced in accidental fires or if the material is incinerated at the end of its useful life. Natural linoleum, made primarily from cork and linseed oil, is a possible substitute, though it's currently manufactured only in Europe. VOCs are also released from linoleum—but these are from minimally processed linseed oil and are not generally considered as harmful as those from petrochemical sources. Nevertheless, some chemically sensitive people may find them problematic. Adhesives used for linoleum must also be screened carefully for toxic offgassing.

Ceramic and porcelain tile have a high embodied energy, but their durability makes them environmentally sound in the long run. Some high-quality ceramic tile incorporates recycled glass. Regionally produced stone flooring is a good natural finish when sealed with low-toxic sealers.

Terrazzo is a long-lasting, nontoxic floorcovering option that uses crushed stone, and sometimes post-consumer recycled glass, in a cementitious matrix. The embodied energy of portland cement is a consideration. Epoxy-based "synthetic terrazzo" may also utilize recycled glass; while the 100%-solids product is considered safe for installers and is benign when cured, bispehonal-A (BPA) is used in the manufacture of epoxy. BPA is a bioaccumulating chemical considered by some experts to be an endocrine disrupter even at minute quantities. Like brominated flame retardants, BPA has been showing up in nature in increasing amounts.

Hardwood flooring from certified well-managed forests may be an excellent environmental choice. Other hardwoods come from forestry operations that may not be environmentally responsible. Tropical hardwoods, in particular, should be avoided unless FSC-certified due to the sensitivity of those ecosystems. Certification to Forest Stewardship Council—FSC—standards involves third-party evaluation and monitoring of sustainable forestry practices. Reclaimed and recycled wood flooring milled from the large timbers of old structures, trestle bridges, or "sinker logs" is another option.

Fast-growing bamboo is manufactured into hardwood-type strip flooring by a number of Southeast Asian companies, offering an intriguing alternative to standard hardwood. Very-low-formaldehyde products are now entering the marketplace, and at least one manufacturer claims to be formaldehyde-free.

Acoustical Underlayment

Acoustical underlayment—which is distinct from flooring underlayment—helps prevent sound transmission through a structure. Use of a sound-deadening sheathing can reduce the need to further control sound transmission with carpeting or rugs.

Homasote 440 SoundBarrier and ComfortBase

Homasote Company
932 Lower Ferry Rd.
P.O. Box 7240
West Trenton, NJ 08628

Toll-free: 800-257-9491
Phone: 609-883-3300
www.homasote.com

Homasote 440 Sound Barrier® and Comfort Base® panels are high-density fiberboard made from 100% recycled wastepaper and a formaldehyde-free paraffin binder, with an R-value of 1.2 for a 1/2" panel. Sound Barrier panels are available in a variety of sizes and thicknesses and are designed to provide sound control as a flooring underlayment and in wall assemblies. Comfort Base is designed for use as a floating underlayment over a concrete slab, has a grooved grid pattern on the underside to provide slab ventilation, and is 1/2" thick. Homasote has been manufacturing building panels from waste papers since 1909.

QuietWood

Quiet Solution
1250 Elko Dr.
Sunnyvale, CA 94089

Toll-free: 800-797-8159
www.quietsolution.com

QuietWood™ sound-control plywood for floors and walls is made with a thin layer of steel embedded in viscoelastic polymer and sandwiched between wood veneers. It provides impressive sound transmission reduction, installs quickly, and results in very little added thickness, relative to the sound control provided. QuietWood is available in thicknesses ranging from 5/8" to 1-3/8".

SoundStop Interior Substrate

Knight-Celotex
One Northfield Plaza
Northfield, IL 60093

Phone: 847-716-8030
www.knightcelotex.com

SoundStop™ interior acoustical substrate from Knight-Celotex is a 1/2" fiberboard that can be used to achieve system STC ratings exceeding 42. Designed to be installed prior to wall or ceiling drywall or plywood underlayment, it is made with 96% recovered fiber (hardwood or sugarcane, depending on which plant manufactures the product), and small percentages of starch and wax. Knight-Celotex also produces SoundStop® Underlayment.

Backing Boards and Underlayments

Underlayment products for flooring serve several functions and can be made from a variety of materials. Environmentally preferable materials for flooring underlayment include natural cork, strawboard, and recycled-paper-based fiberboard. Using underlayment products beneath wood, tile, resilient flooring, or carpet and carpet cushion provides a level surface and helps insulate floors from sound transmission and, to a limited extent, heat loss. Cork rolls and sheets provide particularly high added resilience to the floor system, with significantly less thickness than fiberboard products or a gypsum-cement poured-in-place slab. Use of a sound-deadening underlayment below a hard-surface floor can reduce the need to further control sound transmission with carpeting or rugs.

BetterBoard Tile Backer

Curb Appeal Materials, LTD
3824 N. Johnsburg Rd.
McHenry, IL 60050

Phone: 815-344-7926
www.vortexcomposites.com

BetterBoard™ is a flexible tile backer board for kitchens and other interior building locations with or without high moisture loads. It's made with 100% recycled materials—nylon carpet waste with some commingled plastic from post-consumer and post-industrial sources. The thermoplastic waterproof sheets can be cut with standard tools, screwed, nailed, and glued; they will not rot, deteriorate, or support mold or insects. According to the manufacturer, no waste is generated in the manufacturing process, and the product is recyclable. BetterBoard is a vapor barrier; has 1/4 the weight of traditional backer board; contains no asbestos, gypsum, fiberglass, formaldehyde, or silica; and it doesn't generate dust when cut.

DensArmor Plus and DensShield

G-P Gypsum Corporation
133 Peachtree St. NE
Atlanta, GA 30303

Toll-free: 800-284-5347
Phone: 404-652-4000
www.gp.com/gypsum

G-P Gypsum manufactures the Dens™ line of paperless gypsum board products, which offer excellent mold resistance for residential and commercial construction. Instead of paper facings, the Dens™ products incorporate fiberglass mats on surfaces. This provides moisture resistance and removes a potential food source for mold, but the facing also hinders recyclability, so these products are recommended primarily for moisture prone areas. In particular, DensArmor Plus® panels are designed for interior moisture-prone areas such as basements and residential bathrooms, and DensShield® Tile Backer is a mold-resistant tile backer board.

Fiberock Brand Aqua Tough Panels

USG Corporation
555 West Adams St.
Chicago, IL 60661

Toll-free: 800-874-4968
Phone: 312-436-4000
www.usg.com

Fiberock Interior panels and Sheathing with Aqua Tough are an FGD (flue-gas desulfurization) gypsum and cellulose formulation suitable for a wide range of applications. Interior panels can be used in wet and dry areas as a tile backer board or as a standard drywall panel when mold resistance is required. Fiberock AR and VHI are products that offer an exceptional level of abuse resistance. Fiberock panels have been certified by Scientific Certification Systems (SCS) to contain 95% recycled material, 85% of which is post-industrial recycled gypsum and 10% recycled paper fiber.

Fiberock Brand Aqua Tough Underlayment / Tile Backerboard

USG Corporation
555 West Adams St.
Chicago, IL 60661

Toll-free: 800-874-4968
Phone: 312-436-4000
www.usg.com

Fiberock Underlayment and Tile Backerboard with Aqua Tough Technology are an FGD gypsum and cellulose formulation suitable for a wide range of applications in both wet and dry areas. Fiberock underlayment is a suitable substrate for ceramic tile and composite flooring, while Fiberock Tile Backerboard is specifically for floor and wall applications under ceramic tile (including shower applications). These panels are indentation-resistant and use no adhesives, solvents, or resins; and they have been certified by Scientific Certification Systems (SCS) to contain 95% recycled material, 85% of which is post-industrial recycled gypsum and 10% recycled paper fiber.

Ny-Backer

NYCORE
200 Galleria Pkwy., Ste. 2000
Atlanta, GA 30339

Phone: 770-980-0000
www.nycore.com

Nybacker is a flexible tile backer board for interior building locations with or without high moisture loads. Made with 100% recycled materials (nylon carpet waste with some commingled plastic from post-consumer and post-industrial sources), the thermoplastic waterproof sheets can be cut with standard tools, screwed, nailed, and glued; they will not absorb water, rot, deteriorate, or support mold or insects. According to the manufacturer, no waste is generated in the manufacturing process. Nybacker is one-quarter the weight of cement backer boards; serves as a vapor barrier; contains no asbestos,

gypsum, fiberglass, formaldehyde, or silica; and does not generate dust when cut. It is available in 3x5, 4x4, and 4x8 panels; special orders for large projects are accepted.

Bamboo Flooring

Most bamboo for flooring comes from the Hunan province of China. It's not a food source for pandas, which generally inhabit higher-elevation forests. Despite the long-distance transport of the product to the United States, the durability, hardness, and short regeneration time of bamboo provide justification for using it for flooring instead of conventionally harvested wood. Bamboo is typically processed without preservatives or with benign boric acid, but more toxic preservatives are occasionally used when unprocessed poles are exported. Most bamboo flooring is glued together with urea-formaldehyde binders, which is the primary negative aspect. As the popularity and availability of bamboo increases, so does the need for uniform and credible certification of green attributes. Ideally there would be verification of: (1) low ambient VOC emissions using chamber testing (certified to meet Floorscore or Greenguard), (2) limited use of pesticides and preservatives, (3) growing practices (certified to FSC standards), and (4) manufacturing conditions. GreenSpec listings will be updated to reflect such information as it becomes available. Products listed here are made with binders and adhesives that have ultra-low formaldehyde concentrations (<=0.02 ppm), or have formaldehyde emissions of 0.05ppm or lower using the ASTM E-1333 test for Europe's E1 standard or another roughly equivalent standard (because testing protocols are different, standards are not truly comparable).

Avanti Bamboo Flooring

Central Bamboo Flooring Inc.
2501 Channing Ave.
San Jose, CA 95131

Phone: 408-943-8599
www.centralfloors.com

Central Bamboo Flooring is the sole importer and distributor of Avanti Brand bamboo flooring and molding. The 3-5/8" x 5/8" tongue-and-groove flooring is available unfinished or pre-finished with water-based, non-off-gassing finishes. Avanti offers a variety of patterns, colors, and finishes.

Bamboo Hardwoods Flooring

Bamboo Hardwoods, Inc.
4100 4th Ave. S
Seattle, WA 98134

Toll-free: 800-783-0557
Phone: 206-264-2414
www.bamboohardwoods.com

Bamboo Hardwoods, a U.S. company with a factory in Vietnam, sells both unfinished and prefinished flooring. The unfinished product is vertically laminated, and the prefinished product includes a rubber-tree-wood inner core. These flooring products are manufactured with a melamine adhesive and a boric acid insecticide. The rubberwood used is harvested from over-mature trees on rubber plantations that are out of production. Bamboo Hardwoods also reports that their engineered floor now uses a much harder bamboo (measuring 2048 on the Janka Ball Hardness Test)—the hardest bamboo ever discovered, according to the company.

Bamboo Mountain

Bamboo Mountain, Inc.
110 Pacific Ave. #357
San Francisco, CA 94111

Toll-free: 877-700-1772
Phone: 415-839-7271
www.bamboomountain.com

Bamboo Mountain™, founded in 1997, offers very-low-VOC bamboo flooring in seamless 3' strip, 6' long strip, and 6' plank flooring, along with a trim line that includes heater vent covers, stair treads & riser, and baseboards. All flooring is made with the mid-stalk of Moso bamboo that is harvested on a 6-year cycle, using formaldehyde-free glues in an ISO 9002-certified factory. Bamboo Mountain provides a 25-year warranty.

GreenFloors Bamboo Flooring

GreenFloors
3170 Draper Dr.
Fairfax, VA 22031

Phone: 703-352-8300
www.greenfloors.com

GreenFloors Premium bamboo flooring uses formaldehyde-free glues. A wide variety of lengths, widths, colors and styles (solid, engineered, hand scraped, and stained) are available, including glueless, click-together, floating systems. Veneers and panels are also offered. GreenFloors offers a lifetime structural warranty, and a 25-year finish warranty.

GreenWood Bamboo Flooring

GreenWood Products Company
33049 Calle Aviador, Unit A
San Juan Capistrano, CA 92675

Toll-free: 866-593-4454
Phone: 760-529-0015
www.greenwoodbamboo.com

GreenWood Products Company offers horizontally and vertically laminated bamboo flooring in natural or carbonized colors with a 7-coat aluminum oxide urethane finish. Both styles are 5/8" thick and measure 3-5/8" x 72". The horizontal style is also offered in a 6"-wide version. Formaldehyde emissions are a very low 0.0127 ppm.

JMX Bamboo Molding and Flooring

JMX International Corporation
2123 Porter Lake Dr., Unit H
Sarasota, FL 34240

Toll-free: 866-272-6773
Phone: 941-377-5112
www.jmxbamboo.com

JMX International imports pre-finished bamboo products including flooring and molding in a wide variety of sizes and styles.

Mill Valley Bamboo Flooring

Mill Valley Bamboo Associates
14 E. Sir Francis Drake Blvd.
Larkspur, CA 94939

Toll-free: 877-392-2626
Phone: 415-925-1188
www.mvbamboo.com

Mill Valley Bamboo designs and imports bamboo products from their own factories in China, using only 5-6 year old, fully matured bamboo and non-offgassing, formaldehyde-free, water-based glues and finishes. The exceptionally hard flooring comes in six assorted lengths per box, and can be shipped directly to the site. Custom specifications are available. The company offers 66 styles.

Plyboo Bamboo Flooring

Smith & Fong Company
475 6th St.
S. San Francisco, CA 94103

Toll-free: 866-835-9859
Phone: 415-896-0577
www.plyboo.com

Plyboo® Bamboo Flooring comes either flat or vertical-grained in a natural or amber color. Unfinished or prefinished with aluminum oxide, all flooring measures 5/8" x 3-3/4" x 75" and comes 23.4 ft2 per box. Plyboo is laminated with a low- or zero-VOC adhesive, with formaldehyde emissions testing for the entire product line at 0.3 ppm or below. This flooring is also available as part of their PlybooPure line. PlybooPure products use low-emitting, stable polyisocyanurate as the binder and contain no urea formaldehyde (UF). The company also offers a comprehensive range of trim moldings in stairnosing, threshold, reducer, and baseshoe profiles, and baseboard prefinished in amber or natural color.

Silkroad Bamboo Flooring

K&M Bamboo Products, Inc.
300 Esna Park Dr., Unit 26
Markham, ON L3R 1H3 Canada

Phone: 905-946-8128
www.silkroadflooring.com

K&M Bamboo Products Inc. offers Silkroad™ horizontally or vertically laminated bamboo flooring in natural or carbonized colors, 3-5/8" wide x 5/8" or 1/2" thick, and 36" or 72" long. Also offered are a carbonized composite lamination (3-5/8" wide x 1/2" thick x 36" long) and an amber horizontally-laminated plank (3-5/8" wide x 5/8" thick x 36" long). Accessories include bull-nosing, baseboards, reducers, T-moldings, quarter-rounds, and stair treads. Finish options are 100% UV-cured urethane and aluminum oxide. Silkroad bamboo has a total VOC emission of .017 mg/m2/hr and is the first—and currently the only—flooring product to be certified by the Canadian government's Environmental Choice Program (EcoLogo). K&M also offers bamboo plywood and veneer, as well as cork and FSC-certified maple flooring.

Teragren Bamboo Flooring, Panels, and Veneer

Teragren LLC
12715 Miller Rd. NE, Ste. 301
Bainbridge Island, WA 98110

Toll-free: 800-929-6333
Phone: 206-842-9477
www.teragren.com

Teragren (formerly TimberGrass) manufactures solid strip bamboo flooring in tongue-and-groove or locking system, prefinished or site-finished. All flooring products are available in vertical or flat (horizontal) grains and natural or caramelized standard colors as well as stained cherry, walnut, charcoal and espresso colors. Coatings are water based and solvent free. The company uses the MOSO specie of bamboo which is harvested at maturity at 6 years. Teragren also manufactures coordinating stair parts, flooring accessories and vents, panels and veneer for cabinetry, furniture, interior paneling, countertops, and other interior applications as a direct replacement for wood sheet goods. (Note that while the adhesive used to manufacture the panels and veneer exceeds E1 standards, it is not food grade; if the surface is to be used for food preparation, a food grade sealer is recommended.)

Wellmade Bamboo Flooring

Wellmade
P.O. Box 2704
Wilsonville, OR 97070

Phone: 503-582-0848
www.bamboofloorings.com

Wellmade's bamboo flooring is available 3/8", 1/2", 5/8", and 3/4" thick by 3-5/8" or 3-4/5" wide, and 36", 37-4/5", or 72-3/4" in length. Planks are T&G on all sides, available in natural or carbonized colors, and come prefinished with three coats of UV-cured acrylic or an aluminum oxide lacquer. Also available are wide and narrow molding, stair nosing, stair tread, and base molding in natural or carbonized colors. Be sure to ask for flooring with an ultra-low formaldehyde glue such as DYNO adhesives, since Wellmade makes bamboo flooring with different glues.

Brick Flooring

Brick and stone, particularly if locally produced or salvaged, can provide an extremely long-lasting, low-maintenance, visually interesting floor with low environmental costs. These materials create an unyielding surface that may be hard on joints and feet, however; and uneven floors may collect dirt and debris in low spots and prove difficult or even dangerous for some to traverse. Products listed here are from salvaged materials.

Green Leaf Brick

The Red Tree Group, Inc.
8615 Golf Ridge Dr.
Charlotte, NC 28277

Phone: 704-307-0930
www.greenleafbrick.com

Green Leaf Brick is a fired masonry brick made of 100% recycled materials. In addition to building brick, pavers are also available. Recycled materials include industrial waste from technical ceramic plants, mineral mining operations, and steel manufacturing; post-consumer content includes recycled glass, and incinerated sewage ash. Green Leaf Brick acquires materials from within 500 miles of its Salisbury NC plant, most within 100 miles.

Salvaged Brick

Gavin Historical Bricks
2050 Glendale Rd.
Iowa City, IA 52245

Phone: 319-354-5251
www.historicalbricks.com

Gavin Historical Bricks supplies salvaged bricks and cobblestones recovered from buildings and streets from around the country. Bricks are used in new construction to provide an antique look, as well as for historic restoration projects. Custom brick matching is available. The company also handcuts antique brick into 1/2" floor tile for a variety of applications. Shipping is provided nationwide, though the heavy weight reduces the practicality (and environmental attractiveness) of shipping large quantities long distances.

Thin-Sliced Salvaged Chicago Brick

Vintage Brick Salvage LLC.
1303 Harrison Ave.
Rockford, IL 61104

Toll-free: 800-846-8243
Phone: 847-714-3652
www.bricksalvage.com

Vintage Brick Salvage sells 1/2" and 3/4" thick antique brick that has been thin-sliced from antique common brick for use as flooring, paving, and veneer tile on walls. The brick installs like tile, using thin-set adhesive over a sub floor or backerboard, and can be sealed with polyurethane or a water-based terra cotta sealer. Some split-brick pieces may show saw marks or be flecked with iron deposits. Vintage Brick also sells full-size salvaged bricks and cobblestone pavers.

Carpet Cushion

Carpet cushions may be made from a variety of recycled, natural, and/or synthetic materials. Natural materials include jute fibers and animal hair; synthetic materials include nylon and polypropylene waste from carpet manufacturing, recycled-tire rubber, and rebond polyurethane (reprocessed from virgin prime flexible polyurethane products). As with carpet itself, care should be taken not to expose the cushion to moisture—including long-term moisture from concrete slabs—to minimize the potential for microbial growth. Flexible-foam carpet padding frequently contains brominated flame retardants (BFRs) which have been identified as a growing health and environmental concern. Carpet cushion is used primarily in residential applications.

AcoustiCORK

Amorim Industrial Solutions
26112 110th St.
P.O. Box 25
Trevor, WI 53179

Toll-free: 800-255-2675
Phone: 262-862-2311
www.acousticorkusa.com

AcoustiCORK sheets and rolls are made with cork granules and a polyurethane-based binder. They may be used under a variety of flooring types, such as ceramic tile, natural stone tiles, and hardwood flooring, although an additional board underlayment is advised for use with vinyl sheet and vinyl composition tile. The AcoustiCORK AC 55 Plus product, made with cork sheets and a coconut fiber core, offers higher levels of acoustical performance.

Carpet Padding

Earth Weave Carpet Mills, Inc.
P.O. Box 6120
Dalton, GA 30722

Phone: 706-278-8200
www.earthweave.com

Earth Weave Carpet Mills offers a natural rubber rug gripper padding and a 100% natural untreated wool padding.

Cork Underlayment

Natural Cork, Inc.
1710 N. Leg Ct.
Augusta, GA 30909

Toll-free: 800-404-2675
Phone: 706-733-6120
www.naturalcork.com

Natural Cork's sound control cork underlayment comes in 5/64", 1/8", or 1/4" thicknesses in 4' x 50' rolls or 1/4" and 1/2" thicknesses in 2' x 3' sheets. It is treated with Microban (which contains Triclosan, a widely used antimicrobial additive which may be persistent and toxic in the environment) to prevent the development of mold and bacteria under the floor.

Nova Underlayment

Nova Distinctive Floors
1710 E. Sepulveda Blvd.
Carson, CA 90745

Toll-free: 866-576-2458
www.novafloorings.com

Nova Cork rolled cork underlayment can be used under a wide variety of floorcoverings. It's available as 6 mm-thick 4' x 50" rolls (200 square feet per roll), 6 mm-thick 2' x 3' sheets (300 square feet per carton), and 12 mm-thick 2' x 3' sheets (150 square feet per carton). NovaCork is manufactured in Switzerland.

PL and DublBac Series Carpet Cushion

Leggett & Platt, Inc. - Fairmont Division
2245 W. Pershing Rd.
Chicago, IL 60609

Toll-free: 800-621-6907
Phone: 773-376-1300
www.leggett.com

PL and DublBac Series carpet cushion is made from bonded 100% recycled polyurethane foam from post-industrial and post-consumer sources.

Reliance Carpet Cushion

Reliance Carpet Cushion Division
15902 S. Main St.
Gardena, CA 90248

Toll-free: 800-522-5252
Phone: 323-321-2300

Imperial Carpet Cushion products are made from recycled textile waste fibers. Rather than using a chemical bonding agent, as do most other manufacturers, Reliance uses heat as a bonding agent in the Imperial Cushion products. Inter-Loc, Embassy, Marathon, Ambassador, and the Environmental Performance Collection of products, including Natural Wonder, Performa Bond, Berber Tradition and Broadloom Delight synthetic fiber carpet cushions, are manufactured with 100% post-consumer carpet fiber content. The manufacturer has certified the following recycled-content levels (by weight): total recovered material 100% typical, 100% guaranteed; post-consumer material 0% typic

Rug-Hold 100% Natural

Rug-Hold - Division of Leggett and Platt, Inc.
5070 Phillip Lee Dr.
Atlanta, GA 30336

Toll-free: 800-221-4329
Phone: 404-691-9500
www.rughold.com

Rug-Hold® 100% Natural rug underlayment is made of jute fiber coated with natural rubber. All Rug-Hold products use natural rubber.

UnderFleece

Appleseed Wool Corp.
55 Bell St.
Plymouth, OH 44865

Toll-free: 800-881-9665
Phone: 419-687-9665
www.appleseedwoolcorp.com

UnderFleece™ carpet cushion is made from 100% wool felt needled to a woven jute scrim and contains no glues, dyes, mothproofing, or other chemical treatments.

Whisper Wool Acoustic Underlay

Nature's Acoustics
80 Old East Rd.
Chatsworth, GA 30705

Phone: 706-422-8660
www.naturesacoustics.com

Whisper Wool offers carpet padding as well as acoustic underlayment for laminate, engineered, and hardwood floors made from 100% sheep wool. The underlayment has a clear polypropylene moisture barrier laminate to help prevent mold, fungus, and bacteria growth. Both products feature Sanitized antimicrobial treatment. The 1/8-inch-thick underlayment comes in 3-foot-wide, 33.5-foot-long rolls (covering 100 ft2.). The 1/2"-thick, high-density carpet padding weighs 38 ounces per sq. yard, and comes in 6.5-foot-wide rolls.

Carpet Recycling

Vast quantities of used carpet end up in landfills each year—more than 1.7 million tons, according to recent estimates. Carpet accounts for approximately 1% of all municipal solid waste by weight, and roughly 2% by volume. Programs to recycle carpet waste are, thus, extremely important. Recycling was made easier by the content labeling program instituted in 1996. Some collected carpet is now, or soon will be, recycled into new carpet. Other uses include plastic products for automobile interiors and engine parts, industrial flooring, and parking stops.

OPT3

DPM Enterprises
128 Regional Park Dr.
Kingsport, TN 37660

Phone: 423-349-4129
www.dpmenterprises.net

The Opt3 program recovers used carpet tiles for either reuse through their Recovery Program, or reprocessing through their Recycling Program. Tiles accepted for the Recovery Program are sanitized and refurbished for use in schools, churches, offices, and homes. Tiles not accepted for reuse are recycled into carpet backing systems, components for building materials, and car parts. Tiles that cannot be recycled are used as fuel in a waste-to-energy power plant. Currently, less than 5 percent is used as fuel.

Tarkett Reuse Initiative

Tarkett Commercial
2728 Summer St.
Houston, TX 77007

Toll-free: 800-877-8453
Phone: 713-344-2733
www.tarkett.com

Tarkett's ReUse™ Reclamation Program allows customers to recycle non-installed jobsite waste and samples. Clean, non-installed Tarkett flooring waste is packaged in bags provided by Tarkett and mailed to Alabama or Texas for recycling. Samples are packed in a self-addressed box and postage is prepaid for carry boards and architectural folders. 100% of the returned materials are recycled, and installation waste from heterogeneous sheet, composition tile, luxury tile, and homogeneous sheet and tile, are recycled into new flooring.

Carpet Tile

Carpet tile is an environmentally preferable alternative to carpeting because damaged or stained carpet tiles can be replaced individually without having to replace carpeting on an entire floor. Though primarily used in commercial buildings, carpet tile is beginning to appear for residential applications as well. Products listed here contain recycled content or have other environmental attributes such as low VOC emissions, or certification as a climate-neutral product.

FLOR Terra with Ingeo PLA Fiber

FLOR, Inc.
116 N. York St.
Ste. 300
Elmhurst, IL 60126

Toll-free: 866-281-3567
Phone: 630-516-4250
www.flor.com

The Terra line in Interface's FLOR collection of residential carpet tile products is the first floorcovering to use Ingeo® PLA (polylactic acid) fibers. Cargill Dow's Ingeo is a form of polyester derived from corn. The face fiber in this line is made with one third of Ingeo, while the other twenty lines in this collection use more conventional fibers. The FLOR collection uses a vinyl composite—called Glasbac—made from recycled carpet tiles as a backing.

Cementitious Underlayment

Self-leveling and troweled cementitious underlayments are generally a blend of portland cement and gypsum, typically augmented with VOC-containing polymers and plasticizers, that are used to create a flat, smooth, new surface for subsequent flooring applications. When applied in existing, closed structures, these products can introduce significant moisture as they cure, requiring ventilation. The products listed here contain over 45% recycled material (fly ash), and are ASTME tested zero or low-VOC products.

Fritz Underlayments

Fritz Industries, Inc.
500 Sam Houston Rd.
Mesquite, TX 75149

Toll-free: 800-955-1323
Phone: 972-285-5471
www.fritztile.com

Fritz Industries manufactures non-toxic, zero-VOC, pozzolanic cementitious underlayment products for use in leveling and patching subfloor surfaces before installing floorcoverings. They are made from 45-70% fly ash, sand, and a small amount of proprietary ingredients including polymer material. F-10 is self-leveling underlayment, Poz-Patch® I is a fast-setting (non self-leveling) underlayment, Poz-Patch® II is a underlayment for use on flexible substrates such as plywood, and Poz-Patch® III is a fast-setting skim-coating patch product.

Level-Right

Maxxon Corporation
920 Hamel Rd.
P.O. Box 253
Hamel, MN 55340

Toll-free: 800-356-7887
Phone: 763-478-9600
www.level-right.com

Level-Right® self-leveling, thin-topping cementitious underlayment from Maxxon® (formerly the Gyp-Crete Corporation) is not polymer-modified, resulting in nearly zero VOCs. It also contains over 51% fly ash (which improves certain qualities of the product, but in this case does not reduce the amount of portland cement content). Note that these green attributes do not apply to the entire Level-Right line of products.

Ceramic Tile

Tile is an inherently low-toxic, waterproof, durable finish material for flooring, walls, and other applications. While tile is somewhat energy-intensive to manufacture, the materials involved are readily available and mined with fairly low impact. Products listed here contain post-consumer or post-industrial recycled content.

Debris Series Ceramic Tile and Pavers

Fireclay Tile
495 W. Julian St.
San Jose, CA 95110

Phone: 408-275-1182
www.fireclaytile.com

Fireclay Tile manufactures the Debris Series of handmade tile using post-industrial and post-consumer recycled material. Fireclay's terra cotta body is made from 25% recycled granite dust, 19% broken window panes, and 8.5 % recycled brown and green glass bottles. The company's white clay body contains 47.5% recycled broken window panes and clear glass bottles. The terra cotta tile can be unglazed or glazed. The tiles made with the white clay body have transparent glazes. The glazes do not contain lead.

EcoCycle

Crossville Inc.
P.O. Box 1168
Crossville, TN 38557

Phone: 931-484-2110
www.crossvilleinc.com

Crossville Inc. offers a line of ceramic tile called EcoCycle made from 40% in-house manufacturing scrap generated during the manufacturing process of standard-color porcelain tiles. This manufacturing scrap, which would otherwise be landfilled, is not recycled content as defined by the EPA. The scrap also includes a small percentage of dust from the air and water filtration systems. The tiles measure 12" x 12" with matching 4" x 12" bullnose trim. Available in seven colors, EcoCycle is recommended for interior floors and walls as well as exterior walls.

Eco-Tile

Quarry Tile Company
6328 E. Utah Ave.
Spokane, WA 99212

Phone: 509-536-2812
www.quarrytile.com

Eco-Tile™ is a commercial-grade, glazed ceramic tile made with approximately 70% recycled solid waste as defined by the EPA's CPG program. This waste content is made up of post-consumer recycled glass (about 25%), post-industrial grinding paste from the computer industry, and post-industrial mining waste from the sand and gravel industry (post-industrial content about 45%). The company also utilizes reprocessed glaze waste from their other manufacturing operations. Glaze from overspray, body scrap, and process waste is recycled in a closed-loop, zero-discharge, water reclamation system. Eco-Tile may contain up to 10% by weight of this material. All the recycled content in Eco-Tile comes from within a 10- to 350-mile radius of the plant and replaces virgin materials from as far away as 2,300 miles. Currently produced in over 50 colors and 5 sizes, Eco-Tile must be special-ordered (minimum 300 ft2).

Terra Classic and Terra Traffic

Terra Green Ceramics
1650 Progress Dr.
Richmond, IN 47374

Phone: 765-935-4760
www.terragreenceramics.com

Terra Green Ceramic Tiles are made with 55% post-industrial recycled glass. Terra Classic and Terra Traffic (slip-resistant) are each available in 17 colors, several sizes, and with a wide range of accessories.

Concrete Finishing

Covering concrete with cosmetic layers can increase environmental and financial costs significantly over the lifespan of a structure as compared with using concrete in a structure-as-finish capacity. Polished and densified concrete floors (old or new) combine diamond stone-polishing technology with silicate chemical treatment to provide a significantly better alternative to film and wax coatings—highly durable, nearly maintenance-free, noncombustible... and the improved reflectivity can also reduce lighting requirements.

Ashford Formula

Curecrete Distribution, Inc.
1203 W. Spring Creek Pl.
Springville, UT 84663

Toll-free: 800-998-5664
Phone: 801-489-5663
www.ashfordformula.com

Ashford Formula is a permanent, penetrating concrete hardener, densifier, dustproofer, and sealer for new or existing concrete. As it progressively seals, the concrete becomes watertight but remains breathable and will develop a shine through use or by scrubbing. The product also locks in salts to eliminate the formation of concrete dust. Ashford Formula is water-based, nontoxic, nonflammable, and releases no VOCs. It is effective on concrete, stucco, terrazzo, concrete block, and similar materials. This product is particularly intended for flooring applications.

Certified Green System

VIC International Corporation
231 E. Emory Rd.
Powell, TN 37849

Toll-free: 800-423-1634
Phone: 865-947-2882
www.vicintl.com

VIC International produces concrete grinding and polishing equipment and components for use in producing polished concrete floors. The system uses VIC's grinding machines and specialized densifiers that react with the calcium hydroxide in concrete to achieve a finished floor. Applicable to both new and old concrete slab floors. VIC International provides technical support and complete polishing services along with diamond-grinding/polishing and vacuum machines.

FGS PermaShine Polished Concrete System

L&M Construction Chemicals, Inc.
14851 Calhoun Rd.
Omaha, NE 68152

Toll-free: 800-362-3331
Phone: 402-453-6600
www.fgs-permashine.com

The FGS PermaShine System is a patented dry method of concrete floor or concrete surface restoration using the process of grinding a concrete surface to be resurfaced while extracting and retaining dust during the grinding process. FGS Hardener Plus, a water-based, odorless, penetrating proprietary hardening and densifying solution is applied to the concrete surface after it has been ground to the predetermined degree of smoothness. FGS PermaShine renews existing concrete floors as well as improving new floors. Polishing new concrete should be done after a 28-day curing process. The FGS PermaShine System is patented and is available exclusively through L&M Construction Chemicals, Inc, and only through its dealers and its certified, trained and approved installers.

Induroshine System

W. R. Meadows, Inc.
300 Industrial Dr.
P.O. Box 338
Hampshire, IL 60140

Toll-free: 800-342-5976
Phone: 847-214-2100
www.wrmeadows.com

The Induroshine Concrete Polishing System, appropriate for both new and old concrete slab floors, uses W.R. Meadows' GreenSpec-listed Liqui-Hard zero-VOC concrete densifier and sealer along with the concrete grinding and polishing system from VIC International. W.R. Meadows' Induroshine System uses the same equipment and products as VIC's Certified Green System. W.R. Meadows provides technical support and complete polishing services along with the requisite products.

Liqui-Hard Concrete Densifier and Hardener

W. R. Meadows, Inc.
300 Industrial Dr.
P.O. Box 338
Hampshire, IL 60140

Toll-free: 800-342-5976
Phone: 847-214-2100
www.wrmeadows.com

Liqui-Hard is a zero-VOC concrete hardener and densifier. The silicate-based, colorless liquid reacts with the lime in the concrete to densify and harden new or existing concrete. The product also solidifies the concrete and locks in salts to eliminate dusting and pitting. This product is designed for flooring applications where chemical and abrasion resistance are needed, and can be used for polished concrete.

RetroPlate Concrete Polishing System

Advanced Floor Products, Inc.
P.O. Box 80533
Provo, UT 84605

Toll-free: 888-942-3144
Phone: 801-812-3420
www.retroplatesystem.com

The RetroPlate system grinds, polishes, and densifies old or new concrete floors using grinding machines and sodium silicate treatment to achieve a finished floor. The sodium silicate hardens the concrete, reducing its porosity and contributing to a lasting surface. A uniform finish or a terrazzo look is possible. Coloring can be achieved with acid dyes and, with new concrete, with pigments and colored aggregate.

SureHard Colorless Silcate Liquid

Kaufman Products, Inc.
3811 Curtis Ave.
Baltimore, MD 21226

Toll-free: 800-637-6372
Phone: 410-354-8600
www.kaufmanproducts.net

SureHard is a clear, colorless blend of liquid silicates chemically engineered to react with the lime in concrete, forming an insoluble gel in its pores. On a concrete slab, SureHard provides dustproofing, densifying, sealing, and hardening, as well as waterproofing and increased reflectance. Concrete surfaces treated with SureHard may be diamond polished for a polished concrete floor. SureHard is applied with a water-based solution with no VOC content. It is also non-flammable, low-odor, and non-toxic.

WerkMaster Concrete Polishing System

Werk Industries / Fab-u-Floors Refinishing Services
1448 Charlotte Rd.
North Vancouver, BC V7J 1H2 Canada

Toll-free: 866-373-WERK
Phone: 604-629-8705
www.fab-u-floors.com

The WerkMaster system grinds and polishes concrete, creating a high-gloss floor surface. The system can be used with concrete hardening/densifying compounds, such as sodium silicate, available from other suppliers. Werkmaster Octi-Disc Technology incorporates eight counter-rotating diamond grit discs to achieve a polished surface within 1/8-inch of walls. Together with the WerkMaster HEPA vacuum system, the process is 100% dust free, according to the company. The tools are available in both do-it-yourself and contractor sizes, and work on wood, granite, and marble, as well as terrazzo and concrete. The WerkMaster system is available in North America from Fab-u-Floors Refinishing Services.

Concrete Pigments

Coloring pigments in concrete add architectural interest using very little additional material—turning concrete into finished surfaces, which avoids the need for additional products and coatings, eliminating the environmental impacts associated with manufacturing and maintaining those materials. Products listed here include recycled materials and mineral byproducts of industry.

Davis Colors

Davis Colors
3700 E. Olympic Blvd.
Los Angeles, CA 90023

Toll-free: 800-356-4848
Phone: 323-269-7311
www.daviscolors.com

Davis Colors produces color additives for portland cement-based concrete paving and finished floor surfaces, concrete products, and structures. Made from recycled or reclaimed steel and iron, Davis Colors are added to the concrete mix with the company's Chameleon™ computer-operated automatic dosing system or with Mix-Ready® bags that dissolve when tossed directly into an operating ready-mix truck. With integral color, the high embodied energy of concrete is offset by the dual structural and finish floor role of the colored concrete.

EnvironOxide Pigments

Hoover Color Corporation
2170 Julia Simpkins Rd.
P.O. Box 218
Hiwassee, VA 24347

Phone: 540-980-7233
www.hoovercolor.com

Hoover Color Corporation, in partnership with Iron Oxide Recovery, Inc. (IOR), produces a range of earth-tone pigments made with EnvironOxide™, a natural iron oxide product recovered from abandoned coal mine drainage. Settling ponds and constructed wetlands are used in a patented process to contain the mine runoff. The process yields a premium quality pigment that is nontoxic, nonbleeding, and weather-resistant while cleaning water that would otherwise pollute the receiving stream. The product can be used as a colorant in a wide range of building products, including concrete, cement block, paint, wood stain, and brick. For general information, contact IOR at 412-571-2204; for sales, contact Hoover Color at 540-980-7233. Iron oxide pigments made from EnvironOxide must be specifically requested.

Recycled Glass Aggregates and Powders

American Specialty Glass, Inc.
829 N. 400 W
North Salt Lake, UT 84054

Phone: 801-294-4222
www.americanspecialtyglass.com

American Specialty Glass, Inc., provides recycled-glass aggregate in a range of sizes and colors for terrazzo floors, pavers, and countertops. Sources include post-consumer bottle glass and post-industrial float glass cullet. Glass sand, a substitute for silica sand, is also available, as are powder fines that can be used as concrete coloring agents, providing a different effect than pigments. Polished or unpolished landscaping nuggets in a range of sizes are offered as well.

Cork Flooring

Cork is a natural flooring material that's been used for more than a century. Obtained from the outer bark of the cork oak (Quercus suber), it can be harvested sustainably without killing the tree. The cork regenerates in about 10 years. Grown in Portugal, Algeria, Spain, Morocco, France, Italy, and Tunisia, all cork flooring products available in the U.S. are imported. There's almost no material waste from the manufacturing process, but agglomerating the cork requires binders to hold the ground granules together. Urea-formaldehyde binders should be avoided in favor of urea-melamine, phenol-formaldehyde, polyurethane, or all-natural protein binders. Cork flooring is typically available in a variety of shades in tile form, and in some cases is sandwiched with other flooring materials. It's durable, sound-absorbing, and naturally moisture-, rot-, and mold-resistant. Cork is typically finished with a polyurethane or wax coating, which is periodically reapplied. While cork is naturally fire-resistant, wax finishes reduce this quality. Cork-PVC laminate tiles or cork tiles with a PVC wear layer are not listed in GreenSpec.

Cork Floating Floor and Parquet Tile

Natural Cork, Inc.
1710 N. Leg Ct.
Augusta, GA 30909

Toll-free: 800-404-2675
Phone: 706-733-6120
www.naturalcork.com

Natural Cork Floating Floor™ is a tongue-and-groove cork plank product measuring 1/2" x 11-13/16" x 35-11/16" and is available prefinished with an acrylic coating. The Floating Floor is constructed with a cork surface layer, exterior grade fiberboard core featuring CLIC installation, and cork underlayment. Parquet Tile measures 3/16" x 12" x 12" and is prefinished with an acrylic coating. Parquet Tile can also be purchased unfinished in 3/16" x 12" x 24".

Cork Mosaic Floor Tile

Habitus
166 E. 108th St.
New York, NY 10029

Phone: 212-426-5500
www.habitusnyc.com

These floor tiles are made with circular plugs recycled from the cork-stopper industry, sliced into nominal 1/4" thick, 1" chips, fixed to a 12" x 24" paper-net backing and 1-3/8" chips, fixed to a 24" x 24" paper-net backing. Sheets are glued to the substrate, then grouted. Due to the larger joint size of the 1-3/8' chips, the manufacturer recommends utilizing a sanded grout product. Sealing is required with polyurethane or wax. This product is available unfinished, pre-varnished (water-based), or custom colored (minimum quantities required). According to the manufacturer, the product is durable and suitable for wet areas.

Expanko Cork Tiles

Expanko Cork Co.
1129 West Lincoln Hwy.
Coatesville, PA 19320

Toll-free: 800-345-6202
Phone: 610-380-0300
www.expanko.com

Expanko cork tiles are 12" or 24" square and come in 3/16" and 5/16" thicknesses. They are available in 17 different face patterns either unfinished or finished with a polyurethane or wax coating.

Globus Cork Flooring

Globus Cork
741 E. 136th St.
Bronx, NY 10454

Phone: 718-742-7264
www.corkfloor.com

Globus Cork Flooring is available in a wide range of sizes and shapes (including triangles, hexagons, and baseboard tiles) and comes in more than 40 colors. All pigments, finishes, and adhesives are water based, solvent free, and produce no VOC emissions.

The cork granules are agglomerated with a polyurethane binder. The tiles come with a latex adhesive on their underside and are installed using a second adhesive on the subfloor. Finished with three coats of water-based varnish, the company suggests that a commercial-grade finish coat be applied in the field by the installer.

Nova Cork

Nova Distinctive Floors
1710 E. Sepulveda Blvd.
Carson, CA 90745

Toll-free: 866-576-2458
www.novafloorings.com

Nova Cork™ Floating Floor cork flooring, available in 28 designer patterns, is FSC- and SCS-certified. The 7/16" x 12" x 36" planks snap together with a glueless "Klick" system. They consist of 3 layers—a high-density cork wear layer with a water-based polyurethane finish; a high-density tongue-and-groove fiberboard layer made with recycled fibers; and a low-density cork base layer. This product has a 20-year residential warranty; 10-year commercial. Nova Distinctive Floors is the exclusive North American distributor/importer of Nova Cork, which is manufactured in Switzerland.

ProntoKorQ Floor and Wall Panel

Habitus
166 E. 108th St.
New York, NY 10029

Phone: 212-426-5500
www.habitusnyc.com

ProntoKorQ is a tongue-and-groove floating cork flooring or fixed wall panel that comes in 3/8" x 12" x 36" planks. Cork floor tiles measure 3/16" x 12" x 12". Both products are available in over 40 manufactured patterns and unfinished or prefinished with a water-based varnish. Over 100 custom colors are available.

WE Cork Flooring

WE Cork
16 Kingston Rd., Unit 6
Exeter, NH 03833

Toll-free: 800-666-2675
Phone: 603-778-8558
www.wecork.com

WE Cork Classic Collection cork flooring comes in tiles and planks measuring 12" x 12" x 3/16" and 4" x 36" x 3/16", respectively. The flooring is available in light, medium, dark, or leopard shades and either unfinished, waxed, or in varnished matte. The company also manufactures a line of floating floors, which do not require gluing, and two lines of sound-control underlayment for flooring, WECU Soundless™ and WECU Soundless+™.

Wicanders Natural Cork

Amorim Flooring North America, Inc.
7513 Connelley Dr., Ste. M - Front
Hanover, MD 21076

Toll-free: 800-828-2675
Phone: 410-553-6062
www.wicanders.com

Wicanders Series 100 is a PVC-free floating natural cork flooring system. The tiles are made with a phenolic resin binder and measure 900 x 295 x 10.5 mm (35.4" x 11.6" x 0.4"); they are available in 5 collections with a total of 108 designs. Series 200 is a glue-down version, available in 600 x 300 mm (23.6" x 11.8") and 600 x 600 mm (23.6"-square) tiles, 6 mm (1/4") thick, in more than 100 designs.

Flooring Adhesives

Flooring adhesives can be a major source of indoor air quality problems, often more so than the flooring products they adhere. Water-based adhesives have lower VOC emissions than solvent-based products. While some products are sold as multipurpose, others are specific to a particular application or product (linoleum, for example, requires special adhesives due to its linseed oil content). If a flooring manufacturer recommends a specific low- or zero-VOC, water-based product for use with its material, then use it; otherwise consider a product known to minimize indoor air pollution and check with the flooring product manufacturer to find out whether that product can be used with their flooring material. Some air quality management districts restrict the manufacture, sale, and installation of flooring adhesives that exceed a VOC content of 150 grams per liter. Products listed here are low or zero-VOC, water based and solvent free, or made from natural materials.

#965 Flooring and Tread Adhesive

Johnsonite
16910 Munn Rd.
Chagrin Falls, OH 44023

Toll-free: 800-899-8916
Phone: 440-543-8916
www.johnsonite.com

Johnsonite's #965 is a high-strength, solvent-free, water-based, acrylic latex adhesive. It was formulated for rubber sheet flooring as well as rubber and vinyl stair treads and nosings on porous and nonporous surfaces.

380 Natural All-Purpose Floor Adhesive

Sinan Co. Environmental Products
P.O. Box 857
Davis, CA 95616

Phone: 530-753-3104
www.sinanco.com

Sinan 380 Natural All-Purpose Floor Adhesive is a water-based product made with organic binders for use with cork, wood, linoleum, and carpeting. Sinan products are made from all-natural, primarily plant-based materials, all of which are listed on the packaging.

BioShield Cork Adhesive #16

BioShield Paint Company
3215 Rufina Street
Santa Fe, NM 87507

Toll-free: 800-621-2591
Phone: 505-438-3448
www.bioshieldpaint.com

BioShield Cork Adhesive #16 is a water-based, solvent-free adhesive specially designed for cork flooring.

EcoTimber HealthyBond Adhesive

EcoTimber
1611 4th St.
San Rafael, CA 94901

Toll-free: 888-801-0855
Phone: 415-258-8454
www.ecotimber.com

HealthyBond Adhesive from EcoTimber is used for installation of wood and bamboo flooring. The product's resin-based formula adheres to hardwood, bamboo, cork, plywood, concrete, vinyl, particleboard, and terrazzo, and EcoTimber claims it is strong enough for use with plank flooring. HealthyBond Adhesive is isocynate-free, urethane-free, solvent-free, has low VOC content (7 g/l), and is Greenguard Indoor Air Quality Certified as a low-emitting product.

Envirotec Floor Covering Adhesives

W. F. Taylor Company
11545 Pacific Ave.
Fontana, CA 92337

Toll-free: 800-397-4583
Phone: 909-360-6677
www.wftaylor.com

Envirotec is W. F. Taylor Company's line of nontoxic, solvent-free, low-VOC adhesive products. These products include multipurpose flooring adhesives, carpet adhesives, and cove base adhesives.

Safe-Set Adhesives

Chicago Adhesive Products Co.
1105 S. Frontenac St.
Aurora, IL 60504

Toll-free: 800-621-0220
Phone: 630-679-9100
www.chapco-adhesive.com

Safe-Set products are solvent-free, zero-VOC, nonflammable, nontoxic floor covering adhesives.

Flooring Underlayment

Using underlayment products beneath wood, tile, resilient flooring, or carpet and carpet cushion provides a level surface and helps insulate floors from sound transmission and, to a limited extent, heat loss. Cork rolls and sheets provide particularly high added resilience to the floor system, with significantly less thickness than fiberboard products or a gypsum-cement poured-in-place slab. Use of a sound-deadening underlayment below a hard-surface floor can reduce the need to further control sound transmission with carpeting or rugs. Environmentally preferable materials for flooring underlayment include natural cork, strawboard, and recycled materials. Lauan or other tropical wood based products should be avoided unless FSC certified. Underlayments that use urea-formaldehyde binders or contain other VOC offgassing materials can be an indoor air quality concern. Products listed here are either rapidly renewable (cork or strawboard) or have a recycled content value greater than 40% (80% post industrial, 40% post-consumer). Preference is given to products with no added formaldehyde. In the future, listed products may need to be certified or have other verification that they are low-VOC or formaldehyde-free.

AcoustiCORK

Amorim Industrial Solutions
26112 110th St.
P.O. Box 25
Trevor, WI 53179

Toll-free: 800-255-2675
Phone: 262-862-2311
www.acousticorkusa.com

AcoustiCORK sheets and rolls are made with cork granules and a polyurethane-based binder. They may be used under a variety of flooring types, such as ceramic tile, natural stone tiles, and hardwood flooring, although an additional board underlayment is advised for use with vinyl sheet and vinyl composition tile. The AcoustiCORK AC 55 Plus product, made with cork sheets and a coconut fiber core, offers higher levels of acoustical performance.

Cork Underlayment

Natural Cork, Inc.
1710 N. Leg Ct.
Augusta, GA 30909

Toll-free: 800-404-2675
Phone: 706-733-6120
www.naturalcork.com

Natural Cork's sound control cork underlayment comes in 5/64", 1/8", or 1/4" thicknesses in 4' x 50' rolls or 1/4" and 1/2" thicknesses in 2' x 3' sheets. It is treated with Microban (which contains Triclosan, a widely used antimicrobial additive which may be persistent and toxic in the environment) to prevent the development of mold and bacteria under the floor.

Nova Underlayment

Nova Distinctive Floors
1710 E. Sepulveda Blvd.
Carson, CA 90745

Toll-free: 866-576-2458
www.novafloorings.com

Nova Cork rolled cork underlayment can be used under a wide variety of floorcoverings. It's available as 6 mm-thick 4' x 50" rolls (200 square feet per roll), 6 mm-thick 2' x 3' sheets (300 square feet per carton), and 12 mm-thick 2' x 3' sheets (150 square feet per carton). NovaCork is manufactured in Switzerland.

Subflor

Longlac Wood Industries Inc.
2311 Royal Windsor Dr., Unit 2
Mississauga, ON L5J 1K5 Canada

Toll-free: 866-782-3567
www.subflor.com

Subflor floating floor is made with water-resistant OSB using an MDI binder. An integral HDPE bottom layer has 5/16" corrugations to allow moisture drainage and some airflow. Though designed for installation over concrete slabs, their sound-attenuating properties provide an appropriate flooring system for many applications. This interlocking tongue-and-groove product requires no nails or glue. Subflor has an unfinished OSB surface and comes in 2' x 2' panels; the 7/8" height preserves headroom.

Whisper Wool Acoustic Underlay

Nature's Acoustics
80 Old East Rd.
Chatsworth, GA 30705

Phone: 706-422-8660
www.naturesacoustics.com

Whisper Wool offers carpet padding as well as acoustic underlayment for laminate, engineered, and hardwood floors made from 100% sheep wool. The underlayment has a clear polypropylene moisture barrier laminate to help prevent mold, fungus, and bacteria growth. Both products feature Sanitized antimicrobial treatment. The 1/8-inch-thick underlayment comes in 3-foot-wide, 33.5-foot-long rolls (covering 100 ft2.). The 1/2"-thick, high-density carpet padding weighs 38 ounces per sq. yard, and comes in 6.5-foot-wide rolls.

FSC-Certified Wood Flooring

Certified wood products are verified by a third party as originating from well-managed forests. GreenSpec recognizes the Forest Stewardship Council (FSC) standards as currently the most rigorous and also the only certification system with established chain-of-custody certification to ensure that products used were derived from certified forests. The availability of domestic hardwood from third-party FSC-certified forests makes flooring a great application for certified wood. Products listed here are made of certified wood. However some companies listed here sell both certified and noncertified wood products, or products that have been certified according to different, less stringent environmental standards. To make certain that you get environmentally responsible wood products, be sure to specify your interest in FSC-certified wood.

AltruWood Certified Wood Products

AltruWood, Inc.
P.O. Box 3341
Portland, OR 97208

Toll-free: 877-372-9663
www.altruwood.com

AltruWood, chain-of-custody certified by SGS, only sells and distributes FSC-certified new domestic (including oak, pine, cherry and Douglas Fir) and tropical wood (including Jatoba, Ipe, and Massaranduba). Sourced and shipped from multiple locations, transportation costs and impacts are minimized. A custom cutting service allows the specification of exact sizes and dimensions, minimizing waste. AltruWood also sells reclaimed lumber.

Certified Cherry Flooring

Green River Lumber
29 Locust Hill Rd.
P.O. Box 329
Great Barrington, MA 01230

Phone: 413-528-9000
www.greenriverlumber.com

Green River Certified Cherry Flooring is a solid hardwood flooring milled from well-managed, FSC-certified forests in Pennsylvania. The cherry hardwood flooring is 25/32" thick and comes in 2-1/4", 3", 4", and 5" widths (actual face width).

Certified Hardwood Building Products

Maine Woods Company, LLC
Fish Lake Rd.
P.O. Box 111
Portage, ME 04768

Phone: 207-435-4393
www.mainewoods.net

Maine Woods Company, LLC, owned in part by Seven Islands Land Company, operates a state-of-the-art sawmill in northern Maine producing primarily hard maple and yellow birch lumber and flooring. Smaller quantities of American beech, red maple, and white ash are also produced. A portion of the mill output is FSC-certified.

Certified Lumber, Flooring, Wainscoting, and Veneer

McDowell Lumber Company, Inc.
Rte. 46 S
P.O. Box 148
Crosby, PA 16724

Phone: 814-887-2717
www.mcdowelllumber.com

McDowell Lumber deals in FSC-certified lumber, flooring, wainscoting, and veneer in over 15 species including red oak, cherry, hard and soft maple, ash, and a variety of other hardwoods harvested in Pennsylvania.

Certified Oak Flooring

Smith Flooring
P.O. Box 99
Mountain View, MO 65548

Phone: 417-934-2291
www.smithflooring.com

A portion of Smith Flooring's output consists of FSC-certified oak flooring, available through a national network of distributors. Most is red oak; a small amount of white oak is sometimes available. This flooring meets all NOFMA (Wood Flooring Manufacturers Association) specifications. The solid oak strips are 3/4" thick, available in 2-1/4", 3-1/4" or 1-1/2" faces; all pallets conform to NOFMA standards for average length. Shorts are also available.

Certified Parquet Flooring

Parquet By Dian
16601 S. Main St.
Gardena, CA 90248

Phone: 310-527-3779
www.parquet.com

Parquet By Dian (PBD) received its chain-of-custody SmartWood Certification in September 2001. This square-edged flooring results in a much longer life than traditional tongue-and-groove (T&G) flooring, which can be sanded down only as far as the tongue. In addition, the manufacturer claims they can produce 2 ft2 of parquet from 1 board foot of lumber, whereas manufacturers of T&G can only produce 1 ft2 of 3/4" strip flooring. The 7/16"-thick pieces of FSC-certified wood are preassembled into "tile" sections held together by adhesive sheets of plastic and then installed with polyurethane adhesive. Sealing the perimeter and applying a surface finish results in an installation that is essentially waterproof, according to the manufacturer. PBD flooring can be installed immediately (no acclimation time is required), and the product is available in a large variety of patterns and a number of wood species.

Certified Wood Building Products

West Wind Hardwood, Inc.
P.O. Box 2205
Sidney, BC V8L 3S8 Canada

Toll-free: 800-667-2275
Phone: 250-656-0848
www.westwindhardwood.com

Family-owned and -operated West Wind Hardwood offers locally harvested, FSC-certified custom Douglas fir lumber, timbers, and flooring in clear and vertical grain. Other species, such as hemlock, pine, red oak, birch, and maple may be available, depending on supply. The company also offers SmartWood Rediscovered salvaged woods on request and availability. The dimensions and appearances of salvaged and recycled woods may vary due to the nature of the materials. The company specializes in Douglas fir, and is recognized for custom wood products for less usual applications.

Certified Wood Flooring

A. E. Sampson & Son, Inc.
171 Camden Rd.
Warren, ME 04864

Toll-free: 800-769-6196
Phone: 207-273-4000
www.aesampsonandson.com

A. E. Sampson & Son offers FSC-certified wood flooring in many species, including Eastern White Pine, birch, maple, oak, and ash. Call with specifications.

Certified Wood Flooring

Plaza Hardwood, Inc.
219 W. Manhattan Ave.
Santa Fe, NM 87501

Toll-free: 800-662-6306
Phone: 505-992-3260
www.plzfloor.com

Plaza Hardwood offers FSC-certified maple, birch, cherry, ash, red oak, and white oak flooring.

Certified Wood Flooring

Tembec, Inc., Huntsville Division
80 Old North Rd.
Huntsville, ON P1H 2J4 Canada

Toll-free: 800-461-5386
Phone: 705-789-2371
www.muskokaflooring.com

Tembec's Muskoka wood flooring is produced (on a special-order basis) from FSC-certified maple harvested from lands that the company manages.

Certified Wood Flooring

Whitethorn Construction
545 Shelter Cove Rd.
P.O. Box 400
Whitethorn, CA 95589

Phone: 707-986-7412
www.whitethornconstruction.com

Whitethorn specializes in FSC-certified tan oak flooring, available in varied earth-tones in widths ranging from 2-1/4" to 4-1/4".

Certified Wood Products

Cascadia Forest Goods, LLC
38083 Wheeler Rd.
Dexter, OR 97431

Phone: 541-485-4477
www.cascadiaforestgoods.com

Cascadia Forest Goods (CFG) is a supplier of FSC-certified and recycled forest products, including hardwood and softwood veneers, dimensional lumber and decking, timbers and beams, siding, flooring, paneling, and trim. CFG's woods come from the Pacific Northwest and British Columbia, and include the following species: douglas fir, incense and western red cedar, sitka and englemann spruce, ponderosa and sugar pine, and regional hardwoods (madrone, white and black oak, broadleaf maple, alder, chinkapin, and myrtlewood). FSC-certified and recycled-forest-product flooring species include madrone, white oak, clear vertical grain (CVG) Douglas fir, birch, big-leaf maple, and myrtlewood. CFG also supplies FSC-certified flooring and decking from Central and South America, including Santa Maria, catalox, chechen negro, jobillo, machiche, ramon blanco, sauche, ipe, pucte (ironwood), and others. CFG offers both solid and engineered wood flooring. CFG also supplies both FSC-certified hardwood and softwood veneers and lumber to window and door manufacturers.

Certified Wood Products

Randall Custom Lumber, Ltd.
3530 S.E. Arcadia Rd.
Shelton, WA 98584

Phone: 360-426-8518

Randall Custom Lumber manufactures FSC-certified decking, flooring, hard and softwood lumber, and stair parts. Some of their certified species are ash, red cedar, red alder, Douglas fir, madrone, and maple.

Endura Wood Products

Endura Wood Products, Ltd.
1303 S.E. 6th Ave.
Portland, OR 97214

Phone: 503-233-7090
www.endurawood.com

Endura offers FSC-certified hardwood and softwood flooring, lumber, and decking in a wide variety of exotic and domestic species. Endurawood butcher blocks and countertops are produced from certified woods such as rock maple. Endura also sells reclaimed wood products as well as straw particleboard and agrifiber composite sheet goods.

F.D. Sterritt Certified-Wood Building Products

F.D. Sterritt Lumber Co.
110 Arlington St.
Watertown, MA 02472

Toll-free: 877-635-3362
Phone: 617-923-1480
www.sterrittlumber.com

F.D. Sterritt Lumber sells FSC-certified lumber, plywood, decking, hardwoods, and hardwood flooring. They have a variety of certified species in stock. Additional green building materials available, including low-VOC adhesives, caulking, sealants, and recycled drywall. F.D. Sterritt offers green building product consultations.

FSC-Certified Exotic Hardwood Flooring

JG Architectural Supply
513 Progress Dr., Ste. K
Linthicum, MD 21090

Toll-free: 877-482-4771
Phone: 410-609-6137
www.jgarchitectural.com

JG Architectural Supply carries FSC-Certified hardwood flooring from Paraguay and Bolivia. Prefinished product is kept in stock and unfinished stock is available on a per-order basis. The finish used is free of formaldehyde, heavy metals, insecticides and pesticides. Most of these species have high Janka ratings, making these flooring products many times more dent-resistant than standard oaks.

FSC-Certified Teak Flooring

Unique American Teak
6152 15th St. E
Bradenton, FL 34203

Phone: 941-758-0365
www.uniqueamericanteak.com

Unique American Teak is a direct importer of FSC-certified teak that manufactures and sells pre-finished, natural, and stained solid teak flooring. A three-layer laminate is also offered. Solid wide planks are available in 4-3/4" widths — 3-3/8" available through special order — and sold in a set of random lengths from 12" to 48". Wide engineered is 4-3/4" wide and comes in random lengths of 12" to 84". 1/8" wear layer allows 2 sandings. All materials used contain no added urea-formaldehyde resins.

FSC-Certified Wood Products

Dwight Lewis Lumber / Lewis Lumber Products
30 S. Main St.
P.O. Box 356
Picture Rocks, PA 17762

Toll-free: 800-233-8450
Phone: 570-584-4460
www.lewislp.com

Dwight Lewis Lumber sells FSC-certified moldings, flooring, paneling, and hardwoods, subject to availability. Certified species are cherry, hard and soft maple, and red oak.

Georgian Bay Wet Wood

Georgian Bay Wet Wood Inc.
8520 Highway 93
Midland, ON L4R 4K4 Canada

Phone: 705-526-6912
www.georgianbaywetwood.com

Georgian Bay Wet Wood Inc. recovers submerged old-growth timber from Ontario's Georgian Bay of Lake Huron then mills it to produce veneers, flooring, and lumber. Birch, beech, birds-eye maple, and flame birch are typically recovered. Heritage Timber Veneers are available in two species, Flame Birch and Birds Eye Maple. Heritage Timber Engineered Flooring has a nominal 1/8" (3.2mm) sawn veneer of recovered Maple, Birch, or Oak in 4" wide, random length boards with tongue and groove sides, micro-bevel edges, and a 9mm, 7-ply, FSC-certified Birch plywood core. The flooring is pre-finished with an aluminum oxide, UV-cured, urethane coating. Overall, the product has greater than 70% FSC-certified wood. Georgian Bay Wet Wood's wood products come with a certificate of authenticity that verifies that the product is genuine Georgian Bay Wet Wood.

Harmonized Tropical Wood

Harmonized Wood Products
5500 Prytania St., #143
New Orleans, LA 70115

Toll-free: 877-635-3362
Phone: 504-342-4250
www.harmonizedwood.com

Harmonized Wood Products offers a wide range of FSC-certified tropical hardwood products, specializing in Latin American hardwoods. Products include lumber, timber, decking, flooring, doors, veneer, and custom furniture.

Hoboken Floors

Hoboken Floors
70 Demarest Dr.
Wayne, NJ 07470

Toll-free: 800-222-1068
Phone: 973-694-2888
www.hobokenfloors.com

Hoboken Floors is a large distributor of flooring products that can provide unfinished and prefinished wood flooring from three different FSC-certified Canadian sources. They also distribute multi-ply, laminated flooring products made from certified ash, hackberry, maple, and oak.

Reclaimed Heritage Wood Flooring

Nadurra Wood Corp.
300 Esna Park Dr., Unit 26
Markham, ON L3R1H3 Canada

Phone: 905-947-1488
www.nadurrawood.com

Nadurra Wood Corp. manufactures wide-plank flooring from 12"-thick Douglas Fir timbers salvaged from older Toronto building demolitions. This flooring is FSC-certified and, because it is made from timbers that were originally cut from old-growth trees with very tight grain patterns, the wood tends to be more durable than newly harvested fir, according to the manufacturer. Reclaimed Heritage® Flooring has a unique red and yellow color, often with character markings such as bolt scores, nail holes, and checks that add distinct character. Reclaimed heart pine is also available. Planks come in 4"–10" widths and 1 1/2'–12' random lengths. All dimensions are 3/4"-thick, unfinished, tongue-and-groove (T&G) planks that can be nailed or glued.

SmartChoice Wood Products

Certified Forest Products, LLC.
7 Los Conejos
Orinda, CA 94563

Phone: 925-258-4372
www.certifiedforestproducts.com

Certified Forest Products (CFP) is a distributor of SmartChoice, a collection of FSC-certified and reclaimed wood products from a variety of species including hardwoods, cedar, and redwood. Products include lumber, plywood, decking, siding, flooring, interior and exterior millwork.

Sonic Floor Laminate Flooring

Kronopol Marketing
44 Woodbine Down Blvd.
Rexdale, ON M9W 5R2 Canada

Toll-free: 877-526-9663
Phone: 416-675-1048
www.kronopol.com

European manufacturer Kronopol has entered the U.S. market with Sonic Floor™, an FSC-certified laminate flooring with an integral underpad of felt and rubber that reduces impact noise transmission. The glueless, snap-together, floating floor requires no underlayment, and has very low VOC and formaldehyde emissions. The plank-style flooring comes in 54" lengths for faster installation and fewer visible joints. Sonic Floor for residential and light commercial installations has a 30-year warranty against fading, staining, wear, and "topographical moisture." Sonic Floor Plus Embossed for medium commercial use carries a lifetime limited warranty. Swiss-owned, Poland-based Kronopol is among the world's largest manufacturers of laminate flooring, and is one of only a few manufacturers to have FSC certification for its entire range of products.

Windfall Lumber and Milling

Windfall Lumber and Milling
404 Jefferson St. NE
Olympia, WA 98501

Phone: 360-352-2250
www.windfalllumber.com

Windfall Lumber is a manufacturer and distributor of FSC-certified and Smartwood Rediscovered hardwoods, flooring, millwork, countertops, and timbers.

Wood Floor Resource Group Flooring

Wood Floor Resource Group, LLC
122 Kissel Rd.
Burlington, NJ 08016

Toll-free: 866-457-9374
Phone: 609-589-3100
www.woodfloorrg.com

The Wood Floor Resource Group (WFRG) supplies a comprehensive range of environmentally friendly wood flooring products including FSC-certified wood, salvaged or reclaimed wood, rapidly renewable non-wood materials, and low- or zero-formaldehyde products. The Eco Products Selector on their website allows users to select products based on relevance to LEED Credit or specific environmental attributes, width, color, solid or engineered construction, and whether the product is finished or unfinished. WFRG also provides LEED assistance and other support to customers. WFRG acts as an expert resource to the architectural community and works through major flooring distributors. They also sell flooring directly for personal use by professionals using their services.

Natural Fiber Floor Mats

These mats are made from durable natural fibers in a variety of styles and weaves. Common natural fibers for matting include sisal (often used in wall coverings), jute (used to make rope and burlap bags), and coir (from coconut husks). Natural-fiber mats generally don't have backings or chemical treatments. They're durable but may shed broken fibers, requiring periodic sweeping or vacuuming of the surrounding floor area.

Plain Herringbone-Weave Cocoa Matting

Allied Mat & Matting, Inc.
52-08 Grand Ave.
Maspeth, NY 11378

Toll-free: 800-452-5588
Phone: 718-381-9824
www.alliedmat.com

Plain Herringbone-Weave Cocoa Matting is made from coir fiber and comes in rolls that are 18", 27", 36", 45", 54", 63" or 72" wide and approximately 3/8" thick.

Plastic Flooring

Recycled plastic flooring products are relatively inexpensive, often interlocking, floor tiles that are particularly appropriate in wet areas. Though not always durable enough for heavy traffic areas, plastic flooring is suitable for outdoor showers and certain other utilitarian spaces where easy maintenance and some resilience are required. Textures and open-weave construction also lend slip-resistance to some products. Some offer adhesive-free installation. Products listed here have a recycled content value (equal to post-consumer plus 1/2 pre-consumer) of at least 40%, with many products using 100% post-consumer and/or post-industrial recycled plastic.

Patio Tiles

Renew Resources Ltd.
81 Mack Ave.
Toronto, ON M1L 1M5 Canada

Toll-free: 800-439-5028
Phone: 416-335-4040
www.renewresources.com

Renew Resources offers recycled-plastic tiles made of 100% pre-consumer HDPE, available in grey, taupe, redwood, and cedar. Primarily used over solid surfaces such as rooftops, patios, and balconies, the tiles may also be laid directly on the ground for temporary or permanent yard patios. Available in two sizes: 23" x 23" and 17" x 17".

PlasTEAK Recycled-Plastic Tiles

PlasTEAK
3563 Copley Rd.
P.O. Box 4290
Akron, OH 44321

Toll-free: 800-320-1841
Phone: 330-668-2587
www.plasteak.com

PlasTEAK tiles are made with 100% post-consumer recycled HDPE in a paraffin base—they become more slip-resistant when wet. Locking Tiles are open-weave, 12" x 12" x 3/4", UV-stabilized, interlocking tiles; transitional edge ramps are available. Patio Pads are solid-surface 24" x 24" x 1-1/2" pavers with a decorative appearance. The made-for-function, solid-surface Pro Pads tiles come in two-inch-thick sizes ranging from 24" x 24" to 36" x 48".

Turtle Tiles

Turtle Plastics
7450-A Industrial Pkwy.
Lorain, OH 44053

Toll-free: 800-437-1603
Phone: 440-282-8008
www.turtleplastics.com

Turtle Tiles are open-weave floor tiles made from 50% post-consumer recycled PVC plastic. The interlocking tiles are 3/4" x 12" x 12" and come in 17 solid colors. The manufacturer has certified the following recycled-content levels (by weight): total recovered material 100% guaranteed; post-consumer material 50% guaranteed.

Reclaimed-Wood Flooring

As the demands on forest resources have increased, nonforest sources of wood have grown in importance. Reclaimed-wood flooring is made from timbers salvaged from old buildings, bridges, or other timber structures. It may also be manufactured from logs salvaged from river bottoms, or from trees being removed in urban and suburban areas.

As with other resources, the supply of reclaimed wood is limited. Efficient and appropriate use of reclaimed wood is important for its long-term availability. White pine, longleaf yellow pine, cypress, oak, walnut, and chestnut reclaimed-wood flooring may be available from Eastern and Midwestern suppliers. Western suppliers commonly stock Douglas fir. Plan your needs with plenty of lead time, as availability and pricing fluctuate widely.

AltruWood Reclaimed-Wood Products

AltruWood, Inc.
P.O. Box 3341
Portland, OR 97208

Toll-free: 877-372-9663
www.altruwood.com

AltruWood sells a variety of reclaimed-wood species and products, mostly salvaged from old buildings, barns, factories, warehouses and rivers in the U.S.—principally including domestic pine varieties, Douglas fir, oak, cedar, redwood, chestnut, cypress, and cherry. Products include flooring, timbers, siding, paneling, millwork, and lumber. The company will work with clients to locate recycled lumber from their region. A custom cutting service allows the specification of exact sizes and dimensions, minimizing waste. AltruWood also sells new domestic and tropical FSC-certified wood.

Antique Woods & Colonial Restorations

Antique Woods & Colonial Restorations, Inc.
121 Quarry Rd.
Gouverneur, NY 13642

Toll-free: 888-261-4284
Phone: 610-913-0674
www.vintagewoods.com

Antique Woods & Colonial Restorations, Inc. (formerly Vintage Barns, Woods & Restorations) sells reclaimed and remilled wood products including flooring, siding, millwork, and whole barn frames.

Appalachian Woods

Appalachian Woods, LLC
1240 Cold Springs Rd.
Stuarts Draft, VA 24477

Toll-free: 800-333-7610
Phone: 540-337-1801
www.appalachianwoods.com

Appalachian Woods reclaims and remills timber for a variety of custom millwork applications. Lumber is generally sold rough, but can be provided S4S and S2S. Lumber, flooring, and furniture is available in a variety of species including American chestnut, heart pine, and oak. Appalachian Woods has been a family-run business since 1976.

Barnstormers Reclaimed Hand-Hewn Beams

Barnstormers
166 Malden Tpke.
Saugerties, NY 12477

Phone: 845-661-7989
www.barnstormersflooring.com

Barnstormers sells antique hand-hewn beams from disassembled barns. Species include oak, chestnut, hemlock, and other hardwoods. The company also remills tongue-and-groove barnwood hardwood flooring and siding out of this reclaimed wood, using a technique called "skip planing" to mill the boards while leaving some of the original milling marks for aesthetic purposes.

Craftmark Reclaimed Wood

Craftmark Reclaimed Wood, Inc.
P.O. Box 237
McMinnville, OR 97128

Phone: 503-472-6929
www.craftmarkinc.com

Craftmark Reclaimed Wood, Inc. is a distributor of flooring, decking, paneling, wainscoting, timbers, and specialty wood products such as architectural moldings produced from a wide variety of FSC-certified species. Custom-milling is a specialty. The company is also a manufacturer of wood products from reclaimed timber.

D. Litchfield Reclaimed Wood

D. Litchfield & Co. Ltd.
3046 Westwood St.
Port Coquitlam, BC V3C 3L7 Canada

Toll-free: 888-303-2222
Phone: 604-464-7525
www.dlitchfield.com

Litchfield carries a large, steady supply of all types of reclaimed lumber and beams salvaged through their deconstruction operations.

Durapalm Palm Flooring

Smith & Fong Company
475 6th St.
S. San Francisco, CA 94103

Toll-free: 866-835-9859
Phone: 415-896-0577
www.plyboo.com

Smith & Fong's Durapalm® flooring is made from plantation-grown coconut palm trees that no longer produce coconuts. The 5/8" x 3" tongue-and-groove planks come in 2' to 4' lengths and range from dark to medium-red mahogany in color. They contain no added urea-formaldehyde or VOCs and are available unfinished or prefinished with an 8-coat ceramic/urethane UV-cured finish. Smith & Fong reports that they use only the darker, harder palm for a durable surface (1450 PSI Janka Ball Test, ASTM D1037). Reducer, baseboard, quarter round, and stairnosing and threshold molding are available.

Georgian Bay Wet Wood

Georgian Bay Wet Wood Inc.
8520 Highway 93
Midland, ON L4R 4K4 Canada

Phone: 705-526-6912
www.georgianbaywetwood.com

Georgian Bay Wet Wood Inc. recovers submerged old-growth timber from Ontario's Georgian Bay of Lake Huron then mills it to produce veneers, flooring, and lumber. Birch, beech, birds-eye maple, and flame birch are typically recovered. Heritage Timber Veneers are available in two species, Flame Birch and Birds Eye Maple. Heritage Timber Engineered Flooring has a nominal 1/8" (3.2mm) sawn veneer of recovered Maple, Birch, or Oak in 4" wide, random length boards with tongue and groove sides, micro-bevel edges, and a 9mm, 7-ply, FSC-certified Birch plywood core. The flooring is pre-finished with an aluminum oxide, UV-cured, urethane coating. Overall, the product has greater than 70% FSC-certified wood. Georgian Bay Wet Wood's wood products come with a certificate of authenticity that verifies that the product is genuine Georgian Bay Wet Wood.

Heartwood Reclaimed-Wood Flooring

Heartwood Industries
3658 State Road 1414
Hartford, KY 42347

Phone: 270-298-0084
www.whiskeywood.com

Heartwood is an international distributor of dimension lumber and timbers salvaged from warehouses and whiskey distilleries. They specialize in flooring but also offer custom millwork and moldings in longleaf yellow pine, oak, chestnut, and cypress.

Logs End Reclaimed-Wood Building Products

Logs End Inc.
1520 Triole St.
Ottawa, ON K1B3S9 Canada

Phone: 613-738-7851
www.logsend.com

Logs End, Inc., retrieves sinker logs in Canada's Upper Ottawa Valley area and processes them into lumber and timber, wide-plank flooring, paneling, siding, and trim in standard and custom dimensions. Old-growth, clear pine is typically recovered, though birch, red and white oak, and hard and soft maple are also available. Certificates of authenticity for educational purposes are issued by the company. Logs End lumber and timbers carry Smartwood "Rediscovered" certification.

M. Fine Lumber Company

M. Fine Lumber Company
1301 Metropolitan Ave.
P.O. Box 37 701
Brooklyn, NY 11237

Phone: 718-381-5200
www.mfinelumber.com

M. Fine Lumber Company is a leading supplier of salvaged heavy timber and dimension lumber. Inventory is salvaged from buildings being demolished throughout the U.S. Species include longleaf yellow pine, oak, and Douglas fir.

Michael Evans Natural Resources

Michael Evenson Natural Resources
P.O. Box 157
Petrolia, CA 95558

Phone: 707-629-3506
www.oldgrowthtimbers.com

Natural Resources dismantles buildings and remills salvaged lumber for resale. Available species include redwood, Douglas fir, and western red cedar.

Old Wood Flooring

Old Wood Workshop, LLC.
193 Hampton Rd.
Pomfret Center, CT 06259

Phone: 860-655-5259
www.oldwoodworkshop.com

The Old Wood Workshop offers salvaged and remilled antique flooring as well as salvaged building materials including beams, boards, and joists. Old Wood Workshop also offers custom harvest tables made from reclaimed wood, and architectural antiques such as iron hardware, doors, and fireplace mantles. Remilled chestnut flooring is priced by width. Salvaged flooring in the online inventory is available in limited-size batches only.

Pinocchio's Reclaimed Lumber

Pinocchio's
18651 Hare Creek Ter.
Fort Bragg, CA 95437

Phone: 707-964-6272
www.pinocchioredwood.com

Pinocchio's offers raw and remilled lumber from Douglas fir and redwood in both standard-dimension and custom sizes.

Reclaimed and Urban-Harvested Millwork

Jackel Enterprises
347 Locust St.
Watsonville, CA 95076

Toll-free: 800-711-9663
Phone: 831-768-3880
www.jackelenterprises.com

Jackel Enterprises processes urban and suburban forestry—the low-impact removal of city-owned and back-yard trees, ranch maintenance, and the like. Species include redwood, Douglas fir, Monterey cypress, black acacia, and California black walnut. Jackel also processes forest floor salvage from private parties, primarily old growth redwood, as well as milling recycled hardwoods and softwoods, including Douglas fir, redwood, western red cedar, heart pine, bald cypress, walnut, oak, and hickory. They have recently had their FSC chain-of-custody certification reinstated and will stock certified maple, oak, cherry, Douglas fir, and western red cedar.

Reclaimed Hardwood Flooring

JG Architectural Supply
513 Progress Dr., Ste. K
Linthicum, MD 21090

Toll-free: 877-482-4771
Phone: 410-609-6137
www.jgarchitectural.com

JG Architectural Supply sells reclaimed wood flooring milled from old timbers recovered from historical buildings. Matching moldings and stair treads are also available. Species include heart pine, peroba (Brazilian barnwood), red oak, white oak, wormy chestnut, and wormy maple. Custom reclaimed products with selection for nail holes, saw kerf, and other character marks are available upon request.

Reclaimed Heritage Wood Flooring

Nadurra Wood Corp.
300 Esna Park Dr., Unit 26
Markham, ON L3R1H3 Canada

Phone: 905-947-1488
www.nadurrawood.com

Nadurra Wood Corp. manufactures wide-plank flooring from 12"-thick Douglas Fir timbers salvaged from older Toronto building demolitions. This flooring is FSC-certified and, because it is made from timbers that were originally cut from old-growth trees with very tight grain patterns, the wood tends to be more durable than newly harvested fir, according to the manufacturer. Reclaimed Heritage® Flooring has a unique red and yellow color, often with character markings such as bolt scores, nail holes, and checks that add distinct character. Reclaimed heart pine is also available. Planks come in 4"–10" widths and 1 1/2'–12' random lengths. All dimensions are 3/4"-thick, unfinished, tongue-and-groove (T&G) planks that can be nailed or glued.

Reclaimed-Wood Building Products

Aged Woods / Yesteryear Floorworks Company
2331 E Market St, Ste 6
York, PA 17402

Toll-free: 800-233-9307
Phone: 717-840-0330
www.agedwoods.com

Aged Woods® / Yesteryear Floorworks Company is a full-service mill that uses reclaimed, kiln-dried wood to produce flooring, stair parts, moldings, cabinetry, and paneling. They salvage their materials from barns that are typically between 75 and 200 years old. Available species include American chestnut, longleaf heart pine, maple, cherry, walnut, hemlock, hickory, poplar, pine, and oak. Most of the flooring is 3/4" tongue-and-groove and of random widths and lengths within given ranges. Matching stair parts are available in conjunction with flooring orders.

Reclaimed-Wood Building Products

Conklin's Authentic Antique Barnwood
R.R. 1, Box 70
Susquehanna, PA 18847

Phone: 570-465-3832
www.conklinsbarnwood.com

Conklin's Authentic Antique Barnwood sells hand-hewn beams, barn boards, and flooring "as is" or remilled.

Reclaimed-Wood Building Products

Endura Wood Products, Ltd.
1303 S.E. 6th Ave.
Portland, OR 97214

Phone: 503-233-7090
www.endurawood.com

Endura Wood Products currently has access to over 3.5 million board feet of Douglas fir that is being reclaimed from the old Portland Dry Dock #2. Also available is a limited supply of Douglas fir with a distinct red hue that has been reclaimed from maraschino cherry vats.

Reclaimed-Wood Building Products

General Woodcraft, Inc.
531 Broad St.
New London, CT 06320

Phone: 860-444-9663
www.generalwoodcraftinc.com

General Woodcraft provides wood flooring and other products milled from beams and timbers salvaged from barns and factories built a century ago—often from old-growth timber. Species (as available) include pine, chestnut, and oak.

Reclaimed-Wood Building Products

J. Hoffman Lumber Co.
1330 E. State St.
Sycamore, IL 60178

Phone: 815-899-2260
www.hoffmanlumberco.com

J. Hoffman Lumber Co. is the Midwest's only sawmill company specializing in reclaimed antique heart pine, Douglas fir, and white pine. Reclaimed lumber is remilled into flooring, siding, and other millwork.

Reclaimed-Wood Building Products

Longleaf Lumber
115 Fawcett St.
Cambridge, MA 02138

Toll-free: 866-653-3566
Phone: 617-871-6611
www.longleaflumber.com

Longleaf Lumber, founded in 1997, remills antique timbers into millwork and flooring at the company's sawmill in southern Maine. Longleaf specializes in heart pine, but other salvaged woods such as chestnut, red and white oak, eastern white pine, and maple are also available from buildings dismantled in various locations around the New England region. Longleaf also sells unmilled reclaimed timbers and reclaimed barn siding. In addition to the sawmill, the company operates a retail store at their Cambridge, MA location.

Reclaimed-Wood Building Products

Mayse Woodworking Co.
319 Richardson Rd.
Lansdale, PA 19446

Toll-free: 888-566-4532
Phone: 215-822-8307

Mayse Woodworking offers reclaimed heart pine millwork including flooring, trim, moldings, stair treads, and risers in three styles: American Country, Signature, and Federal. The products are remanufactured from recycled heart pine beams.

Reclaimed-Wood Building Products

Mountain Lumber
6812 Spring Hill Rd.
P.O. Box 289
Ruckersville, VA 22968

Toll-free: 800-445-2671
Phone: 434-985-3646
www.mountainlumber.com

Mountain Lumber reclaims timbers from buildings slated for demolition and ships them to their mill in Virginia for remilling into wide-plank flooring, beams, rough-sawn cabinet lumber, and an extensive range of architectural millwork including stair parts and moldings. Species include heart pine, oak, American chestnut, maple, and elm.

Reclaimed-Wood Building Products

Pioneer Millworks
1180 Commercial Dr.
Farmington, NY 14425

Toll-free: 800-951-9663
Phone: 585-924-9970
www.pioneermillworks.com

Pioneer Millworks remills salvaged wood into flooring and a number of molding profiles, in addition to timbers, cabinetry, stair parts, doors, and trusses. The primary species is longleaf yellow pine; others that are often available include redwood, bald cypress, chestnut, white oak, Douglas fir, and white pine.

Reclaimed-Wood Building Products

Solid Wood Products
3756 Pineridge Dr.
Lac Le Jeune, BC V1S 1Y8 Canada

Phone: 250-320-0936
www.solidwoodpro.com

Solid Wood Products manufactures building and finish products, primarily wide-plank flooring from reclaimed Douglas fir. The one-inch flooring is available in 6" to 14" widths. Also offered are trim, wainscot, panels, and stair parts; timber-frame components including beams, braces, purlins, and rafters; as well as custom furniture.

Reclaimed-Wood Building Products

TerraMai
1104 Firenze St.
P.O. Box 696
McCloud, CA 96057

Toll-free: 800-220-9062
Phone: 530-964-2740
www.terramai.com

TerraMai produces several grades of flooring, ranging from clear tongue-and-groove to rough-cut plank, from reclaimed lumber and tropical hardwoods. All flooring is available in "Character" (with evidence of previous use) and "Select" (clear) grades. Douglas fir, ponderosa pine, and southern yellow pine are among their most popular species. TerraMai also mills various architectural woodwork products from their 700,000-board-foot inventory of reclaimed woods. All of TerraMai's varied products are from reclaimed wood and is FSC certified.

Reclaimed-Wood Building Products

Vintage Material Supply Co.
730 Shady Ln.
Austin, TX 78702

Phone: 512-386-6404
www.vintagematerialsupply.com

Vintage Material Supply Co. offers salvaged wood flooring available "as is" with edges cleaned, as well as new flooring milled from wood recovered from such sources as demolished buildings, ranch recovery, urban logging, and river bottoms. Primary species include old-growth longleaf pine, Tidewater cypress, mesquite, and walnut.

Reclaimed-Wood Building Products

Vintage Timberworks
47100 Rainbow Canyon Rd.
Temecula, CA 92592

Phone: 951-695-1003
www.vintagetimber.com

Vintage Timberworks offers a wide range of reclaimed products made with wood salvaged from buildings in the U.S., Canada, and Australia that are typically at least 70 years old. Typical species include Douglas fir, cedar, and redwood. Reclaimed timber, beams, and flooring are available in a variety of species and are offered "as is," remilled, and/or refinished (distressed, hand-hewed, sandblasted, etc.). Douglas fir and oak flooring can be milled in a wide variety of widths and lengths. Most other species are limited in width and length to available stock.

The company also can arrange for building demolition and material reclamation in the U.S. and Canada.

Reclaimed-Wood Building Products

West Wind Hardwood, Inc.
P.O. Box 2205
Sidney, BC V8L 3S8 Canada

Toll-free: 800-667-2275
Phone: 250-656-0848
www.westwindhardwood.com

Family-owned and -operated West Wind Hardwood offers SmartWood Rediscovered salvaged woods for flooring, planks, lumber, timber, and other applications. The dimensions and appearances of salvaged and recycled woods may vary due to the nature of the materials. The company also offers locally harvested, FSC-certified custom Douglas fir flooring in clear and vertical grain. Other species, such as hemlock, pine, red oak, birch, and maple may be available, depending on supply. The company specializes in Douglas fir, and is recognized for custom wood products for less usual applications.

Reclaimed-Wood Building Products

What It's Worth, Inc.
P.O. Box 162135
Austin, TX 78716

Phone: 512-328-8837
www.wiwpine.com

What It's Worth can provide reclaimed longleaf yellow pine flooring, cabinet stock, and timbers. They also offer tank cyprus (used for water tanks at the turn of the century) cut from salvaged first growth trees. Most of their products are harvested from pre-1900 structures that are being deconstructed.

Reclaimed-Wood Flooring

Antique Speciality Flooring
169 Paridon St.
Springfield, MA 01118

Toll-free: 888-SAVEWOOD
Phone: 413-782-3900
www.antiquespecialtyflooring.com

Antique Speciality Flooring offers reclaimed, random-width wood flooring in tongue-and-groove planks of chestnut, oak, heart pine, white pine, and hemlock.

Reclaimed-Wood Flooring

Carlisle Restoration Lumber
1676 Rte. 9
Stoddard, NH 03464

Toll-free: 800-595-9663
Phone: 603-446-3937
www.wideplankflooring.com

Carlisle Restoration specializes in large-dimension antique flooring, available in heart pine, chestnut, and oak. The "Antique Wood" line provides recycled wood planks. Carlisle also has showrooms in Atlanta, GA, West Hollywood, CA, and Denver CO.

Reclaimed-Wood Flooring

Early New England Restorations
32 Taugwonk Rd., Unit A12
Stonington, CT 06359

Phone: 860-599-4393
www.werestoreoldhomes.com

Early New England Restorations, formerly Horse Drawn Pine, remills pine plank flooring.

Reclaimed-Wood Flooring

Green Mountain Woodworks
P.O. Box 1433
Phoenix, OR 97535

Toll-free: 866-535-5880
www.greenmountainwoodworks.com

Green Mountain Woodworks offers a full line of unique hardwood flooring, emphasizing environmentally responsible, antique reclaimed, and Northwest woods. Green Mountain Woodworks clearly defines the "EcoStatus" of each wood, including FSC-certified, those from ecosystem restoration projects, reclaimed/recycled woods, and woods rescued from low value or waste streams (fire wood and pulp/chip).

Reclaimed-Wood Flooring

Sylvan Brandt
651 E. Main St.
Lititz, PA 17543

Phone: 717-626-4520
www.sylvanbrandt.com

Sylvan Brandt reclaimed-wood flooring is made from resawn beams and barn siding. Tongue-and-groove planks of oak, heart pine, white pine, and hemlock are available.

Reclaimed-Wood Flooring

The Woods Company, Inc.
985 Superior Ave.
Chambersburg, PA 17201

Toll-free: 888-548-7609
Phone: 717-263-6524
www.thewoodscompany.com

The Woods Co. specializes in wide-plank flooring and custom interior millwork made from wood reclaimed from demolished buildings.

Reclaimed-Wood Flooring

Vintage Lumber Co.
1 Council Dr.
P.O. Box 485
Woodsboro, MD 21798

Toll-free: 800-499-7859
www.vintagelumber.com

Since 1973, Vintage Lumber has been reusing historic old wood obtained from dismantled derelict barns to produce reclaimed, antique solid-wood flooring. "The Vintage Collection" uses old beams and boards, ranging in age from 50 to 200 years, which are milled into Vintage and Vintage/Distressed plank flooring. Vintage Lumber mills the lower grades of native Appalachian hardwoods into rustic/character flooring in "The American Country Collection." Both collections are milled in random widths and end-matched in 2' to 10' lengths.

Reclaimed-Wood Flooring and Millwork

Treasured Timbers, Inc.
173 Hunter Lake Rd.
Upper Golden Grove, NB
E2S 3B4 Canada

Phone: 506-849-8016
www.treasuredtimbers.com

Treasured Timbers, Inc. specializes in hardwood plank flooring and millwork made from sinker logs salvaged from the Saint John River.

Reclaimed-Wood Lumber and Products

Armster Reclaimed Lumber Co.
9 Old Post Rd.
Madison, CT 06443

Phone: 203-214-9705
www.woodwood.com

A Reclaimed Lumber Co. salvages wood from old water and wine tanks, mill buildings, bridge timbers, river-recovery log operations, and other sources and custom mills it into a variety of wood products including siding, plank flooring, millwork, paneling, shingles and shakes, stairs parts, and dimension lumber and timber. Available species include red cedar, redwood, beech, black cherry, chestnut, rock maple, red and white oak, Eastern hemlock, Douglas fir, mahogany and Longleaf heart pine. Wood is sourced from all over the country, much of it processed at their Connecticut mill; but the company makes an effort to provide wood that is local to the customer and will make arrangements to process it locally.

Reclaimed-Wood Materials

Big Timberworks
1 Rabel Ln.
P.O. Box 368
Gallatin Gateway, MT 59730

Phone: 406-763-4639
www.bigtimberworks.com

Big Timberworks offers custom-milled, reclaimed lumber and timbers in a variety of species. The company specializes in shipping timber frame houses all over the country for supervised construction but also sells custom-cut, reclaimed wood from their sawmill in Montana for residential and commercial applications such as siding, flooring, and millwork.

Reclaimed-Wood Materials

Black's Farmwood, Inc.
P.O. Box 2836
San Rafael, CA 94912

Toll-free: 877-321-9663
Phone: 415-454-8312
www.blacksfarmwood.com

Black's Farmwood sells reclaimed wood products from deconstructed buildings and river bottoms. Products are available in a variety of species and include salvaged timbers and beams, remilled flooring, and barn siding. The company has a showroom in San Rafael, CA and uses two mills, one in Kentucky and another in New York.

Reclaimed-Wood Millwork

J.L. Powell & Co., Inc.
101 E. Main St.
Whiteville, NC 28472

Toll-free: 800-227-2007
Phone: 910-642-8989
www.plankfloors.com

J.L. Powell & Co. specializes in custom architectural millwork, including stair parts and flooring, produced from reclaimed antique heart pine.

Reclaimed-Wood Products

Albany Woodworks, Inc.
P.O. Box 729
Albany, LA 70711

Toll-free: 1-800-551-1282
Phone: 225-567-1155
www.albanywoodworks.com

Albany Woodworks mills reclaimed woods, including heart pine and heart cypress, into various architectural woodwork products, including flooring, timber, and stair parts. Doors are also offered.

Reclaimed-Wood Products

Architectural Timber and Millwork
49 Mt. Warner Rd.
P.O. Box 719
Hadley, MA 01035

Toll-free: 800-430-5473
Phone: 413-586-3045
www.atimber.com

Architectural Timber and Millwork specializes in custom architectural millwork fabricated from reclaimed wood. They source their materials from different parts of the country, providing a widely varied species inventory. Wide-plank flooring is produced from wood salvaged from existing structures slated for demolition. Species include heart pine, chestnut, and oak.

Reclaimed-Wood Products

Centre Mills Antique Floors
P.O. Box 16
Aspers, PA 17304

Phone: 717-677-9698
www.centremillsantiquefloors.com

Centre Mills Antique Floors salvages, remills, and sells several species and types of wood products, many hand-hewn. Species include chestnut, oak, white pine, and fir. Centre Mills uses the old gristmill, built in 1841, in Centre Mills, Pennsylvania as their storage facility.

Reclaimed-Wood Products

Chestnut Specialists, Inc.
P.O. Box 304
Plymouth, CT 06782

Phone: 860-283-4209
www.chestnutspec.com

Chestnut Specialists dismantles buildings and remills reclaimed timbers for resale in a variety of products, including siding and flooring. Rough timber, planks, and beams in their original milled or hand-hewn condition are also available.

Reclaimed-Wood Products

Crossroads Recycled Lumber
57839 Rd. 225
P.O. Box 928
North Fork, CA 93643

Toll-free: 888-842-3201
Phone: 559-877-3645
www.crossroadslumber.com

Crossroads Recycled Lumber sells raw and remilled salvaged Douglas fir, sugar pine, ponderosa pine, cedar, and redwood lumber, timbers, flooring, paneling, and siding. They also offer doors made from this wood.

Reclaimed-Wood Products

Duluth Timber Co.
P.O. Box 16717
Duluth, MN 55805

Phone: 218-727-2145
www.duluthtimber.com

Duluth Timber reclaims and remills mainly Douglas fir and longleaf yellow pine, but also redwood and cypress. Demolition and salvage of warehouses and sheep-shearing sheds in Australia has yielded a supply of Australian hardwoods such as jarrah and Mountain ash. Duluth has mills in Minnesota and Washington.

Resource Woodworks

Resource Woodworks, Inc.
627 E. 60th St.
Tacoma, WA 98404

Phone: 253-474-3757

Resource Woodworks specializes in Douglas fir, cedar, and redwood timbers salvaged from demolition projects and remilled to custom specifications, including decking, flooring, lumber, timbers, siding, paneling, and millwork.

Re-Tech Wood Products

Re-Tech Wood Products
1324 Russell Rd.
P.O. Box 215
Forks, WA 98331

Phone: 360-374-4141
www.retechwoodproducts.com

Re-Tech reclaims and remills timber for a wide variety of custom millwork and complete custom timber-frame packages for houses. They also make specialty cuts in timber to order.

River-Reclaimed Wood Products

Goodwin Heart Pine Company
106 S.W. 109th Pl.
Micanopy, FL 32667

Toll-free: 800-336-3118
Phone: 352-466-0339
www.heartpine.com

Goodwin manufactures antique wood flooring, millwork, stair parts, paneling, and siding made from antique heart pine and heart cypress logs—200 years old or older—recovered from Southern river bottoms. Flooring, siding, and paneling is kiln-dried, graded, and precision-milled. Decorative wood moldings are architecturally drawn and are designed to classic proportions. Stair parts include solid or laminated treads, and a full range of balusters, newels, and rails. Reclaimed timbers from old buildings are also available.

Trestlewood

Trestlewood
292 N. 2000 W, Ste. A
Lindon, UT 84042

Toll-free: 877-375-2779
Phone: 801-443-4002
www.trestlewood.com

Trestlewood deals exclusively in reclaimed wood. Their wood comes from the Lucin Cutoff railroad trestle, which crosses the Great Salt Lake, and other salvage projects. Trestlewood products include flooring, millwork, timbers, decking, and siding. Available species include Douglas fir, redwood, southern yellow pine, longleaf yellow pine, oak, and other hardwoods.

Urban Hardwoods

Urban Hardwoods
4755 C. Colorado Ave. S
Seattle, WA 98134

Phone: 206-766-8199
www.urbanhardwoods.com

Urban Hardwoods salvages urban trees from within a 50-mile radius of the company and mills them into custom, made-to-order furniture, flooring, and other millwork. Urban Hardwoods continually designs products to make use of manufacturing "fall-down." Remaining waste material is given away or sold as firewood, or is used for heating their facility. The company ships 99% of its products blanket-wrapped; all blankets are reused. Products will be accepted back at the end of their useful life to be refurbished or recycled in the manufacture of new products. The company is SmartWood-certified under the "Redis-covered Wood" category.

Wood Materials from Urban Trees

CitiLog
P.O. Box 685
Pittstown, NJ 08867

Toll-free: 877-248-9564
Phone: 908-735-8871
www.citilogs.com

CitiLog™, also known as D. Stubby Warmbold, is SmartWood-certified for the harvesting of trees in urban areas of New Jersey and Pennsylvania. Wood is sent by rail to Amish craftsmen in central Pennsylvania who take extra care to turn the lesser graded wood into higher quality products such as flooring, lumber, custom architectural millwork, furniture, and kitchen cabinets. Where appropriate, wood is now harvested using horses.

Recycled-Glass Tile

Tile is an inherently low-toxic, durable finish material for flooring, walls, and other applications. Products listed here are specialty tiles produced from recycled glass.

Architectural Accents

Aurora Glass
2345 W. Broadway
Eugene, OR 97402

Toll-free: 888-291-9311
Phone: 541-681-3260
www.auroraglass.org

Aurora Glass Architectural Accents include glass tiles, rosette blocks, sconces, and drawer pulls made from 100% recycled glass. Aurora Glass is a program of St. Vincent de Paul of Lane County, Inc. The glass foundry's profits support homeless and low-income people through emergency services, housing, jobs, training, and other charitable endeavors. The manufacturer has certified the following recycled-content levels (by weight): total recovered material 100% typical, 100% guaranteed; post-consumer material 86% typical, 86% guaranteed.

Blazestone

Bedrock Industries
1401 W. Garfield St.
Seattle, WA 98119

Toll-free: 877-283-7625
Phone: 206-283-7625
www.bedrockindustries.com

Blazestone® tiles are made from 100% recycled glass, most of which is post-consumer content. They come in 2" x 2", 2" x 4", 4" x 4", 5" x 5", 5" x 10", 4" hex sizes, a range of circle shapes, 3.5" x 7" subways, as well as mosaic pieces. Color varies with the recycled glass materials used. Bedrock also makes architectural accents and non-architectural accessories from recycled glass. Three of the 28 colors offered are made exclusively from 100% post-industrial waste. For the others, the manufacturer has certified the following recycled-content levels (by weight): total recovered material 100% typical, 100% guaranteed; post-consumer material 50% typical, 50% guaranteed. The manufacturer has certified the following recycled-content levels (by weight): total recovered material 100% typical, 100% guaranteed; post-consumer material 50% typical, 50% guaranteed.

Oceanside Glasstile

Oceanside Glasstile Co.
2293 Cosmos Ct.
Carlsbad, CA 92011

Toll-free: 877-648-8222
Phone: 760-929-4000
www.glasstile.com

Oceanside produces four styles of tile handcast from 85% post-consumer recycled glass. They are semi-transparent, have an iridescent surface, and are available in a wide range of colors. Tessera is available in 29 colors and 4 sizes. Casa California includes larger-format tiles with a full line of decoratives. Minerali is a specialty tile with wide color variation and a textured surface. Haiku features opal glass with Asian motifs.

Recycled-Glass Tiles

Mellon Glass
1554 Port Mellon Hwy.
Gibsons, BC V0N1V6 Canada

Phone: 604-886-0202
www.mellonglass.com

Mellon Glass (formerly Hot Glass) hand-makes sand-cast, 2" x 2" tiles from 100% post-consumer recycled wine bottles. Colors include green, three shades of blue, clear, and several others. New recycled products for 2007 include 4-foot wide freeblown chandeliers with energy-saving lights.

Recycled-Glass Tiles

Sandhill Industries
6898 S. Supply Rd., Ste. 100
Boise, ID 83716

Phone: 208-345-6508
www.sandhillind.com

Sandhill Industries manufactures wall and floor tile from 100% post-industrial plate glass. The company's manufacturing process can produce both glossy and matte finishes, and results in no wastewater or air emissions. Tiles come in a standard variety of square, bar, and triangle sizes, as well as rail pieces and film-mounted mosaic patterns. A wide assortment of colors, shapes, and textures can be produced by special order. The manufacturer has certified the following recycled-content levels (by weight): total recovered material 100% typical, 100% guaranteed; post-consumer material 0% typical, 0% guaranteed.

UltraGlas

UltraGlas, Inc.
9200 Gazette Ave.
Chatsworth, CA 91311

Toll-free: 800-777-2332
Phone: 818-772-7744
www.ultraglas.com

UltraGlas® is sculpted/embossed, molded architectural glass with 15-30% recycled-glass (cullet) content. A variety of decorative textures, designs, and patterns are available with varying levels of translucency. If so specified, UltraGlas can be made from 100% recycled glass, subject to its availability.

Resilient Sheet Flooring

Natural linoleum is a durable, low-maintenance flooring made from linseed oil, pine rosin, sawdust, cork dust, limestone, natural pigments, and a jute backing—all minimally processed and commonly available materials. Linoleum does not contain significant petroleum-based products or chlorinated chemicals, as does vinyl (PVC) flooring—which is often mistakenly referred to as "linoleum." The ongoing oxidation of linoleic acid in the flooring leads to offgassing of volatile organic compounds (VOCs) that taper off over time, but some argue that linoleum's VOCs, as compared to petroleum-derived VOCs, are a lesser health threat. Recycled-tire rubber provides a highly durable, resilient, slip-resistant, anti-fatigue surface suitable for a variety of flooring requirements. Rubber granules from ground tires may be vulcanized (reformed under high heat using a sulfur additive), or agglomerated with a synthetic binding matrix, such as polyurethane. The rubber and its binders or additives, however, may be significant sources of indoor air pollutants, including VOCs and heavy metals; actual emissions vary widely from product to product. Thus, rubber flooring isn't recommended for most indoor spaces unless there is evidence of low emissions. Indoor/ outdoor spaces, such as entrances and skating rinks, or commercial/industrial areas with high ventilation rates, are potentially excellent applications for these recycled-content products.

DLW Linoleum

Armstrong World Industries, Inc.
2500 Columbia Ave. (17603)
P.O. Box 3001
Lancaster, PA 17604

Toll-free: 877-276-7876
Phone: 717-397-0611
www.armstrong.com

DLW linoleum is made in Germany and comes in a wide variety of colors and styles in both sheet and tile. Tile is available by special order only. Marmorette is available in 2, 2.5 and 3.2 mm thicknesses. Colorette and Uni Walton are available in 2.5 and 3.2 mm thicknesses, and Linorette is 2.5 mm thick. Linodur is a heavy-duty 4 mm product. In 1998, Armstrong World Industries, the largest manufacturer of vinyl flooring (and out of the linoleum industry since the 1970s) purchased DLW, reentering this product field.

Johnsonite Linoleum xf

Johnsonite
16910 Munn Rd.
Chagrin Falls, OH 44023

Toll-free: 800-899-8916
Phone: 440-543-8916
www.johnsonite.com

Johnsonite Linoleum xf is made from wood and cork flour, limestone and linseed oil and comes in a variety of colors. It is comprised of a urethane polymer-based surface treatment with particle reinforcement, solid linoleum core and a jute backing. Johnsonite's Linoleum xf is FloorScore certified, which means it has been independently certified by SCS to comply with the VOC emissions criteria of the California Section 01350 program. Johnsonite claims that their linoleum is made from at least 75% rapidly renewable materials and requires 30% less maintenance than similar products.

Marmoleum and Artoleum

Forbo Linoleum, Inc.
2 Maplewood Dr., Humboldt Industrial Park
P.O. Box 667
Hazleton, PA 18201

Toll-free: 800-842-7839
Phone: 570-459-0771
www.forboflooringNA.com

Forbo, the largest producer of linoleum in the world, operates a sophisticated production facility that helps it meet criteria for the Netherlands Environmental Quality Mark and the Nordic Swan Label. The product also received the Sequoia Award from the U.S. Association of Woodworking and Furnishing Suppliers (AWFS) in recognition of the company's commitment to environmental innovation. A large range of colors and styles is available, including custom-designed borders. Marmoleum® and Artoleum® are available in sheet form. Marmoleum Dual is also available as a 20" x 20" or 13" x 13" tile mounted on a polyester backing to improve dimensional stability. The optional, water-based Topshield finish provides a significant reduction of initial maintenance and chemicals, lowers ongoing cleaning costs, and improves long-term appearance.

Nova Linoleum

Nova Distinctive Floors
1710 E. Sepulveda Blvd.
Carson, CA 90745

Toll-free: 866-576-2458
www.novafloorings.com

Nova Linoleum™comes in 7/16" x 12" x 36" planks or 7/16" x 12" x 12" tiles, and is available in 9 colors. The planks and tiles consist of 3 layers: a 5/64" linoleum wear layer; a high-density fiberboard core; and a 5/64" cork composition layer. This floating floor system snaps together with a glueless "Klick" system. Nova Linoleum is manufactured in Switzerland and includes a 20-year residential warranty; 10-year commercial.

Prontolino

Habitus
166 E. 108th St.
New York, NY 10029

Phone: 212-426-5500
www.habitusnyc.com

Prontolino is a linoleum-cork hybrid flooring product. It comes in 3/8" x 12" x 36" tongue-and-groove planks of natural linoleum laminated onto a thick cork backing. The linoleum surface is available in 9 colors.

Resilient Tile Flooring

Natural linoleum is a durable, low-maintenance flooring made from linseed oil, pine rosin, sawdust, cork dust, limestone, natural pigments, and a jute backing—all minimally processed and commonly available materials. Linoleum does not contain significant petroleum-based products or chlorinated chemicals, as does vinyl (PVC) flooring—which is often mistakenly referred to as "linoleum." The ongoing oxidation of linoleic acid in the flooring leads to offgassing of volatile organic compounds (VOCs) that taper off over time, but some argue that linoleum's VOCs, as compared to petroleum-derived VOCs, are a lesser health threat. Recycled-tire rubber provides a highly durable, resilient, slip-resistant, anti-fatigue surface suitable for a variety of flooring requirements. Rubber granules from ground tires may be vulcanized (reformed under high heat using a sulfur additive), or agglomerated with a synthetic binding matrix, such as polyurethane. The rubber and its binders or additives, however, may be significant sources of indoor air pollutants, including VOCs and heavy metals; actual emissions vary widely from product to product. Thus, rubber flooring isn't recommended for most indoor spaces unless there is evidence of low emissions. Indoor/outdoor spaces, such as entrances and skating rinks, or commercial/industrial areas with high ventilation rates, are potentially excellent applications for these recycled-content products.

CushionWalk Pavers

Dinoflex Manufacturing, Ltd.
5590 - 46th Ave. SE
P.O. Box 3309
Salmon Arm, BC V1E 4S1 Canada

Toll-free: 877-713-1899
Phone: 252-832-7780
www.dinoflex.com

Cushion Walk® Pavers are made from 91% recycled-tire rubber and are designed primarily for covering patios, rooftop decks, and walkways. Paving tiles are available in terra-cotta red, forest green, stone beige, teak brown, and midnight black.

SuperFlexx Paver Tiles, Sports Floor, and SureStep

U.S. Rubber Recycling, Inc.
2225 Via Cerro, Unit B
Riverside, CA 92509

Toll-free: 888-473-8453
Phone: 951-342-0177
www.usrubber.com

SuperFlexx Paver Tiles and Sports Floor are 24" x 24" tiles made from high-density, urethane-bonded primary crumb rubber buffings. The Paver Tiles are available in red, green, or black, and are suitable for indoor/outdoor usage, especially in wet areas. Sports Floor is black tiles decorated with EPDM granules of red, green, blue, or off-white (consisting of 15% of the material's content). SureStep Traffic Tire Tile is made from recycled truck and bus tire linings; this durable flooring is available in 12" x 12" and 12" wide x 25' long rolls. As with other flooring products made from recycled automobile tires, installation is only recommended in semi-enclosed spaces, well-ventilated indoor spaces, or outdoors.

Sheet Carpet

Carpeting is almost ubiquitous in our homes, schools, and office buildings. Almost two billion square yards of carpeting are sold each year, nearly all of it made from petrochemicals. Carpet is a good absorber of sound and impact, yielding a surface associated with comfort. Its absorbent nature, however, also makes it a good medium for holding moisture and harboring dirt, mold, and dust mites. This, along with potential offgassing from the carpet and its adhesive, has led to indoor air quality concerns. Carpet companies are each taking different approaches to improving the environmental profile of their products.

Bio-Floor Collection

Earth Weave Carpet Mills, Inc.
P.O. Box 6120
Dalton, GA 30722

Phone: 706-278-8200
www.earthweave.com

Earth Weave Carpet Mills produces wall-to-wall carpeting and area rugs from 100% biodegradable, all natural materials such as wool, hemp, jute, and natural rubber. Their Bio-Floor line of wool carpeting is nonwoven and uses a 100% biodegradable adhesive to bond the wool to a hemp-cotton primary backing and then a secondary backing of jute fibers. No chemical treatments are used, and color variation is achieved through the selection of naturally pigmented wool.

Natural Design Collection and Natural Textures Collection

Design Materials, Inc.
241 S. 55th St.
Kansas City, KS 66106

Toll-free: 800-654-6451
Phone: 913-342-9796
www.dmikc.com

These carpet collections from Design Materials are made exclusively from natural fibers. Products in the Natural Design Collection are manufactured from sisal, coir, and reed, while those in the Natural Textures Collection are made from sisal, wool, and jute. These carpets come in 13'2"-wide broadloom rolls in a variety of colors, patterns, and weaves.

Natural Fiber Floor Coverings

Sisal Rugs Direct
P.O. Box 313
Excelsior, MN 55331

Toll-free: 888-613-1335
Phone: 952-448-9602
www.sisalrugs.com

Sisal Rugs Direct markets broadloom and area rugs of sisal, sisal/wool blend, seagrass, and mountain grass imported from Brazil, China, and Africa with natural latex-rubber backings.

Nature's Carpet

Colin Campbell & Sons, Ltd.
494 Railway St.
Vancouver, BC V6A 1B1 Canada

Toll-free: 800-667-5001
Phone: 604-734-2758
www.naturescarpet.com

Nature's Carpet, made from 100% New Zealand raw wool, is completely free of chemical residues from all stages of the process—from the washing and spinning of the wool through manufacture of the finished carpet. The line currently consists of six loop-pile carpets in natural wool hues, two loop-pile ribbed products, and one cut-pile carpet with vegetable-dyed colors. The backing is made from jute and strengthened with unbleached cotton. Nature's Carpet uses no moth treatment, uses natural latex rather than synthetic, and has negligible VOC ratings. The carpet has been used extensively for people with chemical sensitivities.

Recycled-Content Residential Carpet

Mohawk Industries, Inc.
160 S. Industrial Blvd.
Calhoun, GA 30701

Phone: 800-622-6227
www.mohawkind.com

Residential polyester Mohawk carpets have 100% recycled-content face fiber from recovery of soda-bottle PET.

Wool and Cotton Carpet

Carousel Carpets
3315 Superior Ln.
Bowie, MD 20715

Phone: 301-262-2650
www.carouselcarpets.com

Carousel produces carpets made from wool, linen, and cotton fibers, with a poly backing. They also make custom carpets and rugs.

Subflooring

Subflooring creates the structural plane of the floor, over which the finish flooring layers are applied. Phenol-formaldehyde (PF) binders are used in plywood, while OSB can be made with PF or the non-formaldehyde-emitting methyl diisocyanate (MDI), a polyurethane binder. Paradoxically, exterior-rated products using PF binders are less of an offgassing concern than interior-grade panels made with urea-formaldehyde. Oriented-strand board (OSB) can be an efficient use of forest resources because it can be produced from small-diameter or low-grade tree species. Wood products can carry the "FSC Mixed" label under a percentage-based standard based on the average certified and non-certified throughput of the facility at which they are made. Products listed here have one or more of the following attributes: FSC-certification; nonformaldehyde binders; nontoxic (to humans) borate insect treatments; or other environmental advantages over conventional OSB and plywood.

4-Way Floor Deck, N.C.F.R., and Firestall Roof Deck

Homasote Company
932 Lower Ferry Rd.
P.O. Box 7240
West Trenton, NJ 08628

Toll-free: 800-257-9491
Phone: 609-883-3300
www.homasote.com

4-Way® Floor Deck, N.C.F.R.®, and Firestall® Roof Deck are structural high-density fiberboard panels made from 100% recycled newspaper, with paraffin binders and additives for pest and fire resistance. Panels are available in a variety of thicknesses. N.C.F.R. is a Class A fire-rated panel for interior and exterior use. 4-Way Floor Deck is a tongue-and-groove multi-ply subfloor that is structural, sound deadening, and moderately insulative (R-2.5/in.). Firestall Roof Deck is a tongue-and-groove Class A fire-rated panel manufactured with 1 to 4 plies of Homasote® and a face ply of N.C.F.R..

AdvanTech OSB

J. M. Huber Wood Products
One Resource Sq.
10925 David Taylor Dr., Ste. 300
Charlotte, NC 28262

Toll-free: 800-933-9220
Phone: 704-547-0671
www.huberwood.com

AdvanTech™ OSB from Huber is an OSB made primarily with formaldehyde-free MDI resin (a small quantity of phenolic resin is added to improve certain properties). Due to its greater moisture resistance than conventional OSB, AdvanTech carries a 50-year warranty. This product has been certified by Greenguard for low emissions.

Certified Pine Plywood

ROMEX World Trade Company, LLC - sales agent for ROM
P.O. Box 1110
Alexandria, LA 71309

Toll-free: 800-299-5174
Phone: 318-445-1973
www.royomartin.com

Roy O. Martin Lumber Management, LLC (ROM) has received Smart-Wood certification for its 585,000 acres of forestland and four mills according to standards of the Forest Stewardship Council (FSC). This is the first FSC certification of any forest management operation in Louisiana. ROM's FSC-certified pine plywood, formerly under the name of SmartCore®, is produced by Martco Plywood in Chopin, Louisiana. Sanded plywood is available in AA, AB, AC, BC, and A-Flat grades in 4' x 8' panels standard thicknesses of 1/4", 11/32", 15/32", 19/32" and 23/32". As is true for the company's OSB plant, some fiber used in the Chopin mill comes from non-company-owned land, but 100% FSC-certified product can be provided. ROM's pine plywood is also available sided with a foil radiant barrier, or printed with the company's new "GRID" panel marking system.

F.D. Sterritt Certified-Wood Building Products

F.D. Sterritt Lumber Co.
110 Arlington St.
Watertown, MA 02472

Toll-free: 877-635-3362
Phone: 617-923-1480
www.sterrittlumber.com

F.D. Sterritt Lumber sells FSC-certified lumber, plywood, decking, hardwoods, and hardwood flooring. They have a variety of certified species in stock. Additional green building materials available, including low-VOC adhesives, caulking, sealants, and recycled drywall. F.D. Sterritt offers green building product consultations.

FSC-Certified Lumber, Plywood, and Products

Potlatch Corporation
601 W. First Ave., Ste. 1600
Spokane, WA 99201

Phone: 509-835-1500
www.potlatchcorp.com

In 2004, Potlatch Corporation became the first publicly traded U.S. timber company to certify timberland according to Forest Stewardship Council (FSC) standards. Potlatch is producing chain-of-custody FSC-certified Hem-Fir and Douglas Fir/Larch framing lumber, inland red cedar decking and siding, and Douglas fir and white fir plywood from three chain-of-custody-certified mills in Idaho. Potlatch has recently added over 400,000 acres of FSC certified timber in Arkansas which supports a chain-of-custody sawmill in Warren, Arkansas. Warren produces dimensional Southern Yellow Pine framing lumber. These products are stamped with the FSC logo when required for specific sales.

Green Board

GreenImports, LLC
P.O. Box 60
North Stonington, CT 06359

Phone: 857-526-6091
www.wwieinc.com

Green Board is made from recycled Tetra Pak beverage cartons and is composed of 75% paper, 20% polyethylene, and 5% aluminum. It is water resistant, termite and borer resistant, and provides insulative and sound proofing qualities. Green Board has a textured surface, and can be formed into curves and other shapes. Marketed as a direct replacement for plywood in any application (including "roofing, boats, cabinets, shipping crates, sheathing, underlayment, furniture"), it can be sawn, molded, cut, glued, screwed, or nailed. Available from the importer by the container-load in 4x8 sheets in 10, 12, or 18 mm thicknesses. Each container holds 676, 250, or 354 sheets of the respective board thicknesses.

Microstrand

Environ Biocomposites, LLC
221 Mohr Dr.
Mankato, MN 56001

Toll-free: 800-324-8187
Phone: 507-388-3434
www.environbiocomposites.com

Microstrand is an industrial-grade replacement for particleboard or plywood, made from rapidly renewable wheat straw and formaldehyde-free polyurethane (MDI) resin. Though 10%–15% lighter than traditional particleboard, the panels offer better strength and impact resistance. The product accepts paints, stains, and lamination, and can be custom-engineered to meet specific requirements, including increased fire-resistance.

Tuff-Strand Certified OSB

ROMEX World Trade Company, LLC - sales agent for ROM
P.O. Box 1110
Alexandria, LA 71309

Toll-free: 800-299-5174
Phone: 318-445-1973
www.royomartin.com

Roy O. Martin Lumber Management, LLC (ROM) has gained FSC-certification of its 585,000 acres of forestland and four mills. In addition to this being the first FSC certification of any forest management operation in Louisiana, ROM has made available the first-ever FSC-certified oriented strand board (OSB). Tuff-Strand® is a fairly conventional OSB produced by the Martco Partnership plant in LeMoyen, Louisiana. The 4' x 8' panels are available in three standard thicknesses: 7/16", 15/32", and 19/32". The mill is fed by up to 70% company-owned timber, and while OSB is typically certified using FSC's partial-content rules, the company can provide 100% FSC-certified product. Tuff-Strand's binder is 100% phenol formaldehyde. FSC-certified Tuff-Strand is also now available sided with a foil radiant barrier, or printed with the company's new "GRID" panel marking system.

Suppressed Wood Flooring

Suppressed wood comes from trees growing in the understory of mature forests—usually where forestry practices have prevented fires, so natural thinning and succession hasn't occurred. It is now generally recognized that overly dense forests increase fire hazard and leave trees vulnerable to insect infestation and disease. These small, slow-growing trees were once regarded as waste, suitable only for fuel and firewood. Attributes of these trees include close grain, fine texture, and small tight knots. This can provide a raw material for joinery, flooring, and panels.

Alpine Grade Douglas Fir Flooring

Green Mountain Woodworks
P.O. Box 1433
Phoenix, OR 97535

Toll-free: 866-535-5880
www.greenmountainwoodworks.com

Green Mountain Woodworks produces this Douglas fir flooring from trees thinned out of overly dense forests in southwest Oregon. Green Mountain Woodworks is associated with the Healthy Forests Healthy Communities Partnership, which works with communities in National Forests to develop locally owned small businesses that make products from the wood recovered during forest restoration. (Timber from National Forests is not eligible for FSC certification.)

Terrazzo

Some terrazzo products include recycled content aggregate material. Be aware that different binders are used in terrazzo products, not all of which are environmentally attractive. The products listed here contain recycled aggregate.

Bio-Glass

Coverings Etc, Inc.
7610 N.E. 4th Ct.
Miami, FL 33138

Phone: 305-757-6000
www.coveringsetc.com

Bio-Glass™ solid surfacing for countertops, walls, floors, and other applications is made from 100% recycled glass, heated and agglomerated under pressure. There are no binders, colorants, fillers, or other admixtures. Depending on color, the product is either pre- or post-consumer, or a blend. The translucent, nonporous material is available as 110-inch by 49-inch slabs, about 3/4 inches thick with a lightly textured, slip-resistant surface; smooth-surfaced slabs are also available, approximately 4 inches thick. The product is currently available in white and light green, with blue, brown, and dark green to follow.

IceStone

IceStone, LLC
63 Flushing Ave., Unit 283, Bldg. 12
Brooklyn Navy Yard
Brooklyn, NY 11025

Phone: 718-624-4900
www.icestone.biz

IceStone is a terrazzo-like material made from a minimum of 75% recycled glass, 17-18% type-3 white portland cement, and small quantities of proprietary ingredients. Although IceStone would not divulge the process they use to avoid the alkali-silica reaction (ASR) that typically affects concrete with glass aggregate, they claim it does not involve the use of epoxy, which is sometimes used for this purpose. IceStone is produced in standard 52.5 x 8' slabs that can be made into large-format tiles, 1-1/4" thick. A 2"-thick product is also available. The slabs are shipped to local stone-finishing companies for cutting, routing, sandblasting, and polishing. IceStone is available in 28 standard colors, based largely on the color of the recycled glass used in the product. The cement matrix can also be pigmented, providing a wide range of color options.

Recycled Glass Aggregates and Powders

American Specialty Glass, Inc.
829 N. 400 W
North Salt Lake, UT 84054

Phone: 801-294-4222
www.americanspecialtyglass.com

American Specialty Glass, Inc., provides recycled-glass aggregate in a range of sizes and colors for terrazzo floors, pavers, and countertops. Sources include post-consumer bottle glass and post-industrial float glass cullet. Glass sand, a substitute for silica sand, is also available, as are powder fines that can be used as concrete coloring agents, providing a different effect than pigments. Polished or unpolished landscaping nuggets in a range of sizes are offered as well.

Recycled Glass for Terrazzo

Heritage Glass, Inc.
130 W. 700 S. Bldg. E
Smithfield, UT 84335

Phone: 435-563-5585
www.heritageglass.net

Heritage Glass offers recycled-glass aggregate in a range of colors and sizes for terrazzo flooring and countertop applications. Sources include post-industrial float glass cullet and post-consumer bottle glass. Heritage also provides 1/2" to 2" recycled-glass aggregate with dulled edges for landscaping applications.

Recycled-Glass "Terrazzo" Tile

Wausau Tile, Inc.
9001 Business Hwy. 51
Rothschild, WI 54474

Toll-free: 800-388-8728
Phone: 715-359-3121
www.wausautile.com

Wausau Tile, one of the largest terrazzo manufacturers in the world, produces a line of terrazzo-like tile from recycled glass (approximately 33% recycled glass by weight) using technology developed by the Civil Engineering Dept. of Columbia University. According to the company, the patented chemical additives result in a much stronger and more water-resistant product than traditional terrazzo.

Thin-Set Tiling

Like tile adhesives, thin-set mortars can have high VOC levels. VOCs contribute to poor indoor air quality (IAQ), and are a major component of smog. Products listed here have low or zero-VOC levels.

D-5 Premium and D-40 Duraflex Thin-Set Mortar

Bostik, Inc.
211 Boston St.
Middleton, MA 01949

Toll-free: 800-366-7837
Phone: 978-777-0100
www.bostik-us.com

D-5 Premium Thin-Set Mortar (formerly D-505+) and D-40™ Duraflex™ are zero-VOC, thin-set tile mortars.

Tiling Adhesive

Adhesives can be a major source of indoor air quality problems, often more so than the products they adhere. Water-based adhesives have lower VOC emissions than solvent-based products. Tile adhesives, like many other adhesives, can have high VOC levels. VOCs contribute to poor indoor air quality (IAQ), and are a major component of smog. Products listed here have low VOC levels.

EcoTimber HealthyBond Adhesive

EcoTimber
1611 4th St.
San Rafael, CA 94901

Toll-free: 888-801-0855
Phone: 415-258-8454
www.ecotimber.com

HealthyBond Adhesive from EcoTimber is used for installation of wood and bamboo flooring. The product's resin-based formula adheres to hardwood, bamboo, cork, plywood, concrete, vinyl, particleboard, and terrazzo, and EcoTimber claims it is strong enough for use with plank flooring. HealthyBond Adhesive is isocynate-free, urethane-free, solvent-free, has low VOC content (7 g/l), and is Greenguard Indoor Air Quality Certified as a low-emitting product.

Envirotec Floor Covering Adhesives

W. F. Taylor Company
11545 Pacific Ave.
Fontana, CA 92337

Toll-free: 800-397-4583
Phone: 909-360-6677
www.wftaylor.com

Envirotec is W. F. Taylor Company's line of nontoxic, solvent-free, low-VOC adhesive products. These products include multipurpose flooring adhesives, carpet adhesives, and cove base adhesives.

Safecoat 3 in 1 Adhesive

American Formulating & Manufacturing (AFM)
3251 Third Ave.
San Diego, CA 92103

Toll-free: 800-239-0321
Phone: 619-239-0321
www.afmsafecoat.com

Safecoat 3 in 1 Adhesive is designed for hard composition—ceramic, vinyl, parquet, formica, and slate—floor and counter tiles. It is a water-based alternative to solvent-based adhesives and has significantly lower VOC content of 44 g/l (82 g/l less water).

Interior Finish & Trim

Particleboard and medium-density fiberboard (MDF) are almost always made with a urea formaldehyde (UF) binder. This is one of the largest in-home sources of formaldehyde gas—a known human carcinogen. These products can offgas for 5 years or more into the living space. UF-based particleboard and MDF are typically used for cabinet boxes, substrates for countertops, shelving, and stair treads. If possible, these materials should be avoided. Any UF-based materials used in a building should be sealed with a low-toxic, low-permeability coating.

A few formaldehyde-free particleboard and MDF products are available, including some made with straw instead of wood fiber. These are made with a urethane-type (MDI) resin. Be aware that MDI is highly toxic before it cures, so its use increases the health risk to factory workers if a manufacturer doesn't have good safety standards. Once cured, MDI-based wood panel products are very stable, without measurable offgassing.

Conventional drywall is quite attractive from an environmental standpoint. It is typically made from 100% recycled paper backing and natural gypsum, which is plentiful and can be low-impact to extract. More and more drywall today contains pre-consumer waste in the form of synthetic gypsum created by sulfur removal systems in the smokestacks of coal-burning power plants. This material is sometimes referred to as flue-gas desulfurization gypsum.

The joint compound used to finish drywall contains synthetic additives that may affect some chemically sensitive people; specialty alternatives are available. Dry-mix, setting-type joint compounds, which are sold in powder form and mixed on site, contain fewer additives.

Cabinets made from nontoxic materials and finishes or solid wood are available. People with chemical sensitivities often find enameled-metal cabinets to be the least problematic.

Clear wood trim materials are increasingly difficult to find (or more expensive), and they place a high demand on virgin timber. On the other hand, this is an application where high-quality wood can be fully seen and celebrated. Finger-jointed trim for painted applications, and veneer-covered, finger-jointed trim for stain applications, are good substitutes.

Whenever possible, woods used in interior finish and trim should be from certified well-managed forests; third-party certification to standards developed by the Forest Stewardship Council (FSC) provides a way that users can verify environmental claims. Currently there are two U.S.-based organizations that certify forest operations (and wood products): Scientific Certifications Systems, and the Rainforest Alliance (SmartWood).

Tropical hardwoods should be avoided unless they come from FSC-certified sustainable sources, as their harvest can cause irreparable damage to tropical rainforests. Only a few of the many species of tropical woods have much commercial value—often large areas of forest are damaged in pursuit of a few trees. The roads left behind by loggers provide access for slash-and-burn farmers and other settlers, so penetration by logging operations is frequently the beginning of a chain of activities that totally destroy the forest. Fortunately, well-managed tropical forests are increasingly becoming certified.

Acoustical Ceilings

Acoustical ceiling materials vary depending on the specific performance criteria desired (e.g., durability, light reflectance, sound absorption, washability, design flexibility, fire resistance). Most common in commercial suspended ceilings are wet-pressed mineral-fiber tiles and panels, typically made from a mixture of waste paper, mineral fiber (which may include slag, a waste product from steel-making), cornstarch, and various other mineral-based components. A number of these products have high recycled content; some, however, may contain low levels of formaldehyde. Fiberglass ceiling panels are also available with recycled content, though the percentage is typically lower than with mineral-fiber products. Most fiberglass ceiling panel products use a phenol-formaldehyde binder. Though far more common in Europe, wood-fiber-based ceiling panel products are also available in the U.S.—these are free of mineral fibers and formaldehyde but are typically more expensive, and they contain no recycled content. Metal ceiling products may or may not include a backing of fiberglass. Products for use in food service facilities, hospitals, or other areas with high sanitary standards have a PVC covering or scrubbable paint finish. Poorly controlled burning of PVC (polyvinyl chloride) may release dioxins and furans. Residential acoustical ceiling panels are not available in as many materials or styles as commercial products.

Acoustical Ceiling Panels and Tiles

USG Corporation
555 West Adams St.
Chicago, IL 60661

Toll-free: 800-874-4968
Phone: 312-436-4000
www.usg.com

USG Interiors manufacturers a range of ceiling products, including acoustical panels that have a high recycled content (up to 78%). Many are made from slag wool (a post-industrial by-product of the steel industry), cornstarch, waste newspaper, and clay. These panels have low VOC emissions, meeting CHPS (Collaborative for High Performance Schools) guidelines. Eight product lines are classified as formaldehyde-free and exceed standards set by the California Office of Environmental Health Hazard Assessment. Other product lines are classified as low-formaldehyde. USG also has a mineral wool ceiling panel recycling program in which old panels are turned into new construction products.

Mineral Fiber and Glass Based Drop-in Ceiling Tile

Armstrong World Industries, Inc.
2500 Columbia Ave. (17603)
P.O. Box 3001
Lancaster, PA 17604

Toll-free: 877-276-7876
Phone: 717-397-0611
www.armstrong.com

Armstrong Ceiling Systems offer a complete line of acoustical ceiling products that include both post-consumer and post-industrial waste, as well as abundant natural materials, including recycled newspaper, mineral wool, perlite, and cornstarch. Armstrong Ceilings offers products that contain up to 82% recycled content. Through its ceiling recycling program, old ceiling tiles are recycled and made into new ones.

Acoustical Wall Finishes

Noise, both from indoor and outside sources, adds to stress and discomfort. A wide range of products are available to help absorb noise and prevent it from spreading.

These wall finishes provide acoustic dampening and may be panelized or trowel-applied products. Products listed here contain recycled content and non-urea formaldehyde binders.

BASWAphon Acoustic Insulation

Sound Solutions Services, LLC
3900 Ben Hur Ave., Ste. 10
Willoughby, OH 44094

Phone: 440-951-6022
www.baswaphonusa.com/

The BASWAphon seamless finish system has acoustic dampening properties and the appearance of plaster or painted drywall. The system, which may be applied to walls or ceilings - including curves, vaults, and domes - is comprised of 5 components: a 32 mm-thick mineral wool supporting panel (74% post-consumer recycled glass and phenol-formaldehyde binder), a factory-applied precoating, and a trowel-applied gap filler containing glass-foam spheres (75% post-consumer recycled glass and vinyl acetate-copolymer binders), and trowel-applied base and top coats (95% recycled marble dust with a vinyl-acetate copolymer binders and acrylic-copolymer binder, respectively). The supporting panels are glued to the substrate with USG Durabond® adhesive. BASWAphon comes in thicknesses of 40 mm and 68 mm and can be colored with integral pigments. The materials for the system are manufactured in Switzerland.

Agfiber Millwork

With similar qualities to wood particleboard and Medium Density Fiberboard (MDF), straw particleboard is made from the stems left over after harvesting the cereal grains, such as wheat, oats, and rice. This is a substitute for paint-grade moldings, offering consistent quality and economy, though it is somewhat rougher and more porous than MDF and does not mill as smoothly. Straw particleboard is made using a non-formaldehyde PMDI binder.

Wheatboard Millwork

CitiLog
P.O. Box 685
Pittstown, NJ 08867

Toll-free: 877-248-9564
Phone: 908-735-8871
www.citilogs.com

CitiLog™ offers custom millwork from formaldehyde-free wheatboard. The company also offers wheatboard cabinetry and doors.

Ceramic Tile

Tile is an inherently low-toxic, waterproof, durable finish material for flooring, walls, and other applications. While tile is somewhat energy-intensive to manufacture, the materials involved are readily available and mined with fairly low impact. Products listed here contain post-consumer or post-industrial recycled content.

Debris Series Ceramic Tile and Pavers

Fireclay Tile
495 W. Julian St.
San Jose, CA 95110

Phone: 408-275-1182
www.fireclaytile.com

Fireclay Tile manufactures the Debris Series of handmade tile using post-industrial and post-consumer recycled material. Fireclay's terra cotta body is made from 25% recycled granite dust, 19% broken window panes, and 8.5 % recycled brown and green glass bottles. The company's white clay body contains 47.5% recycled broken window panes and clear glass bottles. The terra cotta tile can be unglazed or glazed. The tiles made with the white clay body have transparent glazes. The glazes do not contain lead.

EcoCycle

Crossville Inc.
P.O. Box 1168
Crossville, TN 38557

Phone: 931-484-2110
www.crossvilleinc.com

Crossville Inc. offers a line of ceramic tile called EcoCycle made from 40% in-house manufacturing scrap generated during the manufacturing process of standard-color porcelain tiles. This manufacturing scrap, which would otherwise be landfilled, is not recycled content as defined by the EPA. The scrap also includes a small percentage of dust from the air and water filtration systems. The tiles measure 12" x 12" with matching 4" x 12" bullnose trim. Available in seven colors, EcoCycle is recommended for interior floors and walls as well as exterior walls.

Eco-Tile

Quarry Tile Company
6328 E. Utah Ave.
Spokane, WA 99212

Phone: 509-536-2812
www.quarrytile.com

Eco-Tile™ is a commercial-grade, glazed ceramic tile made with approximately 70% recycled solid waste as defined by the EPA's CPG program. This waste content is made up of post-consumer recycled glass (about 25%), post-industrial grinding paste from the computer industry, and post-industrial mining waste from the sand and gravel industry (post-industrial content about 45%). The company also utilizes reprocessed glaze waste from their other manufacturing operations. Glaze from overspray, body scrap, and process waste is recycled in a closed-loop, zero-discharge, water reclamation system. Eco-Tile may contain up to 10% by weight of this material. All the recycled content in Eco-Tile comes from within a 10- to 350-mile radius of the plant and replaces virgin materials from as far away as 2,300 miles. Currently produced in over 50 colors and 5 sizes, Eco-Tile must be special-ordered (minimum 300 ft^2).

Terra Classic and Terra Traffic

Terra Green Ceramics
1650 Progress Dr.
Richmond, IN 47374

Phone: 765-935-4760
www.terragreenceramics.com

Terra Green Ceramic Tiles are made with 55% post-industrial recycled glass. Terra Classic and Terra Traffic (slip-resistant) are each available in 17 colors, several sizes, and with a wide range of accessories.

Certified-Wood Stairs and Railings

FSC-certified wood products are third-party verified as originating from well-managed forests based on Forest Stewardship Council (FSC) standards. Some companies listed here may sell both certified and noncertified products or products certified according to other, less stringent environmental standards. To ensure the use of environmentally responsible wood products, be sure to specify your interest in FSC-certified wood when contacting these companies.

Certified Stair Parts

B.W. Creative Wood Industries Ltd.
23282 River Rd.
Maple Ridge, BC V2W 1B6 Canada

Toll-free: 800-667-8247
Phone: 604-467-5147
www.creativerailing.com

B.W. Creative Wood specializes in stair parts fabricated of FSC-certified white fir.

Certified Wood Products

Randall Custom Lumber, Ltd.
3530 S.E. Arcadia Rd.
Shelton, WA 98584

Phone: 360-426-8518

Randall Custom Lumber manufactures FSC-certified decking, flooring, hard and softwood lumber, and stair parts. Some of their certified species are ash, red cedar, red alder, Douglas fir, madrone, and maple.

Cork Wall Covering

Long used as a wall covering, cork is available in sheets or tiles of various thicknesses. It's tackable, self-healing, durable, sound absorbing, and naturally resistant to moisture, rot, mold, and fire. Obtained from the outer bark of the cork oak Quercus suber, cork can be harvested sustainably without killing the tree.

Natural Cork Wall Tile

Natural Cork, Inc.
1710 N. Leg Ct.
Augusta, GA 30909

Toll-free: 800-404-2675
Phone: 706-733-6120
www.naturalcork.com

Natural Cork Wall Tile is 1/8" thick, 12" high x 24" wide, features a peel-and-stick application, and comes prefinished with a wax coating in 6 patterns.

Tessuto in Sughero/Cork Fabric

Habitus
166 E. 108th St.
New York, NY 10029

Phone: 212-426-5500
www.habitusnyc.com

Cork Fabric wall covering or upholstery is made from a thin layer of cork laminated onto a 50% cotton, 50% polyester backing. It is available in a roll width of 57". Cork Fabric is available in a variety of styles. Custom production is an option.

Countertops

Countertops have particular performance demands because of their high use and exposure to water, especially at the seams of sink cutouts and backsplashes. A variety of suitable countertop products with environmental advantages are available. Ceramic tile or natural linoleum surfaces also offer green countertop options. Products listed here have a recycled content value (equal to post-consumer plus 1/2 pre-consumer) of at least 20% or are made of FSC-certified wood or rapidly renewable materials. Forest Stewardship Council (FSC) certification involves third-party evaluation and monitoring of sustainable forestry practices.

Avonite Surfaces Recycled Collection

Aristech Acrylics LLC
7350 Empire Dr.
Florence, KY 41042

Toll-free: 800-354-9858
Phone: 859-283-1501
www.avonitesurfaces.com

Avonite produces a recycled collection which is made from 40% SCS-certified post-industrial scrap (equal to a recycled content value of 20%), as well as virgin polyester and Aluminium Trihydrate (ATH), which acts as both filler and fire retardant. The recycled material is reclaimed solid surface material from their other product lines. The collection includes 6 patterns and is sold in ½" thick, 36" x 120" sheets. The Kaleidoscope and Cozumel are Class 3 fire rated, while the other four patterns are Class 1 fire rated.

Bio-Glass

Coverings Etc, Inc.
7610 N.E. 4th Ct.
Miami, FL 33138

Phone: 305-757-6000
www.coveringsetc.com

Bio-Glass™ solid surfacing for countertops, walls, floors, and other applications is made from 100% recycled glass, heated and agglomerated under pressure. There are no binders, colorants, fillers, or other admixtures. Depending on color, the product is either pre- or post-consumer, or a blend. The translucent, nonporous material is available as 110-inch by 49-inch slabs, about 3/4 inches thick with a lightly textured, slip-resistant surface; smooth-surfaced slabs are also available, approximately 4 inches thick. The product is currently available in white and light green, with blue, brown, and dark green to follow.

Endura Wood Products

Endura Wood Products, Ltd.
1303 S.E. 6th Ave.
Portland, OR 97214

Phone: 503-233-7090
www.endurawood.com

Endura offers FSC-certified hardwood and softwood flooring, lumber, and decking in a wide variety of exotic and domestic species. Endurawood butcher blocks and countertops are produced from certified woods such as rock maple. Endura also sells reclaimed wood products as well as straw particleboard and agrifiber composite sheet goods.

EQcountertops

VT Industries, Inc.
1000 Industrial Park
Box 490
Holstein, IA 51025

Toll-free: 800-827-1615
Phone: 712-368-4381
www.vtindustries.com

VT Industries manufactures EQcountertops with SkyBlend™ cores made from 100% pre-consumer recycled wood-fiber with a phenol-formaldehyde binder. The countertops use water based biodegradable zero-VOC adhesives, and Greenguard certified laminates.

Greenline

Forefront Designs
1075 Shelley St.
Springfield, OR 97477

Toll-free: 888-245-0075
Phone: 541-747-4884
www.forefrontdesigns.com

Greenline builds cabinets, casework, and countertops using wheatboard structural cores, FSC-certified veneers, high pressure plastic laminates, and various ISO 14001-certified materials. Casework is formaldehyde- and solvent-free and is suitable for laboratories, hospitals, schools, assisted living centers, and other commercial projects. Environmental interior design and consultation are available.

IceStone

IceStone, LLC
63 Flushing Ave., Unit 283, Bldg. 12
Brooklyn Navy Yard
Brooklyn, NY 11025

Phone: 718-624-4900
www.icestone.biz

IceStone is a terrazzo-like material made from a minimum of 75% recycled glass, 17-18% type-3 white portland cement, and small quantities of proprietary ingredients. Although IceStone would not divulge the process they use to avoid the alkali-silica reaction (ASR) that typically affects concrete with glass aggregate, they claim it does not involve the use of epoxy, which is sometimes used for this purpose. IceStone is produced in standard 52.5 x 8' slabs that can be made into large-format tiles, 1-1/4" thick. A 2"-thick product is also available. The slabs are shipped to local stone-finishing companies for cutting, routing, sandblasting, and polishing. IceStone is available in 28 standard colors, based largely on the color of the recycled glass used in the product. The cement matrix can also be pigmented, providing a wide range of color options.

PaperStone Certified

KlipTech Composites
2999 John Stevens Way
Hoquiam, WA 98550

Phone: 360-538-9815
www.paperstoneproducts.com

PaperStone Certified is made with 100% FSC-certified, post-consumer recycled paper. The proprietary water-based resin system uses non-petroleum phenols, including cashew nut shell liquid derivatives. The finished product works easily with a triple-chip, carbide-tipped saw blade and carbide-tipped router bits. It has no detectable free formaldehyde, is Class A fire-rated, heat-resistant to 350 degrees, and stain-resistant. PaperStone comes in 30" and 60" widths, lengths of 8', 10', & 12', with thicknesses ranging from 1/4" - 2". The product is available in a variety of colors. The regular PaperStone product line is made with 50% post-consumer recycled content, versus 100% for PaperStone Certified.

Reclaimed-Wood Building Products

General Woodcraft, Inc.
531 Broad St.
New London, CT 06320

Phone: 860-444-9663
www.generalwoodcraftinc.com

General Woodcraft provides wood flooring and other products milled from beams and timbers salvaged from barns and factories built a century ago—often from old-growth timber. Species (as available) include pine, chestnut, and oak.

Reclaimed-Wood Products

Centre Mills Antique Floors
P.O. Box 16
Aspers, PA 17304

Phone: 717-677-9698
www.centremillsantiquefloors.com

Centre Mills Antique Floors salvages, remills, and sells several species and types of wood products, many hand-hewn. Species include chestnut, oak, white pine, and fir. Centre Mills uses the old gristmill, built in 1841, in Centre Mills, Pennsylvania as their storage facility.

Reclaimed-Wood Products

Duluth Timber Co.
P.O. Box 16717
Duluth, MN 55805

Phone: 218-727-2145
www.duluthtimber.com

Duluth Timber reclaims and remills mainly Douglas fir and longleaf yellow pine, but also redwood and cypress. Demolition and salvage of warehouses and sheep-shearing sheds in Australia has yielded a supply of Australian hardwoods such as jarrah and Mountain ash. Duluth has mills in Minnesota and Washington.

Shetkastone

All Paper Recycling, Inc.
435 W Industrial St.
P.O. Box 38
Le Center, MN 56057

Phone: 507-357-4177
www.shetkastone.com

All Paper Recycling manufactures tables and countertops using a patented process and 100% pre- and post-consumer recycled paper. Shetkastone comes in four standard colors that use a water-based binder. Premium colors are also available and they use a 13% acrylic binder. All products made with Shetkastone that are damaged or at the end of their lifecycle can be recycled back into the manufacturing process, reducing waste. The material has a Class A fire rating without the addition of chemicals and a 400-pound screw test.

Squak Mountain Stone Composite Countertops

Tiger Mountain Innovations, Inc.
14221 N.E. 190th St., Ste. 150
Woodinville, WA 98072

Phone: 425-486-3417
www.tmi-online.com

Squak Mountain Stone™ is a precast, relatively lightweight (14 lbs/sf), paper and cement-based composite with the appearance of natural stone. It is made with post-consumer recycled paper (2.5% by weight), pre-consumer crushed glass and fly ash (49%), and has no steel reinforcement. The cement content is similar to cast concrete. This product is available in five standard colors and several standard sizes including 12" x 12", 30" x 48", and 18" x 72". Factory-sealed with a two-part, water-based sealer, Squak Mountain Stone is appropriate for countertops, tabletops, tiling, and other architectural and decorative applications. Non-pH-neutral cleaning products, cutting, and abrasion may leave marks and damage the sealer. Liquids such as coffee, wine, or oils left on this product for extended periods may cause staining. Hot objects may cause surface darkening, cause micro-cracking, and damage the sealer. Periodic sealer reapplication may be necessary.

Teragren Bamboo Flooring, Panels, and Veneer

Teragren LLC
12715 Miller Rd. NE, Ste. 301
Bainbridge Island, WA 98110

Toll-free: 800-929-6333
Phone: 206-842-9477
www.teragren.com

Teragren (formerly TimberGrass) manufactures solid strip bamboo flooring in tongue-and-groove or locking system, prefinished or site-finished. All flooring products are available in vertical or flat (horizontal) grains and natural or caramelized standard colors as well as stained cherry, walnut, charcoal and espresso colors. Coatings are water based and solvent free. The company uses the MOSO specie of bamboo which is harvested at maturity at 6 years. Teragren also manufactures coordinating stair parts, flooring accessories and vents, panels and veneer for cabinetry, furniture, interior paneling, countertops, and other interior applications as a direct replacement for wood sheet goods. (Note that while the adhesive used to manu-

facture the panels and veneer exceeds E1 standards, it is not food grade; if the surface is to be used for food preparation, a food grade sealer is recommended.)

Urban Hardwoods

Urban Hardwoods
4755 C. Colorado Ave. S
Seattle, WA 98134

Phone: 206-766-8199
www.urbanhardwoods.com

Urban Hardwoods salvages urban trees from within a 50-mile radius of the company and mills them into custom, made-to-order furniture, flooring, and other millwork. Urban Hardwoods continually designs products to make use of manufacturing "fall-down." Remaining waste material is given away or sold as firewood, or is used for heating their facility. The company ships 99% of its products blanket-wrapped; all blankets are reused. Products will be accepted back at the end of their useful life to be refurbished or recycled in the manufacture of new products. The company is SmartWood-certified under the "Rediscovered Wood" category.

Vetrazzo

Vetrazzo
Ford Point, Ste. 1400
1414 Harbour Way S
Richmond, CA 94804

Phone: 510-234-5550
www.vetrazzo.com

Vetrazzo countertops have mixed colors of recycled-glass chips embedded in a masonry binder for a terrazzo-like look. Glass sources include decommissioned traffic lights, windshields, used bottles, and plate glass windows, offering an alternative to virgin materials. To prevent their counter tops from being landfilled, Vetrazzo has implemented a plan to take back and remanufacture used counter tops into new products if they are in good enough condition. Vetrazzo is available in a wide variety of colors and in panels that are 9' x 5' x 1.25". The manufacturer has certified the following recycled-content levels (by weight): total recovered material 90% typical, 80% guaranteed; post-consumer material 90% typical, 80% guaranteed.

Fiberboard and Particleboard Panels

Medium-density fiberboard (MDF) is usually manufactured from sawmill waste and a urea-formaldehyde (UF) binder. Formaldehyde, a known human carcinogen, offgasses from UF binders and can be especially problematic for chemically sensitive individuals. Particleboard is made from larger wood fiber particles than MDF, has a lower density; and doesn't mill as cleanly. Products listed here are low- or zero-formaldehyde, contain FSC-certified wood content, or are made from recovered waste fiber.

Certified Particleboard

Collins Products, LLC
6410 Hwy. 66
Klamath Falls, OR 97601

Toll-free: 800-547-1793
Phone: 541-885-3289
www.collinswood.com

The CollinsWood® line includes FSC-certified western pine particleboard, FSC-certified TruWood® engineered-wood siding and trim, and FSC-certified hardwood and softwood lumber and millwork. In 1993, Collins Pine Company became the first privately owned timber management company to receive FSC certification in the U.S. CollinsWood has been a leader in the forest and wood products certification movement since its inception.

Maplex

Weidmann Electrical Technology, Inc.
One Gordon Mills Way
St. Johnsbury, VT 05819

Phone: 800-242-6748
www.weidmann-industrial.com

Maplex is a dense, strong, bendable, pressed wood fiberboard manufactured without the use of chemical binders. This nontoxic, biodegradable material provides an alternative to formaldehyde-emitting particleboard and MDF products for a variety of interior finish, furniture, and consumer product applications. Maplex can be machined, bent, rolled, formed, punched, and laminated—as well as painted, dyed, stained, and coated. Maplex C (Contour) provides maximum bending or forming, and Maplex P (Performance) provides maximum stability and strength. Weidmann has been manufacturing fiber products since 1877 and is ISO 9001 and ISO 14001 certified.

PrimeBoard

PrimeBoard, Inc.
2441 N. 15th St.
Wahpeton, ND 58075

Phone: 701-642-1152
www.primeboard.com

PrimeBoard® was the first M3-rated particleboard made from wheat straw and a formaldehyde-free binder. Now made from a blend of agricultural-residue fibers, panels are available in a range of thicknesses, sizes, and grades. As of January, 2006, Masonite—the world's largest producer of doors—has purchased Primeboard, and is using most of the output as door core material.

Purekor Particleboard

Panel Source International
23 Rayborn Cres., 2nd Fl.
St. Albert, AB T8N 5B9 Canada

Toll-free: 877-464-7246
Phone: 780-458-1007
www.panelsource.net

Purekor M2 particleboard is made with 100% pre-consumer recycled western softwood and a urea-formaldehyde-free binder by Collins Companies in Klamath Falls, Oregon, for Panel Source International. These panels may be specified with 17.5% FSC-certified content, and an optional melamine lamination. Panel sizes are 4- or 5-feet by 8- or 12-feet, in thicknesses ranging from 1/2" to 1-1/8", and are sold in quantities ranging from 22 to 50, depending on thickness.

Rediscovered Wood Doors

Liberty Valley Doors
6005 Gravenstein Hwy.
Cotati, CA 94931

Phone: 707-795-8040
www.libertyvalleydoors.com

Liberty Valley Doors use reclaimed Douglas Fir beams, joists, and timbers from deconstructed buildings to create entryways and doors. Reclaimed glulams are incorporated into the stiles and rails, providing additional dimensional stability. The cores are formaldehyde-free MDF panels made from 100% recovered wood and use the non-formaldehyde binder methyl diisocyanate (MDI). The units are held together with nontoxic polyvinyl acetate (PVA, white glue) glue and come sanded and unfinished, but can be pre-finished at the factory. They are available with or without arches in one-, two-, or three-panel layouts. Custom thicknesses, widths, and heights are available.

SierraPine Formaldehyde-Free Fiberboard

SierraPine Ltd.
3010 Lava Ridge Ct. #220
Roseville, CA 95661

Toll-free: 800-676-3339
Phone: 916-772-3422
www.sierrapine.com

SierraPine's Medex MDF, for use in interior high-moisture applications, and Medite II MDF, for interior non-structural applications, are manufactured with a polyurethane binder, methyl diisocyanate(MDI), rather than conventional formaldehyde-based resins. SierraPine's newest formaldehyde-free product, Arreis SDF (Sustainable Design Fiberboard), uses the same MDI binder more efficiently to lower cost premiums. SierraPine has earned certification from Scientific Certification Systems (SCS) for using up to 100% recovered and recycled wood fiber for their MDF products.

Fiberboard Millwork

Pressures on timber supply are especially acute for high-visibility, solid-wood products like window sash and molding, which have traditionally been produced from old-growth trees. Medium-density fiberboard (MDF) molding made from post-industrial wood wastes is an excellent substitute for paint-grade moldings. The consistent quality and economical price of MDF moldings is broadening its market share. Some MDF is available with a non-formaldehyde binder.

Certified Veneer-Faced Trim

S. J. Morse Company
Rte. 50
P.O. Box 600
Capon Bridge, WV 26711

Phone: 304-856-3423
www.sjmorse.com

The S. J. Morse Company offers custom-made, veneer-faced trim in a variety of FSC-certified species—four domestics: red oak, white oak, cherry, and maple; three European: steamed beech, sycamore, and eucalyptus; and six relatively unknown Brazilian species: Amapa, Louro Preto, Angelim Fava, Taurari Vermelho, Ucuuba, and Cupiuba. The trim is available in any specified width and can be provided with a clear finish (a water-based option is available) or be left unfinished for custom staining and finishing. FSC-certified, recycled-content, or agrifiber cores are offered, including formaldehyde-free options. Other custom veneer products are also available FSC-certified: window seats, wide window and door jambs, column wraps, wall and ceiling panels, and cabinet door faces.

Medite II and Medex MDF Molding

SierraPine Ltd.
3010 Lava Ridge Ct. #220
Roseville, CA 95661

Toll-free: 800-676-3339
Phone: 916-772-3422
www.sierrapine.com

SierraPine's Medite Division produces MDF moldings made from Medite II, which uses a formaldehyde-free MDI binder. For high-moisture applications, the molding can be produced from Medex, which uses the same binder. SierraPine moldings are manufactured in knot-free, blemish-free, 16' lengths, factory-primed with a water-based paint. SierraPine has earned certification from Scientific Certification Systems (SCS) for using up to 100% recovered and recycled wood fiber for MDF.

Fiberboard Trim

Pressures on timber supply are especially acute for high-visibility, solid-wood products like window sash and molding, which have traditionally been produced from old-growth trees. Medium-density fiberboard (MDF) molding made from post-industrial wood wastes is an excellent substitute for paint-grade moldings. The consistent quality and economical price of MDF moldings is broadening its market share. Some MDF is available with nonformaldehyde binder.

Medite II and Medex MDF Molding

SierraPine Ltd.
3010 Lava Ridge Ct. #220
Roseville, CA 95661

Toll-free: 800-676-3339
Phone: 916-772-3422
www.sierrapine.com

SierraPine's Medite Division produces MDF moldings made from Medite II, which uses a formaldehyde-free MDI binder. For high-moisture applications, the molding can be produced from Medex, which uses the same binder. SierraPine moldings are manufactured in knot-free, blemish-free, 16' lengths, factory-primed with a water-based paint. SierraPine has earned certification from Scientific Certification Systems (SCS) for using up to 100% recovered and recycled wood fiber for MDF.

FSC-Certified Millwork

Certified wood products are verified by a third party as originating from well-managed forests. GreenSpec recognizes the Forest Stewardship Council (FSC) standards as the most rigorous and the only certification system with well-established chain-of-custody certification. Some companies listed here sell both certified and noncertified wood products, or products that have been certified according to different, less stringent environmental standards. To make certain that you get environmentally responsible wood products, be sure to specify your interest in FSC-certified wood.

Certified Lumber, Flooring, Wainscoting, and Veneer

McDowell Lumber Company, Inc.
Rte. 46 S
P.O. Box 148
Crosby, PA 16724

Phone: 814-887-2717
www.mcdowelllumber.com

McDowell Lumber deals in FSC-certified lumber, flooring, wainscoting, and veneer in over 15 species including red oak, cherry, hard and soft maple, ash, and a variety of other hardwoods harvested in Pennsylvania.

Certified Millwork

Anderson-Tully
1725 N. Washington St.
P.O. Box 38
Vicksburg, MS 39180

Phone: 601-629-3283
www.andersontully.com

Anderson-Tully Company (ATCO) received its FSC certification from SmartWood after years of uncertified but well-managed forestry practices. Anderson-Tully has long been offering an extensive number of species (with cottonwood and hackberry leading the list) due to its practice of finding markets for lesser-used tree species rather than eliminating them.

Certified Millwork

Les Produits Forestiers Becesco
2900, 95ieme Rue
St-Georges, QC G6A 1E3 Canada

Phone: 418-227-3671

Les Produits Forestiers Becesco is a certified hardwood lumber supplier milling oak, beech, birch, hard maple, and soft maple.

Certified Paneling and Millwork

Architectural Millwork Mfg. Co.
2125 Cross St.
P.O. Box 2809
Eugene, OR 97402

Toll-free: 800-685-1331
Phone: 541-689-1331
www.archmillwork.com

Architectural Millwork produces finished and unfinished FSC-certified stock and custom molding and paneling (including radius paneling and millwork) for commercial and residential projects. Custom panels may utilize any available core. Moldings may be up to 11-1/4" wide; custom profiles and pattern-matching are achieved with in-house knife grinding. Paint-grade MDF millwork (from sawmill byproduct) is also available.

Certified Wood Moldings

Colonial Craft
501 Main St.
Luck, WI 54853

Toll-free: 800-289-6653
Phone: 715-472-2223
www.colonialcraft.com/architecturalmouldings.html

Colonial Craft offers FSC-certified hardwood moldings. All other Colonial Craft products, including architectural moldings, can be produced from certified wood upon request.

Certified Wood Products

Cascadia Forest Goods, LLC
38083 Wheeler Rd.
Dexter, OR 97431

Phone: 541-485-4477
www.cascadiaforestgoods.com

Cascadia Forest Goods (CFG) is a supplier of FSC-certified and recycled forest products, including hardwood and softwood veneers, dimensional lumber and decking, timbers and beams, siding, flooring, paneling, and trim. CFG's woods come from the Pacific Northwest and British Columbia, and include the following species: douglas fir, incense and western red cedar, sitka and englemann spruce, ponderosa and sugar pine, and regional hardwoods (madrone, white and black oak, broadleaf maple, alder, chinkapin, and myrtlewood). FSC-certified and recycled-forest-product flooring species include madrone, white oak, clear vertical grain (CVG) Douglas fir, birch, big-leaf maple, and myrtlewood. CFG also supplies FSC-certified flooring and decking from Central and South America, including Santa Maria, catalox, chechen negro, jobillo, machiche, ramon blanco, sauche, ipe, pucte (ironwood), and others. CFG offers both solid and engineered wood flooring. CFG also supplies both FSC-certified hardwood and softwood veneers and lumber to window and door manufacturers.

CollinsWood FSC-Certified Wood Products

The Collins Companies
1618 S.W. First Ave., Ste. 500
Portland, OR 97201

Toll-free: 800-329-1219
Phone: 503-417-7755
www.collinswood.com

The CollinsWood line includes FSC-certified western pine particleboard, FSC-certified TruWood engineered (hardboard) siding and trim, and FSC-certified hardwood and softwood lumber and millwork. TruWood products are made under FSC's partial-content rules (with an actual certified fiber content of 32%), and use a phenol formaldehyde binder. Millwork includes cherry, red oak, soft maple and poplar interior millwork, including casing, base, chair rail, crown, etc. In 1993, Collins Pine Company became the first privately owned timber management company to receive FSC certification in the U.S. CollinsWood has been a leader in the forest and wood products certification movement since its inception.

F.D. Sterritt Certified-Wood Building Products

F.D. Sterritt Lumber Co.
110 Arlington St.
Watertown, MA 02472

Toll-free: 877-635-3362
Phone: 617-923-1480
www.sterrittlumber.com

F.D. Sterritt Lumber sells FSC-certified lumber, plywood, decking, hardwoods, and hardwood flooring. They have a variety of certified species in stock. Additional green building materials available, including low-VOC adhesives, caulking, sealants, and recycled drywall. F.D. Sterritt offers green building product consultations.

FSC-Certified Wood Products

Dwight Lewis Lumber / Lewis Lumber Products
30 S. Main St.
P.O. Box 356
Picture Rocks, PA 17762

Toll-free: 800-233-8450
Phone: 570-584-4460
www.lewislp.com

Dwight Lewis Lumber sells FSC-certified moldings, flooring, paneling, and hardwoods, subject to availability. Certified species are cherry, hard and soft maple, and red oak.

Reclaimed and Urban-Harvested Millwork

Jackel Enterprises
347 Locust St.
Watsonville, CA 95076

Toll-free: 800-711-9663
Phone: 831-768-3880
www.jackelenterprises.com

Jackel Enterprises processes urban and suburban forestry—the low-impact removal of city-owned and back-yard trees, ranch maintenance, and the like. Species include redwood, Douglas fir, Monterey cypress, black acacia, and California black walnut. Jackel also processes forest floor salvage from private parties, primarily old growth redwood, as well as milling recycled hardwoods and softwoods, including Douglas fir, redwood, western red cedar, heart pine, bald cypress, walnut, oak, and hickory. They have recently had their FSC chain-of-custody certification reinstated and will stock certified maple, oak, cherry, Douglas fir, and western red cedar.

Windfall Lumber and Milling

Windfall Lumber and Milling
404 Jefferson St. NE
Olympia, WA 98501

Phone: 360-352-2250
www.windfalllumber.com

Windfall Lumber is a manufacturer and distributor of FSC-certified and Smartwood Rediscovered hardwoods, flooring, millwork, countertops, and timbers.

FSC-Certified Wood Paneling

Certified wood products are third-party verified as originating from well-managed forests based on Forest Stewardship Council (FSC) standards. Some companies listed here may sell both certified and noncertified products or carry other types of certification that don't qualify for GreenSpec. To ensure the use of environmentally responsible wood products, be sure to specify your interest in FSC-certified wood when contacting these companies.

Certified Panel Products

Mt. Baker Plywood
2929 Roeder Ave.
Bellingham, WA 98225

Phone: 360-733-3960
www.mtbakerplywood.com

Mt. Baker Plywood manufactures FSC-certified panel products.

Certified Paneling and Millwork

Architectural Millwork Mfg. Co.
2125 Cross St.
P.O. Box 2809
Eugene, OR 97402

Toll-free: 800-685-1331
Phone: 541-689-1331
www.archmillwork.com

Architectural Millwork produces finished and unfinished FSC-certified stock and custom molding and paneling (including radius paneling and millwork) for commercial and residential projects. Custom panels may utilize any available core. Moldings may be up to 11-1/4" wide; custom profiles and pattern-matching are achieved with in-house knife grinding. Paint-grade MDF millwork (from sawmill byproduct) is also available.

Certified Wood Products

Cascadia Forest Goods, LLC
38083 Wheeler Rd.
Dexter, OR 97431

Phone: 541-485-4477
www.cascadiaforestgoods.com

Cascadia Forest Goods (CFG) is a supplier of FSC-certified and recycled forest products, including hardwood and softwood veneers, dimensional lumber and decking, timbers and beams, siding, flooring, paneling, and trim. CFG's woods come from the Pacific Northwest and British Columbia, and include the following species: douglas fir, incense and western red cedar, sitka and englemann spruce, ponderosa and sugar pine, and regional hardwoods (madrone, white and black oak, broadleaf maple, alder, chinkapin, and myrtlewood). FSC-certified and recycled-forest-product flooring species include madrone, white oak, clear vertical grain (CVG) Douglas fir, birch, big-leaf maple, and myrtlewood. CFG also supplies FSC-certified flooring and decking from Central and South America, including Santa Maria, catalox, chechen negro, jobillo, machiche, ramon blanco, sauche, ipe, pucte (ironwood), and others. CFG offers both solid and engineered wood flooring. CFG also supplies both FSC-certified hardwood and softwood veneers and lumber to window and door manufacturers.

CollinsWood FSC-Certified Wood Products

The Collins Companies
1618 S.W. First Ave., Ste. 500
Portland, OR 97201

Toll-free: 800-329-1219
Phone: 503-417-7755
www.collinswood.com

The CollinsWood line includes FSC-certified western pine particleboard, FSC-certified TruWood engineered (hardboard) siding and trim, and FSC-certified hardwood and softwood lumber and millwork. TruWood products are made under FSC's partial-content rules (with an actual certified fiber content of 32%), and use a phenol formaldehyde binder. Millwork includes cherry, red oak, soft maple and poplar interior millwork, including casing, base, chair rail, crown, etc. In 1993, Collins Pine Company became the first privately owned timber management company to receive FSC certification in the U.S. CollinsWood has been a leader in the forest and wood products certification movement since its inception.

EarthSource Forest Products

EarthSource Forest Products/Plywood and Lumber Sales, Inc.
1618 28th St.
Oakland, CA 94608

Toll-free: 866-549-9663
Phone: 510-208-7257
www.earthsourcewood.com

EarthSource Forest Products, a division of Plywood and Lumber Sales, Inc., sells FSC-certified hardwood plywood and lumber of the following species: maple, cherry, red oak, white oak, ash, Honduras mahogany, walnut, machiche, amapola, and many more. EarthSource also sells salvaged and rediscovered lumber such as fir, redwood, and hickory.

FSC-Certified Wood Products

Menominee Tribal Enterprises
Hwy. 47 N
P.O. Box 10
Neopit, WI 54150

Phone: 715-756-2311
www.mtewood.com

Menominee Tribal Enterprises (MTE) offers a full line of certified wood products harvested from the 220,000-acre Menominee Forest. MTE is continuing its development of value-added products from the 16 wood species harvested. Menominee forest lands were the first certified to FSC standards in North America.

FSC-Certified Wood Wall and Ceiling Paneling

Wood Ceilings
25310 Jeans Rd.
Veneta, OR 97487

Phone: 541-935-9663
www.woodceilings.com

Wood Ceilings—formerly Pacific Wood Systems—crafts architectural suspended ceiling panel systems and wall paneling of FSC-certified woods including black cherry, western hemlock, red oak, maple, mahogany, and teak (when available).

SkyBlend UF-Free Particle Board

Roseburg Forest Products
P.O. Box 1088
Roseburg, OR 97470

Toll-free: 800-245-1115
Phone: 541-679-3311
www.rfpco.com

Roseburg SkyBlend™ is a general-use particleboard produced with phenol-formaldehyde (PF) binder instead of the industry-standard urea-formaldehyde (UF) binder. The company claims formaldehyde emissions of about 0.01 parts per million (ppm) under standard test conditions—comparable to natural levels in outdoor air. It is Green Cross-certified by Scientific Certification Systems (SCS) as being made from 100% recycled wood fibers (pre-consumer waste from lumber mills). The wood fiber is not FSC-certified. The particleboard core is tinted light blue for field identification. SkyBlend™ is available in industrial grade only, in seven thicknesses from 1/4" to 1-1/8". Standard dimensions for most thicknesses are 49" x 97", while the 3/4" and 1-1/8" panels are also available in larger sizes. Custom dimensions may be available for large orders.

SkyPly

Roseburg Forest Products
P.O. Box 1088
Roseburg, OR 97470

Toll-free: 800-245-1115
Phone: 541-679-3311
www.rfpco.com

SkyPly veneer-core hardwood plywood, from Roseburg Forest Products, is available in three different urea formaldehde-free adhesive combinations. They use phenol formaldehyde adhesive alone for paint-grade and laminates, phenol formaldehde plus water-based polyvinyl acetate glue (PVA, or white glue) for surface veneers to prevent bleed-through, and PVA alone. SkyPly plywoods are available with a Forest Stewardship Council (FSC)-certified veneer cores in all ANSI face and back grades.

Gypsum Board

Gypsum board, or drywall, is typically made with 100% recycled, unbleached paper facings that are bonded without adhesives onto a gypsum core. Though mined virgin gypsum is still widely used in gypsum board production, recycled and synthetic gypsum comprise an increasing portion of product manufacturing. Recycled gypsum board is derived from in-plant scrap and some clean construction waste; advances in recycling technology allow separation of the paper from the core so that each may be recycled separately. Synthetic, or flue-gas, gypsum is a waste product obtained from stack scrubbers that remove sulfur from coal-fired power plant emissions. (In these scrubbers, calcium carbonate is converted to calcium sulfate, or gypsum.) Synthetic gypsum may replace up to 100% of the natural gypsum in drywall. Reducing waste is an important consideration in green building projects; 54"-wide gypsum board may allow more efficient wall coverage in rooms with 9' ceilings. Be aware that paper facings may provide a medium for mold growth in conditions of high humidity and low air circulation; some drywall is made with integral cellulose or fiberglass fibers instead of paper facing to eliminate mold risk. These products, however, are less recyclable. Products listed here are manufactured by companies with at least one U.S. plant operating or planned that uses 100% synthetic gypsum. Additionally, some products listed here are designed to eliminate mold risk.

DensArmor Plus and DensShield

G-P Gypsum Corporation
133 Peachtree St. NE
Atlanta, GA 30303

Toll-free: 800-284-5347
Phone: 404-652-4000
www.gp.com/gypsum

G-P Gypsum manufactures the Dens™ line of paperless gypsum board products, which offer excellent mold resistance for residential and commercial construction. Instead of paper facings, the Dens™ products incorporate fiberglass mats on surfaces. This provides moisture resistance and removes a potential food source for mold, but the facing also hinders recyclability, so these products are recommended primarily for moisture prone areas. In particular, DensArmor Plus® panels are designed for interior moisture-prone areas such as basements and residential bathrooms, and DensShield® Tile Backer is a mold-resistant tile backer board.

Fiberock Brand Aqua Tough Panels

USG Corporation
555 West Adams St.
Chicago, IL 60661

Toll-free: 800-874-4968
Phone: 312-436-4000
www.usg.com

Fiberock Interior panels and Sheathing with Aqua Tough are an FGD (flue-gas desulfurization) gypsum and cellulose formulation suitable for a wide range of applications. Interior panels can be used in wet and dry areas as a tile backer board or as a standard drywall panel when mold resistance is required. Fiberock AR and VHI are products that offer an exceptional level of abuse resistance. Fiberock panels have been certified by Scientific Certification Systems (SCS) to contain 95% recycled material, 85% of which is post-industrial recycled gypsum and 10% recycled paper fiber.

Gold Bond Gypsum Wallboard

National Gypsum Company
2001 Rexford Rd.
Charlotte, NC 28211

Toll-free: 800-628-4662
Phone: 704-365-7300
www.national-gypsum.com

National Gypsum manufactures Gold Bond® gypsum wallboard with synthetic gypsum in some plants.

G-P Gypsum Board

G-P Gypsum Corporation
133 Peachtree St. NE
Atlanta, GA 30303

Toll-free: 800-284-5347
Phone: 404-652-4000
www.gp.com/gypsum

G-P Gypsum operates 18 manufacturing plants for gypsum board. The Wheatfield, Indiana and Tacoma, Washington plants use synthetic gypsum, while the remaining plants use varying amounts of recycled gypboard. The manufacturer has certified the following recycled-content levels (by weight): total recovered material 8% typical, 6% guaranteed; post-consumer material 0% typical, 0% guaranteed.

QuietRock

Quiet Solution
1250 Elko Dr.
Sunnyvale, CA 94089

Toll-free: 800-797-8159
www.quietsolution.com

QuietRock™ sound-control drywall for walls and ceilings is made with a thin layer of steel embedded in viscoelastic polymer that is formulated with near-zero emissions of VOCs and sandwiched between sheets of gypsum drywall. It provides impressive sound transmission reduction, installs quickly, and results in very little increase in wall thickness, compared with other sound-control options. QuietRock is available in thicknesses ranging from 5/8" to 1-7/16".

Sheetrock Brand Gypsum Panels

USG Corporation
555 West Adams St.
Chicago, IL 60661

Toll-free: 800-874-4968
Phone: 312-436-4000
www.usg.com

Sheetrock® Brand Gypsum Panels are USG's brand of standard drywall products. USG uses flue-gas desulfurization (FGD) gypsum, an industrial waste product derived from pollution-control equipment at coal-fired power plants, in its standard drywall products—over 3 million tons of it in 2004, more than any other wallboard supplier. However, this content changes from plant to plant and even day to day at any one plant due to availability. The recycled content of USG boards nationwide for 2004 was over 37% by weight, according to the company; over 32% was recaptured gypsum. All USG wallboard uses 100% post-consumer recycled paper. USG has seven plants that make panels with over 97% recycled content, and an additional seven plants use a blend of natural gypsum and FGD gypsum.

Temple-Inland Gypsum

Temple-Inland Forest Products
303 S. Temple Dr.
P.O. Drawer N
Diboll, TX 75941

Toll-free: 800-231-6061 x5008
Phone: 972-467-3499
www.templeinland.com

Temple-Inland produces over 60% of its wallboard using synthetic gypsum derived from flue-gas desulphurization. All wallboard coming from their Tennessee and Arkansas plants has an SCS-certified recycled content of 99% with the exception of sheathing and moisture-resistant wallboard, which is certified to contain 95% recycled content. Wallboard can be specified from these plants and comes with endtapes designating production source. The manufacturer has certified the following recycled-content levels (by weight): total recovered material 99% typical, 95% guaranteed; post-consumer material 6% typical, 4% guaranteed.

Gypsum Board Accessories

Using drywall clips at corners and partition-wall intersections allows a reduction in steel or wood studs, saving resources and reducing costs. Used at corners, drywall clips allow slight movement of drywall panels to accommodate expansion and contraction of framing members, minimizing cracking and call-backs. In addition, drywall clips and stops do not take up space that insulation could occupy in wall cavities where interior partitions meet exterior walls. Products listed here are accessories for gypsum board construction that have various environmental features or benefits in use such as drywall clips or "stops."

ButtHanger and EZ-Backer

Wilco Tools, Inc.
1122 Siddonsburg Rd.
Mechanicsburg, PA 17055

Toll-free: 888-292-1002
Phone: 717-766-4594
www.butthanger.com

The ButtHanger, a simple device made from wood strapping and metal cross pieces, eliminates the single most problematic aspect of interior finish work—the drywall butt joint. By enabling the laying out and hanging of board finish ends to space rather than to framing, the Butthanger bends the butt ends inward about 1/8". This changes a labor-intensive and difficult 3'-wide mud joint into a quick and easy 1'-wide one while both reducing cut-off waste and joint compound used for butt joints. EZ-Backer is an all-steel commercial version of the ButtHanger.

DC1 Drywall Clip

USP Structural Connectors
14305 Southcross Dr., Ste. 200
Burnsville, MN 55306

Toll-free: 800-328-5934
www.uspconnectors.com

The DC1 Drywall Clip is a galvanized steel clip that is installed with nails and reduces the need for wood blocking on top plates, end walls, and corners.

No-Nail and Stud Claw

Stud Claw USA
5370 Chestnut Ridge Rd.
Orchard Park, NY 14127

Phone: 716-662-7877
www.studclaw.com

No-Nail™ is a sheet metal drywall clip that creates floating corners. It friction-fits to one sheet of drywall and grips the adjoining sheet with its own spurs. This clip can accommodate non-right-angle applications such as cathedral ceilings. The Stud Claw is a metal wire clip that grips two-by wood framing with spurs and also facilitates floating corners. Two sizes are available: GC-15 (1-1/2") for single top plates and studs, and GC-30 (3") for double plates.

PowerSand and QuikSand Sanding Blocks

Earthstone International
101 S. Coit Rd., Ste. 36-319
Richardson, TX 75080

Toll-free: 888-994-6327
www.goearthstone.com

Earthstone PowerSand, made with limestone and 90% post-consumer recycled glass, are self-sharpening, pumice-like blocks or discs that attach to palm-sized power sanders or electric drills (with mount adapters). QuikSand is a hand-held, wet-or-dry version of the product made with limestone and 96% post-consumer recycled glass. In addition to smoothing wood, they can be used to remove finishes from most substrates without the need for stripping chemicals. The PowerSand blocks produce less airborne dust than sandpaper, and the porous material won't clog or rip. One block is the equivalent of several sheets of sandpaper, so fewer change-outs are required.

Prest-on Cornerbacks

Prest-on Company
312 Lookout Pt.
Hot Springs, AR 71913

Toll-free: 800-323-1813
Phone: 501-767-3855
www.prest-on.com

Prest-on's steel Cornerbacks are "pressed" onto the drywall and nailed or screwed to the structural member. This product is not designed for floating corners.

Simpson Drywall Stop (DS)

Simpson Strong-Tie Connectors
5956 W. Las Positas Blvd.
P.O. Box 10789
Pleasanton, CA 94588

Toll-free: 800-999-5099
Phone: 925-560-9000
www.strongtie.com

The Simpson Drywall Stop (DS) is a galvanized steel product that installs with nails.

The Nailer

The Millennium Group, Inc.
2300 W. Eisenhower Blvd.
Loveland, CO 80537

Toll-free: 800-280-2304
Phone: 970-663-1200
www.thenailer.com

The Nailer® is a 100% recycled-content, high-density polyethylene (HDPE) plastic drywall stop or backer. The Nailer installs with flat-head nails or staples and the standard component "Tec" screw for steel studs. Drywall may be screwed or glued to The Nailer or may simply be floated behind the adjacent drywall sheet. The Nailer allows for full-size friction fit insulation in wall cavities and can reduce cracking due to truss uplift.

Gypsum Board Taping and Finishing

Products listed here are accessories for gypsum board taping and finishing that have various environmental features or benefits in use such as low-VOC joint compounds.

Murco M100 Joint Compound

Murco Wall Products
2032 N. Commerce
Fort Worth, TX 76164

Toll-free: 800-446-7124
Phone: 817-626-1987
www.murcowall.com

Murco Wall Products manufactures a powdered all-purpose joint cement and texture compound formulated with inert fillers and natural binders only. It does not contain any preservatives or slow-releasing compounds and is zero-VOC. M100 mixes easily with tap water.

Plastic Paneling

Recycled plastic paneling is an appropriate use for some of the various post-consumer plastic materials entering the waste stream in particular, high-density polyethylene (HDPE) from milk and detergent bottles. Plastic materials are resistant to water and microbial growth, making them appropriate for wet locations such as bathrooms and industrial or agricultural facilities. The plastic paneling products listed here have a recycled content value (equal to % post-consumer plus 1/2 % pre-consumer) of at least 45%, with many products using 100% post-consumer recycled plastic.

Bedford Technology Recycled-Plastic Products

Bedford Technology, LLC
2424 Armour Rd.
P.O. Box 609
Worthington, MN 56187

Toll-free: 800-721-9037
Phone: 507-372-5558
www.plasticboards.com

Bedford Technology offers plastic lumber and other products made with post-consumer recycled HDPE and LDPE. Their lumber is available in a variety of dimensions, including 5/4 decking, two-by, and large timbers up to 12x12, in black, brown, gray, and cedar with other colors available. Parking stops and speed bumps are also offered, as well as plastic paneling that can be used as a substitute for plywood. Bedford's ForeSite Designs(R) line of recycled-plastic site furnishings includes picnic tables, benches, and waste receptacles. The manufacturer has certified the following recycled-content levels (by weight): total recovered material 99% typical, 99% guaranteed; post-consumer material 65% typical, 50% guaranteed.

EPS Recycled-Plastic Lumber and Outdoor Furniture

Engineered Plastic
Systems
885 Church Rd.
Elgin, IL 60123

Phone: 847-289-8383
www.epsplasticlumber.
com

Engineered Plastic Systems (EPS) Bear Board plastic lumber is typically made from a minimum 51% post-consumer recycled HDPE and is available in a variety of sizes and colors, with a smooth or wood-grain finish. Fiberglass-reinforced structural plastic lumber is also available. Their plastic landscape timbers (from the same feedstock) are available in a wide variety of colors and sizes. Durapoly plastic "plywood" is available in white and gray, in thicknesses ranging from 1/4" to 1-1/2". All of these products are covered by a 50-year limited warranty.

Ny-Board

NYCORE
200 Galleria Pkwy., Ste. 2000
Atlanta, GA 30339

Phone: 770-980-0000
www.nycore.com

Ny-Board is a strong, flexible, skid-resistant sheeting made from 100% recycled nylon carpet waste from post-consumer and post-industrial sources. The flexible, waterproof sheets can be cut with standard saws, screwed, nailed, glued, and painted; they don't rot, deteriorate, or support mold or insects. According to the manufacturer, no waste is generated in the manufacturing process, and the product is recyclable. Ny-Board is available in 1/8", 1/4" or 3/8" thicknesses and in 4x4 or 4x8 sheets. Other sizes are available by special order. Uses are wide-ranging, including protective wall and floor liners, foundation guards, dock surfacing, and sign backing. Considerations include thermal expansion and possible cold-weather brittleness. The manufacturer offers a 30-year warranty.

Phonotherm 200

BOSIG, Inc.
2125 Center Ave., Ste. 507
Fort Lee, NJ 07024

Phone: 201-302-6081
www.bosig.com

Phonotherm® 200 has the appearance of particleboard, but is made with compressed recycled residuals from the rigid polyurethane foam industry—resulting in a board product that is waterproof, free of swell and decay, and recyclable, and that offers better insulation values than wood-based or solid plastic boards. Damp and wet applications such as bathrooms, kitchen, facades, doors, and windows are appropriate. Phonotherm may be used as a subfloor. It can be milled with normal carbide tools; contains no formaldehyde; and is vapor permeable.

PlasTEAK Plastic Paneling

PlasTEAK
3563 Copley Rd.
P.O. Box 4290
Akron, OH 44321

Toll-free: 800-320-1841
Phone: 330-668-2587
www.plasteak.com

PlasTEAK is made with 100% post-consumer recycled HDPE in a paraffin base—the boards become more slip-resistant when wet. Boatboard extruded HDPE panels meet the requirements of marine and outdoor environments. Limarpa is a lightweight alternative to plywood, also appropriate for marine use. PlasTEAK also makes UV-stabilized, 1' x 4' x 1.25"-thick, recycled-plastic grates for such applications as boardwalks, dune walkovers, nature walks, and floating docks; these grates provide 60% light and visual penetration for such uses as boardwalks, dune walkovers, and nature walks. Trim and lumber goods are available as well.

Plastic Paneling

Taylors Recycled Plastic Products Inc.
581 County Road 28
Bailieboro, ON K0L 1B0 Canada

Toll-free: 877-939-6072
Phone: 705-939-6072
www.taylorsplastic.com

Taylors Recycled Plastic Products, Inc. produces 100% recycled plastic sheeting primarily from post-consumer recycled plastic as a direct replacement for plywood in nonstructural indoor and outdoor applications. It comes in square-edged 4' x 8' sheets with a smooth matt surface in off-white and gray. Available thicknesses range from 1/4" to 1-3/4". Custom colors and sizes are available on volume orders.

Plastic Panels

Coon Manufacturing, Inc.
78 N.E. 115th St.
P.O. Box 108
Spickard, MO 64679

Toll-free: 800-843-1532
Phone: 660-485-6299
www.coonmfginc.com

Coon Manufacturing markets their recycled plastic products for agricultural construction applications. Their 100% plastic sheet goods are rugged, smooth or corrugated, recycled high-density polyethylene panels available in various sizes. Coon complements their white panels with plastic molding products and stainless steel hardware. Coon also manufactures 100% recycled septic tanks and trash containers.

Plastic Panels

Iowa Plastics, Inc.
322 N. Main Ave.
Sioux Center, IA 51250

Phone: 712-722-0692

Iowa Plastics manufactures 4' x 8' panels in thicknesses from 1/16" to 1/2". Panels come in white and black and are made from 98% post-consumer recycled HDPE. Custom sizes are also available. The manufacturer has certified the following recycled-content levels (by weight): post-consumer material 98% typical, 98% guaranteed.

Plastic Panels

Reprocessed Plastics, Inc.
609 County Rd. 82 NW
Garfield, MN 56332

Phone: 320-834-2293
www.gipo-rpi.com

RPI's plastic panels (formerly called EcoPanels) are extruded sheets made from 100% recycled HDPE. Depending upon specific color patterns, the sheets contain 0-50% post-industrial recycled HDPE, with the balance being post-consumer recycled. This product is available in 10 custom colors as well as black and white, and measure 4' x 8' in thicknesses from 1/8" to 3/4". They can be cut, sanded, routed, milled, drilled and otherwise handled with conventional wood and metal working tools and machines. In addition, the material can be shaped by thermoforming and welding.

Recycled-Plastic Panels

Plastic Lumber Yard, LLC
220 Washington St.
Norristown, PA 19401

Phone: 610-277-3900
www.plasticlumberyard.com

Plastic Lumber Yard, LLC manufactures plastic sheeting from 100% recycled plastic. The black or white panels come in 4' x 8' sheets in 1/8", 1/4", 3/8", and 1/2" thicknesses and 4' x 10' sheets in a 1/2" thickness.

Sandhill Plastics Sheeting

Sandhill Plastics
119 W. 19th St.
Kearney, NE 68847

Toll-free: 800-644-7141
Phone: 308-236-5025
www.sandhillplastics.com

Sandhill Plastics manufactures plastic sheeting of 100% post-consumer HDPE used primarily for agricultural applications. Standard sheets measure 4' x 8' in thicknesses ranging from 1/16" to 5/8".

Prefinished Paneling

The following products are an eclectic assortment of prefinished panels that offer an alternative to traditional prefinished paneling. Products listed here are made with recycled content, low-emitting binders, agricultural-waste fiber such as straw, rapidly renewable materials such as bamboo, and/or FSC-certified wood.

Bamboo Veneer and Paneling

DMVP Timber Bamboo Ltd.
De Marowijne 43
ZWAAG The Netherlands

Phone: 0031-229-265732
www.dmvpbamboo.com

DMVP's standard veneers have a cellulose fleece backing, which is bonded with a D3 water resistant PVAC glue. The cellulose backing can endure temperatures above 220 degrees Celsius.

In addition to single-ply veneers, DMVP produces multi-layer veneer panels by laminating multiple layers of veneer under high temperature, producing panels 1.5 mm or thicker.

DMVP also offers sandwich panels, with bamboo veneers laminated onto core panels, such as chipboard, plywood, MDF, or HDF.

DMVP is a joint venture between Hangzhou Liuzhuang floor Co., Ltd. and MVP International BV. MVP delivers veneer from the Netherlands to customers in Europe and the USA. DMVP distributes in the US, through various distributors, including M Bohlke Veneer Corporation of Fairfield, Ohio and General Woods & Veneers Ltd. of Québec, Canada.

Canfor PanelWOODS

Canfor Panel and Fibre
430 Canfor Ave.
New Westminster, BC V3L 5G2 Canada

Toll-free: 800-363-8873
Phone: 604-521-9650
www.canforpfd.com

Panelwoods interior decorative hardboard panels are certified by SCS as being made with 100% recycled and recovered wood fibers. One-half of the raw material is from post-consumer waste; most of the rest comes from byproducts from the forest industry. The binder is a fully cured phenolic resin (no urea formaldehyde), and water-based paints are used in the finishing process. The panels are embossed or printed to simulate various stone, brick, and wood surfaces. They are available in 4-by-8-foot panels, and in wainscot-height. The panels have a flame-spread rating of 150 (US Class C, Canada Class 3).

DesignWall, NovaCork, and Burlap Panels

Homasote Company
932 Lower Ferry Rd.
P.O. Box 7240
West Trenton, NJ 08628

Toll-free: 800-257-9491
Phone: 609-883-3300
www.homasote.com

DesignWall®, NovaCork®, and Burlap Panels all consist of a Homasote 100% recycled newspaper fiber and paraffin binder substrate with various decorative coverings. DesignWall is a substrate of Class A fire-rated N.C.F.R. board wrapped in Class A fire-rated Guilford of Maine fabric covering. NovaCork is available as a Class A board and is covered with cork veneer. Burlap Panels are standard 440 Homasote covered with burlap. All three products are available in 4' x 8' and 4' x 10' panels.

EarthSource Forest Products

EarthSource Forest Products/Plywood and Lumber Sales, Inc.
1618 28th St.
Oakland, CA 94608

Toll-free: 866-549-9663
Phone: 510-208-7257
www.earthsourcewood.com

EarthSource Forest Products, a division of Plywood and Lumber Sales, Inc., sells FSC-certified hardwood plywood and lumber of the following species: maple, cherry, red oak, white oak, ash, Honduras mahogany, walnut, machiche, amapola, and many more. EarthSource also sells salvaged and rediscovered lumber such as fir, redwood, and hickory.

Environ Biocomposite, Dakota Burl, and Biofiber Wheat

Environ Biocomposites, LLC
221 Mohr Dr.
Mankato, MN 56001

Toll-free: 800-324-8187
Phone: 507-388-3434
www.environbiocomposites.com

Environ is a biocomposite panel containing recycled newsprint, soy flour, pigment, and a water-based catalyst that converts the soy flour into a resin, creating a material that looks like granite and works like hardwood. It is not appropriate for moisture-prone applications. Dakota Burl composite panels are made primarily from post-process, sunflower-seed hulls. Biofiber panels are made from finely chopped post-harvest wheat straw combined with a high-performance urethane resin. All the panels come in standard 4' x 8' sheets in 1/2", 3/4", and 1" thicknesses.

Kirei Board

Kirei USA
1805 Newton Ave.
San Diego, CA 92113

Phone: 619-236-9924
www.kireiusa.com

Kirei™ board, made with waste sorghum fiber, is a lightweight substitute for wood-panel products and is appropriate for use in cabinetry and furniture, store displays, restaurant and office interiors, wall treatments, and flooring for low-traffic areas. The nonformaldehyde MDI binder (similar to that used in most straw-particleboard panels) is more water-resistant than the common urea-formaldehyde binder. Though not friable, the product has a soft surface that may require wood-putty filling and sealing. The irregular pattern is very striking and popular with designers. Kirei board is 3' x 6' and comes in 10, 20 or 30 mm thicknesses.

MeadowBoard Straw Panels

Meadowood Industries, Inc.
P.O. Box 257
Belmont, CA 94002

Phone: 650-637-0539
www.meadowoodindustries.com

MeadowBoard™ is a formaldehyde-free rye grass straw panel available in 4' x 8' sheets from 1/8" to 1" thick. This coarse-textured interior finish material can be custom-molded into various shapes. Meadowood is not an M3-rated structural panel product. Rye grass straw is an agricultural waste product from grass seed production.

Plyboo Bamboo Paneling, Plywood, and Veneer

Smith & Fong Company
475 6th St.
S. San Francisco, CA 94103

Toll-free: 866-835-9859
Phone: 415-896-0577
www.plyboo.com

Plyboo® tambour, fabric-backed, flexible paneling is available in a 3/16" x 48" x 96" size with either a sanded or "raw" surface. Sanded comes prefinished or unfinished in an amber or natural color. The "raw" paneling, which retains the outside skin of the bamboo and has a more rustic appeal, comes unfinished in a natural green/yellow, black, or amber color. Plyboo bamboo plywood comes in a variety of dimensions and sizes; in amber or natural color; and with either vertical or flat grain. Plyboo bamboo veneer has a vertical pattern in amber or natural color in 0.6 mm x 12" x 98". There is also a 1/8" bamboo veneer in a 48" x 96" size with a plywood backing. Veneers are provided with either paper or fleece backing. Playboo's plywood and veneers are also available as part of their PlybooPure line. These products use low-emitting, stable polyisocyanurate as the binder and contain no added urea formaldehyde.

SkyBlend UF-Free Particle Board

Roseburg Forest Products
P.O. Box 1088
Roseburg, OR 97470

Toll-free: 800-245-1115
Phone: 541-679-3311
www.rfpco.com

Roseburg SkyBlend™ is a general-use particleboard produced with phenol-formaldehyde (PF) binder instead of the industry-standard urea-formaldehyde (UF) binder. The company claims formaldehyde emissions of about 0.01 parts per million (ppm) under standard test conditions—comparable to natural levels in outdoor air. It is Green Cross-certified by Scientific Certification Systems (SCS) as being made from 100% recycled wood fibers (pre-consumer waste from lumber mills). The wood fiber is not FSC-certified. The particleboard core is tinted light blue for field identification. SkyBlend™ is available in industrial grade only, in seven thicknesses from 1/4" to 1-1/8". Standard dimensions for most thicknesses are 49" x 97", while the 3/4" and 1-1/8" panels are also available in larger sizes. Custom dimensions may be available for large orders.

Teragren Bamboo Flooring, Panels, and Veneer

Teragren LLC
12715 Miller Rd. NE, Ste. 301
Bainbridge Island, WA 98110

Toll-free: 800-929-6333
Phone: 206-842-9477
www.teragren.com

Teragren (formerly TimberGrass) manufactures solid strip bamboo flooring in tongue-and-groove or locking system, prefinished or site-finished. All flooring products are available in vertical or flat (horizontal) grains and natural or caramelized standard colors as well as stained cherry, walnut, charcoal and espresso colors. Coatings are water based and solvent free. The company uses the MOSO specie of bamboo which is harvested at maturity at 6 years. Teragren also manufactures coordinating stair parts, flooring accessories and vents, panels and veneer for cabinetry, furniture, interior paneling, countertops, and other interior applications as a direct replacement for wood sheet goods. (Note that while the adhesive used to manufacture the panels and veneer exceeds E1 standards, it is not food grade; if the surface is to be used for food preparation, a food grade sealer is recommended.)

Tricel Honeycomb

Tricel Corp.
2100 Swanson Ct.
Gurnee, IL 60031

Toll-free: 800-352-3300
Phone: 847-336-1321
www.tricelcorp.com

Tricel Honeycomb recycled-content paper core panels have either plywood, foil, or paper board exteriors bonded with phenolic resins.

Unicor

National Shelter Products, Inc.
50 S.E. Bush St.
Issaquah, WA 98027

Toll-free: 800-552-7775
Phone: 425-557-7968
www.nationalshelter.com

Unicor™ wallboard is made from recycled corrugated containers and bottle carrier stock from the beverage industry bonded with PVA (white glue) adhesive. Unicor is mainly used as a sheathing panel in RV, manufactured housing, and residential construction applications. It is not rated for use as a shear panel.

Reclaimed-Wood Millwork

As the demands on forest resources have increased, nonforest sources of wood have grown in importance. Reclaimed wood is usually salvaged from buildings slated for demolition, abandoned railroad trestles, and "sinker logs" that sank decades ago during river-based log drives. It can also be from trees that have been recently harvested from urban or suburban areas (such as disease-killed trees). Reclaimed wood is often available in species, coloration, and wood quality not available in newly harvested timber. In some cases, reclaimed wood suppliers have only limited quantities with matching coloration or weathering patterns; ample lead time and accurate materials estimates can help ensure the availability of the desired wood. Lowering the uniformity standards for finished wood can also increase the potential for use of reclaimed wood. As with other resources, the supply of reclaimed wood is limited. Efficient and appropriate use of reclaimed wood is important for its long-term availability. Be aware that reclaimed wood may contain lead paint; testing is recommended if lead paint residue is suspected.

Reclaimed and Urban-Harvested Millwork

Jackel Enterprises
347 Locust St.
Watsonville, CA 95076

Toll-free: 800-711-9663
Phone: 831-768-3880
www.jackelenterprises.com

Jackel Enterprises processes urban and suburban forestry—the low-impact removal of city-owned and back-yard trees, ranch maintenance, and the like. Species include redwood, Douglas fir, Monterey cypress, black acacia, and California black walnut. Jackel also processes forest floor salvage from private parties, primarily old growth redwood, as well as milling recycled hardwoods and softwoods, including Douglas fir, redwood, western red cedar, heart pine, bald cypress, walnut, oak, and hickory. They have recently had their FSC chain-of-custody certification reinstated and will stock certified maple, oak, cherry, Douglas fir, and western red cedar.

Reclaimed-Wood Flooring and Millwork

Treasured Timbers, Inc.
173 Hunter Lake Rd.
Upper Golden Grove, NB
E2S 3B4 Canada

Phone: 506-849-8016
www.treasuredtimbers.com

Treasured Timbers, Inc. specializes in hardwood plank flooring and millwork made from sinker logs salvaged from the Saint John River.

Reclaimed-Wood Materials

Big Timberworks
1 Rabel Ln.
P.O. Box 368
Gallatin Gateway, MT 59730

Phone: 406-763-4639
www.bigtimberworks.com

Big Timberworks offers custom-milled, reclaimed lumber and timbers in a variety of species. The company specializes in shipping timber frame houses all over the country for supervised construction but also sells custom-cut, reclaimed wood from their sawmill in Montana for residential and commercial applications such as siding, flooring, and millwork.

Reclaimed-Wood Millwork

J.L. Powell & Co., Inc.
101 E. Main St.
Whiteville, NC 28472

Toll-free: 800-227-2007
Phone: 910-642-8989
www.plankfloors.com

J.L. Powell & Co. specializes in custom architectural millwork, including stair parts and flooring, produced from reclaimed antique heart pine.

Recycled-Glass Tile

Tile is an inherently low-toxic, durable finish material for flooring, walls, and other applications. Products listed here are specialty tiles produced from recycled glass.

Architectural Accents

Aurora Glass
2345 W. Broadway
Eugene, OR 97402

Toll-free: 888-291-9311
Phone: 541-681-3260
www.auroraglass.org

Aurora Glass Architectural Accents include glass tiles, rosette blocks, sconces, and drawer pulls made from 100% recycled glass. Aurora Glass is a program of St. Vincent de Paul of Lane County, Inc. The glass foundry's profits support homeless and low-income people through emergency services, housing, jobs, training, and other charitable endeavors. The manufacturer has certified the following recycled-content levels (by weight): total recovered material 100% typical, 100% guaranteed; post-consumer material 86% typical, 86% guaranteed.

Blazestone

Bedrock Industries
1401 W. Garfield St.
Seattle, WA 98119

Toll-free: 877-283-7625
Phone: 206-283-7625
www.bedrockindustries.com

Blazestone® tiles are made from 100% recycled glass, most of which is post-consumer content. They come in 2" x 2", 2" x 4", 4" x 4", 5" x 5", 5" x 10", 4" hex sizes, a range of circle shapes, 3.5" x 7" subways, as well as mosaic pieces. Color varies with the recycled glass materials used. Bedrock also makes architectural accents and non-architectural accessories from recycled glass. Three of the 28 colors offered are made exclusively from 100% post-industrial waste. For the others, the manufacturer has certified the following recycled-content levels (by weight): total recovered material 100% typical, 100% guaranteed; post-consumer material 50% typical, 50% guaranteed. The manufacturer has certified the following recycled-content levels (by weight): total recovered material 100% typical, 100% guaranteed; post-consumer material 50% typical, 50% guaranteed.

Oceanside Glasstile

Oceanside Glasstile Co.
2293 Cosmos Ct.
Carlsbad, CA 92011

Toll-free: 877-648-8222
Phone: 760-929-4000
www.glasstile.com

Oceanside produces four styles of tile handcast from 85% post-consumer recycled glass. They are semi-transparent, have an iridescent surface, and are available in a wide range of colors. Tessera is available in 29 colors and 4 sizes. Casa California includes larger-format tiles with a full line of decoratives. Minerali is a specialty tile with wide color variation and a textured surface. Haiku features opal glass with Asian motifs.

Recycled-Glass Tiles

Mellon Glass
1554 Port Mellon Hwy.
Gibsons, BC V0N1V6 Canada

Phone: 604-886-0202
www.mellonglass.com

Mellon Glass (formerly Hot Glass) hand-makes sand-cast, 2" x 2" tiles from 100% post-consumer recycled wine bottles. Colors include green, three shades of blue, clear, and several others. New recycled products for 2007 include 4-foot wide freeblown chandeliers with energy-saving lights.

Recycled-Glass Tiles

Sandhill Industries
6898 S. Supply Rd., Ste. 100
Boise, ID 83716

Phone: 208-345-6508
www.sandhillind.com

Sandhill Industries manufactures wall and floor tile from 100% post-industrial plate glass. The company's manufacturing process can produce both glossy and matte finishes, and results in no wastewater or air emissions. Tiles come in a standard variety of square, bar, and triangle sizes, as well as rail pieces and film-mounted mosaic patterns. A wide assortment of colors, shapes, and textures can be produced by special order. The manufacturer has certified the following recycled-content levels (by weight): total recovered material 100% typical, 100% guaranteed; post-consumer material 0% typical, 0% guaranteed.

UltraGlas

UltraGlas, Inc.
9200 Gazette Ave.
Chatsworth, CA 91311

Toll-free: 800-777-2332
Phone: 818-772-7744
www.ultraglas.com

UltraGlas® is sculpted/embossed, molded architectural glass with 15-30% recycled-glass (cullet) content. A variety of decorative textures, designs, and patterns are available with varying levels of translucency. If so specified, UltraGlas can be made from 100% recycled glass, subject to its availability.

Residential Cabinetry

Environmental features to look for with residential casework include FSC-certified or salvaged wood, recovered-fiber wood products, agrifiber panels, low-formaldehyde wood products, and low-VOC finishes. (Certification to Forest Stewardship Council—FSC—standards involves third-party evaluation and monitoring of sustainable forestry practices.) In some cases metal cabinets, which typically do not offgas, may be a good choice for those with chemical sensitivities. However, because of the lifecycle costs associated with mining and production, metal cabinets are generally not considered an environmentally preferred product.

Custom Furniture and Cabinets

NePalo Cabinetmakers
4328 Redwood Hwy., Ste. 400
San Rafael, CA 94903

Phone: 415-491-1403
www.NePalo.com

NePalo Cabinetmakers offers high-end custom furniture and cabinets made with FSC-certified hardwoods and FSC-certified, formaldehyde-free panels (in cherry, maple, and mahogany). Their products are made with waterproof, solvent-free glue and use environmentally responsible, hand-rubbed finishes, including linseed oil and beeswax. NePalo products can be shipped anywhere in the continental US.

FSC-Certified Cabinetry

Silver Walker Studios
P.O. Box 70667
Richmond, CA 94807

Phone: 510-215-1266
www.silverwalker.com

Silver Walker Studios provides custom-designed cabinetry in a variety of styles and finishes using only FSC-certified wood. The products use only low-VOC glues and finishes and are free of added formaldehyde.

FSC-Certified Cabinetry

Young Furniture Mfg., Inc.
35 River Rd.
Bow, NH 03225

Phone: 603-224-8830
www.youngfurnituremfg.com

Young Furniture manufactures unfinished FSC-certified eastern white pine, soft maple, and poplar cabinets, entertainment centers, and built-ins for kitchens, bathrooms, and living rooms. Solid wood backs and drawer bottoms can be used in place of plywood upon request. All cabinets are manufactured from domestic wood harvested and processed within a 500-mile radius of the manufacturing facility. Panels are joined with Franklin Adhesives Multibond 2000, a low-VOC (4.44 g/l) adhesive with no added formaldehyde. Direct jobsite delivery is available throughout the northeast U.S., with delivery to other regions upon special request.

Furniture and Kitchen Cabinetry from Urban Trees

CitiLog
P.O. Box 685
Pittstown, NJ 08867

Toll-free: 877-248-9564
Phone: 908-735-8871
www.citilogs.com

CitiLog™, also known as D. Stubby Warmbold, is SmartWood-certified for the harvesting of trees in urban areas of New Jersey and Pennsylvania. Wood is sent by rail to Amish craftsmen in central Pennsylvania who take extra care to turn the lesser graded wood into higher quality products such as flooring, lumber, custom architectural millwork, furniture, and kitchen cabinets. Where appropriate, wood is now harvested using horses.

Green Leaf Cabinetry

Green Leaf Cabinetry, LLC
P.O. Box 110875
Cleveland, OH 44111

Toll-free: 877-422-2463
www.greenleafcabinetry.com

Cabinet King's Green Leaf series uses PrimeBoard® agrifiber particleboard (made from agricultural residue fibers and a formaldehyde-free binder) for sides, tops, bottoms, backs, shelving, and drawer bottoms, and FSC-certified wood for frames and drawers (sides and backs). Finishes are either Safecoat® Acrylacq or PrimeBoard's all-paper-based melamine. Forbo Marmoleum® will also soon be available as a countertop option. Adhesives are water-based. Cabinet King is also a dealer for cabinets made by other companies, as well as a line of green building products including PrimeBoard, Marmoleum, Safecoat finishes, Titebond® solvent-free construction adhesive, and Bonded Logic recycled-cotton insulation.

Neil Kelly Naturals Collection

Neil Kelly Cabinets
2636 N.W. 26th Ave.
Ste. 200
Portland, OR 97210

Phone: 503-335-9207
www.neilkellycabinets.com

The Neil Kelly "Naturals Collection" is an award-winning cabinet line that features formaldehyde-free wheatboard case material, low-VOC finishes, and optional FSC-certified lumber doors/drawers. Unlimited customization and virtually any desired upgrade are available.

Reclaimed-Wood Building Products

Aged Woods / Yesteryear Floorworks Company
2331 E Market St, Ste 6
York, PA 17402

Toll-free: 800-233-9307
Phone: 717-840-0330
www.agedwoods.com

Aged Woods® / Yesteryear Floorworks Company is a full-service mill that uses reclaimed, kiln-dried wood to produce flooring, stair parts, moldings, cabinetry, and paneling. They salvage their materials from barns that are typically between 75 and 200 years old. Available species include American chestnut, longleaf heart pine, maple, cherry, walnut, hemlock, hickory, poplar, pine, and oak. Most of the flooring is 3/4" tongue-and-groove and of random widths and lengths within

given ranges. Matching stair parts are available in conjunction with flooring orders.

Schiffini Eco Panel Cabinets

Schiffini USA Sales
51 Locust Ave.
Ste. 201
New Canaan, CT 06840

Phone: 203-966-3234
www.schiffini.it

Designer-kitchen manufacturer Schiffini is a member of the Consorzio Pannello Ecologico, a group of companies employing panels made from FSC-certified, 100% post-consumer recycled wood. The reclaimed wood travels primarily by rail from a network of 30 European collection centers to the manufacturing facility in Italy. Formaldehyde emissions from the UF resin achieve European class E1 (releasing =0.13 mg/m3 air). Schiffini uses these panels for most of their wall-mount and base cabinets; the panels are mechanically fastened, without glue. Many of Schiffini's designs use facing components made from virgin aluminum, which has high embodied energy; those lines are not specified here.

Wheatboard Cabinets

CitiLog
P.O. Box 685
Pittstown, NJ 08867

Toll-free: 877-248-9564
Phone: 908-735-8871
www.citilogs.com

CitiLog™ offers cabinets made with formaldehyde-free wheatboard cores veneered in North American hardwoods or South American tropical woods, both FSC-certified. Wheatboard is similar to MDF and wood particleboard but is made with wheat stems left over after grain harvesting. These cabinets can be custom-manufactured to meet particular specifications. CitiLog also offers wheatboard millwork and doors.

Wheatcore Doors and Cabinets

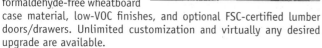

Humabuilt Healthy Building Solutions
2305-C Ashland St. #511
Ashland, OR 97520

Phone: 541-488-0931
www.humabuilt.com

Humabuilt Wheatcore Doors are available in a wide variety of styles, sizes, wood-veneer species, and paint-grade finishes. The core is made from chopped wheat straw bound with waterproof, nonformaldehyde, MDI binder. These doors contain 85% rapidly renewable resource by volume. Lag-bolt construction at the door edges strengthens the styles and rails. Ultra-low-VOC water-based adhesives are used for joining components and veneers. The competitively priced doors have a lifetime warranty to the original owner and a 5-year commercial warranty. Humabuilt Wheatcore production cabinets are available in a wide variety of styles, sizes, and wood-veneer species. These production cabinets are KCMA certified.

Textile Wall Coverings

Because large amounts of adhesive may be needed for some special wall coverings, low-VOC adhesives are a high priority. Products listed here include unusual wall covering products with recycled content or made of natural materials.

Abaca Wallcovering

Silk Dynasty Inc.
875 Maude Ave., Unit 1
Mountain View, CA 94043

Phone: 650-903-0078
www.silkdynasty.com

Silk Dynasty makes wallcovering from Abaca (banana plant fiber) that has been processed by hand, woven on hand looms, and held in place by cotton thread. Abaca is a fast-growing plant grown without synthetic fertilizer or pesticides that can be harvested several times a year, and it is biodegradable. These wallcoverings have a Class A fire rating and are available in a variety of colors and textures.

No-Flame Sisal Wallcovering

Design Materials, Inc.
241 S. 55th St.
Kansas City, KS 66106

Toll-free: 800-654-6451
Phone: 913-342-9796
www.dmikc.com

A natural fiber obtained from the Agave plant (Agave sisalana), sisal can be woven into durable, resilient, sound-absorbing, and tackable fabrics and textiles of various thicknesses. Its hydroscopic property helps modify a room's humidity without conducting static electricity. It can be directly applied to concrete masonry walls and other surfaces with a trowel-on adhesive. The sisal fiber for this product is treated with borax for fire retardance, dyed, spun into yarn, and woven into sheets with a boucle weave construction. The end-product is available in 12 colors. Design Materials also offers a zero-VOC adhesive.

Plaster in a Roll and Faster Plaster Underliner

Flexi-Wall Systems
208 Carolina Dr.
P.O. Box 89
Liberty, SC 29657

Toll-free: 800-843-5394
Phone: 864-843-3104
www.flexiwall.com

Plaster in a Roll™ is a 35-mil-thick jute fabric wall covering impregnated with gypsum plaster and a factory-applied clear coating. It comes in 48"-wide rolls and can be applied to any rigid wall or ceiling surface. It is available in two textures: Classics, available in 16 colors; and Images, available in 10 colors. Flexi-Wall Adhesive #500, used to adhere the product to the surface, also crystallizes the gypsum. Faster Plaster™ Underliner is a similar 50-mil wall liner designed to be adhered to concrete or masonry as a substrate for painting, plastering, or application of a finish wall covering.

Wall Covering

Textile and vinyl wall coverings are commonly used in commercial buildings for sound control and durability. Paper and vinyl "wallpaper" is widely used in homes. Avoiding vinyl (PVC) products is environmentally desirable for several reasons: interior finishes containing PVC can be a significant source of VOCs (tests have shown that VOC levels do drop off dramatically within weeks after installation); during disposal at the end of the wall covering's useful life, toxins (including dioxin) may be released if the material is incinerated improperly; combustion of PVC during accidental building fires can produce both dioxin and hydrochloric acid; phthalate plasticizers in many vinyl products, including wall coverings, are also increasingly being identified as health concerns, particularly due to their ability to mimic natural hormones; finally, most vinyl wall coverings have very low moisture permeability, and there is potential for mold growth if moisture is trapped behind these wall coverings. Using low-VOC adhesives is another important step in establishing good indoor air quality. Products listed here are synthetic and natural-fiber alternatives to PVC-based wall coverings.

DuraWeave

Roos International Ltd. Inc.
1020 N.W. 6th St., Ste. H
Deerfield Beach, FL 33442

Toll-free: 800-888-2776
Phone: 954-429-3883
www.roosintl.com

DuraWeave™ Wallcovering is a woven glass textile wall covering. Designed to be painted, DuraWeave is available in a large variety of textures and patterns and is washable (when painted), nontoxic, nonflammable, and repairable. DuraWeave allows walls to breathe and is particularly resistant to mold and mildew in high-moisture areas. DuraWeave can be applied to nearly all wall surfaces, providing additional reinforcement and bridging minor imperfections and cracks.

Innvironments Collection

Innovations in Wallcoverings, Inc.
150 Varick St.
New York, NY 10013

Toll-free: 800-227-8053
Phone: 212-807-6300
www.innovationsusa.com

The Innvironments® Collection is comprised of breathable, Class A fire-rated wall coverings manufactured from materials such as sisal, cellulose, honeysuckle vines, and cork using water soluble inks that contain no heavy metals. The Allegory® Series, which has a Type II wall covering rating, is made from 50% wood fiber and 50% spun-woven polyester. Because Allegory is permeable, it avoids IAQ problems associated with nonpermeable wall coverings associated with PVC-based products.

Moment

Roos International Ltd. Inc.
1020 N.W. 6th St., Ste. H
Deerfield Beach, FL 33442

Toll-free: 800-888-2776
Phone: 954-429-3883
www.roosintl.com

Moment is a sturdy (Type I) nonwoven, breathable wall covering designed expressly as an alternative to vinyl wall covering. A protective finish resists grease and stains while providing a scrubbable surface. Moment contains 38% cellulose fiber, 37% polyester, and 25% acrylic polymers; is entirely free of PVC and chlorine; and may be fully recycled. Moment is available in a range of 40 colors and carries a Class A fire rating.

Rauhsaser

Better Wall System
P.O. Box 567
Kenora, ON P9N 3X5 Canada

Toll-free: 800-461-2130
Phone: 807-548-2130

Rauhsaser (Rough Fiber), a thick wallpaper designed to be painted, is made from recycled paper with a wood chip texture. Five patterns are available. This product was previously sold in the U.S. under the name CoverAge.

Texturglas

Roos International Ltd. Inc.
1020 N.W. 6th St., Ste. H
Deerfield Beach, FL 33442

Toll-free: 800-888-2776
Phone: 954-429-3883
www.roosintl.com

Texturglas is a PVC-free woven glass textile wall covering that is durable, flame-retardant, washable (when painted), and repairable. Texturglas allows walls to breath and is suitable for high-moisture areas to reduce the risk of mold and mildew. This product can be applied to nearly all wall surfaces providing additional reinforcement and bridging minor imperfections and cracks. Available in a large variety of patterns and textures, Texturglas can be painted approximately 8 times without losing its texture and provides an estimated service life of over 30 years.

The South Seas Collection

Newcastle Fabrics Corp.
80 Wythe Ave.
Brooklyn, NY 11211

Toll-free: 800-404-5560
Phone: 718-782-5560
www.newcastlefabrics.com

The South Seas Collection is a series of wall coverings made from hand-woven natural fibers in a wide variety of patterns.

Wall Covering Adhesives

A large quantity of adhesive is required for wall coverings, especially when highly porous materials such as sisal are installed. Testing a small area of the covering with the chosen adhesive is recommended to determine whether offgassing or unpleasant odors will be a problem; this is especially important if any building occupants suffer from chemical sensitivity. Products listed here are low-VOC adhesives.

389 Natural Wallpaper Adhesive

Sinan Co. Environmental Products
P.O. Box 857
Davis, CA 95616

Phone: 530-753-3104
www.sinanco.com

Sinan 389 Natural Wallpaper Adhesive is sold in powder form to be mixed with water. It is suitable for up to medium-weight paper-based wall coverings. Sinan products are made from all-natural, primarily plant-based materials, all of which are listed on the packaging.

Wood Veneer

Products listed here come from FSC-certified or rapidly renewable sources. GreenSpec recognizes the Forest Stewardship Council (FSC) standards as the most rigorous and the only certification system with well-established chain-of-custody certification.

Bamboo Veneer and Paneling

DMVP Timber Bamboo Ltd.
De Marowijne 43
ZWAAG The Netherlands

Phone: 0031-229-265732
www.dmvpbamboo.com

DMVP's standard veneers have a cellulose fleece backing, which is bonded with a D3 water resistant PVAC glue. The cellulose backing can endure temperatures above 220 degrees Celsius.

In addition to single-ply veneers, DMVP produces multi-layer veneer panels by laminating multiple layers of veneer under high temperature, producing panels 1.5 mm or thicker.

DMVP also offers sandwich panels, with bamboo veneers laminated onto core panels, such as chipboard, plywood, MDF, or HDF.

DMVP is a joint venture between Hangzhou Liuzhuang floor Co., Ltd. and MVP International BV. MVP delivers veneer from the Netherlands to customers in Europe and the USA. DMVP distributes in the US, through various distributors, including M Bohlke Veneer Corporation of Fairfield, Ohio and General Woods & Veneers Ltd. of Québec, Canada.

Certified Lumber, Flooring, Wainscoting, and Veneer

McDowell Lumber Company, Inc.
Rte. 46 S
P.O. Box 148
Crosby, PA 16724

Phone: 814-887-2717
www.mcdowelllumber.com

McDowell Lumber deals in FSC-certified lumber, flooring, wainscoting, and veneer in over 15 species including red oak, cherry, hard and soft maple, ash, and a variety of other hardwoods harvested in Pennsylvania.

Certified Wood Products

Cascadia Forest Goods, LLC
38083 Wheeler Rd.
Dexter, OR 97431

Phone: 541-485-4477
www.cascadiaforestgoods.com

Cascadia Forest Goods (CFG) is a supplier of FSC-certified and re-cycled forest products, including hardwood and softwood veneers, dimensional lumber and decking, timbers and beams, siding, flooring, paneling, and trim. CFG's woods come from the Pacific Northwest and British Columbia, and include the following species: douglas fir, incense and western red cedar, sitka and englemann spruce, ponderosa and sugar pine, and regional hardwoods (madrone, white and black oak, broadleaf maple, alder, chinkapin, and myrtlewood). FSC-certified and recycled-forest-product flooring species include madrone, white oak, clear vertical grain (CVG) Douglas fir, birch, big-leaf maple, and myrtlewood. CFG also supplies FSC-certified flooring and decking from Central and South America, including Santa Maria, catalox, chechen negro, jobillo, machiche, ramon blanco, sauche, ipe, pucte (ironwood), and others. CFG offers both solid and engineered wood flooring. CFG also supplies both FSC-certified hardwood and softwood veneers and lumber to window and door manufacturers.

FSC-Certified Wood Products

Menominee Tribal Enterprises
Hwy. 47 N
P.O. Box 10
Neopit, WI 54150

Phone: 715-756-2311
www.mtewood.com

Menominee Tribal Enterprises (MTE) offers a full line of certified wood products harvested from the 220,000-acre Menominee Forest. MTE is continuing its development of value-added products from the 16 wood species harvested. Menominee forest lands were the first certified to FSC standards in North America.

Georgian Bay Wet Wood

Georgian Bay Wet Wood Inc.
8520 Highway 93
Midland, ON L4R 4K4 Canada

Phone: 705-526-6912
www.georgianbaywetwood.com

Georgian Bay Wet Wood Inc. recovers submerged old-growth timber from Ontario's Georgian Bay of Lake Huron then mills it to produce veneers, flooring, and lumber. Birch, beech, birds-eye maple, and flame birch are typically recovered. Heritage Timber Veneers are available in two species, Flame Birch and Birds Eye Maple. Heritage Timber Engineered Flooring has a nominal 1/8" (3.2mm) sawn veneer of recovered Maple, Birch, or Oak in 4" wide, random length boards with tongue and groove sides, micro-bevel edges, and a 9mm, 7-ply, FSC-certified Birch plywood core. The flooring is pre-finished with an aluminum oxide, UV-cured, urethane coating. Overall, the product has greater than 70% FSC-certified wood. Georgian Bay Wet Wood's wood products come with a certificate of authenticity that verifies that the product is genuine Georgian Bay Wet Wood.

Plyboo Bamboo Paneling, Plywood, and Veneer

Smith & Fong Company
475 6th St.
S. San Francisco, CA 94103

Toll-free: 866-835-9859
Phone: 415-896-0577
www.plyboo.com

Plyboo® tambour, fabric-backed, flexible paneling is available in a 3/16" x 48" x 96" size with either a sanded or "raw" surface. Sanded comes prefinished or unfinished in an amber or natural color. The "raw" paneling, which retains the outside skin of the bamboo and has a more rustic appeal, comes unfinished in a natural green/yellow, black, or amber color. Plyboo bamboo plywood comes in a variety of dimensions and sizes; in amber or natural color; and with either vertical or flat grain. Plyboo bamboo veneer has a vertical pattern in amber or natural color in 0.6 mm x 12" x 98". There is also a 1/8" bamboo veneer in a 48" x 96" size with a plywood backing. Veneers are provided with either paper or fleece backing. Playboo's plywood and veneers are also available as part of their PlybooPure line. These products use low-emitting, stable polyisocyanurate as the binder and contain no added urea formaldehyde.

Teragren Bamboo Flooring, Panels, and Veneer

Teragren LLC
12715 Miller Rd. NE, Ste. 301
Bainbridge Island, WA 98110

Toll-free: 800-929-6333
Phone: 206-842-9477
www.teragren.com

Teragren (formerly TimberGrass) manufactures solid strip bamboo flooring in tongue-and-groove or locking system, prefinished or site-finished. All flooring products are available in vertical or flat (horizontal) grains and natural or caramelized standard colors as well as stained cherry, walnut, charcoal and espresso colors. Coatings are water based and solvent free. The company uses the MOSO specie of bamboo which is harvested at maturity at 6 years. Teragren also manufactures coordinating stair parts, flooring accessories and vents, panels and veneer for cabinetry, furniture, interior paneling, countertops, and other interior applications as a direct replacement for wood sheet goods. (Note that while the adhesive used to manufacture the panels and veneer exceeds E1 standards, it is not food grade; if the surface is to be used for food preparation, a food grade sealer is recommended.)

Wood-Alternative Trim

This Space is Available for Your Notes

Pressures on timber supply are especially acute for high-visibility, solid-wood products like window sash and molding, which have traditionally been produced from old-growth trees. Molding made from plastic wastes is an excellent substitute for paint-grade moldings.

Timbron Molding

Timbron International, Inc.
1333 N. California Blvd., Ste. 545
Walnut Creek, CA 94596

Phone: 925-943-1632
www.timbron.com

Timbron produces interior molding in a variety of profiles made from at least 90% recycled polystyrene, along with small quantities of a coloring agent, a UV stabilizer, and a foaming agent. Timbron has earned certification from Scientific Certification Systems (SCS) for using a minimum of 75% post-consumer and 15% pre-consumer recycled material in its molding products, and claims the products are zero-VOC and recyclable. Timbron is highly durable, waterproof, termite-proof, paintable (though also suitable unpainted as white), and fully workable with carpentry tools.

Wood-Veneer Paneling

FSC-certified wood veneer panels are made with certified veneers on various cores. The greenest cores are made from certified wood, recovered wood, or straw particleboard. Wood products can carry the "FSC Mixed" label under a percentage-based standard based on actual product content or the average certified and non-certified throughput of the facility at which they are made. Urea-formaldehyde (UF), phenol-formaldehyde (PF), and methyl diisocyanate (MDI) binders are used in these materials, though UF is currently most common. UF binders can offgas significant concentrations of formaldehyde gas, a known carcinogen and an indoor air quality concern.

EarthSource Forest Products

EarthSource Forest Products/Plywood and Lumber Sales, Inc.
1618 28th St.
Oakland, CA 94608

Toll-free: 866-549-9663
Phone: 510-208-7257
www.earthsourcewood.com

EarthSource Forest Products, a division of Plywood and Lumber Sales, Inc., sells FSC-certified hardwood plywood and lumber of the following species: maple, cherry, red oak, white oak, ash, Honduras mahogany, walnut, machiche, amapola, and many more. EarthSource also sells salvaged and rediscovered lumber such as fir, redwood, and hickory.

Caulks & Adhesives

Caulks and adhesives are applied wet, and then dry or cure in place. During that process a carrier evaporates, leaving the active agents in place. For most products this carrier was traditionally a volatile organic solvent that turned into an airborne volatile organic compound (VOC) as it evaporated. Air quality regulations and health concerns have driven a shift toward waterborne products. Evaporating water isn't a health concern, though other components of the coating or adhesive still generally release some VOCs.

Caulks and adhesives have their greatest effect on indoor air quality during and immediately after installation. The health hazard is particularly acute for installers. Most conventional products offgas VOCs, formaldehyde, and other chemicals that are added to enhance the performance or extend shelf-life of the product. Little scientific data is available on the health effects of many of these chemicals—and even less on the effects of exposure to a *combination* of such chemicals that may occur in buildings. Quality substitutions, which are lower in toxicity or nontoxic, are available for all of these products.

Even so-called zero-VOC materials may still release small amounts of organic compounds. People with chemical sensitivities should always test these products before applying them on their projects, or having them applied by workers. Aside from solvents with well-known health effects (such as benzene, toluene, or xylene), the scientific community offers little guidance on the distinction between acceptable and problematic VOCs.

In most categories, the *GreenSpec* criteria for "low-VOC" products is 50 grams per liter, which is well below even the most stringent VOC regulations in California.

Glue-down carpets and resilient flooring should be applied only with low-VOC adhesives. Alternative carpet fastening methods should also be considered—these include:

- tackless strips, commonly used in residential settings;

- a hook-and-loop (Velcro®-type) tape system that allows sections of carpet to be lifted and re-attached as needed;

- peel-and-stick adhesive systems, such as those used on modular carpet tiles—the acrylic adhesives used on tiles are generally considered safer.

Caulk Joint Sealants

Environmental considerations for caulking materials include durability, potentially hazardous ingredients, and VOC content.

Chem-Calk 600 & 2000

Bostik, Inc.
211 Boston St.
Middleton, MA 01949

Toll-free: 800-366-7837
Phone: 978-777-0100
www.bostik-us.com

Chem-Calk 600 is a white, paintable, water based, siliconized acrylic latex caulk for general purpose architectural sealing. It is appropriate for interior and limited exterior applications, has 39 g/l VOC, and is available in tubes and 5-lb buckets. Chem-Calk 2000 is a modified single-component polyurethane caulk that is solvent- and isocyanate-free. This non-silicone, elastomeric sealant is moisture-curable and is appropriate for exterior architectural applications. It has less than 30 g/l VOC, and is available in tubes and in sausage packs that limit the amount of waste from empty tubes (ten 20-ounce sausage packs generate the same waste as one 10-ounce tube).

Liquid Nails Brand Supercaulk and Painter's Caulk

Macco Adhesives
15885 W. Sprague Rd.
Strongsville, OH 44136

Toll-free: 800-634-0015
Phone: 440-297-7304
www.liquidnails.com

Liquid Nails® Brand Super Caulk (LC130) is a water-based acrylic latex sealant that has a VOC content of 26.1 g/l. Liquid Nails Brand Painter's Caulk (LC135) is a water-based acrylic latex sealant that has a VOC content of 70 g/l.

Pecora Sealants

Pecora Corporation
165 Wambold Rd.
Harleysville, PA 19438

Toll-free: 800-523-6688
Phone: 215-723-6051
www.pecora.com

AC-20® + Silicone is a one-part, water-based acrylic/silicone sealant with a VOC content of 31 g/l. It is available in 11 standard colors. Pecora 864, 890, and 895 are all one-part silicone sealants with VOC contents of 12 g/l. Urexpan® NR-200 (two-part) and Urexpan NR-201 (one-part) are both polyurethane traffic-grade sealants. Both parts of NR-200 are zero-VOC. Pro-Silsct 1, at less than 15 g/l VOCs, is a one-part hybrid polymer sealant used for sealing perimeters, expansion joints, EIFS, etc.

Phenoseal and Sealant

Phenoseal
2400 Boston St., Ste. 200
Baltimore, MD 21224

Toll-free: 800-543-3840
www.phenoseal.com

Phenoseal is a vinyl acetate homopolymer-based adhesive caulk. (Note that vinyl acetate does not contain chlorine, so is very different from PVC.) This product is often tolerated by the environmentally sensitive. Uncured Phenoseal can be cleaned up with water. Sealant is a water-based acrylic latex window and door sealant.

Quick Shield VOC-Free Sealant

Geocel Corporation
P.O. Box 398
Elkhart, IN 46515

Toll-free: 800-348-7615
Phone: 574-264-0645
www.geocelusa.com

Quick Shield is a white, one-part, quick-setting, interior/exterior flexible sealant that contains no VOCs. It is resistant to water within 5 minutes and is paintable within 10 minutes. Quick Shield bonds to wood, aluminum, brick, and concrete without a primer. It cleans up with water, is mold- and mildew-resistant, and is rated to last 50 years.

Tremflex 834 and Tremco Spectrem 1

Tremco, Inc.
3735 Green Rd.
Company City
Beachwood, OH 44122

Toll-free: 800-852-8173
Phone: 216-292-5000
www.tremcosealants.com

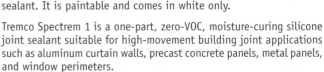

Tremflex 834 is a water-based, siliconized acrylic latex sealant with a VOC content of 13.7 g/l. It is mildew-resistant and can be used in bathrooms and kitchens, as well as for general interior and exterior caulking, as a back bedding glazing compound, and as an acoustical sealant. It is paintable and comes in white only.

Tremco Spectrem 1 is a one-part, zero-VOC, moisture-curing silicone joint sealant suitable for high-movement building joint applications such as aluminum curtain walls, precast concrete panels, metal panels, and window perimeters.

Duct Mastic

Duct leakage is a major problem with forced-air heating or air-conditioning systems. When ducts are run outside of the conditioned space, heating and cooling efficiencies may be cut in half due to leakage. Tightly sealed ducting is extremely important in ensuring high energy efficiency of forced-air HVAC equipment. Experts strongly recommend duct mastics—not duct tape—for sealing ducts.

Air Duct Closure Systems and Air Duct Sealants

RCD Corporation
2850 Dillard Rd.
Eustis, FL 32726

Toll-free: 800-854-7494
Phone: 352-589-0099
www.rcdmastics.com

RCD Corporation is a leading manufacturer of low-VOC air duct sealants, mastics, and weather barrier coatings.

Duct Sealants

Hardcast, Inc.
900 Hensley Ln.
P.O. Box 1239
Wylie, TX 75098

Toll-free: 800-527-7092
Phone: 888- 229-0199
www.hardcast.com

Hardcast manufactures a line of VOC-free and water-based duct sealants.

UNI-MASTIC 181 Duct Sealer

McGill Airseal Corporation
2400 Fairwood Ave.
Columbus, OH 43207

Toll-free: 800-624-5535
Phone: 614-443-5520
www.mcgillairseal.com

Uni-Mastic™ 181 duct sealer is a water-based product that is designed to remain flexible over time in applications including sheet-metal, flexible, and fiberglass duct. It is UL181 listed and contains antimicrobial agents that remain effective after curing.

Foam Joint Sealants

The challenge of sealing building envelopes against air infiltration is made easier with foam sealants. Look for products with blowing agents that are non-ozone-depleting and have low global-warming potential. Be aware that a label "no CFCs" is not the same as "ozone-safe"; HCFC propellants/blowing agents, while not as bad as CFCs, still deplete ozone. Foam sealants are commonly available in high-expanding and low-expanding formulations; low-expanding foam is the material of choice for sealing window and door rough openings—it performs significantly better than fiberglass and will be less likely than high-expanding foams to swell the openings (which can make opening and closing difficult). Foam sealants are useful in many applications, especially in building renovation. Some products are available only in disposable cans; the use of bulk tanks and reusable dispensing guns can reduce the environmental costs of using these sealants by minimizing waste.

CF 116 Grip Filler Foam

Hilti, Inc.
P.O. Box 21148
Tulsa, OK 74121

Toll-free: 866-445-8827
Phone: 918-252-6000
www.us.hilti.com

CF 116 is a single-component, polyurethane-based foam sealant propelled by HFC-134a, propane, and isobutane blowing agents. This minimally expanding product is dispensed from a can with a reusable gun. According to the company, one can is equivalent to 46 ten-ounce tubes of caulk.

PurFil 1G

Todol Products
25 Washington Ave.
P.O. Box 398
Natick, MA 01760

Toll-free: 800-252-3818
Phone: 508-651-3818
www.todol.com

PurFil 1G uses HFC-134a as its propellant and a mix of propane and isobutane as the blowing agent. It is available in disposable cans with application guns.

Touch'n Foam

Convenience Products
866 Horan Dr.
Fenton, MO 63026

Toll-free: 800-325-6180
Phone: 636-349-5333
www.convenienceproducts.com

Touch'n Foam is an HCFC-free foam sealant that uses a mixture of propane and isobutane as the blowing agent. It is available in triple-expanding or low-expanding formulations in disposable cans.

Preformed Joint Seals

Quality weatherstripping and gaskets are very important in achieving airtight, low-energy buildings. Specialized gaskets can also be used as a moisture-control strategy, as in the "Airtight Drywall Approach" for light-frame construction.

Weatherstripping and Gaskets

M-D Building Products
4041 N. Santa Fe Ave.
Oklahoma City, OK 73118

Toll-free: 800-654-8454
Phone: 405-528-4411
www.mdteam.com

M-D manufactures a wide range of weatherstripping and weatherization products.

Weatherstripping and Gaskets

Resource Conservation Technology, Inc.
2633 N. Calvert St.
Baltimore, MD 21218

Toll-free: 800-477-7724
Phone: 410-366-1146
www.conservationtechnology.com

Resource Conservation Technology specializes in building gaskets, weatherstripping, and air barriers.

Wood, Plastic, and Composite Fastenings

Adhesives are a significant potential source of indoor air quality concerns, so these products should be selected with care. Water-based adhesives have lower VOC emissions than solvent-based products. While some are sold as multipurpose, others are specific to particular applications. If a manufacturer recommends a low- or zero-VOC, water-based product for use with its material, then use that product; otherwise consider one known to minimize indoor air pollution. Products included here have VOC levels of 50 grams per liter or less. With mechanical fasteners, look for recycled content.

Construction Adhesives

ITW TACC
56 Air Station Industrial Pk.
Rockland, MA 02370

Toll-free: 800-503-6991
www.itwtacc.com

ITW TACC offers waterbased construction adhesive, duct sealant, and lag seal. T1168 is a multipurpose, nonflammable, synthetic-latex-emulsion, mastic-type construction adhesive particularly formulated for field-gluing subflooring; also appropriate for wallboard, paneling, and drywall, according to the manufacturer. (One surface must be porous.) It is also sold as Job Site Brand Miracle SFA-1168 Water Base; it contains 22.9 g/l of VOCs.

Maze Nails

Maze Nails
100 Church St.
Peru, IL 61354

Toll-free: 800-435-5949
www.mazenails.com

Maze Nails are made from domestic remelted steel in all standard and most specialty nail styles and sizes. Maze's Stormguard line of nails is galvanized with a double hot-dipped zinc coating for extra durability.

Speed Grip

Geocel Corporation
P.O. Box 398
Elkhart, IN 46515

Toll-free: 800-348-7615
Phone: 574-264-0645
www.geocelusa.com

Speed Grip construction adhesive—with a 100% VOC-free, chemically reactive formula—is suitable for use on a variety of porous and nonporous surfaces including plastic, wood, concrete, brick, plasterboard, carpet, and metal. This adhesive is intended for applications such as panel installation, sheathing, windows, and other building components. Speed Grip cleans up with water.

Titebond Solvent-Free Construction Adhesive

Franklin International
2020 Bruck St.
Columbus, OH 43207

Toll-free: 800-877-4583
Phone: 614-443-0241
www.titebond.com

Titebond® is a solvent-free, nonflammable construction adhesive that contains 6.6 g/l VOCs. Its performance is equivalent to conventional adhesives and can be used on most common building materials. Titebond complies with the requirements of the APA, AFG-01 test for subfloors as well as ASTM C557. It costs about 10% more than conventional solvent-based adhesives. Titebond is available in 10.5-ounce and 29-ounce sizes. The company also produces specialized solvent-free adhesives for such applications as subflooring, drywall, cove-base, and acoustical ceiling tile.

This Space is Available for Your Notes

Paints & Coatings

Paints and coatings are applied as a fluid, and they dry or cure in place. During that process a carrier evaporates, leaving the active agents in place. For most products this carrier was traditionally a volatile organic solvent that turned into an airborne volatile organic compound (VOC) as it evaporated. Air quality regulations and health concerns have driven a shift toward waterborne products. Evaporating water isn't a health concern, though other components of the coating or adhesive still generally release some VOCs.

Paints and coatings have their greatest effect on indoor air quality during and immediately after installation. The health hazard is particularly acute for installers. Most conventional products offgas VOCs, and other chemicals that are added to enhance the performance or extend shelf-life of the product. Little scientific data is available on the health effects of many of these chemicals—and even less on the effects of exposure to a *combination* of such chemicals that may occur in buildings. Quality substitutions, which are lower in toxicity or nontoxic, are available for all of these products.

Even so-called zero-VOC materials may still release small amounts of organic compounds. People with chemical sensitivities should always test these products before applying them on their projects, or having them applied by workers. Alternatives to conventional paints made from plant-based solvents may also release significant amounts of VOCs, but many people find these compounds less objectionable than those derived from petrochemicals. Aside from solvents with well-known health effects (such as benzene, toluene, or xylene), the scientific community offers little guidance on the distinction between acceptable and problematic VOCs.

In certain categories, the *GreenSpec* criteria for "low-VOC" products is 50 grams per liter, which is well below even the most stringent VOC regulations in California.

While wet-applied products emit the most VOCs immediately after curing, some continue to *offgas* such compounds for a long time. In addition, VOCs emitted during curing can become attached to other surfaces in the space, especially fabrics, and then be re-emitted over time. To reduce this problem, painting should be done with soft surfaces covered and direct ventilation provided until the coating is dry.

For wood-floor finishes, waterborne polyurethane is suggested. It contains no crosslinking agent—a type of chemical that adds hardness but is toxic. Waterborne finishes have been tested for durability, and many wear comparably to solvent-based ones. Installers often prefer waterborne finishing products because they dry quickly, allowing several coats to be applied in one day.

Coatings for Steel

Paints, rust inhibitors, and other coatings for steel have traditionally been lead-based and/or very high in VOCs. A few environmentally preferable products exist.

MetalCoat Acrylic Metal Primer

American Formulating & Manufacturing (AFM)
3251 Third Ave.
San Diego, CA 92103

Toll-free: 800-239-0321
Phone: 619-239-0321
www.afmsafecoat.com

MetalCoat Acrylic Metal Primer is a thermoplastic emulsion primer fortified with rust-inhibiting pigments. It is designed for use on steel, aluminum, and galvanized metal but is not recommended for copper. The product contains no hazardous chemicals and has a low-VOC content of 44 g/l (88 less water).

Decorative Finishes

Decorative finishes are typically high-grade, multicolored and/or textured coatings for interior and exterior applications. Textures and colors are achieved by proprietary mixtures of pigments, oils, and inorganic fillers. Such products offer a durable and environmentally preferable alternative to common vinyl wall coverings, which offgas plasticizers and pose heightened health risks during a fire or end-of-life incineration. Products listed here are waterborne and have relatively low-VOC content.

Aglaia Natural Finishes

Ecohaus
4121 1st Ave. South
Seattle, WA 98134

Toll-free: 800-281-9785
Phone: 206-682-7332
www.ecohaus.com

Aglaia Natural Finishes are biodegradable, plant- and mineral-based products free of petrochemicals and artificial resins. Available in Germany since the late 1960s and now being imported into North America, a variety of interior paints, stains, plasters, and texture coats are also offered. Note than some Aglaia products may have relatively high VOC levels (from plant-based materials), though others have zero VOC content.

Ferroxton-W, Crafton and Crafton Plus

Bollen International, Inc.
9218 Viscount Row
Dallas, TX 75247

Toll-free: 800-248-4808
Phone: 214-631-9300
www.bolleninternational.com

Ferroxton-W is a water-based metallic coating with a foundry-like texture for exterior or interior spray-on applications over metal, brick, concrete, sheetrock, or plaster. It has a VOC content of less than 60 g/l. Crafton and Crafton Plus are odorless, multicolor, water-based emulsion interior paints designed to provide a soft, fabric-like texture and can be applied to any substrate.

Exterior Paints

Paints for exterior surfaces may be listed here for a number of reasons, including minimal offgassing and superior durability. Included are mineral silicate paints that chemically react with mineral surfaces (stucco, plaster, concrete, etc.) in a process called petrification to form a highly durable finish. Mineral silicate paints can also be used indoors. Some listings may exceed 50 grams of VOC per liter; this threshold is anticipated to be adjusted down in future editions.

Best Duracryl Exterior Paint

Best Paint, Inc.
1728 Fourth Ave. S
Seattle, WA 98134

Phone: 206-783-9938
www.bestpaintco.com

Best Paint's Duracryl Exterior Paint is a 100% acrylic resin formula, which contains a low-toxic zinc compound for mold and mildew protection. Best Paint's water-based formula contains less than 50 g/l VOC (less water) and is manufactured for interior and exterior applications with a semi-gloss or eggshell finish. Duracryl Exterior Primer is also available. Suitable for wood, stucco, masonry, primed metal, and other typical surfaces.

Eco-House Mineral Silicate Paint

Eco-House, Inc.
P.O. Box 220, Stn. A
Fredericton, NB E3B 4Y9 Canada

Toll-free: 877-326-4687
Phone: 506-366-3529
www.eco-house.com

Eco-House, Inc. was the first manufacturer to produce mineral silicate paints in North America. The binder is potassium silicate dissolved in water (also known as "waterglass"), which petrifies when it chemically reacts with lime. Used on plaster, concrete, and other mineral surfaces, this product is not suitable for wood, metal, or any flexible surface. According to Eco-House, silicate paints are solvent-free, completely odorless after 1-2 days, made from widely available materials (water, quartz sand, potash, lime, and silicate minerals), naturally antimicrobial (not requiring fungicides), noncombustible at any temperature, and extremely durable.

Ecological Interior/Exterior Paint

Innovative Formulations Corporation
1810 S. Sixth Ave.
Tucson, AZ 85713

Phone: 520-628-1553
www.innovativeformulations.com

Ecological Paint is a line of professional-quality, odor-free, interior/exterior, zero-VOC, hypo-allergenic, water-based acrylic urethanes containing no known hazardous, toxic, or carcinogenic materials. Available with or without a mold inhibitor in semi-gloss, high-gloss, eggshell, satin, and flat. Clay paint and "direct-to-metal" paint are also available.

EverKote 300

Edison Coatings, Inc.
3 Northwest Dr.
Plainville, CT 06062

Toll-free: 800-697-8055
Phone: 860-747-2220
www.edisoncoatings.com

EverKote 300 is a waterborne, inorganic mineral-silicate coating made with a potassium silicate binder, sometimes known as "waterglass," that forms a chemical bond (petrifies) with suitable substrates. It is appropriate for application on calcareous stone (such as limestone or marble), masonry, concrete, cement plaster, ceramics, as well as on iron and other metals. EverKote 300 is extremely durable, non-flammable, UV-resistant, breathable, and naturally antimicrobial. It is available in two grades: low-viscosity, semi-transparent Penetral; and medium-viscosity, opaque Patinar. EverKote 300 comes in a flat (matte) finish in 900 standard colors; custom color matching is also available.

Heritage Series Coatings

Fuhr Industrial
6780 Exchange
Mansfield, TX 76063

Toll-free: 800-558-7437
Phone: 817-225-0083
www.fuhrinternational.com

Fuhr International's Heritage Series Low to Zero VOC Coatings include stains, sealers, and primers. Their waterbased stain is an acrylic wood stain for interior and exterior use suitable for a wide variety of applications, including kitchen cabinets, decks, and windows and doors. High Solids Clear Coat and Wax Seal & Finish waterbased acrylic products for interior and exterior wood substrates were designed for the kitchen cabinet industry and exceed KCMA finish-coat testing requirements with proper application. Sanding Sealer is a water-based acrylic sanding sealer designed as a companion product for their zero-VOC line.

Keim Mineral Silicate Paint

Cohalan Company, Inc.
102 Savannah Road
Lewes, DE 19958

Phone: 302-684-3299
www.keimmineralsystems.com

Keim Mineral Systems invented mineral silicate paints in Bavaria (Germany) in 1878, and Keim paints are widely used around the world today. The binder is potassium silicate dissolved in water (also known as "waterglass"). This is combined with inorganic fillers and natural earth oxide to produce an inorganic "liquid stone" finish through a process of petrification. Durability in excess of 100 years has been reported, according to Keim. Used on plaster, concrete, and other mineral surfaces; not suitable for wood, metal, or any flexible surface.

Available in both exterior and interior products, with 370 standard colors and over 38,000 recorded custom colors available. Keim mineral silicate paints are solvent-free, odorless, nontoxic, vapor-permeable, naturally resistant to fungi and algae, noncombustible, light-reflective, resistant to acid rain, and extremely durable. Keim Mineral Systems carries ISO 14001 certification.

Rodda Zero-VOC Paint

Rodda Paint
6107 N. Marine Dr.
Portland, OR 97203

Toll-free: 800-452-2315
Phone: 503-737-6033
www.roddapaint.com

Rodda Paint's Horizon line includes 42 different products in various finishes for interior, exterior, and priming applications. The interior products are nominally zero-VOC, with less than one gram of VOCs per liter. The Horizon line also includes the first exterior paint that meets Green Seal's GS-11 standard for coatings. Rodda is a founding member of the Oregon Natural Step Network, a statewide group of businesses working towards environmental sustainability.

Safecoat Exterior Satin Enamel

American Formulating & Manufacturing (AFM)
3251 Third Ave.
San Diego, CA 92103

Toll-free: 800-239-0321
Phone: 619-239-0321
www.afmsafecoat.com

Safecoat Exterior Satin Enamel contains no ammonia, formaldehyde, ethylene glycol, mildewcides, or fungicides. This premium exterior paint has a VOC content of 17 g/l (42 g/l less water), virtually no odor during application and none when dry, and a satin sheen. It is suitable for use on wood, stucco, aluminum, vinyl, and fully-cured concrete.

Silacote Mineral Silicate Paint

Silacote USA LLC
11265 Limekiln Rd.
Grass Valley, CA 95949

Toll-free: 800-249-1881
www.silacote.com

Silacote Mineral Silicate Paint is made from natural inorganic compounds such as quartz, other minerals, and mineral colorants with a potassium silicate binder. It is suitable for coating inorganic substrates such as concrete, lime plaster, marble, natural stone, brick, and new gypsum wallboard. For interior and exterior applications, Silacote is breathable, nontoxic, noncombustible, zero-VOC (including colorants), and will not support mold growth. This water-based product chemically bonds (petrifies) with the substrate, producing a coating with a life expectancy of 25 to 30+ years, according to the manufacturer. Silacote forms a microcrystalline structure that reflects light and heat. Fully tintable, with a large number of colors available; colors not affected by UV or acid rain.

Exterior Stains and Finishes

VOC emissions are the primary concern with exterior stains and finishes. Products listed here have low VOC levels, are derived from natural oils, or are biodegradable.

9400 and 9400W Impregnant

Palmer Industries, Inc.
10611 Old Annapolis Rd.
Frederick, MD 21701

Toll-free: 800-545-7383
Phone: 301-898-7848
www.palmerindustriesinc.com

9400 Impregnant is a water-repellent, UV-protective coating for masonry, concrete, and other cementitious materials, formulated without solvents for minimal toxicity. 9400W is a variant for wood surfaces.

BioShield Exterior Stains and Finishes

BioShield Paint Company
3215 Rufina Street
Santa Fe, NM 87507

Toll-free: 800-621-2591
Phone: 505-438-3448
www.bioshieldpaint.com

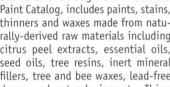

The BioShield product line, available online and through the BioShield Paint Catalog, includes paints, stains, thinners and waxes made from naturally-derived raw materials including citrus peel extracts, essential oils, seed oils, tree resins, inert mineral fillers, tree and bee waxes, lead-free dryers and natural pigments. Thinners are derived from low-toxic, non-petroleum-based ingredients.

Broda Pro-Tek-Tor

CBR Products
#102 - 876 Cordova DVSN
Vancouver, BC V6A 3R3
Canada

Toll-free: 888-311-5339
Phone: 604-254-3325
www.cbrproducts.com

Broda Pro-Tek-Tor Natural Oil Wood Finish is an oil-based, waterborne, non-film-forming, penetrating wood finish. This product needs only soap and water cleanup and is available in clear, transparent, semi-transparent, and semi-solid formulations. Mold and mildew resistance is provided by liquid microbiocides with low acute oral toxicity.

Envirolast XT

E3 Coatings, Inc.
813 Harbor Blvd. #163
Sacramento, CA 95691

Phone: 916-669-8498
www.envirolast.com

Envirolast XT™ is a zero-VOC, waterborne oil/alkyd emulsion sealer for interior and exterior wood surfaces. It provides a transparent, semi-transparent, or semi-solid pigmented finish, and may be applied over most existing wood finishes.

GCP 1000

Genesis Coatings, Inc.
2780 La Mirada Dr., Ste. D
Vista, CA 92081

Toll-free: 800-533-4273
Phone: 760-599-6011
www.genesiscoatings.com

GCP 1000 coating is an odorless, water-based, zero-VOC, two-part aliphatic polyurethane designed to be a high-performance general maintenance coating that is resistant to scuff marks and other unwanted markings. Genesis Coatings has also developed nontoxic, biodegradable graffiti removers: Graffiti Gold Remover, Graffiti Eaze Away, and Graffiti Terminator.

Heritage Series Coatings

Fuhr Industrial
6780 Exchange
Mansfield, TX 76063

Toll-free: 800-558-7437
Phone: 817-225-0083
www.fuhrinternational.com

Fuhr International's Heritage Series Low to Zero VOC Coatings include stains, sealers, and primers. Their waterbased stain is an acrylic wood stain for interior and exterior use suitable for a wide variety of applications, including kitchen cabinets, decks, and windows and doors. High Solids Clear Coat and Wax Seal & Finish waterbased acrylic products for interior and exterior wood substrates were designed for the kitchen cabinet industry and exceed KCMA finish-coat testing requirements with proper application. Sanding Sealer is a water-based acrylic sanding sealer designed as a companion product for their zero-VOC line.

Safecoat DuroStain

American Formulating & Manufacturing (AFM)
3251 Third Ave.
San Diego, CA 92103

Toll-free: 800-239-0321
Phone: 619-239-0321
www.afmsafecoat.com

Safecoat® DuroStain is a premium fast-curing, flat-finish, semi-transparent interior/exterior wood stain. It contains no aniline dyes, gilsonite, asphalt, aromatic solvents, or formaldehyde, and has a VOC content of 100 g/l (349 g/l less water).

SoySeal Wood Sealer

Natural Soy, LLC
P.O. Box 489
123 N. Orchard St.
Brooklyn, IA 52211

Toll-free: 888-606-9559
Phone: 641-522-9559
www.soyclean.biz

SoySeal is a water-based, nontoxic, nonflammable sealer suitable for exposed wood surfaces. It contains no VOCs or other known user hazards and cleans up with water. This product spreads water rather than beading it, which reduces the risk of UV magnification and damage, according to Natural Soy. Coverage is 150 to 300 ft2. This product complies with ASTM C-672 and is also used to seal concrete. It is available in 1-, 5-, 55-, and 250-gallon containers.

Timber Pro Natural Wood Stains

Timber-Pro UV
2232 E. Burnside
Portland, OR 97214

Toll-free: 888-888-6095
Phone: 503-232-1705
www.timberprocoatings.com

Timber Pro Natural Wood Stains are waterborne, non-petroleum, plant-oil based finishes containing less than 93 g/l of VOCs. The Crystal Urethane product line is also made with rapidly renewable plant oils (safflower and tall oil), with VOC levels of 145 g/l. These finishes are appropriate for use on cedar, redwood, cypress, pine, fir, and all products made from softwoods such as log homes, wood siding, decks, fences, and shakes and shingles.

Weather-Bos Finishes

Weather-Bos International
316 California Ave., Ste. 1082
Reno, NV 89509

Toll-free: 800-664-3978
www.weatherbos.com

Weather-Bos transparent finishes are made from natural, nontoxic vegetable oils and resins as well as other natural ingredients. These finishes are low-odor, water-reducible, nonflammable, and free of harmful fungicides. The small amount of pigment in some formulas provides UV protection. The Boss™ is the company's original all-purpose wood finish; Deck Boss™ protects and weatherproofs wood decks; and Log Boss™ is for use on log homes.

Zar Exterior Polyurethane

United Gilsonite Laboratories (UGL)
P.O. Box 70
Scranton, PA 18501

Toll-free: 800-845-5227
Phone: 570-344-1202
www.ugl.com

Zar Exterior Water-Based Polyurethane is an amber-colored protective finish for exterior wood surfaces as well as fiberglass and metal entry doors. The product contains ultraviolet-radiation inhibitors to provide additional protection from UV rays.

Interior Paints

A primary consideration for most interior paints is their potential impact on occupant health. To this end, very-low-VOC or zero-VOC paints are generally preferred, though some chemically sensitive people find that even these can be difficult to tolerate. Note that liquid carriers (including water and exempt VOCs) are usually excluded when stating VOC levels, which are expressed as grams of VOC per liter of VOC-plus-paint-solids. Most zero-VOC paints still use colorant systems that contain VOCs, so custom-coloring will increase emissions. Some paints are made from minimally processed plants and minerals; while these products may contain relatively high levels of VOCs, they may not be as troublesome as the compounds released from petrochemical-based paints. Products listed here contain less than 50 grams of VOCs per liter and may include other environmental features.

Aglaia Natural Finishes

Ecohaus
4121 1st Ave. South
Seattle, WA 98134

Toll-free: 800-281-9785
Phone: 206-682-7332
www.ecohaus.com

Aglaia Natural Finishes are biodegradable, plant- and mineral-based products free of petrochemicals and artificial resins. Available in Germany since the late 1960s and now being imported into North America, a variety of interior paints, stains, plasters, and texture coats are also offered. Note than some Aglaia products may have relatively high VOC levels (from plant-based materials), though others have zero VOC content.

Air-Care Odorless Paints

Coronado Paint Company
308 Old County Rd.
Edgewater, FL 32132

Toll-free: 800-883-4193
Phone: 386-428-6461
www.coronadopaint.com

The Air-Care line consists of Odorless Acrylic Primer, Odorless Acrylic Flat, Odorless Acrylic Eggshell, and Low Odor Acrylic Semi-Gloss. All these formulations are zero-VOC, though colorants add some VOCs.

American Pride High Performance, Low VOC

Southern Diversified Products, LLC
2714 Hardy St.
Hattiesburg, MS 39401

Toll-free: 1-888-714-9422
Phone: 601-264-0442
www.americanpridepaint.com

Southern Diversified Products is manufacturing a line of interior latex paints called "American Pride" that is based on technology by polymer science researchers at the University of Southern Mississippi. American Pride has a VOC content of 0-5 g/l and virtually no smell, allowing interior painting without evacuating a building or providing additional ventilation. The paint is the second to be certified under the paint standard by the independent nonprofit Green Seal and, according to the organization, performs well compared to other high-end interior latex paints, while being priced competitively with them. American Pride's flat white has a scrub rating of 2,500 strokes (ASTM D2486-89), while its eggshell white withstood 3,100 strokes. The paints are currently for sale at independent dealers throughout the United States.

Best Paints

Best Paint, Inc.
1728 Fourth Ave. S
Seattle, WA 98134

Phone: 206-783-9938
www.bestpaintco.com

Best Paint's Interior and Breathe-EZ products are Zero VOC, with no biocide and low to no odor. They are available in flat, satin, eggshell, and semi-gloss in a wide range of colors.

BioShield Interior Paint

BioShield Paint Company
3215 Rufina Street
Santa Fe, NM 87507

Toll-free: 800-621-2591
Phone: 505-438-3448
www.bioshieldpaint.com

The BioShield product line, available online and through the BioShield Paint Catalog, includes paints, stains, thinners and waxes made from naturally-derived raw materials including citrus peel extracts, essential oils, seed oils, tree resins, inert mineral fillers, tree and bee waxes, lead-free dryers and natural pigments. Thinners are derived from low-toxic, non-petroleum-based ingredients.

Devoe Wonder Pure, Dulux LifeMaster, Prep & Prime

ICI Paints
15885 W. Sprague Road
Strongsville, OH 44136

Toll-free: 800-984-5444
Phone: 216-344-8000
www.iciduluxpaints.com

The Wonder-Pure line of Devoe Paint, manufactured by Glidden, is zero-VOC. The line includes primer, interior flat, eggshell, and semi-gloss. They are available only through independent Glidden dealers. LifeMaster interior latex paints have zero-VOC content and are available in flat, eggshell, and semi-gloss finishes. Prep & Prime Odor-Less Primer Sealer is a zero-VOC tintable primer and sealer for interior use. Prep & Prime Vapor Barrier Interior Primer/Sealer is a latex primer-sealer formulated to reduce the permeability of wall surfaces. It is low-VOC (85 g/l) and tintable; it may also be topcoated with latex or alkyd paints of any finish. This product has a perm rating of 0.6 when applied at a coverage rate of 400 ft2/gal to smooth surfaces, which compares favorably with the performance of a 2-mil-thick sheet of medium-density polyethylene.

Eco-Spec

Benjamin Moore & Co.
101 Paragon Dr.
Montvale, NJ 07645

Toll-free: 866-708-9181
Phone: 201-573-9600
www.benjaminmoore.com

Eco-Spec® is a low-VOC 100% acrylic latex interior paint available in primer/sealer, flat, eggshell, and semi-gloss. The product line is for the professional contractor market.

EnviroKote Interior Low Odor Paint

Frazee Paint
6625 Miramar Rd.
San Diego, CA 92121

Toll-free: 800-477-9991
Phone: 858-626-3600
www.frazeepaint.com

EnviroKote paint is a very-low-VOC acrylic latex available in flat, eggshell, and semi-gloss formulations. White and medium-tint base paints are available.

EnviroSafe Paint

EnviroSafe Paint Company
HC 32 Box 122
Uvalde, TX 78801

Toll-free: 888-281-6467
www.envirosafepaint.com

EnviroSafe zero-VOC paints are available in flat, satin, and semi-gloss for interior use, and satin for exterior use. The product line uses a grapefruit-derived low-toxic preservative, so shelf life is guaranteed for only one year.

Eurolux Waterborne Paints and Varnishes

Fine Paints of Europe
P.O. Box 419
Woodstock, VT 05091

Toll-free: 800-332-1556
Phone: 802-457-2468
www.finepaintsofeurope.com

Eurolux waterborne varnishes and acrylic paints are made in Holland. The varnishes have less than 60 g/l VOCs, and the paints less than 30 g/l. These are durable, high-quality coatings at a premium price.

Everfresh Paint

Mercury Paint Corporation
4808 Farragut Rd.
Brooklyn, NY 11203

Toll-free: 800-858-8787
Phone: 718-469-8787
www.mercurypaint.com

Mercury Paint's Everfresh zero-VOC 100% acrylic latex interior paint is available in primer (5900), flat (6900), eggshell (9150), and semi-gloss (8900). Everfresh paint is free of lead, mercury and chromate compounds. Colorants may contain VOCs.

Gold Label Premium Enviro Paints

Spectra-tone Paint Company
1595 E. San Bernardino Ave.
San Bernardino, CA 92408

Toll-free: 800-272-4687
Phone: 909-478-3485
www.spectra-tone.com

Gold Label Premium Enviro Paints for interior use are VOC-free and come in flat (#410), low-lustre enamel (#8800), and semi-gloss (#9900). The product line is made with a terpolymer resin that may not be as durable as acrylic latex resins.

Harmony Interior Latex Coating

The Sherwin-Williams Company Stores Group
101 Prospect Ave. NW
Cleveland, OH 44115

Toll-free: 800-524-5979
Phone: 216-566-2000
www.sherwin-williams.com

Harmony Interior Latex Flat, Eg-Shel, Semi-Gloss, and Primer provide a durable, low-odor, anti-microbial, interior paint system formulated without silica. These products can be used, without typical odor complaints, in occupied areas because of the very low odor during application and drying. The Harmony line contains zero-VOCs.

Heritage Series Coatings

Fuhr Industrial
6780 Exchange
Mansfield, TX 76063

Toll-free: 800-558-7437
Phone: 817-225-0083
www.fuhrinternational.com

Fuhr International's Heritage Series Low to Zero VOC Coatings include stains, sealers, and primers. Their waterbased stain is an acrylic wood stain for interior and exterior use suitable for a wide variety of applications, including kitchen cabinets, decks, and windows and doors. High Solids Clear Coat and Wax Seal & Finish waterbased acrylic products for interior and exterior wood substrates were designed for the kitchen cabinet industry and exceed KCMA finish-coat testing requirements with proper application. Sanding Sealer is a water-based acrylic sanding sealer designed as a companion product for their zero-VOC line.

Kelly-Moore Enviro-Cote

Kelly-Moore Paint Co.
5101 Raley Blvd.
Sacramento, CA 95838

Toll-free: 800-874-4436
Phone: 916-921-0165
www.kellymoore.com

Kelly-Moore Enviro-Cote acrylic satin enamel paint is zero-VOC, their Acry-prime has a maximum VOC content of 15 g/l, semi-gloss enamel has a maximum VOC content of 6 g/l, and flat finish paints have VOC contents of less than 13 g/l.

Kurfees Fresh Air

Progress Paint Manufacturing Co., Inc.
201 E. Market St.
P.O. Box 33188
Louisville, KY 40202

Toll-free: 800-626-6407
Phone: 502-587-8685
www.progresspaint.com

Kurfees Fresh Air interior paint has a calculated maximum VOC content of 24 g/l and is available in flat, eggshell, and satin finishes or as primer.

Milk Paint

Old Fashioned Milk
Paint Co.
436 Main St.
P.O. Box 222
Groton, MA 01450

Toll-free: 866-350-6455
Phone: 978-448-6336
www.milkpaint.com

Milk Paint is a powdered paint made from casein (milk protein) mixed with lime, clay, and earth pigments. Water is added to make a pint, quart, or gallon size. It is available in 20 historical colors, which can be blended or tinted. Milk Paint is marketed primarily as a paint for wood furniture or other porous surfaces such as bare masonry; however, different additives and clear sealers can be used to enhance durability and adhesion to nonporous surfaces. Although Milk Paint contains a natural mildewcide, the use of a clear sealer over the paint in damp areas such as bathrooms is recommended to prevent waterspotting and for washability. In fall 2007 a new line of organic milk paint specifically for walls is being introduced, called SafePaint, which sticks to many surfaces such as painted and primed walls and new sheetrock with joint compound, and has greater water resistance than the traditional formula for porous surfaces.

Murco LE-1000 and GF-1000

Murco Wall Products
2032 N. Commerce
Fort Worth, TX 76164

Toll-free: 800-446-7124
Phone: 817-626-1987
www.murcowall.com

Murco paints are water-based, low-VOC, latex products for interior use, popular with chemically sensitive individuals. Available in flat (GF-1000) and high-gloss (LE-1000).

Natural Paints

Sinan Co. Environmental Products
P.O. Box 857
Davis, CA 95616

Phone: 530-753-3104
www.sinanco.com

Sinan natural interior paint products include primers, a professional wall paint (satin only), and a milk paint in powder form. Manufactured in white, they can be tinted using a concentrate available in 8 earth-tone colors. Sinan products are made from all-natural, primarily plant-based materials, all of which are listed on the packaging.

Pure Performance

PPG Architectural Finishes
One PPG Pl.
Pittsburgh, PA 15272

Toll-free: 800-441-9695
Phone: 412-434-3131
www.ppgaf.com

PPG Architectural Finishes sells Pure Performance zero-VOC interior latex paint under its Pittsburgh Paints brand. A full range of sheens can be tinted to any Pittsburgh Paints color (tints contribute a minimal amount of VOCs—2 g/l maximum). Pure Performance, which replaced the company's second-to-the-top Wallhide line, is the first paint certified under the Green Seal standard and meets the special "Class A" rating reserved for zero-VOC paints. PPG claims that the Pure Performance line, made with vinyl acetate ethylene resin, is the first to offer zero-VOC with no compromise on durability and at a price similar to that of conventional paints.

Rodda Zero-VOC Paint

Rodda Paint
6107 N. Marine Dr.
Portland, OR 97203

Toll-free: 800-452-2315
Phone: 503-737-6033
www.roddapaint.com

Rodda Paint's Horizon line includes 42 different products in various finishes for interior, exterior, and priming applications. The interior products are nominally zero-VOC, with less than one gram of VOCs per liter. The Horizon line also includes the first exterior paint that meets Green Seal's GS-11 standard for coatings. Rodda is a founding member of the Oregon Natural Step Network, a statewide group of businesses working towards environmental sustainability.

Safecoat Interior Paints

American Formulating & Manufacturing (AFM)
3251 Third Ave.
San Diego, CA 92103

Toll-free: 800-239-0321
Phone: 619-239-0321
www.afmsafecoat.com

Safecoat Zero-VOC interior paints in flat, eggshell, and semi-gloss have little odor when wet and none when dry. None of these paints contains formaldehyde, ammonia, crystalline silica, or ethylene glycol, and they are tinted using zero-VOC colorants. Safecoat Enamels are low-VOC, do not contain extenders, heavy-metal drying agents, formaldehyde, acetone, or heavy-duty preservatives. They are available in a variety of finishes and can be tinted to virtually any color. Safecoat paints have long been used by people with chemical sensitivities.

Sico Design Paints

Sico, Inc.
2505 de la Metropole
Longueuil, QC J4G 1E5 Canada

Toll-free: 800-463-7426
www.sico.ca

Sico, Inc.'s Design product—made up of Cashmere, Chamois, and Shantung—is a line of odor-free, zero-VOC paints. This 100% acrylic latex paint is available in a range of finishes in 1,680 colors, and is certified by Green Seal®. Sico paints are primarily distributed in Canada.

The Real Milk Paint Co.

The Real Milk Paint Co. LLC
11 West Pumping Station Rd.
Quakertown, PA 18951

Toll-free: 800-339-9748
Phone: 215-538-3886
www.realmilkpaint.com

The Real Milk Paint Company's Real Milk Paint is derived from purified milk protein, lime, natural fillers, and nontoxic lead-free pigments. Real Milk Paint comes ready to be mixed with water for a desired consistency from thin wash to thick paint. Once mixed with water, the paint will remain usable from 2 to 4 weeks. Real Milk Paint is virtually odorless during application and drying, and contains no VOCs.

Yolo Colorhouse Paint

YOLO Colorhouse LLC
1001 S.E. Water Ave., Ste. 140
Portland, OR 97214

Toll-free: 877-493-8275
www.yolocolorhouse.com

YOLO Colorhouse is a collection of Green-Seal-certified, zero-VOC, latex interior paint, available in primer, flat, satin, and semigloss. 40 colors are offered, with poster-sized swatches available for purchase.

Zero-VOC Premium Interior Line

Olympic Paint and Stain
PPG Architectural Finishes, Inc.
PPG World Headquarters, One PPG Place
Pittsburgh, PA 15272

Toll-free: 800-441-9695
Phone: 412-434-3131
www.ppg.com

Olympic's zero-VOC Premium Interior Paint, made by PPG Architectural Finishes, is available at Lowes Hardware Centers and includes four standard sheens and two specialty interior paints. 1,224 standard colors are available as well as custom colors to match other paints. The paint is Green Seal certified, meeting Green Seal's GS-11 standard for coatings.

Interior Stains and Finishes

In recent years, polyurethane and other clear interior finishes have dramatically decreased the amount of volatile organic compounds (VOCs) that they offgas. Waterborne polyurethanes are becoming common alternatives to conventional solvent-based products. Low-VOC stains are also becoming available. Products listed here have low VOC levels, are derived from natural materials, are biodegradable, or have exceptional durability.

Aglaia Natural Finishes

Ecohaus
4121 1st Ave. South
Seattle, WA 98134

Toll-free: 800-281-9785
Phone: 206-682-7332
www.ecohaus.com

Aglaia Natural Finishes are biodegradable, plant- and mineral-based products free of petrochemicals and artificial resins. Available in Germany since the late 1960s and now being imported into North America, a variety of interior paints, stains, plasters, and texture coats are also offered. Note than some Aglaia products may have relatively high VOC levels (from plant-based materials), though others have zero VOC content.

Aqua ZAR

United Gilsonite Laboratories (UGL)
P.O. Box 70
Scranton, PA 18501

Toll-free: 800-845-5227
Phone: 570-344-1202
www.ugl.com

Aqua ZAR® Water-Based Polyurethane is a low-odor, nonyellowing, clear interior wood finish available in gloss and satin. According to the manufacturer, Aqua Zar's fast-drying, low-odor formula resists most household chemicals and abrasions.

BioShield Interior Stains and Finishes

BioShield Paint Company
3215 Rufina Street
Santa Fe, NM 87507

Toll-free: 800-621-2591
Phone: 505-438-3448
www.bioshieldpaint.com

The BioShield product line, available online and through the BioShield Paint Catalog, includes paints, stains, thinners and waxes made from naturally-derived raw materials including citrus peel extracts, essential oils, seed oils, tree resins, inert mineral fillers, tree and bee waxes, lead-free dryers and natural pigments. Thinners are derived from low-toxic, non-petroleum-based ingredients.

Envirolast XT

E3 Coatings, Inc.
813 Harbor Blvd. #163
Sacramento, CA 95691

Phone: 916-669-8498
www.envirolast.com

Envirolast XT™ is a zero-VOC, waterborne oil/alkyd emulsion sealer for interior and exterior wood surfaces. It provides a transparent, semi-transparent, or semi-solid pigmented finish, and may be applied over most existing wood finishes.

Eurolux Waterborne Paints and Varnishes

Fine Paints of Europe
P.O. Box 419
Woodstock, VT 05091

Toll-free: 800-332-1556
Phone: 802-457-2468
www.finepaintsofeurope.com

Eurolux waterborne varnishes and acrylic paints are made in Holland. The varnishes have less than 60 g/l VOCs, and the paints less than 30 g/l. These are durable, high-quality coatings at a premium price.

Heritage Series Coatings

Fuhr Industrial
6780 Exchange
Mansfield, TX 76063

Toll-free: 800-558-7437
Phone: 817-225-0083
www.fuhrinternational.com

Fuhr International's Heritage Series Low to Zero VOC Coatings include stains, sealers, and primers. Their waterbased stain is an acrylic wood stain for interior and exterior use suitable for a wide variety of applications, including kitchen cabinets, decks, and windows and doors. High Solids Clear Coat and Wax Seal & Finish waterbased acrylic products for interior and exterior wood substrates were designed for the kitchen cabinet industry and exceed KCMA finish-coat testing requirements with proper application. Sanding Sealer is a waterbased acrylic sanding sealer designed as a companion product for their zero-VOC line.

Land Ark Wood Finishes

Land Ark Wood Finishes
213 Townes Rd.
N. Augusta, SC 29860

Phone: 803-279-4116

Land Ark wood finishes are formulated for use on timber frames as well as both exterior and interior finish applications. These finishes—including tung oil, linseed oil, beeswax, D-limonene (cold-pressed from orange peels), and resin (from pine trees)—have no chemical additives, petroleum products, or heavy-metal driers and are completely biodegradable.

OSMO Hardwax Oil

Environmental Home Center
4121 1st Ave. S
Seattle, WA 98134

Toll-free: 800-281-9785
Phone: 206-682-7332
www.environmentalhomecenter.com

OSMO Hardwax Oil®, formerly known as OS Hardwax Oil, is a penetrating floor finish made from natural vegetable oils and waxes, and contains no biocides or preservatives. Because OSMO is very high in solids, it can be applied in only two coats and is very durable. The finish may also be spot-repaired.

Penofin

Performance Coatings, Inc.
360 Lake Mendocino Dr.
P.O. Box 1569
Ukiah, CA 95482

Toll-free: 800-736-6346
Phone: 707-462-3023
www.penofin.com

Penofin is a low-VOC, semi-transparent, penetrating oil finish. The main ingredient is Brazilian rosewood oil—made from the harvested nut of this tree, not the wood. Performance Coatings reduced the VOC levels of Penofin in advance of the 2002 standard of 250 g/l adopted in California, and the product also meets all National AQ standards.

Pure Tung Oil

The Real Milk Paint Co. LLC
11 West Pumping Station Rd.
Quakertown, PA 18951

Toll-free: 800-339-9748
Phone: 215-538-3886
www.realmilkpaint.com

The Real Milk Paint Company's 100% Pure Tung Oil contains no petroleum distillates or other additives and has a light, nutty odor. Tung oil, which comes from the seed of the tung tree, is a suitable treatment for wood and stone, forming a tough, flexible, water- and alkali-resistant coating. Pure Tung Oil produces a nontoxic finish that is suitable for food preparation surfaces. Other applications include children's toys and furniture, wooden instruments, and wood paneling and molding. A light coating on metal surfaces acts as an effective rust inhibitor.

Safecoat Clear Finishes

American Formulating & Manufacturing (AFM)
3251 Third Ave.
San Diego, CA 92103

Toll-free: 800-239-0321
Phone: 619-239-0321
www.afmsafecoat.com

Hard Seal is a clear finish for highly porous surfaces including bare wood, cabinetry, vinyl or porous tile, or previously painted surfaces; it forms a tight membrane to reduce offgassing from walls, ceilings, and floors. Hard Seal is formaldehyde-free, nonflammable, low-odor, and has a VOC content below 72 g/l (less water). It is not for use on surfaces subject to standing water, heavy moisture, or unsealed particleboard. Acrylacq is a clear, water-based replacement for solvent-based lacquers that creates a hard, high-gloss or satin finish over wood, galvanized or properly primed metal, or plastics. AcriGlaze is a clear, odorless, mildew-resistant mixing medium and finish for faux finishing, sealing pigmented plaster, or restoring old finishes.

Safecoat Safe Seal and SafeChoice Carpet Seal

American Formulating & Manufacturing (AFM)
3251 Third Ave.
San Diego, CA 92103

Toll-free: 800-239-0321
Phone: 619-239-0321
www.afmsafecoat.com

Safe Seal is a clear sealer designed to limit offgassing from particleboard and other manufactured wood products containing formaldehyde. It lends water repellency and serves as the base coat for adhesives and finishes on porous surfaces, including wood and concrete products. SafeChoice® Carpet Seal is designed to help prevent the offgassing from synthetic carpet backing and adhesives. Applied directly after shampooing carpet, Carpet Seal cures into a clear membrane. According to the company, Carpet Seal is odorless and remains effective for up to a year, depending on traffic and cleaning frequency. It cannot be applied to wool carpet.

Sinan 160 Series Natural Stain

Sinan Co. Environmental Products
P.O. Box 857
Davis, CA 95616

Phone: 530-753-3104
www.sinanco.com

Sinan products are made from all-natural, primarily plant-based materials, all of which are listed on the packaging. Sinan 160 Series Natural Stain is available in 12 earth-tone colors and can be thinned using purified water.

Sutherland Welles Low-Toxic Wood Finishes

Sutherland Welles Ltd.
P.O. Box 180
North Hyde Park, VT 05665

Toll-free: 800-322-1245
Phone: 802-635-2700
www.tungoilfinish.com

Sutherland Welles Low-Toxic Wood Finishes are polymerized tung oils with natural Di-Citrusol™ solvent and reduced chemical driers. The products are botanicals, free of petroleum distillates, and are available in various lustres and as a sealer. Performance and coverage of the low-toxic products are comparable to those features of conventional lines, according to the company. Millie's All Purpose Penetrating Wood Oil is formulated with polymerized tung oil, Di-Citrusol™ and beeswax; no chemical driers are added. All the botanical products are formulated from 99.4% tree-derived raw materials that also contribute to ozone renewing. The Di-Citrusol™ is formulated using oil extracted from discarded citrus peels used by the juice industry.

Tried & True Wood Finishes

Tried & True Wood Finishes
14 Prospect St.
Trumansburg, NY 14886

Phone: 607-387-9280
www.triedandtruewoodfinish.com

Tried & True™ Wood Finishes are made from polymerized linseed oil through a proprietary heat treatment process. Original Wood Finish includes beeswax. Varnish Oil includes varnish resin (hardened tree sap). All are nontoxic with zero VOCs and no heavy-metal driers. The ingredients are derived from renewable agricultural resources. By contrast, conventional "boiled" linseed oil finishes typically include toxic, heavy-metal drying agents.

Tried & True finishes are appropriate for a wide range of applications from interior millwork to fine furniture. Application labor costs are similar to those for conventional products. The Danish Oil Finish may also be used as a rammed-earth floor finish, while the Varnish Oil may be used as a concrete countertop sealant as well as a sealer for terra cotta and thrown-tile products.

Mastic Removers

Products listed here include low-VOC, nontoxic, and biodegradable mastic removers.

BEAN-e-doo Mastic Remover

Franmar Chemical, Inc.
P.O. Box 5565
Bloomington, IL 61702

Toll-free: 800-538-5069
Phone: 309-452-7526
www.franmar.com

FranMar's BEAN-e-doo® Mastic Remover is made from soybeans to remove ceramic tile mastic, asbestos mastic, and carpet mastic. BEANedoo Mastic Remover has no odor, is nontoxic, noncaustic, 100% biodegradable, and rinses with water.

Moisture Proofing

Products listed here help prevent moisture from penetrating the envelope.

Astec Coatings

Insulating Coatings Corp. (ICC)
103 Main St.
Binghamton, NY 13905

Toll-free: 800-223-8494
Phone: 607-723-1727
www.icc-astec.com

Astec Coatings are water-based ceramic, elastomeric building coatings with superior energy performance. White Astec coatings reflect solar radiation, as does the ceramic radiant barrier within the coating. ICC products are applied with a paint roller or spray equipment.

QuickFlash Weatherproofing Products

QuickFlash Weatherproofing Products, Inc.
4129 Wagon Trail Ave.
Las Vegas, NV 89118

Toll-free: 800-963-6886
Phone: 702-614-6100
www.quickflashproducts.com

A line of products from QuickFlash offers prefabricated thermoplastic flashing for exterior wall protrusions on buildings, including plumbing, electrical, gas, and HVAC penetrations. The polyethylene or rubber panels friction fit around a protrusion, helping prevent moisture, air, and insect entry. A variety of products in QuickFlash's plumbing and HVAC lines accommodate 1/2- and 3/4-inch pipes, up to 4" and 6" sheet metal duct. The electrical line offers specific solutions for single-gang, pancake, and round boxes, as well as depth variations for different exterior cladding. The products carry a 10-year warranty.

Mold-Resistant Coatings

Mold can compromise both human health and the integrity of building materials. It is generally preferable to design and maintain structures in a way that prevents moisture accumulation, and thereby control and mold growth. However surface-applied mold-resistant coatings are increasingly available, and there are certain applications, such as in bathrooms, where such coatings are appropriate. Care must be taken to ensure that surface applied coatings will not introduce different indoor air quality or environmental problems.

American MoldGuard

American MoldGuard, Inc.
30200 Rancho Viejo Rd., Ste. G
San Juan Capistrano, CA 92675

Toll-free: 877-665-3482
Phone: 949-240-5144
www.americanmoldguard.com

American MoldGuard offers a mold-inhibiting treatment program for new construction utilizing a proprietary, non-volatizing, non-migrating antimicrobial silicon polymer—a highly permeable, water-stabilized organosilane that inhibits the growth of mold, mildew, algae, and bacteria without the use of heavy metals or other conventional toxins. Certified applicators treat surfaces during three phases of construction: the first application occurs prior to drywall installation and treats all interior structural surfaces; a second application occurs after drywall is installed and prior to painting; the third application happens after all interior surfaces have been finished. The company provides a 10-year prevention warranty against mold infestation.

Concrobium Mold Control

Siamons International
36 Meteor Dr.
Toronto, ON M9W 1A4 Canada

Toll-free: 866-811-4148
Phone: 416-213-0219
www.concrobium.com

Concrobium Mold Control is a surface-applied product that, when dry, produces a thin polymeric film that surrounds and encapsulates microbes, inhibiting mold growth. Concrobium Mold Control is odorless and colorless, contains no bleach, ammonia, acids or volatile organic compounds (VOCs), and can be applied by hand-spray, paintbrush, roller, immersion, or airless sprayer. Larger areas can be professionally treated using a cold fogging machine. The product is EPA-registered as a Fungistat and Mildewstat.

Other Plastering

Lime plasters have slightly lower embodied energy than portland-cement-based plasters, and they don't include petroleum-based ingredients, as acrylic plasters do. Integral natural pigments obviate the need for painting. Products listed here include natural lime plasters and wall coatings made from ingredients such as clay, sand, and cellulose.

Adobe and Earth Plasters

Clay Mine Adobe, Inc.
6401 W. Old Ajo Hwy.
Tucson, AZ 85735

Phone: 520-578-2222
www.claymineadobe.com

Clay Mine Adobe, founded in 1996, manufactures adobe block with a custom portland cement stabilizer, wheat straw (optional), and washed coarse aggregate admixture. Clay Mine adobe block requires no sealing and retains the authentic look of unstabilized adobe. It is available in a variety of standard as well as custom sizes and natural custom colors including a burnt adobe look. Clay plaster, cement-stabilized and unstabilized in a variety of earth tones, is also available in 95-pound bags.

Aglaia Natural Finishes

Ecohaus
4121 1st Ave. South
Seattle, WA 98134

Toll-free: 800-281-9785
Phone: 206-682-7332
www.ecohaus.com

Aglaia Natural Finishes are biodegradable, plant- and mineral-based products free of petrochemicals and artificial resins. Available in Germany since the late 1960s and now being imported into North America, a variety of interior paints, stains, plasters, and texture coats are also offered. Note than some Aglaia products may have relatively high VOC levels (from plant-based materials), though others have zero VOC content.

American Clay Earth Plaster

American Clay Enterprises, LLC
8724 Alameda Park Dr., NE
Albuquerque, NM 87113

Toll-free: 866-404-1634
Phone: 505-243-5300
www.americanclay.com

American Clay is a 100% natural earth plaster veneer made from clay, aggregates (including 65-75% post-industrial recycled marble dust), nontoxic mineral pigments, and a boric acid mold inhibitor. Designed for interior use, the product can be applied to many substrates (including painted surfaces, though a primer is required). American Clay Earth Plaster is breathable, humidity controlling, and flexible, and is not for areas that come into direct contact with water, such as shower stalls (areas subject to splashing can be sealed to resist damage). Available in 40 standard colors; custom colors may be ordered. American Clay Earth Plaster is mixed with water to apply and can be rewet and reworked indefinitely if left unsealed. Produced in New Mexico exclusively with U.S.-sourced materials. No water or heat is used in production, it is shipped dry, and virtually no waste is generated, according to the company.

Armourcoat Polished Plaster

Armourcoat USA
4629 S 136th St.
Omaha, NE 68137

Toll-free: 888-368-5893
Phone: 402-896-2005
www.armourcoat.com

Armourcoat Polished Plaster is a zero-VOC, durable, decorative troweled finish. The marble powders used as the main ingredient are byproducts from the manufacture of marble slabs and tiles. The product is vapor-permeable, making it particularly well-suited to old or historic buildings.

Dimensions Plasters

Dimensions Plaster
1967 W. 9th St., Ste. B
Riviera Beach, FL 33404

Toll-free: 877-242-8935
www.dimensionsplaster.com

Dimensions Plaster sells non-toxic, VOC-free, lime plasters and primers from Italy. The plasters come in five finishes, which are made by adding marble dust and talc, clay, sand, and vegetable oils, such as linseed oil, to the lime plaster. Dimensions Plaster also sells 14 mineral pigments for use with the plaster and their lime paints. The limestone is from family-owned quarries in Italy, and profits are returned annually to the communities where they do business. The product is designed for the professional plastering contractor.

St. Astier Natural Hydraulic Lime

TransMineral USA, Inc.
201 Purrington Rd.
Petaluma, CA 94952

Phone: 707-769-0661
www.limes.us

St. Astier Natural Hydraulic Lime, or NHL, is a 100% natural product that has been in production since 1851. St. Astier NHL Mortar is widely used in the restoration of old buildings. This natural hydraulic lime mortar imported from France allows stone to "breathe" naturally. Used in construction as plaster, stucco, mortar, and paint, its high level of vapor exchange and mineral composition can help reduce the risk of mold development and dry rot. NHL products are highly permeable, elastic, low shrinking, zero VOC, self-healing, and recyclable. Transmineral USA also offers Le Decor Selection, a line of high-end, all-natural interior/exterior limestone finishes which require trained installers and crushed limestone aggregate imported from France instead of the domestically available aggregate used for the St. Astier NHL products.

Terramed

Med Imports
1710 N. Leg Ct.
Augusta, GA 30909

Toll-free: 866-363-6334
Phone: 706-733-6120
www.medimports.net

Med Imports is the North American distributor for Terramed, an all-natural interior wall coating made from clay, sand, and cellulose. Terramed is available in 12 colors that are derived from clays from the Mediterranean plate of Europe. The product is shipped dry and mixed with water prior to application.

Tierrafino Clay Plaster

Hopper Handcrafted Specialty Finishes
8240 East Gelding Drive
Suite 110
Scottsdale, AZ 85260

Phone: 480-609-7555
www.hopperfinishes.com

Tierrafino® is a 100% natural clay interior finish made from colored sands and clays mined from European quarries. The product contains no pigment or chemical additives. Mother of pearl or straw can be mixed in to add interest. Because Tierrafino sets mechanically and not chemically, it may be reworked over and over again and the surface refreshed by wiping down with a wet sponge and rubbing with a soft brush. Tierrafino is available in several colors, which can be changed after installation by applying fresh Tierrafino powder with a wet sponge. The manufacturer claims the finish is suitable for areas of high humidity, though use should be avoided where it can come in contact with streams of water or excessively wet walls, such as in cellars.

Tobias Stucco

Tobias Stucco Interior Wall Finish, Inc.
608 Fifth St.
Santa Rosa, CA 95404

Phone: 707-577-8196
www.tobiasstucco.com

Tobias Stucco is a non-toxic, odor-free, virtually VOC-free, trowelled-on wall finishing product. The limestone-and-sand-based product can be used as an alternative to paint or plaster and applied to most building substrates. Tobias Stucco is available in a variety of colors and can be applied to provide various textures. The product is designed for the professional plastering contractor and is sold in quart, gallon, and 5-gallon containers through a national sales network of building supply distributors, and independent sales reps.

Paint Removers

Conventional paint strippers, including those containing methylene chloride, are notoriously hazardous and should be avoided. Less-hazardous alternatives are becoming increasingly available. Products listed here are low-VOC, nontoxic, and/or biodegradable.

Soy-Gel

Franmar Chemical, Inc.
P.O. Box 5565
Bloomington, IL 61702

Toll-free: 800-538-5069
Phone: 309-452-7526
www.franmar.com

Soy Gel is a soy-based paint remover suitable for stripping urethanes, polyurethanes, and all paints, including lead-based paint. The product contains methylated soybean oil and mild surfactants, N-Methyl-2-Pyrolidone.

Radiant Barrier Paints

When they face a heat source, radiant barriers work by reflecting heat. When faced away from a heat source, radiant barriers function primarily by virtue of their low emissivity. This means that the surface does not radiate heat well. A radiant-barrier surface on roof sheathing, for example, heats up from the sunlight striking the roof, but that heat energy is not readily emitted into the attic space—so that attic remains cooler. This is why the radiant barrier seems to "reflect" heat back out of the building. An air space is required on at least one side of a radiant barrier in order for it to function as designed. Radiant barriers in attics are most beneficial in reducing cooling loads; their effectiveness in reducing heating loads is more limited. When comparing low-emissivity aluminized paints, look for the lowest emissivity (which corresponds to the highest reflectivity), and low VOC levels. Do not rely on "effective" or "equivalent" R-values, which are only relevant in certain climates or under certain conditions.

E-Barrier Coating

The Sherwin-Williams Company Stores Group
101 Prospect Ave. NW
Cleveland, OH 44115

Toll-free: 800-524-5979
Phone: 216-566-2000
www.sherwin-williams.com

E-Barrier reflective coating for commercial or residential attic decking contains microscopic metal particles to create a low-e surface. Its emissivity when applied over wood is 0.32, and is 0.29 when applied over metal. The VOC content is under 300 g/l —below the 500 g/l limit for metallic pigmented coatings under California Rule 1113. It can be applied with brush, roller, or sprayer. A 2" minimum air space between E-Barrier and the next substrate is required for maximum effectiveness, according to the manufacturer. Energy savings will vary depending upon building materials, home location, and conditions.

Lo/Mit-II

SOLEC-Solar Energy Corp.
129 Walters Ave.
Ewing, NJ 08638

Phone: 609-883-7700
www.solec.org

Lo/Mit-II is a low-emissivity, silicone emulsion radiant barrier paint for interior use. Compared to similar products, it has an unusually low VOC content of 43 g/l, offering an emissivity of 0.21 to 0.26, depending on the substrate. Installs with standard spray equipment, low-nap rollers, or fine-bristle brushes. In buildings, low-e coatings are typically applied to the underside of roof sheathing, and are particularly helpful when retrofitting poorly insulated ceilings.

Recycled Paints

Some recycled paints are commingled paints from partially used containers, often collected under municipal waste programs. These are sometimes referred to as consolidated or reusable paint and are typically sold as primers because the color is variable. Other recycled paints are collected and reprocessed or remanufactured to achieve higher quality and consistency. The two resulting products are generally very different. The better recycled paint brands have sophisticated testing and quality control.

Amazon Select Recycled Paint

Amazon Environmental, Inc.
6688 Doolittle Ave.
Riverside, CA 92503

Phone: 951-588-0206
www.amazonpaint.com

Amazon Select Recycled Paint is available in whipped white, ivory white, concrete gray, tawny beige, and chocolate brown. Custom colors are available upon request. Recover Brand recycled paint is sold exclusively through Dunn-Edwards Paint Co. in California, Colorado, Nevada, Texas, Arizona, and New Mexico. Amazon Select is sold directly through the manufacturer in all markets. The manufacturer has certified the following recycled-content levels (by weight): total recovered material 95% typical, 50% guaranteed; post-consumer material 95% typical, 50% guaranteed.

E-Coat Recycled Latex Paint

Kelly-Moore Paint Co.
5101 Raley Blvd.
Sacramento, CA 95838

Toll-free: 800-874-4436
Phone: 916-921-0165
www.kellymoore.com

E-Coat is an interior/exterior line of paint made from recycled latex paint. Typically available in a flat finish, semi-gloss is also available by special order. Seven standard colors are available, as well as a wide range of custom colors. The manufacturer has certified the following recycled-content levels (by weight): total recovered material 80% typical, 50% guaranteed; post-consumer material 80% typical, 50% guaranteed.

Local Color Recycled Latex Paint

The Environmental Depot
1021 Redmond Rd.
Williston, VT 05495

Phone: 802-872-8100
www.cswd.net

Local Color recycled latex paint is made from 100% recycled, filtered latex paint that has been sorted by color and reblended. The cost is less than half the price of new paint, and quality satisfaction is guaranteed. Local Color interior and exterior paints are available for purchase at the Vermont Environmental Depot in a variety of colors including off-white, tan, green, gray, and blue. All paint is eggshell finish.

VRI Remanufactured Latex Paint

Visions Paint Recycling, Inc.
4481 Kilzer Ave.
McClellan, CA 95652

Toll-free: 800-770-7664
Phone: 916-564-9121
www.visionsrecycling.com

Visions Recycling, Inc. (VRI) produces recycled latex paint from post-consumer (contractor overstock and city and county paint collection sites) and secondary recycled sources (mistints and overstock from factory and store-level distributors). Minimum post-consumer/secondary recycled content is 50%. The paint is checked for quality, sorted, and reblended with virgin materials and additives to produce a high-resin paint that the company claims is comparable in quality to major brands of virgin, one-coat latex paints for roughly one-third the cost. The paints are available for interior and exterior applications, and they come in flat, eggshell, and semi-gloss in twelve stock colors (custom colors are available upon request). VRI also manufactures a low VOC recycled paint made from zero VOC slurry and recycled content. The average VOC content is 17.25 grams/litre.

Traffic Coatings

Most traffic coatings are urethane- or epoxy-based and have high VOC content. Products listed here have VOC content well below the federal VOC content limit of 700 grams per liter.

DynoSeal Waterproofing Sealer

American Formulating & Manufacturing (AFM)
3251 Third Ave.
San Diego, CA 92103

Toll-free: 800-239-0321
Phone: 619-239-0321
www.afmsafecoat.com

DynoSeal is an asphaltic emulsion waterproof sealer with a VOC content of less than 100 g/l for use on foundations and other wet applications. The product containers have over 90% post-consumer recycled-plastic content. The Dyno line of AFM coatings also includes driveway sealers and UV-stabilized rooftop coatings.

Vapor-Retarding Coatings

Vapor retarders are generally sheet goods added to either the interior (cold climates) or exterior (hot and particularly hot humid climates) to restrict moisture moving by diffusion into wall, roof and foundation assemblies. Products listed here usually have superior performance in terms of variable vapor permeability based on their water content. Note that the placement of vapor retarders should always be done in the context of the vapor permeabilities of all the other components of the assembly and their vapor permeability, and the designated direction for drying of the assembly.

MemBrain Smart Vapor Retarder

CertainTeed Corporation
750 E. Swedesford Rd.
P.O. Box 860
Valley Forge, PA 19482

Toll-free: 800-233-8990
Phone: 610-341-7000
www.certainteed.com

MemBrain™ Smart Vapor Retarder is made from a transparent polyamide-based (Nylon-6) material, which changes permeability according to relative humidity and can increase the drying potential of closed building envelope systems. The 2-mil-

thick, high-tensile-strength sheeting is as strong as a 6-mil sheet of polyethylene. Its moisture permeability varies from less than 1 perm at low relative humidity to more than 20 perms at high (95%) relative humidity. MemBrain is intended for use in heating and mixed climates, and is not suitable for cooling climates with high outdoor humidity or in buildings with high constant indoor relative humidity. Interior finish materials and cavity-fill insulation must also be highly permeable.

Water-Repellent Coatings

Fluid-applied waterproofing is commonly made of polyurethane-based or hot rubberized-asphalt materials. Products listed here have low VOC content, recycled content, exceptional durability, or some combination of these product attributes.

DynoSeal Waterproofing Sealer

American Formulating & Manufacturing (AFM)
3251 Third Ave.
San Diego, CA 92103

Toll-free: 800-239-0321
Phone: 619-239-0321
www.afmsafecoat.com

DynoSeal is an asphaltic emulsion waterproof sealer with a VOC content of less than 100 g/l for use on foundations and other wet applications. The product containers have over 90% post-consumer recycled-plastic content. The Dyno line of AFM coatings also includes driveway sealers and UV-stabilized rooftop coatings.

Rub-R-Wall Foundation Waterproofing

Rubber Polymer Corp.
1135 W. Portage Trl. Ext.
Akron, OH 44313

Toll-free: 800-860-7721
Phone: 330-945-7721
www.rpcinfo.com

Rub-R-Wall® foundation waterproofing is made from synthetic rubber. This product is spray-applied under high pressure (3,000 psi) and temperature (140 to 160 degrees F) by factory-certified professionals. The resulting rubber coating requires protection from backfilling with either 1/4" EPS foam or a woven geotextile. Rub-R-Wall has a lifetime limited warranty for residential applications and a 10-year warranty for commercial applications.

Water Repellents

Water repellents are clear liquid products that are usually solvent- or water-based silicone, acrylic, silane or siloxane based. Products listed here have VOC content well below the federal VOC content limit of 700 grams per liter for this category of products.

9400 and 9400W Impregnant

Palmer Industries, Inc.
10611 Old Annapolis Rd.
Frederick, MD 21701

Toll-free: 800-545-7383
Phone: 301-898-7848
www.palmerindustriesinc.com

9400 Impregnant is a water-repellent, UV-protective coating for masonry, concrete, and other cementitious materials, formulated without solvents for minimal toxicity. 9400W is a variant for wood surfaces.

Ashford Formula

Curecrete Distribution, Inc.
1203 W. Spring Creek Pl.
Springville, UT 84663

Toll-free: 800-998-5664
Phone: 801-489-5663
www.ashfordformula.com

Ashford Formula is a permanent, penetrating concrete hardener, densifier, dustproofer, and sealer for new or existing concrete. As it progressively seals, the concrete becomes watertight but remains breathable and will develop a shine through use or by scrubbing. The product also locks in salts to eliminate the formation of concrete dust. Ashford Formula is water-based, nontoxic, nonflammable, and releases no VOCs. It is effective on concrete, stucco, terrazzo, concrete block, and similar materials. This product is particularly intended for flooring applications.

Concrete & Masonry Cleaner and Sealer

Envirosafe Manufacturing Corporation
7634-B Progress Cir.
W. Melbourne, FL 32904

Toll-free: 800-800-5737
www.envirosafemfg.com

Trojan Masonry Sealer, a penetrating sealer for permanently waterproofing masonry, is a water-dispersed polyester polymer that dries to form a monolithic barrier filling voids and coating the interior particles of concrete to block moisture transmission. Trojan Masonry Sealer releases no VOCs, is nontoxic, nonflammable, noncaustic, and is suitable for use indoors or out on concrete, cement, brick, stucco, plaster, mortar, terrazzo, and most natural stones. Envirosafe NuLook Concrete & Masonry Cleaner #40-44 is a fluid-applied cleaner that removes dirt, oil, and stains from concrete. NuLook is biodegradable, noncarcinogenic, and water-soluble with a pH of less than 1.0. NuLook Gel is slightly more viscous for vertical surfaces. Envirosafe also has a production plant in Wenatchee, Washington.

Deck-O-Shield

W. R. Meadows, Inc.
300 Industrial Dr.
P.O. Box 338
Hampshire, IL 60140

Toll-free: 800-342-5976
Phone: 847-214-2100
www.wrmeadows.com

Deck-O-Shield is a ready-to-use, zero-VOC, water-based sealer and water repellent for use on natural stone, concrete, brick, stucco, and masonry surfaces. Deck-O-Shield is designed for use in or around swimming pools, providing a clear finish and also inhibiting the penetration of salts into the surface, reducing whitening or staining.

Enviroseal

BASF Corporation
889 Valley Park Dr.
Shakopee, MN 55379

Toll-free: 800-433-9517
www.corporate.basf.com

The Enviroseal® product line consists of single-component, water-based, water-repellent clear sealers. The VOC contents of these products is below 350 g/l. Enviroseal 20 and Enviroseal 40 are patented, penetrating silane sealers for concrete and masonry. Enviroseal 7 is an economical, blended silane/siloxane penetrating sealer for concrete, brick masonry, stucco, and many natural stones. Enviroseal Double 7 for Brick is a high-performance sealer developed for dense, vertical masonry surfaces such as hard-burnt brick, and also concrete, stone, and stucco. Enviroseal Surface Guard is a protective sealer designed to repel water and oils from horizontal interior masonry surfaces. The Enviroseal product line was formerly produced by Degussa Building Systems acquired by BASF in March of 2006.

Intraseal

Conspec
4226 Kansas Ave.
Kansas City, KS 66106

Toll-free: 800-348-7351
Phone: 913-279-4800
www.conspecmkt.com

Intraseal is a penetrating, water-based, reactive siliconate concrete sealer, hardener, and dustproofer. Its VOC content is below 100 g/l. This product is for use on concrete floors.

Penetrating Waterstop

American Formulating & Manufacturing (AFM)
3251 Third Ave.
San Diego, CA 92103

Toll-free: 800-239-0321
Phone: 619-239-0321
www.afmsafecoat.com

Safecoat® Penetrating WaterStop is a zero-VOC sealer that increases water-repellency on brick walls, concrete foundations, stucco, stone, and most unglazed tile. It is nonflammable and free of formaldehyde and hazardous ingredients.

Seal-Krete Sealers

Seal-Krete, Inc.
Convenience Products
306 Gandy Rd.
Auburndale, FL 33823

Toll-free: 800-323-7357
Phone: 863-967-1535
www.seal-krete.com

Seal-Krete Original Waterproofing Sealer (SKWPS) is a water-based, very-low-VOC (less than 8 g/l), strong-binding, clear acrylic, penetrating sealer/primer for interior and exterior concrete and masonry surfaces. The product is available in 10% solids and 25% solids formulations. Seal-Krete Masonry Sealer is a waterborne, nonyellowing, clear acrylic emulsion sealer that can be used on both concrete and wood floors. It has a VOC content below 100 g/l. These sealers are for above-grade applications.

Seal-Once

New Image Coatings, LLC
150 Dow St.
Manchester, NH 03101

Phone: 603-669-8786
www.seal-once.com

Seal-Once™ is a water-based penetrating waterproofer for wood, concrete, masonry, and composite decking. It is colorless, UV-resistant, and paintable and contains no heavy metals, petroleum distillates, solvents, or VOCs. Seal-Once protects against mold, mildew, and freeze-thaw cycles and resists salts, chlorides, and UV damage yet allows water vapor to pass through. Clear and tinted formulas are available, as well as marine and industrial grades. The manufacturer claims the compound will not leach; is safe for aquatic environments; and will protect horizontal surfaces for 6 years and vertical surfaces for ten years.

SoySeal Wood Sealer

Natural Soy, LLC
P.O. Box 489
123 N. Orchard St.
Brooklyn, IA 52211

Toll-free: 888-606-9559
Phone: 641-522-9559
www.soyclean.biz

SoySeal is a water-based, nontoxic, nonflammable sealer suitable for exposed wood surfaces. It contains no VOCs or other known user hazards and cleans up with water. This product spreads water rather than beading it, which reduces the risk of UV magnification and damage, according to Natural Soy. Coverage is 150 to 300 ft2. This product complies with ASTM C-672 and is also used to seal concrete. It is available in 1-, 5-, 55-, and 250-gallon containers.

Weather-Bos Sealers

Weather-Bos International
316 California Ave., Ste. 1082
Reno, NV 89509

Toll-free: 800-664-3978
www.weatherbos.com

Weather-Bos sealers are made from natural, nontoxic vegetable oils and resins as well as other natural ingredients. These sealers are low-odor, water-reducible, nonflammable, and free of harmful fungicides. The small amount of pigment in some formulas provides UV protection. Masonry Boss™ waterproofs and protects brick, adobe, concrete, tile, and stone.

Waterproof Coatings for Concrete and Masonry

While most conventional concrete sealers and waterproofing agents have very high VOCs, some products react with the concrete or otherwise provide a seal without resorting to solvents that emit VOCs. Products listed here contain zero VOCs, either nominally or actually.

Aquafin-IC Crystalline Waterproofing

Aquafin, Inc.
505 Blue Ball Rd., Bldg. 160
Elkton, MD 21921

Toll-free: 888-482-6339
Phone: 410-392-2300
www.aquafin.net

Aquafin-IC is a penetrating, inorganic, cementitious material used to permanently waterproof and protect new or existing structurally sound concrete and concrete masonry by reacting with moisture and free lime in the concrete. Aquafin-IC resists strong hydrostatic pressure and can be used in both interior and exterior below-grade applications. It is "breathable," nontoxic, releases no VOCs, and is suitable for potable water storage applications. Aquafin-IC may take up to a month to reach full waterproofing potential.

Concrete & Masonry Cleaner and Sealer

Envirosafe Manufacturing Corporation
7634-B Progress Cir.
W. Melbourne, FL 32904

Toll-free: 800-800-5737
www.envirosafemfg.com

Trojan Masonry Sealer, a penetrating sealer for permanently waterproofing masonry, is a water-dispersed polyester polymer that dries to form a monolithic barrier filling voids and coating the interior particles of concrete to block moisture transmission. Trojan Masonry Sealer releases no VOCs, is nontoxic, nonflammable, noncaustic, and is suitable for use indoors or out on concrete, cement, brick, stucco, plaster, mortar, terrazzo, and most natural stones. Envirosafe NuLook Concrete & Masonry Cleaner #40-44 is a fluid-applied cleaner that removes dirt, oil, and stains from concrete. NuLook is biodegradable, noncarcinogenic, and water-soluble with a pH of less than 1.0. NuLook Gel is slightly more viscous for vertical surfaces. Envirosafe also has a production plant in Wenatchee, Washington.

Xypex Concentrate

Xypex Chemical Corporation
13731 Mayfield Pl.
Richmond, BC V6V 2G9 Canada

Toll-free: 800-961-4477
Phone: 604-273-5265
www.xypex.com

Xypex Concentrate is a nontoxic powder consisting of portland cement, very fine treated silica sand, and various active proprietary chemicals. Mixed with water to form a slurry, it penetrates the pores of concrete and masonry structures, plugging them with a nonsoluble crystalline formation that becomes an integral part of the structure. This product is approved for use on potable water structures and contains no VOCs. Xypex Concentrate is available in powder form in 20-lb. pails, 60-lb. pails, and 50-lb. bags. Other formulations for the protection and waterproofing of concrete are available. Xypex products also protect reinforcing steel.

This Space is Available for Your Notes

Mechanical Systems/HVAC

Heating, ventilation, and air-conditioning (HVAC) are the "engine" that drives the comfort systems in most structures. They directly consume the largest portion of energy in buildings—which makes them critically important from an environmental standpoint. Additionally, good indoor air quality, to a significant extent, depends on the ventilation they provide, while a problematic mechanical system can create and distribute indoor pollutants.

The first place to look to minimize the impact of a mechanical system isn't the equipment, however; it's the building's design and construction. Careful, integrated design and optimal levels of insulation can minimize the need for supplemental heating, ventilation, or air-conditioning. In situations where a central mechanical system is still necessary, an efficient building envelope can reduce the size of that system. A high-performance domestic water heater is fully capable of supplying heat to a very well-insulated house in most U.S. climates.

In a well-designed building, distribution requirements are also greatly reduced—offering tremendous potential savings in both first cost and operating costs. Houses with very well-insulated walls and high-performance windows, for example, may no longer require heat distribution at the exterior walls to provide comfort. Short duct runs to the closest point in each room save a great deal of money and space, and reduce the potential for wasteful air leakage from the duct system (which should be sealed with duct mastic, not duct tape, at all joints).

After reducing the loads that a mechanical system must meet, it's important to size the system carefully to meet the remaining loads. An oversized system wastes money and materials initially and then operates wastefully, because heating and cooling equipment is at its most efficient when operating at full capacity.

Mechanical equipment should be as efficient as possible, durable, and installed for ease of regular maintenance. As is common practice with heating and cooling, fresh air should be provided to each occupied space and distributed to avoid pockets of trapped, stale air.

To avoid the risk of backdrafting toxic flue gases such as carbon monoxide into a home, only sealed-combustion equipment should be used in houses.

Many air-conditioning systems still rely on HCFC refrigerants, which destroy the ozone layer if allowed to escape. These are being phased out in favor of non-ozone-depleting alternatives. The system efficiency, potential for refrigerant leakage, and ozone-depletion potential of the refrigerant should all be considered when choosing an air-conditioning system.

Good controls are also important. They should have setback options to adjust temperature and fresh air setpoints according to occupancy levels and time of day, and be easy to understand and use. "Smart" microprocessor-driven controllers with occupancy-detecting sensors can "learn" the activity of a household over time, activating mechanical equipment.

A mechanical system also requires careful *commissioning* to ensure optimal operation. During commissioning, mechanical equipment is checked for proper operation, distribution systems are balanced, and controls are all checked. All too often, careless mistakes in installation and set-up result in poor system performance. Without a commissioning process, these mistakes might not be caught for years. Commissioning is important in both commercial buildings and homes. Clear, thorough documentation is critical to ensure proper ongoing maintenance and operation of systems of any size.

Biomass for woodstoves, pellet stoves, wood-chip boilers, and other combustion devices is renewable as long as production of that biomass is sustainable—that is, as long as harvesting doesn't outpace regeneration or stress the ecosystems. Some of these heating systems can generate significant amounts of air pollution, however, so appropriate pollution controls such as catalytic converters or secondary burn chambers should always be incorporated.

Air Conditioning Equipment

The two most important issues with compressor-based cooling systems are energy efficiency and potential ozone depletion from refrigerants. Most unitary equipment now uses R-22, an HCFC, as the refrigerant. This refrigerant is slated for phaseout by 2020. A few units use HFC refrigerants, which do not affect the ozone layer but are greenhouse gases that contribute to global warming if released to the atmosphere. Seasonal energy efficiency ratio (SEER) ratings compare cooling capacity (in Btu) to energy inputs (in watts) and are helpful in evaluating central air-conditioner performance. One ton of cooling capacity represents the ability to remove 12,000 Btu of heat per hour. Also consider the moisture-removal capability of air-conditioning equipment.

Affinity 8T Air Conditioner

York International Corp.
5005 York Dr.
Unitary Products Group
Norman, OK 73069

Toll-free: 877-874-7378
Phone: 405-364-4040
www.yorkupg.com

The Affinity 8T Series line offers up to 18-SEER residential systems in sizes ranging from 2 to 5 tons. The quiet, two-stage design allows improved part-load efficiency; increased demand triggers full capacity. These units are available with R-410A refrigerant. The compressor has a ten-year warranty; the parts warranty is five years.

Allegiance 18

American Standard Heating and Air Conditioning
6200 Troup Hwy.
Tyler, TX 75711

Toll-free: 888-556-0125
Phone: 903-581-3499
www.americanstandardair.com

American Standard (the parent company of Trane) offers the Allegiance® 18 Ultra Efficiency Air Conditioner with a variable-speed fan and Dual Duration™ compressors that provide two-stage cooling: a smaller compressor handles most of the work, but on the hottest days a larger compressor takes over. With a SEER rating of up to 18.9, these are among the highest-efficiency central air conditioners available. They are available in 2.5 to 5 tons, and have a ten-year warranty. These units use ozone-depleting R-22 refrigerant.

Infinity Central Air Conditioners

Carrier Corp.
Carrier Parkway
P.O. Box 4808
Syracuse, NY 13221

Toll-free: 800-227-7437
Phone: 315-432-6000
www.carrier.com

The Infinity™ line from Carrier includes the company's most efficient central air conditioner, with SEER ratings from 16 to 21. These 2- to 5-ton, two-speed units use Carrier's Puron refrigerant (R-410a), which is a blend of three different HFCs. Carrier offers a 5-year limited warranty on parts, and a ten-year limited warranty on the compressor.

Rheem RASL Prestige Series

Rheem Manufacturing Company
101 Bell Rd.
Montgomery, AL 36117

Toll-free: 800-432-8373
Phone: 334-260-1500
www.rheem.com

The RASL Prestige Series from Rheem features ozone-safe R-410A refrigerant and SEER ratings up to 18. The manufacturer uses durable Copeland® Scroll® compressors and on-board safety circuitry to protect against damage cause by improper refrigerant levels. Certain models employ two-speed ECM fan motors. The nominal size is 3 ton (10.5 kW). An on-demand dehumidification terminal can be matched with an optional air handler for greater humidity control. This product is offered with a ten-year warranty.

XC21 Air Conditioners

Lennox Industries, Inc.
2100 Lake Park Blvd
Richardson, TX 75080

Toll-free: 800-953-6669
Phone: 972-497-5000
www.lennox.com

XC21 Air Conditioner uses non-ozone-depleting R410A refrigerant, and with models up to 20.50 SEER, it's one of the highest-rated central air conditioning units available. It carries a 10-year limited compressor warranty, and a 5-year limited warranty on covered components. Though it is non-ozone-depleting, HFC refrigerant R410A is a significant greenhouse gas that, like HCFC, contributes to global warming.

XL19i Air Conditioners

Trane Residential Systems
6200 Troup Hwy.
Tyler, TX 75707

Phone: 903-581-3200
www.trane.com

Trane's 2.5-ton XL19i two-stage air conditioner is a highly efficient unit which, when coupled with an optional air-handler, achieves a SEER rating of up to 19.5. The 3-ton unit, with the optional air-handler, is rated up to SEER 19; the 4- and 5-ton units, similarly enhanced, can deliver 17 and 16.5 SEER, respectively. The XL19i uses R-22 refrigerant. The manufacturer's limited warranty covers compressor, coil, and internal functional parts for ten years.

Air Outlets and Inlets

These listings include passive air inlets and outlets used in HVAC systems, as well as fresh-air make-up inlets that replace air removed by exhaust-only ventilation systems.

Fresh 80 and Reton 80 Passive Air Inlets

Therma-Stor LLC
P.O. Box 8680
Madison, WI 53708

Toll-free: 800-533-7533
Phone: 608-222-5301
www.thermastor.com

Fresh 80 and Reton 80 through-the-wall passive air inlets supply controlled trickle ventilation for tight buildings. A single unit is designed to supply fresh air for up to 270 ft2 of floor area. Both are available in a larger "100" version, supplying more fresh air for a given indoor-outdoor pressure difference.

Speedi-Boot

Applied Applications International Inc.
500 Colorado St.
Kelso, WA 98626

Toll-free: 866-794-7900
Phone: 360-577-0876
www.speediboot.com

The Speedi-Boot™ boot hanger for air-supply ducts is a mounting system that allows air supply boots (the termination that connects a round duct to a rectangular grill opening) to be tightly sealed to a ceiling, wall, or subfloor. This product also helps keep dust and debris out of the duct system during construction. It comes with protective cardboard covers that are easily removed after construction is completed. The adjustable hanger installs between joists, trusses, or studs. A foam gasket provides a tight seal to the drywall or subfloor, reducing air leakage. The Speedi-Boot is available in 15 sizes, is designed for both residential and commercial construction, and works with wood or steel framing.

Trickle Ventilators

Titon Inc.
P.O. Box 241
Granger, IN 46530

Phone: 574-271-9699
www.titon.com

Titon produces a range of trickle ventilators designed to suit a variety of window applications, including retrofits. Tests indicate that IAQ is improved with little negative effect on energy costs. The moving air also helps to reduce condensation mold.

Air-to-Air Energy Recovery Ventilation

Heat-Recovery Ventilators (HRVs) and Energy-Recovery Ventilators (ERVs) are mechanical air-exchange systems that can capture up to 90% of the heat content from stale indoor air being exchanged for fresh outside air. These products work by passing the air streams through a heat-exchange core, generally made with multiple aluminum or plastic plates. HRVs capture heat from the outgoing air during heating season to warm the incoming air; and in cooling season, heat from the incoming air is transferred to the outgoing air to help prevent warming the building while providing fresh air. ERVs also provide humidity conditioning using a desiccant wheel or plates made of a permeable material; these help retain indoor moisture during the heating season and exclude it during the cooling season. The efficiency of the heat exchange is dependent on both the equipment and the climate. Most systems are balanced: the same volume of air is exhausted and taken in.

Aprilaire Energy Recovery Ventilator

Aprilaire
1015 E. Washington Ave.
P.O. Box 1467
Madison, WI 53701

Toll-free: 800-334-6011
Phone: 608-257-8801
www.aprilaire.com

The Aprilaire Energy Recovery Ventilator (formerly PerfectAire® Fresh Air Exchanger) uses an Energy Max® enthalpic-type air exchanger to recover approximately 77% of the heat in outgoing air and to control moisture, according to the company. Aprilaire also offers a full line of indoor air quality products, such as programmable thermostats, whole-house humidifiers, zoning, and high-efficiency air cleaners.

AquaMaster Q100

Vebteck Research
30 Riviera Dr.
Markham, ON L3R 5M1 Canada

Phone: 905-479-4048
www.ekocomfort.com

The AquaMaster Q100 is a joint development effort from Vebteck Research, Nutech Energy Systems, and Fleetline Products that offers integrated high-efficiency space heating (forced air or hydronic), domestic water heating, and continuous whole-house, heat-recovery ventilation (HRV) under a single, unified control system. The small system—it has a 4' x 2' footprint—includes a high-efficiency, low-mass, low-water-volume boiler (natural gas, propane, or fuel oil); a single, multi-speed, ECM blower; and an aluminum HRV core. The AquaMaster is a product of the eKOCOMFORT® consortium, a partnership of Canadian manufacturers and governmental agencies developing efficient, gas-fired, module-based units integrating space heating, ventilation, and domestic hot water.

AVS Solo and AVS Duo

Venmar Ventilation Inc.
550 Lemire Blvd.
Drummondville, QC J2C 7W9 Canada

Toll-free: 800-567-3855
Phone: 819-477-6226
www.venmar.ca

Previously known as VanEE, Venmar is the leading manufacturer of advanced ventilation equipment. The company manufactures energy-efficient ventilation equipment including enthalpic wheels, HRVs, and ERVs. Venmar's residential products include the AVS Solo, an HRV, and the AVS Duo, an ERV, meaning that it also reclaims moisture in the air stream. The company offers an extensive line of controls for maintaining comfortable, healthy indoor environments.

Broan Fresh Air Systems

Broan-NuTone LLC
926 W. State St.
P.O. Box 140
Hartford, WI 53027

Toll-free: 800-558-1711
Phone: 262-673-4340
www.broan.com

Broan offers Fresh Air Systems ERVs and HRVs along with appropriate controls for enhancing indoor air quality while maintaining comfort and energy efficiency.

Enerboss HRV/Air Handler

Nu-Air Ventilation Systems
P.O. Box 2758
Windsor, NS B0N 2T0 Canada

Phone: 902-798-2261
www.nu-airventilation.com

The Enerboss integrated HRV/air handler for residential or light-commercial installations couples with a boiler to provide space heating and ventilation. With an optional evaporator coil, the Enerboss will couple with a split system's compressor to also meet cooling loads. A ½-hp ECM motor provides continuous circulating air and ventilation, and provides fresh air to the ERV. An independent exhaust fan serves the HRV. Circulating and ventilating air are filtered separately. The manufacturer claims 69% sensible recovery efficiency in continuous mode, and 71% at high speed. The heat output is 40,000 – 80,000 Btu/hr, and the design air temperature rise is 45°F. Electric draw (heating, 900 – 1150 cfm airflow) is 345 W; circulation draw, at 350 cfm, is 109 W.

Energy Recovery Ventilator

BossAire Inc.
2929 West Park Dr.
Owatonna, MN 55060

Phone: 507-451-3524
www.bossaire.com

Boss Aire manufactures ERVs for many sizes of residential buildings and for light commercial and industrial buildings.

Heat Recovery Ventilators

American Aldes Ventilation Corp.
4537 Northgate Ct.
Sarasota, FL 34234

Toll-free: 800-255-7749
Phone: 941-351-3441
www.americanaldes.com

American Aldes Ventilation offers a wide range of engineered ventilation products, including Heat Recovery Ventilators (HRV) and Energy Recovery Ventilators (ERV). Their residential HRVs are designed for spaces ranging from 1,100 to 8,000 ft2. The 200S residential ERV designed for climates with long cooling seasons and moderately cold winters, where the temperature remains above 0 degrees F. Commercial Heat/Energy Recovery Ventilators rated for 450-2900 CFM are also available.

Lifebreath Clean Air Furnace

Nutech Brands, Inc.
511 McCormick Blvd.
London, ON N5W 4C8 Canada

Phone: 519-457-1904
www.lifebreath.com

The Clean Air Furnace combines a Heat Recovery Ventilator with an Air Handler. The combination heating system provides constant ventilation and a steady stream of warm air to create a temperature-steady, healthy home environment. The combination heating system is available in hydronic or electric models, and offers up to 90% efficiency. Features include a high-efficiency heating coil and ECM motor. Add-on cooling capacities range from 2 tons to 5 tons, with heating outputs ranging from 25,000 to 120,000 Btu/H (hydronic), and 17,000 to 75,000 Btu/H (electric).

Lifebreath Heat Recovery Ventilators

Nutech Brands, Inc.
511 McCormick Blvd.
London, ON N5W 4C8 Canada

Phone: 519-457-1904
www.lifebreath.com

Lifebreath residential HRVs range in capacity from 95 to 300 cfm. All have a high-efficiency aluminum heat exchanger core. Heat exchange effectiveness ranges from 80 to 90%, according to the company. Commercial models, designed to be integrated into HVAC systems, range in size from 500 to 2,500 cfm. Nutech also makes a 200 cfm Lifebreath for hot, humid climates that exchanges moisture in the core in addition to heat, reducing dehumidification costs.

Lossnay ERVs

Mitsubishi Electric Sales Canada Inc.
4299 14th Ave.
Markham, ON L3R 0J2

Phone: 905-475-7728
www.mitsubishielectric.ca

Mitsubishi Electric Canada, under the Lossnay brand, offers commercial and residential ERVs that can be installed as part of their City Multi product line, or as independently operating units. For light-commercial use, ceiling suspended mounting is available. Mitsubishi Electric also supplies the Lossnay ERV core to RenewAire for their products.

Perfect Window Fresh Air Ventilator

Honeywell Home & Building Controls
P.O. Box 524
Minneapolis, MN 55440

Toll-free: 800-328-5111
Phone: 612-951-1000
yourhome.honeywell.com

The Honeywell Perfect Window™ line of Fresh Air Ventilator Systems includes HRVs and ERVs.

RenewAire ERVs

RenewAire
4510 Helgesen Drive
Madison, WI 53718

Toll-free: 800-627-4499
Phone: 608-221-4499
www.renewaire.com

RenewAire, formerly under the Lossnay name for Mitsubishi Electric, manufactures a full line of commercial and residential ERVs. Among the residential units, the EV 130 is rated at 130 cfm and the EV 200 is rated at 200 cfm with 73% and 76% energy recovery efficiencies, respectively. These units can be installed stand-alone or tied into a furnace.

UltimateAir RecoupAerator

Stirling Technology, Inc.
178 Mill St.
Athens, OH 45701

Toll-free: 800-535-3448
Phone: 740-594-2277
www.ultimateair.com

The UltimateAir™ RecoupAerator® 200DX ERV system from Stirling Technology has a heat-recovery efficiency of up to 96% and employs a brushless DC, high-efficiency, variable-speed, ECPM motor. The system efficiently delivers 70 ft3 per minute (cfm) using 34 watts to 210 cfm using 200 watts. The low-cfm efficiency is the highest in the industry, owing to the ECPM motor. The system comes with washable MERV 8 filters and a five-year warranty. Optional features include an economizer module; a CO2 sensor that boosts airflow when carbon dioxide levels are elevated; a pressure sensor that reacts to maintain the owner-set indoor pressure; and HEPA (high-efficiency particulate air) filtration (which increases electrical use significantly). A window unit appropriate for single offices and apartments, Model SW-120, is also available.

Ventilation Products

Fantech
1712 Northgate Blvd.
Sarasota, FL 34234

Toll-free: 800-747-1762
Phone: 506-743-9500
www.fantech.net

Fantech manufactures ventilation products with energy recovery cores for residential, commercial, and industrial buildings.

Bathroom Vent Fans

Exhaust fans are an important component of today's tightly sealed buildings. Unless there's a central ventilation system, kitchen and bathroom spot-ventilators may be the only mechanical ventilation system in a house. To increase the likelihood that fans will be used, they should be quiet. Products listed here have sone ratings no higher than 1.5. ("Sone" is a measure of loudness; one sone is about as loud as a common residential refrigerator.)

Broan-Nutone Fans

Broan-NuTone LLC
926 W. State St.
P.O. Box 140
Hartford, WI 53027

Toll-free: 800-558-1711
Phone: 262-673-4340
www.broan.com

Broan-NuTone produces a number of quiet bathroom fans for residential and commercial applications. The Ultra Silent™ series of residential bathroom fans operate at 0.3-1.4 sones depending on size (50-150 CFM). The Ultra Quiet Humidity Sensing Fan operates at 0.9 sones (110 CFM), and detects rapid rises in humidity for automated start with an adjustable auto shut-off time. LoSone Select Ventilators are quiet continuous-operation commercial ventilators, with the 100/150 CFM model rated at 0.9 Sones. The SmartSense line communicates with other fans in a home, over existing power lines, to control the house-wide ventilation rate.

Panasonic Exhaust Fans

Panasonic Consumer Electronics Building Department
Panazip 4A-6
One Panasonic Way
Secaucus, NJ 07094

Toll-free: 866-292-7292
www.panasonic.com

Panasonic, the first company to introduce a truly quiet bathroom fan, remains an industry leader with a full line of very quiet high-efficiency ceiling, wall, and inline exhaust fans. The WhisperGreen™ series use an improved DC motor and are 70 - 400% more energy efficient than minimum Energy Star® standards. Automated variable speed controls, CFM optimization, and motion sensors enhance performance for spot or whole-house ventilation systems.

Ultra-QuieTTest

NuTone, Inc.
4820 Red Bank Rd.
Cincinnati, OH 45227

Toll-free: 888-336-6151
Phone: 513-527-5100
www.nutone.com

NuTone produces the Ultra-QuieTTest® line of bathroom fans.

Central Cooling Equipment

Most air conditioning systems are compressor based, requiring refrigerants that may affect the ozone layer or contribute to climate change, and using lots of energy. In dry climates evaporative coolers are an option. Products listed here provide cooling in unique ways, for instance by capturing cool night air.

NightBreeze

Davis Energy Group
123 C St.
Davis, CA 95616

Phone: 530-753-1100
www.davisenergy.com

The NightBreeze ventilation cooling system—composed of a special vent damper, an advanced thermostat, sensors, and a highly efficient air handler—integrates with a home's mechanical system to provide ventilative cooling with pre-filtered night air. The system runs an efficient, variable-speed, electronically commutated motor (ECM) during off-peak hours to quietly circulate cool night air, storing the cooling energy in the home's thermal mass. Depending on the climate, this system can reduce or eliminate the need for daytime compression-cycle air conditioning. The system can also provide heat, either with hot-water coils in the base of the air handler (supplied by the home's domestic hot water system or a dedicated tankless water heater), or through an add-on control system that enables use of the NightBreeze with a compatible forced-air furnace.

Condensing Boilers

Condensing boilers capture and cool the combustion gases that are normally vented. Water condenses from those combustion byproducts, which releases additional heat and raises the overall efficiency of the system.

Baxi Luna Condensing Boilers

Marathon International
1815 Sismet Rd.
Mississauga, ON L4W 1P9 Canada

Phone: 905-602-5360
www.wallhungboilers.com

Marathon International is the North American distributor for the Baxi line of boilers and water heating products from Britain. The Luna wall-hung, condensing boiler is a gas-fired, sealed-combustion, direct-venting boiler for home heating applications. (One model in the line will also supply domestic hot water.) Btu/hr deliveries range from as low as 32,804 to as high as 221,789, with efficiencies up to 97%. Multiple boilers can be ganged together to share a common venting system while increasing Btu output for commercial applications. Circuitry-based anti-freeze protection comes standard.

FCX Oil-Fired Condensing Boiler

Monitor Products, Inc.
P.O. Box 3408
Princeton, NJ 08543

Toll-free: 800-524-1102
Phone: 732-329-0900
www.monitorproducts.com

The FCX is a small, oil-fired condensing boiler measuring 33-1/2" H x 23" W x 24-1/2" D with a Btu output of 76,100 and an application efficiency of 95%. The unit (which produces heat and domestic hot water) contains a primary, noncondensing heat exchanger coupled to a stainless steel condensing secondary heat exchanger. The FCX is approved as a sealed combustion device and can be fitted to take combustion air from the outside via a concentric vent.

MZ Boiler

Monitor Products, Inc.
P.O. Box 3408
Princeton, NJ 08543

Toll-free: 800-524-1102
Phone: 732-329-0900
www.monitorproducts.com

Monitor is the U.S. distributor for the fully condensing gas-fired MZ Boiler. All three models are wall-mounted and perform with up to 97.7% efficiency (minimum of 90%, according to the company). The units offer spark ignition, sealed combustion, and zero clearance, and use only 108 watts of electricity to operate. The MZ25S (the only unit of the three to provide both heat and domestic hot water) and the MZ25C have 94,000 Btu/hr input. The MZ40C has 142,500 Btu/hr input in two 71,000 Btu stages (high/low fire). These hydronic heat sources meet German "Blue Angel" environmental standards.

Prestige Condensing Boilers

Triangle Tube
1 Triangle Ln.
Blackwood, NJ 08012

Phone: 856-228-8881
www.triangletube.com

The Prestige line of gas-fired, fully condensing, wall-mounted, modulating boilers for space heating or domestic water heating adjust in response to the room thermostat, supply and return water temperature, flue temperature, domestic hot water thermostat, and outdoor temperature to provide up to 96% efficiency in low-temperature applications. Three models are available with outputs ranging from 93,000 to 226,000 Btu/hr.

Q95M-200 Modulating Condensing Boiler

Dunkirk
85 Middle Rd.
Dunkirk, NY 14048

Phone: 877-386-5475
www.dunkirk.com

Dunkirk's Q95M-200 gas-fired, modulating, condensing boiler has an AFUE of 95%. Rather than cycling on and off, the sealed-combustion boiler modulates from 80,000 to 200,000 BTUs/hour to meet real-time load requirements.

Quantum Series Boilers

ECR International, Inc.
2201 Dwyer Ave.
Utica, NY 13501

Phone: 315-797-1310
www.ecrinternational.com

The Q95-200M condensing, gas-fired, residential hot water boiler features a cast aluminum heat exchanger and an AFUE of 95%. Via a second heat exchanger, hot flue gases heat conden- sate which is used to saturate and heat combustion air so that 90+% efficiencies can be obtained at return water temperatures up to 160 degrees F. The system is most efficient (up to 98%), however, with lower tem- perature water returns such as with radiant systems. The boiler offers sealed combustion and direct venting. PVC exhaust piping requires 0" clearance to combustible construction. The other unit in the series, the Quantum 90 (AFUE 90%), is similar but does not use condensate to heat and saturate combustion air. According to the manufacturer, both units substantially reduce CO and NOx emissions (acid rain and smog components)—to less than 10 ppm for the Q95-200M and 30 ppm for the Quantum 90.

Vitodens 200 Wall-Mounted Boiler

Viessmann Manufacturing Co. (U.S.) Inc.
45 Access Rd.
Warwick, RI 02886

Toll-free: 800-288-0667
Phone: 401-732-0667
www.viessmann-us.com

Vitodens 200 is a wall-mounted, gas-fired, condensing boiler with efficiencies of up to 95.2% AFUE. This small, quiet, low-emission, zero-clearance, sealed-combustion unit can be installed in a living space. The five models have a maximum input ranging from 91,000 to 230,000 Btu/hr. The smaller WB2-24 and -32 models have a variable- speed pump for low electrical consumption and precise heating, and the WB2 6-24C has a plate-type heat exchanger to supply domestic hot water in addition to space heating. Up to four of the larger WB2-44 and -60 models can be ganged together for light-commercial applications.

Convection Heating and Cooling

In highly energy-efficient homes and small commercial buildings, it is often possible to satisfy all heating demands with space heaters rather than a central, distributed heating system. Prod- ucts listed here include high-efficiency, quiet space heaters.

EnergySaver Ductless Heater

Rinnai
103 International Dr.
Peachtree City, GA 30269

Toll-free: 800-621-9419
Phone: 678-829-1700
www.rinnai.us

The EnergySaver by Rinnai is an 84%-efficient, sealed-combustion space heater. It is 20% more efficient than typical American through- the-wall gas space heaters.

Laser Vented Heaters

Toyotomi U.S.A., Inc.
604 Federal Rd.
Brookfield, CT 06804

Phone: 203-775-1909
www.toyotomiusa.com

The four models in the sealed-combustion Laser kerosene heater line from Toyotomi offer heating efficiencies ranging from 90 to 93% (AFUE rating of 87.7%) while providing outputs from 5,200 to 40,000 Btu/hr. The units have heat-circulation fans and require 120-volt AC power, generating a preheating load of 260-280 watts, and a burning load of 42-76 watts. An external fuel tank is usually required. Units feature electronic ignition (no pilot light), setback thermostat, au- tomatic safety shutoff, and power failure recovery. The cabinet stays cool to the touch.

Oil Miser Space Heaters

Toyotomi U.S.A., Inc.
604 Federal Rd.
Brookfield, CT 06804

Phone: 203-775-1909
www.toyotomiusa.com

The only oil-fired, sealed-combustion space-heating system in North America, Oil Miser model OM-22 from Toyotomi has an AFUE rating of 90%, with output ranging from 8,000 to 22,000 Btu/hr. An external fuel tank is required (No. 1 or No. 2 fuel oil). The unit has a heat- circulation fan and requires 120-volt AC power for a preheating load of 275 watts and a burning load of 46 watts. Units feature setback thermostat, automatic safety shutoff, and power failure recovery. The cabinet stays cool to the touch.

Space Heaters

Monitor Products, Inc.
P.O. Box 3408
Princeton, NJ 08543

Toll-free: 800-524-1102
Phone: 732-329-0900
www.monitorproducts.com

Monitor space heaters are gas-, LPG-, or kerosene-fired, direct-vented, through-the-wall units with 83% efficiencies.

Dampers

Quality dampers and other air duct accessories are a crucial part of most large HVAC systems.

Wax-Actuator Dampers

Keenan & Meier
5191 Stump Rd.
Plumsteadville, PA 18949

Toll-free: 866-326-7371
Phone: 215-766-3010
www.kmdampers.com

Keenan & Meier manufactures a variety of passive ventilation dampers that use a phase-changing wax actuator to open and close the damper. The damper starts to open at 60 degrees Fahrenheit and becomes fully open at 80 degrees, as the paraffin wax turns to liquid and increases in volume, pushing out a piston that operates the damper. The damper uses no electricity and is made from approximately 60% post-industrial recycled aluminum. These dampers are an alternative to both motor-operated dampers requiring electricity and manually opened spring-mounted dampers.

Duct Mastic

Duct leakage is a major problem with forced-air heating or air-conditioning systems. When ducts are run outside of the conditioned space, heating and cooling efficiencies may be cut in half due to leakage. Tightly sealed ducting is extremely important in ensuring high energy efficiency of forced-air HVAC equipment. Experts strongly recommend duct mastics—not duct tape—for sealing ducts.

Air Duct Closure Systems and Air Duct Sealants

RCD Corporation
2850 Dillard Rd.
Eustis, FL 32726

Toll-free: 800-854-7494
Phone: 352-589-0099
www.rcdmastics.com

RCD Corporation is a leading manufacturer of low-VOC air duct sealants, mastics, and weather barrier coatings.

Duct Sealants

Hardcast, Inc.
900 Hensley Ln.
P.O. Box 1239
Wylie, TX 75098

Toll-free: 800-527-7092
Phone: 888- 229-0199
www.hardcast.com

Hardcast manufactures a line of VOC-free and water-based duct sealants.

UNI-MASTIC 181 Duct Sealer

McGill Airseal Corporation
2400 Fairwood Ave.
Columbus, OH 43207

Toll-free: 800-624-5535
Phone: 614-443-5520
www.mcgillairseal.com

Uni-Mastic™ 181 duct sealer is a water-based product that is designed to remain flexible over time in applications including sheet-metal, flexible, and fiberglass duct. It is UL181 listed and contains antimicrobial agents that remain effective after curing.

Evaporative Air-Cooling Equipment

Modern residential and commercial evaporative coolers are more efficient and use much less water than their "swamp cooler" predecessors. In hot dry climates, they can provide significant energy savings over even the best compressor-based cooling systems without the use of refrigerants and with cost-competitive initial prices. They also lower peak demand on the electrical grid. Evaporative coolers use the latent heat of evaporation to cool air in areas of low-humidity. The difference between the "dry bulb" and the "wet bulb" temperature indicates how much cooling is possible (with 100% humidity, the dry- and wet-bulb temperatures are the same). Most modern evaporative coolers are direct systems that bring moist cool air straight into the building, but there are also indirect systems, which use an air-to-air heat exchanger to provide cool air without raising indoor humidity, and direct/indirect systems which are two-stage coolers that can deliver air that is cooler than the wet-bulb temperature. Cooling efficiency is measured by the "saturation effectiveness" whereas the California Energy Commission's Evaporative Cooler Efficiency Ratio (ECER) provides a standardized measure of both cooling and energy efficiency. Products listed here must have saturation effectiveness of at least 80% under all operating conditions and a mechanism for effective cleaning with minimal water use (for example, a sump-dump system). The ECER is listed when available, and a high ECER rating may become a requirement for listing when its use becomes more common.

Aerocool Pro Series Evaporative Coolers

Phoenix Manufacturing, Inc
3655 E. Roeser Rd.
Phoenix, AZ 85040

Phone: 602-437-1034
www.evapcool.com

The Pro Series residential-scale direct evaporative coolers include programmable thermostats and high-efficiency cooling media that provides over 90% saturation effectiveness. Models are available with industry-standard cfm ratings of 4800 and 6800, with multiple discharge orientations. These coolers include a Pro-clean system that drains and washes the unit daily. The pro-clean system is an optional add-on to PMI's other residential and commercial evaporative coolers.

Breezair Elite EX Series

Seeley International Corporation
1202 N. 54th Ave.
Bldg. 2 Ste. 117
Phoenix, AZ 85043

Phone: 602-353-8066
www.seeleyinternational.com

The Breezair Elite EX direct evaporative cooler comes with a water manager that monitors mineral content in the water, adjusting water supply appropriately to reduce water use and cleaning requirements as compared to a standard continuous-bleed process. The cooler drains automatically when not in use, allowing the cooling media to dry out and minimize risk of mold growth. A remote control adjusts the variable-speed fan motor to regulate temperature.   Breezair's full line of coolers have been ECER tested. The Elite EX comes in 5500 and 7500 industry standard cfm ratings. The EX155V has an ECER of 32.9 and media saturation effectiveness of 85.6% and the EX275V has an ECER of 33.3 and media saturation effectiveness of 87.4%.

Coolerado

Coolerado, LLC
4700 W. 60th Ave., Unit 3
Arvada, CO 80003

Phone: 303-375-0878
www.coolerado.com

The Coolerado Cooler is an all-indirect system that, like other evaporative air conditioners, relies on the latent heat of vaporization for cooling. Unlike other systems, the Coolorado does not introduce moisture into the building, and thus can be used in conjunction with conventional compression-cycle air conditioning. The Coolerado R600 delivers four to six tons of cooling with electricity consumption of 1,200 watts—750 watts if specified with an electronically commutated motor (ECM). Water consumption is comparable to or slightly lower than that of direct evaporative coolers—as much as 12 gallons per hour at peak load, but typically averaging about 4 gallons per hour over the cooling season.

MasterCool Contractor and HC Series

AdobeAir, Inc.
1450 E. Grant St.
Phoenix, AZ 85034

Toll-free: 877-595-3827
Phone: 602-257-0060
www.adobeair.com

The MasterCool® Contractor® and HC Series direct evaporative coolers have a 90% saturation effectiveness with 12" cooling pads. The systems have automatic thermostat controls and automatically drain every 6 hours of operation. Models are available with industry standard cfm ratings of 4200, 4800, 5500, and 6500, with multiple discharge orientations and mounting options.

Furnaces

Furnaces heat air that is then distributed through ducting and warm-air registers. These listings include the highest-efficiency, sealed-combustion furnaces and high-efficiency multi-fuel or wood-only furnaces. A multi-fuel furnace uses several sources of energy such as wood, wood-pellets, coal, oil, or gas, with oil or gas operating as backup. One can also purchase wood-only furnaces and boilers without the fossil-fuel backup, or interconnect an "add-on" wood system with an existing oil or gas system. Well-designed biomass-fueled furnaces have very high combustion efficiencies, reducing particulate emissions to less than half of the levels of the best wood stoves. When wood is locally available and can be harvested sustainably, it has no net impact on global warming.

Gas furnaces listed here must have at least 94% annual fuel utilization efficiency (AFUE). Multifuel systems are listed with system efficiencies of at least 80% using wood and 85% with gas or oil. Multi-fuel systems still lack standardized testing for efficiency and preference is given to systems which provide certification or other verification of testing procedures.

Amana AMV9 Gas Furnace

Amana Heating and Air Conditioning
1810 Wilson Pkwy.
Fayetteville, TN 37334

Phone: 800-647-2982
www.amana-hac.com

Amana's AMV9 two-stage, variable-speed gas furnace has an efficiency of up to 96% AFUE. Heating capacity ranges from 30,800 to 109,000 Btu/hr. These furnaces are available in a variety of airflow configurations. Amana offers a lifetime warranty on the heat eschanger and recuperative coil, and five years on the balance of the system.

Diamond 90 and Diamond 95 ULTRA

York International Corp.
5005 York Dr.
Unitary Products Group
Norman, OK 73069

Toll-free: 877-874-7378
Phone: 405-364-4040
www.yorkupg.com

The Diamond 90 gas-fired, sealed-combustion furnace has an efficiency of up to 94.3% AFUE. This condensing-type furnace is suitable for commercial and residential installation. The Diamond 90 has a primary and secondary heat exchanger to maximize efficiency. The Diamond 95 Ultra comes with a variable-speed fan.

Encore NC 1450

Vermont Castings
1000 E. Market St.
Huntington, IN 46750

Toll-free: 800-227-8683
www.vermontcastings.com

The Encore NC 1450 is a cast-iron, non-catalytic wood stove with emissions of 0.7 grams per hour (gph), which is lower than most catalytic wood stoves and pellet stoves. The 40,000 Btu/hour (max.) stove uses Vermont Casting's EVERBURN combustion technology. It is the lowest-emitting wood stove that has been certified by the U.S. Environmental Protection Agency (EPA), and it handily meets the strict Washington State emission limit of 4.5 gph for non-catalytic wood stoves. (For catalytic stoves, the limit is 2.5 gph.) A slightly larger Defiant NC 1610 has emissions nearly as low and produces up to 60,000 Btu/hour.

Infinity Series

Carrier Corp.
Carrier Parkway
P.O. Box 4808
Syracuse, NY 13221

Toll-free: 800-227-7437
Phone: 315-432-6000
www.carrier.com

Carrier's Infinity™ gas furnaces features a smart microprocessor control center and variable-speed motors that minimize electrical usage. Sealed combustion protects indoor air quality and reduces noise. Models in this series range in heating capacity from 40,000 to 154,000 Btu per hour. The 58MVB, with an efficiency of up to 96.6% AFUE, is Carrier's most efficient gas furnace. It has a variable-speed fan, 4-way multipoise, and advanced humidity-removal capabilities.

Plus 90 High-Efficiency Furnaces

Bryant Heating & Cooling Systems
7310 W. Morris St.
Indianapolis, IN 46231

Toll-free: 800-428-4326
Phone: 317-243-0851
www.bryant.com

Bryant's Plus 90i and Plus 95i series of gas furnaces has AFUEs ranging from to 95.0 to 96.6%. Heating capacities from its two-stage gas valve range from 40,000/120,000 Btu/hr. These furnaces have variable-speed fans and advanced humidity-control technology, and are available in upflow, downflow, or horizontal airflow configurations.

UltraMAX III

ECR International, Inc.
2201 Dwyer Ave.
Utica, NY 13501

Phone: 315-797-1310
www.ecrinternational.com

Olsen's UltraMAX III high-efficiency furnaces are available in heating capacities ranging from 47,000 to 95,000 Btu/hr. The GTH 85 and GTH 100 models have efficiencies of up to 95% AFUE. GTH 50 and GTH 70 have efficiencies of up to 94% AFUE.

Heat Pumps

Heat pumps are similar to air conditioners—but in addition to removing heat, they can reverse their cycle to pump heat into a building when needed. Heat pumps use electricity as the energy input; the heat source is the outside air, the ground, or a body of water. Air-source heat pumps use the outdoor air as the heat source or heat sink. Air-source heat pump heating efficiency is measured as the Heating Seasonal Performance Factor (HSPF), which is the ratio of thermal energy output (in Btu) to electrical energy input (in watt-hours) over a heating season. Similarly derived, the cooling performance of air-source heat pumps is typically measured as the seasonal energy efficiency rating (SEER). Ground-source heat pumps utilize the earth's more stable temperatures as the heat source and heat sink; performance is typically measured as the coefficient of performance (COP)—the instantaneous ratio of energy input in Btus to energy output in Btus. Since the temperatures are usually more moderate underground, geothermal systems typically cost less to operate than conventional heat pumps. Water-source heat pumps are like ground-source heat pumps but use a body of water as the heat source and sink. Some heat pumps can provide water heating in addition to heating and cooling.

Acadia Combined Heating and Cooling System

Hallowell International
110 Hildreth St.
Bangor, ME 04401

Phone: 207-990-5600
www.gotohallowell.com

Hallowell's Acadia™ Combined Heating and Cooling System is a multistage air source heat pump that uses patented Opti-Cycle technology to allow the system to continue its heating performance well below zero degrees without the use of resistance heat backup. Its performance rivals many geothermal heat pumps. The Hallowell heat pump uses non-ozone-depleting refrigerant R-410a and cooling mode operation efficiency is comparable to many dedicated unitary air conditioners.

Affinity 8T Heat Pump

York International Corp.
5005 York Dr.
Unitary Products Group
Norman, OK 73069

Toll-free: 877-874-7378
Phone: 405-364-4040
www.yorkupg.com

The Affinity 8T line of heat pumps from York offers up to 18 SEER (cooling) and 9.4 HSPF (heating) in sizes ranging from 2 to 5 tons. The quiet, two-stage design allows improved part-load efficiency; increased demand triggers full capacity. These units are available with non-ozone-depleting R-410A refrigerant. The compressor has a ten-year warranty; the parts warranty is five years.

Ground-Source Heat Pumps

ClimateMaster
7300 S.W. 44th St.
Oklahoma City, OK 73179

Toll-free: 800-299-9747
Phone: 405-745-6000
www.climatemaster.com

ClimateMaster is one of the largest producers of ground-source heat pumps.

Ground-Source Heat Pumps

ECONAR Energy Systems Corp.
19230 Evans St.
Elk River, MN 55330

Toll-free: 800-432-6627
Phone: 763-241-3110
www.econar.com

The ColdClimate™ GeoSource® 2000 line of ground-source heat pumps are designed for residential (1 to 6 tons) and commercial (8 to 10 tons) applications. These self-contained units have a 25 degrees F design point for regions with higher numbers of heating degree days per year.

Ground-Source Heat Pumps

WaterFurnace International, Inc.
9000 Conservation Way
Fort Wayne, IN 46809

Toll-free: 800-222-5667
Phone: 260-478-5667
www.waterfurnace.com

WaterFurnace International manufactures and distributes Envision, E Series, Premier, and Versatec commercial, institutional, and residential lines of ground-source geothermal heat pumps for retrofit or new construction. Water-Furnace produces both water-to-air and water-to-water units with 3/4- to 30-ton capacities. Envision and E Series lines use R410-A refrigerant that does not deplete the ozone layer. Wholly owned subsidiary LoopMaster, Inc. is an earth loop contractor.

Heritage Heat Pumps

American Standard Heating and Air Conditioning
6200 Troup Hwy.
Tyler, TX 75711

Toll-free: 888-556-0125
Phone: 903-581-3499
www.americanstandardair.com

American Standard (the parent company of Trane) offers the Heritage® line of heat pumps. They use a variable-speed fan and Dual Duration™ compressors that provide two-stage cooling: a smaller compressor handles most of the work, but on the hottest days a larger compressor takes over. With SEER ratings of up to 18.9, and HSPF ratings up to 9, these are among the highest-efficiency air-sourced heat pumps available. They are available in 1.5 to 5 tons, and have a ten-year warranty. Some units use ozone-depleting R-22 refrigerant; others use ozone-safe R410A.

Infinity Heat Pumps

Carrier Corp.
Carrier Parkway
P.O. Box 4808
Syracuse, NY 13221

Toll-free: 800-227-7437
Phone: 315-432-6000
www.carrier.com

The Infinity™ line of heat pumps from Carrier has SEER ratings up to 19, and up to 9 HSPF. These 2- to 5-ton, two-speed units use Carrier's Puron ozone-safe R-410a refrigerant , which is a blend of three different HFCs. Carrier offers a 5-year limited warranty on parts, and a 10-year limited warranty on the compressor.

Quantum Plus 698b Heat Pump

Bryant Heating & Cooling Systems
7310 W. Morris St.
Indianapolis, IN 46231

Toll-free: 800-428-4326
Phone: 317-243-0851
www.bryant.com

Bryant produces the Quantum Plus™ 698b heat pump using non-ozone-depleting Puron™ refrigerant. The heat pump features a quiet fan and pump, two speeds, a SEER rating of 16, HSPF of 8.5, plus a 10-year warranty on the compressor and 5 years on everything else. The 650A heat pump also uses Puron™ refrigerant, has a SEER of 13.0 to 14.5, and the same warranty as the 698b.

Water-Source Heat Pump

FHP Manufacturing
601 N.W. 65th Ct.
Ft. Lauderdale, FL 33309

Phone: 954-776-5471
www.fhp-mfg.com

The EV and ES Two Stage Series EnviroMiser water-source heat pump is among FHP's most efficient and one of the first ground-source/water-source heat pumps to use the non-ozone-depleting refrigerant R-410a, an HFC mixture.

XL Series Heat Pump

Trane Residential Systems
6200 Troup Hwy.
Tyler, TX 75707

Phone: 903-581-3200
www.trane.com

Trane's Weatherton® XL Series of dual-compressor, air-source heat pumps have up to 17.9 SEER (cooling value), and up to 9.05 HSPF (heating value). They are available in 1.5- to 5-ton units. The manufacturer's limited warranty covers compressor, coil, and internal functional parts for 10 years. Some units use ozone-depleting R22 refrigerant; others use R410A.

XP19 Heat Pump

Lennox Industries, Inc.
2100 Lake Park Blvd
Richardson, TX 75080

Toll-free: 800-953-6669
Phone: 972-497-5000
www.lennox.com

The XP19 heat pump has a two-stage operation that saves energy by running at low speed 80% of the time. The XP19 uses non-ozone-depleting R410A refrigerant and at 18.6 SEER (cooling) and 9.3 HSPF (heating), it's one of the highest-rated heat pumps available. It carries a 10-year limited compressor warranty and a 5-year limited warranty on covered components. Though HFC refrigerant R410A is non-ozone-depleting, it, like HCFC, is a significant greenhouse gas that contributes to global warming.

Heating Boilers

Boilers heat water in hydronic heating systems; the heat is distributed through baseboard radiators (convectors), panel radiators, or radiant-floor piping. These listings include the highest-efficiency oil- or gas-fired boilers and products, as well as biomass-fired and multi-fuel alternatives. (Well-designed biomass-fueled boilers have very high combustion efficiencies, reducing particulate emissions to less than half of the levels of the best wood stoves.) Boilers listed here have system efficiencies of at least 87% for oil, 94% for gas, and 80% for wood (Multifuel boilers must be at least 85% efficient when using fossil fuels). Preference is given to systems that provide certification or other verification of standardized testing procedures. Some water heaters—especially electronic-ignition on-demand water heaters—can also be used as boilers for heating, particularly in very-low-energy buildings.

AquaMaster Q100

Vebteck Research
30 Riviera Dr.
Markham, ON L3R 5M1 Canada

Phone: 905-479-4048
www.ekocomfort.com

The AquaMaster Q100 is a joint development effort from Vebteck Research, Nutech Energy Systems, and Fleetline Products that offers integrated high-efficiency space heating (forced air or hydronic), domestic water heating, and continuous whole-house, heat-recovery ventilation (HRV) under a single, unified control system. The small system—it has a 4' x 2' footprint—includes a high-efficiency, low-mass, low-water-volume boiler (natural gas, propane, or fuel oil); a single, multi-speed, ECM blower; and an aluminum HRV core. The AquaMaster is a product of the eKOCOMFORT® consortium, a partnership of Canadian manufacturers and governmental agencies developing efficient, gas-fired, module-based units integrating space heating, ventilation, and domestic hot water.

Dryair Hydronic Construction Heater

Dryair Inc.
1095 N. Main St.
Bowling Green, OH 43402

Toll-free: 866-354-8546
Phone: 419-354-8546
www.dryair.us

The Dryair System uses a portable central heating plant and a low-pressure hydronic circulation system with remote heat exchangers to provide temporary, thermostatically-controlled heat for construction areas. The heat plant (individual models are fueled by propane or natural gas, or diesel / light oil) is located outdoors; no fumes, water vapor, or other combustion by-products are added to the conditioned space. Eliminating the supplemental ventilation required for conventional construction heat sources can reduce heating fuel use by half. Two sizes of fan/coil powered heat exchangers (120v) deliver an average of 80,000 or 200,000 Btu/h. Hose-type line heat exchangers transfer heat by conduction and radiation for ground thaw, frost prevention, and curing applications. These systems may also provide total structure dryout in disaster or accident mitigation situations.

G115 Sealed-Combustion Oil Boilers

Buderus
50 Wentworth Ave.
Londonderry, NH 03053

Toll-free: 800-283-3787
Phone: 603-552-1100
www.buderus.net

The smallest three models in this German hydronic boiler line are among the only true sealed-combustion, oil-fired residential boilers on the market. They are noted for their quiet operation and 86% combustion efficiency. A sophisticated "Logamatic" optional control module allows boiler water temperature control based on outside temperature (outdoor reset), plus priority control for indirect water heating. Buderus also makes indirect water heater tanks.

HeatManager Heating Boiler Economizer

R. W. Beckett Corporation
P.O. Box 1289
Elyria, OH 44036

Toll-free: 800-645-2876
Phone: 440-327-1060
www.beckettcorp.com

R. W. Beckett guarantees that its HeatManager Model 7512 will reduce oil, natural gas, or propane consumption by at least 10% in most residential boiler heating systems (sized up to 300,000 Btu, and if the boiler temperature regularly exceeds 150 degrees F during the heating season). The economizing microprocessor works with the existing boiler controls, adjusting firing patterns and boiler water temperature according to system load. Cycling may be reduced by 30%. This aftermarket product is optimally used in multi-zoned systems and also works with domestic hot water systems.

MPO Oil-Fired Boiler

Burnham Corporation
P.O. Box 3079
Lancaster, PA 17604

Toll-free: 888-432-8887
Phone: 717-397-4701
www.burnham.com

The MPO™ oil-fired, noncondensing, hydronic boiler is available in four sizes with GPH burner capacities ranging from 0.6 to 1.65, and and DOE Heating Capacities (MBH) from 74 to 203. All four models have an 87% AFUE, and are available in natural draft or direct vent. These boilers can be used for residential or light commercial applications, or installed in tandem for larger applications.

Multi-Fuel and Wood Boilers

Tarm USA, Inc.
5 Main St.
P.O. Box 285
Lyme, NH 03768

Toll-free: 800-782-9927
Phone: 603-795-2214
www.woodboilers.com

The HS-Tarm Excel 2000 Boiler is a multi-fuel boiler and domestic water heater that operates at over 80% efficiency on wood and 85% on oil. It has fully automatic controls to maintain the wood fire and the oil or gas backup that will automatically turn on the oil or gas burner when the wood fire dies down. The Excel 2000 burns very cleanly and generates very little ash for clean up.

The HS-Tarm Solo Plus-MKII boiler and domestic hot-water heater uses substantially less wood than conventional boilers and outdoor water stoves and also has a very clean burn. Three sizes are available with outputs from 100,000 to 198,000 Btu/hr.

Polaris Heating Systems

American Water Heater Company
500 Princeton Rd.
Johnson City, TN 37601

Toll-free: 800-937-1037
Phone: 423-283-8000
www.americanwaterheater.com

Polaris Heating Systems are high-efficiency, combination water and residential space-heating products. The gas-fired unit has a submerged stainless steel flue that transfers combustion energy to the water with 95+% efficiency. Polaris heaters are available in 34-, 50-, and 100-gal. sizes with outputs of 100,000 to 199,000 Btu/hr and energy factors of 0.86.

System 2000

Energy Kinetics
51 Molasses Hill Rd.
Lebanon, NJ 08833

Toll-free: 800-323-2066
www.energykinetics.com

System 2000, for residential and light commercial applications, has an AFUE rating of 87% and steady state efficiency of 99%. This integrated system provides multi-zone control of warm air, radiant heat, hydronic baseboard, and domestic hot water, as well as heating capabilities for pools or spas. It uses oil or natural gas or propane.

Humidity Control Equipment

Many of the most significant indoor air quality problems in buildings relate to moisture. While preventing rain penetration, plumbing leaks, wicking of moisture from the soil, and unvented moisture sources are the top priorities, it is sometimes also necessary to remove unwanted moisture from indoor air. Products listed here include high-efficiency dehumidification products.

Santa Fe, Ultra-Aire, and Hi-E Dry Dehumidifiers

Therma-Stor LLC
P.O. Box 8680
Madison, WI 53708

Toll-free: 800-533-7533
Phone: 608-222-5301
www.thermastor.com

Therma-Stor manufactures a range of high-efficiency dehumidifiers for residential and commercial use. Residential products include the Sante Fe and Ultra-Aire APD (air purifying dehumidifier), which provide air filtration in addition to dehumidification. For commercial applications, Therma-Stor offers the Hi-E Dry line of dehumidifiers.

HVAC Air Cleaning Devices

Air filtration is an important part of HVAC design. Quality products should have high filtration efficiency over a range of particle sizes, be energy-efficient (low pressure drop across filters), and durable. Measures of filtration defined by ASHRAE standards include arrestance efficiency, dust-spot efficiency, and Minimum Efficiency Reporting Value (MERV) ratings. High-efficiency particulate air (HEPA) filters are designed to capture extremely fine particulates but require increased duct pressure, which may necessitate an oversized mechanical system. Some lower-efficiency filters use recycled materials or are washable.

Airguard Air Filters

Airguard, Inc.
3807 Bishop Ln.
P.O. Box 32578
Louisville, KY 40232

Toll-free: 866-247-4827
Phone: 502-969-2304
www.airguard.com

Airguard produces a wide range of air filtration products, including rigid-cell filters with MERV 13 and higher ratings and HEPA filters. The company's Permalast® latex-coated natural-fiber (hog's hair) media and foam media, both with arrestance values of 60-70% (MERV 1-2), can be washed for repeated use but are only suitable for filtering the coarsest particulates. StreamLine™ filters, with arrestance values of 85-95% (MERV 5-6), are produced primarily from post-consumer recycled polyester fiber. Variflow filters, including the Compact Series, which rely on ultrafine fiberglass and wet-laid paper filtration, are available with dust-spot efficiencies of 60-95% (MERV 11-14).

CX3000 Air Purifier

Continental Fan Manufacturing
203 Eggert Rd.
Buffalo, NY 14215

Toll-free: 800-779-4021
Phone: 716-842-0670
www.continentalfan.com

The CX3000 whole-house air purification system will filter and clean up to 3,000sf (with a rated maximum airflow of 2,170 cfm). The system has an electrostatic MERV-11 Filter and a UVC light that activates a photo-catalytic Titanium Dioxide catalyst to destroy a wide variety of pollutants. The expected service life of the filter and UVC lamp is 6 months and 1 year, respectively. The CX3000 has computerized electronic controls, service lights that indicate when it is time to change filters and UVC lights, and a power rating of 45 watts.

Filtera Air Filters

Filtera
12999 Murphy Rd., Ste I-1
Stafford, TX 77477

Toll-free: 888-933-0100
Phone: 281-933-1100
www.filtera.com

Filtera offers mini-pleat air filters with efficiencies up to MERV 14 in 2- and 4-inch frames; these filters are available in UL Class 1 and 2. High-velocity, 12"-deep mini-pleat V-cell filters are also offered. The polypropylene media in these pleated filters doesn't support mold or bacteria, and doesn't corrode or degrade in humid conditions. Custom sizes are available. UL Class 2 HEPA glass-fiber gasketed filters—including high-temperature, high capacity, and turbine style—are also available in wood or metal frames.

High-Efficiency Air Filters

AAF International
10300 Ormsby Park Pl., Ste. 600
Lousiville, KY 90223

Toll-free: 888-223-2003
www.aafintl.com

The VariCel V (MERV 15) high capacity mini-pleat V-bank filter from AAF International replaces MERV 14 filters with minimal increase in resistance, up to 750 FPM. Their DriPak 2000 non-supported pocket filters are available in MERV 14 and 15. These UL Class 1 synthetic-media filters are available in a wide range of sizes.

High-Efficiency Air Filters

Camfil Farr
One North Corporate Dr.
Riverdale, NJ 07457

Toll-free: 866-422-6345
Phone: 973-616-7300
www.camfilfarr.com

Camfil Farr offers a variety of types, sizes, and styles of air filters rated up to MERV 15 including pleated, mini-pleat, and V-bank filters, UL Class 1 and 2, and carbon filters offering 95% odor removal efficiency with a low pressure drop. Packaged prefilters, roll media, and specialty filters are also available.

High-Efficiency Air Filters

Glasfloss Industries
400 South Hall St.
P.O. Box 150469
Dallas, TX 75315

Phone: 214-741-7056
www.glasfloss.com

Glasfloss offers a variety of types and sizes of air filters rated up to MERV 14, including UL Class 1 and 2 filters. Z-Pak pleated filters have plastic or fiberglass media in 6" and 12" depths for mixed- and high-velocity systems; the pleated fiberglass-media Magna line, also in 6" and 12" depths, has turbine, high-temperature, and HEPA options; the mini-pleated Puracell fiberglass line offers up to MERV 14 in a 4" depth, as well as a 12" V-pack filter model; and bag filters are available in plastic media (Excel line) and fiberglass (PuraPak line).

High-Efficiency Air Filters

Tri-Dim Filter Corp.
93 Industrial Dr.
Louisa, VA 23093

Toll-free: 800-458-9835
Phone: 540-967-2600
www.tridim.com

Tri-dim offers air filters from MERV 5 to MERV 20 and HEPA/ULPA in a range of types, sizes, and depths, including pleated, mini-pleat, V-cell, rigid box, and bag in fiberglass and synthetic media. Packaged prefilters, roll media, and bulk pads are also available.

Photox Air Purification Systems

Zentox Corporation
310-G Ed Wright Ln.
Newport News, VA 23606

Phone: 757-369-9870
www.zentox.com

The Photox™ is a stand-alone air purification system that removes VOCs and microorganisms (including bacteria, virus, and mold spores; urine and fecal odors; carbon monoxide and hydrogen sulfide; cooking odors and musty air; cleaning solvents, paint odors, and formaldehyde) from indoor air through photocatalytic oxidation. The system does not generate or make use of ozone. Photox 500 is for rooms up to 40' x 50', moving up to 500 cfm with an 180W draw. Photox 100 is for rooms up to 20' x 20', moving 50 to 100 cfm with a 25W draw. Annual replacement of the 32-watt fluorescent UV lamps and air filters is required.

HVAC Air Handlers

Indoor central-station air-handling units are prefabricated assemblies that work in conjunction with space conditioning systems to perform such functions as air circulation and filtration, humidity control, and ventilation air mixing. Additional functions may include air quality monitoring and heat recovery.

NightBreeze

Davis Energy Group
123 C St.
Davis, CA 95616

Phone: 530-753-1100
www.davisenergy.com

The NightBreeze ventilation cooling system—composed of a special vent damper, an advanced thermostat, sensors, and a highly efficient air handler—integrates with a home's mechanical system to provide ventilative cooling with pre-filtered night air. The system runs an efficient, variable-speed, electronically commutated motor (ECM) during off-peak hours to quietly circulate cool night air, storing the cooling energy in the home's thermal mass. Depending on the climate, this system can reduce or eliminate the need for daytime compression-cycle air conditioning. The system can also provide heat, either with hot-water coils in the base of the air handler (supplied by the home's domestic hot water system or a dedicated tankless water heater), or through an add-on control system that enables use of the NightBreeze with a compatible forced-air furnace.

HVAC Ducts and Casings

Air-supply and return ducts can be a medium for mold growth or (with insulated ducts) a source of fiber-shedding, both of which can pose significant indoor air quality concerns. Products listed here allow easy duct cleaning, or protect against mold growth or fiber-shedding.

Cotton-Insulated Semi-Flex Ducts

Payless Insulation, Inc.
1331 Seamist Dr.
Houston, TX 77008

Phone: 713-868-1021
www.superiorairducts.com

Superior Air Ducts™ R8 Cotton Insulated Semi Flex Ducts are integrally insulated round ducts made with 85% post-industrial recycled cotton fibers. The jacket is reflective metallized mylar; the inner core is made with clear mylar sheets encapsulating a steel wire helix. As with most flexible ducts, the inner surface is not smooth, so more fan energy will be needed than with a smooth-surfaced duct. Designed for low to medium operating pressures, these ducts are resistant to mold and bacteria, are Class A fire-rated, and have a 10-year warranty. The 2.2 lb/ft3 cotton walls are indicated by the manufacturer to be 2" thick, for an R-value of 8. These ducts are available in 12.5' and 25' sections in a dozen different diameters ranging from 2" to 20". The cotton fiber is supplied by Bonded Logic, Inc.

Dryer-Ell

In-O-Vate Technologies, Inc.
810 Saturn St., Ste. 21
Jupiter, FL 33477

Toll-free: 888-443-7937
Phone: 561-743-8696
www.dryerbox.com

The Dryer-Ell™ dryer-duct elbow is a 4"-diameter, large-radius elbow with a smooth interior that is designed to reduce friction in dryer venting systems. The elbow reduces the need for a booster fan and increases the allowable duct length by about five feet, compared with standard elbows (based on ASHRAE methodology for calculating friction loss).

ToughGard

CertainTeed Corporation
750 E. Swedesford Rd.
P.O. Box 860
Valley Forge, PA 19482

Toll-free: 800-233-8990
Phone: 610-341-7000
www.certainteed.com

CertainTeed's ToughGard™ fiberglass duct board is a ducting material with integral insulation. At 75 degrees F, the company claims an R-value of 4.3 for 1" board, 6.5 for 1-1/2" board, and 8.7 for 2" board. To prevent fiber shedding, ToughGard has both a nonwoven composite interior facing of textile fiberglass and polypropylene, and a reinforced foil-laminate exterior facing. The material's ship-lap design helps minimize air leakage at joints. This product carries the Greenguard certification for low emissions.

HVAC Fans

Fans for air circulation, air distribution, and exhaust and key components of most mechanical systems, and major users of energy. For optimal efficiency fans should be properly sized and controlled with efficient motors and drives. In residences, unless there's a central ventilation system, kitchen and bathroom spot-ventilators may be the only mechanical ventilation system in a house. To increase the likelihood that fans will be used, they should be quiet. To be included in GreenSpec, bathroom ventilators must have sone ratings no higher than 1.5. ("Sone" is a measure of loudness; one sone is about as loud as a common residential refrigerator.) Quiet kitchen range-hood fans are much more difficult to find; often the best option is to use a remote, in-line fan. Ceiling fans are designed to mix air in a room and provide airflow for enhanced comfort—they do not provide fresh air.

F. R. Series Fans

Fantech
1712 Northgate Blvd.
Sarasota, FL 34234

Toll-free: 800-747-1762
www.fantech.net

Fantech's in-line duct fans are often specified where minimizing noise is a high priority. These in-line fans range in size from 122 cfm to 649 cfm, 4" to 10" duct diameter, with energy consumption from 19 W to 241 W. Smaller products are generally used for residential applications; larger for commercial. Fantech's F.R. Series fans carry a 5-year warranty.

Gossamer Wind Ceiling Fans

King of Fans, Inc.
1951 N.W. 22nd St.
Ft. Lauderdale, FL 33311

Toll-free: 800-330-3267
Phone: 954-484-7500
www.king-of-fans.com

King of Fans is now manufacturing the energy-efficient Gossamer Wind Ceiling Fans for Home Depot's Hampton Bay label. Tests have shown that the production models are 40-50% more energy-efficient than conventional fans.

Inline Exhaust Duct Fans

Continental Fan Manufacturing
203 Eggert Rd.
Buffalo, NY 14215

Toll-free: 800-779-4021
Phone: 716-842-0670
www.continentalfan.com

Continental Fan Manufacturings AXC inline centrifugal duct fans for residential, commercial, and industrial applications offer quiet, efficient operation with high exhaust capacities, and are particularly appropriate where long vent runs are required. These fans use backward-curved impellers and infinitely variable RPM motors to meet versatile air-moving needs. With the fan and motor above the plane of the ceiling, operating noise is significantly dampened. Pressure, fan speed, dehumidistat, and timer controls are available, as well as backdraft dampers. For dryer venting applications - such as in apartment complexes - the pressure switch is preferable to using a timer in terms of energy conservation.

Quiet-Vent

Therma-Stor LLC
P.O. Box 8680
Madison, WI 53708

Toll-free: 800-533-7533
Phone: 608-222-5301
www.thermastor.com

Quiet-Vent is a multiport, central exhaust ventilation system designed to quietly, effectively, and automatically ventilate airtight homes.

Thermal Equalizers

Avedon Engineering, Inc.
811 S. Sherman St.
Longmont, CO 80501

Phone: 303-772-2633
www.airius.us

Airius Thermal Equalizers reduce heating and cooling energy needs through air destratification in rooms with 10- to 60-foot ceilings. The turbines "drill" air down in a column, keeping floor and ceiling temperatures within three degrees of each other in conditioned spaces. Power consumption for the different models ranges from 14 to 110 watts, with the most common using 35 watts. Product selection is based on ceiling height and area coverage. Larger models feature highly efficient electronically commutated motors (ECM).

Ventilation and Airflow Equipment

Tamarack Technologies, Inc.
320 Main Street
P. O. Box 963
Buzzards Bay, MA 02532

Toll-free: 800-222-5932
Phone: 508-759-4660
www.tamtech.com

Tamarack Technologies produces specialized ventilators and ventilation controllers. Among its innovative products are the sophisticated whole-house ventilators (HV 1000 and HV 1600-Gold). These fans have motorized, insulated covers that seal the exhaust opening tightly when the units are not in operation.

HVAC Insulation

Air-supply and return ducts can be a medium for mold growth or (with insulated ducts) a source of fiber-shedding, both of which can pose significant indoor air quality concerns. Products listed here allow easy duct cleaning, or protect against mold growth or fiber-shedding. Also included are specialized insulation products for piping and other mechanical equipment. For hydronic heating pipes that experience high temperature (over 150 degrees F), inexpensive foam-plastic pipe insulation sleeves may not be adequate; high-temperature pipe insulation is required.

Cotton Insulating Duct Wrap

Payless Insulation, Inc.
1331 Seamist Dr.
Houston, TX 77008

Phone: 713-868-1021
www.superiorairducts.com

Superior R8 Cotton Duct Wrap™ is an insulating HVAC duct wrap for commercial or residential applications. It is made with 85% post-industrial fibers (2.2 lbs/ft3 density, borax-treated cotton) bonded to a metallized mylar jacket and is resistant to fungus, bacteria, fire, and moisture. Standard available size is 2" thick x 25' long x 5' wide. The cotton fiber is supplied by Bonded Logic, Inc.

Knauf Air-Handling Insulation Products

Knauf Insulation
One Knauf Dr.
Shelbyville, IN 46176

Toll-free: 800-825-4434
Phone: 317-398-4434
www.knaufusa.com

Knauf air-handling insulation products, including duct wrap, duct board, duct liner, and plenum liner contribute minimal levels of formaldehyde and other pollutants to the indoor environment. Duct wrap rolls are available with a variety of facings, including PSK (polypropylene-scrim-kraft); duct liner rolls have an airstream surface mat facing of tightly bonded fiberglass. Duct board is available with a nonwoven mat face; the rigid plenum liner has a polymer overspray on the airstream side.

ToughGard

CertainTeed Corporation
750 E. Swedesford Rd.
P.O. Box 860
Valley Forge, PA 19482

Toll-free: 800-233-8990
Phone: 610-341-7000
www.certainteed.com

CertainTeed's ToughGard™ fiberglass duct board is a ducting material with integral insulation. At 75 degrees F, the company claims an R-value of 4.3 for 1" board, 6.5 for 1-1/2" board, and 8.7 for 2" board. To prevent fiber shedding, ToughGard has both a nonwoven composite interior facing of textile fiberglass and polypropylene, and a reinforced foil-laminate exterior facing. The material's ship-lap design helps minimize air leakage at joints. This product carries the Greenguard certification for low emissions.

Instrumentation and Control for HVAC

Good HVAC instrumentation and control systems are important for maintaining high levels of comfort as well as energy savings.

Aprilaire Ventilation Control System

Aprilaire
1015 E. Washington Ave.
P.O. Box 1467
Madison, WI 53701

Toll-free: 800-334-6011
Phone: 608-257-8801
www.aprilaire.com

The Aprilaire Ventilation Control System works in conjunction with an included Aprilaire motorized damper as part of a home's heating/cooling system. The controller monitors interior humidity and outdoor air temperature; user-adjustable controls react to this information, allowing homeowners to manage the quantity and quality of fresh air being brought into the home. Setpoints for high and low outdoor temperature and high indoor humidity override the system to prevent increased heating, cooling, and dehumidification loads; and the system will ventilate only during a heating cycle when outdoor temperatures are below 20 degrees F.

HK2000 Fresh Air / Economizer

EWC Controls, Inc.
385 Hwy. 33
Englishtown, NJ 07726

Toll-free: 800-446-3110
www.ewccontrols.com

The Ultra-Zone HK2000 Fresh Air and Economizer panel from EWC helps minimize HVAC loads while maintaining indoor comfort levels and providing controlled air changes. EWC makes a wide range of HVAC zone controls for commercial and residential applications with multi-stage, dual-fuel, and heat pump compatibility. The company also provides a range of dampers, pressure regulators, registers, diffusers, and thermostats. Avoid thermostats containing mercury switches.

Hunter Set & Save

Hunter Fan Co.
2500 Frisco Ave.
Memphis, TN 38114

Toll-free: 888-830-1326
Phone: 901-743-1360
www.hunterfan.com

Hunter Fan manufactures a full line of programmable digital and mechanical thermostats.

Invisible Service Technician

Invisible Service Technicians, LLC
502 TechneCenter Dr., Ste. B
Milford, OH 45150

Phone: 513-248-0900
www.istmonitor.com

The Invisible Service Technician (IST) is a data acquisition and monitoring system for residential and light-commercial HVAC&R applications. It monitors heating, cooling, and refrigeration equipment using a system of electronic sensors and the HVAC&R unit's control board, transmitting any problems to a central monitoring facility. Measured data includes various temperatures, pressure differentials, control signals, and any on-board fault-detection processes in the native HVAC&R control system. The IST is powered by the 24-volt power circuit of the HVAC&R system and requires a (non-dedicated) working phone line to transmit performance data. This system can reduce the increased energy use and environmental impacts caused by poorly functioning equipment.

Programmable Thermostats

Honeywell Home & Building Controls
P.O. Box 524
Minneapolis, MN 55440

Toll-free: 800-328-5111
Phone: 612-951-1000
yourhome.honeywell.com

Honeywell produces a wide range of programmable thermostats, including a line of microprocessor-controlled electronic thermostats for heating and/or cooling. This series allows for programmed temperature setbacks and for gradual temperature recovery. Several models are available for replacement and new installation applications.

Wax-Actuator Dampers

Keenan & Meier
5191 Stump Rd.
Plumsteadville, PA 18949

Toll-free: 866-326-7371
Phone: 215-766-3010
www.kmdampers.com

Keenan & Meier manufactures a variety of passive ventilation dampers that use a phase-changing wax actuator to open and close the damper. The damper starts to open at 60 degrees Fahrenheit and becomes fully open at 80 degrees, as the paraffin wax turns to liquid and increases in volume, pushing out a piston that operates the damper. The damper uses no electricity and is made from approximately 60% post-industrial recycled aluminum. These dampers are an alternative to both motor-operated dampers requiring electricity and manually opened spring-mounted dampers.

Masonry Fireplaces

Burning wood creates significant pollution. Emissions of particulates, carbon monoxide, VOCs, and methane are significantly greater from wood stoves than from any other common heating fuel. However, when wood is locally available and can be harvested sustainably, it has no net impact on global warming—because the carbon emissions from combustion are more than compensated for by growing trees. Thus, if wood is burned in a manner that minimizes pollution, it can be a good fuel choice. Products listed here have superior burning efficiencies and reduced particulate emissions in comparison even the best wood stoves. The high thermal mass of masonry heaters and biomass-fueled boiler systems can more effectively capture, store, and release heat over time. The downside of a high-mass masonry heater is that the heat of a freshly lit fire may not be felt in the

living space until several hours later. In passive solar homes this may make temperature regulation difficult.

Moberg Fireplaces

Moberg Fireplaces, Inc.
Cellar Building
1124 N.W. Couch St. Ste. 300
Portland, OR 97209

Phone: 503-227-0547
www.mobergfireplaces.com

FireSpaces is a dealer and manufacturer of masonry fireplaces. They also manufacture the masonry Moberg MRC and the Modern Rumford Masonry Fireplace Kit.

Temp-Cast Enviroheat Masonry Heater Kits

Temp-Cast
3409 Yonge St.
P.O. Box 94059
Toronto, ON M4N 3R1 Canada

Toll-free: 800-561-8594
Phone: 416-322-5197
www.tempcast.com

Temp-Cast is a modular masonry heater core kit featuring corner, 'see through,' and bake-oven models. Temp-Cast provides manuals detailing appropriate chimney construction with each masonry heater kit. Masonry materials for the chimney and the heater's exterior are sourced separately.

Tulikivi

Tulikivi U.S., Inc.
P.O. Box 7547
Charlottesville, VA 22906

Toll-free: 800-843-3473
www.tulikivi.com

Tulikivi's masonry heaters, available in over 25 different models, are made from soapstone quarried in Finland. Tulikivi masonry heaters produce a hot, clean-burning fire and efficiently transfer the fire's heat to the living space.

Mastic Removers

Products listed here include low-VOC, nontoxic, and biodegradable mastic removers.

BEAN-e-doo Mastic Remover

Franmar Chemical, Inc.
P.O. Box 5565
Bloomington, IL 61702

Toll-free: 800-538-5069
Phone: 309-452-7526
www.franmar.com

FranMar's BEAN-e-doo® Mastic Remover is made from soybeans to remove ceramic tile mastic, asbestos mastic, and carpet mastic. BEANedoo Mastic Remover has no odor, is nontoxic, noncaustic, 100% biodegradable, and rinses with water.

Packaged Water Chillers

Products listed here either use ozone-safe refrigerants or have failsafe systems to prevent the escape of refrigerant.

SunChiller

Sun Chiller
220 S. Kenwood St., Ste. 305
Glendale, CA 91205-1671

Phone: 818-240-4500
www.sunchiller.com

The SunChiller provides air cooling as a primary output, with space and water heating also possible. The system uses vacuum-tube heat-pipe solar thermal collectors to heat water, which drives an absorption chiller to provide cooling. Water serves as the "refrigerant," avoiding the use of ozone-depleting compounds. A SunChiller can be used in a hybrid system to provide space heating and water heating in addition to absorption cooling. The system can be configured to provide solar-powered absorption cooling during electrical peak hours, with a more conventional electric chiller taking over during lower-cost off-peak hours. The system combines vacuum-tube solar-thermal collectors, an insulated storage tank, a single-effect water-heated absorption chiller, a cooling tower, an energy management system, and air handler. It is available as an integrated system for commercial buildings requiring air conditioning capacity of at least 10 tons.

Powered Attic Exhaust Fans

Attic fans are used for whole-house exhaust and airflow or for heat removal from attics. In certain climates, attic fans can be used very effectively for night-flush cooling—in which household air is replaced with cooler air during the nighttime hours.

Attic Ventilation System

SolarAttic, Inc.
15548 95th Cir. NE
Elk River, MN 55330

Phone: 763-441-3440
www.solarattic.com

SolarAttic produces an electronic attic temperature switch for attic ventilation in all seasons. This product is used to automate ventilation equipment; it is compatible with existing fans or can be a part of a SolarAttic system.

Cyclone Solar Fan

Solar Dynamics, Inc.
212 Gateway Dr.
Ottumwa, IA 52501

Toll-free: 800-775-2134
Phone: 817-676-6192
www.solardynamicsinc.com

The Cyclone solar powered attic fan is powered by a 20-watt photovoltaic panel and moves up to 1275 cfm of air. Its compact, low-profile design allows it to be used to reduce extreme heat build-up and condensation in a variety of locations. The fan is available with self flash, curb mount, and gable mount flashing for pitched or flat roof applications. The 'Remote' systems separate the panel from the fan for more flexible installation, and the turbine retrofit solar fan is designed to fit the base assembly of any 12" turbine fan.

Fan-Attic

NuLight Solutions
1350 Dell Ave., Ste. 202
Campbell, CA 95008

Toll-free: 877-326-2884
Phone: 408-369-7447
www.fan-attic.com

The Fan-Attic™, (formerly available from Sun Tunnel Skylights and SteelTile Distributing), is a PV-powered roof ventilator fan that can move up to 800 cfm. This product is used instead of (or in addition to) ridge or gable vents. This solar-powered fan works hardest when ventilation is needed most and saves on installation costs because electrical wiring is not necessary.

Solar Attic Fan

Natural Light Energy Systems
10821 N. 23rd Ave., Ste. 1
Phoenix, AZ 85029

Toll-free: 800-363-9865
www.solaratticfan.com

Natural Light has roof-top and gable-mounted fans with either 10-watt or 20-watt PV panels built into the fan housing. The 10-watt fans are rated to move 850 cfm; the 20-watt fans 1,350. This product is used instead of (or in addition to) ridge or gable vents. This solar-powered fan works hardest when ventilation is needed most and saves on installation costs because electrical wiring is not necessary.

SolarCool Attic Vent

Air Vent, Inc.
4117 Pinnacle Point Drive,
Suite 400
Dallas, TX 75211

Phone: 800-247-8368
www.airvent.com

The SolarCool roof-mounted attic vent from Air Vent, Inc., is a low-profile, galvanized steel dome with a high-efficiency 24-volt DC motor powered by a small solar panel. The photovoltaic panel is mounted either on an adjustable bracket directly on the vent dome or up to 10 feet away, allowing it to be positioned for optimal solar exposure. No auxiliary electricity is required. A gable-mounted version is also available. This model mounts in the gable end of the house and the panel mounts on the roof. Both models ventilate up to 800 cfm for attics up to 1,200 ft2, and come with a 5-year limited warranty and 2-Year Replacement Plus™ protection.

Solar-Powered Attic Vents

Attic Breeze
4582 Kingwood Dr.
Ste. E-154
Kingwood, TX 77345

Toll-free: 877-288-4234
www.atticbreeze.net

Attic Breeze's solar-powered attic ventilation fans are rated to move 1,350 cfm using a 20-watt PV panel that can be mounted on the fan housing or remotely. The fan is available in either a galvanized steel or painted finish. This product is used instead of (or in addition to) ridge or gable vents. This solar-powered fan works hardest when ventilation is needed most and saves on installation costs because it does not need to be wired into the building's electrical system.

SunRise Attic Fans

SunRise Solar
P.O. Box 53
St. John, IN 46373

Phone: 219-558-2211
www.sunrisesolar.net

SunRise fans come in three models, named according to their rate airflow in cubic feet per minute (cfm): SunRise 850, SunRise 1050, and SunRise 1250. Each has photovoltaic panels built into the fan cover, so the fan must be installed with good solar orientation for optimal performance. The 850 cfm unit has 11 watts of thin-film PV; the other two have 15-watt and 20-watt crystalline PV under tempered glass. This product is used instead of (or in addition to) ridge or gable vents. This solar-powered fan works hardest when ventilation is needed most and saves on installation costs because electrical wiring is not necessary.

Space Heaters

Products listed here include high-performance panel radiators.

Hydronic Panel Radiators

Buderus
50 Wentworth Ave.
Londonderry, NH 03053

Toll-free: 800-283-3787
Phone: 603-552-1100
www.buderus.net

Buderus Solidoflux-N panel radiators deliver hydronic heat and may interfere with furniture placement less than baseboard radiators. Panel radiators are available in heights of 12", 20", and 24" and depths of 2-1/2" and 4". They can be fitted with optional individual thermostats and diverter valves to provide individual zoning. Flexible PEX polyethylene piping can be used in place of copper.

Hydronic Panel Radiators

Runtal North America
187 Neck Rd.
P.O. Box 8278
Ward Hill, MA 01835

Toll-free: 800-526-2621
Phone: 978-373-1666
www.runtalnorthamerica.com

Runtal panel and baseboard radiators are designed to operate at lower temperatures than conventional hydronic radiators (convectors). Therefore, a high percentage of the heat will be delivered through radiation rather than convection. The room's mean radiant temperature may be higher, and the thermostat set point (air temperature) can be kept somewhat lower with comparable comfort. Thus, some energy savings can be achieved. Runtal also manufactures the Omnipanel® radiator for bathrooms, which provides additional radiator area. The company's electric Omnipanel may be justified if its use allows whole-house thermostats to be kept lower. Runtal is a Swiss company.

Plumbing

Access to fresh water is one of the world's major geo-political issues, yet in most of the U.S. we still use drinking-quality water as if it were free and unlimited. A substantial portion of this usage happens in buildings where leaky plumbing drips it away, and fixtures designed decades ago use exorbitant quantities. In some areas of North America, water is drawn from ground and surface sources at unsustainable rates—in other words, withdrawals from aquifers exceeding annual recharge rates. For much of the year, for example, the Colorado River no longer reaches the Gulf of California. In the U.S., we currently withdraw over 300 billion gallons of fresh water per day from streams, reservoirs, and wells. Even in places where the water supply has traditionally not been a concern, problems are appearing as populations grow or precipitation patterns change (perhaps due to global climate change).

Toilet flushing uses over 4 billion gallons of water per day in the U.S. alone. While older toilets use about 4 gallons per flush, modern toilets conform to the requirements of the Energy Policy Act of 1992 and use no more than 1.6 gallons per flush (gpf). Simply replacing those older toilets with the new ones has been found to reduce a household's overall water use between 10% and 30%. Some toilets use less water—or even none at all. *GreenSpec* includes toilets that provide exceptional flush performance as determined by the Maximum Performance (MaP) testing protocol. Other water-saving designs, devices, and systems are also included. The Energy Policy

Act of 1992 also mandates that showerheads and faucets can use no more than 2.5 gallons per minute (gpm); some models use substantially less. Retrofitting these devices in older buildings is usually a very easy and extremely cost-effective investment.

Consumption of potable water can also be reduced by recycling graywater for nonpotable uses, such as irrigation and toilet flushing; however, these systems may be prohibited by local health codes. In most of California it is legal to use graywater for landscape irrigation, provided the system is designed to meet certain conditions.

The drain on limited water supplies can also be reduced by harvesting rainwater. On some of the Virgin Islands, rainwater-storing cisterns provide the primary water supply to most homes. In parts of the U.S., it is not uncommon for collected rainwater to be used for landscape irrigation, toilet flushing, laundry, and other nonpotable uses. For use as potable water, collected rainwater should be filtered and disinfected.

The other end of the plumbing system is wastewater disposal. Many conventional wastewater treatment systems, including both large municipal systems and private on-site septic systems, are inefficient and/or expensive. Alternative technologies are available for systems of all sizes: from composting toilets and recirculating sand filters, to ecological wastewater treatment systems that rely on enhanced biological treatment processes.

Composting Toilet Systems

Composting toilets convert human waste into nutrient-rich fertilizer for nonfood plants, rather than mixing the waste with potable water and flushing it down the drain. The advantages of composting toilets include dramatic reductions in water use, reduced groundwater pollution or sewage-treatment impacts, and a recycling of nutrients. Some composting chambers can be used with microflush toilets, though most are nonflush. Proper sizing is critical for effective composting; a model with undersized capacity won't function appropriately. If composting toilets are used, graywater treatment and disposal still need to be addressed.

Clivus Multrum Composting Toilet Systems

Clivus Multrum, Inc.
15 Union St.
Lawrence, MA 01840

Toll-free: 800-425-4887
Phone: 978-725-5591
www.clivusmultrum.com

Clivus Multrum popularized the composting toilet in the U.S. and is still one of the most widely recognized manufacturers. The company offers a range of composting toilets for various applications, from small residences to large public facilities. All include a composting chamber below one or more toilet fixtures. In addition to waterless models, Clivus offers a foam flush fixture that uses a soap solution and 3 oz. of water for flushing. Electricity is required for ventilation and moistening systems. Design, installation, and maintenance services are available.

Ecotech Carousel

Ecological Engineering Group
50 Beharell St.
Concord, MA 01742

Phone: 978-369-3951
www.ecological-engineering.com

The EcoTech Carousel is a "batch" composting toilet that processes waste faster and more completely without raking. Available from Gaiam Real Goods.

Envirolet Cleantech Sanitation

Sancor Industries Ltd.
140-30 Milner Ave.
Scarborough, ON M1S 3R3 Canada

Toll-free: 800-387-5126
Phone: 416-299-4818
www.envirolet.com

Sancor'd Envirolet composting toilets are available as waterless self-contained, waterless, and low water models with a separate composting chamber below; a 0.2 liter vacuum-powered nano-flush model with composting system beside; or above in-bathroom toilets. Available in non-electric, 12-volt DC, and 120-volt AC. Envirolet™ has been sold worldwide since 1977.

Equaris Biomatter Resequencing Converter

Equaris Corporation
15711 Upper 34th St. S
P.O. Box 6
Afton, MN 55001

Phone: 651-337-0261
www.equaris.com

Equaris Corporation, formerly AlasCan, Inc., manufactures a composting toilet system that operates as part of a system of integrated technologies to separate toilet and organic kitchen wastes from the wastewater stream at the source. Solid waste is deposited into the Equaris Biomatter Resequencing Converter (BMRC), where 90-95% of the toilet and organic wastes are biologically converted into odorless carbon dioxide and water vapor; the remaining 5-10% can be used safely as a soil amendment. The toilets used with this system require one cup of water or less per flush. Graywater is treated aerobically in the Equaris Greywater Treatment System utilizing a small continuously operating 67-watt linear air compressor to filter and remove most pollutants. This system eliminates septic tanks and reduces leachfields or mounds by 40-90%, according to the manufacturer. The water can then be diverted through the Equaris Water Recycling System to produce potable water using reverse osmosis, ozone and UV treatment, and physical filtration.

ExcelAerator

Bio-Sun Systems, Inc.
7088 Rte. 549
Millerton, PA 16936

Toll-free: 800-847-8840
Phone: 570-537-2200
www.bio-sun.com

Bio-Sun composting toilet systems can serve multiple toilets. The ExcelAerator™ system extracts by-product gasses from the composting chamber and also injects air directly into the waste piles for accelerated decomposition. A vent extraction device is incorporated which simultaneously removes byproduct gases.

Nepon Foam Flush Toilet

Nepon-USA
P.O. Box 127
North Andover, MA 01845

Toll-free: 866-396-3766
Phone: 978-794-4810
www.neponusa.com

The Nepon foam-flush toilet for ultra-low-flush or composting toilet applications uses a biodegradable soap solution and 3 ounces of water for each flush. An electric air pump aerates the soap, generating a foam of soap bubbles. The foaming action provides lubrication, prevents splashing and streaking, and keeps the toilet bowl clean. This toilet design relies on a physical trapway, as the flushing system does not accommodate the internal water-trap found in conventional toilets. Nepon offers a flush-accumulator system to allow this toilet to be used with conventional plumbing in retrofit applications.

Phoenix Composting Toilet

Advanced Composting Systems
195 Meadows Rd.
Whitefish, MT 59937

Toll-free: 888-862-3854
Phone: 406-862-3854
www.compostingtoilet.com

Phoenix Composting Toilet systems are used in residential and public-facility applications such as parks and recreation areas. They have mixing tines for aerating the compost and a system for recycling leachate. The only electrical load is a 12-volt DC, 5-watt exhaust fan.

Sun-Mar Composting Toilet

Sun-Mar Corp.
600 Main St.
Tonawanda, NY 14150 Canada

Toll-free: 888-341-0782
Phone: 905-332-1314
www.sun-mar.com

Sun-Mar offers over 20 different models of composting toilets, some self-contained and others with a separate composting chamber below. In general, composting toilets with separate compost chambers have proven more reliable. Any composting toilet must be correctly sized and installed, and appropriately maintained, in order to function properly.

Domestic Water Heat Exchangers

In the building industry, "domestic" water includes all potable water, whether in a residence or any kind of commercial building. A number of different opportunities exist to use waste heat for heating water. With refrigeration and air-conditioning equipment, waste heat is typically captured through desuperheating. Desuperheaters are most common in commercial settings, but equipment is available for residential use as well. To be cost-effective, a significant cooling load must support desuperheating operation—in homes, this means those in southern climates, and in commercial buildings this applies to businesses such as supermarkets that have large, year-round cooling and refrigeration loads. Waste heat from fuel-fired boilers can also be recovered for water heating. The heat content of wastewater can be recovered as well, using several different heat exchange technologies; the greater the surface area of contact between the two fluids, the more efficiently heat recovery can be achieved (but this must be balanced against the risk of blockage). Wastewater heat recovery systems are available for both commercial and residential applications.

GFX Wastewater Heat Reclaimer

The GFX Store
P.O. Box 75386
Colorado Springs, CO 80970

Phone: 209-814-8253
www.gfxtechnology.com

The GFX (gravity film exchange) drainline heat recovery device is a section of 2", 3" or 4" copper wastewater drainpipe wrapped by a coil of 1/2" copper supply line. Fresh water coming in through the supply line is warmed by the film of warm water descending the inner surface of the waste pipe. The GFX is available in various lengths and configurations for residential, institutional, and industrial uses. When hot water is being drawn, energy savings are obtained, and the heating capacity of water heaters extended.

HRP - Heat Recovery Option

FHP Manufacturing
601 N.W. 65th Ct.
Ft. Lauderdale, FL 33309

Phone: 954-776-5471
www.fhp-mfg.com

Florida Heat Pump makes a Heat Recovery Option or desuperheater that uses a heat exchanger to capture the waste heat from air conditioning units. The captured heat is then used for domestic water heating. System capacities are appropriate for both residential and commercial applications. Installation is appropriate where air conditioning loads are significant.

Power-Pipe Drainwater Heat Recovery

RenewABILITY Energy Inc.
60 Baffin Place, Unit 2
Waterloo, ON N2V 1Z7 Canada

Toll-free: 877-606-5559
Phone: 519-885-0283
www.power-pipe.biz

The Power-Pipe™ installs in a vertical plumbing drain stack, recovering heat energy from draining water to warm an incoming cold water supply. As liquid drains, it clings to the inner surface of the copper pipe due to surface tension; part of the draining water's thermal energy is transferred to incoming water line (squared copper for maximum contact area) coiled around the stack. The heat transfer is most effective with equal drain and incoming flow volumes. Multiple units may be used in parallel for large flows. The energy savings potential can be significant, particularly in commercial or institutional applications with showers, laundry, dishwashing, boiler blowdown, etc. The Power-Pipe can also be effective in residential applications, and is approved for potable water.

Domestic Water Heaters

The most efficient domestic water heaters include electronic-ignition gas-fired on-demand models, direct-contact commercial water heaters, heat-pump water heaters, and advanced combination space- and water-heating systems. (All electric resistance water heaters have the inefficiencies and fuel-source pollution concerns inherent to electric power generation.) Some water heaters—especially electronic-ignition on-demand water heaters—can also be used as boilers for heating, particularly in very-low-energy buildings. Other factors to consider include indoor air quality (in terms of combustion gases) and the ozone-depletion impacts associated with refrigerants for heat pumps and blowing agents for storage tank insulation. On-demand water heaters have no standby losses or storage tank insulation concerns, and some models have sealed combustion and no pilot lights. Gas-fired condensing storage-tank type water heaters have fuel efficiencies greater than 90% and use a variety of types of insulation. Heat-pump water heaters have tremendous efficiencies, but these are still very uncommon. In combined or integrated systems, efficiencies are boosted by uniting space heating and/or cooling into a single system that includes water heating. In almost every type of high-efficiency water heater there are issues of rate-of-use, climate, and maintenance that require consideration to make the appropriate selection for optimal results.

AquaMaster Q100

Vebteck Research
30 Riviera Dr.
Markham, ON L3R 5M1 Canada

Phone: 905-479-4048
www.ekocomfort.com

The AquaMaster Q100 is a joint development effort from Vebteck Research, Nutech Energy Systems, and Fleetline Products that offers integrated high-efficiency space heating (forced air or hydronic), domestic water heating, and continuous whole-house, heat-recovery ventilation (HRV) under a single, unified control system. The small system—it has a 4' x 2' footprint—includes a high-efficiency, low-mass, low-water-volume boiler (natural gas, propane, or fuel oil); a single, multi-speed, ECM blower; and an aluminum HRV core. The AquaMaster is a product of the eKOCOMFORT® consortium, a partnership of Canadian manufacturers and governmental agencies developing efficient, gas-fired, module-based units integrating space heating, ventilation, and domestic hot water.

Baxi Niagara Tankless Water Heater

Marathon International
1815 Sismet Rd.
Mississauga, ON L4W 1P9 Canada

Phone: 905-602-5360
www.wallhungboilers.com

Marathon International is the North American distributor for the Baxi line of boilers and water heating products from Britain. The Niagara tankless water heater is a zero-clearance, direct-venting, gas-fired unit with sealed combustion and electronic ignition. The rated heat output is 95,540 Btu/hr (77 degree F rise at 3 gpm), and the rated efficiency is 85.5.

Bosch ProTankless Water Heaters

Bosch Water Heating
340 Mad River Park
Waitsfield, VT 05673

Toll-free: 866-330-2725
Phone: 802-496-4436
www.protankless.com

The Bosch ProTankless line of gas-fired, tankless water heaters offer efficiencies up to 87%. The ProTankless 635ES and 635ESO water heaters supply two hot water outlets simultaneously at a combined rate of 6 gpm. The heaters can also be fueled by either natural gas or propane, and have an electronic ignition, digital temperature control, an energy factor of 0.85, and a 15-year warranty. Model ES contains a sealed-combustion unit for indoor installation that can be vented horizontally or vertically. Model ESO has built-in freeze protection to 5°F for exterior installation.

Demand Water Heaters

Low Energy Systems, Inc.
4975 E. 41st Ave.
Denver, CO 80216

Toll-free: 800-873-3507
Phone: 303-781-9437
www.tanklesswaterheaters.com

Low Energy Systems is a specialized distributor of Paloma and Takagi demand gas hot water heaters. Homeowner-friendly maintenance kits, and solar thermal systems and components, are also available.

Flash and Mobius Tankless Water Heaters

Takagi Industrial Co. USA, Inc.
5 Whatney
Irvine, CA 92618

Toll-free: 888-882-5244
Phone: 949-770-7171
www.takagi-usa.com

Takagi's Flash T-H1, T-K2, T-KD20, T-KJr., and T-K3 tankless gas water heaters are suited for residential and commercial applications and have no pilot, so standby losses are negligible. They do use electricity for a power burner and power vent. The Mobius T-M1 is a tankless, pilotless, computer-controlled gas water heater. Up to 20 units can be operated by a single control module, and several control modules can be linked together, making the Mobius practical for offices, hotels, hospitals, and other large facilities. The T-K1S pilotless, demand water heater is designed for single-use residential or commercial applications. Takagi's T-K3 is designed to fit between wall studs, with up to four units interconnected to provide hot water to larger homes. The T-K3 saves water by activating at a flow of .5 gpm instead of .75 gpm, providing hot water quicker to bathroom faucets and other low-use fixtures.

Indirect Water Heater Tanks

Buderus
50 Wentworth Ave.
Londonderry, NH 03053

Toll-free: 800-283-3787
Phone: 603-552-1100
www.buderus.net

The S, ST, L, and LT domestic hot water tanks allow water heating by a gas- or oil-fired boiler. Unlike most domestic indirect water heater tanks, the Buderus uses non-ozone-depleting rigid foam. Because the unit is made in Germany, there are environmental impacts of shipping to consider.

Multi-Fuel and Wood Boilers

Tarm USA, Inc.
5 Main St.
P.O. Box 285
Lyme, NH 03768

Toll-free: 800-782-9927
Phone: 603-795-2214
www.woodboilers.com

The HS-Tarm Excel 2000 Boiler is a multi-fuel boiler and domestic water heater that operates at over 80% efficiency on wood and 85% on oil. It has fully automatic controls to maintain the wood fire and the oil or gas backup that will automatically turn on the oil or gas burner when the wood fire dies down. The Excel 2000 burns very cleanly and generates very little ash for clean up.

The HS-Tarm Solo Plus-MKII boiler and domestic hot-water heater uses substantially less wood than conventional boilers and outdoor water stoves and also has a very clean burn. Three sizes are available with outputs from 100,000 to 198,000 Btu/hr.

Noritz Tankless Water Heaters

Noritz America Corp.
11160 Grace Ave.
Fountain Valley, CA 92708

Toll-free: 866-766-7489
Phone: 714-433-2905
www.noritz.com

Noritz, a manufacturer of gas-fired, tankless, on demand water heaters, offers a full line of electronic-ignition, wall-hung models for residential and commercial applications. Models range in output from 190,000 Btu/hour up to 380,000 Btu/hour, with options for ganging multiple units for large commercial applications. Minimum output ranges from 21,000 to 25,000 Btu/hour; efficiencies are 80-85%. Direct-vent, sealed-combustion configurations are recommended for most applications (specify DV models). Residential products carry a 10-year warranty on the heat exchanger and 3-year warranty on all other parts; commercial products carry a 3-year warranty on all parts, including heat exchanger.

Oil Miser Water Heaters

Toyotomi U.S.A., Inc.
604 Federal Rd.
Brookfield, CT 06804

Phone: 203-775-1909
www.toyotomiusa.com

The only oil-fired, sealed-combustion, on-demand water heating systems in North America, Oil Miser Water Heater models OM-148 and BS-36UFF from Toyotomi have efficiency ratings of 88%. Both models provide up to 148,000 Btu/hr—the OM-148 consuming fuel at a rate of 1.05 gal/hr, and the BS-36UFF at 1.1 gal/hr. An external fuel tank is required (No. 1 or No. 2 fuel oil for the OM-148; ASTM No. 1-K Grade

Kerosene or No. 1 Fuel Oil for BS-36UFF). The units require 120-volt AC power for ignition loads of 110 watts (no pilot light) and 98 watts while operating. Units may be direct- or chimney-vented and offer overheat protection, ignition safety, and no-water shutoff.

Phase III Indirect Water Heaters

Triangle Tube
1 Triangle Ln.
Blackwood, NJ 08012

Phone: 856-228-8881
www.triangletube.com

Phase III indirect-fired water heaters, available in residential and commercial models, work in conjunction with a boiler to provide domestic hot water. The tank-in-tank design, insulated with HCFC-free polyurethane foam, provides an average lifespan in excess of 20 years, faster recovery rates than conventional water heaters, and reduced fuel use. Commercial models are compatible with high-pressure, seawater, desalination, and deionized water applications and can be manifolded to meet service hot water needs.

Phoenix Solar Water Heater

Heat Transfer Products, Inc.
120 Braley Rd.
P.O. Box 429
East Freetown, MA 02717

Toll-free: 800-323-9651
Phone: 508-763-8071
www.htproducts.com

The Phoenix Solar Water Heater provides a heat exchanger to transfer heat from solar collectors (or other alternative sources), along with a back-up gas burner that operates at 97% thermal efficiency. The gas burner is located halfway up the tank and a solar heat exchanger is located at the bottom, keeping water at the bottom of the tank cooler and maximizing the solar collector's efficiency. The Phoenix comes with auxiliary hook-ups so it can be connected to air handlers or radiant heating systems. These units are available in 80- or 110-gallon corrosion-resistant 316L-grade stainless steel tanks that are wrapped in two-inch non-HCFC polyurethane foam insulation. The unit is direct-vent and rated for zero clearance from combustible surfaces.

Polaris Heating Systems

American Water Heater Company
500 Princeton Rd.
Johnson City, TN 37601

Toll-free: 800-937-1037
Phone: 423-283-8000
www.americanwaterheater.com

Polaris Heating Systems are high-efficiency, combination water and residential space-heating products. The gas-fired unit has a submerged stainless steel flue that transfers combustion energy to the water with 95+% efficiency. Polaris heaters are available in 34-, 50-, and 100-gal. sizes with outputs of 100,000 to 199,000 Btu/hr and energy factors of 0.86.

Prestige Condensing Boilers

Triangle Tube
1 Triangle Ln.
Blackwood, NJ 08012

Phone: 856-228-8881
www.triangletube.com

The Prestige line of gas-fired, fully condensing, wall-mounted, modulating boilers for space heating or domestic water heating adjust in response to the room thermostat, supply and return water temperature, flue temperature, domestic hot water thermostat, and outdoor temperature to provide up to 96% efficiency in low-temperature applications. Three models are available with outputs ranging from 93,000 to 226,000 Btu/hr.

Rheem Pronto! Tankless Gas Water Heaters

Rheem Manufacturing Company
101 Bell Rd.
Montgomery, AL 36117

Toll-free: 800-432-8373
Phone: 334-260-1500
www.rheem.com

The Rheem Pronto!™ series Tankless Water Heaters for natural or LP gas feature electronic ignition, power venting, low NOx emissions, electric freeze protection, and an exclusive oxygen-depletion-sensor safety device and overheat limiter. Model 4.2 has an input rating from 31,500 to 118,000 Btu/hr, delivering 4.2 gallons per minute with a 45-degree temperature rise at a 0.81 energy factor. Model 7.4 has an input rating of 19,000 to 199,900 Btu/hr and delivers 7.4 gallons at a 45-degree temperature rise with an 0.82 energy factor.

Rinnai Tankless Water Heaters

Rinnai
103 International Dr.
Peachtree City, GA 30269

Toll-free: 800-621-9419
Phone: 678-829-1700
www.rinnai.us

The Rinnai 2532FFU is a forced-combustion, tankless water heater with electronic ignition. The heater can deliver up to 8.5 GPM. Highly sophisticated freeze protection is provided, allowing exterior installation in freezing climates. 5.3 GPM and 9.8 GPM models are also available. Wall-mounted units can save up to 16 ft2 of floor space.

System 2000

Energy Kinetics
51 Molasses Hill Rd.
Lebanon, NJ 08833

Toll-free: 800-323-2066
www.energykinetics.com

System 2000, for residential and light commercial applications, has an AFUE rating of 87% and steady state efficiency of 99%. This integrated system provides multi-zone control of warm air, radiant heat, hydronic baseboard, and domestic hot water, as well as heating capabilities for pools or spas. It uses oil or natural gas or propane.

Vitodens 200 Wall-Mounted Boiler

Viessmann Manufacturing Co. (U.S.) Inc.
45 Access Rd.
Warwick, RI 02886

Toll-free: 800-288-0667
Phone: 401-732-0667
www.viessmann-us.com

Vitodens 200 is a wall-mounted, gas-fired, condensing boiler with efficiencies of up to 95.2% AFUE. This small, quiet, low-emission, zero-clearance, sealed-combustion unit can be installed in a living space. The five models have a maximum input ranging from 91,000 to 230,000 Btu/hr. The smaller WB2-24 and -32 models have a variable-speed pump for low electrical consumption and precise heating, and the WB2 6-24C has a plate-type heat exchanger to supply domestic hot water in addition to space heating. Up to four of the larger WB2-44 and -60 models can be ganged together for light-commercial applications.

Water and Gas Safety Valve

Taco, Inc.
1160 Cranston St.
Cranston, RI 02920

Phone: 401-942-8000
www.taco-hvac.com

WAGS is a leak-detection and shut-off valve for domestic water heaters. This mechanical valve sits in a drip pan under the water heater. If leaking water accumulates to a level of 3/4", a water-soluble fiber element dissolves, releasing a piston that closes the flow of water to the tank and, in gas-fired heaters, breaking a fuse to shut off the gas supply. The system has the potential to provide savings from eliminating water leakage as well as any resulting mold growth or damage. Once activated in a leak, the valve must be replaced.

Domestic Water Piping

The three major materials currently used in supply piping in North America are copper, chlorinated polyvinyl chloride (CPVC), and cross-linked polyethylene (XLPE or, more commonly, PEX). CPVC has toxic manufacturing intermediaries, requires the use of hazardous solvents for welding the joints, and can generate highly toxic dioxins in the case of accidental fire or improper incineration. Copper's environmentally intensive extraction and manufacturing process make it an even worse performer in terms of life-cycle environmental and human health impacts, according to recent studies. In contrast, XLPE and Polypropylene (PP) are 'clean' hydrocarbons, provided harmful additives are not used for application-specific properties. Products listed here are made of nonhalogenated plastics that contain no heavy metals or brominated flame retardants.

Fusiotherm Piping

Aquatherm Inc.
2097 Ironton Blvd.
Provo, UT 84603

Phone: 801-805-6657
www.aquathermpipe.com

Fusiotherm® piping from Aquatherm Piping Systems is an exceptionally strong, non-PVC piping for pressurized applications such as potable water distribution and hydronic heating. The polypropylene pieces are heat-joined in the field with an electric fusing tool to create truly monolithic plumbing systems without the use of solvents or glues. Fusiotherm is available in a wide range of diameters from 16 mm to 160 mm (0.63" to 6.29") in three wall-thickness ratios (SDR classifications); over 400 fittings are available. Introduced in the U.S. in 2003, the product has been used in Europe for three decades with great success. Fusiotherm® piping was awarded ESR 1613 listing by the International Code Council in September 2005.

Graywater Systems

Graywater is defined either as all wastewater other than that from toilets, or as wastewater from baths, showers, lavatories, and clothes washers (not including kitchen sinks and dishwashers). In some states, codes allow graywater to be collected and used for below-ground landscape irrigation. Products listed here are used in graywater systems.

Aqus System

Watersaver Technologies LLC
13400 U.S. Highway 42, Ste. 214
Prospect, KY 40059

Toll-free: 502-741-1859
Phone: 502-550-1506
www.watersavertech.com

The Aqus System from Watersaver Technologies captures graywater from a bathroom sink in a 5.5-gallon reservoir that is housed inside the vanity. The device filters the water and controls bacteria with disinfection tablets, and pumps it to the toilet tank, where it replaces the use of fresh, potable water. The system works with toilet tanks of any size, but it will not work with pressurized toilet tank systems. Watersaver estimates that installation will take 1–2 hours, and will save 10–20 gallons of water a day in a two-person household. The product was introduced in 2006, following testing that began in 2004.

BioGreen

BioGreen System (Pacific) Ltd.
#4 11443 Kingston St.
Maple Ridge, BC V2X 0Y6 Canada

Phone: 604-460-0203
www.biogreensystems.com

BioGreen is a biological wastewater treatment system for use in rural and suburban areas and recreational facilities without a central sewage system.

Brac Systems

Brac Systems
3571 Ashby
Ville St-Laurent
Montreal, QC H4R 2K3 Canada

Toll-free: 866-494-2722
Phone: 514-856-2722
www.bracsystems.com

The Brac Graywater Recycling System treats water from showers, bathing, and laundry, and reuses it for toilet flushing or irrigation. According to the manufacturer, the system operates seamlessly with the existing plumbing, and will reduce a household's water usage by approximately one-third. The W-200 has a 53-gallon tank and is sized for homes with 5 or fewer people. The W-325 holds 86 gallons for households of 6 or more. Larger systems can be custom-designed. The filter requires manual cleaning every two to four weeks; the tank requires draining and cleanout two or three times per year. The manufacturer recommends using a chlorinated toilet cleaning tablet or bromine/chlorine tablet every other month; GreenSpec recommends exploring alternatives to chlorine-based sanitizers. These systems carry a two-year guarantee, which can be extended to five years for a small fee.

Envirosink

Bismart Distributors, Inc.
2790 McKenzie Ave
Surrey, BC V4A 3H4 Canada

Toll-free: 888-663-4950
Phone: 604-596-5894
www.envirosink.com

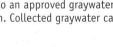

The Envirosink® is a secondary kitchen sink that drains to an approved graywater system instead of a sewage or septic system. Collected graywater can then be used for landscape irrigation.

Graywater Treatment Systems

Clivus Multrum, Inc.
15 Union St.
Lawrence, MA 01840

Toll-free: 800-425-4887
Phone: 978-725-5591
www.clivusmultrum.com

Clivus Multrum custom-designs greywater irrigation systems for commercial and residential applications.

Recirculating Wastewater Garden

Ecological Engineering Group, Inc.
508 Boston Post Rd.
Weston, MA 02493

Toll-free: 866-432-6364
Phone: 978-369-9440
www.ecological-engineering.com/

Ecological Engineering Group, Inc. is an engineering design and consulting firm specializing in alternative on-site wastewater treatment systems including graywater systems such as Recirculating Wastewater Garden.

ReWater System

ReWater Systems, Inc.
P.O. Box 210171
Chula Vista, CA 91921

Phone: 619-421-9121
www.rewater.com

The ReWater® System is a graywater irrigation system comprised of two primary sections. A self-cleaning filter captures and pressurizes the water, which is then released through either a surface or subsurface drip irrigation network, depending on your state code. An electronic controller operates all 156 filtration and irrigation functions with 21 stations capable of being programmed for fresh water or drip of recycled water, with four independent irrigation programs. The electronic controller adds supplemental fresh water to recycling stations when required by the programs.

Irrigation

Over half of urban water use in the U.S. is for landscape irrigation. Before researching irrigation systems, consider water-saving landscapes with drought-hardy native plantings to reduce or eliminate water, energy, and chemical use. If irrigation is needed, high-tech, permanent irrigation systems that monitor soil and atmospheric conditions can save a great deal of water simply by not running when irrigation isn't needed. Drip irrigation systems release measured quantities of water directly to the soil surrounding the intended plants instead of spraying an entire area, using water more efficiently and greatly reducing evaporative loss. Look for products with intelligent sensing, long warranties that indicate good durability, and such environmental features as recycled content. Consider integrated systems that re-use water that would otherwise be sent down the drain.

Fiskars Soaker Hose and Sprinkler Hose

Fiskars, Inc. - Fiskars Garden Tools
780 Carolina St.
Sauk City, WI 53583

Toll-free: 800-500-4849
www.fiskars.com

Fiskars Soaker Hose and Sprinkler Hose, formerly Moisture Master, are products that contain 65% post-consumer recycled rubber from tires.

Graywater Treatment Systems

Clivus Multrum, Inc.
15 Union St.
Lawrence, MA 01840

Toll-free: 800-425-4887
Phone: 978-725-5591
www.clivusmultrum.com

Clivus Multrum custom-designs greywater irrigation systems for commercial and residential applications.

ReWater System

ReWater Systems, Inc.
P.O. Box 210171
Chula Vista, CA 91921

Phone: 619-421-9121
www.rewater.com

The ReWater® System is a graywater irrigation system comprised of two primary sections. A self-cleaning filter captures and pressurizes the water, which is then released through either a surface or subsurface drip irrigation network, depending on your state code. An electronic controller operates all 156 filtration and irrigation functions with 21 stations capable of being programmed for fresh water or drip of recycled water, with four independent irrigation programs. The electronic controller adds supplemental fresh water to recycling stations when required by the programs.

WeatherTRAK

HydroPoint Data Systems, Inc.
1726 Corporate Cir.
Petaluma, CA 94954

Toll-free: 800-362-8774
Phone: 707-769-9696
www.weathertrak.com

The WeatherTRAK irrigation control systems (available in commercial and residential models) automatically create watering schedules based on parameters that include plant and soil types, sun exposure, and slope. Each watering zone is subsequently adjusted automatically each day based on analyzed NOAA weather data received from HydroPoint's ET Everywhere™ satellite communications service, which eliminates the need for a standalone weather station by delivering geographically specific weather data. Remote management and monitoring via the internet is available. The system is also compatible with rain sensors that can override watering instructions (i.e., not irrigate if the ground is wet).

Rainwater Harvesting

Rainwater harvesting is the practice of collecting and using rainwater, most commonly from roofs. Use of collected rainwater can provide building owners with high-quality soft water for irrigation and potable uses, reduce pressure on water-treatment plants, and reduce stormwater runoff and flooding. To use as potable water, filtration and purification are necessary.

Rainwater Catchment Components

Rain Harvesting Pty, Ltd
28-34 Reginald St.
Rocklea, Brisbane, QLD 4106 Australia

Phone: +61 7 3248 9600
www.rainharvesting.com

Rain Harvesting Pty Ltd. offers rainwater catchment components including gutter screens, rainheads, first flush diverters, flap valves, filter pits, vermin-proof screens, and overflow valves. A 144-page introductory handbook is also available describing the processes, materials, and uses of rainwater harvesting. Most components offered are made with stainless steel and PVC. No recycled plastic is used in manufacturing these components due to the potential for lead contamination of potable water; only lead-free virgin resins are used. Orders made at their website are drop-shipped from Australia. North American support is provided via the internet and e-mail.

Rainwater Catchment Systems

Northwest Water Source
P.O. Box 2766
Friday Harbor, WA 98250

Phone: 360-378-8252

Northwest Water Source offers components and equipment as well as design and consulting for both residential and commercial rainwater catchment and harvesting systems. The company imports European rainfall catchment equipment and stormwater infiltration technology from Germany and Holland. Equipment includes European-made stainless steel demand pumping systems that don't require a pressure tank; UV water purification and filtration; and a variety of water storage tanks including above- and below-ground rotationally molded polyethylene and custom-made in-ground units consisting of a polyethylene "endoskeleton" covered by a welded sheet polypropylene.

Rainwater Catchment Systems

Rain Man Waterworks
P.O. Box 972
Dripping Springs, TX 78620

Phone: 512-858-7020
www.rainharvester.com

Rain Man Waterworks builds and installs turnkey rainwater catchment systems. The company is also a supplier of components used for rainwater catchment systems.

Rainwater Collection and Filtration Systems

Resource Conservation Technology, Inc.
2633 N. Calvert St.
Baltimore, MD 21218

Toll-free: 800-477-7724
Phone: 410-366-1146
www.conservationtechnology.com

Resource Conservation Technology, Inc. provides residential and commercial rainwater collection, filtration, and storage systems. In a typical installation, water from a building's downspouts is piped underground through a central filter to the storage tanks. System capacities range from hundreds to thousands of gallons, and a system may include additional pumps, controls, and disinfection systems tailored to the application.

Rainwater Harvesting Components

Water Filtration Company
1205 Gilman St.
Marietta, OH 45750

Toll-free: 800-733-6953
Phone: 740-373-6953
www.waterfiltrationcompany.com

Water Filtration Company offers rainwater-catchment parts and accessories. The Filtering Roofwasher installs between the downspout and cistern to remove dirt and debris from water collected from a roof, and can greatly improve the quality of cistern water and significantly increase the time between cistern cleanings. The Filtering Roofwasher is often used in conjunction with Water Filtration's Floating Cistern Filter, which reduces the final filtration loads. Filter elements for the Floating Cistern Filter need replacement approximately every one to two years. Additional filtration or sterilization is usually required for potable water applications.

Smart-Valve Rainwater Diverter

FloTrue International Corp
5516 Yale St.
Metairie, LA 70003

Phone: 504-338-3727
www.flotrue.com

Smart-Valve is a kit that transforms an off-the-shelf pipe fitting into a low-cost first-flush diverter valve for roofwater catchment systems. The amount of water diverted is adjustable.

The Garden Watersaver

Watersaver Products Company
8260 Dalemore Rd.
Richmond, BC V7C 2A8 Canada

Phone: 604-274-6630
www.gardenwatersaver.com

The Garden Watersaver is an automatic rainwater collection system that installs on a downspout from the roof's gutter to divert a percentage of this water to a barrel or other container for later use in a garden or other applications.

Residential Faucets, Showerheads, and Controls

Many conservation efforts—in industrial, commercial, and residential settings—are making significant improvements in water-use efficiency. These advances are also reducing our wastewater treatment burden and expense. Products listed here dispense water efficiently or improve controllability of the water supply. To qualify for GreenSpec, showerheads must have a flow of 1.75 gallons per minute or less; bathroom faucets, 1.5 gallons per minute or less. Kitchen faucets may be up to 2.5 gallons per minute, but should be installed with foot or other controls to prevent long periods of running.

Bricor Elite Series Showerheads

Bricor Southwest
205 FM2722
P.O. Box 312024
New Braunfels, TX 78132

Phone: 830-624-7228
www.bricor.com

Bricor Elite Series showerheads have a small hole on the side of the throat that generates a vacuum, pulling air into the showerhead. This aerates the water, boosting the pressure. According to the company, this venturi-induction technology increases the shower intensity by 1.75 times over other conventional low-flow systems. There are seven 1.5 gpm models to choose from. Other flow rates are possible with custom orders. For multilevel buildings, the company can provide custom-manufactured showerheads for each floor to provide consistent flow throughout the building.

Croma 1-Jet EcoAIR Showerhead

Hansgrohe, Inc.
1490 Bluegrass Lakes Pkwy.
Alpharetta, GA 30004

Toll-free: 800-488-8119
www.hansgrohe-usa.com

The Croma 1-Jet EcoAIR showerhead uses proprietary air injection technology to achieve a forceful spray with 1.6 gpm instead of the industry-standard 2.5 gpm. Surrounding air is drawn into the center of the showerhead using the Venturi effect, infusing air into the water stream in a 3:1 air-to-water ratio. Water is delivered through 50 no-clog silicone spray channels. The Rub-It™ system allows for easy removal of mineral deposits and debris from the face of the showerhead. Croma EcoAIR showerheads are available in Chrome and Brushed Nickel.

D'Mand Hot Water Delivery System

Uponor
5925 148th St. W
Apple Valley, MN 55124

Toll-free: 800-321-4739
www.uponor-usa.com

Uponor (formerly Wirsbo) offers the D'mand Hot Water Delivery System, an electronically activated water-pumping system that quickly delivers hot water to a fixture while returning water that has been sitting in the hot-water pipes back to the hot-water tank. The pump may be activated on demand by pushing a button near the fixture or by a motion sensor. The system switches off when hot water reaches the temperature sensor on the pump at the fixture. Aside from quicker hot water delivery, benefits include energy savings (especially compared with continuous-circulation or timer-based circulation hot-water loops) and the elimination of water waste while waiting for hot water. In retrofit applications, the cold-water line serves as the return line; in new construction, a third plumbing line is usually installed.

ETL Low-Flow Showerheads

Energy Technology Laboratories
2351 Tenaya Dr.
Modesto, CA 95354

Toll-free: 800-344-3242
Phone: 209-529-3546
www.etlproducts.com

The Oxygenics® line of showerheads, made with DuPont Delrin® 500P acetal resin, employs a venturi air-induction design using a single, centered orifice—rather than a lot of small holes in the face of the showerhead—and stationary fins to break the spray into pulsating droplets. Showerheads in the Oxygenics line are rated to use from 1.5 to 2.5 gpm and are optimized for different water pressures. The products achieve remarkably satisfying shower force and are guaranteed for life never to clog.

Foot-Operated Sink Valve

Step-Flow, Inc.
2361 Campus Dr. #99
Irvine, CA 92612

Toll-free: 888-783-7356
www.stepflow.com

Step Flow is a retrofit (or OEM) foot-operated valve system, which converts any sink from hand operation to foot operation. This foot-pedal faucet control uses a sheathed flex cable for the pedal-to-valve controller so that no plumbing extends to the foot pedal. "Hands free" usage of sinks results in a sanitary application and conserves water.

Foot-Pedal Faucet Controls

T&S Brass and Bronze Works, Inc.
2 Saddleback Cv.
P.O. Box 1088
Travelers Rest, SC 29690

Toll-free: 800-476-4103
Phone: 864-834-4102
www.tsbrass.com

T&S Brass manufactures double- and single-pedal, wall- and floor-mounted, foot-operated water faucet controls. Each pedal may be set up to control hot, cold, or tempered water. (For tempered water, conventional hand controls can be used to set the temperature balance and flow volume, and the pedal used to turn the flow on and off.) Hands-free operation saves water and encourages sanitary sink conditions. Water savings are significant but difficult to quantify.

H-11 and H-12 Water-Efficient Showerheads

Leonard Valve Company
1360 Elmwood Ave.
Cranston, RI 02910

Toll-free: 888-222-1208
Phone: 401-461-1200
www.leonardvalve.com

Leonard Valve Company's H-11 and H-12 Showerheads use 1.75 gallons per minute, 30% below the standard 2.5 gpm. Both models use ABS for the showerhead. The H-11 has a chrome plated arm and flange design. The H-12 has chrome plated brass construction and vandal resistant screws.

Low-Flow Showerhead

Ecotech Water, LLC
7121 Gulf Blvd.
St. Pete Beach, FL 33706

Toll-free: 877-341-9500
www.ecotechwater.com

Ecotech's Low-Flow Showerhead uses patented aeration technology to produce a forceful stream of water while using only 1 gallon per minute (gpm). Air is drawn in through a small hole in the throat of the showerhead and mixes with the water, significantly increasing the water pressure. Along with water savings compared with standard 2.5 gpm showerheads, low-flow showerheads, such as this, save energy used for heating water. According to the manufacturer, this showerhead can often compensate for low water pressure commonly found in larger apartment buildings.

Low-Flow Sink Aerator

Ecotech Water, LLC
7121 Gulf Blvd.
St. Pete Beach, FL 33706

Toll-free: 877-341-9500
www.ecotechwater.com

Ecotech's Low-Flow Sink Aerator for lavatory faucets incorporates a patented aeration technology that pulls air in through the side of the unit, boosting pressure while reducing flow to .33 gallons per minute (gpm)–significantly less than the 2.5 gpm federal standard for lavatory faucets. Aerators can be installed for a fraction of the cost of replacing faucets, providing a cost-effective way to save both water and energy.

Metlund Hot Water D'MAND System

ACT, Inc. Metlund Systems
3176 Pullman St., Ste. 119
Costa Mesa, CA 92626

Toll-free: 800-638-5863
Phone: 714-668-1200
www.gothotwater.com

Metlund Hot Water D'mand System is an electronically controlled valve and pumping system that rapidly distributes hot water from the water heater to fixtures in a home or commercial building. This system can operate either with a return line or by the existing cold-water line. The Metlund System pumps cold tapwater back to the water heater and delivers hot water instead, saving otherwise wasted water and shortening the wait for hot water. Because it circulates the water only on demand, this system avoids the energy penalties of continuously circulating systems. The Metlund System can also be activated by either a low-voltage remote button or a motion sensor.

Pedalworks and Footworks

Pedal Valves, Inc.
13625 River Rd.
Luling, LA 70070

Toll-free: 800-431-3668
Phone: 985-785-9997
www.pedalvalve.com

Footworks and Pedalworks are unique, single-pedal faucet controllers. The Footworks product is for commercial applications and bolts into the floor beneath the sink; the residential Pedalworks controller is installed in the base of a kitchen cabinet or bathroom vanity. The conventional hand controls are used to set the temperature balance between hot and cold water, and the foot pedal is used to turn the flow on and off. A lock-on button allows the water to be left running when necessary. Water savings are significant but difficult to quantify. In applications such as hospitals (when water is often left running while surgeons scrub their hands and arms) and commercial kitchens, water savings can be dramatic. The products also help with hygiene and productivity.

Taco Hot Water D'MAND System

Taco, Inc.
1160 Cranston St.
Cranston, RI 02920

Phone: 401-942-8000
www.taco-hvac.com

The Taco D'MAND® System is an electronically activated water-pumping system that quickly delivers hot water to a fixture while returning water that has been sitting in the hot-water pipes back to the hot-water tank. The pump may be activated on demand by pushing a button near the fixture or by remote control. The system switches off when hot water reaches the temperature sensor on the pump at the fixture. Aside from quicker hot water delivery, benefits include energy savings and the elimination of water waste while waiting for hot water. In retrofit applications, the cold-water line serves as the return line; in new construction, a third plumbing line is usually installed.

Tapmaster

Tapmaster Incorporated
20175 Township Rd. 262
Calgary, AB T3P 1A3 Canada

Toll-free: 800-791-8117
Phone: 403-275-5554
www.tapmaster.ca

Tapmaster is a foot- or knee-activated switch that controls the flow to a faucet. The conventional hand controls are used to set the temperature balance and flow volume between hot and cold water, and the foot switch is used to turn the flow on and off. A lock-on button allows the water to be left running when necessary. Water savings are significant but difficult to quantify, as they depend on user habits. Tapmaster is widely used in dental offices for hygienic reasons, as well as homes. Easy installation with no electronics or wires, pressure tank, bulky mechanical devices, or ongoing maintenance.

The Chilipepper Appliance

Chilipepper Systems
4623 Hasting Pl.
Lake Oswego, OR 97035

Toll-free: 800-914-9887
Phone: 209-401-8888
www.chilipepperapp.com

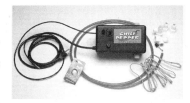

The Chilipepper Appliance is an on-demand water circulation device that speeds the availability of hot water at the tap. This energy- and money-saving appliance is easily mounted at the most remote tap. The 115-volt pump moves cold water out of the hot-water line and back to the water heater via the cold-water line. The Chilipepper is activated by either a wireless remote or a wired controller.

Water-Conserving Fixtures

Niagara Conservation Corp.
45 Horsehill Rd.
Cedar Knolls, NJ 07927

Toll-free: 800-831-8383
Phone: 973-829-0800
www.niagaraconservation.com

Niagara Conservation Corporation offers water- and energy-conserving products including showerheads, toilets, toilet retrofit kits, faucet aerators, light bulbs, and weatherization products. They also produce a patented tamperproof, flapperless, 1.6-gal. toilet suitable for both 10" and 12" rough-ins.

Water-Efficient Showerheads

Delta Faucet Company
55 East 111th St.
P.O. Box 40980
Indianapolis, IN 46280

Toll-free: 800-345-3358
Phone: 317-848-1812
www.deltafaucet.com

Delta Faucet Company offers water-efficient showerheads with H2Okinetic Technology™ that use only 1.6 gallons per minute yet deliver a satisfying shower. The showerhead provides 36% water savings over standard 2.5 gpm showerheads; this saves both water and energy (for heating water). The showerhead produces water droplets that are fairly large, resulting in good heat retention and body wetting. Most low-flow showerheads either create very small droplets or aerate the water.

Zurn AquaSpec Foot Pedal Valves

Zurn Plumbing Products Group
5900 Elwin Buchanan Dr.
Sanford, NC 27330

Toll-free: 800-997-3876
Phone: 919-775-2255
www.zurn.com

Zurn® both single-pedal and double-pedal AquaSpec® foot pedal valves that provide hands-free faucet operation (model numbers Z85100 and Z85500 respectively). A wall-mounted knee-control product (Z85700) and several specialized faucet controls are also available. In commercial kitchens, hospitals, and homes foot- and knee-control valves for faucets can save water for allowing users to save water by faucets on and off easily without altering the temperature mix.

Zurn AquaSpec Low-Flow Showerheads

Zurn Plumbing Products Group
5900 Elwin Buchanan Dr.
Sanford, NC 27330

Toll-free: 800-997-3876
Phone: 919-775-2255
www.zurn.com

Zurn® offers a variety of AquaSpec® showerheads (produced for the company by other manufacturers) that use less than the federally mandated maximum of 2.5 gallons per minute. The Z7000-S3-EWS is a 1.5 gpm, chrome-finish showerhead with brass ball joint connector and volume control with integral tamper-resistant flow control.

Residential Lavatories and Sinks

Products listed here contain recycled content or can contribute to innovative wastewater treatment practices, such as graywater separation.

Envirosink

Bismart Distributors, Inc.
2790 McKenzie Ave
Surrey, BC V4A 3H4
Canada

Toll-free: 888-663-4950
Phone: 604-596-5894
www.envirosink.com

The Envirosink® is a secondary kitchen sink that drains to an approved graywater system instead of a sewage or septic system. Collected graywater can then be used for landscape irrigation.

Residential Toilets

Since 1992, federal law has mandated that nearly all new toilets use no more than 1.6 gallons per flush (gpf)– the exception being commercial blow-out toilets, which are still allowed to use 3.5 gallons in some states. As toilet flushing is the largest single use of water in most residential and commercial buildings (accounting for up to 40% of residential use), water savings from toilet replacement is very significant. In addition to improvements to the traditional gravity system, pressure- and vacuum-assisted flushing systems have been developed that offer superior performance, albeit with the addition of some noise. Dual-flush toilets have been available for years overseas and are now making inroads in the U.S. These save additional water by making two flushes available: one for solid wastes and a lower-volume flush for liquids and paper. Products listed here must meet the minimum standards of the Uniform North American Requirements (UNAR) for toilets, which includes elements of the Maximum Performance (MaP) flush-quality testing protocol

and Los Angeles Supplementary Purchase Specification (SPS), which discourages the use of toilets that might be adjusted to use significantly more water. Products listed here use at least 20% less than the federal minimum of 1.6 gallons (6 liters) per flush– that is, 1.28 gallons (4.8 liters) or less. The toilet must also evacuate at least 250 grams of solid waste per flush, as tested under the Maximum Performance (MaP) protocol. Toilets that are included without MaP testing are extremely low-water use or have other unique green features. For dual-flush toilets, we factor water savings by averaging the high and low volume flush levels. Other factors considered in GreenSpec evaluations include bowl washing effectiveness and water surface area.

American Standard FloWise Toilet

American Standard
One Centennial Plaza
P.O. Box 6820
Piscataway, NJ 08855

Toll-free: 800-442-1902
Phone: 732-980-3000
www.americanstandard-us.com

The FloWise™ toilet, introduced in 2005 by American Standard, uses advanced design to achieve very good flush performance with just 1.28 gallons—20% savings compared with a standard 1.6 gpf toilet. The toilet relies on the Champion flush technology, which uses a 3" flush valve and a 2-3/8" trapway to achieve a high-velocity, forceful flush. On the MaP tests, the FloWise is rated at 550 grams—more than twice the minimum acceptable rating of 250 grams.

AquaSaver

The Fuller Group, Inc.
3461 Summerford Ct.
Marietta, GA 30062

Phone: 770-565-8539

AquaSaver is a small, inexpensive, adjustable, water-saving device for gravity-flush, tanked toilets. The product is a plastic manifold that clips over the toilet's overflow pipe. It saves 15-25% of water per flush without impeding the flushing ability of the toilet. It does this by diverting some of the excess refill water that typically overfills the toilet bowl, keeping it in the toilet tank. It saves more water in older, less-efficient toilets. Sales are primarily in bulk to large institutions or water-conservation contractors.

Caroma Caravelle and Reflections Dual-Flush Toilets

Caroma USA, Inc.
2650 N.E. Aurora Dr.
Hillsboro, OR 97124

Toll-free: 800-605-4218
Phone: 503-681-2720
www.caromausa.com

Caroma USA, the North American subsidiary of Australian Caroma International Pty Ltd, offers a variety of two-button, dual-flush 1.6/0.8 gpf toilets. All units feature full 4" trapways. When MaP-tested at the high-volume flush, the Caravelle 270 and One-Piece each removed 500 grams, while the Caravelle 305 and Reflections 270 each removed 650 grams—resulting in grams-per-liter flushes between 90 and 110. The

best results came from the Caravelle 270 ADA, which evacuated 800 grams, for a grams-per-liter rating of 133.

Eclipse Mariner II Pressure-Assist Toilets

St. Thomas Creations
9393 Waples St., Ste 120
San Diego, CA 92121

Phone: 858-812-2550
www.stthomascreations.com

The 1.0 gpf Eclipse Mariner II ™ pressure-assist toilet uses Sloan's Flushmate IV operating system. A supply line with a minimum water pressure of 25 psi is required. Two models were tested using the MaP (Maximum Performance) protocol in May 2004: both had a 5.9-liter flush volume; the elongated rim model removed 500 grams of solids for a grams-per-liter rating of 85, while the round-front model evacuated 465 grams for a rating of 79.

Escale Dual Flush Toilet

Kohler Co.
444 Highland Dr.
Kohler, WI 53044

Toll-free: 800-456-4537
Phone: 920-457-4441
www.kohler.com

The Escale is a dual-flush, flapperless, gravity-flush toilet from Kohler, offering users the choice of a 1.6-gallon or 0.8-gallon flush. The two-button flush actuator is integrated into the tank lid.

EverGreen 1.2 GPF Toilet

VitrA USA
305 Shawnee North Dr., Ste. 600
Suwanee, GA 30024

Phone: 770-904-6830
www.vitra-usa.com

EverGreen high-efficiency toilets use 1.2 gpf and are capable of disposing of 800 grams of solids based on third-party MaP testing. These quiet, gravity-flush toilets meet ADA requirements and come with either an elongated bowl (model number 5195) or round front (5196), in 10, 12, and 14 inch rough-in dimensions. EverGreen toilets are available with Vitra's glazing technologies: VitraHygiene uses silver ions to make the treated surface resistant to bacteria, and VitraClean improves surface tension to resists staining and make cleaning easier.

FlushMate IV

Sloan Valve Company
10500 Seymour Ave.
Franklin Park, IL 60131

Toll-free: 800-982-5839
Phone: 847-671-4300
www.sloanvalve.com

The FlushMate IV pressure-assisted toilet flushing mechanism is a water-conserving (1.0 gpf) flush mechanism produced by the Sloan Valve Company. The FlushMate IV uses an airtight flushometer vessel inside the toilet tank (a tank-within-a-tank configuration). The inner tank is pressurized by the incoming clean water after the toilet is flushed—as it refills, air becomes compressed at the top of the tank. The next time the toilet is used, this pressure provides a high-velocity flush that very effectively evacuates wastes and prevents clogging.

Gerber Ultra Flush 1.1-Gallon & Dual Flush Toilets

Gerber Plumbing Fixtures LLC
2500 Internationale Pkwy.
Woodridge , IL 60517

Phone: 630-754-0183
www.gerberonline.com

Gerber's Ultra Flush line of pressure-assist toilets includes dual-flush and 1.1-gallon models that returned impressive performances in third-party MaP testing. All used about 3.5 liters of measured flush volume (at high flush, in the case of dual-flush models); the dual-flush models evacuated 1000 grams (at high-flush—about 290 grams per liter), while the 1.1-gallon models evacuated 800 grams (about 230 grams per liter). Rear-discharge models of both are available. These toilets, which use pressure-assist technology by WDI International, do not meet LA SPS non-tampering requirements.

Happy D Dual-Flush Toilets

Duravit USA, Inc.
1750 Breckinridge Pkwy., Ste. 500
Duluth, GA 30096

Toll-free: 888-387-2848
Phone: 770-931-3575
www.duravit.com

The Happy D dual-flush, gravity-type designer toilet from Duravit is available in floor-mounted and wall-mounted models. Both models removed 600 grams of solids under the MaP testing protocol. The average full-flush volume for the floor-mount model was 1.45 gallons; the wall-mount model averaged 1.51 gallons. Both averaged 0.8 gallon reduced flushes. These toilets meet LADWP SPS requirements. All Duravit wall-mounted toilets are dual-flush.

Ifo Cera Dual-Flush Toilets

DEA Bathroom Machineries
495 Main St.
Murphys, CA 95247

Toll-free: 800-255-4426
Phone: 209-728-2031
www.deabath.com

Ifo toilets have a 50-year track record in Sweden, and theirs were among the first water-conserving toilets to gain acceptance in the American market. Their dual-flush Cera line offers users the choice of a 1.6-gallon full flush, or a 0.8-gallon half-volume flush. Note that Ifo toilets are constructed to European plumbing conventions and require a 4" rough-in rather than 12" or 14", or accommodation for rear-outlet. Retrofitting existing plumbing may not be feasible; refer to rough-in diagrams before ordering. The flush performance of these toilets has not been tested by the MaP (Maximum Performance) protocol; these toilets are included for their water-saving attribute.

Kohler 1.1-Gallon, Pressure-Assist Toilets

Kohler Co.
444 Highland Dr.
Kohler, WI 53044

Toll-free: 800-456-4537
Phone: 920-457-4441
www.kohler.com

Highline and Wellworth 1.1-gpf toilets from Kohler use the Sloan FlushMate IV flushing system, which was recognized by BuildingGreen as a 2004 Top-10 Green Building Product. Kohler used advanced "noise-mapping and frequency analysis technology" to make these among the quietest pressure-assist toilets on the market. The Highline removed 1000 grams of solids per flush under third-party MaP testing.

Kohler 1.28 GPF, Gravity-Flush Toilets

Kohler Co.
444 Highland Dr.
Kohler, WI 53044

Toll-free: 800-456-4537
Phone: 920-457-4441
www.kohler.com

The Cimarron, Highline, and Archer high-efficiency toilets (HET) from Kohler with Class Five EcoSmart flush technology uses 1.28 gallons per flush. These gravity-flush toilets feature a flapperless flush tower, and meet the requirement for programs offering rebates on HETs. These toilets also passed certification to bear the EPA's WaterSense label.

Mancesa Cyclone 4

Mancesa (Division of Mansfield Plumbing Products, LLC)
150 First St.
P.O. Box 620
Perrysville, OH 44864

Toll-free: 877-850-3060
Phone: 419-938-5211
www.mancesa.com

The 1.1-gallon-per-flush Cyclone 4, from Colombian manufacturer Mancesa (a Mansfield brand), uses Sloan's Flushmate IV® pressure-assist flushing system. In MaP testing, it evacuated 650 grams with a measured flush of 3.6 liters—removing over 180 grams per liter of flush water. This toilet has a 2" trapway and an 8.5" x 10.25" water surface area.

Mansfield EcoQuantum and QuantumOne Toilets

Mansfield Plumbing Products, LLC
150 E. 1st St.
P.O. Box 620
Perrysville, OH 44864

Toll-free: 877-850-3060
Phone: 419-938-5211
www.mansfieldplumbing.com

The pressure-assisted, dual-flush EcoQuantum line from Mansfield provides either a 1.6-gallon or 1.1-gallon flush, depending on whether the flush lever is pushed up or pressed down. Under MaP testing using the 1-gallon flush setting, models evacuated between 825 and 925 grams with measured flush volumes of 3.4 liters—grams-per-liter removal of 250 to 270. These toilets use the EcoFlush™ Dual Flushing Technology system. The QuantumOne one-gallon per flush line uses Flushmate IV™ pressure-assist technology; with a measured flush volume of 3.1 liters, models yielded grams-per-flush levels of 170 to 217 (525 to 675 grams).

Metzi 0.6 gpf Toilet

Bogo Global
3525 Ellicott Mills Dr., Ste. A
Ellicott City, MD 21043

Phone: 410-465-1841
www.bogoglobal.com

The Metzi toilet uses 0.6 gallons per flush. The patented South Korean technology uses a straight pipe with an odor prevention trap instead of a siphoning system. The performance of the Metzi toilet has not been tested by the MaP (Maximum Performance) protocol, but is included for its very low water consumption.

Peerless Pottery-The Predator

Peerless Pottery
P.O. Box 145
Rockport, IN 47635

Toll-free: 800-457-5785
www.peerlesspottery.com

Manufactured by Capizzi, Peerless Pottery offers two models (ADA and low-profile) in the Predator line that meet GreenSpec standards. Both use Sloan's FlushMate® technology to achieve 1.1-gallon flushes. In MaP testing, the ADA model evacuated 500 grams with a measured flush volume of 3.7 liters (135 grams per liter). The low-profile model evacuated 400 grams with 3.1 liters (129 grams per liter). These toilets do not meet LA SPS non-tampering requirements.

Pressure-Assisted Low-Flush Toilets

Microphor
452 E. Hill Rd.
Willits, CA 95490

Toll-free: 800-358-8280
Phone: 707-459-5563
www.microphor.com

Microphor produces air-assisted toilets, including the Microflush® toilets that use 0.5 gpf. Compressed air is used to assist flushing. Noise may be a concern. Microflush is also available in a 12-volt DC version. The flush performance of these toilets has not been tested by the MaP (Maximum Performance) protocol; these toilets are included in GreenSpec for their water-saving attribute.

Sanicompact Macerating Toilet

SFA Saniflo, Inc.
105 Newfield Ave.
Ste. A, Raritan Center
Edison, NJ 08837

Toll-free: 1-800-571-8191
www.saniflo.com

The Sanicompact 1.1-gallon-per-flush macerating toilet uses a 1" diameter discharge pipe, and can be installed in tight spaces as well

as below-grade. A switch activates the flush sequence that fills and washes the toilet bowl with water, pumps the effluent to the macerator, and then pumps the discharge away. Effluent can be pumped a maximum of 9 feet vertically, or 100 feet horizontally. Saniflow offers a number of other macerating toilet and plumbing systems as well.

Sterling Dual-Flush Toilets

Kohler Co.
444 Highland Dr.
Kohler, WI 53044

Toll-free: 800-456-4537
Phone: 920-457-4441
www.kohler.com

The Rockton and Karston are dual-flush, flapperless, gravity-fed toilets from Sterling (a Kohler brand), offering users the choice of a 1.6 gal. or 0.8 gal. flush. The two-button flush actuator is integrated into the tank lid. The Waste Removal Performance Measure for the Karston Dual Force EL, using the MaP (Maximum Performance) protocol, was 400 grams using 1.6 gallons; the Rockton evacuated 325 grams. These toilets are on the Los Angeles Department of Water and Power's SPS-Certified Ultra-Low-Flush Toilet list.

TOTO Aquia Dual-Flush Toilet

TOTO USA, Inc.
1155 Southern Rd.
Morrow, GA 30260

Phone: 770-282-8686
www.totousa.com

The Aquia™ dual-flush toilet, introduced to the North American market in 2005, uses 1.6 gallons at the full flush and 0.9 gallons at the low flush. The company estimates that a typical family of four will save approximately 7,000 gallons of water per year over a standard 1.6 gallon-per-flush toilet. Unlike other TOTO gravity-flush toilets, this is a wash-down design, which like other TOTO toilets is highly clog-free. The toilet successfully removed 800 grams of test media at full flush, based on standardized MaP testing. The toilet is offered in six colors.

Turbo Capizzi

Capizzi
413 Interamerica Blvd.
WH1, PMB-006-225
Laredo, TX 78045

Toll-free: 866-250-8833
www.capizzi.com

The Turbo Capizzi high-efficiency toilet, which has an 8" x 9.5" water surface area, uses less than one gallon per flush. A fully glazed 2-1/8" (2" ballpass) trapway and Flushmate IV pressure-assist siphon-jet flush provide reliable performance. The low-profile, low-profile ADA, and high-profile models performed well under MaP testing, evacuating 400 - 500 grams with measured flush volumes between 3.1 and 3.7 liters—about 130 grams per liter, give or take a few grams. The Turbo Capizzi high-profile model meets LA SPS non-tampering specifications. These toilets have limited lifetime warranties; the Sloan Flushmate flush mechanism has a five-year warranty.

VitrA Dual Flush Toilet

VitrA USA
305 Shawnee North Dr., Ste. 600
Suwanee, GA 30024

Phone: 770-904-6830
www.vitra-usa.com

European manufacturer VitrA offers two floor-mounted, dual-flush toilets that use 1.6 gallons at full flush and 0.8 gallons at low flush. The round front dual-flush model removed 475 grams of solids at full flush under third-party MaP testing. The elongated dual flush model, removed 800 grams of solids at full flush.

Vortens Dali, Rhodas DF, Tornado, and Delfos

Vortens U.S. Office
1498 Brookpark Dr.
Mansfield, OH 44906

Toll-free: 800-471-5129
www.vortens.com

The One Piece Delfos, Dali and Rhodas dual-flush toilets from Mexican manufacturer Sanitarios Lamosa S.A. de C.V. offer 1.0 or 1.6 gallon flushes. The flush performances were MaP-tested as having evacuated 400 and 550 grams respectively, with measured flush volumes of 5.5 and 6 liters. With high- and low-flush volumes averaged, the grams-per-liter removal was 80 and 110. In the same test, the Tornado and Tornado ADA pressure-assisted 1.1-gallon-flush toilet used a measured flush volume of 4 liters to evacuate 700 grams—175 grams per liter.

Zurn EcoVantage Dual-Flush Toilet

Zurn Plumbing Products Group
5900 Elwin Buchanan Dr.
Sanford, NC 27330

Toll-free: 800-997-3876
Phone: 919-775-2255
www.zurn.com

The Zurn® EcoVantage™ dual-flush toilet uses a pressure tank that flushes with either 1.6 or 1.0 gallons. This two-piece toilet, elongated-bowl toilet is manufactured for Zurn by WDI. Air is compressed in a sealed tank during the refill; when flushed, a high-velocity, forceful flush is produced. The EcoVantage features a 2-1/8" fully glazed trapway, siphon-jet flush action, a "large" water surface area, and "ultra-quiet" flush action, according to the manufacturer. Available in both standard height and ADA-compliant height (17"). This toilet evacuated 1000 grams with a GreenSpec-adjusted water use of 1.35 gallons per average flush in MaP testing.

Residential Urinals

Products listed here are low-water-use urinals for residential use.

Mister Miser Urinal

Mister Miser Urinal
1800 W. Roscoe, Ste. 325
Chicago, IL 60657

Phone: 773-975-8170
www.mistermiser.net

Designed primarily for residential use, the 10-ounce (1-1/4 cup) flush Mister Miser urinal—made of ABS with a porcelain-like coating—installs at any height between 2x4 studs. A hinged cover folds down for use; the silent flush activates when the lid is closed, providing adequate surface wash and enough liquid to evacuate the built-in P-trap. The manufacturer offers a 5-year warranty. Made in Chicago. This product returned to the market in 2006, after being unavailable for a number of years.

Sanitary Waste and Vent Piping

Most sanitary drain waste and vent (DWV) piping used today is made from PVC or ABS plastic. Both of these have toxic manufacturing intermediaries and require the use of hazardous solvents for welding the joints. PVC can also generate highly toxic dioxins in the case of accidental fire or improper incineration. Cast iron, the traditional DWV pipe material, has high recycled content, but the scrap metal is melted primarily with coke, and the toxic and carcinogenic emissions from coke manufacture makes cast iron worse than available plastic alternatives on a life-cycle basis. Vitrified clay pipe can be used in buildings as drain pipe but is more commonly used for larger-diameter sewage applications (where it competes with concrete and PVC); although heavy and labor-intensive, vitrified clay is the most durable waste and sewage piping material. Finally, there are some polyolefin (polyethylene and polypropylene) plastic pipes that can be used for drainage and venting. If plastic piping products are being chosen, look for recycled content. Products listed here now include vitrified clay pipe, but lower-impact plastic DWV piping will be listed if and when it becomes available.

Industry Representation

National Clay Pipe Institute
P.O. Box 759
Lake Geneva, WI 53147

Phone: 262-248-9094
www.ncpi.org

The National Clay Pipe Institute represents the manufacturers of vitrified clay waste and sewer pipe. Clay pipe is the environmentally preferable, highly durable, corrosion-resistant alternative to PVC sewer pipe.

Vitrified Clay Pipe

Building Products Company
4850 W. Buckeye Rd.
Phoenix, AZ 85043

Phone: 602-269-8314
www.mcpind.com

Building Products Company is a manufacturer of vitrified clay pipe for waste line and sewage piping.

Vitrified Clay Pipe

Gladding, McBean & Co.
P.O. Box 97
Lincoln, CA 95648

Toll-free: 800-776-1133
Phone: 916-645-3341
www.gladdingmcbean.com

Gladding McBean is a manufacturer of vitrified clay pipe for waste line and sewage piping.

Vitrified Clay Pipe

Mission Clay Products
P.O. Box 549
Corona, CA 92878

Toll-free: 800-795-6067
Phone: 951-277-4600
www.missionclay.com

Mission Clay Products is a manufacturer of vitrified clay pipe for waste line and sewage piping. Diameters range from 4" to 40". The company has plants located in California, Kansas, Arizona, and Texas.

Vitrified Clay Pipe

Superior Clay Corp.
P.O. Box 352
Uhrichsville, OH 44683

Toll-free: 800-848-6166
Phone: 740-922-4122
www.superiorclay.com

Superior Clay is a manufacturer of vitrified clay pipe, with available diameters ranging from 3" to 30".

Vitrified Clay Pipe

The Logan Clay Products Co.
P.O. Box 698
Logan, OH 43138

Toll-free: 800-848-2141
Phone: 740-385-2184
www.loganclaypipe.com

The Logan Clay Products Co. is a manufacturer of vitrified clay pipe for waste line and sewage piping.

Swimming Pool Plumbing Systems

Products listed here include specialized systems to use solar thermal energy for pool water heating.

Heliocol Solar Pool-Heating Systems

Heliocol
13620 49th St. N
Clearwater, FL 33762

Phone: 727-572-6655
www.heliocol.com

Heliocol manufactures unglazed polypropylene, solar pool-heating systems.

Solar Collectors

Integrated Solar LLC
2030 W. Pinnacle Peak Rd.
Phoenix, AZ 85027

Toll-free: 800-927-2326
Phone: 805-928-1881
http://radcosolar.com/about.html

Integrated Solar LLC manufactures Radco glazed flat-plate solar collectors and Radco complete drainback solar water-heating systems for areas with freezing weather conditions. The company also produces a line of Radco unglazed solar pool-heating systems.

Solar Collectors

Sealed Air Corp. - Solar Pool Heating
200 Riverfront Boulevard
Elmwood Park, NJ 07407

Toll-free: 201-791-7600
Phone: 510-887-8090
www.sealedair.com

Sealed Air Corporation is primarily in the packaging business but also produces a line of flat-plate solar collectors for pool heating.

Solar Pool-Heating Systems

Aquatherm Industries, Inc.
1940 Rutgers University Blvd.
Lakewood, NJ 08701

Toll-free: 800-535-6307
Phone: 732-905-9002
www.warmwater.com

Aquatherm produces unglazed polypropylene collectors designed for pool heating. These are used with existing conventional filtration systems to circulate pool water through the collectors then back into the pool. Most systems utilize an automatic temperature control. The swimming pool serves as the heat-storage reservoir.

Solar Pool Heating Systems

Fafco, Inc.
435 Otterson Dr.
Chico, CA 95928

Toll-free: 800-994-7652
Phone: 530-332-2100
www.fafco.com

Fafco is the oldest manufacturer of solar water-heating equipment in the U.S.—since 1969. The company manufactures a line of pool-heating systems.

Water Filtering

Products included here are used to purify water. Such systems can help to ensure high-quality drinking water. Some are also key components of rainwater harvesting systems.

ECO-Nomad

Architectural & Community Planning Inc.
261 Albany St.
Winnipeg, MB R3G 2A9 Canada

Phone: 204-831-0216
www.economad.com

The ECO-Nomad™ combined mechanical utility container provides utility services to off-grid locations by creating a self-contained, integrated micro-infrastructure, including potable water storage and purification, biological wastewater treatment, water and space heating, electrical supply, and fire protection. All functions can be remotely monitored. The portable 8′ x 8′ x 16′ utility container can be transported by road, rail, water, or air. Designed for extreme winter conditions, uses include remote residential, tourism, or commercial facilities; temporary mining or logging camps; disaster relief; and remote airports and weather stations.

SolAqua Water Distillation

SolAqua
P.O. Box 4976
El Paso, TX 79914

Phone: 915-383-1485
www.solaqua.com

SolAqua sells passive-solar water distillation systems that provide purified distilled water without electricity, pumps, chemicals, or boiling. Products include the Rainmaker 550, which produces a maximum of 1.5 gallons of distilled water per day, do-it-yourself installation plans and kits, and community-size solar distiller arrays. SolAqua also provides consulting and installation for large systems.

Solar Cube

Spectra Watermachines
20 Mariposa Rd.
San Rafael, CA 94901

Phone: 415-526-2780
www.spectrawatermakers.com

The Spectra Solar Cube is a solar- and wind-powered water purification and/or desalination system that can provide both pure drinking water and electricity for small villages, resorts, or disaster relief. The system's 1 kW wind generator and 1.2 kW PV panel provide power to an inverter/charger that keeps the 100 Amp-hour battery pack charged, and powers the 900 W filtration system. The system can provide extra power in 24V DC, or convert it to 110 or 220V AC. Each subsystem can be removed from the cube for accessibility and easy maintenance. The SSW 3500 Spectra Solar Seawater System produces 3500 liters/day of fresh water from saline water. The SSBW 6500 Spectra Solar Brackish Water System provides from 3500–6500 liters/day, depending on the salinity of the feed water. These systems use Spectra's patented clark pump reverse osmosis desalinization system. The SFWS 15,000 Spectra Solar Fresh Water System can purify 15,000 liters/day from almost any non-saline water source using an ultra filtration purification system from GE to remove virus and bacteria without the use of harsh or toxic chemicals.

Solar Turtle

Solar Turtle, Inc.
4901 Cactus Wren Ave.
Tucson, AZ 85746

Phone: 520-883-3356

The Solar Turtle is a photovoltaic power supply and water purification system mostly used for remote cabins and RVs. These systems include 120-watt panels, deep-cycle batteries, an inverter, and General Ecology's SeaGull IV water purification systems. The system can output up to 720 W DC or 2,500 W AC. Most Solar Turtle units include custom features to match customer needs.

SunRay-30 and SunRay-1000

Safe Water Systems
1600 Kapiolani Blvd., Ste. 721
Honolulu, HI 96814

Phone: 808-949-3123
www.safewatersystems.com

The SunRay-30 and SunRay-1000 can provide inexpensive microbial water purification without electricity, pumps, chemicals, or boiling. The SunRay-30 is comprised of a black, double-walled HDPE collector covered by two layers of transparent acrylic glazing. Up to 3.5 gal. of untreated water is poured into the unit and placed in the sun; when pasteurization is complete, an indicator will change color. The SunRay-1000 is designed to purify approximately 260 gal. of water a day in sunny climates, utilizes a flat plate collector, a high-efficiency heat exchanger, and a fail-safe thermal control valve. On cloudy days, or at night, an optional backup burner can use any form of combustible fuel. Neither unit can be used in freezing temperatures.

UV Water Disinfection Systems

Siemens Water Technologies, Inc.
80 Commerce Dr.
Allendale, NJ 07401

Phone: 201-760-0586
www.water.siemens.com

Siemens Water Technologies manufactures and markets ultraviolet (UV) water disinfection systems for residential, commercial, and industrial use and also supplies replacement parts and service. UV purification is suitable for disinfecting water that is microbially contaminated. In certain situations, it may be necessary to pretreat water with another filtration system to remove impurities which can interfere with UV light transmission.

Water Storage Tanks

Tanks for storing potable water supplies should be drainable, cleanable, and durable.

Plastic Cistern Liners

Thompson Plastics Melita
P.O. Box 456
Melita, MB R0M 1L0 Canada

Toll-free: 866-522-3241

Thompson cistern liners are made of polyethylene sheeting seam-welded to fit loosely into a round tank or rectangular cavity used to hold liquid, usually water. These liners are appropriate for rainwater storage.

Rainwater Catchment Systems

Northwest Water Source
P.O. Box 2766
Friday Harbor, WA 98250

Phone: 360-378-8252

Northwest Water Source offers components and equipment as well as design and consulting for both residential and commercial rainwater catchment and harvesting systems. The company imports European rainfall catchment equipment and stormwater infiltration technology from Germany and Holland. Equipment includes European-made stainless steel demand pumping systems that don't require a pressure tank; UV water purification and filtration; and a variety of water storage tanks including above- and below-ground rotationally molded polyethylene and custom-made in-ground units consisting of a polyethylene "endoskeleton" covered by a welded sheet polypropylene.

Rainwater Collection and Filtration Systems

Resource Conservation Technology, Inc.
2633 N. Calvert St.
Baltimore, MD 21218

Toll-free: 800-477-7724
Phone: 410-366-1146
www.conservationtechnology.com

Resource Conservation Technology, Inc. provides residential and commercial rainwater collection, filtration, and storage systems. In a typical installation, water from a building's downspouts is piped underground through a central filter to the storage tanks. System capacities range from hundreds to thousands of gallons, and a system may include additional pumps, controls, and disinfection systems tailored to the application.

Vertical Above-Ground Storage Tanks

Holloway Welding & Piping Co.
820 W. Forest Grove Rd.
Allen, TX 75002

Toll-free: 800- 548-3134
Phone: 972-562-5033
www.hollowaywp.com

Holloway Welding & Piping supplies storage tanks for use with rainwater catchment systems.

Water Cistern and Storage Tanks

Snyder Industries
4700 Fremont St.
P.O. Box 4583
Lincoln, NE 68504

Phone: 402-467-5221
www.snydernet.com

Snyder's NuConCept above- and below-ground water storage tanks are rotationally molded with a variety of polyethylene materials, including FDA- and NSF 61-approved high-density (HDLPE) and cross-linked high-density (XLPE) resins. May be used as rainwater catchment cisterns.

Water Storage Tanks

Norwesco, Inc.
4365 Steiner St.
P.O. Box 439
St. Bonifacius, MN 55375

Phone: 800-328-3420
www.norwesco.com

Norwesco's seamless polyethylene storage tanks range from 12 to 15,000 gallons and are manufactured using resins meeting FDA specifications to ensure safe storage of potable water. Applicable tanks are also NSF-approved. Appropriate for rainwater catchment cisterns.

This Space is Available for Your Notes

This Space is Available for Your Notes

Electrical

The plastic insulation and jacketing on electric and data wire and cable can contain lead, plasticizers, flame retardants, and chemicals that may be toxic. Polyvinyl chloride (PVC) and fluoropolymers (Teflon®) are commonly used on wire and cable. Toxic compounds may be released in the event of fire or as the wire jacketing deteriorates over time. Wires and cables are available with nonhalogenated insulation and jacketing and with no heavy metals.

Electrical current flow creates electromagnetic fields (EMFs), which—according to some experts—may cause a range of adverse health effects. While many studies have been conducted, these health concerns have yet to be proven to the satisfaction of mainstream scientists. Due to the uncertainty surrounding this issue, it makes sense to take steps to minimize exposure to such fields, as long as these measures aren't expensive (a strategy referred to as "produce avoidance"). Such measures might include locating main electrical service lines away from occupied areas and specifying that wiring be installed in such a way as to minimize EMFs. Electronics may also be sensitive to EMFs, so rooms with computers and other such equipment should be designed with that in mind.

Alternative Energy Balance of Systems Components

Inverters convert the direct-current (DC) power produced by the renewable energy system into alternating-current (AC) power needed for most conventional appliances or for feeding site-generated electricity into the power grid. Other power-conditioning equipment, controllers, batteries, and mounting equipment are also included here.

Fronius Grid-Tied PV Inverters

Fronius USA LLC
10421, Ste. 1100
Solar Electronics Division
Brighton, MI 48116

Phone: 810-220-4414
www.fronius-USA.com

Fronius manufactures high-efficiency, lightweight, DC-to-AC inverters for residential-scale PV power applications. Most are used for grid-connected applications. The IG line of products has a wide DC-voltage range (150-450 V), and an LCD data display, with a maximum output power ranging from 2.0 to 5.1 kW. The Fronius USA Solar Electronics Division is a branch of the German company Fronius International GmbH.

GE Solar Systems and Modules

GE Energy
231 Lake Dr.
Newark, DE 19702

Toll-free: 866-750-3150
www.gepower.com

GE offers a range of solar electric power systems for residential, commercial, and industrial applications as well as polycrystal PV modules ranging from 66 watts to 200 watts. Grid-tied, remote, or building integrated systems for new construction or retrofit applications are available. In 2004 GE purchased Astropower, thus entering the photovoltaics industry.

GridPoint Connect Backup PV System

GridPoint Inc.
2020 K Street NW
Ste. 550
Washington, DC 20006

Phone: 202-903-2100
www.gridpoint.com

GridPoint Connect provides the balance-of-system (everything but the solar panel array) for a grid-connected PV backup power system. Gridpoint Connect combines the electronics, inverter, charge controllers, recyclable batteries, computer, and other needed components, in a single 'plug-and-play' device. This device connects to the main circuit breaker panel, PV array, communication line, and secure load panel (on which critical circuits are placed). The GridPoint Connect system ensures batteries are fully charged and supplies local power needs, feeding excess power to the grid. If the grid is down, the Connect system will power critical loads from the solar array and/or battery pack.

Inverters

Xantrex Technology
5916 195th St. NE
Arlington, WA 98223

Toll-free: 888-800-1010
Phone: 360-435-8826
www.xantrex.com

Xantrex Technology, formerly Trace Engineering, manufactures energy-efficient DC-to-AC inverters for residential, commercial, mobile, remote, and emergency applications. These are the most widely used inverters for PV and wind power systems. Inverters specially designed for feeding power into the electric grid are available.

Outback Power System Components

OutBack Power Systems
19009 62nd Ave. NE
Arlington, WA 98223

Phone: 360-435-6030
www.outbackpower.com

Outback Power Systems provides balance-of-system components including inverters, solar charge controllers, communication managers, and a range of other components and accessories for stand-alone, grid-tied, or backup photovoltaic power systems. Outback's FLEXware integration hardware allows horizontal or vertical mounting orientations for locations with limited wall space and can accommodate a wide range of power system sizes.

PV Controllers

Solar Converters Inc.
558 Massey Road, Unit 1
Guelph, ON N1K 1B4 Canada

Phone: 519-824-5272
www.solarconverters.com

Solar Converters Inc. is a designer and manufacturer of highly efficient power control products for the renewable energy field. Included among the products the company has developed are Linear Current Boosters, Battery Equalizers, Power Tracker™ charge controllers with Maximum Power Point Tracking (MPPT), Cathodic Protection Controllers, Generator Starters, Battery Desulphators, Constant Voltage Pump Drivers, Voltage Controlled Switches, Solar Lighting Controllers, DC-DC Converters, and more.

Smart Power M-Series Solar Power Conversion

Beacon Power Corporation
65 Middlesex Rd.
Tyngsboro, MA 01879

Toll-free: 888-938-9112
Phone: 978-694-9121
www.beaconpower.com

Beacon Power Corporation introduced the Smart Power line of inverters in 2003, with inverter technology acquired from Advanced Energy, Inc. (previously of Wilton, New Hampshire). The M-Series is a 4000- or 5000-watt grid connected solar inverter capable of operating during grid outages, providing true sine wave backup power to critical loads. The product includes the charge controller, inverter and switchgear all in one outdoor-rated enclosure. The company claims 90% efficiency at full output and 93% efficiency at 50% output.

Solar Controllers

Heliotrope PV, LLC
3766 Kathryn Ave. Unit C
P.O. Box 696
Springfield, OR 97477

Phone: 541-726-1091
www.heliotrope-pv.com

Heliotrope PV manufacturers electronic charge controllers for PV systems. Though marketed to recreational vehicle users, they are appropriate for any small PV system.

Solaris 3500XP

Alpha Technologies, Inc.
3767 Alpha Way
Bellingham, WA 98226

Phone: 360-647-2360

The Solaris 3500XP system is an integrated 3.5 kW inverter and uninterruptible power supply (UPS) for grid-tied and off-grid photovoltaic applications. The system has a CEC rated efficiency of 91% and the company claims the system maintains its rated output over an operating temperature range of -20 to 50 degrees C. The system is designed to support either 120/240 or 208 VAC output and can include an optional 48 volt DC input for use with a DC generator or additional batteries.

Solectria Grid-Tied PV Inverters

Solectria Renewables LLC
360 Merrimack St.
Building 9, 2nd Fl.
Lawrence, MA 01843

Phone: 978-683-9700
www.solren.com

Solectria manufactures a line of high-efficiency DC-to-AC inverters for residential and commercial PV power applications, especially grid-connected systems. The products cover systems from 12-500kW and can include an optional internet-connected data logger and monitoring system. Solectria also manufactures inverters for connected or 'mini-grid' distributed generation with input from fuel cells, batteries, ICE, or heat engines. Solectria also provides engineering services and custom products for any 1-500kW distributed generation system.

Steca Solar Charge Controllers

SunWize Technologies
1155 Flatbush Rd.
Kingston, NY 12401

Toll-free: 800-817-6527
Phone: 845-336-0146
www.sunwize.com

SunWize distributes Steca electronic charge controllers for PV systems. The Sunwize Steca controller is a self-learning controller that uses an advanced control algorithm combining battery temperature, battery voltage, and load discharge rate to determine the true battery state of charge(SOC), automatically adjusting for the capacity and age of the battery.

SunEarth Solar Equipment

SunEarth, Inc.
8425 Almeria Ave.
Fontana, CA 92335

Phone: 909-434-3100
www.sunearthinc.com

SunEarth, Inc., a manufacturer of solar water-heating equipment since 1978, produces flat-plate solar collectors, ICS and thermosiphon water-heating systems, and ancillary components including residential and commercial racking systems for both solar water heating and PV systems.

Sunny Boy Inverters

SMA America, Inc.
12438 Loma Rica Dr.
Grass Valley, CA 95945

Phone: 530-273-4895
www.sma-america.com

SMA America offers 2,500-, 1,800-, and 700-watt inverters designed for residential-scale photovoltaic applications. These German-made inverters carry a 5-year warranty and are being specified by some of the leading PV system designers today. The company also offers a larger, 125 kW inverter, as well as PV control and monitoring equipment.

UniRac PV Mounting Systems

UniRac, Inc.
1411 Broadway Blvd. NE
Albuquerque, NM 87102

Phone: 505-242-6411
www.unirac.com

UniRac produces systems for mounting PV modules. SolarMount® is a system of components for flat and tilted roofs. SolarMount/S-5! is designed for easy installation on standing-seam metal roofs. SunFrame offers building integration, a low-profile and a choice of finishes. PoleTops are ground mounting systems. U-LA is for arrays of 3-kW or more. UniRac recycles all solid waste and purchases recycled materials when available, including 20-25% post-consumer recycled aluminum and 75% recycled steel. In addition, most shipping materials are salvaged or have recycled-content.

Batteries for Alternative Energy Systems

Lead-acid batteries designed for use in solar applications are included here because of their application. Lead is a toxic heavy metal and should be recycled.

Deep-Cycle, Lead-Acid Batteries

Surrette Battery Company Limited
1 Station Rd.
P.O. Box 2020
Springhill, NS B0M 1X0 Canada

Toll-free: 800-681-9914
Phone: 902-597-3767
www.surrette.com

Surrette Battery Company Limited manufactures specialty batteries. The deep-cycle, lead-acid batteries for solar applications feature dual containers to withstand rough handling and prevent acid leakage. These batteries have a ten-year warranty, and an expected life of 15 years. Surrette is the parent company of the Rolls Battery Company in the U.S.

GridPoint Connect Backup PV System

GridPoint Inc.
2020 K Street NW
Ste. 550
Washington, DC 20006

Phone: 202-903-2100
www.gridpoint.com

GridPoint Connect provides the balance-of-system (everything but the solar panel array) for a grid-connected PV backup power system. Gridpoint Connect combines the electronics, inverter, charge controllers, recyclable batteries, computer, and other needed components, in a single 'plug-and-play' device. This device connects to the main circuit breaker panel, PV array, communication line, and secure load panel (on which critical circuits are placed). The GridPoint Connect system ensures batteries are fully charged and supplies local power needs, feeding excess power to the grid. If the grid is down, the Connect system will power critical loads from the solar array and/ or battery pack.

Solaris 3500XP

Alpha Technologies, Inc.
3767 Alpha Way
Bellingham, WA 98226

Phone: 360-647-2360

The Solaris 3500XP system is an integrated 3.5 kW inverter and uninterruptible power supply (UPS) for grid-tied and off-grid photovoltaic applications. The system has a CEC rated efficiency of 91% and the company claims the system maintains its rated output over an operating temperature range of -20 to 50 degrees C. The system is designed to support either 120/240 or 208 VAC output and can include an optional 48 volt DC input for use with a DC generator or additional batteries.

Building Integrated Photovoltaic Roofing

Photovoltaics (PV) enable the direct conversion of sunlight into electricity. Some PV modules are integrated into building components, such as roofing and wall glazings—these are often referred to as building-integrated photovoltaics (BIPV).

Sunslates

Atlantis Energy Systems, Inc.
4517 Harlin Dr.
Sacramento, CA 95826

Phone: 916-438-2930
www.atlantisenergy.org

Atlantis Energy Systems produces Sunslates®, which serve as both a roofing product and a solar-electric power source. Sunslates are fiber-cement shingles into which PV cells have been laminated. Each shingle has a plug-in wiring connection.

UNI-SOLAR PV Shingles and Standing Seam Panels

United Solar Ovonic LLC
3800 Lapeer Rd.
Auburn Hills, MI 48326

Toll-free: 800-843-3892
Phone: 248-475-0100
www.uni-solar.com

Uni-Solar Ovonic LLC PV Shingles and Standing Seam Roofing Panels are installed much like conventional roofing products. They generate electricity while protecting the structure from weather. PV Shingles, measuring 86.4" x 12" with 7 tabs, are interspersed among conventional 3-tab shingles. Standing Seam Panels are available for laminating onto conventional roofing or as a PV-integrated, standing-seam product. Lead wires from each shingle or panel enter the structure through drilled holes in the roof decking. Uni-Solar roofing products use triple-junction amorphous silicon technology.

Data Cables

Working toward the goal of eliminating halogenated flame retardants must not result in elevated fire risk. Products listed are not necessarily plenum rated (the highest fire-resistant rating). Lower-rated products may need to be installed in metal conduit to provide fire separation, and/or changes such as fire-resistant construction detailing and sprinkler use must be incorporated as directed by code. While the use of metal conduit is likely to be more expensive, it also simplifies remodeling. In addition there is growing concern about lead-dust from old cables, and new regulations are requiring removal of old wiring to reduce potential fire-loads. Use of metal conduit is a preventative measure against these concerns.

Products listed here must be free of heavy metals and halogens (ie containing no chlorinated, brominated, or florinated substances) This means that Greenspec will not include cable products that contain PVC, chlorinated polyethylene, FEP, or brominated flame retardants and that products will meet the EU RoHS standards to be free of lead, cadmium, hexavalent chromium, and mercury as well as for flame retardants.

Zero-Halogen RoHS-Compliant Data Cables

Berk-Tek
132 White Oak Rd.
New Holland, PA 17557

Phone: 717-354-6200
www.berktek.com

Berktek, a division of Nexans, supplies a full line of riser-rated compliant data cables compliant with RoHS, the European Union's rules on hazardous substances in electrical equipment. A low-smoke, zero-halogen option is available by special request for a range of cable types. The company can provide low-smoke, zero-halogen, Category-6 cable, but requires a 25,000-foot minimum order.

Lighting Controls and Building Automation

Optimizing lighting systems is a complex task involving daylighting and building design issues, careful lamp and fixture selection, and advanced lighting control. The environmental and financial benefits can be significant. Well-designed systems provide high-quality light where and when it's needed, with reduced energy consumption and maintenance costs. Lighting control systems can be as basic as a bathroom light occupancy sensor or as complex as a whole-building, computer-controlled energy management system that handles lighting, HVAC equipment, and sometimes other functions, such as security.

Decora Wall Switch Occupancy Sensors

Leviton Manufacturing Co. Ltd.
59-25 Little Neck Pkwy.
Little Neck, NY 11362

Toll-free: 800-824-3005
Phone: 718-229-4040
www.leviton.com

Decora® Wall Switch Occupancy Sensors are passive infrared sensors that control lighting based upon detected motion. Leviton manufactures wall- and ceiling-mounted, infrared and ultrasonic, commercial and residential occupancy sensors, and lighting control systems.

GreenSwitch

GreenSwitch LLC
225 Columbia Ave.
Chapin, NC 29036

Toll-free: 1-803-932-0210
www.greenswitch.tv

GreenSwitch is a wireless system that controls lighting and other electronic devices by use of a "master" switch that controls several designated "slave" switches, receptacles (wall outlets), and thermostats. With the master switch on ("occupied" mode), a wireless signal provides power to lighting and appliances and adjusts the HVAC to predetermined settings. When the master switch is shut off ("unoccupied" mode), a signal is sent to the slave components, turning off lights and lowering the thermostat. Lights and other systems can be turned on and off manually, overriding the GreenSwitch. The system can reduce the "phantom" power use by home electronics when the house is not occupied by cutting the power to the receptacles used by this equipment.

Isolé Plug Load Control

Watt Stopper/Legrand
2800 De La Cruz Blvd.
Santa Clara, CA 95050

Toll-free: 800-879-8585
Phone: 408-988-5331
www.wattstopper.com

The Isolé IDP-3050 Plug Load Control from The Watt Stopper consists of an eight-outlet power strip with surge protection and a passive infrared (PIR) personal occupancy sensor. The occupancy sensor controls six of the eight outlets and is recommended for computer monitors, task lights, printers, personal electric space heaters, and fans. Computers and fax machines should be plugged into uncontrolled outlets.

LightHAWK-MT

Hubbell Building Automation, Inc.
9601 Dessau Rd., Bldg. 1
Austin, TX 78754

Toll-free: 888-698-3242
Phone: 512-450-1100
www.hubbell-automation.com

The LightHAWK-MT™ occupancy sensor combines passive infrared, ultrasonic, and photocell sensors in one unit to optimize lighting control for energy savings. Hubbell Building Automation, Inc., which was formed by the joining of Mytech Corporation and Unenco, produces a full line of occupancy sensors and controls.

Occupancy Sensors and Lighting Controls

Watt Stopper/Legrand
2800 De La Cruz Blvd.
Santa Clara, CA 95050

Toll-free: 800-879-8585
Phone: 408-988-5331
www.wattstopper.com

Watt Stopper/Legrand manufactures occupancy sensors and controls for lighting and HVAC equipment in commercial and residential buildings. Products include automatic wall switches, ceiling- and wall-mount sensors, outdoor motion sensors, and sensors for special applications. They include a range of sensing technologies, such as passive infrared, ultrasonic, and dual technology. In addition, Watt Stopper/Legrand manufactures lighting control panels, daylighting controls, bi-level HID controls, and plug load controls.

Sensor Switch Occupancy Sensors

Sensor Switch, Inc.
900 Northrop Rd.
Wallingford, CT 06492

Toll-free: 800-727-7483
Phone: 203-265-2842
www.sensorswitch.com

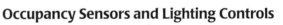

Sensor Switch, Inc. is a leading manufacturer of passive infrared (PIR) and passive dual-technology (PDT) occupancy sensor and photosensor daylighting controls for lighting. Products are available for both commercial and residential applications. PDT combines PIR with sound detection, providing four times the detection reliability, according to the company, and enabling lights to be reactivated by voice if the lights accidentally go out. Sensor Switch also offers a sensor that works on all electrical systems worldwide with a 20-year guaranteed life. Manufactured in the U.S.

Microturbines

Microturbines use natural gas, propane, or other fuels to generate electricity on-site. The same principle is used as for large gas turbines at power plants, but microturbines are much smaller and, thus, designed for distributed power production (producing power where it is needed). When combined with cogeneration equipment—heat exchangers that make use of otherwise-wasted thermal energy—the overall efficiency of microturbines can be increased to over 60%. Microturbines have a number of applications, including off-grid generation, utility peak-shaving, emergency back-up power, and combined heat and power (cogeneration) at restaurants, commercial laundries, hospitals, manufacturing plants, and office buildings with dehumidification or absorption cooling systems.

Warm Air Freewatt System

Climate Energy
93 West St.
Medfield, MA 02052

Phone: 508-359-4500
www.climate-energy.com

Climate Energy's Warm Air Freewatt System is the first residential-sized combined heat and power system in the USA. A low-emission natural gas Honda engine generator produces 1.2 kW of electricity and 11,000 Btu/hr of useful heat, resulting in a combined efficiency of 81%. The generator operates fairly continuously during the heating season, with the waste heat captured and distributed. During periods of high heating demand, the Olsen UltraMax III gas furnace provides 47,000 to 143,000 Btu/hr of additional heat at 95% AFUE efficiency. The system is quieter than a typical warm air furnace, according to the manufacturer. The Climate Energy system is set up to be grid-connected and has an Internet connection for remote monitoring and potential control by the utility company under 'dispatchable load' arrangements. It is also compatible with conventional central air conditioning systems.

Photovoltaic Collectors

Photovoltaics (PV) enable the direct conversion of sunlight into electricity. Some PV modules are integrated into building components, such as roofing and wall glazings—these are often referred to as building-integrated photovoltaics (BIPV). Packaged Solar Equipment includes "plug-and-play" systems that include all of the necessary components.

Blue Link Photovoltaic Systems

Solar Market
25 Limerick Rd.
Arundel, ME 04046

Toll-free: 877-785-0088
www.solarmarket.com

The Blue Link 480 grid-connected photovoltaic system from Solar Market™ is a complete, ground-mounted, plug-and-play unit with a rated power production of 480 watts DC. A steel mounting rack supports the solar panels, inverter, and electrical disconnects; a 25' cable for the intertie is included. Installation takes about 30 minutes. A licensed electrician may be required to connect the unit into a home's load center; check with the local electric utility for any additional requirements or restrictions. The array measures 5' x 8'; the system weighs 140 pounds. The PV panels (manufactured by BP Solar) are guaranteed for 25 years; the balance of the system carries a 5-year warranty.

GE Solar Systems and Modules

GE Energy
231 Lake Dr.
Newark, DE 19702

Toll-free: 866-750-3150
www.gepower.com

GE offers a range of solar electric power systems for residential, commercial, and industrial applications as well as polycrystal PV modules ranging from 66 watts to 200 watts. Grid-tied, remote, or building integrated systems for new construction or retrofit applications are available. In 2004 GE purchased Astropower, thus entering the photovoltaics industry.

Industry Representation

Solar Energy Industries Association
805 15th St. NW, Ste. 510
Washington, DC 20005

Phone: 202-682-0556
www.seia.org

The Solar Energy Industries Association (SEIA) is the national trade association of solar energy manufacturers, dealers, distributors, contractors, and installers. SEIA's primary mission is to expand the use of solar technologies in the global marketplace. Membership exceeds 500 companies providing solar thermal and solar electric products and services.

PV Modules

BP Solar
630 Solarex Ct.
Frederick, MD 21703

Phone: 301-698-4200
www.bpsolar.com

BP Solar is one of the world's largest solar electric companies, with manufacturing plants in the U.S., Spain, Australia, and India. They manufacture, design, market, and install a wide range of crystalline silicon solar electric products. The highest percentage of BP Solar's sales are to homeowners, builders, and businesses, and they are the largest supplier to the rural infrastructure market, where solar is the core power source for off-grid communities. In 1999, BP-Amoco acquired Solarex and folded it into BP's PV Division to form BP Solar.

PV Modules

Evergreen Solar, Inc.
138 Bartlett St.
Marlboro, MA 01752

Phone: 508-357-2221
www.evergreensolar.com

Evergreen Solar is a manufacturer of PV modules and the innovator of the String Ribbon™ method of producing solar cells. This technique uses approximately half the amount of silicon as the industry norm. The company manufactures panels suitable for both grid-tied and off-grid installations and offers a 20-year warranty on all its products. Evergreen products are available through various distributors.

PV Modules

First Solar, LLC
4050 E. Cotton Ctr. Blvd., Ste. 6-68
Phoenix, AZ 85040

Phone: 602-414-9300
www.firstsolar.com

First Solar develops and manufactures Cadmium Telluride (CdTe) thin-film photovoltaic modules. First Solar has invested heavily in developing advanced, high-volume manufacturing processes that are considered essential to achieving the low cost required to make solar electricity economically viable across a broad range of applications.

PV Modules

Sharp Electronics Corp. - Solar Systems Division
5901 Bolsa Ave.
Huntington Beach, CA 92647

Toll-free: 800-BE-SHARP
Phone: 630-378-3357
www.sharpusa.com

Sharp Electronics Corporation, a worldwide leader in solar electric technology, offers single-crystal and polycrystalline PV panels. Available modules range from 62 to 208 watts for grid-tied or stand-alone systems. Sharp modules carry a 25-year warranty. Product introductions planned for the future include green, golden brown, and light blue PV cells; triangular modules; AC modules; and thin-film, virtually transparent modules.

PV Modules

Shell Solar
4650 Adohr Ln.
Camarillo, CA 93011

Toll-free: 800-272-6765
Phone: 805-482-6800
www.shell.com/solar/

Shell Solar is one of the world's largest manufacturers of PV modules, producing single-crystal, multi-crystal, and CIS thin-film modules. Shell also offers EarthSafe™ PV kits for residential and commercial installations. These solar electric rooftop kits include mounting hardware, inverter, and 25-year warranty panels. Shell Solar was previously Siemens Solar (and before that Arco Solar) before Shell acquired Siemens in April 2002.

PV Systems

Kyocera Solar, Inc.
7812 E. Acoma Dr.
Scottsdale, AZ 85260

Toll-free: 800-223-9580
Phone: 480-948-8003
www.kyocerasolar.com

Kyocera is one of the world's largest manufacturers of polycrystal PV modules.

Renewable Energy Equipment

RWE Schott Solar, Inc.
2260 Lava Ridge Ct., Ste. 102
U.S. Sales & Marketing
Roseville, CA 95661

Toll-free: 888-457-6527
Phone: 916-774-3000
www.us.schott.com

RWE Schott Solar Inc. (RSS), formerly Schott Applied Power, is a leading manufacturer and distributor of solar power components and systems. RSS produces the world's largest solar power module available, the ASE 300. RSS serves a diverse market including grid-connected residential and commercial systems, and grid-independent agricultural, governmental and utility applications. RWE Schott Solar Inc. is a joint venture of the RWE Group, a global multi-utility concern with core businesses in electricity, gas, water, waste management, and recycling.

Schüco Photovoltaic Modules

SCHÜCO, LP
240 Pane Rd.
Newington, CT 06111

Toll-free: 877-472-4826
Phone: 860-666-0505
www.schuco-usa.com

Schüco offers three models of permanently sealed polycrystalline PV modules that are manufactured and tested to meet international quality standards. Model S 125-SP (49.13" x 31.61") has a rated output of 125 W; S 158-SP (62.2" x 31.5") is 158 W; and S 170-SPU (62.2" x 31.5") is 170 W. Schüco provides a 5-year product guarantee, and a performance guarantee of 90% output at 12 years, and 80% at 25 years. These products are manufactured in Germany.

Solar Turtle

Solar Turtle, Inc.
4901 Cactus Wren Ave.
Tucson, AZ 85746

Phone: 520-883-3356

The Solar Turtle is a photovoltaic power supply and water purification system mostly used for remote cabins and RVs. These systems include 120-watt panels, deep-cycle batteries, an inverter, and General Ecology's SeaGull IV water purification systems. The system can output up to 720 W DC or 2,500 W AC. Most Solar Turtle units include custom features to match customer needs.

Sunslates

Atlantis Energy Systems, Inc.
4517 Harlin Dr.
Sacramento, CA 95826

Phone: 916-438-2930
www.atlantisenergy.org

Atlantis Energy Systems produces Sunslates®, which serve as both a roofing product and a solar-electric power source. Sunslates are fiber-cement shingles into which PV cells have been laminated. Each shingle has a plug-in wiring connection.

Suntech Silicon Solar Modules

Solar Resources
771 Shrewsbury Ave., Ste. 105
Shrewsbury, NJ 07702

Phone: 732-758-1600
www.solarresources.com

Solar Resources distributes PV panels manufactured in China by Suntech Power, which has quickly risen to become one of the world's largest PV manufacturers.

UNI-SOLAR PV Shingles and Standing Seam Panels

United Solar Ovonic LLC
3800 Lapeer Rd.
Auburn Hills, MI 48326

Toll-free: 800-843-3892
Phone: 248-475-0100
www.uni-solar.com

Uni-Solar Ovonic LLC PV Shingles and Standing Seam Roofing Panels are installed much like conventional roofing products. They generate electricity while protecting the structure from weather. PV Shingles, measuring 86.4" x 12" with 7 tabs, are interspersed among conventional 3-tab shingles. Standing Seam Panels are available for laminating onto conventional roofing or as a PV-integrated, standing-seam product. Lead wires from each shingle or panel enter the structure through drilled holes in the roof decking. Uni-Solar roofing products use triple-junction amorphous silicon technology.

Raceway and Boxes for Electrical Systems

Penetrations in exterior walls—such as dryer vents and electrical service entrances—are common sources of air infiltration into buildings. Standard electrical boxes, although they don't penetrate the exterior of the building envelope, can be significant sources of air leakage. Products included here are airtight electrical boxes designed for use in exterior walls.

Air-Vapor Barrier Box

Low Energy Systems Supply Co., Inc.
W. 1330 Happy Hollow Rd.
Campbellsport, WI 53010

Phone: 920-533-8690
www.lessco-airtight.com

Low Energy Systems Supply Co. (LESSCO) manufactures special boxes in which electrical receptacle boxes can be mounted. Caulk sealant is used to seal the wire penetrations into the LESSCO box, and contractors tape is used to seal box flanges to the air barrier (polyurethane film).

Wind Energy Equipment

Most large wind-power systems are installed in centralized wind farms, with the power fed into electric utility grids. Included here are smaller wind turbines that are more appropriate for individual homes or commercial buildings. Like PV systems, these generators may be designed for use in grid-tied or off-grid applications.

AIR and Whisper Series Wind Turbines

Southwest Windpower
1801 W. Rt. 66
Flagstaff, AZ 86001

Phone: 928-779-9463
www.windenergy.com

Southwest Windpower manufactures 400-, 900-, 1,000- and 3,000-watt wind turbines for on- and off-grid residential and industrial power generation. The 400-watt unit can also be used to power telecommunication stations, and the 1,000-watt unit can be used to pump water.

ARE Wind Generators

Abundant Renewable Energy
22700 N.E. Mountain Top Rd.
Newberg, OR 97132

Phone: 503-538-8298
www.abundantRE.com

ARE wind generators are manufactured in Oregon, USA, and distributed worldwide by Abundant Renewable Energy. The ARE110 wind generator is rated at 2,500 watts and is available in 48-volt models for battery-charging applications and in a high-voltage model for grid-connect systems. The ARE442 is rated at 10,000 watts and is available as a grid-connect system.

BWC Excel Wind Turbines

Bergey Windpower Co., Inc.
2200 Industrial Blvd.
Norman, OK 73069

Phone: 405-364-4212
www.bergey.com

Bergey Windpower manufactures three models of wind generators for residential and small-scale commercial applications. The BWC XL.1 is rated at 1,000 watts, the BWC Excel-R is rated at 7,500 watts, and the BWC Excel-S is rated at 10,000 watts.

Jacobs 31-20 Wind Turbine

Wind Turbine Industries Corp.
16801 Industrial Cir. SE
Prior Lake, MN 55372

Phone: 952-447-6064
www.windturbine.net

Wind Turbine Industries' Jacobs 31-20 generator is rated at 20,000 watts. Jacobs wind turbines range in size from 10kW to 20kW, with rotor sizes ranging from 23 ft. (7m) to 29 ft. (8.8 m). These systems can provide power for a broad range of applications, which include Grid Intertie (utility bill reduction) or off-grid/remote battery charging. Other Jacobs turbines (also known as "Jakes" and made in the 1930s) are no longer manufactured but, due to their exceptional durability, are still widely available as used and rebuilt machines.

OY Windside Turbines

Tangarie Energy LLC
18 Deer Path
Hillsborough, NJ 08844

Toll-free: 866-994-6500
www.tangarie-energy.com

Tangarie Energy is the U.S. distributor for vertical wind turbines produced by OY Windside Production Ltd. of Finland. Designed for power production in extreme conditions, these turbines are also appropriate for a variety of other on and off-grid applications including population centers, parks, and residences. The soundless (0 db) turbine is safe for birds and bats and have been used as part of power-generating sculptures. The Windside is not affected by turbulent wind, can generate even in freezing and snowy conditions, and starts to generate power at wind speeds as low as 1.5 m/s (3.3 mph) to 2.8 m/s (6.2 mph), depending on model, and can operate at wind speeds as high as 30 m/s (66 mph), 40 m/s (88 mph), or 60 m/s (132 mph) depending on model.

Skystream 3.7

Southwest Windpower
1801 W. Rt. 66
Flagstaff, AZ 86001

Phone: 928-779-9463
www.windenergy.com

The Skystream 3.7™ is a grid-connected, residential-sized 1.8 kW wind turbine that is designed for quiet operation at low wind-speeds. The 12-foot diameter, curved-blade rotor starts producing power at a wind speed of 8 mph and reaches full output at 20 mph. The wind turbine can be mounted on a 35 ft single pole, with towers up to 110 ft available. At an average windspeed of 12 mph, the Skystream 3.7 will produce about 400 kWh per month. The complete installed system costs approximately $7,000 to $10,000, including generator, controls, inverter, and tower.

Urban-Appropriate Wind Turbines

WES Canada
2952 Thompson Rd.
P.O. Box 552
Smithville, ON L0R 2A0
Canada

Phone: 905-957-8791
www.windenergysolutions.ca

WES Canada, in partnership with manufacturer WES Netherlands, offers the Tulipo—a medium-sized, low-noise, low-RPM 2.5 kW wind turbine appropriate for building-integrated urban installations. Larger 80- and 250-kW commercial turbines are also available. These turbines were formerly manufactured under the name Lagerway.

Wind Turbines

Proven Energy, Ltd.
Wardhead Park
Stewarton, Ayrshire KA3 5LH Scotland, UK

Phone: +44 (0)1560 485 570
www.provenenergy.com

Proven Energy, Ltd. manufactures four turbine models, rated at 2,500 watts (2,500-5,000 kWh annual output), 6,000 watts (6,000-12,000 kWh annual output) and 15,000 watts (15,000-30,000 kWh annual output). Proven Energy has three American distributors: Lake Michigan Wind and Sun can be reached by phone at 920-743-0456 and is online at www.windandsun.com; Solar Wind Works can be reached by phone at 530-582-4503 and is online at www.solarwindworks.com; Remote Power Inc. can be reached by phone at 907-457-4299 and is online at www.remotepowerinc.com.

This Space is Available for Your Notes

This Space is Available for Your Notes

Lighting

Lighting is a major user of electricity. Besides using electricity, electric lighting also generates heat, contributing to cooling loads that are generally met by using more electricity for air-conditioning. Thus, improving the energy efficiency of lighting has benefits that go beyond the direct electricity savings by the lighting products.

Fluorescent lamps are three to four times more efficient than incandescent lamps. Quality fluorescent lamps today provide far better light quality than the older lamps that often produced a bluish cast. Electronically ballasted fluorescent lighting also doesn't generate the hum and flicker that many people find objectionable in older, magnetically ballasted fluorescent lighting. Both straight-tube fluorescent and compact-fluorescent lamps (CFLs) are widely available. In general, thinner-diameter fluorescent lamps offer higher efficacy (lumens per watt) than larger-diameter lamps. LED (light-emitting diode) light sources are also being introduced and are approaching the efficacy of fluorescent lamps. The highly focusable nature of LEDs enable significant energy savings in certain applications. Unlike fluorescent, metal halide, sodium, and other high-intensity discharge (HID) lamps, LEDs do not contain mercury.

Older magnetic ballasts for fluorescent lighting may contain highly toxic PCBs or the less toxic but also problematic DEHP; these should be handled carefully and disposed of properly when changing or servicing fixtures. Fluorescent lamps (as well as all HID lamps) also contain small amounts of the toxic metal mercury. These lamps should never be landfilled or incinerated but instead be recycled by a company that reclaims the mercury. Some new lamps are available with mercury levels far below the industry average, and these should be used whenever possible.

Daylighting strategies must be carefully designed if they're to result in net energy savings. In commercial buildings, savings often don't accrue unless there are automatic controls; but in homes, those controls may not be as necessary to achieve savings. Daylight also introduces heat that can increase cooling loads (though daylight's ratio of heat to light is less than that of all common artificial light sources). Daylight can also cause problems with glare. In spite of these potential pitfalls, daylighting is a valuable strategy for saving energy and improving the well-being of occupants.

Compact Fluorescent Lamps

Replacing standard incandescent light bulbs with compact-fluorescent lamps (CFLs) can slash electrical consumption in homes and offices where incandescent lighting is widely used. Most CFLs use roughly one-third as much electricity as incandescent bulbs with comparable output. By more efficiently converting electrical energy into light, CFLs generate less heat—which can reduce cooling loads, particularly in commercial buildings. In reducing electrical usage, CFLs also reduce associated carbon dioxide, sulfur dioxide, and nitrous oxide emissions. CFL technology continues to evolve; there are many types to choose from, including straight-tube, folded-tube, and twisted-tube. As CFLs have shrunk in size, they have become suitable for most light fixtures that were designed for incandescent light bulbs. Advances in light quality, lamp durability, and dimming technology have also been significant. Most manufacturers offer 15- and 20-watt models; larger lamps are also available. The average life of CFLs is eight to ten times that of incandescent bulbs. Cold-cathode compact fluorescent lamps use a cold, rather than hot, cathode to release electrons in the fluorescent tube. While this takes somewhat more electricity, the lamps turn on instantly, can operate at very low temperatures, can be fully dimmed (down to about 5%), can blink on and off, and have a very long lifetimes.

Cold Cathode Specialty Lamps

Technical Consumer Products, Inc.
325 Campus Dr.
Aurora, OH 44202

Toll-free: 800-324-1496
www.tcpi.com

TCP's cold-cathode fluorescent lamps are particularly appropriate for specialty applications where cold operation, dimming or blinking operation, and long life are important. Using from 2 to 8 watts, TCP's cold-cathode bulbs are rated at 25,000 hours and come in many colors, finishes, sizes, and configurations including A-lamp, globes, R20's, torpedo and flame tipped bulbs. The lamps are an useful as a replacement for low- and mid-wattage incandescents.

Compact Fluorescent Lamps

Lights of America
611 Reyes Dr.
Walnut, CA 91789

Toll-free: 800-321-8100
Phone: 909-594-7883
www.lightsofamerica.com

Lights of America manufactures twisted-tube, straight-tube, and other electronic-ballasted fluorescent lamps. Durability concerns have been raised with certain LOA products.

Compact Fluorescent Lamps

Link USA International, Inc.
1420 Decision St., Ste. C
Vista, CA 92081

Phone: 760-599-1280
www.linklights.net

Link USA produces several sizes of compact, spiral, and covered CFLs for indoor/outdoor use.

Compact Fluorescent Lamps

Osram Sylvania
100 Endicott St.
Danvers, MA 01923

Toll-free: 800-544-4828
Phone: 978-777-1900
www.sylvania.com

Osram Sylvania offers a full line of CFLs, both with and without integral ballasts.

Compact Fluorescent Lamps

U.S. WAY Building Systems
P.O. Box 10080
Chicago, IL 60610

Phone: 773-338-9688
www.uswaycorp.com

U.S. WAY Lighting offers CFLs in 14 styles and a variety of wattages and color temperatures. Hi-Output up to 300 watts, 21600 lumens, 1,500-watt incandescent equivalent and Hi-Power T5 fixtures and tubes up to 80W, 7000 lumens each. Lamps achieve 95% illumination at start up with full brightness within 3 seconds.

Dimmable Cold Cathode Fluorescent Lamps and Cans

Axiom Power Corp.
1000 N. Green Valley Pkwy, Ste. 440274
Green Valley Ranch, NV 89074

Phone: 702-430-8917
www.axiompowercorp.com

Axiom manufactures cold-cathode fluorescent lamps (CCFLs) for drop-in replacement of A19, PAR38, and GU10 bulbs, as well as GX-53 style CCFLs and recessed can and track lighting fixtures for CCFL and LED lamps designed to meet the requirements of California Title 24. Like other CCFLs, Axiom lamps are slightly less efficient than regular CFLs, and are particularly appropriate where cold operation, dimming or blinking operation, and long life are important. Using from 5 to 18 watts, Axiom's CCFLs have a lifetime of 25,000 to 50,000 hours, a warm white color temperature of 2700K, and a color rendering index (CRI) of > 80. The A19 and GU10 bulbs have an efficacy of 60 lumens per watt (LPW). The GX-53 dimmable bulbs have efficacies of 50-70 LPW.

Fresh2Ti

Technical Consumer Products, Inc.
325 Campus Dr.
Aurora, OH 44202

Toll-free: 800-324-1496
www.tcpi.com

Fresh2Ti is a line of compact fluorescent lamps from TCP, available in 14, 23, and 27 watts, that, in addition to providing light, have a titanium dioxide coating that breaks down odors through a photocatalytic reaction when the lamp is on. This is a better alternative to air fresheners and they may help to destroy unhealthy air pollutants. These CFLs have a 10,000-hour rated life, and their air cleaning properties are expected to last for up to 3 years. The bulb has a color temperature of 2700°K, a color rendering index (CRI) of 82, and initial efficacy of 57 to 70 lumens per watt. TCP provides a full line of CFLs, including many that are Energy Star listed (though the Fresh2Ti are not Energy Star CFLs) and products with A-19 screw-base, TCX base, 2-pin and 4-pin base, and the new GU24 base.

GE CFL and Induction Lamps

GE Lighting
1975 Noble Rd., Nela Park
Cleveland, OH 44112

Toll-free: 800-255-1200
Phone: 216-266-2121
www.gelighting.com

GE Lighting manufactures a full line of CFLs, with and without integral ballasts. Dimmable integral-ballast CFLs are available. The GE Genura lamp is marketed as a compact fluorescent lamp, but is really an induction lamp. The 23-watt Genura offers longer life than standard CFLs (15,000 hours) in an R30 reflector style. The lamp is designed for indoor use and screws into a standard A-type socket and is designed to replace a 65-watt R30 incandescent lamp. Initial output of 1,100 lumens, or 48 lumens per watt, with 25% lumen drop-off over its life. The power factor is relatively low at 0.55 and the total harmonic distortion fairly high at 130%. The lamp should not be used on dimming circuits.

Greenlite Compact Fluorescent Lamps

Greenlite Lighting Corporation USA
10 Corporate Park, Ste. 100
Irvine, CA 92606

Toll-free: 800-930-2111
Phone: 949-261-5300
www.greenliteusa.com

Greenlite manufactures a wide range of compact fluorescent lamps including Dimmable and 3-Way Spirals. The company's 13-watt "Mini" Spiral is nearly comparable in size to a standard incandescent bulb.

Lumatech Compact Fluorescent Lamps

Lumatech Corporation
2 Marlen Dr.
Hamilton, NJ 08691

Toll-free: 800-932-0637
Phone: 609-689-3122
www.carpenterlighting.com

Lumatech manufactures a variety of CFLs, including the Reflect-A-Star, Microlamp, and new twist lamps. The twist lamps are available from 11 to 32 watts, the latter producing 1900 lumens (the highest output of any twist lamp).

Maxlite Compact Fluorescent Lamps

MaxLite SK America, Inc.
80 Little Falls Rd.
Fairfield, NJ 07004

Toll-free: 800-555-5629
Phone: 973-244-7300
www.maxlite.com

MaxLite SK America manufactures CFLs with integral electronic ballasts.

Micro-Brite Cold-Cathode CFL

Litetronics International, Inc.
4101 W. 123rd St.
Aslip, IL 60803 USA

Toll-free: 800-860-3392
Phone: 708-389-8000
www.litetronics.com

The Litetronics Micro-Brite CFLs are rated at 18,000 to 25,000 hours and are available in various colors, sizes, and shapes. Using from 2 to 8 watts, these CFLs have very thin 1/8-inch (T1) fluorescent tubes and integral ballasts. Their efficacy ranges from 38 to 43 lumens per watt for the white lamps. The relatively low light output limits applicability for general illumination, but they are very effective for sign lighting and specialized applications where cold operation, blinking operation, and long life are important.

Philips Compact Fluorescent Lamps

Philips Lighting Company
200 Franklin Square Dr.
P.O. Box 6800
Somerset, NJ 08875

Toll-free: 800-555-0050
Phone: 732-563-3000
www.lighting.philips.com/nam

Philips Lighting Company produces a full line of CFLs, both with and without integral ballasts, including the Philips Marathon™ line of compact fluorescent bulbs. Lamps in the Marathon line are guaranteed for at least 6,000 hours and are the first CFLs to have the look of standard incandescents. These high-efficacy lamps offer a high color rendering index (CRI) and the energy-saving benefits associated with compact fluorescent technology. Philips introduced CFL lamps.

Sunpark Twisted-Tube CFLs

Sunpark Electronic Corp.
1850 W. 205th St.
Torrance, CA 90501

Toll-free: 866-478-6775
Phone: 310-320-7880
www.sunpkco.com

Sunpark Electronic Corp. produces several sizes of compact, twisted-tube CFLs.

TCP Compact Fluorescent Lamps

Technical Consumer Products, Inc.
325 Campus Dr.
Aurora, OH 44202

Toll-free: 800-324-1496
www.tcpi.com

TCP manufactures a full range of energy-efficient compact fluorescent lamps, such as integral ballast and modular ballast configurations, reflector lamps, spiral- and folded-tube configurations, and candelabra-base lamps.

Twisted-Tube CFLs

Star Lighting Products
11350 Brookpark Rd.
Cleveland, OH 44130

Toll-free: 800-392-3552
Phone: 216-433-7500
www.starlightingproducts.com

Star Lighting Products offers several sizes of compact, twisted-tube CFLs.

Westinghouse Compact Fluorescent Lamps

Westinghouse Lighting Corporation
12401 McNulty Rd.
Philadelphia, PA 19154

Toll-free: 800-999-2226
Phone: 215-671-2000
www.westinghouselighting.com

Westinghouse Lighting Corporation offers a full line of compact fluorescent lamps (CFLs), including integral-ballast, screw-in and plug-in CFL replacements. The company offers dimming, three-way, photo-sensing, full-spectrum, globe, interior flood, and exterior flood CFLs—most in various sizes and wattages. All Westinghouse CFLs are Energy Star-rated.

Exterior Lighting

Outdoor lighting is common around buildings. Incandescent, metal halide, and high-pressure sodium are the most common outdoor lighting options. Environmental issues include lamp efficacy (lumens per watt), luminaire efficiency, controllability of the light source, potential for PV power, and control of light pollution. To control light pollution, full-cutoff luminaires should be specified.

Dark-Sky Compliant CFL Lamps

Bulbrite Industries, Inc.
145 W. Commercial Ave.
Moonachie, NJ 07074

Toll-free: 800-528-5555
Phone: 201-531-5900
www.bulbrite.com

Bulbrite offers CFL lamps with standard screw bases and integrated hoods that prevent light trespass, complying with light fixture standards of the International Dark Sky Association. These lamps do not require a fixture to control illumination patterns. The 15-watt integral-fixture lamps provide 60 lumens per watt.

Full-Cutoff Luminaires

Gardco Lighting
1611 Clovis Barker Rd.
San Marcos, TX 78666

Toll-free: 800-227-0758
Phone: 512-753-1000
www.sitelighting.com

Gardco Lighting produces a wide range of full-cutoff luminaires for various lamp types.

Full-Cutoff Luminaires

Kim Lighting
P.O. Box 60080
City of Industry, CA 91716

Phone: 626-968-5666
www.kimlighting.com

Kim Lighting produces a wide range of full-cutoff luminaires for various lamp types.

Full-Cutoff Luminaires

Sterner Lighting Systems, Inc.
701 Millennium Blvd.
Greenville, SC 29607

Toll-free: 864-678-1000
www.sternerlighting.com

Sterner Lighting produces a wide range of full-cutoff luminaires for various lamp types.

Outdoor Solar Lighting

OkSolar
1 Birch Meadow Dr.
Hadley, MA 01035

Phone: 347-624-5693
www.oksolar.com

OkSolar manufactures solar lighting including fluorescent, low-pressure sodium, and LED lighting for parking lots, walkways, streets, and other outdoor areas. The lights include all components except mounting poles. OkSolar also manufactures multi-LED replacement lamps that can be used in standard lamp sockets.

Solar Street Lighting

Quality Solar Concepts Inc.
47 Tea Rose Meadow
Rockport , NY 14420

Phone: 585-278-3773
www.solar4me.com

Quality Solar Concepts manufacturers and distributes photovoltaic-powered outdoor lighting, including street lights, walkway lights, parking lights, and area lights. Fixtures are engineered to be used with either LED or compact fluorescent lamps. Quality Solar Concepts is also distributor for a wide range of other alternative energy components and systems.

SoLed Solar-Powered LED Outdoor Luminaires

SolarOne Solutions
51 Marble St.
Framingham, MA 01702

Toll-free: 877-527-6461
Phone: 508-620-7652
www.solarone.net

SolarOne® produces Dark-Sky-compliant, solar-powered, LED outdoor lighting systems, including overhead and directional pathway lighting, bus-shelter lighting, and custom and designer systems. Systems typically include solar panels, an adjustable panel-mounting system, LED lamps, battery and enclosure, solar charge controller, and MC2 advanced lighting controls with remote control. A variety of lamp and power packages are available.

Sonne Solar-Powered Outdoor Luminaire

Selux Corporation
5 Lumen Ln.
P.O. Box 1060
Highland, NY 12528

Toll-free: 800-735-8927
Phone: 845-691-7723
www.selux.com/usa

Sonne solar-powered Type III full-cutoff luminaires from Selux come equipped with 80W or 120W solar panels, mounted singly or in pairs on a fully tilting and rotating mount for maximum solar exposure. One or two 12V, 82AH sealed gel batteries power a compact fluorescent lamp rated at 18, 26, 32, or 42 watts, providing initial lumens between 1250 and 3200. A regulator/controller prevents overcharging and backflow; senses and remembers dusk and dawn time; and may be programmed to illuminate during set periods of time relative to sunrise and sunset. A motion detector is optional. Steel parts are hot-dip galvanized; some parts are made with recycled ABS.

SunWize Designer Lighting Systems

SunWize Technologies
1155 Flatbush Rd.
Kingston, NY 12401

Toll-free: 800-817-6527
Phone: 845-336-0146
www.sunwize.com

The SunWize Designer Lighting Systems for street, security, parking lot, or path lighting include battery packs and all other components except the mounting pole. The luminaires are available with either low-pressure sodium or fluorescent lamps.

The GlareBuster

Lighting by Branford
727 Boston Post Rd.
Guilford, CT 06437

Toll-free: 888-994-5273
www.theglarebuster.com

The GlareBuster GB-1000 and GB-2000 are light-pollution-controlling, full-cutoff exterior floodlight fixtures for residential and light commercial applications. Reduced glare allows better visibility beyond the illumination source, and more focused 100% downlighting decreases light trespass (direct-beam light leaving the property) and light pollution. The GB-2000 includes a 26w, GU-24 CFL bulb. These fixtures accommodate standard compact fluorescent lamps and other bulb options. These products are commonly available at hardware, lighting, and electrical supply stores. The International Dark Sky Association (IDA) has awarded their "Dark Sky Friendly" seal to the GlareBuster.

Fluorescent Lamps

Fluorescent lamps have long been preferable to incandescent lighting, relative to energy efficiency. New developments with fluorescent technology, including the high-efficacy T5 lamps, have pushed the energy efficiency envelope further. Recently, attention has also been paid to the mercury content of fluorescents and the consequences of mercury releases into the environment. As with all resource use and pollution issues, reduction is the best way to limit the problem. Even with low-mercury lamps, however, recycling of old lamps remains a high priority.

Neolite CFLs

Litetronics International, Inc.
4101 W. 123rd St.
Aslip, IL 60803 USA

Toll-free: 800-860-3392
Phone: 708-389-8000
www.litetronics.com

Neolite CFLs from Litetronics are ultra-compact CFLs using thinner-than-normal, T2 fluorescent tubes wrapped in tight spirals. The smallest of these, a 10-watt lamp producing 635 lumens (in warm-white color) with an efficacy of 63.5 lumens per watt, is just 3.74 inches in total length from the tip of the screw-base to the tip of the spiraled fluorescent tube. Other sizes available: 13, 15, 20, and 23 watts. The largest has an efficacy of 72 lpw and is 4.76 inches in total length. Rated life is 10,000 hours, and the color rendering index (CRI) is 82. Neolite lamps are Energy Star rated.

Panasonic Compact Fluorescent Lamps

Panasonic Consumer Electronics
Building Department
Panazip 4A-6
One Panasonic Way
Secaucus, NJ 07094

Toll-free: 866-292-7292
www.panasonic.com

Panasonic manufactures CFLs with integral electronic ballasts, including plug-ins and screw-ins.

SILHOUETTE T5 Lamps

Philips Lighting Company
200 Franklin Square Dr.
P.O. Box 6800
Somerset, NJ 08875

Toll-free: 800-555-0050
Phone: 732-563-3000
www.lighting.philips.com/nam

The Silhouette T5 and Silhouette T5 High Output fluorescents are available in a variety of popular wattages (ranging from 14 to 80 watts), with an average rated life of 20,000 hours. They are particularly suitable for offices, retail stores, hotels, schools, and hospitals, especially where small fixtures are required.

Induction Lamps

Induction lighting offers an extremely long life, fairly high-efficacy, instant-on lighting alternative to incandescent and metal halide lamps. Most products are designed for outdoor applications and hard-to-reach indoor applications. Induction lamps work by using electrical energy to create an alternating magnetic field to induce gas discharge in mercury vapor without the use of electrodes; phosphor coatings convert the UV light into white light, as with fluorescent lamps. Induction lamp systems include a high-frequency generator, a power coupler, and a lamp, so most products can only be used in specialized fixtures. There is moderate lumen depreciation over time. Like fluorescent lamps (including CFLs), induction lamps contain mercury so should be recycled.

GE CFL and Induction Lamps

GE Lighting
1975 Noble Rd., Nela Park
Cleveland, OH 44112

Toll-free: 800-255-1200
Phone: 216-266-2121
www.gelighting.com

GE Lighting manufactures a full line of CFLs, with and without integral ballasts. Dimmable integral-ballast CFLs are available. The GE Genura lamp is marketed as a compact fluorescent lamp, but is really an induction lamp. The 23-watt Genura offers longer life than standard CFLs (15,000 hours) in an R30 reflector style. The lamp is designed for indoor use and screws into a standard A-type socket and is designed to replace a 65-watt R30 incandescent lamp. Initial output of 1,100 lumens, or 48 lumens per watt, with 25% lumen drop-off over its life. The power factor is relatively low at 0.55 and the total harmonic distortion fairly high at 130%. The lamp should not be used on dimming circuits.

Osram Sylvania Induction Lighting

Osram Sylvania
100 Endicott St.
Danvers, MA 01923

Toll-free: 800-544-4828
Phone: 978-777-1900
www.sylvania.com

The Endura® induction lamps from Osram (described as "electrodeless fluorescent" lighting by Osram) and the Icetron® lamps from Sylvania offer high efficacy (70-80 lumens per watt) long-life exterior lighting. 70-watt (6,500 lumen), 100-watt (8,000 lumen), and 150-watt (12,000 lumen) products are available in 3500 and 4100°K color temperatures. Lamps are rated for 100,000 hours, have CRI ratings of 80, and offer reliable ignition at temperatures as low as −40°F. Endura and Icetron lamps are warranted for 5 years.

Philips QL Induction Lighting

Philips Lighting Company
200 Franklin Square Dr.
P.O. Box 6800
Somerset, NJ 08875

Toll-free: 800-555-0050
Phone: 732-563-3000
www.lighting.philips.com/nam

The Philips QL induction lamps offer fairly high efficacy (65-70 lumens per watt) lighting for exterior luminaires. 55-watt (3500 lumen) and 85-watt (6000 lumen) products are available for both 120- and 240-volt applications. Lamps are rated for 100,000 hours with a 50% failure rate and 60,000 hours with a 10% failure rate (based on 4,000 burning hours per year), have CRI ratings of 80, are available in three color temperatures (2700, 3000, and 4000°K), and operate at very low temperatures (rated to −13°F). QL lamps are warranted for 5 years.

Interior Luminaires

Many innovative, energy-efficient luminaires are available, most of which are primarily relevant to commercial buildings. Environmental characteristics to consider include fluorescent lamp use, effective reflectors, and application-appropriate design. Fluorescent high-bay fixtures can replace conventional HID lighting in gymnasiums, warehouses, and other high-ceiling spaces, offering both direct energy savings and the benefit of instant-on (so they are more likely to be turned off).

CFL Fixtures

Technical Consumer
Products, Inc.
325 Campus Dr.
Aurora, OH 44202

Toll-free: 800-324-1496
www.tcpi.com

Technical Consumer Products (TCP) produces many types of table and floor lamps, ceiling fixtures, and outdoor and portable fixtures. TCP's electronically ballasted CFL torchieres have a 65-watt T6 lamp configuration and 3-way light levels (30/36/65 W) in polished brass, matte black, glossy white, and brushed steel; average lamp life is 10,000 hours, and average ballast life is 50,000 hours. TCP also produces complete retrofit kits to change an existing recessed-can fixture into an energy-efficient CFL system. The replaceable lamp lasts for 10,000 hours, while the ballast lasts 50,000 hours.

CFL Recessed Downlights

Juno Lighting, Inc.
1300 S. Wolf Rd.
Des Plaines, IL 60017

Toll-free: 800-367-5866
Phone: 847-827-9880
www.junolighting.com

Juno Lighting manufactures an extensive line of commercial-quality recessed downlights using CFLs. All models have separate ballasts—most electronic—with plug-in twin-tube, quad-tube, or triple-tube CFLs. Fixtures designed for lamp wattages of 13 to 42 are available. Some fixtures have the CFL oriented vertically, others horizontally. Full photometric data are available for all fixtures.

CFL Torchieres

Catalina Lighting
18191 N.W. 68th Ave.
Miami, FL 33015

Toll-free: 800-966-7074
Phone: 305-558-4777
www.catalinalighting.com

Catalina Lighting offers energy-efficient, torchiere-style floor lamps that use a single 55-watt fluorescent bulb.

CFL Torchieres

Good Earth Lighting
122 Messner Dr.
Wheeling, IL 60090

Toll-free: 800-291-8838
Phone: 847-808-1133
www.goodearthlighting.com

Good Earth Lighting produces energy-efficient, fluorescent torchiere standing fixtures.

Fluorescent Light Fixtures

Sunpark Electronic Corp.
1850 W. 205th St.
Torrance, CA 90501

Toll-free: 866-478-6775
Phone: 310-320-7880
www.sunpkco.com

Sunpark Electronics produces a wide range of compact-fluorescent and linear-tube fluorescent lamp fixtures, including fluorescent torchieres, ceiling fixtures, recessed downlights, table lamps, floor lamps, outdoor fixtures, and under-counter fixtures. Electronic ballasts are also available.

Frankie Goes Fluorescent, Parallel Universe, Lulu, Flipster and Fibonacci Series

Fire & Water Lighting/David Bergman Architect
241 Eldridge St., Ste. 3R
New York, NY 10002

Phone: 212-475-3106
www.cyberg.com

Most Fire & Water fluorescent lighting fixtures are green both from a materials standpoint and an energy efficiency standpoint. Fibonacci, Flipster, Lulu, and Frankie Goes Fluorescent fixtures use the newest Energy Star pin-based CFL's with replaceable ballasts. Some models can be alternatively ordered with dimmable, integral ballast screw-base CFLs. Frankie Goes Fluorescent ceiling, wall and table fixtures are made of 100% recycled glass (post-consumer content varies) and Environ™, a composite of soy flour and recycled paper. The Lulu series, available in table, floor, wall, and ceiling versions, is made of 50% post-consumer recycled plastic. Fibonacci's shades are made with formaldehyde free, 70-100% post-industrial recycled wood, and process chlorine-free (PCF) paper liners. Flipster's shades are made with up to 40% recycled content resin. Both are available in table, floor, wall, and ceiling models. The Parallel Universe series (floor, table, wall and ceiling) incorporates recycled and sustainable materials, and utilizes pin-based dimmable (dedicated) CFLs.

Studio A CFL Lighting

American Fluorescent
2345 Ernie Krueger Cir.
Waukegan, IL 60087

Phone: 847-249-5970
www.americanfluorescent.com

American Fluorescent's STUDIO A collections offer decorative and energy-efficient lighting options for kitchen, hallway, and bath. Many of American Fluorescent's lights are Energy Star rated. LED fixtures also available.

LED Lighting

LEDs (light-emitting diodes) have been improving in light quality and efficacy (lumens of light output per watt of electrical consumption) at a rapid pace. The highest-efficacy LEDs today produce about 50 lumens per watt, more than twice the efficacy of incandescent and halogen lamps. Although fluorescent lamps have higher efficacy than today's LEDs, the ability to more precisely focus LED light output can enable LED luminaires to outperform fluorescents in certain applications. LEDs also have a very long life (30,000 to 50,000 hours) and they are the only common non-incandescent light source that does not rely on mercury vapor.

Enbryten LED Luminaires

Permlight Products, Inc.
422 W. Sixth St.
Tustin, CA 92780

Phone: 714-508-0729
www.permlight.com

Enbryten™ LED luminaires from Permlight Products use high-efficacy, white LEDs (light-emitting diodes) in a wide variety of luminaire styles. The replaceable LED modules allow easy replacement as needs change, as LED output drops over time, or as LEDs improve in quality and light output. The LEDs currently available in the Enbryten series provide up to 50 lumens per watt. Products are available in pendant, downlight, sconce, and step luminaires for both residential and commercial applications. These luminaires work on standard dimming circuits.

LED Custom Lighting Solutions

Color Kinetics, Inc.
10 Milk St., Ste. 1100
Boston, MA 02108

Toll-free: 888-385-5742
Phone: 617-423-9999
www.colorkinetics.com

Color Kinetics, part of Philips Lighting, provides LEDs in a variety of color options for both residential and commercial applications. The company combines LED light sources with controllers, power supplies, software, and peripherals to create energy-efficient, customizable architectural lighting effects for everything from retail displays to massive commercial exteriors. The company touts its IntelliWhite as providing attractive white light that is consistent from one fixture to the next and dimmable. This lighting was designed to replace traditional lighting for use in hard-to-reach areas where replacement or maintenance is difficult; where heat buildup could be a problem; or where vibration could damage fixtures.

LR6 Downlights

LED Lighting Fixtures, Inc.
617 Davis Dr., Ste. 200
Keystone Technology Park VI
Morrisville, NC 27560

Phone: 919-991-0700
www.llfinc.com

LED Light Fixtures, Inc. offers the LR6 LED downlight that uses 12 watts to provide 650 lumens, for a measured efficacy of 54 lumens per watt, which is better than CFL downlights. The lamp also has a color rendering index (CRI) of 92, significantly better than most CFLs. LLF achieves this performance by using both red and green LEDs behind a diffuser, while most "white" LEDs achieve the white light by coating blue LEDs with a yellow phosphor. The product is designed to fit into standard 6" recessed cans and is available with Edison screw-base and the newer GU-24 mount. Fins in the cast-aluminum housing help with heat dissipation.

LSGC LEDs

Lighting Science Group Corporation
2100 McKinney Ave., Ste. 1555
Dallas, TX 75201

Phone: 214-382-3630
www.lsgc.com

Lighting Science Group Corporation (LSGC) manufactures LED floodlights and decorative lamps in a variety of styles, light outputs, and standard bases. Lamps are available in cool white, warm white, and amber, with G11 accent lighting available in a variety of other colors. LSGC also manufactures a low bay fixture using LEDs to replace HID lighting in warehouses, parking garages, and other applications that require widely distributed, glare free light.

saviLED Lamps

Nexxus Lighting, Inc.
9400 Southridge Park Ct., Ste. 200
Orlando, FL 32819

Phone: 407-857-9900
www.nexxuslighting.com

Nexxus Lighting manufactures SaviLED lamps, a comprehensive line of commercial and decorative LED lamps in a variety of styles, light outputs, and standard bases. The LEDs currently used in the SaviLED series provide over 45 lumens per watt. The lamps are available in cool and warm white, with G11 accent lighting available in a variety of other colors.

Special Purpose Lighting

These listings include heavy-duty work lights using high-efficiency compact fluorescent lamps, as well as other efficient solutions for special purpose lighting needs.

Limelite

EI Products
55 Second St.
Maxwell, TX 78656

Phone: 512-357-2776
www.limelite.com

Limelite® is a lime green electroluminescent exit light with a current draw of 0.2 W.

SideKick Worklytes

Crescent-Stonco
2345 Vauxhall Rd.
Union, NJ 07083

Toll-free: 800-334-2212
Phone: 908-964-7000
www.stoncolighting.com

Stonco Lighting has introduced a line of portable CFL worklights and cord reels under the name SideKick™. These energy-efficient worklights reduce heat buildup and the risk of contact with hot surfaces. SideKick WorkLytes come in a range of styles for a variety of applications. Included in the series is the Ratchet Lyte™, which ratchets into 8 positions and gives 60-watt light output from a 13-watt quad CFL. Also available is the 13-watt fluorescent Lyte Rover Cordless WorkLyte, which converts any extension cord into a portable light source.

Appliances

Appliances are significant ongoing users of energy and potable water. Federal standards for some appliances are helping to ensure that certain new appliances will be far more efficient than models they are replacing, but some manufacturers offer products that significantly exceed federal standards. Many of the most efficient appliances come from Europe, where energy is more expensive than in North America.

Horizontal-axis clothes washing machines have long been the standard among commercial-quality washers and in Europe. They use much less water than the typical American top-loader, are gentler on the clothes, use less detergent, wash more effectively, and—because they spin faster— remove more of the moisture from a load of laundry, which reduces the amount of energy needed for drying. For years these models were almost impossible to find in the U.S., but now most major American manufacturers are producing them. Although more expensive than standard top-loaders, the extra cost of a horizontal-axis washer will be covered by detergent savings alone—even before the water savings, energy savings (by using less hot water and reducing drying time), and wear-and-tear on clothing are factored in.

As with other appliances, seek out an efficient dishwasher that meets the convenience and feature requirements—and don't use energy-guzzling features, such as heat drying, when it isn't necessary. Most models have a water-saving cycle that should be used for lightly soiled dishes or partial loads (though it usually makes the most sense to wash only full loads). Note that hand-washing dishes may use more water and energy than a dishwasher, depending on how one does the hand-washing.

Driven by national standards, the energy efficiency of refrigerators has improved greatly over the past few decades. Unfortunately, a common practice when buying a new refrigerator is to keep the older one for storing beer and soda; this practice should be avoided. In general, refrigerators in the 16- to 20-cubic-foot range tend to be most efficient (because these are the most popular sizes, this is where manufacturers invest the most R&D funding), as are those with freezers on top or bottom instead of side-by-side. Avoid extra convenience features like ice-makers unless they'll *really* get used.

For ranges and cooktops, electric elements should be preferred over gas simply to avoid the toxic byproducts of gas combustion in the house. If a gas appliance is used, an effective, exhausting vent-hood (rather than one that simply filters and recirculates the air) should be used whenever the burners are on. As quiet a range-hood fan as possible should be selected to increase the likelihood that it will be used by occupants. Halogen electric elements provide the instant-on, instant-off performance that many cooks seek in a gas range.

Most gas ovens use a significant amount of electricity because they have a glow-bar that is on continuously in order to reignite the gas flame immediately if it is blown out somehow. In fact, a microwave oven can use less electricity to bake a potato than a gas oven! While microwaves are a more efficient way to cook, there are some concerns about the possible leakage of microwaves if the door seals aren't perfect.

Residential Dishwashers

Most of the energy consumed by dishwashers is used to heat the water; therefore, water-efficient dishwashers are also energy-efficient. As with other home appliances, national energy standards have catalyzed the development of more efficient dishwashers. As a measure of efficiency, the Energy Factor (EF) describes energy performance under carefully defined conditions, and provides a basis of comparison among different models. The national energy standard requires all regular size dishwashers to have an energy factor of at least 0.46. The Energy Star program qualifies dishwashers exceeding that standard by at least 25% (EF of 0.58). Products listed here must exceed the national minimum energy standard by at least 60%, with an EF of 0.74 or higher.

Ariston Dishwashers

Ariston Appliances US
3027 E. Sunset, Ste. 101
Ultra 8 International
Las Vegas, NV 89120

Toll-free: 888-426-0845
www.aristonappliances.us

Six dishwasher models in the Elegance and Premier lines from Italian manufacturer Ariston exceed U.S. federal minimum energy standards by 74%—all have an EF of 0.8 and are rated at 270 kWh per year. Features may vary by model and affect overall energy use. As of March 2007, Ariston model numbers meeting GreenSpec standards include: LI640, LI670, LI700, L63, LL64, AND LL65.

Asko Dishwashers

AM Appliance Group - Asko
P.O. Box 851805
Richardson, TX 75085

Toll-free: 800-898-1879
Phone: 972-644-8595
www.askousa.com

Swedish manufacturer Asko offers 15 dishwasher models in their D3000 line that are among the most energy-efficient available, with energy factors as high as 1.11—which is 141% better than minimum federal energy standards. As of March 2007, Asko model numbers (followed parenthetically by kWh/year, EF, and %-better than federal minimum standard) meeting GreenSpec standards include: D3232 (278, 0.77, 67.00%); D3112 and D3121 (278, 0.78, 70.00%); D3122, D3331, and D3432 (242, 0.89, 93.00%); D3251FI, D3251HD, D3251XLFI, D3251XLHD, D3252, and D3451 (231, 0.93, 102.00%); D3531XLFI, D3531XLHD, and D3731 (194, 1.11, 141.00%). Features may vary between models, and affect overall electric use.

Bosch Dishwashers

BSH Home Appliances Corp.
5551 McFadden Ave.
Huntington Beach, CA 92649

Toll-free: 800-944-2904
Phone: 714-901-6600
www.boschappliances.com

In their Integra and Evolution lines of dishwashers, Bosch offers over a dozen models with energy factors of at least 0.74 (rated at 290 kWh/year), which is 61% better than the Energy Star standard. Features such as soil sensing may vary between models, and affect overall electric use. The 800 Series SHE98M Evolution Dishwasher is rated at just 190 kWh per year of electricity consumption, an Energy Factor of 1.14 (148% higher than the federal standard in the U.S. and 73% higher than the Energy Star requirement), and a very low noise level of 42 dB. This dishwasher is also available in the Integra line as the SMX98M model. Bosch is the only appliance manufacturer with 100% of applicable products currently meeting Energy Star standards.

Danby Designer Dishwashers

Danby Products Inc.
P.O. Box 669
Findlay, OH 45839

Toll-free: 800-26-DANBY
Phone: 419-425-8627
www.danby.com

Canadian company Danby offers built-in model DDW1802W, and portable version DDW1805W. Both have an energy factor of 0.77, which is 67% better than the minimum federal energy standard for dishwashers. Low water consumption settings offer 3.8-gallon washes. Features may affect overall energy use. Manufactured in China.

Equator Dishwashers

Equator Corporation
2801 W. Sam Houston Pkwy. North, Ste. 150
Houston, TX 77080

Toll-free: 800-935-1955
Phone: 713-464-3422
www.equatorappliance.com

Equator offers model CD400, a compact dishwasher with an energy factor of 1.09, which is 76% better than the Energy Star standard. It's rated at 196 kWh/year. Equator dishwashers are made in Germany. Dishwashers may have features such as soil sensing that can affect overall electric use.

Eurotech Dishwashers

AM Appliance Group - Eurotech
P.O. Box 851805
Richardson, TX 75085

Toll-free: 800-898-1879
Phone: 972-644-8595
www.eurotechappliances.com

Eurotech, a division of Texas-based AM Appliance Group, manufactures four GreenSpec-qualifying models. All are 61% better than the minimum federal energy standards for dishwashers, with a 0.74 EF. As of March 2007, Eurotech model numbers meeting GreenSpec standards include: EDW242C, EDW254E, EDW274E, and EDW294. Features vary between models, and may affect overall electric use.

Fisher & Paykel / DCS Dishwashers

Fisher & Paykel
5900 Skylab Rd.
Huntington Beach, CA 92647

Toll-free: 888-936-7872
www.usa.fisherpaykel.com

Fisher & Paykel's DishDrawer (model DD603-USA), made in New Zealand, is a double-drawer dishwasher with an energy factor of 0.72, rated at 189 kWh/year, 97% better than the Energy Star threshold. DCS, recently acquired by Fisher & Paykel, offers model DD124, which has the same statistics. Dishwashers may have features such as soil sensing that can affect overall electric use.

Gaggenau Dishwashers

Gaggenau USA / Canada
780 Dedham St.
Canton, MA   02021

Toll-free: 800-828-9165
www.gaggenau.com

Gaggenau, a Bosch luxury brand, offers four models with 0.74 EF (61% higher than the Energy Star baseline), rated at 290 kWh/year. As of March 2007, model numbers include DF241760, DF290760, DF291760, and DI291730. Note that dishwashers may have features such as soil sensing that can affect overall electric use.

GE Dishwashers

GE Appliances
9500 Williamsburg Office Plz.
General Electric Answer Center
Louisville, KY   40222

Toll-free: 800-626-2000
www.geappliances.com

As of March 2007, GE has one dishwasher that meets GreenSpec's standard. Their model GSM18**J in the Monogram line is rated at 282 kWh operating electricity per year; with an EF of 0.76, it's 65% better than the minimum Energy Star standard for dishwashers. Optional features may affect overall energy use.

Kenmore Dishwashers

Sears
3333 Beverly Rd.
Hoffman Estates, IL   60179

Toll-free: 800-349-4358
www.sears.com

Sears offers a Kenmore compact dishwasher in the Elite line (model 1332*) that exceeds the Energy Star minimum standard by 110%, with an EF of 1.30 and an estimated energy use of 174 kWh/year. As of March 2007, only Asko has more efficient dishwashers listed in GreenSpec. Kenmore dishwashers are made in the U.S.A. by Electrolux. Certain features such as soil-sensing may affect overall energy use.

KitchenAid Dishwashers

KitchenAid
701 Main St.
P.O. Box 218
St. Joseph, MI   49085

Toll-free: 800-422-1230
www.kitchenaid.com

KitchenAid's compact, single-drawer dishwasher model KUDD01S in their Architect line exceeds Energy Star's minimum threshold by 97%, with an Enegy Factor (EF) of 1.22 and an estimated annual energy use

of 189 kWh. As of March 2007, this is the only KitchenAid dishwasher meeting GreenSpec's standard. Certain features, such as soil-sensing, may affect overall energy use.

LG Dishwashers

LG Appliances
1000 Sylvan Ave.
Englewood Cliffs, NJ   07632

Toll-free: 800-243-0000
www.lgappliances.com

LG Electronics standard-sized dishwasher model LDF881#** has an Energy Factor (EF) of 0.75, which is 63% better than the Energy Star baseline. It is projected to used 285 kWh of electricity per year. As of March 2007, this is the only LG dishwasher meeting GreenSpec's standard. Certain features, such as soil-sensing, may affect overall energy use.

Siemens Dishwashers

Siemens Home Appliances
5551 McFadden Ave.
Huntington Beach, CA   92649

Toll-free: 888-474-3636
Phone: 714-901-6600
www.siemens-home.com

In its hiDefinition line, Siemens offers dishwasher models SL33A00-2UC, -5UC, and - 6UC; and SL34A01-2UC, -5UC, and -6UC. These dishwashers have an Energy Facor (EF) of 0.79 and an estimated annual energy use of 270 kWh, exceeding the Energy Star minimum by 72%. Certain dishwasher features, such as soil-sensing, may affect overall energy use.

Thermador Dishwashers

Thermador
5551 McFadden Ave.
Huntington Beach, CA   92649

Toll-free: 800-656-9226
www.thermador.com

Thermador dishwasher models DWHD64C*, DWHD94B-F, -P, and -S have an energy factor of 0.74, which is 61% better than the Energy Star minimum, and are projected to use 290 kWh/year. Certain features, such as soil sensing, may affect overall electric use. Thermador dishwashers are manufactured in the U.S.

Viking Dishwashers

Viking Range Corporation
111 Front St.
Greenwood, MS   38930

Toll-free: 888-845-464
Phone: 662-455-1200
www.vikingrange.com

Viking dishwasher models DFUD042 and DFUD142 each have an energy factor of 0.92, which is 100% better than the minimum Energy Star standard for dishwashers. Certain features may affect overall energy use. Made in the U.S.

Residential Laundry Appliances

Manufacturers have made tremendous strides in increasing the energy efficiency of clothes washers in recent years. This has been aided by U.S. Department of Energy (DOE) minimum efficiency standards, the federal Energy Star program, and efforts of the Consortium for Energy Efficiency (CEE). Energy Star standards require a minimum Modified Energy Factor (MEF) of 1.72 and a maximum Water Factor (WF) of 8.0. The higher the MEF, the more efficient the washer is in the entire laundry cycle (including drying; the MEF factors in Remaining Moisture Content—RMC—to predict dryer energy use). The WF is a measure of the number of gallons of water used per cubic foot of laundry. A significant amount of the energy used for clothes washing is for heating the water—so clothes washers that use less water are usually more energy efficient. Some manufacturers also offer condensing dryers; these do not require exterior venting, and they release all generated heat inside the building (an advantage in the winter but a disadvantage in the summer). The primary problem with single units that both wash and dry laundry in a common drum is that the volume required for drying a load of laundry is larger than the volume required for washing—so when one drum has to serve both needs, the wash volume is reduced. Condensing dryers can also increase water consumption by running cold water through condensation coils. Products listed here have a minimum MEF of 1.85, and a maximum WF of 5.0.

Ariston Clothes Washers & Washer-Dryers

Ariston Appliances US
3027 E. Sunset, Ste. 101
Ultra 8 International
Las Vegas, NV 89120

Toll-free: 888-426-0845
www.aristonappliances.us

As of March 2007, Italian manufacturer Ariston offers a clothes washer (model AW120) and a washer-dryer (model AWD120) that exceed minimum federal standards by 52%. These models both have an MEF of 1.92 and a WF of 5. These 1.92 cubic-foot appliances are projected to use 143 kWh and 3763 gallons of water per year.

Bosch Clothes Washers

BSH Home Appliances Corp.
5551 McFadden Ave.
Huntington Beach, CA 92649

Toll-free: 800-944-2904
Phone: 714-901-6600
www.boschappliances.com

Bosch offers ten large-capacity (3.31 cubic feet), horizontal-axis clothes washers that qualify for GreenSpec as of March, 2007. These models exceed federal standards by 69% to 93%, with MEF ratings of 2.13 to 2.43, and WF ratings of 4.1 to 4.7. Annual water use, based on standard assumptions, ranges from 5268 to 6150 gallons of water per year, and annual electricity use ranges from 146 to 182 kWh. Models numbers (and MEF numbers) include: WFMC2100UC (2.13),

WFMC6400UC (2.2), WFMC1001UC (2.24), WFMC4300UC (2.31), WFMC3301UC (2.4), WFMC330SUC (2.4), WFMC4301UC (2.4), WFMC2201UC (2.43), WFMC6401UC (2.43), WFMC640SUC (2.43). Features may vary between models, and some features may affect overall energy use.

Dryer-Ell

In-O-Vate Technologies, Inc.
810 Saturn St., Ste. 21
Jupiter, FL 33477

Toll-free: 888-443-7937
Phone: 561-743-8696
www.dryerbox.com

The Dryer-Ell™ dryer-duct elbow is a 4"-diameter, large-radius elbow with a smooth interior that is designed to reduce friction in dryer venting systems. The elbow reduces the need for a booster fan and increases the allowable duct length by about five feet, compared with standard elbows (based on ASHRAE methodology for calculating friction loss).

Equator Clothes Washers

Equator Corporation
2801 W. Sam Houston Pkwy. North, Ste. 150
Houston, TX 77080

Toll-free: 800-935-1955
Phone: 713-464-3422
www.equatorappliance.com

Two residential laundry products from Equator Corporation qualified for GreenSpec as of March, 2007. Models EZ 3612 CEE (combination washer and ventless dryer) and EZ 1612 V are 1.92 cubic foot capacity machines that exceed federal standards by 52% and 62% respectively, with MEFs of 1.92 and 2.04, and WFs of 5 and 4.9. Estimated annual water and electrical use is 3763 gallons for the 3612, 3650 gallons for the 1612; and 143 or 135 kWh respectively. These appliances are made in Italy.

Inline Exhaust Duct Fans

Continental Fan Manufacturing
203 Eggert Rd.
Buffalo, NY 14215

Toll-free: 800-779-4021
Phone: 716-842-0670
www.continentalfan.com

Continental Fan Manufacturings AXC inline centrifugal duct fans for residential, commercial, and industrial applications offer quiet, efficient operation with high exhaust capacities, and are particularly appropriate where long vent runs are required. These fans use backward-curved impellers and infinitely variable RPM motors to meet versatile air-moving needs. With the fan and motor above the plane of the ceiling, operating noise is significantly dampened. Pressure, fan speed, dehumidistat, and timer controls are available, as well as backdraft dampers. For dryer venting applications - such as in apartment complexes - the pressure switch is preferable to using a timer in terms of energy conservation.

Kenmore Clothes Washers

Sears
3333 Beverly Rd.
Hoffman Estates, IL 60179

Toll-free: 800-349-4358
www.sears.com

With 31 models qualifying for GreenSpec as of March 2007, the Kenmore brand—manufactured for Sears by Electrolux and Whirlpool—impresses. The most efficient models overall include the 3.29 CF 4708#60** and 4709#60**, which exceed Energy Star standards by 89%: a 2.38 MEF, and 4.1 WF, estimated to use 173 kWh and 5288 gallons of water per year. Compare other Kenmore models to these using the yellow EnergyGuide label.

Kitchen Aid Clothes Washers

KitchenAid
701 Main St.
P.O. Box 218
St. Joseph, MI   49085

Toll-free: 800-422-1230
www.kitchenaid.com

As of March 2007, Kitchen Aid offers two high-end, 3.3-cubic-foot clothes washers meeting GreenSpec the threshold. Model KHWV01R* exceeds energy Star standards by 66%, offering an MEF of 2.09, a WF of 4.2, estimated annual water use of 5485 gallons, and estimated annual electric use of 214 kWh. Models KHWS01P#** and KHWS02R*+ exceed Energy Star by 47%, with 1.85 MEF, 4.3 WF, using an estimated 5524 gallons and 311 kWh per year. Use of certain features may affect overall energy use.

LG Clothes Washers

LG Appliances
1000 Sylvan Ave.
Englewood Cliffs, NJ 07632

Toll-free: 800-243-0000
www.lgappliances.com

LG Appliances offers 23 models qualifying for GreenSpec as of March 2007—among them the most efficient clothes washers to date, exceeding federal standards by up to 97%. (Siemens and Whirlpool have a couple slightly more efficient models.) offer The most efficient model is WM268#H**, the 3.47 CF "SteamWasher," with a 2.48 MEF, 3.5 WF, and estimated annual electric and water use of 171 kWh and 4690 gallons. Compare the yellow EnergyGuide labels on other LG models using this one as a benchmark. These appliances are manufactured in Korea. Use of certain features on clothes washers may affect their overall water and energy consumption.

Maytag Clothes Washers

Maytag Appliances
403 W. Fourth St. N
P.O. Box 39
Newton, IA 50208

Toll-free: 888-462-9824
Phone: 641-792-7000
www.maytag.com

Maytag's Neptune line includes two GreenSpec-qualifying models in their Epic line as of March 2007: MFW9700S#** and MFW9600S*+. Respectively, they exceed federal standards by 68% and 55%. MEFs are 2.12 and 1.95; WFs are 4.4 and 4.5; estimated annual kWh, 212 and 218; estimated annual water use, 5649 and 5855 gallons. These machines are manufactured by Maytag in the U.S. Certain features may affect overall water and energy use.

Miele Clothes Washers

Miele, Inc.
9 Independence Way
Princeton, NJ 08540

Toll-free: 800-843-7231
Phone: 609-419-9898
www.mieleusa.com

Miele offers seven German-made clothes washers that qualify for GreenSpec. Two 3.07 CF models (W4800 and W4840) exceed federal minimum thresholds by 90%, with 2.4 MEF and 4.2 WF; 186 kWh and 5091 gallons of water estimated use annually. 2.08 CF models W1203, W1213, and W1215 are rated at 2.04 MEF, 4.4 WF, 127 kWh and 3547 gallons per year... 62% better than the federal minimum. The small 1.73 CF models W1113 and W1119 exceed federal standards by 67%, with 2.11 MEF, 4.5 WF, using an estimated 113 kWh and 3045 gallons of water annually. Certain features may be included that, when used, may affect overall energy and water use.

Samsung Clothes Washers

Samsung Electronics
105 Challenger Rd.
Ridgefield Park, NJ 07660

Phone: 201-229-5000
www.samsungusa.com

Samsung offers six horizontal-axis clothes washers that meet GreenSpec's criteria. All have 3.29 cubic feet of capacity, and a 3.9 WF. Annual electric use estimates range from 210 to 220 kWh per year, with MEFs of either 2.01 or 2.06, depending on model. These products exceed federal minimum standards by 60% to 63%. Model numbers are WF206***, WF306BHW, WF306LAW, WF316***, WF326LAS, and WF326LAW.

Siemens Clothes Washer

Siemens Home Appliances
5551 McFadden Ave.
Huntington Beach, CA 92649

Toll-free: 888-474-3636
Phone: 714-901-6600
www.siemens-home.com

Siemens Home Appliances offers three 3.31-cubic-foot models that qualify for GreenSpec. WFXD8400UC is estimated to use 178 kWh and 5,839 gallons of water per year, with a 2.2 MEF and 4.5 WF, making it 75% better than the federal minimum standard. WFXD840AUC is estimated to use 176 kWh and 5,268 gallons of water per year, with a 2.43 MEF and 4.1 WF, making it 93% better than the federal minimum standard. WFXD5201UC is estimated to use 182 kWh and 5,514 gallons of water per year, with a 2.57 MEF and 4.3 WF, making it 104% better than the federal minimum standard.

Splendide Clothes Washer-Dryers

Splendide
15650 S.E. 102nd Ave.
P.O. Box 427
Clackamas, OR 97015

Toll-free: 800-356-0766
www.splendide.com

Splendide offers models WDC6200CEE and WD2100, washer-dryer combos that exceed federal standards by 52%. Each has a capacity of 1.92 cubic feet and a WF of 5 and 4.9 respectively, with 1.92 MEF. Estimated annual water use is about 3700 gallons, with a corresponding annual electric use of 143 kWh. Certain features may affect overall energy use. The 6200 has an integral ventless dryer; the 2100's dryer is vented.

Whirlpool Clothes Washers

Whirlpool Corporation
2000 N. Hwy. M-63
Benton Harbor, MI 49022

Toll-free: 800-253-1301
www.whirlpool.com

Whirlpool offers a dozen models that qualify for GreenSpec as of April, 2007. All offer 3 cubic feet capacity (give or take .30 cubic feet), have MEF numbers around 2 and WF numbers between 4 and 5; annual water and electric use is estimated to be 5300 – 5900 gallons and 170 – 285 kWh. They range between 57% and 113% better than federal standards; the most efficient models are WFW9400T*#**, WFW9600T*#**, and WFW9200T*#**. Certain features may affect overall water and energy use. These washers are made in Europe by Whirlpool.

Residential Refrigerators and Freezers

The energy efficiency of refrigerators has improved dramatically in the last several decades. National standards have helped reduce the energy use of refrigerators to less than one-third that of pre-1973 models; and in the short amount of time since 2001, the energy use of conventional refrigerators has dropped by 40%. Developments in refrigerator design, including increased insulation, tighter door seals, and more efficient compressors, are continuing that trend. Different options and freezer compartment configurations affect energy use. A side-by-side refrigerator-freezer with such amenities as through-the-door ice service and automatic defrost may use nearly 40% more energy than a top-freezer, manual-defrost, basic model. Products listed here must exceed the federal minimum standard by at least 20% in the full-sized and apartment-sized category. Compact refrigerators—less than 7.75 cubic feet of volume, and less than 36" tall—must exceed the minimum federal standard by 30% or more. Also listed here are super-efficient refrigerators that are usually sold for use in off-grid houses; these generally haven't qualified for Energy Star because the companies are too small to be required to submit to testing.

Absocold Compact Refrigerators

Absocold Corporation
P.O. Box 1545
Richmond, IN 47375

Toll-free: 800-843-3714
www.absocold.com

Absocold offers one compact refrigerator that qualifies for GreenSpec as of April, 2007. Model ARD298C*10R/L, with a top freezer, exceeds federal standards by 31%. It has partial defrost, an adjusted volume (freezer volume x 1.5 + refrigerator volume) of 3.34 cubic feet and projected annual electric consumption of 290 kWh. (Note that even though compact refrigerators may be much better than federal standards, they can still use more than two-thirds as much energy as a top-efficiency full-size refrigerator with nearly four times the interior volume.)

Amana Refrigerators

Amana
403 W. 4th St. N
Maytag Customer Service
Newton, IA 50208

Toll-free: 800-843-0304
www.amana.com

Amana offers three side-by-side models projected to use 580 kWh/year: 20% less energy than federal standards for models of the type, just reaching the GreenSpec threshold. These models (ASD2626HE*, ASD2627KE*, and ASD2628HE*) are automatic defrost and include through-the-door ice, and are among the largest residential refrigerators listed in GreenSpec, with an adjusted volume (freezer volume x 1.5 + refrigerator volume) of 31.76 cubic feet. The bottom-freezer, ice-dispensing model AFD2535DE* is 26% better than the minimum federal standard, estimated to use 505 kWh per year for its 29.4 cubic feet of adjusted volume. Other bottom-freezer models paradoxically use less energy, but are only 20% - 21% above the federal minimum standard - due to the machinations of considering features like through-the-door ice dispensing. Always compare energy-use data on the yellow EnergyGuide labels. These other models numbers include ABB1922FE*, ABB2522FE*, ABL1922FE*, ABL2522FE*, ABR1922FE*, ABR2522FE*, ABB2222FE*, ABL2222FE*, and ABR2222FE*.

Avanti Apartment-Sized Refrigerators

Avanti Products
10880 N.W. 30th St.
Miami, FL 33172

Toll-free: 800-323-5029
Phone: 305-592-7830
www.avantiproducts.com

Avanti offers three apartment-sized refrigerator models that meet GreenSpec's requirements. Models BCA902W and RM901W are single-door, refrigerator-only configurations. The former has automatic defrost, a volume of 8.87 cubic feet, and uses 32% less energy than federal standards, at 247 kWh/year. The second model listed is a manual-defrost unit with a volume of 8.7 cubic feet; it uses 29% less energy than federal standards, at 230 kWh/year. (Note that the unit that uses less energy is actually rated as less in excess of federal standards, which don't use a single formula in establishing energy thresholds for refrigerators. Adjustments are made for features and size—which is confusing at best and misleading at worst. When in doubt, read the EnergyGuide label, which presents energy consumption in a neutral way.) Avanti also offers model 1201W-1: a single-door refrigerator/freezer with manual defrost. The volume is 11 cubic feet; the adjusted volume (freezer volume x 1.5 + refrigerator volume) is 11.69 cubic feet. Estimated annual energy use is 277 kWh.

Conserv

Equator Corporation
2801 W. Sam Houston Pkwy. North, Ste. 150
Houston, TX 77080

Toll-free: 800-935-1955
Phone: 713-464-3422
www.equatorappliance.com

Conserv™ is a specialized very-low-energy-usage refrigerator designed for homes with or without connection to the utility grid. A Danish product formerly marketed as Vestfrost™, the manual-defrost Conserv is built with all recyclable parts, CFC-free foam and refrigerant, and separate compressors for the refrigerator and freezer.

Frigidaire Refrigerators

Electrolux Home Products
P.O. Box 212378
Martinez, GA 30917

Toll-free: 800-374-4432
Phone: 706-651-1751
www.frigidaire.com

Frigidaire, an Electrolux company, has two GreenSpec-qualifying refrigerator-freezers as of December, 2005. Models FRT21KR7E* and FRT21FR7E* exceed federal standards by 28%. They have top freezer compartments, auto defrost, and through-the-door ice service. Estimated annual electric use is 432 kWh. Volume is 20.6 cubic feet.

GE Refrigerators

GE Appliances
9500 Williamsburg Office Plz.
General Electric Answer Center
Louisville, KY 40222

Toll-free: 800-626-2000
www.geappliances.com

General Electric produces 20 models that just achieve GreenSpec's criteria by exceeding federal energy standards by 20%. They are all automatic-defrost, bottom-freezer units, none with through-the-door ice; volumes are all either approximately 19.5 or 22.25 cubic feet. Projected energy use for models with volumes of 19.5 ft3 is 453 kWh/year; for those with 22.5 ft3, 464 kWh/year. 19.5-foot models include GBS20KBR**, PDS20MBR, PDS20MCR, PDS20SBR, PDS20SCR, GB*20******, GBS20HBS**, GDL20KCS**, GDS20KBS**, GDS20KCS**, GDS20SBS**, GDS20SCS**, and SDL20KCS**; 22.25-foot models include GBS22HBR**, GBS22HCR**, PDS22MBR, PDS22MCR, PDS22SBR, PDS22SCR, and GBS22KBR**.

Jenn-Air Refrigerators

Jenn-Air
403 W. 4th St. N.
Newton, IA 50208

Toll-free: 800-688-1100
Phone: 641-792-7000
www.jennair.com

Jenn-Air, a Maytag brand, offers eight models that meet GreenSpec's requirements (as of April, 2007). These models are all in side-by-side configuration, have automatic defrost, and just meet the GreenSpec threshold by exceeding federal energy standards by 20%. Projected energy use ranges from 510 to 580 kWh/year. Models JCB2280HE*, JCB2282HT*, and JCB2285HES have 21.47 cubic feet of volume, no ice dispenser, and the lowest estimated energy use of the models in this listing. Models JSD2690HE*, JSD2695KE*, JSD2695KG*, and JSD2697KE* have 25.6 cubic feet, through-the-door ice, and 580 kWh/year estimated electric use. Models JCD2290HE*

is 21.57 cubic feet, has through-the-door ice, and is rated at 537 kWh/year.

Kenmore Refrigerators

Sears
3333 Beverly Rd.
Hoffman Estates, IL 60179

Toll-free: 800-349-4358
www.sears.com

Sears offers a whopping 29 full-size models under the Kenmore brand that qualify for GreenSpec (as of December, 2005)—18 in top-freezer configuration, and 11 side-by-side. All are 20-21% better than federal standards, with the exception of one side-by, which is 23%, and two 28% top-freezers. All have automatic defrost; the side-by-side models have ice service, while all but two of the top-freezers don't (and in part because of that have lower annual electric use projections). The lowest energy use numbers (387 kWh/year) are for models 7490*40* and 7491*40*, top-freezers with 18.79 cubic feet; the highest energy use numbers (581 kWh/year) are for models 5460*30*, 5656*40*, and 5657*40*, side-by-sides with over 25.5 cubic feet. (It's revealing to note that the models exceeding federal standards by 28%—7682*40* and 7683*40*—are the smallest top-freezers included in this listing; but they have through-the-door ice dispensers, and are projected to use 569 kWh/year. The federal standards include multiple adjustments for features and size—which is confusing at best and misleading at worst. When in doubt, read the EnergyGuide label, which presents energy consumption data in a neutral way.) A list of all qualifying Kenmore models as of December, 2005: 7491*40*, 7490*40*, 7499*40*, 7592*40*, 7390*30*, 7498*40*, 7594*40*, 7398*30*, 6398*30*, 7393*30*, 6397*30*, 7397*30*, 7682*40*, 7683*40*, 7420*40*, 7421*40*, 7428*40*, 7429*40*, 4432*40*, 5420*30*, 5637*40*, 5636*40*, 5520*40*, 5521*40*, 5561*40*, 5560*40*, 5656*40*, 5657*40*, and 5460*30*. Most of these models are manufactured for Sears by Whirlpool.

KitchenAid Refrigerators

KitchenAid
701 Main St.
P.O. Box 218
St. Joseph, MI 49085

Toll-free: 800-422-1230
www.kitchenaid.com

KitchenAid, a Whirlpool brand, offers four side-by-side, automatic defrost models with through-the-door ice that exceed federal energy standards for refrigerators of this class with the same options by 20%. These models each have volumes of 23.05 cubic feet, and are projected to use 557 kWh/year. The model numbers are KSBP23IN**0*, KSBS23IN**0*, KSCS23FS**0*, and KSCS23IN**0*. Six auto-defrost bottom-freezers are also available - 20.46 cubic feet, 453 kWh per year - models KBLC36FT*0*, KBLO36FT*0*, KBLS36FT*0*, KBRO36FT*0*, KBRS36FT*0*, and KRBC36FT*0*.

LG Refrigerators

LG Appliances
1000 Sylvan Ave.
Englewood Cliffs, NJ 07632

Toll-free: 800-243-0000
www.lgappliances.com

LG Electronics model LSC2696#** is an automatic defrost, side-by-side refrigerator-freezer with through-the-door ice. It has a volume of 25.51 cubic feet, and is projected to use 565 kWh/year, exceeding by 22% the federal standard for refrigerators of this size with the same features. Model LRD*20731** is an auto-defrost bottom-freezer without ice service; it has a volumes of 19.74 cubic feet, is projected to use 440 kWh/year, 23% better than the federal standard for refrigerators of this size with the same features. Similar model LFX25970** has 24.7 cubic feet of volume and uses 515 kWh/year, yet is rated as 25% better than the federal minimum standard - because it has a larger adjusted volume and an ice-dispensing feature, which changes the efficiency formula. Always compare the projected energy usage on the yellow EnergyGuide labels.

Maytag Refrigerators

Maytag Appliances
403 W. Fourth St. N
P.O. Box 39
Newton, IA 50208

Toll-free: 888-462-9824
Phone: 641-792-7000
www.maytag.com

Maytag manufactures nine side-by-side, automatic defrost refrigerator models with ice dispensing that each exceed the federal standards for similar refrigerators by 20%. Models MCB2256HE*, MCD2257HE*, and MCD2257KE* each have about 21.5 cubic feet of volume, using between 510 - 537 kWh/year. Models MSD2656KE*, MSD2656KG*, MS-D2657HE*, MSD2659KE*, MSD2660KE*, and MSD2660KG* each have a volume of 25.6 and a 727 kWh/year estimate. Thirteen bottom-freezer models (MBF1956KE*, MBF2556KE*, MBL1956KE*, MBL2556KE*, MBR1956KE*, MBR2556KE*, MB2216PUA*, MBF2255KE*, MBF2256KE*, MBL2255KE*, MBL2256KE*, MBR2255KE*, and MBR2256KE*) have volumes ranging from 18.5 - 25 cubic feet, using between 560 - 595 kWh/year.

Microfridge Compact Refrigerators

MicroFridge
10 Walpole Park S
Walpole, MA 02081

Toll-free: 800-994-0165
Phone: 508-660-9200
www.microfridge.com

Microfridge® offers several compact units. Model MHRA-4E is a single-door, 4-cubic-foot-capacity, auto-defrost refrigerator-freezer projected to use 241 kWh/year. Models MF-3XPNTPS, MF-3XPNTP, MF-3XNTP, MF-3XNTPS, and MFR-3** all have identical attributes: 2.9 cubic feet capacity in a top-freezer configuration, 31% better than federal standards for units of this size and type—estimated to use 290 kWh/year. (Note that although these refrigerators are up to

31% better than federal standards, they still uses about two-thirds as much energy as a top-efficiency full-size refrigerator with nearly four times the interior volume.)

Monogram Refrigerators

GE Appliances
9500 Williamsburg Office Plz.
General Electric Answer Center
Louisville, KY 40222

Toll-free: 800-626-2000
www.geappliances.com

Monogram, a brand of GE, offers three side-by-side units for the built-in market that meet the GreenSpec threshold. Models ZIS360NR and ZISS360NRS both have a volume of 21.62 cubic feet, are automatic defrost, have through-the-door ice service, and a projected energy use of 547 kWh/year; they exceed minimum federal standards by 20%. Bottom-freezer model ZICP360S, an ice-dispensing auto-defrost, is 27% better than the federal minimum standard: 485 kWh/year with an adjusted volume of 24.37 cubic feet.

Summit Compact Refrigerators

Summit Appliance Division - Felix Storch, Inc.
770 Garrison Ave.
Bronx, NY 10474

Phone: 718-893-3900
www.summitappliance.com

Summit Appliances offers its compact two-door, top-freezer model CP-35*. With a volume of 3.34 cubic feet and a projected energy use of 290 kWh/year, it exceeds the federal standard for refrigerators of its type by 31%. The refrigerator compartment is auto-defrost; the freezer is manual. (Note that although this refrigerator is 31% better than federal standards, it still uses about two-thirds as much energy as a top-efficiency full-size refrigerator with nearly four times the interior volume.)

Sun Frost Refrigerators

Sun Frost
P.O. Box 1101
Arcata, CA 95518

Phone: 707-822-9095
www.sunfrost.com

Sun Frost produces refrigerators and freezers with extremely low energy use. Model R-19 is an auto-defrost, passive (fanless), single-door, refrigerator-only model. It has a total volume of 16.14 cubic feet and a projected energy use of 204 kWh/year—exceeding the federal standard by 53%. Models RF-12 and RF-16 have a two-door, top-freezer configuration with volumes of 10.12 and 14.31 cubic feet, respectively. Projected electric use for these fanless units is 171 kWh/year for the RF-12 (51% better than the federal standard), and 254 kWh/year (36% better) for the RF-16. Both have auto-defrost refrigerators and manual-defrost freezers. All models are available in 12- and 24-volt DC, and 110- and 220-volt AC. They are particularly suitable for homes not connected to the utility grid.

SunDanzer

SunDanzer
11135 Dyer Ste. C
El Paso, TX 79934

Phone: 915-821-0042
www.sundanzer.com

SunDanzer produces small, DC-powered refrigerators and freezers with extremely low energy use. All SunDanzer freezers and refrigerators have 11" (4.3 cm) of polyurethane insulation, an aluminum interior, a galvanized steel exterior, a patented low-frost system, and a drain hole at the bottom for easy cleaning. The brushless, thermostatically controlled DC compressor runs on either 12 or 24 volts and operates with ozone-safe HFC-134a refrigerant. In most climates, a single 75-watt photovoltaic module will generate enough power to run a freezer. The chest style refrigerators and freezers are available in 165 liter (5.8 cubic feet) and 225 liter (8 cubic feet) capacities. The units are custom-manufactured for SunDanzer by Electrolux at a factory in Hungary and are particularly suitable for homes not connected to the utility grid.

Whirlpool Refrigerators

Whirlpool Corporation
2000 N. Hwy. M-63
Benton Harbor, MI 49022

Toll-free: 800-253-1301
www.whirlpool.com

Whirlpool models GC3SHE*N*0*, GC3PHE*N*0*, and EC3JHA*R*0* are side-by-side refrigerator-freezers with through-the-door ice dispensers and automatic defrost. They have a capacity of 23.07 cubic feet, with a projected energy use of 557 kWh/year. Model ED2GTG*N*0* is slightly smaller unit (21.8 cubic feet) with similar attributes. Projected energy use is 572 kWh/year. These units all exceed federal standards for similar models by 20%. Whirlpool also makes a number of other GreenSpec-approved units sold under Kenmore and KitchenAid labels.

This Space is Available for Your Notes

This Space is Available for Your Notes

Furniture & Furnishings

The introduction of furnishings that offgas hazardous chemicals can undo all the care given to using "clean" building materials. Furniture and furnishings incorporate many separate products and all of the issues that go with them. As a result, they can be a significant source of IAQ problems—coming from binders in wood composites such as particleboard, from finishes used on the products, from flame retardants used in foam cushions, and from adhesives used to assemble the products. Those items incorporating fabric, such as upholstered furniture and workstations, can also collect dirt and airborne contaminants, releasing them later.

Most of the plastic laminates used on inexpensive furniture is made from phenolic resins. These compounds are somewhat toxic to work with but relatively stable—and they're easy to keep clean after manufacture.

Hardwoods—especially tropical hardwoods—used in furniture manufacture should be third-party certified according to Forest Stewardship Council (FSC) standards to ensure that they were harvested in an environmentally responsible manner. FSC certification involves third-party evaluation and monitoring of sustainable forestry practices.

Most fabrics used on commercial furniture and work-stations are primarily polyester. Wool is a durable and attractive natural alternative, though it is sometimes treated with toxic mothproofing agents. The polyurethane foam padding used in furniture generally contains poly-brominated diphenol ethers (PBDEs), which are bioaccumulating relatives of PCBs. These flame retardants are released into the building as the foam padding ages.

Furniture should be as simple as possible, with a minimum of different materials, and it should be assembled with mechanical fasteners rather than adhesives to facilitate end-of-life recycling.

Some innovative designers have produced lines of furniture made from various recycled materials and with high recyclability.

Bedroom Furnishings

Products listed here are produced from recycled materials, from organic cotton, or without chlorine bleaches and other hazardous chemicals.

Cotton Futons

Futon Man
5280 N.W. Hwy. 99 W
Corvallis, OR 97330

Phone: 541-753-6395
www.fatfuton.com

Natural Life Furnishings manufactures futons with untreated cotton and wool with a poly layer made from recycled plastic. Futon mattresses can be made from organic cotton on request.

Natural Fiber Bedding and Mattresses

Vivètique
11911 Clark Street
Arcadia, CA 91006

Toll-free: 800-365-6563
www.vivetique.com

Vivètique natural-fiber mattresses are available in three types: standard cotton, organic cotton, hemp, and an organic cotton/wool blend. Organic cotton mattresses are made without the use of fire-retardant chemicals and, therefore, require a doctor's prescription showing chemical sensitivity to purchase. The organic cotton/wool blend mattress contains naturally fire-resistant wool. Organic cotton and wool pillows and wool mattress covers and comforters are also available.

Wellspring Futon Mattresses and Covers

Rising Star...Stellar Home Furnishings
35 N.W. Bond St.
Bend, OR 97701

Toll-free: 800-828-6711
Phone: 541-382-4221
www.risingstarfurniture.com

Wellspring Futon Mattresses are made with 100%-recycled PET fiber batt, and cases are made from 100% organic cotton or a 50/50 cotton/polyester blend.

FSC-Certified Wood Furniture

Products listed here are produced using wood certified under standards established by the Forest Stewardship Council (FSC). Certification to FSC standards involves third-party evaluation and monitoring of sustainable forestry practices. SmartWood and Scientific Certification Services are the primary FSC-accredited third-party certifying organizations in North America.

Certified Hardwood Furniture

Berkeley Mills
2830 Seventh St.
Berkeley, CA 94710

Toll-free: 877-426-4557
www.berkeleymills.com

Berkeley Mills is a manufacturer of high-end custom and limited-production furniture available in FSC-certified hardwoods including cherry and maple. Distribution is nationwide though primarily on the West Coast.

Certified Hardwood Furniture

Cotswold Furniture Makers
904 Sawyer Rd.
Whiting, VT 05778

Phone: 802-623-8400
www.cotswoldfurniture.com

Cotswold Furniture Makers offers handcrafted home and office furniture. Pieces are typically made from American black cherry from FSC-certified sources. Other hardwoods—such as oak, maple, and walnut—may be offered but may not be available FSC-certified.

Certified Wood Furniture

Beeken Parsons
1611 Harbor Rd.
Shelburne Farms
Shelburne, VT 05482

Phone: 802-985-2913
www.beekenparsons.com

Beeken Parsons offers Vermont Forest Furniture, a line of FSC-certified forest furniture handcrafted out of character wood incorporating knots, grain textures, and colors that reflect the life of the tree and "tell the story of the forest." Character Wood often comes from trees that are relegated to such low-value uses as firewood and paper pulp. Increasing the value of these trees will help to offset the costs of responsible forest stewardship. Beeken Parsons has been designing and building custom furniture for more than 20 years. Its shop is located at historic Shelburne Farms in Shelburne, Vermont.

Certified Wood Furniture

Island Pond Woodproducts Inc.
306 Meadow St.
P.O. Box 236
Island Pond, VT 05846

Phone: 802-723-6611
www.islandpondwoodproducts.com

Founded by displaced workers after a multinational furniture manufacturer shut its doors on a local plant, employee-owned Island Pond Woodproducts produces handcrafted residential, business, and institutional furniture from locally harvested FSC-certified lumber or sustainably harvested lumber.

Certified Wood Furniture

South Cone Trading Company
19038 S. Vermont Ave.
Gardena, CA 90248

Toll-free: 800-466-7282
Phone: 310-538-5797
www.southcone.com

South Cone Trading Company is an FSC-certified furniture manufacturer with factories in Lima, Peru and Santa Fe, Argentina. The company offers a variety of home furnishings sold nationwide through approximately 300 independently owned retail stores and also sells to hotels and resorts on a contract basis. South Cone is the founder of PaTS (Partnerships and Technology for Sustainability), a nonprofit organization pursuing sustainable development in the Peruvian rainforest through the implementation of market-driven forms of forest conservation.

Certified Wood Furniture

The Joinery
4804 S.E. Woodstock Blvd.
Portland, OR 97206

Toll-free: 800-259-6762
Phone: 503-788-8547
www.thejoinery.com

The Joinery hand-crafts a wide variety of home and office furniture with lines reflecting Mission, Shaker, Asian, and French styles. FSC-certified hardwood, mostly cherry, is used in 75% of their work. Custom orders are commonly filled. The Joinery guarantees its furniture for life.

Certified Wood Furniture

Wiggers Custom Furniture
173 Reach Industrial Park Rd.
Port Perry, ON L9L 1B2 Canada

Phone: 905-985-1128
www.wiggersfurniture.com

Wiggers Custom Furniture manufactures individually crafted casegoods, desks, tables, consoles, and wall hung consoles made from FSC-certified woods. Wiggers Custom Furniture is one of the first custom furniture makers in the world to become FSC-certified.

Environmental Language Furniture

Environmental Language
Four 2 Five Park Barrington Dr.
Barrington, IL 60010

Phone: 847-382-9285
www.el-furniture.com

Environmental Language offers high-end home furniture made with locally reclaimed wood, rapidly renewable materials, and wood which can be specified as FSC for a 10% upcharge. Upholstered products are made with natural latex, organic cotton, wool, and jute with 100% organic materials also specified for a 10% upcharge. El furniture uses non-toxic low-VOC finishes and adhesives. El collections include tables, chairs, stools, sofas, sleepers, desks, nightstands and dressers.

Low Toxicity Furniture

Karp Woodworks
136 Fountain St.
Ashland, MA 01721

Phone: 508-881-7000
www.karpwoodworks.com

Karp Woodworks specializes in building custom furniture for chemically sensitive people. Low-VOC finishes are used, as well as organic cotton and special batting for upholstered designs.

Modular Furniture

IKEA, North American Service Office
496 W. Germantown Pike
Plymouth Meeting, PA 19462

Phone: 610-834-0180
www.ikea.com

Swedish-based IKEA has taken a number of steps to reduce the environmental impact of its modular, build-it-yourself furniture products. An FSC member, IKEA's long term goal is to have all wood used in its products certified by the Forest Stewardship Council (FSC) or an equivalent program. Currently all high-value tropical wood species must originate from forests certified by the FSC. PVC has been eliminated in all products except the isolating plastic of electric cables, and the company is looking to find an alternative for this as well. Bromine fire-retardants have been eliminated entirely. IKEA uses water-based and UV-cured coatings, powder coatings for metal components, and white and hot-melt glues. A line of air-filled seating products is available as well.

Furniture

Furniture is made from a wide variety of materials, and may be both resource-intensive to produce and contribute to poor indoor air quality. Products listed here have features such as being made from recycled materials or certified wood; having "green" upholstery; safety from an indoor-air-quality standpoint; design-for-disassembly and refurbishment or recycling; and avoiding materials with high environmental burdens (brominated flame retardants, plasticizers, PVC, etc.).

Furniture, Fabrics, and Accessories

Q Collection
915 Broadway, Ste. 1001
New York, NY 10010

Phone: 212-529-1400
www.qcollection.com

Q Collection's furniture, fabrics, and accessories for home and office are made without formaldehydes, polyurethanes, brominated flame retardants, or other commonly used and potentially hazardous chemicals and organic pollutants. The fabric line is 100% biodegradable and made with nontoxic dyes. Wood is from certified sources (including, but not exclusively, FSC); the company is pursuing chain-of-custody certification under FSC, which will allow it to sell products carrying the FSC label. Q Collection also provides green accessories, such as ceramics, pillows, and throws.

Natural Fiber Fabrics

Natural fibers such as cotton, linen, ramie, wool, silk, jute, and hemp are traditional fabric materials. Unlike their polymer-based replacements, natural fibers require little energy to process and are biodegradable—but they may have other environmental impacts. Cotton is typically grown with significant chemical fertilizer and pesticide use, although the availability of organically grown cotton is increasing. Silk and wool, both animal products, are obtained primarily from overseas sources; both are prone to moth attack and microbial growth, so are often treated with chemicals. Hemp and jute, also primarily from overseas sources, are relatively resistant to pests, both as plants and after manufacture into fabrics. Natural dyes are sometimes used with these fabrics, but synthetic dyes are more commonly employed for greater color retention. Natural-fiber fabrics may be used as furniture upholstery, workstation fabrics, draperies, etc.

Cotton Plus

Organic Cotton Plus, Inc.
822 Baldridge St.
O'Donnell, TX 79351

Phone: 806-428-3345
www.organiccottonplus.com

Cotton Plus fabrics are made from organically grown cotton fiber, woven into chambray, twill, canvas, and flannel. In addition to natural-color cotton fabrics, some fabrics are dyed using low-impact processing.

Foxfibre Colorganic Fabric

Vreseis Ltd.
P.O. Box 69
Guinda, CA 95637

Phone: 530-796-3007
www.vreseis.com

Vreseis manufactures upholstery fabrics from Foxfibre® Colorganic® organic cotton, which has been selectively bred and grown to produce cotton in shades of green, brown, and natural off-white. The brown color is naturally flame-retardant, though additional chemicals have to be added to meet most commercial standards.

Furniture, Fabrics, and Accessories

Q Collection
915 Broadway, Ste. 1001
New York, NY 10010

Phone: 212-529-1400
www.qcollection.com

Q Collection's furniture, fabrics, and accessories for home and office are made without formaldehydes, polyurethanes, brominated flame retardants, or other commonly used and potentially hazardous chemicals and organic pollutants. The fabric line is 100% biodegradable and made with nontoxic dyes. Wood is from certified sources (including, but not exclusively, FSC); the company is pursuing chain-of-custody certification under FSC, which will allow it to sell products carrying the FSC label. Q Collection also provides green accessories, such as ceramics, pillows, and throws.

Portable Partitions, Screens, and Panels

Moveable partition systems allow spaces to be easily reconfigured, thus reducing cost and environmental impact. Products listed here have recycled content, certified wood, low-VOC content, and other green attributes.

Bulletin Board

Forbo Linoleum, Inc.
2 Maplewood Dr., Humboldt Industrial Park
P.O. Box 667
Hazleton, PA 18201

Toll-free: 800-842-7839
Phone: 570-459-0771
www.forboflooringNA.com

Bulletin Board is a colored, 1/4"-thick, granulated linoleum-cork composite product sold in full-size sheets for use as tack panels, or as a decorative finish for furniture, doors, or moveable partitions. Bulletin Board is durable, washable, low-glare, and will not warp or crumble. It is available in 12 solid colors.

Reclaimed-Wood Furniture

Products listed here have significant wood content that was reclaimed or salvaged from other uses (barns and buildings slated for demolition, for example). Some of these products use salvaged wood sources that have been certified through the SmartWood Rediscovered Wood Program.

Antique Woods & Colonial Restorations

Antique Woods & Colonial Restorations, Inc.
121 Quarry Rd.
Gouverneur, NY 13642

Toll-free: 888-261-4284
Phone: 610-913-0674
www.vintagewoods.com

Antique Woods & Colonial Restorations, Inc. (formerly Vintage Barns, Woods & Restorations) sells reclaimed and remilled wood products including flooring, siding, millwork, and whole barn frames.

Appalachian Woods

Appalachian Woods, LLC
1240 Cold Springs Rd.
Stuarts Draft, VA 24477

Toll-free: 800-333-7610
Phone: 540-337-1801
www.appalachianwoods.com

Appalachian Woods reclaims and remills timber for a variety of custom millwork applications. Lumber is generally sold rough, but can be provided S4S and S2S. Lumber, flooring, and furniture is available in a variety of species including American chestnut, heart pine, and oak. Appalachian Woods has been a family-run business since 1976.

Barnstormers Reclaimed Hand-Hewn Beams

Barnstormers
166 Malden Tpke.
Saugerties, NY 12477

Phone: 845-661-7989
www.barnstormersflooring.com

Barnstormers sells antique hand-hewn beams from disassembled barns. Species include oak, chestnut, hemlock, and other hardwoods. The company also remills tongue-and-groove barnwood hardwood flooring and siding out of this reclaimed wood, using a technique called "skip planing" to mill the boards while leaving some of the original milling marks for aesthetic purposes.

Furniture and Kitchen Cabinetry from Urban Trees

CitiLog
P.O. Box 685
Pittstown, NJ 08867

Toll-free: 877-248-9564
Phone: 908-735-8871
www.citilogs.com

CitiLog™, also known as D. Stubby Warmbold, is SmartWood-certified for the harvesting of trees in urban areas of New Jersey and Pennsylvania. Wood is sent by rail to Amish craftsmen in central Pennsylvania who take extra care to turn the lesser graded wood into higher quality products such as flooring, lumber, custom architectural millwork, furniture, and kitchen cabinets. Where appropriate, wood is now harvested using horses.

Millennium Oak

Ecologic, Inc.
921 Sherwood Dr.
Lake Bluff, IL 60044

Toll-free: 800-899-8004
Phone: 847-234-5855
www.ecoinc.com

Ecologic's Millennium Oak furnishings are made from recycled, plantation-grown hardwood with an oak color. The product line includes beds and lofts, desks, dressers, nightstands, and bookcases.

Reclaimed-Wood Building Products

Endura Wood Products, Ltd.
1303 S.E. 6th Ave.
Portland, OR 97214

Phone: 503-233-7090
www.endurawood.com

Endura Wood Products currently has access to over 3.5 million board feet of Douglas fir that is being reclaimed from the old Portland Dry Dock #2. Also available is a limited supply of Douglas fir with a distinct red hue that has been reclaimed from maraschino cherry vats.

Reclaimed-Wood Building Products

Solid Wood Products
3756 Pineridge Dr.
Lac Le Jeune, BC V1S 1Y8 Canada

Phone: 250-320-0936
www.solidwoodpro.com

Solid Wood Products manufactures building and finish products, primarily wide-plank flooring from reclaimed Douglas fir. The one-inch flooring is available in 6" to 14" widths. Also offered are trim, wainscot, panels, and stair parts; timber-frame components including beams, braces, purlins, and rafters; as well as custom furniture.

Reclaimed-Wood Building Products

Vintage Log and Lumber, Inc.
Glen Ray Rd.
Rt. 1, Box 2F
Alderson, WV 24910

Toll-free: 877-653-5647
Phone: 304-445-2300
www.vintagelog.com

Vintage Log and Lumber salvages the materials in log cabins and timber-frame barns in Kentucky, Ohio, Pennsylvania, and West Virginia. The company's inventory includes salvaged redwood, chestnut, oak, pine, and poplar boards, beams, flooring, and split rails. They also sell complete hand-hewn log cabins and timber-frame barns, as well as architectural salvage items.

Reclaimed-Wood Building Products

Vintage Material Supply Co.
730 Shady Ln.
Austin, TX 78702

Phone: 512-386-6404
www.vintagematerialsupply.com

Vintage Material Supply Co. offers salvaged wood flooring available "as is" with edges cleaned, as well as new flooring milled from wood recovered from such sources as demolished buildings, ranch recovery, urban logging, and river bottoms. Primary species include old-growth longleaf pine, Tidewater cypress, mesquite, and walnut.

River-Reclaimed Wood Products

Goodwin Heart Pine Company
106 S.W. 109th Pl.
Micanopy, FL 32667

Toll-free: 800-336-3118
Phone: 352-466-0339
www.heartpine.com

Goodwin manufactures antique wood flooring, millwork, stair parts, paneling, and siding made from antique heart pine and heart cypress logs—200 years old or older—recovered from Southern river bottoms. Flooring, siding, and paneling is kiln-dried, graded, and precision-milled. Decorative wood moldings are architecturally drawn and are designed to classic proportions. Stair parts include solid or laminated treads, and a full range of balusters, newels, and rails. Reclaimed timbers from old buildings are also available.

Salvaged-Wood Furniture

Clayoquot Crafts
1336 Chesterman Beach Rd.
Tofino, BC V0R 2Z0 Canada

Toll-free: 877-522-3327
Phone: 250-725-3990
www.clayoquotcrafts.com

Clayoquot Crafts hand-builds furniture suitable for outdoor or indoor use from Western Red Cedar or Alder locally salvaged from discards remaining after logging operations. Clayoquot Crafts is located in Tofino, British Columbia, Canada.

Urban Hardwoods

Urban Hardwoods
4755 C. Colorado Ave. S
Seattle, WA 98134

Phone: 206-766-8199
www.urbanhardwoods.com

Urban Hardwoods salvages urban trees from within a 50-mile radius of the company and mills them into custom, made-to-order furniture, flooring, and other millwork. Urban Hardwoods continually designs products to make use of manufacturing "fall-down." Remaining waste material is given away or sold as firewood, or is used for heating their facility. The company ships 99% of its products blanket-wrapped; all blankets are reused. Products will be accepted back at the end of their useful life to be refurbished or recycled in the manufacture of new products. The company is SmartWood-certified under the "Rediscovered Wood" category.

Wooden Duck Reclaimed Furniture

The Wooden Duck
2919 Seventh St.
Berkeley, CA 94710

Toll-free: 866-848-3575
Phone: 510-848-3575
www.thewoodenduck.com

The Wooden Duck offers furniture, including custom work, made with reclaimed California Douglas fir or imported reclaimed teak. Their product lines are sold to the wholesale market and through their retail store, which also features the work of local craftspeople working exclusively with reclaimed wood.

Recycled-Content Furniture

Conventional furniture may offgas formaldehyde and VOCs, and is often very resource-intensive to produce. A number of innovative furniture products have been introduced in recent years made with both high recycled content and low emitting materials. Products listed here are have high recycled content, and are produced from materials that will not compromise indoor air quality.

Danko Chairs & Benches

Danko Design Initiative
839 McKinzie St.
York, PA 17403

Phone: 717-309-3731
www.peterdanko.com

Danko offers recycled-content furniture, most of which incorporates frames of structural ply-bent veneers (which provide higher yields of usable wood from a log than does solid lumber). Veneer laminations are made with water-based adhesives. Recycled materials, including post-industrial automotive seat belt material, are used for seat suspension and padding. As of March, 2006, the company is migrating to FSC certified wood veneer, and indicates that all their products will be free of added formaldehyde, isocyanates, and brominated flame retardants.

ECO+Plus

Ecologic, Inc.
921 Sherwood Dr.
Lake Bluff, IL 60044

Toll-free: 800-899-8004
Phone: 847-234-5855
www.ecoinc.com

Ecologic designs and manufactures furniture of recycled HDPE. Founded in 1992 to manufacture better college dormitory furniture, the company also makes products for other markets, including federal and municipal office buildings and fire stations. Eco+Plus is an attractive line of desks, bookcases, lofts, beds and bunks, dressers, nightstands, and wardrobes. Products generally do not require tools for assembly.

Pulp Furniture

Poesis Design
126 Lime Rock Rd.
Lakeville, CT 06039

Phone: 860-542-5152
www.poesisdesign.com

The Pulp Armchair (31" x 31" x 26", cube-shaped with upholstered cushions) is made of recycled newspaper blended with water and wax, and is designed with maple or walnut trim. FSC-certified wood may be specified. Pulp end tables, coffee tables, beds, bureaus, and file cabinets are also available.

Salvaged-Metal-Parts Furnishings

Resource Revival, Inc.
P.O. Box 440
Mosier, OR 97040

Toll-free: 800-866-8823
Phone: 503-282-1449
www.resourcerevival.com

Resource Revival crafts furniture, door and window grates, and other items from discarded bicycle parts and other recycled materials. Additional products include clocks, desk accessories, picture frames, promotional items and corporate gifts, trophies and awards. All items are handmade. The manufacturer has certified the following recycled-content levels (by weight): total recovered material 90% typical, 90% guaranteed; post-consumer material 90% typical, 90% guaranteed.

Shetkastone

All Paper Recycling, Inc.
435 W Industrial St.
P.O. Box 38
Le Center, MN 56057

Phone: 507-357-4177
www.shetkastone.com

All Paper Recycling manufactures tables and countertops using a patented process and 100% pre- and post-consumer recycled paper. Shetkastone comes in four standard colors that use a water-based binder. Premium colors are also available and they use a 13% acrylic binder. All products made with Shetkastone that are damaged or at the end of their lifecycle can be recycled back into the manufacturing process, reducing waste. The material has a Class A fire rating without the addition of chemicals and a 400-pound screw test.

Residential Cabinetry

Environmental features to look for with residential casework include FSC-certified or salvaged wood, recovered-fiber wood products, agrifiber panels, low-formaldehyde wood products, and low-VOC finishes. (Certification to Forest Stewardship Council—FSC—standards involves third-party evaluation and monitoring of sustainable forestry practices.) In some cases metal cabinets, which typically do not offgas, may be a good choice for those with chemical sensitivities. However, because of the lifecycle costs associated with mining and production, metal cabinets are generally not considered an environmentally preferred product.

Custom Furniture and Cabinets

NePalo Cabinetmakers
4328 Redwood Hwy., Ste. 400
San Rafael, CA 94903

Phone: 415-491-1403
www.NePalo.com

NePalo Cabinetmakers offers high-end custom furniture and cabinets made with FSC-certified hardwoods and FSC-certified, formaldehyde-free panels (in cherry, maple, and mahogany). Their products are made with waterproof, solvent-free glue and use environmentally responsible, hand-rubbed finishes, including linseed oil and beeswax. NePalo products can be shipped anywhere in the continental US.

FSC-Certified Cabinetry

Silver Walker Studios
P.O. Box 70667
Richmond, CA 94807

Phone: 510-215-1266
www.silverwalker.com

Silver Walker Studios provides custom-designed cabinetry in a variety of styles and finishes using only FSC-certified wood. The products use only low-VOC glues and finishes and are free of added formaldehyde.

FSC-Certified Cabinetry

Young Furniture Mfg., Inc.
35 River Rd.
Bow, NH 03225

Phone: 603-224-8830
www.youngfurnituremfg.com

Young Furniture manufactures unfinished FSC-certified eastern white pine, soft maple, and poplar cabinets, entertainment centers, and built-ins for kitchens, bathrooms, and living rooms. Solid wood backs and drawer bottoms can be used in place of plywood upon request. All cabinets are manufactured from domestic wood harvested and processed within a 500-mile radius of the manufacturing facility. Panels are joined with Franklin Adhesives Multibond 2000, a low-VOC (4.44 g/l) adhesive with no added formaldehyde. Direct jobsite delivery is available throughout the northeast U.S., with delivery to other regions upon special request.

Furniture and Kitchen Cabinetry from Urban Trees

CitiLog
P.O. Box 685
Pittstown, NJ 08867

Toll-free: 877-248-9564
Phone: 908-735-8871
www.citilogs.com

CitiLog™, also known as D. Stubby Warmbold, is SmartWood-certified for the harvesting of trees in urban areas of New Jersey and Pennsylvania. Wood is sent by rail to Amish craftsmen in central Pennsylvania who take extra care to turn the lesser graded wood into higher quality products such as flooring, lumber, custom architectural millwork, furniture, and kitchen cabinets. Where appropriate, wood is now harvested using horses.

Green Leaf Cabinetry

Green Leaf Cabinetry, LLC
PO. Box 110875
Cleveland, OH 44111

Toll-free: 877-422-2463
www.greenleafcabinetry.com

Cabinet King's Green Leaf series uses PrimeBoard® agrifiber particleboard (made from agricultural residue fibers and a formaldehyde-free binder) for sides, tops, bottoms, backs, shelving, and drawer bottoms, and FSC-certified wood for frames and drawers (sides and backs). Finishes are either Safecoat® Acrylacq or PrimeBoard's all-paper-based melamine. Forbo Marmoleum® will also soon be available as a countertop option. Adhesives are water-based. Cabinet King is also a dealer for cabinets made by other companies, as well as a line of green building products including PrimeBoard, Marmoleum, Safecoat finishes, Titebond® solvent-free construction adhesive, and Bonded Logic recycled-cotton insulation.

Neil Kelly Naturals Collection

Neil Kelly Cabinets
2636 N.W. 26th Ave.
Ste. 200
Portland, OR 97210

Phone: 503-335-9207
www.neilkellycabinets.
com

The Neil Kelly "Naturals Collection" is an award-winning cabinet line that features formaldehyde-free wheatboard case material, low-VOC finishes, and optional FSC-certified lumber doors/drawers. Unlimited customization and virtually any desired upgrade are available.

Reclaimed-Wood Building Products

Aged Woods / Yesteryear Floorworks Company
2331 E Market St, Ste 6
York, PA 17402

Toll-free: 800-233-9307
Phone: 717-840-0330
www.agedwoods.com

Aged Woods® / Yesteryear Floorworks Company is a full-service mill that uses reclaimed, kiln-dried wood to produce flooring, stair parts, moldings, cabinetry, and paneling. They salvage their materials from barns that are typically between 75 and 200 years old. Available species include American chestnut, longleaf heart pine, maple, cherry, walnut, hemlock, hickory, poplar, pine, and oak. Most of the flooring is 3/4" tongue-and-groove and of random widths and lengths within given ranges. Matching stair parts are available in conjunction with flooring orders.

Schiffini Eco Panel Cabinets

Schiffini USA Sales
51 Locust Ave.
Ste. 201
New Canaan, CT 06840

Phone: 203-966-3234
www.schiffini.it

Designer-kitchen manufacturer Schiffini is a member of the Consorzio Pannello Ecologico, a group of companies employing panels made from FSC-certified, 100% post-consumer recycled wood. The reclaimed wood travels primarily by rail from a network of 30 European collection centers to the manufacturing facility in Italy. Formaldehyde emissions from the UF resin achieve European class E1 (releasing =0.13 mg/m3 air). Schiffini uses these panels for most of their wall-mount and base cabinets; the panels are mechanically fastened, without glue. Many of Schiffini's designs use facing components made from virgin aluminum, which has high embodied energy; those lines are not specified here.

Wheatboard Cabinets

CitiLog
P.O. Box 685
Pittstown, NJ 08867

Toll-free: 877-248-9564
Phone: 908-735-8871
www.citilogs.com

CitiLog™ offers cabinets made with formaldehyde-free wheatboard cores veneered in North American hardwoods or South American tropical woods, both FSC-certified. Wheatboard is similar to MDF and wood particleboard but is made with wheat stems left over after grain harvesting. These cabinets can be custom-manufactured to meet particular specifications. CitiLog also offers wheatboard millwork and doors.

Wheatcore Doors and Cabinets

Humabuilt Healthy Building Solutions
2305-C Ashland St. #511
Ashland, OR 97520

Phone: 541-488-0931
www.humabuilt.com

Humabuilt Wheatcore Doors are available in a wide variety of styles, sizes, wood-veneer species, and paint-grade finishes. The core is made from chopped wheat straw bound with waterproof, nonformaldehyle, MDI binder. These doors contain 85% rapidly renewable resource by volume. Lag-bolt construction at the door edges strengthens the styles and rails. Ultra-low-VOC water-based adhesives are used for joining components and veneers. The competitively priced doors have a lifetime warranty to the original owner and a 5-year commercial warranty. Humabuilt Wheatcore production cabinets are available in a wide variety of styles, sizes, and wood-veneer species. These production cabinets are KCMA certified.

Storage Shelving

Products listed here have recycled content, low-VOC coatings, or other green features.

Dura-Shelf, Dunnage Rack, and Modular-Kart

Structural Plastics Corp.
3401 Chief Dr.
Holly, MI 48442

Toll-free: 800-523-6899
Phone: 810-953-9400
www.plastictreegrates.com

Structural Plastics specializes in recycled HDPE plastic products for commercial and industrial shelving and storage. Dura-Shelf™ and Dunnage Rack™ are bulk-storage and display-shelving systems. Modular-Kart™ is a similar product with wheels in the form of a multilevel mobile cart. The manufacturer has certified the following recycled-content levels (by weight): total recovered material 82% typical, 82% guaranteed.

Tackboards

Cork is the traditional, natural solution for vertical tackable surfaces, and it remains an excellent green option. Cork is obtained from the outer bark of the cork oak tree (Quercus suber). After harvesting, the bark regenerates and can be harvested again in about 10 years. The substrate for some tackboards is made from recycled paper and paraffin. Products listed here are made with natural cork.

Bulletin Board

Forbo Linoleum, Inc.
2 Maplewood Dr., Humboldt Industrial Park
P.O. Box 667
Hazleton, PA 18201

Toll-free: 800-842-7839
Phone: 570-459-0771
www.forboflooringNA.com

Bulletin Board is a colored, 1/4"-thick, granulated linoleum-cork composite product sold in full-size sheets for use as tack panels, or as a decorative finish for furniture, doors, or moveable partitions. Bulletin Board is durable, washable, low-glare, and will not warp or crumble. It is available in 12 solid colors.

Dodge Cork Rolls and Sheets

ECORE International
715 Fountain Ave.
Lancaster, PA 17601

Toll-free: 866-883-7780
Phone: 717-295-3400
www.ecoreintl.com

Dodge Cork comes in 36" x 36" and 28" x 50" sheets and 36", 42" or 48"-wide rolls. Roll thickness available from 1/32" to 1/4". Sheet thickness available from 1/32" to 1"

Tub and Shower Doors

Products listed here have high recycled content and other environmental attributes.

UltraGlas

UltraGlas, Inc.
9200 Gazette Ave.
Chatsworth, CA 91311

Toll-free: 800-777-2332
Phone: 818-772-7744
www.ultraglas.com

UltraGlas® is sculpted/embossed, molded architectural glass with 15-30% recycled-glass (cullet) content. A variety of decorative textures,

designs, and patterns are available with varying levels of translucency. If so specified, UltraGlas can be made from 100% recycled glass, subject to its availability.

Window Shades

Window shades, blinds, and other treatments can control daylight penetration and significantly reduce heat loss or heat gain through windows. In commercial buildings, engineered window shading installations can be part of an integrated design strategy addressing glare, heat gain, and solar penetration. In residential buildings, insulating window blinds and quilts may be appropriate retrofits for older, leaky windows, when window replacement can't be justified. In new construction or when replacement can be justified, installing high-performance windows is usually a better option than investing in energy-conserving blinds or shades.

Duette Window Shades

Hunter Douglas Window Covering
1 Duette Way
Broomfield, CO 80020

Toll-free: 800-789-0331
Phone: 303-466-1848
www.hunterdouglas.com

Duette shades from Hunter Douglas offer significantly better energy performance than standard shades because of their unique accordion-fold design. When lowered, the fabric opens up providing pockets of trapped air. The Duette Architella line is a honeycomb-within-a-honeycomb design that creates multiple pockets of insulating trapped air, providing improved noise reduction and thermal resistance--up to R-7.7--for the 1.25-inch opaque version, which includes a reflective layer to boost energy performance.

Earthshade Natural Fiber Window Treatments

Earthshade Natural Window Fashions
P.O. Box 1003
Great Barrington, MA 01230

Toll-free: 866-528-5443
www.earthshade.com

Made from mostly wildcrafted grasses and reeds grown without the use of fertilizers or pesticides, Earthshade custom window treatments are handwoven in Mexico and assembled in Texas. The materials are handharvested, sundried, and if treated at all, bathed in hydrogen peroxide to meet import regulations. Glues are water-based, and the only finishes are a water-based stain on one pattern (others are baked to achieve their color) and an optional water-based flame retardant for commercial spaces. Nylon cords are used to operate the shades though the company is currently testing hemp as a replacement. Earthshade offers a comprehensive collection of PVC-, urea-formaldehyde-, and halogen-free fabrics for Spring, Clutch, or motorized roler shades. Earthshade natural window treatments are available in 10 operating styles and come with the industry standard lifetime limited warranty making them suitable for both contract and residential applications.

Handwoven Collection

Hartmann & Forbes
P.O. Box 1149
Tualatin, OR 97062

Toll-free: 888-582-8780
Phone: 503-692-9313
www.hfshades.com

Hartmann & Forbes produces handwoven window coverings made from natural materials, such as reeds, grasses, bamboos, and cotton string. The PapyrusWeave™ line includes woven roman shades, draperies, rollershades, and a panelscreen that operates on a track. There is no glue used in the weave; non-chlorine polyvinyl acetate (PVA) glue is used in assembly of the finished product. Hartmann&Forbes also has a Take-Back Initiative™ to collect and recycle used shades.

Sailshade Window Coverings

Sailshade/Cloth Construction
P.O. Box 3935
Westport, MA 02790

Phone: 508-677-3160
www.sailshadeyourhome.com

Sailshade® multilayer window coverings are estimated by the manufacturer to provide R-8 insulating values in combination with a double-glazed window. When not in use, they fold compactly in a "self-creating valance" to maximize solar gain. The standard face fabric is minimally processed 100% cotton twill (washed, but no chemical finishes); 100% hemp linen is an available option, or customer's own material may be supplied. The blackout lining is non-PVC (Roc-lon), and an interior layer of Reflectix® insulation is standard.

Shading Solutions

Lutron Electronics Co., Inc.
7200 Suter Rd.
Coopersburg, PA 18036

Toll-free: 888-588-7661
Phone: 610-282-3800
www.lutron.com

Lutron offers manual and motorized shading systems for residential and commercial interiors. A number of PVC- and halogen-free fabrics—made with various combinations of fiberglass, acrylic, cotton, and polyester—are available. Openness ranges from blackout to 10 percent, in widths from 69 to 92 inches. Lutron shading systems are designed for easy integration with electric lighting controls from the same company.

Warm Window Insulated Shade System

The Warm Company
5529 186th Place SW
Lynnwood, WA 98037

Phone: 425-248-2424
www.warmcompany.com

The Warm Window Insulated Shade System (previously Window Quilt) is an insulating blind for windows. Blinds roll up at the top of the window, and the edges fit into a track, making the blind fairly airtight. The product makes the most sense for older windows; with new construction or when windows are being replaced, investing in super-high-performance windows generally makes more sense. The Warm Company finalized the acquisition of Window Quilt®, a Vermont company, in early 2006.

Warm Windows

Cozy Curtains
4295 Duncan Dr.
Missoula, MT 59802

Toll-free: 800-342-9955
www.cozycurtains.com

Warm Windows® is a custom-made insulating Roman-shade system which folds above the window when not in use. The shades are made up of 4 layers: High Density Dacron Holofil II®, a polyethylene moisture vapor barrier, metalized Mylar®, and the customer's choice of fabric. The company reports an R-value of 7.69 for installations over single-pane and 8.69 over double-pane windows. Shades attach to a board over the window frame with Velcro® and are pulled up and down with a cord. Magnetic strips around the frame and concealed within the shade provide a magnetically tight seal. Cozy Curtains also offers individual components for sale for do-it-yourselfers.

This Space is Available for Your Notes

Renewable Energy

Renewable energy sources offer environmentally attractive alternatives to fossil fuels and nuclear power. Although no energy system can claim to be 100% pollution free, renewables are orders of magnitude better than our conventional energy systems. The U.S. Department of Energy estimates that the annual influx of accessible renewable resources in the U.S. is more than 200 times the total amount of energy used. Technologies for converting these energy sources into electricity or usable heat are improving in efficiency and dropping in price.

The simplest way to utilize renewable energy in buildings is with climate-responsive design—passive solar heating in winter, summertime cooling with natural ventilation, and daylighting.

The field of building-integrated photovoltaics (BIPV) is expanding dramatically, with enormous arrays of PV panels on large, institutional buildings and smaller arrays integrated into individual homes. These typically come in the form of panels that can be wall- or roof-mounted, though PV panels that serve a dual role as glazing and power production are now also available. Solar-domestic hot water systems have quick paybacks in climates where sophisticated freeze-control systems aren't needed.

In colder climates the paybacks are longer, but such systems can still be a very worthwhile investment.

While large-scale hydroelectric facilities are associated with some significant environmental problems (most notably the displacement of humans and other species, and the interruption of fish migration), carefully sited small-scale hydropower may be a good option.

The Union of Concerned Scientists estimates that wind power could supply one-fifth of U.S. electricity demand. Small, home-based wind machines range in output from 250 watts to 10 kilowatts (compared to utility-sized wind turbines can product more than 750 kilowatts of power).

One issue affecting many renewable energy sources is that their power production varies with the time of day and season. In some cases, the peak production actually matches peak demand—for example, photovoltaic systems generate the most electricity on hot days, when cooling loads are highest. In other cases, different forms of energy storage are needed to match the energy demand with energy production.

Alternative Energy Balance of Systems Components

Inverters convert the direct-current (DC) power produced by the renewable energy system into alternating-current (AC) power needed for most conventional appliances or for feeding site-generated electricity into the power grid. Other power-conditioning equipment, controllers, batteries, and mounting equipment are also included here.

Fronius Grid-Tied PV Inverters

Fronius USA LLC
10421, Ste. 1100
Solar Electronics Division
Brighton, MI 48116

Phone: 810-220-4414
www.fronius-USA.com

Fronius manufactures high-efficiency, lightweight, DC-to-AC inverters for residential-scale PV power applications. Most are used for grid-connected applications. The IG line of products has a wide DC-voltage range (150-450 V), and an LCD data display, with a maximum output power ranging from 2.0 to 5.1 kW. The Fronius USA Solar Electronics Division is a branch of the German company Fronius International GmbH.

GE Solar Systems and Modules

GE Energy
231 Lake Dr.
Newark, DE 19702

Toll-free: 866-750-3150
www.gepower.com

GE offers a range of solar electric power systems for residential, commercial, and industrial applications as well as polycrystal PV modules ranging from 66 watts to 200 watts. Grid-tied, remote, or building integrated systems for new construction or retrofit applications are available. In 2004 GE purchased Astropower, thus entering the photovoltaics industry.

GridPoint Connect Backup PV System

GridPoint Inc.
2020 K Street NW
Ste. 550
Washington, DC 20006

Phone: 202-903-2100
www.gridpoint.com

GridPoint Connect provides the balance-of-system (everything but the solar panel array) for a grid-connected PV backup power system. Gridpoint Connect combines the electronics, inverter, charge controllers, recyclable batteries, computer, and other needed components, in a single 'plug-and-play' device. This device connects to the main circuit breaker panel, PV array, communication line, and secure load panel (on which critical circuits are placed). The GridPoint Connect system ensures batteries are fully charged and supplies local power needs, feeding excess power to the grid. If the grid is down, the Connect system will power critical loads from the solar array and/or battery pack.

Inverters

Xantrex Technology
5916 195th St. NE
Arlington, WA 98223

Toll-free: 888-800-1010
Phone: 360-435-8826
www.xantrex.com

Xantrex Technology, formerly Trace Engineering, manufactures energy-efficient DC-to-AC inverters for residential, commercial, mobile, remote, and emergency applications. These are the most widely used inverters for PV and wind power systems. Inverters specially designed for feeding power into the electric grid are available.

Outback Power System Components

OutBack Power Systems
19009 62nd Ave. NE
Arlington, WA 98223

Phone: 360-435-6030
www.outbackpower.com

Outback Power Systems provides balance-of-system components including inverters, solar charge controllers, communication managers, and a range of other components and accessories for stand-alone, grid-tied, or backup photovoltaic power systems. Outback's FLEXware integration hardware allows horizontal or vertical mounting orientations for locations with limited wall space and can accommodate a wide range of power system sizes.

PV Controllers

Solar Converters Inc.
558 Massey Road, Unit 1
Guelph, ON N1K 1B4 Canada

Phone: 519-824-5272
www.solarconverters.com

Solar Converters Inc. is a designer and manufacturer of highly efficient power control products for the renewable energy field. Included among the products the company has developed are Linear Current Boosters, Battery Equalizers, Power Tracker™ charge controllers with Maximum Power Point Tracking (MPPT), Cathodic Protection Controllers, Generator Starters, Battery Desulphators, Constant Voltage Pump Drivers, Voltage Controlled Switches, Solar Lighting Controllers, DC-DC Converters, and more.

Smart Power M-Series Solar Power Conversion

Beacon Power Corporation
65 Middlesex Rd.
Tyngsboro, MA 01879

Toll-free: 888-938-9112
Phone: 978-694-9121
www.beaconpower.com

Beacon Power Corporation introduced the Smart Power line of inverters in 2003, with inverter technology acquired from Advanced Energy, Inc. (previously of Wilton, New Hampshire). The M-Series is a 4000- or 5000-watt grid connected solar inverter capable of operating during grid outages, providing true sine wave backup power to critical loads. The product includes the charge controller, inverter and switchgear all in one outdoor-rated enclosure. The company claims 90% efficiency at full output and 93% efficiency at 50% output.

Solar Controllers

Heliotrope PV, LLC
3766 Kathryn Ave. Unit C
P.O. Box 696
Springfield, OR 97477

Phone: 541-726-1091
www.heliotrope-pv.com

Heliotrope PV manufacturers electronic charge controllers for PV systems. Though marketed to recreational vehicle users, they are appropriate for any small PV system.

Solaris 3500XP

Alpha Technologies, Inc.
3767 Alpha Way
Bellingham, WA 98226

Phone: 360-647-2360

The Solaris 3500XP system is an integrated 3.5 kW inverter and uninterruptible power supply (UPS) for grid-tied and off-grid photovoltaic applications. The system has a CEC rated efficiency of 91% and the company claims the system maintains its rated output over an operating temperature range of -20 to 50 degrees C. The system is designed to support either 120/240 or 208 VAC output and can include an optional 48 volt DC input for use with a DC generator or additional batteries.

Solectria Grid-Tied PV Inverters

Solectria Renewables LLC
360 Merrimack St.
Building 9, 2nd Fl.
Lawrence, MA 01843

Phone: 978-683-9700
www.solren.com

Solectria manufactures a line of high-efficiency DC-to-AC inverters for residential and commercial PV power applications, especially grid-connected systems. The products cover systems from 12-500kW and can include an optional internet-connected data logger and monitoring system. Solectria also manufactures inverters for connected or 'mini-grid' distributed generation with input from fuel cells, batteries, ICE, or heat engines. Solectria also provides engineering services and custom products for any 1-500kW distributed generation system.

Steca Solar Charge Controllers

SunWize Technologies
1155 Flatbush Rd.
Kingston, NY 12401

Toll-free: 800-817-6527
Phone: 845-336-0146
www.sunwize.com

SunWize distributes Steca electronic charge controllers for PV systems. The Sunwize Steca controller is a self-learning controller that uses an advanced control algorithm combining battery temperature, battery voltage, and load discharge rate to determine the true battery state of charge(SOC), automatically adjusting for the capacity and age of the battery.

SunEarth Solar Equipment

SunEarth, Inc.
8425 Almeria Ave.
Fontana, CA 92335

Phone: 909-434-3100
www.sunearthinc.com

SunEarth, Inc., a manufacturer of solar water-heating equipment since 1978, produces flat-plate solar collectors, ICS and thermosiphon water-heating systems, and ancillary components including residential and commercial racking systems for both solar water heating and PV systems.

Sunny Boy Inverters

SMA America, Inc.
12438 Loma Rica Dr.
Grass Valley, CA 95945

Phone: 530-273-4895
www.sma-america.com

SMA America offers 2,500-, 1,800-, and 700-watt inverters designed for residential-scale photovoltaic applications. These German-made inverters carry a 5-year warranty and are being specified by some of the leading PV system designers today. The company also offers a larger, 125 kW inverter, as well as PV control and monitoring equipment.

UniRac PV Mounting Systems

UniRac, Inc.
1411 Broadway Blvd. NE
Albuquerque, NM 87102

Phone: 505-242-6411
www.unirac.com

UniRac produces systems for mounting PV modules. SolarMount® is a system of components for flat and tilted roofs. SolarMount/S-5! is designed for easy installation on standing-seam metal roofs. SunFrame offers building integration, a low-profile and a choice of finishes. PoleTops are ground mounting systems. U-LA is for arrays of 3-kW or more. UniRac recycles all solid waste and purchases recycled materials when available, including 20-25% post-consumer recycled aluminum and 75% recycled steel. In addition, most shipping materials are salvaged or have recycled-content.

Batteries for Alternative Energy Systems

Lead-acid batteries designed for use in solar applications are included here because of their application. Lead is a toxic heavy metal and should be recycled.

Deep-Cycle, Lead-Acid Batteries

Surrette Battery Company Limited
1 Station Rd.
P.O. Box 2020
Springhill, NS B0M 1X0 Canada

Toll-free: 800-681-9914
Phone: 902-597-3767
www.surrette.com

Surrette Battery Company Limited manufactures specialty batteries. The deep-cycle, lead-acid batteries for solar applications feature dual containers to withstand rough handling and prevent acid leakage. These batteries have a ten-year warranty, and an expected life of 15 years. Surrette is the parent company of the Rolls Battery Company in the U.S.

GridPoint Connect Backup PV System

GridPoint Inc.
2020 K Street NW
Ste. 550
Washington, DC 20006

Phone: 202-903-2100
www.gridpoint.com

GridPoint Connect provides the balance-of-system (everything but the solar panel array) for a grid-connected PV backup power system. Gridpoint Connect combines the electronics, inverter, charge controllers, recyclable batteries, computer, and other needed components, in a single 'plug-and-play' device. This device connects to the main circuit breaker panel, PV array, communication line, and secure load panel (on which critical circuits are placed). The GridPoint Connect system ensures batteries are fully charged and supplies local power needs, feeding excess power to the grid. If the grid is down, the Connect system will power critical loads from the solar array and/ or battery pack.

Solaris 3500XP

Alpha Technologies, Inc.
3767 Alpha Way
Bellingham, WA 98226

Phone: 360-647-2360

The Solaris 3500XP system is an integrated 3.5 kW inverter and uninterruptible power supply (UPS) for grid-tied and off-grid photovoltaic applications. The system has a CEC rated efficiency of 91% and the company claims the system maintains its rated output over an operating temperature range of -20 to 50 degrees C. The system is designed to support either 120/240 or 208 VAC output and can include an optional 48 volt DC input for use with a DC generator or additional batteries.

Building Integrated Photovoltaic Roofing

Photovoltaics (PV) enable the direct conversion of sunlight into electricity. Some PV modules are integrated into building components, such as roofing and wall glazings—these are often referred to as building-integrated photovoltaics (BIPV).

Sunslates

Atlantis Energy Systems, Inc.
4517 Harlin Dr.
Sacramento, CA 95826

Phone: 916-438-2930
www.atlantisenergy.org

Atlantis Energy Systems produces Sunslates®, which serve as both a roofing product and a solar-electric power source. Sunslates are fiber-cement shingles into which PV cells have been laminated. Each shingle has a plug-in wiring connection.

UNI-SOLAR PV Shingles and Standing Seam Panels

United Solar Ovonic LLC
3800 Lapeer Rd.
Auburn Hills, MI 48326

Toll-free: 800-843-3892
Phone: 248-475-0100
www.uni-solar.com

Uni-Solar Ovonic LLC PV Shingles and Standing Seam Roofing Panels are installed much like conventional roofing products. They generate electricity while protecting the structure from weather. PV Shingles, measuring 86.4" x 12" with 7 tabs, are interspersed among conventional 3-tab shingles. Standing Seam Panels are available for laminating onto conventional roofing or as a PV-integrated, standing-seam product. Lead wires from each shingle or panel enter the structure through drilled holes in the roof decking. Uni-Solar roofing products use triple-junction amorphous silicon technology.

Masonry Fireplaces

Burning wood creates significant pollution. Emissions of particulates, carbon monoxide, VOCs, and methane are significantly greater from wood stoves than from any other common heating fuel. However, when wood is locally available and can be harvested sustainably, it has no net impact on global warming—because the carbon emissions from combustion are more than compensated for by growing trees. Thus, if wood is burned in a manner that minimizes pollution, it can be a good fuel choice. Products listed here have superior burning efficiencies and reduced particulate emissions in comparison even the best wood stoves. The high thermal mass of masonry heaters and biomass-fueled boiler systems can more effectively capture, store, and release heat over time. The downside of a high-mass masonry heater is that the heat of a freshly lit fire may not be felt in the living space until several hours later. In passive solar homes this may make temperature regulation difficult.

Moberg Fireplaces

Moberg Fireplaces, Inc.
Cellar Building
1124 N.W. Couch St. Ste. 300
Portland, OR 97209

Phone: 503-227-0547
www.mobergfireplaces.com

FireSpaces is a dealer and manufacturer of masonry fireplaces. They also manufacture the masonry Moberg MRC and the Modern Rumford Masonry Fireplace Kit.

Temp-Cast Enviroheat Masonry Heater Kits

Temp-Cast
3409 Yonge St.
P.O. Box 94059
Toronto, ON M4N 3R1 Canada

Toll-free: 800-561-8594
Phone: 416-322-5197
www.tempcast.com

Temp-Cast is a modular masonry heater core kit featuring corner, 'see through,' and bake-oven models. Temp-Cast provides manuals detailing appropriate chimney construction with each masonry heater kit. Masonry materials for the chimney and the heater's exterior are sourced separately.

Tulikivi

Tulikivi U.S., Inc.
P.O. Box 7547
Charlottesville, VA 22906

Toll-free: 800-843-3473
www.tulikivi.com

Tulikivi's masonry heaters, available in over 25 different models, are made from soapstone quarried in Finland. Tulikivi masonry heaters produce a hot, clean-burning fire and efficiently transfer the fire's heat to the living space.

Packaged Solar Heating Equipment

These "plug-and-play" systems include all of the necessary components for solar thermal systems. A wide range of technologies are employed for solar water heating, including integral-collector storage (ICS) systems, evacuated-tube collector systems, and flat-plate collector systems.

Architectural Solar-Hydronic System

Dawn Solar Systems, Inc.
183 Route 125, Ste. A-7
Brentwood, NH 03833

Toll-free: 866-338-2018
Phone: 603-642-7899
www.dawnsolar.com

The Dawn Solar System® uses looped hydronic tubing concealed in a one-inch layer between the roof or wall sheathing and the exterior finish material to capture solar heat. The collector system has a 25-year warranty and can be designed as an integrated system to produce heated air, water, and electricity from the same roof or wall area. The system is pre-engineered for each application. In cold climates, a closed-loop glycol system is recommended. The system qualifies for government energy incentives.

CopperSun

Sun Systems, Inc.
2030 W. Pinnacle Peak Rd.
Phoenix, AZ 85027

Toll-free: 800-777-6657
Phone: 623-869-7652
www.sunsystemsinc.com

Sun Systems manufactures the CopperSun™ integral collector storage (ICS) solar water heater. The unit is designed for integration into a roof, with flush mounting and a flashing kit for roofing right up to the textured-glass cover plate. Systems are available with either a 40- or 50-gallon capacity. The company is primarily pursuing the new-home builder market in the Sun Belt, as the CopperSun system is not appropriate for heavy-freeze climates.

ECO-Nomad

Architectural & Community Planning Inc.
261 Albany St.
Winnipeg, MB R3G 2A9 Canada

Phone: 204-831-0216
www.economad.com

The ECO-Nomad™ combined mechanical utility container provides utility services to off-grid locations by creating a self-contained, integrated micro-infrastructure, including potable water storage and purification, biological wastewater treatment, water and space heating, electrical supply, and fire protection. All functions can be remotely monitored. The portable 8' x 8' x 16' utility container can be transported by road, rail, water, or air. Designed for extreme winter conditions, uses include remote residential, tourism, or commercial facilities; temporary mining or logging camps; disaster relief; and remote airports and weather stations.

Flat-Plate Water Heating Systems

ACR Solar International Corporation
5840 Gibbons Dr., Ste. G
Carmichael, CA 95608

Phone: 916-481-7200
www.solarroofs.com

The Skylite 10-01 is a lightweight, easy-to-ship solar water heater that weighs only 19 pounds. SolarRoof also offers offers a number of closed- and open-loop kits with DC or AC pumps and all the fittings, including systems for hard freeze climates. The company is known for its Fireball solar water heating products.

Gobi Solar Collectors and Helio-Pak Solar Water Heater

Heliodyne, Inc.
4910 Seaport Ave.
Richmond, CA 94804

Phone: 510-237-9614
www.heliodyne.com

Heliodyne is a manufacturer of flat-plate solar collectors and heat-transfer systems for residential and commercial water heating.

Renewable Energy Equipment

Solar Energy, Inc.
5191 Shawland Rd.
Jacksonville, FL 32254

Phone: 904-786-6600
www.solarenergy.com

Solar Energy Inc. (SEI) is a manufacturer and distributor of a variety of solar water-heating systems for commercial or residential applications. The turnkey, drainback SUN HoM system has one or more roof-integrated flat-plate solar collectors and uses a controller and pump to circulate a heat-transfer fluid. When the pump shuts off, water drains to an insulated reservoir to protect from freezing. Solar Energy also sells other alternative energy systems including PV and wind power.

Solahart Solar Water Heating Systems

Rheem Water Heating
101 Bell Rd.
Montgomery, AL 36117

Phone: 334-260-1586
www.rheem.com

Solahart's Free Heat series is a closed-circuit thermosiphoning solar water-heating system utilizing a heat-transfer fluid that circulates around a jacketed water tank. The Free Heat series comes with a 10-year warranty in a range of tank sizes and panel configurations. It is designed for use in virtually any climate. Other models, also available in various sizes, have specific design criteria—including the J series for areas with medium to good solar radiation, poor water quality, or frost conditions; the KF series for low to medium solar radiation, poor water quality, or frost or snow conditions; and the L series for frost-free areas with medium to high solar radiation and relatively clean water supplies. The J and KF series have a five-year warranty. The L series has a 10 year warranty. Solahart is a division of Rheem Water Heating.

Solar Collectors

Integrated Solar LLC
2030 W. Pinnacle Peak Rd.
Phoenix, AZ 85027

Toll-free: 800-927-2326
Phone: 805-928-1881
http://radcosolar.com/about.html

Integrated Solar LLC manufactures Radco glazed flat-plate solar collectors and Radco complete drainback solar water-heating systems for areas with freezing weather conditions. The company also produces a line of Radco unglazed solar pool-heating systems.

Solar Collectors

R&R Services Solar Supply
922 Austin Ln., Bldg. D
Honolulu, HI 96817

Phone: 808-842-0011

R&R Services Solar Supply is a manufacturer of copper-tube/absorber flat-plate collectors. The company packages solar water-heating systems for sale throughout Hawaii.

Solar Water Heating

EnerWorks Inc.
252 Hamilton Crescent
P.O. Box 9
Dorchester, ON N0L 1G0 Canada

Phone: 519-268-6500
www.enerworks.com

The Solar Hot Water Appliances from EnerWorks provide auxiliary hot water heating for washing, cooking, and space conditioning. These systems utilize low-flow, natural convection for long-term reliability, reduced first cost, and lower operating cost. The system consists of one or more flat-plate solar collector panels, fluid transfer lines, a stainless steel heat transfer module (designed to fit on any new or existing electric storage-type water heater), and a controller. The manufacturer claims average energy savings of 50% for full-year operation in southern Ontario and Northern U.S., and up to 100% for seasonal installations.

Solar Water-Heating Systems

SCHÜCO, LP
240 Pane Rd.
Newington, CT 06111

Toll-free: 877-472-4826
Phone: 860-666-0505
www.schuco-usa.com

Schüco manufactures solar water-heating systems with a controller and pump to circulate a heat-transfer fluid. The system allows for air-purging without accessing the panels. Panels have anodized aluminum hardware and frames. The Solar Thermal Slim Line package is the basic model with two installation options for pitched roofs. The Premium Line has higher system efficiency and a wide range of frame colors and installation options. Schüco also offers custom systems for large installations, apartment buildings, and swimming pools. These products are manufactured in Germany.

Solar Water-Heating Systems

Thermo Dynamics Ltd.
101 Frazee Ave.
Dartmouth, NS B3B-1Z4 Canada

Phone: 902-468-1001
www.thermo-dynamics.com

Thermo Dynamics manufactures a full range of solar water-heating systems with liquid flat-plate, glazed collectors with fused copper tubing and aluminum absorbers. The company also produces the Solar Pump™—a PV-powered pump—and a thermosiphoning heat exchanger.

SUN HoM Solar Hot Water System

Solar Energy, Inc.
5191 Shawland Rd.
Jacksonville, FL 32254

Phone: 904-786-6600
www.solarenergy.com

SUN HoM DHW is a solar water heating system appropriate for all climates. The active-indirect, drainback system uses a propylene glycol mixture (or plain water in non-freezing climates) in the collector panels, and transfers the heat from that fluid to the domestic water using a heat exchanger. When the sun isn't out, the system shuts down. Unlike thermosiphoning systems, this one uses small electric pumps; the hot water storage tanks (available in 80 or 120 gallon sizes) don't need to be above, or even particularly near, the collector panels. The system lends itself well to retrofit applications.

SunChiller

Sun Chiller
220 S. Kenwood St., Ste. 305
Glendale, CA 91205-1671

Phone: 818-240-4500
www.sunchiller.com

The SunChiller provides air cooling as a primary output, with space and water heating also possible. The system uses vacuum-tube heat-pipe solar thermal collectors to heat water, which drives an absorption chiller to provide cooling. Water serves as the "refrigerant," avoiding the use of ozone-depleting compounds. A SunChiller can be used in a hybrid system to provide space heating and water heating in addition to absorption cooling. The system can be configured to provide solar-powered absorption cooling during electrical peak hours, with a more conventional electric chiller taking over during lower-cost off-peak hours. The system combines vacuum-tube solar-thermal collectors, an insulated storage tank, a single-effect water-heated absorption chiller, a cooling tower, an energy management system, and air handler. It is available as an integrated system for commercial buildings requiring air conditioning capacity of at least 10 tons.

SunCoil

Taylor Munro Energy Systems Inc.
11-7157 Honeyman St.
Delta, BC V4G 1E2 Canada

Phone: 604-946-4433
www.taylormunro.com

The SunCoil from Taylor Munro Energy Systems is an active solar water heating system for residential or commercial installations. According to the manufacturer, residential SunCoil systems in temperate climates are typically designed to meet 50-60% of the total annual hot water demand, with up to 100% provided during peak summer performance and more supplemental heat needed during the rest of the year. In tropical climates, the SunCoil can provide 80-100% of the hot water demand. Multiple panels can be used to provide institutional water heating for showers and other domestic use, as well as for pools, hatcheries, and process water. The SunCoil system can also be designed for combined water and space heating.

SunEarth Solar Equipment

SunEarth, Inc.
8425 Almeria Ave.
Fontana, CA 92335

Phone: 909-434-3100
www.sunearthinc.com

SunEarth, Inc., a manufacturer of solar water-heating equipment since 1978, produces flat-plate solar collectors, ICS and thermosiphon water-heating systems, and ancillary components including residential and commercial racking systems for both solar water heating and PV systems.

Sunwell

Taylor Munro Energy Systems Inc.
11-7157 Honeyman St.
Delta, BC V4G 1E2 Canada

Phone: 604-946-4433
www.taylormunro.com

The Sunwell three-season batch (or integral collector storage – ICS) solar water heater from Taylor Munro Energy Systems consists of a stainless steel tank and a parabolic reflector inside an insulated, glazed housing. It is most commonly used as a preheater for a conventional water heater. It runs on line water pressure; no additional pump, tank, or heat exchanger is required. According to the manufacturer, the system can provide up to 100% of a family's water heating energy load in non-freezing climates and up to 40% in freezing climates. The unit should not be used during freezing seasons.

Winston Series CPC Collector

Solargenix Energy, LLC
2101-115 Westinghouse Blvd.
Raleigh, NC 27604

Phone: 919-871-0423
www.solargenix.com

The Winston Series CPC Collector from Solargenix Energy is a residential and commercial solar water-heating system. The basic system is comprised of 12 small compound parabolic collectors (CPC) which focus light onto absorber tubes through which heat-transfer fluid is piped. One to three collectors are commonly used for residential solar water-heating systems, depending on the size of the hot water storage tank. A roof-integrated thermosiphoning configuration is possible with new construction. The collectors carry a 10-year warranty. The system's heat exchanger, SOLPAC, is also available as a separate item. Coupled with one or more solar collectors, it prepackages the components needed to convert existing electric or gas water heaters into solar water-heating systems.

Photovoltaic Collectors

Photovoltaics (PV) enable the direct conversion of sunlight into electricity. Some PV modules are integrated into building components, such as roofing and wall glazings—these are often referred to as building-integrated photovoltaics (BIPV). Packaged Solar Equipment includes 'plug-and-play' systems that include all of the necessary components.

Blue Link Photovoltaic Systems

Solar Market
25 Limerick Rd.
Arundel, ME 04046

Toll-free: 877-785-0088
www.solarmarket.com

The Blue Link 480 grid-connected photovoltaic system from Solar Market™ is a complete, ground-mounted, plug-and-play unit with a rated power production of 480 watts DC. A steel mounting rack supports the solar panels, inverter, and electrical disconnects; a 25' cable for the intertie is included. Installation takes about 30 minutes. A licensed electrician may be required to connect the unit into a home's load center; check with the local electric utility for any additional requirements or restrictions. The array measures 5' x 8'; the system weighs 140 pounds. The PV panels (manufactured by BP Solar) are guaranteed for 25 years; the balance of the system carries a 5-year warranty.

GE Solar Systems and Modules

GE Energy
231 Lake Dr.
Newark, DE 19702

Toll-free: 866-750-3150
www.gepower.com

GE offers a range of solar electric power systems for residential, commercial, and industrial applications as well as polycrystal PV modules ranging from 66 watts to 200 watts. Grid-tied, remote, or building integrated systems for new construction or retrofit applications are available. In 2004 GE purchased Astropower, thus entering the photovoltaics industry.

Industry Representation

Solar Energy Industries Association
805 15th St. NW, Ste. 510
Washington, DC 20005

Phone: 202-682-0556
www.seia.org

The Solar Energy Industries Association (SEIA) is the national trade association of solar energy manufacturers, dealers, distributors, contractors, and installers. SEIA's primary mission is to expand the use of solar technologies in the global marketplace. Membership exceeds 500 companies providing solar thermal and solar electric products and services.

PV Modules

BP Solar
630 Solarex Ct.
Frederick, MD 21703

Phone: 301-698-4200
www.bpsolar.com

BP Solar is one of the world's largest solar electric companies, with manufacturing plants in the U.S., Spain, Australia, and India. They manufacture, design, market, and install a wide range of crystalline silicon solar electric products. The highest percentage of BP Solar's sales are to homeowners, builders, and businesses, and they are the largest supplier to the rural infrastructure market, where solar is the core power source for off-grid communities. In 1999, BP-Amoco acquired Solarex and folded it into BP's PV Division to form BP Solar.

PV Modules

Evergreen Solar, Inc.
138 Bartlett St.
Marlboro, MA 01752

Phone: 508-357-2221
www.evergreensolar.com

Evergreen Solar is a manufacturer of PV modules and the innovator of the String Ribbon™ method of producing solar cells. This technique uses approximately half the amount of silicon as the industry norm. The company manufactures panels suitable for both grid-tied and off-grid installations and offers a 20-year warranty on all its products. Evergreen products are available through various distributors.

PV Modules

First Solar, LLC
4050 E. Cotton Ctr. Blvd., Ste. 6-68
Phoenix, AZ 85040

Phone: 602-414-9300
www.firstsolar.com

First Solar develops and manufactures Cadmium Telluride (CdTe) thin-film photovoltaic modules. First Solar has invested heavily in developing advanced, high-volume manufacturing processes that are considered essential to achieving the low cost required to make solar electricity economically viable across a broad range of applications.

PV Modules

Sharp Electronics Corp. - Solar Systems Division
5901 Bolsa Ave.
Huntington Beach, CA 92647

Toll-free: 800-BE-SHARP
Phone: 630-378-3357
www.sharpusa.com

Sharp Electronics Corporation, a worldwide leader in solar electric technology, offers single-crystal and polycrystalline PV panels. Available modules range from 62 to 208 watts for grid-tied or stand-alone systems. Sharp modules carry a 25-year warranty. Product introductions planned for the future include green, golden brown, and light blue PV cells; triangular modules; AC modules; and thin-film, virtually transparent modules.

PV Modules

Shell Solar
4650 Adohr Ln.
Camarillo, CA 93011

Toll-free: 800-272-6765
Phone: 805-482-6800
www.shell.com/solar/

Shell Solar is one of the world's largest manufacturers of PV modules, producing single-crystal, multi-crystal, and CIS thin-film modules. Shell also offers EarthSafe™ PV kits for residential and commercial installations. These solar electric rooftop kits include mounting hardware, inverter, and 25-year warranty panels. Shell Solar was previously Siemens Solar (and before that Arco Solar) before Shell acquired Siemens in April 2002.

PV Systems

Kyocera Solar, Inc.
7812 E. Acoma Dr.
Scottsdale, AZ 85260

Toll-free: 800-223-9580
Phone: 480-948-8003
www.kyocerasolar.com

Kyocera is one of the world's largest manufacturers of polycrystal PV modules.

Renewable Energy Equipment

RWE Schott Solar, Inc.
2260 Lava Ridge Ct., Ste. 102
U.S. Sales & Marketing
Roseville, CA 95661

Toll-free: 888-457-6527
Phone: 916-774-3000
www.us.schott.com

RWE Schott Solar Inc. (RSS), formerly Schott Applied Power, is a leading manufacturer and distributor of solar power components and systems. RSS produces the world's largest solar power module available, the ASE 300. RSS serves a diverse market including grid-connected residential and commercial systems, and grid-independent agricultural, governmental and utility applications. RWE Schott Solar Inc. is a joint venture of the RWE Group, a global multi-utility concern with core businesses in electricity, gas, water, waste management, and recycling.

Schüco Photovoltaic Modules

SCHÜCO, LP
240 Pane Rd.
Newington, CT 06111

Toll-free: 877-472-4826
Phone: 860-666-0505
www.schuco-usa.com

Schüco offers three models of permanently sealed polycrystalline PV modules that are manufactured and tested to meet international quality standards. Model S 125-SP (49.13" x 31.61") has a rated output of 125 W; S 158-SP (62.2" x 31.5") is 158 W; and S 170-SPU (62.2" x 31.5") is 170 W. Schüco provides a 5-year product guarantee, and a performance guarantee of 90% output at 12 years, and 80% at 25 years. These products are manufactured in Germany.

Solar Turtle

Solar Turtle, Inc.
4901 Cactus Wren Ave.
Tucson, AZ 85746

Phone: 520-883-3356

The Solar Turtle is a photovoltaic power supply and water purification system mostly used for remote cabins and RVs. These systems include 120-watt panels, deep-cycle batteries, an inverter, and General Ecology's SeaGull IV water purification systems. The system can output up to 720 W DC or 2,500 W AC. Most Solar Turtle units include custom features to match customer needs.

Sunslates

Atlantis Energy Systems, Inc.
4517 Harlin Dr.
Sacramento, CA 95826

Phone: 916-438-2930
www.atlantisenergy.org

Atlantis Energy Systems produces Sunslates®, which serve as both a roofing product and a solar-electric power source. Sunslates are fiber-cement shingles into which PV cells have been laminated. Each shingle has a plug-in wiring connection.

Suntech Silicon Solar Modules

Solar Resources
771 Shrewsbury Ave., Ste. 105
Shrewsbury, NJ 07702

Phone: 732-758-1600
www.solarresources.com

Solar Resources distributes PV panels manufactured in China by Suntech Power, which has quickly risen to become one of the world's largest PV manufacturers.

UNI-SOLAR PV Shingles and Standing Seam Panels

United Solar Ovonic LLC
3800 Lapeer Rd.
Auburn Hills, MI 48326

Toll-free: 800-843-3892
Phone: 248-475-0100
www.uni-solar.com

Uni-Solar Ovonic LLC PV Shingles and Standing Seam Roofing Panels are installed much like conventional roofing products. They generate electricity while protecting the structure from weather. PV Shingles, measuring 86.4" x 12" with 7 tabs, are interspersed among conventional 3-tab shingles. Standing Seam Panels are available for laminating onto conventional roofing or as a PV-integrated, standing-seam product. Lead wires from each shingle or panel enter the structure through drilled holes in the roof decking. Uni-Solar roofing products use triple-junction amorphous silicon technology.

Solar Concentrating Collectors

High-temperature solar thermal systems typically use parabolic reflectors to concentrate the solar energy and heat-transfer fluids other than water.

Winston Series CPC Collector

Solargenix Energy, LLC
2101-115 Westinghouse Blvd.
Raleigh, NC 27604

Phone: 919-871-0423
www.solargenix.com

The Winston Series CPC Collector from Solargenix Energy is a residential and commercial solar water-heating system. The basic system is comprised of 12 small compound parabolic collectors (CPC) which focus light onto absorber tubes through which heat-transfer fluid is piped. One to three collectors are commonly used for residential solar water-heating systems, depending on the size of the hot water storage tank. A roof-integrated thermosiphoning configuration is possible with new construction. The collectors carry a 10-year warranty. The system's heat exchanger, SOLPAC, is also available as a separate item. Coupled with one or more solar collectors, it prepackages the components needed to convert existing electric or gas water heaters into solar water-heating systems.

Solar Flat-Plate Collectors

These listings include flat-plate solar collectors used for water and space heating. Building-integrated transpired collectors are also included here.

Air-Heating Solar Collector

Sunsiaray
4414 N. Washburn Rd.
Davison, MI 48423

Phone: 810-653-3502
www.sunsiaray.com

Sunsiaray Solar Manufacturing produces air-heating solar collectors.

Gobi Solar Collectors and Helio-Pak Solar Water Heater

Heliodyne, Inc.
4910 Seaport Ave.
Richmond, CA 94804

Phone: 510-237-9614
www.heliodyne.com

Heliodyne is a manufacturer of flat-plate solar collectors and heat-transfer systems for residential and commercial water heating.

Heliocol Solar Pool-Heating Systems

Heliocol
13620 49th St. N
Clearwater, FL 33762

Phone: 727-572-6655
www.heliocol.com

Heliocol manufactures unglazed polypropylene, solar pool-heating systems.

ProgressivTube Passive Water-Heating Systems

Thermal Conversion Technology
101 Copeland St.
Jacksonville, FL 32204

Phone: 904-358-3720
www.tctsolar.com

Thermal Conversion Technology produces the ProgressivTube® line of integral collector-storage (ICS) systems with 4"-diameter copper pipes in a glass-glazed collector. The collectors are typically for solar preheating of water and are used extensively in Caribbean and Hawaiian hotels. Founded in 1974, the company has sold thousands of the current ProgressiTube® line since its introduction in 1982.

Skyline Solar Thermal Collectors and Systems

SolarRoofs.com Inc.
5840 Gibbons Dr., Ste. G
Carmichael, CA 95608

Toll-free: 888-801-9060
Phone: 916-481-7200
www.solarroofs.com

SolarRoofs.com Inc. manufactures lightweight flat-plate solar water heating systems and collectors. Its Skyline collectors have copper piping and absorber plates with polycarbonate Twinwall glazing. Collectors are available in 26 architectural colors, are SRCC and FSEC certified, and carry an independent structural certification to withstand 150 mph wind. The company offers a variety of systems for different climates, including drain-back and closed-loop with integral PV-powered pump/controller.

SOL 25 and Storage Tank

Stiebel Eltron
17 West St.
West Hatfield, MA 01088

Toll-free: 800-582-8423
Phone: 413-247-3380
www.stiebel-eltron-usa.com

Stiebel Eltron manufactures the SOL 25 Plus flat plate solar collectors and SB/SBB Plus storage tanks for solar water-heating systems. The Berlin, Germany based company has manufacturing plants in Holzminden, Germany and Tailand. The solar collector selective absorber surface is chromium oxide, which offers high performance, but carries significant environmental burdens. The storage tanks are insulated with three inches of polyurethane foam and available in four sizes (39 to 109 gallons) and with one or two heat exchangers.

Solar Collectors

Integrated Solar LLC
2030 W. Pinnacle Peak Rd.
Phoenix, AZ 85027

Toll-free: 800-927-2326
Phone: 805-928-1881
http://radcosolar.com/about.html

Integrated Solar LLC manufactures Radco glazed flat-plate solar collectors and Radco complete drainback solar water-heating systems for areas with freezing weather conditions. The company also produces a line of Radco unglazed solar pool-heating systems.

Solar Collectors

R&R Services Solar Supply
922 Austin Ln., Bldg. D
Honolulu, HI 96817

Phone: 808-842-0011

R&R Services Solar Supply is a manufacturer of copper-tube/absorber flat-plate collectors. The company packages solar water-heating systems for sale throughout Hawaii.

Solar Pool-Heating Systems

Aquatherm Industries, Inc.
1940 Rutgers University Blvd.
Lakewood, NJ 08701

Toll-free: 800-535-6307
Phone: 732-905-9002
www.warmwater.com

Aquatherm produces unglazed polypropylene collectors designed for pool heating. These are used with existing conventional filtration systems to circulate pool water through the collectors then back into the pool. Most systems utilize an automatic temperature control. The swimming pool serves as the heat-storage reservoir.

Solar Pool-Heating Systems

Fafco, Inc.
435 Otterson Dr.
Chico, CA 95928

Toll-free: 800-994-7652
Phone: 530-332-2100
www.fafco.com

Fafco is the oldest manufacturer of solar water-heating equipment in the U.S.—since 1969. The company manufactures a line of pool-heating systems.

Solar Thermal Flat-Plate Collectors

Alternate Energy Technologies
1057 N. Ellis Rd., Unit 4
Jacksonville, FL 32254

Toll-free: 800-874-2190
Phone: 904-781-8305
www.aetsolar.com

Alternate Energy Technologies is a manufacturer of copper-tube, flat-plate collectors with a nontoxic collector coating.

Solar Water-Heating Systems

Thermo Dynamics Ltd.
101 Frazee Ave.
Dartmouth, NS B3B-1Z4 Canada

Phone: 902-468-1001
www.thermo-dynamics.com

Thermo Dynamics manufactures a full range of solar water-heating systems with liquid flat-plate, glazed collectors with fused copper tubing and aluminum absorbers. The company also produces the Solar Pump™—a PV-powered pump—and a thermosiphoning heat exchanger.

SunEarth Solar Equipment

SunEarth, Inc.
8425 Almeria Ave.
Fontana, CA 92335

Phone: 909-434-3100
www.sunearthinc.com

SunEarth, Inc., a manufacturer of solar water-heating equipment since 1978, produces flat-plate solar collectors, ICS and thermosiphon water-heating systems, and ancillary components including residential and commercial racking systems for both solar water heating and PV systems.

SunMate Hot Air Solar Panel

Environmental Solar Systems
119 West St.
Methuen, MA 01844

Phone: 978-975-1190
www.environmentalsolarsystems.com

Sunmate® is a side-mounted residential solar thermal collector constructed of aluminum, double-sealed glass, and polyisocyanurate insulation. A 100 CFM, 7W fan on an automatic thermostat pulls cool air from the home, channels it through the absorber plate, and circulates hot air back into the home. Sunmate can also be used for fresh air intake in tight houses. One panel heats up to 300 square feet, and panels can be installed in parallel.

Solar Heating Balance of System Components

These listings include specialized components and materials for solar thermal systems other than the actual panels or collectors.

Phoenix Solar Water Heater

Heat Transfer Products, Inc.
120 Braley Rd.
P.O. Box 429
East Freetown, MA 02717

Toll-free: 800-323-9651
Phone: 508-763-8071
www.htproducts.com

The Phoenix Solar Water Heater provides a heat exchanger to transfer heat from solar collectors (or other alternative sources), along with a back-up gas burner that operates at 97% thermal efficiency. The gas burner is located halfway up the tank and a solar heat exchanger is located at the bottom, keeping water at the bottom of the tank cooler and maximizing the solar collector's efficiency. The Phoenix comes with auxiliary hook-ups so it can be connected to air handlers or radiant heating systems. These units are available in 80- or 110-gallon corrosion-resistant 316L-grade stainless steel tanks that are wrapped in two-inch non-HCFC polyurethane foam insulation. The unit is direct-vent and rated for zero clearance from combustible surfaces.

SOL 25 and Storage Tank

Stiebel Eltron
17 West St.
West Hatfield, MA 01088

Toll-free: 800-582-8423
Phone: 413-247-3380
www.stiebel-eltron-usa.com

Stiebel Eltron manufactures the SOL 25 Plus flat plate solar collectors and SB/SBB Plus storage tanks for solar water-heating systems. The Berlin, Germany based company has manufacturing plants in Holzminden, Germany and Tailand. The solar collector selective absorber surface is chromium oxide, which offers high performance, but carries significant environmental burdens. The storage tanks are insulated with three inches of polyurethane foam and available in four sizes (39 to 109 gallons) and with one or two heat exchangers.

Solar Hydronic Check Valves, Differential Thermostats

Heliotrope Thermal
4910 Seaport Ave.
Richmond, CA 94804

Phone: 510-237-9614
www.heliotropethermal.com

Heliotrope Thermal offers low-resistance spring/ball brass check valves designed for the high temperatures and pressures of solar domestic hot water systems. The cleanable valves have sweat-union connections, silicone O-rings, and can be Installed on vertical or horizontal lines. Delta-T electronic controllers are differential-temperature thermostats designed to regulate the operation of solar hydronic heating systems by monitoring collector and storage temperatures and automating pumps or blowers appropriately. They can also provide system freeze protection, and high- or low-limit shut-offs. Heliotrope Thermal, like Heliotrope PV, is a successor to Heliotrope General, a branch of Heliodyne, Inc.

Solar Pumping Components

Solarnetix Inc.
777 Warden Ave.
Toronto, ON M1L4C3 Canada

Phone: 416-699-6746
www.solarnetix.com

Solarnetix is the North American distributor of hydronic heat and solar pumping components made by the German company, Pommerening Armaturenwerk (PAW GmbH & Co. KG). Components range from brass check valves and flow gauges to complete distribution systems designed for the high temperatures and pressures of solar domestic hot water systems. Neatly packaged in insulated wall-mount packs.

Solar Water Storage Tanks

Morley Manufacturing
P.O. Box 1540
Cedar Ridge, CA 95924

Phone: 530-477-6527

Morley manufactures storage tanks used for solar water-heating systems.

Solar Water Storage Tanks

Vaughn Manufacturing Corporation
26 Old Elm St.
P.O. Box 5431
Salisbury, MA 01952

Toll-free: 800-282-8446
Phone: 978-462-6683
www.vaughncorp.com

Vaughn Manufacturing produces stone-lined storage tanks specifically for solar water heating systems. Vaughn tanks have removable copper-finned heat exchangers enabling periodic cleaning of the coil to maintain maximum performance. The tanks—which are lined with centrifugally applied Hydrastone for corrosion protection—come in 65-, 80-, and 115-gallon capacities, and can also be made to custom dimensions.

Viessmann Solar Water-Heating System

Viessmann Manufacturing Company Inc.
750 McMurray Rd.
Waterloo, ON N2V 2G5 Canada

Toll-free: 800-387-7373
Phone: 519-885-6300
www.viessmann.ca

Viessmann manufactures solar water-heating components which can be purchased separately, or together as part of a fully integrated system package. Components include a number of different collectors and storage tanks, pumps, controllers, and balance-of-system components. Viessmann offers a lower-cost Vitosol 100 flat-plate solar collector and the Vitosol 300 evacuated-tube solar collector. Both hot water tanks, the stainless-steel Vitocell B 300 and the more economical steel Vitocell B 100, use HCFC-free polyurethane insulation and have dual heat exchanger coils that accommodate both solar and conventional-boiler heat input.

Winston Series CPC Collector

Solargenix Energy, LLC
2101-115 Westinghouse Blvd.
Raleigh, NC 27604

Phone: 919-871-0423
www.solargenix.com

The Winston Series CPC Collector from Solargenix Energy is a residential and commercial solar water-heating system. The basic system is comprised of 12 small compound parabolic collectors (CPC) which focus light onto absorber tubes through which heat-transfer fluid is piped. One to three collectors are commonly used for residential solar water-heating systems, depending on the size of the hot water storage tank. A roof-integrated thermosiphoning configuration is possible with new construction. The collectors carry a 10-year warranty. The system's heat exchanger, SOLPAC, is also available as a separate item. Coupled with one or more solar collectors, it prepackages the components needed to convert existing electric or gas water heaters into solar water-heating systems.

Solar Vacuum-Tube Collectors

Evacuated tubes offer higher efficiencies and better performance in cold weather than conventional flat-plate collectors, though cost is typically higher.

Apricus Evacuated-Tube Solar Collectors

Maine Green Building Supply
111 Fox St.
Portland, ME 04101

Phone: 207-780-1500
www.mainegreenbuilding.com

Apricus manufactures evacuated-tube solar collectors in Nanjing, China for worldwide distribution. The borosilicate twin-glass vacuum tubes passively track the sun (because of their round shape). A selective coating on the inner tube provides minimal reflection and maximum solar-radiation absorption, while the vacuum reduces heat losses via conduction and convection. If the vacuum is ever lost, the silver-colored barium layer at the end of the tube, acquired during manufacture, will turn white, allowing the faulty tube to be identified and replaced. The copper heat pipes use a phase change fluid to effect one-way heat flow to the header pipe. Water is intermittently pumped through the header pipe where it absorbs heat. The system has a 10-year limited warranty, and Apricus is ISO 9001 certified.

Sunda Evacuated-Tube Solar Collectors

Sun Spot Solar & Heating, Inc.
PO Box 55
Delaware Water Gap, PA 18327

Phone: 570-422-1292
www.sssolar.com

Sun Spot Solar offers the Seido line of evacuated-tube solar collectors manufactured by Beijing Sunda Solar Energy Technology Co., Ltd. These collectors use an aluminum solar absorber plate mounted in a long glass vacuum tube; the vacuum reduces heat losses via conduction and convection. Heat is transferred from the absorber plate to a small "heat pipe," which acts as a heat-exchanger in a fluid-filled manifold. The fluid in the heating circuit does not flow through the collectors. The vacuum tubes are made with low-iron tempered glass designed to withstand 35mm (1.38 inch) hail. The tubes have a six-year warranty.

SunTube Collector

Sun Utility Network, Inc.
4952 Coringa Dr.
Los Angeles, CA 90042

Phone: 323-478-0866
www.sunutility.com

Sun Utility Network is the U.S. distributor of NEG's SunTube evacuated-tube solar water-heating systems. SunTube panels can be used for residential and commercial water heating, space heating and cooling, water pasteurization, and desalination applications.

Thermomax Evacuated-Tube Solar Collectors

Aurora Energy Inc./
Thermo Technologies
9009 Mendenhall Ct.,
Ste. E
Columbia, MD 21045

Phone: 410-997-0778
www.thermomax.com

Thermo Technologies (formerly Advanced Solar Technologies) is the east-coast U.S. distributor for Thermomax, a European company with manufacturing facilities in Italy, Northern Ireland, and Wales. Thermomax produces an evacuated-tube solar collector system using heat-pipe technology to transfer heat to a manifold. (Heat pipes use a phase-change fluid to effect one-way heat flow, obviating the need for complex controls.) Standard-sized tubes are ganged together to produce any size system from small residential to large commercial and are typically configured into a closed-loop antifreeze system. The selective absorber surface is an environmentally friendly Tinox® titanium nitride oxide coating from Germany. Thermo Technologies also offers balance-of-system components and design services.

Swimming Pool Plumbing Systems

Products listed here include specialized systems to use solar thermal energy for pool water heating.

Heliocol Solar Pool-Heating Systems

Heliocol
13620 49th St. N
Clearwater, FL 33762

Phone: 727-572-6655
www.heliocol.com

Heliocol manufactures unglazed polypropylene, solar pool-heating systems.

Solar Collectors

Integrated Solar LLC
2030 W. Pinnacle Peak Rd.
Phoenix, AZ 85027

Toll-free: 800-927-2326
Phone: 805-928-1881
http://radcosolar.com/about.html

Integrated Solar LLC manufactures Radco glazed flat-plate solar collectors and Radco complete drainback solar water-heating systems for areas with freezing weather conditions. The company also produces a line of Radco unglazed solar pool-heating systems.

Solar Collectors

Sealed Air Corp. - Solar Pool Heating
200 Riverfront Boulevard
Elmwood Park, NJ 07407

Toll-free: 201-791-7600
Phone: 510-887-8090
www.sealedair.com

Sealed Air Corporation is primarily in the packaging business but also produces a line of flat-plate solar collectors for pool heating.

Solar Pool-Heating Systems

Aquatherm Industries, Inc.
1940 Rutgers University Blvd.
Lakewood, NJ 08701

Toll-free: 800-535-6307
Phone: 732-905-9002
www.warmwater.com

Aquatherm produces unglazed polypropylene collectors designed for pool heating. These are used with existing conventional filtration systems to circulate pool water through the collectors then back into the pool. Most systems utilize an automatic temperature control. The swimming pool serves as the heat-storage reservoir.

Solar Pool-Heating Systems

Fafco, Inc.
435 Otterson Dr.
Chico, CA 95928

Toll-free: 800-994-7652
Phone: 530-332-2100
www.fafco.com

Fafco is the oldest manufacturer of solar water-heating equipment in the U.S.—since 1969. The company manufactures a line of pool-heating systems.

Wind Energy Equipment

Most large wind-power systems are installed in centralized wind farms, with the power fed into electric utility grids. Included here are smaller wind turbines that are more appropriate for individual homes or commercial buildings. Like PV systems, these generators may be designed for use in grid-tied or off-grid applications.

AIR and Whisper Series Wind Turbines

Southwest Windpower
1801 W. Rt. 66
Flagstaff, AZ 86001

Phone: 928-779-9463
www.windenergy.com

Southwest Windpower manufactures 400-, 900-, 1,000- and 3,000-watt wind turbines for on- and off-grid residential and industrial power generation. The 400-watt unit can also be used to power telecommunication stations, and the 1,000-watt unit can be used to pump water.

ARE Wind Generators

Abundant Renewable Energy
22700 N.E. Mountain Top Rd.
Newberg, OR 97132

Phone: 503-538-8298
www.abundantRE.com

ARE wind generators are manufactured in Oregon, USA, and distributed worldwide by Abundant Renewable Energy. The ARE110 wind generator is rated at 2,500 watts and is available in 48-volt models for battery-charging applications and in a high-voltage model for grid-connect systems. The ARE442 is rated at 10,000 watts and is available as a grid-connect system.

BWC Excel Wind Turbines

Bergey Windpower Co., Inc.
2200 Industrial Blvd.
Norman, OK 73069

Phone: 405-364-4212
www.bergey.com

Bergey Windpower manufactures three models of wind generators for residential and small-scale commercial applications. The BWC XL.1 is rated at 1,000 watts, the BWC Excel-R is rated at 7,500 watts, and the BWC Excel-S is rated at 10,000 watts.

Jacobs 31-20 Wind Turbine

Wind Turbine Industries Corp.
16801 Industrial Cir. SE
Prior Lake, MN 55372

Phone: 952-447-6064
www.windturbine.net

Wind Turbine Industries' Jacobs 31-20 generator is rated at 20,000 watts. Jacobs wind turbines range in size from 10kW to 20kW, with rotor sizes ranging from 23 ft. (7m) to 29 ft. (8.8 m). These systems can provide power for a broad range of applications, which include Grid Intertie (utility bill reduction) or off-grid/remote battery charging. Other Jacobs turbines (also known as "Jakes" and made in the 1930s) are no longer manufactured but, due to their exceptional durability, are still widely available as used and rebuilt machines.

OY Windside Turbines

Tangarie Energy LLC
18 Deer Path
Hillsborough, NJ 08844

Toll-free: 866-994-6500
www.tangarie-energy.com

Tangarie Energy is the U.S. distributor for vertical wind turbines produced by OY Windside Production Ltd. of Finland. Designed for power production in extreme conditions, these turbines are also appropriate for a variety of other on and off-grid applications including population centers, parks, and residences. The soundless (0 db) turbine is safe for birds and bats and have been used as part of power-generating sculptures. The Windside is not affected by turbulent wind, can generate even in freezing and snowy conditions, and starts to generate power at wind speeds as low as 1.5 m/s (3.3 mph) to 2.8 m/s (6.2 mph), depending on model, and can operate at wind speeds as high as 30 m/s (66 mph), 40 m/s (88 mph), or 60 m/s (132 mph) depending on model.

Skystream 3.7

Southwest Windpower
1801 W. Rt. 66
Flagstaff, AZ 86001

Phone: 928-779-9463
www.windenergy.com

The Skystream 3.7™ is a grid-connected, residential-sized 1.8 kW wind turbine that is designed for quiet operation at low wind-speeds. The 12-foot diameter, curved-blade rotor starts producing power at a wind speed of 8 mph and reaches full output at 20 mph. The wind turbine can be mounted on a 35 ft single pole, with towers up to 110 ft available. At an average windspeed of 12 mph, the Skystream 3.7 will produce about 400 kWh per month. The complete installed system costs approximately $7,000 to $10,000, including generator, controls, inverter, and tower.

Urban-Appropriate Wind Turbines

WES Canada
2952 Thompson Rd.
P.O. Box 552
Smithville, ON L0R 2A0
Canada

Phone: 905-957-8791
www.windenergysolutions.ca

WES Canada, in partnership with manufacturer WES Netherlands, offers the Tulipo—a medium-sized, low-noise, low-RPM 2.5 kW wind turbine appropriate for building-integrated urban installations. Larger 80- and 250-kW commercial turbines are also available. These turbines were formerly manufactured under the name Lagerway.

Wind Turbines

Proven Energy, Ltd.
Wardhead Park
Stewarton, Ayrshire KA3 5LH Scotland, UK

Phone: +44 (0)1560 485 570
www.provenenergy.com

Proven Energy, Ltd. manufactures four turbine models, rated at 2,500 watts (2,500-5,000 kWh annual output), 6,000 watts (6,000-12,000 kWh annual output) and 15,000 watts (15,000-30,000 kWh annual output). Proven Energy has three American distributors: Lake Michigan Wind and Sun can be reached by phone at 920-743-0456 and is online at www.windandsun.com; Solar Wind Works can be reached by phone at 530-582-4503 and is online at www.solarwindworks.com; Remote Power Inc. can be reached by phone at 907-457-4299 and is online at www.remotepowerinc.com.

This Space is Available for Your Notes

This Space is Available for Your Notes

Distributors & Retailers

Green building products are increasingly available from mainstream distributors and building suppliers, but only a few U.S. cities are fortunate enough to have specialized green building suppliers that stock a significant range of products. In most places, green building products that aren't available through mainstream suppliers will need to be purchased directly from the manufacturer, by mail order, or from regional distributors specializing in those products. Specialized distributors and retailers of green building products are addressed here.

Distributors/Retailers, Energy Conservation

The companies listed here specialize in energy conservation products, including lighting, weatherization materials, and specialized energy-conserving products.

Energy-Efficient Lighting

Fred Davis Corp.
120 N. Meadows Rd.
Medfield, MA 02052

Toll-free: 800-497-2970
Phone: 508-359-3610

Fred Davis Corporation is a national wholesaler of energy-efficient lighting. The company offers thousands of products including: compact, low-mercury, and T8/T5 fluorescent lamps; electronic ballasts; energy-efficient fixtures; and LED exit signs.

Lighting, Ventilation, and Weatherization

Energy Federation Incorporated
40 Washington St., Ste. 2000
Westborough, MA 01581

Toll-free: 800-876-0660
Phone: 508-870-2277
www.efi.org

Energy Federation Incorporated (EFI) is a retailer and wholesaler of energy-efficient lighting, ventilation, and weatherization products.

Renewable Energy & Energy Conservation

Gaiam Real Goods
13771 South Highway 101
Hopland, CA 95449

Toll-free: 888-507-2561
Phone: 800-919-2400
www.realgoods.com

Gaiam Real Goods sells a broad range of energy-conserving, alternative energy, and environmental-living products through its catalogs and retail stores. Real Goods catalogs are available by mail upon request or can be accessed on their website. Real Goods and Jade Mountain merged in 2001 to become the largest provider of renewable energy systems (solar, wind, and hydro) in the world. These companies have been involved with solarizing more than 50,000 homes since 1978.

Renewable Energy Equipment

Solardyne.com
Solar Dynamics LLC
5806 N. Williams Ave.
Portland, OR 97217

Phone: 503-830-8739
www.solardyne.com

Solardyne is an online retailer of renewable energy equipment and high-efficiency appliances including solar and wind power systems and components, solar lighting, solar water pumps, tankless water heaters, and super efficient refrigerators, freezers, and washers.

Ventilation and Energy-Conserving Products

Shelter Supply, Inc.
151 E. Cliff Rd., Ste. 30
Burnsville, MN 55337

Toll-free: 800-762-8399
Phone: 952-516-3400
www.sheltersupply.com

Shelter Supply offers products for better indoor air quality and greater energy efficiency. Shelter Supply specializes in residential building ventilation products.

Weatherization and Energy-Conservation Products

AM Conservation Group, Inc.
2301 Charleston Regional Pkwy.
Charleston, SC 29492

Toll-free: 800-777-5655
Phone: 843-971-1414
www.amconservationgroup.com

AM Conservation Group, Inc. introduces, manufactures, markets, and distributes a wide array of products for weatherization, as well as water and energy conservation.

Weatherization and Energy-Conservation Products

Positive Energy
P.O. Box 7568
Boulder, CO 80306

Toll-free: 800-488-4340
www.positive-energy.com

Positive Energy publishes a catalog of hard-to-find energy saving products at wholesale prices. The selection includes products for ventilation, sealing, lighting, water saving, and water and air purification.

Distributors/Retailers, FSC-Certified Wood

Distributors of FSC-certified wood products are subject to the same rigor of inspections as manufacturers and land managers. "Chain-of-custody certification" is the term used to describe the documentation of certified-wood product sourcing, processing, handling, and distribution. Accurate paperwork and careful separation of certified and noncertified wood must be maintained for compliance with FSC standards.

AltruWood Certified Wood Products

AltruWood, Inc.
P.O. Box 3341
Portland, OR 97208

Toll-free: 877-372-9663
www.altruwood.com

AltruWood, chain-of-custody certified by SGS, only sells and distributes FSC-certified new domestic (including oak, pine, cherry and Douglas Fir) and tropical wood (including Jatoba, Ipe, and Massaranduba). Sourced and shipped from multiple locations, transportation costs and impacts are minimized. A custom cutting service allows the specification of exact sizes and dimensions, minimizing waste. AltruWood also sells reclaimed lumber.

Craftmark Reclaimed Wood

Craftmark Reclaimed Wood, Inc.
P.O. Box 237
McMinnville, OR 97128

Phone: 503-472-6929
www.craftmarkinc.com

Craftmark Reclaimed Wood, Inc. is a distributor of flooring, decking, paneling, wainscoting, timbers, and specialty wood products such as architectural moldings produced from a wide variety of FSC-certified species. Custom-milling is a specialty. The company is also a manufacturer of wood products from reclaimed timber.

EarthSource Forest Products

EarthSource Forest Products/Plywood and Lumber Sales, Inc.
1618 28th St.
Oakland, CA 94608

Toll-free: 866-549-9663
Phone: 510-208-7257
www.earthsourcewood.com

EarthSource Forest Products, a division of Plywood and Lumber Sales, Inc., sells FSC-certified hardwood plywood and lumber of the following species: maple, cherry, red oak, white oak, ash, Honduras mahogany, walnut, machiche, amapola, and many more. EarthSource also sells salvaged and rediscovered lumber such as fir, redwood, and hickory.

EcoTimber

EcoTimber
1611 4th St.
San Rafael, CA 94901

Toll-free: 888-801-0855
Phone: 415-258-8454
www.ecotimber.com

EcoTimber® offers a wide range of domestic and tropical wood flooring from ecologically sound sources. EcoTimber products include reclaimed and FSC-certified woods, as well as a full line of bamboo flooring products. Prefinished, floating and formaldehyde-free floors are available.

Edensaw Woods

Edensaw Woods Ltd.
211 Seton Rd.
Port Townsend, WA 98368

Toll-free: 800-745-3336
Phone: 360-385-7878
www.edensaw.com

Edensaw Woods' selection of FSC-certified wood includes alder, ash, cherry, Honduras mahogany, maple, poplar, and red and white oak; and for decking, purpleheart, tigerwood, and ipe, as well as many species of FSC-certified domestic hardwood plywood. Edensaw also has a location in Kent, Washington.

Endura Wood Products

Endura Wood Products, Ltd.
1303 S.E. 6th Ave.
Portland, OR 97214

Phone: 503-233-7090
www.endurawood.com

Endura offers FSC-certified hardwood and softwood flooring, lumber, and decking in a wide variety of exotic and domestic species. Endurawood butcher blocks and countertops are produced from certified woods such as rock maple. Endura also sells reclaimed wood products as well as straw particleboard and agrifiber composite sheet goods.

J.E. Higgins Lumber Company

J.E. Higgins Lumber Company
240 Littlefield Rd.
S. San Francisco, CA 94080

Toll-free: 800-241-1883
Phone: 925-245-4300
www.higlum.com

J.E. Higgins Lumber sells FSC-certified hardwood, plywood, and flooring.

North American Wood Products

North American Wood Products, Inc.
7204 Durham Rd. #800
Portland, OR 97224

Phone: 503-620-6655
www.nawpi.com

North American Wood Products, chain-of-custody certified according to FSC standards, matches wood suppliers with buyers requiring specific species, grades, colors dimensions, or cuts. Products include hardwood and softwood lumber, veneers, dimension stock, and panels.

Northland Forest Products

Northland Forest Products
16 Church St.
P.O. Box 369
Kingston, NH 03848

Phone: 603-642-3665
www.northlandforest.com

Northland Forest Products carries FSC-certified kiln-dried Northern and Appalachian hardwood lumber for flooring and architectural millwork, as well as fixed widths, special widths, and figured woods. Species include cherry, maple, ash, yellow birch, red oak, mahogany, eastern white pine, white oak, eucalyptus grandis and others, depending on availability.

Reclaimed-Wood Building Products

TerraMai
1104 Firenze St.
P.O. Box 696
McCloud, CA 96057

Toll-free: 800-220-9062
Phone: 530-964-2740
www.terramai.com

TerraMai produces several grades of flooring, ranging from clear tongue-and-groove to rough-cut plank, from reclaimed lumber and tropical hardwoods. All flooring is available in "Character" (with evidence of previous use) and "Select" (clear) grades. Douglas fir, ponderosa pine, and southern yellow pine are among their most popular species. TerraMai also mills various architectural woodwork products from their 700,000-board-foot inventory of reclaimed woods. All of TerraMai's varied products are from reclaimed wood and is FSC certified.

Windfall Lumber and Milling

Windfall Lumber and Milling
404 Jefferson St. NE
Olympia, WA 98501

Phone: 360-352-2250
www.windfalllumber.com

Windfall Lumber is a manufacturer and distributor of FSC-certified and Smartwood Rediscovered hardwoods, flooring, millwork, countertops, and timbers.

Distributors/Retailers, Green Building Materials

Certain green building materials can be found in most lumberyards and home centers; a few building supply centers in the U.S. specialize in green products. Among the broad selection of products offered by these companies are low-toxic paints and finishes, cabinets, flooring products, formaldehyde-free panels, and FSC-certified lumber. In most cases, online or print catalogs are available with listings of the products offered. In addition

to sourcing products, these companies have knowledgeable sales experts. A few have buildings that serve as demonstrations of high-performance green building.

Amicus Green Building Center

Amicus Green Building Center
4080A Howard Ave.
Kensington, MD 20895-2465

Phone: 301-571-8590
www.amicusgreen.com

The Amicus Green Building Center offers a wide range of environmentally responsible building and finishing materials, including paints, panel products, water conservation products, and flooring materials. Design support is also available through their sister company, Amicus Design and Build.

BC Energy

BC Energy
357 Warbler Pl.
Nanaimo, BC V9R 6Y8 Canada

Toll-free: 888-714-4545
Phone: 250-714-4545
www.bcenergy.net

BC Energy provides energy-efficient, environmentally preferable products for home builders, including ICFs, SIPs, engineered wood, HVAC, water heaters, windows, lighting, and finishes. In addition to selling products, the company offers design, certification, and supply of energy-optimized home packages.

Bettencourt Green Building Supplies

Bettencourt Green Building Supplies
70 N. 6th St.
Brooklyn, NY 11211

Toll-free: 800-883-7005
Phone: 718-218-6737
www.bettencourtwood.com

Bettencourt Green Building Supplies provides sheet goods such as Plyboo®, Kirei Board, Environ®, Dakota Burl™, Durapalm®, and FSC-certified hardwood plywood to designers, architects, contractors and homeowners on the East Coast. Bettencourt is based in Brooklyn, NY with an office outside Boston. In late 2005, the company planned to begin stocking eco-friendly and low-VOC finishes soon.

BigHorn Materials

BigHorn Materials
1221 Blue River Pkwy.
Silverthorne, CO 80498

Phone: 970-513-1575
www.bighornace.com

In business for 18 years and offering green building products for four years, BigHorn Materials supplies general building materials and hardware, sustainable forest products, CFLs, and set-back thermostats. The company caters mainly to contractors but serves the general public as well.

Building For Health Materials Center

Building For Health Materials Center
102 Main St.
P.O. Box 113
Carbondale, CO 81623

Toll-free: 800-292-4838
Phone: 970-963-0437
www.buildingforhealth.com

The Building For Health Materials Center is a centrally located, nation-wide supplier of healthy, environmentally conscious building products for consumers and contractors. The company states that each product is evaluated in relationship to environmental impact and human health effects. Catalogs are available upon request.

Eco-Products, Inc.

Eco-Products, Inc.
3640 Walnut St.
Boulder, CO 80304

Phone: 303-449-1876
www.ecoproducts.com

Eco-Products primarily supplies exterior and interior finish materials, composite decking, and household items and equipment. The company currently serves Colorado and neighboring states but is expanding to serve the national market.

Eco-Wise Building Supplies

Eco-Wise
110 W. Elizabeth St.
Austin, TX 78704

Phone: 512-326-4474
www.ecowise.com

Eco-wise Building Supplies carries a wide variety of green building materials, including such items as rainwater catchment systems, cotton insulation, recycled-glass tiles, reclaimed woods, plant-based finishes, milk paint, recycled-content carpeting, bamboo flooring, and Energy Star® appliances.

Environmental Building Supplies

Ecohaus
4121 1st Ave. South
Seattle, WA 98134

Toll-free: 800-281-9785
Phone: 206-682-7332
www.ecohaus.com

Environmental Building Supplies, which recently merged with Environmental Home Center (EHC), sells environmental building materials and interior finishes to trade professionals and to both residential and commercial end-users. Products include flooring and floorcoverings, FSC-certified and salvaged wood, finishes, cabinetry, tiles, and furniture. The company distributes to retailers as well as offers products to the public from their showroom location in Portland, Oregon. Environmental Building Supplies also has a second retail location in Bend, Oregon.

Environmental Home Center

Environmental Home Center
4121 1st Ave. S
Seattle, WA 98134

Toll-free: 800-281-9785
Phone: 206-682-7332
www.environmentalhomecenter.com

Environmental Home Center sells a wide variety of environmental building products to trade professionals, dealers, and commercial and residential customers across the country through their showroom and call center in Seattle, as well as through the company's website. Wholesale pricing is available to trade professionals.

F.D. Sterritt Certified-Wood Building Products

F.D. Sterritt Lumber Co.
110 Arlington St.
Watertown, MA 02472

Toll-free: 877-635-3362
Phone: 617-923-1480
www.sterrittlumber.com

F.D. Sterritt Lumber sells FSC-certified lumber, plywood, decking, hardwoods, and hardwood flooring. They have a variety of certified species in stock. Additional green building materials available, including low-VOC adhesives, caulking, sealants, and recycled drywall. F.D. Sterritt offers green building product consultations.

Green Building Finishing Materials

EcoHome Improvement
2619 San Pablo Ave.
Berkeley, CA 94702

Phone: 510-644-3500
www.ecohomeimprovement.com

Ecohome Improvement offers environmentally responsible finishing materials including flooring, cabinetry, countertops, tiles, paints, stains, and sealants. Ecohome Improvement also offers design services.

Green Building Supply

Green Building Supply
508 N. 2nd St.
Fairfield, IA 52556

Toll-free: 800-405-0222
Phone: 641-469-5558
www.greenbuildingsupply.com

Green Building Supply offers hundreds of name-brand, sustainable, and energy-efficient construction products for residential and commercial projects, including non-toxic paints, stains, sealers, cleaners, furniture and cabinetry; eco-countertops; air and water purification/grey water equipment; water-efficient toilets and waterless urinals; linoleum, cork and bamboo flooring; wool carpeting; cotton insulation. Contact the company for a catalog.

Green Depot

Green Depot
1 Ivy Hill Rd.
Brooklyn, NY 11211

Toll-free: 800-238-5008
Phone: 718-782-2991
www.greendepot.com

Environmental Construction Outfitters of NY offers a full line of environmental and hypoallergenic building products. They cater to the needs of the chemically sensitive. Home inspections and consultations on greening homes and workplaces are available.

Hayward Corporation

Hayward Corporation
10 Ragsdale Dr., Ste. 100
Monterey, CA 93940

Phone: 831-643-1900
www.haywardlumber.com

Hayward Corporation, formerly Hayward Lumber, with eight building supply centers in California, is reported to have the largest stock of certified lumber in the country. They also carry an expanding stock of other green building materials, including high-performance windows, ACQ- and borate-treated lumber, cotton insulation, and wood alternatives. In 2000, the company began producing its own line of FSC-certified roof trusses, now manufactured in a solar-powered LEED Gold facility.

Livingreen

Livingreen
218 Helena Ave.
Santa Barbara, CA 93101

Toll-free: 866-966-1319
Phone: 805-966-1319
www.livingreen.com

Livingreen offers environmentally sustainable building and finishing materials, accessories, and retail products highlighting natural and recycled alternatives to standard building materials. The company's two stores provide product samples for both homeowners and trade professionals. As a resource center, Livingreen maintains a green bookstore and provides consultation and information on design, energy and water conservation, and product searches for home, work, and marine environments.

Maine Green Building Supply

Maine Green Building Supply
111 Fox St.
Portland, ME 04101

Phone: 207-780-1500
www.mainegreenbuilding.com

Maine Green Building Supply offers a range of hand-chosen heating systems, solar thermal, insulation, finishing products, and other green building materials that meet high environmental standards for commercial and residential applications.

Natural Home Products.com

Natural Home Products.com
461 Sebastopol Ave.
Santa Rosa, CA 95401

Toll-free: 800-373-4548
Phone: 707-571-1229
www.naturalhomeproducts.com

Natural Home Products.com carries an extensive line of natural floor coverings and flooring. The company also sells organic paints and wood finishes, as well as organic-cotton sheets and wool bedding.

Planetary Solutions

Planetary Solutions
2030 17th St.
P.O. Box 1049
Boulder, CO 80302

Phone: 303-442-6228
www.planetearth.com

Planetary Solutions caters to contractors, the design professions, and the general public in the Rocky Mountain region with a range of environmentally sound products including cork flooring, linoleum, 100% natural wool and recycled PET plastic carpet, reclaimed and FSC-certified wood flooring, bamboo flooring, recycled-glass tile, and natural paints and finishes.

Refuge Sustainable Building Center

Refuge Sustainable Building Center
714 E. Mendenhall
Bozeman, MT 59715

Phone: 406-585-9958
www.refugebuilding.com

Refuge Sustainable Building Center offers a wide range of environmental building materials as well as non-toxic household products and sustainable building books. Products include FSC-certified and salvaged wood, siding, sheathing, and flooring; bamboo and cork flooring; recycled roofing and glass tiles; caulking; plasters; cotton insulation; dual-flush toilets; and low-VOC finishes and adhesives. Refuge also hosts environmental building workshops.

SolSource

SolSource, Inc.
5919 N. Broadway
Denver, CO 80216

Phone: 303-297-1874
www.solsourceinc.com

SolSource is a distributor of high-performance green building materials and systems through a network of dealers in the Rocky Mountain region. Lines include a range of renewable energy, roofing, SIP, and ICF products, as well as finishes.

The New England Green Building Center

New England Green Building Center
21 Conwell St.
Provincetown, MA 02657

Phone: 508-487-0150
www.negreen.com

The New England Green Building Center, a division of Conwell ACE Hardware and Lumber, stocks a variety of environmentally preferable building products, including energy-efficient products, solar equipment, and cleaning supplies. FSC-certified wood products are available upon request. Products can be shipped or delivered throughout the Northeast.

Truitt & White Lumber Company

Truitt & White Lumber Company
642 Hearst Ave.
Berkeley, CA 94710

Toll-free: 877-600-1470
Phone: 510-841-0511
www.truittandwhite.com

Since 1946, builder's supply store Truitt & White has committed to developing and promoting green products and practices. Environmentally preferable products, such as FSC-certified wood, low-VOC paints and caulks, and energy-efficient items, are clearly labeled throughout the store, making them easy to find. Truitt & White is a founding member and sponsor of educational nonprofit Bay Area Build It Green.

Distributors/Retailers, Renewable Energy Equipment

Most of these companies supply a wide range of renewable energy equipment, including photovoltaic systems, solar water-heating equipment, batteries, and inverters. A few also supply wind-energy and micro-hydro equipment.

Renewable Energy & Energy Conservation

Gaiam Real Goods
13771 South Highway 101
Hopland, CA 95449

Toll-free: 888-507-2561
Phone: 800-919-2400
www.realgoods.com

Gaiam Real Goods sells a broad range of energy-conserving, alternative energy, and environmental-living products through its catalogs and retail stores. Real Goods catalogs are available by mail upon request or can be accessed on their website. Real Goods and Jade Mountain merged in 2001 to become the largest provider of renewable energy systems (solar, wind, and hydro) in the world. These companies have been involved with solarizing more than 50,000 homes since 1978.

Renewable Energy Equipment

AEE Solar
1155 Redway Dr.
P.O. Box 339
Redway, CA 95560

Toll-free: 800-777-6609
Phone: 707-923-2277
www.aeesolar.com

AEE Solar offers solar, wind, hydro, and balance-of-system products for renewable energy systems, as well as pumps, lighting, and appliances. AEE Solar sells only to resale-licensed dealers, contractors, and installers.

Renewable Energy Equipment

Backwoods Solar Electric Systems
1589 Rapid Lightning Creek Rd.
Sandpoint, ID 83864

Phone: 208-263-4290
www.backwoodssolar.com

A company of six solar-electric technicians who own and operate solar-electric homes powered by the products in their catalog, Backwoods Solar Electric Systems has been in business since 1978. The company is catalog-based (web and print) and is dedicated to serving remotely located homeowners/builders.

Renewable Energy Equipment

Carmanah Technologies Corporation
Building 4, 203 Harbour Rd.
Victoria, BC V9A 3S2 Canada

Toll-free: 877-722-8877
Phone: 250-380-0052
www.carmanah.com

Carmanah's Solar Power Systems Group was formed through the purchase of Soltek Powersource, Ltd. in July 2005. A wide range of photovoltaic equipment and systems is offered, including remote, grid-connected, and emergency backup power for industry, commercial, and residential installations. Carmanah packages and integrates PV and balance-of-systems components, such as their Green Gridtie™ Solar Power System for residential applications. The company also manufacturers and markets solar LED hazard lighting and LED illuminated signs.

Renewable Energy Equipment

Creative Energy Technologies
2872 State Rte. 10
Summit, NY 12175

Phone: 518-287-1428
www.cetsolar.com

Founded in 1999, Creative Energy Technologies (CET) offers a wide range of renewable and energy-efficient equipment through its online catalog. The company operates a store in Summit, New York, from which they also offer workshops and an energy audit weatherization service. According to CET, they test all the products they offer to verify the claims of the manufacturers and will provide free technical support for the life of a purchased product.

Renewable Energy Equipment

EA Energy Alternatives Ltd.
5-4217 Glanford Ave.
Victoria, BC V8Z 4B9 Canada

Toll-free: 800-265-8898
Phone: 250-727-0522
www.energyalternatives.ca

Energy Alternatives offers solar, wind, hydro, and balance-of-systems products for renewable energy systems, as well as pumps, lighting, appliances, and books.

Renewable Energy Equipment

Electron Connection
P.O. Box 203
Hornbrook, CA 96044

Toll-free: 800-945-7587
www.electronconnection.com

In business and producing its own power since 1976 (with its owner utilizing renewable energy since 1970), Electron Connection designs, sells, installs, and maintains renewable energy systems. The company does not publish a paper catalog but provides information about some products on its website. Manufacturers' literature is also provided on products determined to be suitable for a specific customer's needs. Electron Connection is fully licensed, bonded, and insured to install and service renewable energy systems in California and Oregon. The company also maintains a worldwide network of Electron Connection dealer/installers.

Renewable Energy Equipment

Energy Outfitters, Ltd.
543 N.E. E St.
Grants Pass, OR 97526

Toll-free: 800-467-6527
Phone: 541-476-4200
www.energyoutfitters.com

In business since 1991, Energy Outfitters is a renewable energy distributor supplying products either as components or assembled systems, and offering technical design services for a wide range of renewable energy products and systems including PV, wind, and micro-hydro. The company also distributes a variety of photovoltaic modules from BP, GE, Isofoton, and Mitsubishi.

Renewable Energy Equipment

Mr.Solar.com
P.O. Box 1506
Cockeysville, MD 21030

Phone: 410-308-1599
www.mrsolar.com

Mr.Solar.com designs and sells PV systems using BP, Siemens, Kyocera, Trace, and Solarex components for residential and commercial use. Small wind systems, water pumps, fans, appliances, and balance-of-systems equipment are also available.

Renewable Energy Equipment

New England Solar Electric, Inc.
401 Huntington Rd.
P.O. Box 435
Worthington, MA 01098

Toll-free: 800-914-4131
www.newenglandsolar.com

New England Solar Electric, formerly Fowler Solar Electric, offers renewable energy equipment and systems from a 96-page catalog and product guide. The company also publishes the Solar Electric Independent Home book.

Renewable Energy Equipment

Northern Arizona Wind & Sun, Inc.
4091 East Huntington Dr.
Flagstaff, AZ 86004

Toll-free: 800-383-0195
Phone: 928-526-8017
www.solar-electric.com

In business selling and installing solar electric systems since 1979, Northern Arizona Wind & Sun offers renewable energy equipment through its catalog, an online store, and a retail location in Flagstaff.

Renewable Energy Equipment

RWE Schott Solar, Inc.
2260 Lava Ridge Ct., Ste. 102
U.S. Sales & Marketing
Roseville, CA 95661

Toll-free: 888-457-6527
Phone: 916-774-3000
www.us.schott.com

RWE Schott Solar Inc. (RSS), formerly Schott Applied Power, is a leading manufacturer and distributor of solar power components and systems. RSS produces the world's largest solar power module available, the ASE 300. RSS serves a diverse market including grid-connected residential and commercial systems, and grid-independent agricultural, governmental and utility applications. RWE Schott Solar Inc. is a joint venture of the RWE Group, a global multi-utility concern with core businesses in electricity, gas, water, waste management, and recycling.

Renewable Energy Equipment

SBT Designs
3881 Wilkes Street
Pace, FL 32571

Phone: 210-872-4615

SBT Designs' Alternative Energy Catalog includes design guides, product descriptions, and prices on solar modules, wind generators, and a variety of renewable energy products.

Renewable Energy Equipment

Solar Energy, Inc.
5191 Shawland Rd.
Jacksonville, FL 32254

Phone: 904-786-6600
www.solarenergy.com

Solar Energy Inc. (SEI) is a manufacturer and distributor of a variety of solar water-heating systems for commercial or residential applications. The turnkey, drainback SUN HoM system has one or more roof-integrated flat-plate solar collectors and uses a controller and pump to circulate a heat-transfer fluid. When the pump shuts off, water drains to an insulated reservoir to protect from freezing. Solar

Energy also sells other alternative energy systems including PV and wind power.

Renewable Energy Equipment

Solar Works, Inc.
64 Main St.
Montpelier, VT 05602

Toll-free: 800-339-7804
Phone: 802-223-7804
www.solarworksinc.com

Solar Works, Inc. is a renewable energy systems integrator and contractor providing solar electric (photovoltaic), solar thermal and wind power systems for clients worldwide. Founded in 1980, Solar Works is also active in commercializing new technologies and developing renewable energy programs for both public and private sector clients. The company's corporate headquarters are located in Montpelier, VT.

Renewable Energy Equipment

Solardyne.com
Solar Dynamics LLC
5806 N. Williams Ave.
Portland, OR 97217

Phone: 503-830-8739
www.solardyne.com

Solardyne is an online retailer of renewable energy equipment and high-efficiency appliances including solar and wind power systems and components, solar lighting, solar water pumps, tankless water heaters, and super efficient refrigerators, freezers, and washers.

Renewable Energy Equipment

Southwest Photovoltaic Systems, Inc.
212 E. Main
Tomball, TX 77375

Toll-free: 800-899-7978
Phone: 281-351-0031
www.southwestpv.com

In business since 1986, Southwest PV Systems designs and supplies PV, wind, and hybrid-power systems. The company offers training seminars on-site and maintains a large in-stock distribution warehouse.

Renewable Energy Equipment

Sunnyside Solar, Inc.
1014 Green River Rd.
Guilford, VT 05301

Phone: 802-254-4670
www.sunnysidesolar.com

Sunnyside Solar, Inc., founded in 1979, is a small, family-owned firm specializing in photovoltaic electric systems. The company provides design, engineering, sales, installation, service, and education in the field of off- and on-grid residential and commercial photovoltaic installations.

Renewable Energy Equipment

TerraTek Environmental Solutions
4805 Alton Place
Courtenay, BC V9N 8H7 Canada

Toll-free: 877-335-1415
Phone: 250-897-3877
www.terratek.ca

TerraTek Environmental Solutions sells and installs renewable energy systems for grid-connected and off-grid systems, specializing in solar, wind and micro-hydro on Vancouver Island, the Gulf Islands, and the Coastal Mainland area of western Canada. Lighting and off-grid appliances are also offered.

Solar Energy Solutions

groSolar
(formerly Global Resource Options)
Corporate Headquarters
White River Junction, VT 05001

Toll-free: 800-374-4494
www.grosolar.com

groSolar, previously Global Resource Options, sells and installs solar electric systems for residential and commercial markets in locations across the country. In late 2006, groSolar acquired Oregon-based Energy Outfitters, with distribution offices in Grants Pass Oregon as well as Calgary, Alberta and Barrie, Ontario, making groSolar one of North America's largest solar energy distribution and installation companies.

Solar Street Lighting

Quality Solar Concepts Inc.
47 Tea Rose Meadow
Rockport , NY 14420

Phone: 585-278-3773
www.solar4me.com

Quality Solar Concepts manufacturers and distributes photovoltaic-powered outdoor lighting, including street lights, walkway lights, parking lights, and area lights. Fixtures are engineered to be used with either LED or compact fluorescent lamps. Quality Solar Concepts is also distributor for a wide range of other alternative energy components and systems.

Distributors/Retailers, Used Building Materials

Clearly, reusing building materials can be environmentally advantageous. The companies listed here commonly have varying selections of doors, windows, cabinets, brick, stone, wood flooring, and plumbing fixtures. Also check the Yellow Pages under "salvage" for local suppliers. Avoid the use of old, inefficient windows in exterior envelopes, plumbing fixtures that don't meet current water conservation standards, or appliances such as refrigerators with poor efficiencies. In these cases, new products will save more than the environmental costs of their manufacture. Testing for lead paint is recommended for items such as salvaged doors and millwork. Raw, unsealed wood can be a source of lead dust in a building even if lead paint has been removed. If lead paint residue is found or suspected, the wood should be sealed after paint is stripped.

Bent Nail

Bent Nail
31255 Wheel Ave.
Abbotsford, BC V2T 6H1 Canada

Toll-free: 877-850-2691
Phone: 604-850-2691
www.bentnail.org

Bent Nail offers 60,000 sf of salvaged and new construction and renovation stock including lumber, doors, plumbing, windows, bathtubs, and lighting. All salvaged lumber is denailed and resawn as needed.

Green Building Resource Guide

Salvaged Building Materials Exchange
P.O. Box 3808
Redwood City, CA 94064

www.greenguide.com/exchange/

The salvaged building materials exchange section of this website is set up for sellers and buyers to connect by way of free listings.

Industry Representation

Building Materials Reuse Association
545 Ridge Ave.
State College, PA 16803

www.ubma.org

The Building Materials Reuse Association (formerly the Used Building Materials Association) is the nonprofit North American organization representing firms that deconstruct buildings, retail used building materials, or both. Its website gives current contact information for all members nationwide.

Jack's New & Used Building Materials

Jack's New & Used Building Materials
4912 Still Creek Ave.
Burnaby, BC V5C 4E4 Canada

Phone: 604-299-2967
www.jacksused.com

Jack's New & Used Building Materials offers thousands of items, including new and used doors, windows, cabinets, plumbing, electrical, lumber, stained glass, skylights, architectural antiques, and more.

Liz's Antique Hardware

Liz's Antique Hardware
453 S. La Brea
Los Angeles, CA 90036

Phone: 323-939-4403
www.lahardware.com

Liz's Antique Hardware refurbishes and sells salvaged door, cabinet, and window hardware, lighting, and other building materials. Their Los Angeles showroom has over 1 million pieces of original hardware circa 1850 to 1970. The company also offers a hardware matching service for hard-to-find original hardware.

Materials Exchange

Vermont Business Materials Exchange
1580 Barber Pond Rd.
Pownal, VT 05261

Toll-free: 800-895-1930
Phone: 802-823-9399
www.vbmx.org

Vermont Business Materials Exchange (VBMX) is a free service that connects businesses or institutions that have surplus commercial materials with other businesses or individuals who can put the materials to good use. VBMeX maintains a database of available and wanted materials, and publicizes the listings in the form of "classified ads" through their website, specialized listserves and Vermont Business magazine. The database normally contains about 150 active listings of materials offered free or at low cost, updated daily. Materials include surplus wood and plastic materials, construction salvage, and containers, among other items.

ReNew Building Materials & Salvage

ReNew Building Materials & Salvage, Inc.
16 Town Crier Dr. #2
Putney Rd. (opposite Shell)
Brattleboro, VT 05301

Phone: 802-246-2400
www.renewsalvage.org

ReNew Building Materials & Salvage is a non-profit, environmentally-driven store offering used, surplus, and salvaged building materials including doors, windows, kitchen cabinets, hardware, plumbing, electrical, lumber, appliances, and tools. Stock is derived from donations and deconstruction projects. They also offer an expanding selection of new green products and materials. Profits support other local initiatives and organizations.

Salvaged and Sustainably Harvested Wood Search Engine

Woodfinder
P.O. Box 493
Springtown, PA 18081

Toll-free: 877-933-4637
www.woodfinder.com

Woodfinder can be used to locate both salvaged and sustainably harvested wood. Their database contains over 400 suppliers.

Salvaged Architectural Antiques

North Shore Architectural Antiques
616 - 2nd Ave.
Two Harbors, MN 55616

Phone: 218-834-0018
www.north-shore-architectural-antiques.com

North Shore Architectural Antiques salvages antique residential and commercial building materials. The company operates a retail showroom and will deliver regionally and ship anywhere.

Surrey New & Used Building Materials

Surrey New & Used Building Materials, Inc.
17861-64th Ave.
Surrey, BC V3S 1Z3 Canada

Toll-free: 877-570-8733
Phone: 604-576-8488
www.surreynewandused.com

For over 40 years, Surrey New & Used Building Materials has offered salvaged windows, doors, hardware, plumbing, woodwork, cupboards and cabinets, appliances, lighting, electrical, lumber and structural materials, commercial and industrial salvage.

Used Building Materials

1st Saturday Construction Salvage
7010 S.R. 43
Spencer, IN 47460

Phone: 812-876-6347

1st Saturday deconstructs small buildings and carries everything from lumber to doors to stained glass. Open Saturdays.

Used Building Materials

American Salvage
7001 N.W. 27th Ave.
Miami, FL 33147

Phone: 305-691-7001
www.americansalvage.com

A source for general home furnishing items, American Salvage carries a wide variety of finished building components such as paneled doors and specialty windows.

Used Building Materials

Austin Habitat for Humanity Re-Store
310 Comal, Ste. 101
Austin, TX 78702

Phone: 512-478-2165
www.re-store.com

The Austin Re-Store carries a broad range of salvaged building materials in part supplied by deconstruction activities of the local Habitat for Humanity affiliate.

Used Building Materials

Building Materials Resource Center
100 Terrace St.
Boston, MA 02120

Phone: 617-442-2262
www.bostonbmrc.org

The Building Materials Resource Center (BMRC) is a nonprofit organization that accepts donations of good quality used and surplus building materials and offers them for a modest fee to the general public. A generous discount is offered to low- to moderate-income homeowners (proof of income is required) and nonprofit organizations. BMRC maintains a 6,000 ft2 retail location and also offers workshops, in-home consults, a lending library, and other homeowner-assistance services. Donations to the BMRC are tax-deductible on the estimated fair market value of the item.

Used Building Materials

Center for ReSource Conservation
1702 Walnut St.
Boulder, CO 80302

Phone: 303-441-3278
www.conservationcenter.org

ReSource is a program of the Center for ReSource Conservation to salvage and resell building materials from construction and demolition projects. Available materials include lumber, door, window, and cabinet packages as well as architectural artifacts including timbers, hardwood flooring, and other items of significance. ReSource also now offers a complete line of millwork and flooring from reclaimed timbers.

Used Building Materials

Odom Reusable Building Materials
5555 Brentwood Ave.
Grawn, MI 49637

Phone: 231-276-6330
www.odomreuse.com

Odom salvages and deconstructs commercial and residential buildings and sells lumber, cabinets, doors, windows, and a variety of fixtures to the public at a retail warehouse.

Used Building Materials

Rejuvenation
1100 S.E. Grand Ave.
Portland, OR 97214

Toll-free: 888-401-1900
Phone: 503-238-1900
www.rejuvenation.com

Encompassing over 5,000 ft^2, the Salvage Department of the Rejuvenation store in Portland, OR offers a wide variety of salvaged architectural products. The company's Restoration Department refurbishes, repairs, and sells antique lighting fixtures. Rejuvenation is also a manufacturer of period lighting fixtures, including a line equipped with energy-efficient CFLs and small electronic ballasts. The company has taken a number of steps to reduce its environmental impact. Rejuvenation also has a store in Seattle, WA.

Used Building Materials

Rejuvenation Seattle
2910 1st Ave. S
Seattle, WA 98134

Toll-free: 888-401-1900
Phone: 206-382-1901
www.rejuvenation.com

Rejuve Seattle, a branch of Rejuvenation in Portland, OR, offers a wide variety of salvaged architectural products at its 6,000 ft2 facility. The company's Restoration Department refurbishes, repairs, and sells antique lighting fixtures. Rejuvenation is also a manufacturer of period lighting fixtures, including a line equipped with energy-efficient CFLs and small electronic ballasts. The company has taken a number of steps to reduce its environmental impact.

Used Building Materials

Renovators ReSource
6040 Almon St.
Halifax, NS B3K 1T8 Canada

Toll-free: 877-230-7700
Phone: 902-429-3889
www.renovators-resource.com

Renovators ReSource stocks a wide variety of quality used building materials, including entire dismantled buildings, and carries a line of furniture and household items elegantly designed from used building materials.

Used Building Materials

Reuse Development Organization
c/o The Loading Dock
2 N. Kresson St.
Baltimore, MD 21224

Phone: 410-558-3625
www.redo.org

Reuse Development Organization is a national nonprofit organization providing technical assistance in reuse, deconstruction, and building materials salvaging. It's a great information resource for all types of secondhand consumer products as well as building materials, office equipment, and furniture.

Used Building Materials

Second Use Building Materials
7953 Second Ave. S
Seattle, WA 98108

Phone: 206-763-6929
www.seconduse.com

Second Use salvages and sells reusable building materials from their well-stocked retail yard in Seattle, WA.

Used Building Materials

South Puget Sound Habitat for Humanity
210 Thurston Ave.
Olympia, WA 98501

Phone: 360-753-1575
www.spshabitat.org

South Puget Sound Habitat for Humanity is a nonprofit organization donating all profits from the sale of a wide variety of used building supplies to Habitat for Humanity. The company operates a 5,500 sq. ft. retail space known as the Builders' ReStore in downtown Olympia stocked with everything from vintage, one-of-a-kind items to new and surplus materials. Purchases help to fund the construction of safe, decent, affordable homes for Habitat for Humanity's partner families in Thurston County.

Used Building Materials

The Brass Knob and The Back Doors Warehouse
2311 18th St. NW
Washington, DC 20009

Phone: 202-332-3370
www.thebrassknob.com

The Brass Knob and The Back Doors Warehouse offer salvaged building supplies, carrying everything from salvaged antique hardware to chandeliers, stained glass, and radiators. The two locations are within walking distance of each other, with The Back Doors Warehouse carrying larger items in greater volume.

Used Building Materials

The Rebuilding Center of Our United Villages
3625 N. Mississippi Ave.
Portland, OR 97227

Phone: 503-331-1877
www.rebuildingcenter.org

The Rebuilding Center accepts and carries lumber, doors, windows, cabinets, sinks, tubs, toilets, carpets, and more. The Rebuilding Center also offers deconstruction services for commercial and residential structures.

Used Building Materials

The ReUse Center
2801 21st Ave. S
Minneapolis, MN 55407

Phone: 612-724-2608
www.greeninstitute.org

Run by the Green Institute, The ReUse Center supplies its retail operations through a partner deconstruction business and as a donation-based resale business.

Used Building Materials

Urban Ore, Inc.
900 Murray St.
Berkeley, CA 94710

Phone: 510-841-7283
www.urbanore.citysearch.com

One of the oldest used building materials retail operations in the country, Urban Ore carries large quantities of a wide variety of exterior and interior building materials.

Used Building Materials

Used Building Materials Exchange
RecycleNet Corporation
P.O. Box 24017
Guelph, ON N1E 6V8 Canada

Phone: 519-767-2913
build.recycle.net/exchange/index.html

Used Building Materials Exchange (UBM) is a free worldwide information exchange for those companies and individuals who buy/sell/trade used building materials.

Used Building Materials

Whole House Building Supply
1955 Pulgas Ave.
E. Palo Alto, CA 94303

Phone: 650-856-0634
www.driftwoodsalvage.com

Whole House Building Supply offers a complete range of used building materials, fixtures, cabinetry, and architectural elements, including virgin growth redwood. Their website pictures these quality materials as well as uses of salvaged building materials.

This Space is Available for Your Notes

This Space is Available for Your Notes

Miscellaneous

- Air Quality Monitoring and Assessment
- Communication Wiring
- Detection and Alarm
- Electricity Metering
- Facility Remediation
- Outdoor Trash and Recycling Receptacles
- Pest Control Devices
- Recycling Equipment
- Recycling Programs
- Wood Products Certification and Information

Air Quality Monitoring and Assessment

Alerting building occupants about toxins or contaminants is important in many situations. With some toxins, an immediate warning is needed; with others, long-term exposure is the concern.

Air Ion Counter

AlphaLab, Inc.
1280 S. 300 W
Salt Lake City, UT 84101

Toll-free: 800-658-7030
Phone: 801-487-9492
www.trifield.com

AlphaLab's handheld, battery-operated Air Ion Counter detects natural and artificial ions, including radon gas.

IAQ Test Kit

Aerotech P&K
1501 W. Knudsen Dr.
Phoenix, AZ 85027

Toll-free: 800-651-4802
Phone: 623-780-4800
www.aerotechpk.com

Aerotech provides a wide array of sampling devices for measuring IAQ, including Zefon Air-O-Cell Cassettes for gathering mold and bioaerosol samples. Samples are returned to Aerotech for analysis. Aerotech also supplies and rents equipment for gathering specimens.

IAQ Test Kits

Air Quality Sciences, Inc.
2211 Newmarket Pkwy., Ste. 106
Marietta, GA 30067

Toll-free: 800-789-0419
Phone: 770-933-0638
www.aqs.com

Air Quality Sciences produces a variety of IAQ test kits to screen for molds and other allergens, as well as VOCs and formaldehyde. These self-administered kits are simple to use and fairly economical. Results are analyzed by AQS, including comparisons to existing standards, and delivered in an easy-to-read report.

Communication Wiring

Working toward the goal of eliminating halogenated flame retardants must not result in elevated fire risk. Products listed are not necessarily plenum rated (the highest fire-resistant rating). Lower-rated products may need to be installed in metal conduit to provide fire separation, and/or changes such as fire-resistant construction detailing and sprinkler use must be incorporated as

directed by code. While the use of metal conduit is likely to be more expensive, it also simplifies remodeling. In addition there is growing concern about lead-dust from old cables, and new regulations are requiring removal of old wiring to reduce potential fire-loads. Use of metal conduit is a preventative measure against these concerns. Products listed here must be free of heavy metals and halogens (ie containing no chlorinated, brominated, or florinated substances). This means that Greenspec will not include cable products that contain PVC, chlorinated polyethylene, FEP, or brominated flame retardants and that products will meet the EU RoHS standards to be free of lead, cadmium, hexavalent chromium, and mercury as well as for flame retardants.

Zero-Halogen RoHS-Compliant Data Cables

Berk-Tek
132 White Oak Rd.
New Holland, PA 17557

Phone: 717-354-6200
www.berktek.com

Berktek, a division of Nexans, supplies a full line of riser-rated compliant data cables compliant with RoHS, the European Union's rules on hazardous substances in electrical equipment. A low-smoke, zero-halogen option is available by special request for a range of cable types. The company can provide low-smoke, zero-halogen, Category-6 cable, but requires a 25,000-foot minimum order.

Detection and Alarm

Alerting building occupants about toxins or contaminants is important in many situations. With some toxins, an immediate warning is needed; with others, long-term exposure is the concern. Detecting water leaks contributes to occupant health by allowing steps to be taken to stop mold before it starts, as well as protecting the health and longevity of the building itself.

Air Check Radon Test

Air Check, Inc.
1936 Butler Bridge Rd.
Fletcher, NC 28732

Toll-free: 800-247-2435
Phone: 828-684-0893
www.radon.com

Air Check offers a series of radon test kits, each designed for different exposure times. The company provides fully certified analysis of mailed-in air samples for as little as $10 per test. Air Check performs same-day tests upon receipt of samples and provides a complete written report describing the results and their implications for indoor air quality.

Atwood CO Alarm

Atwood Mobile Products
1120 N. Main St.
Elkhart, IN 46514

Phone: 574-264-2131
www.atwoodmobile.com

Atwood Mobile Products' CO alarm is certified by the Canadian Standards Association, which includes specifications for both alarm longevity and time-of-manufacture testing. Atwood uses a patented electrochemical technology to alert building occupants to the presence of carbon monoxide. According to the company, the sensor is more accurate, more energy efficient, and less sensitive to humidity than competing models. A digital display updates CO levels every 30 seconds and indicates battery and sensor conditions. The unit requires 3 AAA batteries. A picture-frame leg allows installation in various locations. The Canadian Standards Association certifies Atwood CO alarms for use in RVs.

Detec Moisture Detection and Monitoring Systems

Detec Systems, LLC
711 St. Helens Ave.
Suite 201
Tacoma, WA 98402

Phone: 253-272-3262
www.detecsystems.com

Detec Systems offers a real-time, automated moisture intrusion monitoring system for building envelopes and roof systems. The detection system uses a proprietary moisture-detection tape with copper conductors and stainless steel probes which can be installed in nearly 100% of the building envelope. Zones of tape are connected to onsite sensor modules that communicate with Detec's central monitoring center. The Detec system is primarily used in commercial, institutional and multi-family/residential buildings. The system can monitor any type of building structure, including wood-frame, non-combustible steel construction, window wall, curtain wall and concrete. The technology was originally developed for the telecom industry, and has been used to monitor cable routes for moisture intrusion since the early '80s.'

Floodstopper Leak Detection and Control

FirstSmart Sensor Corp.
1460 Pandosy St., Ste. 201
Kelowna, BC V1Y 1P3 Canada

Toll-free: 800-660-1522
Phone: 250-763-5694
www.thefloodstopper.com

The Floodstopper™ from FirstSmart Sensor Corporation is designed to stop plumbing overflows on the spot. It uses sensors placed at floor level near toilets, washing machines, and other potential flood sources. These sensors are connected (with wires or via a wireless link) to a central controller and an automatic shutoff valve.

H2ORB

Aqua One Technologies, Inc.
14726 Golden West, Ste. J
Westminster, CA 92683

Phone: 714-898-7016
www.aquaone.com

The H2Orb is a simple leak-detection system for toilets that includes both bowl and tank sensors. When either sensor detects a flow problem, a wireless signal is sent to the controller which shuts off water flow to the toilet, sounds an alarm, and identifies the problem on its LCD screen. The unit is powered by a battery with a five-year expected life.

Low Level CO "Health" Monitor

CO-Experts, Div. of G. E. Kerr Companies, Inc.
19299 Katrina Ln.
Eldridge, MO 65463

Toll-free: 888-443-5377
Phone: 417-426-5504
www.coexperts.com

The Low Level (LL) CO Monitor displays carbon monoxide (CO) levels as low as 10 ppm, audible and visual warnings at 10, 25, 35, 50, & 70 ppm with immediate, automatic hush & hush overrides at all levels. Unlike most CO detectors, these monitors (in addition to sensing higher levels) are designed to alert occupants to low levels of CO that may be harmful, but not necessarily fatal, so that corrective measures may be taken. Most CO detectors sound an alarm only after much higher levels are sustained for a protracted period of time. The CO-Experts Low Level Monitors take a CO reading every second, then averages 5 readings, updating the display and audible alarm every 5 seconds. The monitor provides 1 ppm resolution. The reasons for diagnostic failure warnings are shown on the display as well as CO exposure data storage timelines, peak, time of peak, duration of CO exposure, and the resulting COHB in the blood stream. If not cleared by owner, the stored data will be retained for 2 years & 8 months. The sensor is fully monitored and provides end of life warning. The unit comes with a 1-year warranty and a 5 year expected lifetime. An annual calibration and warranty renewal service is available for an additional charge.

Nighthawk CO Detector

Kidde Safety
1394 S. Third St.
Mebane, NC 27302

Toll-free: 800-880-6788
www.kidde.com

The Nighthawk CO detector uses electrochemical technology to alert building occupants to the presence of carbon monoxide (CO). The Canadian Standards Association certifies Kidde's Nighthawk CO detectors for use in homes.

Radon Control Equipment

Infiltec Radon Control Supply
108 S. Delphine Ave.
P.O. Box 1125
Waynesboro, VA 22980

Toll-free: 888-349-7236
Phone: 540-943-2776
www.infiltec.com

Infiltec Radon Control distributes and installs radon-control equipment.

The Professional Radon Gas Test Kit

Pro-Lab, Inc.
1675 N. Commerce Pkwy.
Weston, FL 33326

Phone: 954-384-4446
www.prolabinc.com

Each EPA-recognized Pro-Lab test kit comes with a pair of radon detectors. The detectors use liquid scintillation technology with silica-gel desiccants, so they require only 96 hours of exposure before they are sealed and sent back to the lab for analysis. Results will be returned within one week; express 2-day analysis is also available. Pro-Lab also offers kits to detect pesticides, molds, carbon monoxide, asbestos, and bacteria in water, paints, dust, and on surfaces.

Electricity Metering

Electrical metering equipment provides valuable diagnostic information on building energy loads and usage, from plug loads to whole building energy systems. Some products in this section are also specifically designed to be educational tools.

Brand Digital Power Meter

Brand Electronics
421 Hilton Rd.
Whitefield, ME 04353

Toll-free: 888-433-6600
Phone: 207-549-3401
www.brandelectronics.com

The Brand Digital Power Meter monitors energy usage of 120-volt AC plug loads (up to 1,850 watts). It calculates instantaneous watts, accumulated kWh, and monthly cost. The higher-end models also display peak demand, power factor, and volt-amps, and are capable of datalogging and transferring data to a PC (Win 95/98/XP). Other models are available for multichannel metering, including 240-volt and DC channels. All models measure accurate (+/-2%) wattage—including power factor—by sampling volts and amps at 4 kHz.

Kill A Watt

P3 International Corporation
132 Nassau St.
New York, NY 10038

Phone: 212-346-7979
www.p3international.com

The Kill A Watt™ energy monitor records appliance electrical consumption by kilowatt-hour within 0.2% accuracy and shows it in a large LCD display by the hour, day, week, month, or up to a year. Also displays volts, amps, watts, hertz, and volt-amps. It is more affordable than most energy-monitoring products on the market.

Watts Up?

Electronic Educational Devices, Inc.
3090 S. Jamaica Ct. #306
Denver, CO 80014

Toll-free: 877-928-8701
Phone: 303-282-6410
www.doubleed.com

Watts Up? electricity monitors show users the electricity usage of any 120-volt AC load. The monitor displays 16 values including watts, current volts, duty cycle, and dollars and cents based upon a specified electricity rate. The Pro version records this data, and with a PC interface, provides graphs of the collected data over time. Watts up? is an educational tool that is also useful for people planning their off-the-grid energy needs.

Facility Remediation

Asbestos and lead are among the most common hazardous materials encountered in older buildings. Use of asbestos as an insulating and fireproofing material, and lead as a primary ingredient in paint, ended in the 1970s as awareness of these dangers grew. Lead and asbestos remediation in buildings should generally be done by professionals, through either removal or encapsulation. Fluorescent lighting products—lamps as well as older ballasts—should also be disposed of only through specialized recycling facilities, some of which are listed here. All fluorescent lamps (as well as mercury-vapor and other high-intensity-discharge-HID-lamps) contain elemental mercury, which is a very serious environmental contaminant. Fluorescent lighting ballasts made prior to 1979 contain significant quantities of PCB (polychlorinated biphenyls)—each ballast containing 0.6 to 1 ounce—which is highly toxic and bioaccumulates in natural systems. Before sending fluorescent lamps and ballasts to out-of-town recycling facilities, check with your local solid-waste agency; many handle lamps and ballast disposal through toxic waste collection programs. Products listed here aid in managing lead and asbestos with minimal additional environmental and health risks.

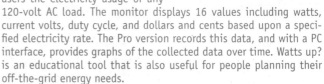

A-B-C and L-B-C

Fiberlock Technologies, Inc.
150 Dascomb Rd.
Andover, MA 01810

Toll-free: 800-342-3755
Phone: 978-623-9987
www.fiberlock.com

A-B-C® (Asbestos Binding Compound) is a high-solids asbestos encapsulant. This product can be used for effective in-place management of asbestos hazards.

L-B-C® (Lead Barrier Compound) is an elastomeric-thermoplastic water-based copolymer paint for lead encapsulation. L-B-C is available for indoor and outdoor applications in 1-, 5-, and 55-gallon containers.

AeRO 30 Dry Ice Blasting System

Cold Jet, LLC
455 Wards Corner Rd.
Loveland, OH 45140

Toll-free: 800-337-9423
Phone: 513-831-3211
www.coldjet.com

Cold Jet's AeRO 30 system is configured specifically for disaster remediation contractors and used for removing mold and fire-damage from building surfaces. The dry ice evaporates immediately, greatly reducing the clean-up and disposal costs compared with sandblasting. It is more energy intensive to produce and handle, however. The AeRO 30 uses 1.5 pounds of dry ice per minute, along with 50 to 150 cfm of compressed air at 80 psi, depending on the nozzle used. Dry ice for the system can be purchased from a regional supplier (prices range from 35 to 45 cents per pound, according to Cold Jet) or manufactured on site using Cold Jet's dry ice production equipment. (The company's P325 dry ice maker draws about 17 kW to make 300 lbs. of dry ice per hour, or about 18 lbs per kWh.)

LeadCheck

HybriVet Systems, Inc.
P.O. Box 1210
Framingham, MA 01701

Toll-free: 800-262-5323
Phone: 508-651-7881
www.leadcheck.com

HybriVet Systems offers several tests for lead in paint, soil, and water, as well as tests for other heavy metal pollutants. LeadCheck® swabs are a quick means of detecting lead in paint and other materials.

LeadLock and AsbestoSafe

Global Encasement, Inc.
132 – 32ND St.
Union City, NJ 07087

Toll-free: 800-266-3982
Phone: 201-902-9770
www.encasement.com

AsbestoSafe® and LeadLock™ are water-based, low-VOC, protective acrylic coatings for long-term, in-place management of asbestos and lead-based paint. Both products provide waterproofing yet allow water vapor to pass through the protective coating, and both are highly impact- and seismic-resistant. One of the most impressive characteristics of Global Encasement's PrepLESS Primer is that it can eliminate and/or minimize surface preparation prior to the application of TopCoats.

Safe Encasement Systems

SAFE Encasement Systems
8689 W. Sahara Blvd., Ste. 160
Las Vegas, NV 89117

Toll-free: 888-277-8834
Phone: 702-360-6111
www.safeencasement.com

Safe Encasement Systems manufactures a two-step encasement process for in-place abatement of lead-based paint and asbestos-fibers. SE-110 Penetrating Stabilizer, also available with corrosion inhibitors or mold-resisting additive, is a clear primer suitable for penetrating and sealing friable fibrous insulation materials and damaged paint surfaces. SE-110 can be used for interior and exterior applications on a variety of surfaces. When dry, SE-110 is followed by the application of SE-120 Protective Skin, a high-solids, 100% acrylic coating available with or without a mold-resisting additive. Both the Stabilizer and Protective Skin are water-based, nontoxic, nonflammable, zero-VOC formulations that clean up with soap and water.

Outdoor Trash and Recycling Receptacles

Enabling homeowners and commercial building occupants to be good environmental stewards is important. Systems that make it easy to recycle wastes should be provided in houses, apartment buildings, offices, and institutions. Recycled plastic receptacles are most commonly made from either HDPE or commingled plastics. Recycled commingled plastics may have slightly inconsistent properties, but this is a lower-grade waste material that is generally more of a disposal problem. Products listed here contain recycled content.

2nd Site Systems

Victor Stanley, Inc.
P.O. Drawer 330
Dunkirk, MD 20754

Toll-free: 800-368-2573
Phone: 301-855-8300
www.victorstanley.com

2nd Site Systems utilizes a patented slat design of 100% recycled plastic lumber reinforced with recycled steel bar. Products include park benches, picnic tables, and trash receptacles.

Barco Recycled-Content Products

Barco Products
11 N. Batavia Ave.
Batavia, IL 60510

Toll-free: 800-338-2697
Phone: 630-879-0084
www.barcoproducts.com

Barco Products offers site furnishings, landscape timbers, and traf-fic devices made with recycled content, including dozens of styles of picnic tables and park benches made with recycled commingled HDPE and LDPE averaging 40% post-consumer, as well as planters and waste receptacles made from recycled HDPE (90 to 100% post-consumer). Landscape Timbers are made from 100% recycled com-mingled HDPE and LDPE, sized as railroad ties with premolded holes for rebar reinforcement and interlocking edges for stacking stability. Each timber weighs 42 lbs, about half that of most plastic landscape timbers. 100% recycled tire rubber speed bumps and 100% recycled plastic speed bumps are offered, and colored wheel stops made of 95% recycled commingled HDPE and LDPE. Gray wheel stops contain 85% recycled PVC. Bollards are made from 96% recycled commingled LDPE and HDPE (50%–80% post-industrial).

Bedford Technology Recycled-Plastic Products

Bedford Technology, LLC
2424 Armour Rd.
P.O. Box 609
Worthington, MN 56187

Toll-free: 800-721-9037
Phone: 507-372-5558
www.plasticboards.com

Bedford Technology offers plastic lumber and other products made with post-consumer recycled HDPE and LDPE. Their lumber is available in a variety of dimensions, including 5/4 decking, two-by, and large timbers up to 12x12, in black, brown, gray, and cedar with other colors available. Parking stops and speed bumps are also offered, as well as plastic paneling that can be used as a substitute for plywood. Bedford's ForeSite Designs(R) line of recycled-plastic site furnishings includes picnic tables, benches, and waste receptacles. The manufacturer has certified the following recycled-content levels (by weight): total recovered material 99% typical, 99% guaranteed; post-consumer material 65% typical, 50% guaranteed.

Benches, Picnic Tables, and Recycling Receptacles

Eagle One Site Furnishings
1340 N. Jefferson St.
Anaheim, CA 92807

Toll-free: 800-448-3160
Phone: 714-983-0050
www.eagleoneproducts.com

EagleOne Site Furnishings offers site amenities, including benches, picnic tables, and recycling receptacles, made from recycled HDPE plastic.

Benches, Picnic Tables, Waste Receptacles, and Planters

Kay Park Recreation Corp.
1301 Pine St.
P.O. Box 477
Janesville, IA 50647

Phone: 319-987-2313
www.kaypark.com

Kay Park Recreation manufactures picnic tables, benches, waste receptacles, and planters containing 96% post-consumer recycled commingled plastics.

Conservancy Series - Benches, Picnic Tables, and Recycling Receptacles

Florida Playground and Steel Co.
4701 S. 50th St.
Tampa, FL 33619

Toll-free: 800-444-2655
Phone: 813-247-2812
www.fla-playground.com

Conservancy Series benches, picnic tables, and recycling receptacles are made from recycled plastic/wood composite materials and steel.

Earthcare Series

Litchfield Industries
4 Industrial Dr.
Litchfield, MI 49252

Toll-free: 800-542-5282
Phone: 517-542-2988
www.litchfieldindustries.com

The Earthcare Series of site furnishings is made from 100% post-consumer recycled plastic. The Series includes picnic tables, benches, and trash receptacles.

Eco Outdoor Series

Ecologic, Inc.
921 Sherwood Dr.
Lake Bluff, IL 60044

Toll-free: 800-899-8004
Phone: 847-234-5855
www.ecoinc.com

Ecologic is a large producer of furniture based on recycled HDPE plastic. They have an extensive range of outdoor furniture suitable for residential and public spaces, ranging from individual Adirondack chairs and ottomans to tables, benches, trash receptacles (designed to take standard Rubbermaid inserts), and fan trellises. Some of these products contain recycled steel to add stiffness. The entire line is manufactured with 97.5% recycled content. UV protection is integral to the plastic in each component.

Pilot Rock Site Furnishings

R. J. Thomas Manufacturing Co., Inc.
P.O. Box 946
Cherokee, IA 51012

Toll-free: 800-762-5002
Phone: 712-225-5115
www.pilotrock.com

Pilot Rock Site Furnishings are made from recycled HDPE and LDPE plastic. The Pilot Rock line includes benches, picnic tables, waste receptacles, and car stops. The manufacturer has certified the following recycled-content levels (by weight): total recovered material 100% typical, 100% guaranteed; post-consumer material 75% typical, 60% guaranteed.

Recycle Design Site Furnishings

Trimax Building Products, Inc.
2600 W. Roosevelt Rd.
Chicago, IL 60608

Toll-free: 866-987-4629
www.trimaxbp.com

The award-winning Recycle Design site furnishings are made with Durawood PE plastic lumber that contains 90% post-consumer recycled HDPE by weight, and steel or aluminum structural components. The Recycle Design line includes benches, picnic tables, and waste receptacles.

Recycled-Plastic Products

American Recycled Plastic, Inc.
1500 Main St.
Palm Bay, FL 32905

Toll-free: 866-674-1525
Phone: 321-674-1525
www.itsrecycled.com

American Recycled Plastic manufactures a range of products from recycled HDPE, including lumber and timbers, car stops, speed bumps and humps, and vehicle barriers. They also offer a wide variety of recycled-HDPE site furnishings, including benches, outdoor tables, waste receptacles, mailboxes, planters, custom wildlife structures, and bicycle racks. The manufacturer has certified the following recycled-content levels (by weight): total recovered material 100% typical, 100% guaranteed; post-consumer material 80% typical, 80% guaranteed.

Recycled-Plastic Site Amenities

DuMor, Inc.
P.O. Box 142
Mifflintown, PA 17059

Toll-free: 800-598-4018
Phone: 717-436-2106
www.dumor.com

DuMor offers a wide array of site amenities made from recycled HDPE plastic lumber. Products include benches, picnic tables, planters, and waste receptacles. The HDPE used in DuMor's recycled plastic furnishings is derived from post-consumer bottle waste resulting in a product that is more than 90% recycled. The manufacturer has certified the following recycled-content levels (by weight): total recovered material 95% typical, 95% guaranteed; post-consumer material 95% typical, 95% guaranteed.

Recycled-Plastic Site Amenities

The Plastic Lumber Company, Inc.
115 W. Bartges St.
Akron, OH 44311

Toll-free: 800-886-8990
Phone: 330-762-8989
www.plasticlumber.com

The Plastic Lumber Company offers site furnishings, playground equipment, and signage made with recycled plastic. Commercial-grade benches, picnic tables, and waste receptacles/recycling centers are available in a variety of color combinations and are made with 97% post-consumer recycled content. Signage products have a post-industrial recycled content level up to 40% depending on color selection. (The Digital DeSigns line of signs does not contain recyled content).

Site Furnishings

Doty & Sons Concrete Products, Inc.
1275 E. State St.
Sycamore, IL 60178

Toll-free: 800-233-3907
www.dotyconcrete.com

Doty & Sons Concrete Products uses recycled HDPE plastic in its precast concrete site amenities, including benches and table sets, recycling and waste receptacles.

Site Furnishings and Materials

Inteq Corp.
35800 Glen Dr.
Eastlake, OH 44095

Phone: 440-953-0550
www.4-inteqcorp.com

Inteq's benches and picnic tables are made from recycled HDPE plastic. Tables are either standard 6' or 8' length or hexagonal. Benches come in a variety of styles and can be custom designed. Inteq's waste receptacles and planters contain recycled HDPE plastic and are available in many styles including custom production. All are offered in a variety of colors. Recycled content is up to 100% (minimum 20% post-consumer). Inteq nonstructural landscape timbers are available in multiple colors up to 12' in length in standard sizes of 4x4, 4x6, and 6x6. Decking and railing material is also made from recycled HDPE plastic and is available in multiple colors.

Pest Control Devices

Termite control in buildings has traditionally been accomplished with pesticides—in the past with chlordane and heptachlor, and more recently with chlorpyrifos. With all of these pesticides no longer in use because of health and environmental concerns, there's tremendous interest in alternatives. Products listed here include totally nontoxic termite barrier systems as well as less toxic, or more precisely targeted, chemical treatments. Termite barriers and full-control bait systems are generally quite expensive.

Basaltic Termite Barrier

Ameron Hawaii
2344 Pahounui Dr.
P.O. Box 29968
Honolulu, HI 96820

Phone: 808-832-9200
www.ameronhawaii.com

Basaltic Termite Barrier is a regionally available product made from basaltic aggregates (a coarse sand) on the Hawaiian Islands. These aggregates, when graded to a specific size, shape, and weight, form an effective, nontoxic barrier to standard subterranean and Formosan termite entry. The aggregates are too large and heavy for termites to move and the spaces between too small to move through.

Exterra

Ensystex, Inc.
P.O. Box 2587
Fayetteville, NC 28302

Toll-free: 888-398-3772
www.exterra.com

The Exterra® Termite Interception and Baiting System is similar to the Sentricon System, using a chitin synthesis-inhibitor called diflubenzuron. A unique feature of Exterra's bait station, the Labyrinth, is the ability to install pesticide in the bait core without disturbing termites feeding on the bait box perimeter.

Mite-Out

Hohmann & Barnard, Inc.
30 Rasons Ct.
P.O. Box 5270
Hauppauge, NY 11788-0270

Phone: 631-234-0600
www.h-b.com

Mite-Out from Hohmann & Barnard is a soft copper termite flashing adhered to a closed-cell polyethylene foam sill seal, providing termite protection while contributing to the airtightness of the building envelope in a location that can be troublesome to detail. The flexible, asphalt-free product is compatible with any adhesive, caulk, or sealant. Mite-Out is available in 8-, 10-, and 12-inch widths, in 50-foot long rolls.

Roach and Ant Baits

Blue Diamond, LLC
P.O. Box 953
Rogersville, TN 37857

Phone: 423-585-6312
www.bluediamonddistribution.com

Blue Diamond offers a number of dustless roach and ant baits in paste or gel formulations for residential, commercial, and industrial applications. The manufacturer claims that insects cannot build up

resistance to the boric acid in these products, while they can with many chemical insecticides. The baits are spot-applied, odorless, noncombustible, and effective for a year after application. These products work outdoors, but must be protected from rain. The roach baits are not available in all U.S. states.

Sentricon Termite Colony Elimination System

Dow AgroSciences, LLC
9330 Zionsville Rd.
Indianapolis, IN 46268

Toll-free: 800-352-6776
www.sentricon.com

The Sentricon® Termite Colony Elimination System eliminates termites with a highly targeted noviflumuron-based bait. This bait is considered to be highly targeted because worker termites carry it back to the colony to feed others. The chemical affects chitin formation in termites. In a management-intensive approach that limits environmental impact, the noviflumuron pesticide is employed only when regularly inspected bait stations reveal termite activity. The Sentricon System is offered as part of an ongoing service contract.

Termimesh System

Termimesh, LLC
9519 N IH 35
Austin, TX 78753

Phone: 512-997-0066
www.termimesh.com

The Termimesh™ System is a termite barrier from Australia made from a tight-weave stainless steel mesh. Proper installation of Termimesh may avoid the repeated application of pesticides. Currently this system is available only in a few Southern states.

Recycling Equipment

Enabling commercial and public building and campus occupants to be good environmental stewards is important. Systems that make it easy to recycle wastes should be provided in offices, institutions, parks, and other public spaces. Many of the products described here are themselves made from recycled waste materials.

Curbside or Work-Area Recycling Bins

Microphor
452 E. Hill Rd.
Willits, CA 95490

Toll-free: 800-358-8280
Phone: 707-459-5563
www.microphor.com

Microphor recycling bins, made from plastic, are designed for curbside or office-paper recycling. These stackable bins have large handles and measure 12-1/4" x 12-1/2" x 20-1/2". Standard colors are white, navy blue, blue, red, green, and yellow.

Feeny Lidded Waste and Recycle and Rotary Recycling Center

Knape & Vogt Manufacturing Company
2700 Oak Industrial Dr. NE
Grand Rapids, MI 49505

Toll-free: 800-253-1561
Phone: 616-459-3311
www.knapeandvogt.com

Knape & Vogt offers two products for residential recyclable collection. The Feeny Lidded Waste and Recycle is intended for base cabinet applications; it has up to 3 bins and rolls out. The Feeny Rotary Corner Recycling Center has 3 bins and works like a lazy susan.

Recycling Equipment

Recy-CAL Supply Co.
42597 De Portola Rd.
Temecula, CA 92592

Toll-free: 800-927-3873
Phone: 951-302-7585
www.recy-cal.com

Recy-CAL Supply is a distributor of recycling containers, waste receptacles, and mobile collection containers. Many styles and sizes of products from more than 30 manufacturers are available to fit various needs, budgets, and decors.

Recycling Programs

Rechargeable nickel-cadmium (Ni-Cad) batteries have become ubiquitous on building sites. Despite their durability, they do wear out; the health and environmental risks posed by the heavy-metal content of Ni-Cad batteries makes their recycling a very high priority, so programs for recycling them are included here.

Ni-Cad Battery Recycling

Inmetco
One Inmetco Dr.
Ellwood City, PA 16117

Phone: 724-758-2800
www.inmetco.com

Inmetco maintains a nationwide battery recycling program for nickel-cadmium, nickel-metal-hydride, zinc, alkaline, lithium-ion, and nickel-iron batteries.

Wood Products Certification and Information

Forest certification in North America is conducted primarily by two third-party certifying organizations: SmartWood and Scientific Certification Systems (SCS). SmartWood and SCS certify forest lands and chain-of-custody forest products based on Forest Stewardship Council (FSC) standards.

Forest Stewardship Council

Forest Stewardship Council - US
1155 30th St. NW, Ste. 300
Washington, DC 20007

Toll-free: 877-372-5646
Phone: 202-342-0413
www.fscus.org

The Forest Stewardship Council (FSC) is a nonprofit international organization committed to the conservation, restoration, and protection of the world's working forests through standards setting and accreditation. Founded in 1993, FSC is comprised of more than 600 members from 70 countries, including major environmental groups like Greenpeace and World Wildlife Fund, social organizations representing indigenous peoples and forest workers, and progressive forest-management and wood-products companies. The FSC checkmark-and-tree logo indicates that wood and wood products bearing the logo came from a well-managed forest. The FSC is the only forest certification standards program recognized in evaluating wood products for GreenSpec.

Scientific Certification Systems

Scientific Certification Systems
2000 Powell St., Ste. 1350
Emeryville, CA 94608

Phone: 510-452-8000
www.scscertified.com

Scientific Certification Systems (SCS) is an independent certification organization that offers a range of services. SCS certifies manufacturers' claims of building product attributes such as recycled and recovered content and absence of added formaldehyde. The company also conducts life-cycle impact assessments and the certification of environmentally preferable products such as paints, carpets, technologies, services, and electricity. In addition, SCS is accredited by the FSC to certify well-managed forests and conduct chain-of-custody certification for forest products based on FSC standards.

SmartWood

SmartWood
65 Millet St., Ste. 201
Goodwin-Baker Bldg.
Richmond, VT 05477

Phone: 802-434-5491
www.smartwood.org

SmartWood is the sustainable forestry program of the Rainforest Alliance, an international conservation organization that works to protect ecosystems and the people and wildlife that depend on them by transforming land use practices, business practices, and consumer behavior. Established in 1989, SmartWood was the first certification program in the world and is accredited by the Forest Stewardship Council. SmartWood's headquarters is located in Richmond, Vermont.

This Space is Available for Your Notes

This Space is Available for Your Notes

This Space is Available for Your Notes

Index of Products & Manufacturers

ABOUT THE EDITORS

Alex Wilson is president of BuildingGreen and serves as executive editor of *Environmental Building News*, a monthly newsletter on environmentally responsible building design and construction, and as coeditor of the *GreenSpec®* product directory. Prior to starting his own company in 1985 (now BuildingGreen), he was executive director of the Northeast Sustainable Energy Association for five years. Alex has written about energy-efficient and environmentally responsible design and construction for more than 25 years and is author, coauthor or editor of several books and manuals, including *Greening Federal Facilities* (U.S. Dept. of Energy, 2nd Edition, 2001), *The Consumer Guide to Home Energy Savings* (ACEEE, 9th edition, 2007), *Green Development: Integrating Ecology and Real Estate* (John Wiley & Sons, 1998), and *Your Green Home* (New Society, 2006). He has also written hundreds of articles for other publications, including *Fine Homebuilding, Architectural Record, The Construction Specifier, Landscape Architecture,* and *Popular Science.* Alex served on the board of the U.S. Green Building Council from 2000 through 2005, and he is a trustee of the Vermont Chapter of The Nature Conservancy.

Mark Piepkorn is associate editor of *Environmental Building News*, products researcher for *GreenSpec®*, and contributor to the online resource *BuildingGreen Suite*, all publications of BuildingGreen He is also the products editor for *GreenSource*, the member publication of the U.S. Green Building Council, for which BuildingGreen is a content partner. His knowledge of conventional and alternative construction methods, materials, and building science—in applications as diverse as underground structures, vernacular timber construction, and earthen techniques, as well as the rehabilitation and remodeling of conventional structures—lends an interesting and important perspective to the understanding of the roles of manufactured products and materials in our built and conditioned environments. Active in the natural building movement, Mark has also been the editor of *The Last Straw*, an international newsletter about straw-bale construction and natural building.

NEW SOCIETY PUBLISHERS

ENVIRONMENTAL BENEFITS STATEMENT

New Society Publishers has chosen to produce this book on recycled paper made with **100% post-consumer waste**, processed chlorine free, and old-growth free.

For every 5,000 books printed, New Society saves the following resources:[1]

95	Trees
8,620	Pounds of Solid Waste
9,484	Gallons of Water
12,371	Kilowatt Hours of Electricity
15,670	Pounds of Greenhouse Gases
67	Pounds of HAPs, VOCs, and AOX Combined
24	Cubic Yards of Landfill Space

[1]Environmental benefits are calculated based on research done by the Environmental Defense Fund and other members of the Paper Task Force who study the environmental impacts of the paper industry. Contact the EDF for more information on this environmental benefits statement, a copy of their report, and the latest updates on their data.